Intellectuals and the State in Modern China

The Transformation of Modern China Series
James E. Sheridan, General Editor

The Fall of Imperial China
Frederic Wakeman, Jr.

China in Disintegration
The Republican Era in Chinese History, 1912–1949
James E. Sheridan

Mao's China
A History of the People's Republic
Maurice Meisner

Intellectuals and the State in Modern China
A Narrative History
Jerome B. Grieder

Chinese Foreign Policy *
A Conceptual History
Mark Mancall

* In preparation.

Intellectuals and the State in Modern China

A Narrative History

Jerome B. Grieder

THE FREE PRESS
A Division of Macmillan, Inc.
NEW YORK

Collier Macmillan Publishers
LONDON

The Free Press
A Division of Macmillan, Inc.
866 Third Avenue, New York, N.Y. 10022

Collier Macmillan Canada, Inc.

First Free Press Paperback Edition 1983

Printed in the United States of America

printing number paperback

  2 3 4 5 6 7 8 9 10

printing number hard cover

1 2 3 4 5 6 7 8 9 10

Library of Congress Cataloging in Publication Data

Grieder, Jerome B.
  Intellectuals and the state in modern China.

  (The Transformation of modern China)
  Bibliography: p.
  1. China—Intellectual life—1644-1912. 2. China—
Intellectual life—1912-1949. I. Title. II. Series:
Transformation of modern China.
DS754.14.G74   951   81-66436
ISBN 0-02-912810-2   AACR2
ISBN 0-02-912670-3 pbk.

For Elsa

Contents

Preface

A traveler to the People's Republic of China today visits a revolution now more than a generation old. He sees a country vastly changed from what it was when that revolution came to power in 1949; or a generation before that, when the Nationalist government held sway; or a century earlier still, when the imperial Confucian regime was in the initial stages of its long and fatal decline. China's recent history has set a permanent mark upon the country and its people. The aspiration to modernity shows itself in reservoirs and dams, railroads and bridges, the great sweep of power lines across the countryside or the fragile thread of an electric wire that carries light to a remote rural village, smoky factory stacks, the graceless bulk of industrial plants, the sprawling monotony of modern apartment blocks. The people look healthier than one remembers them, more uniform—and more uniformly prosperous—than the fading photographs of an earlier time portray them. One can easily believe, as one is urged to do, that they are better fed, and better doctored, and in general better served by their government; nor is one likely to be as painfully aware as one once was of the appalling social chasm that divided privilege from unprivilege.

But still one knows that this is China, and nowhere else. One flies over a landscape still unique: the patchwork tapestry of fields and paddy in central and south China, the endless dry and dusty highlands of the north. There are the familiar canals and rivers of rural China as it exists in memory; there, the ponderous square-sailed junks and agile sampans; there, the clustered village houses, ancient gray stone and modern yellow stucco side-by-side along the narrow lanes. And the countryside itself is a stage as lively with human activity as it has been—or so we are inclined to imagine—since time began for China: as vital in its energies, as varied in its forms, and even more crowded.

As with what is visible, so it is too with the hidden landscape of the mind. The narrative that follows stresses the changes that have transformed this interior landscape almost beyond recognition since the early decades of the nineteenth century, fundamentally altering the sense the Chinese have of themselves and of China's place in the world. Yet, more frequently than one might expect, as we survey the changing sense of social purpose and individual responsibility, of assumptions concerning the good life, and attitudes toward the community and the self, our attention will be caught by a glimpse of something that is somehow familiar. We cannot say that the spirit of modern Chinese history is aptly characterized by the phrase "change within tradition" often used to epitomize the long centuries of dynastic history, for little remains that one can appropriately label "traditional." But neither can one deny that China itself remains distinctively Chinese in its social personality.

* * *

"May you live in interesting times!" So says a proverbial Chinese curse. The years that this narrative focuses upon, from the early nineteenth century into the middle of the twentieth, have indeed been "interesting times" for most of the Chinese intellectuals whose thoughts and lives carry the burden of our tale. We are dealing here with a conspicuous minority which was sufficiently perceptive and pensive to be aware of the push of change and the tug of tradition, and sufficiently well-educated and self-confident to hold and express opinions about the circumstances in which it found itself. This is a loose and unanalytical definition of the term "intellectuals," not as a social or economic class, nor as those whose vocations are strictly scholastic, but as a procession of thoughtful, responsive, and expressive individuals. Since their ideas emerge out of, and are expressed in the context of, the experiences and perceptions of particular lives, I have tried—at least in my treatment of the major protagonists—to convey some sense of the individuals behind the ideas, in terms of family background, education, temperament, attitudes, prejudices—whatever, in short, embodies an intellectual persuasion and gives it life and personality. And since their motive, virtually without exception, was not simply to react to a situation but to persuade others to their view of what should be done about it, I have allowed the protagonists to speak for themselves as much as possible: even in translation, the message written to be read carries an authority that no paraphrastic synthesis can achieve. I have also tried to preserve this persuasive intent in my translations, even if this meant in some cases favoring rather free renderings of the original language—without, I hope, doing violence to its meaning.

This account has been written primarily to provoke—and I hope partially to satisfy—the interest of the general reader who wishes to share something of an absorbing but largely unfamiliar historical experience. The scholar who has made a special study of modern China will find few surprises here, in respect to the cast of characters, the *mise en scène*, or the plot of the drama. To the best of my knowledge, however, the story has not been told in the panoramic manner in which it is set forth here—and I hope that even those who differ with me on points of interpretation, or who take exception to the perspective from which I view one or another individual or issue, will agree that it is a story deserving of a wider audience. China's modern history should be considered not merely as an exotic fragment in the background of our understanding of "the modern world," but as a historical experience that provides important insights into the way in which familiar ideas and expectations can be translated into unfamiliar contexts in this unprecedentedly ecumenical age, and thus as something that belongs to all of us.

Errors of commission, of which doubtless there are many, will I trust be called to my attention by interested readers. Of omissions attributable to the constraints of theme, space, or ignorance I am myself (in a number of cases, at least) painfully aware. This does not pretend to be, in any comprehensive or systematic way, a history of modern Chinese thought or modern Chinese culture. It is an exploration of certain concerns, as these were perceived and expressed by thinkers "whose lives are devoted to the shaping of public opinion," as Hu Shih characterized himself and others in 1919. An account of this kind is necessarily selective; and selection implies criteria which determine what, or who, will be included or excluded. I have not attempted to devise a single unifying theme around which to arrange the individuals about whom I am writing: their characters and ideas are too diverse to submit to such treatment. The reader may nevertheless discern, in the pages that follow, a general preoccupation with a certain range of intellectual problems—or, I might better say, a particular sort of intellectual endeavor: the search for what Ortega called "liberty of spirit . . . intellectual power . . . measured by its capacity to dissociate ideas traditionally inseparable."* In the twentieth century—especially with the emergence of the "New Culture" in the teens and twenties, and in its aftermath—this endeavor reaches the point of articulation, and becomes a part of the ongoing history of Chinese liberalism and Chinese radicalism. I suggest, however, that one may also assess the significance of nineteenth-century reform, and of the radical politics of the first decade of this century, in light of this rather general concern.

Many intellectuals who labored mightily to sustain the tradition of philosophical and scholarly discourse, even in untraditional terms, but who did not elect to publish their opinions on broader issues of political

---

* José Ortega y Gasset, *The Revolt of the Masses* (New York: W. W. Norton & Co., 1957), p. 42.

and cultural significance, are not accorded here the attention they would merit in a more generously proportioned history. Harder to justify, by my own criteria, is the fact that I have not dealt with modern Chinese literary personalities, with the exception of Lu Hsun, who seems always to stand as a case apart. Many of the intellectuals who do figure in these pages emphasized the importance of literature as a means of influencing public standards of opinion and behavior; from the beginning, the "new literature" that has emerged out of China's revolutionary crisis has been strongly inspired by pedagogic and social as well as aesthetic and individual motives. But to deal properly with this dimension of modern Chinese intellectual history would involve complex questions of style and substance, and, among other issues, an analysis of the literary polemics of the revolutionary period. All this would require not only more space than I have at my disposal, but also a knowledge, and an educated critical judgment, which I cannot claim to possess.

For the transcription of Chinese names and terms I have retained the still familiar Wade–Giles system of romanization, rather than the *pinyin* system that has been officially promulgated by the government of the People's Republic. This fidelity to a relic of the imperialist past is not intended as a political reproach. It does, however, express my own disappointment at a missed opportunity. The purpose of any system of romanization is—or should be—to render the sounds of a nonroman orthography or, as is the case with Chinese, a nonphonetic written language, accessible in a form which is as nearly as possible a self-evident guide to correct pronunciation. A system of romanization is not a code, in other words, but a device designed to permit the reader to approximate, with reasonable confidence, the sounds of the original language. The Yale system accomplishes this admirably, for English-speaking readers, but unfortunately it has never achieved general acceptance. Until recently, the Wades–Giles system has been almost universally found in English-language scholarly and popular literature. Anyone familiar with it knows that it does not satisfy the definition given above; but neither does the *pinyin* system, by (in my opinion) a wider margin of deviation. I strongly suspect that the uninitiated reader of English will feel more at ease, for example, in the presence of Tz'u Hsi, the Dowager Empress of the Ch'ing dynasty, as Wade–Giles has it, than with her formidable *pinyin* counterpart, Cixi, the Dowager Empress of the Qing dynasty. It should be a matter of more general protest than it has been, I think, that the authority of the Peking government was not brought to bear in behalf of a system more rather than less sensible, from the point of view of the average reader, than the systems that *pinyin* is intended to replace. As a concession to the powers that be, however, I have cross-indexed Chinese names and terms according to both Wade–Giles and *pinyin*, and a pronunciation guide to both systems is appended.

Acknowledgments

A book of this kind draws heavily, and gratefully, on existing literature in the field, both scholarly and interpretive. Many of my debts will be evident from the notes; others are mentioned in the bibliography. To acknowledge, or even to recognize, all of them is beyond my power. But to some I owe particular thanks. To my former teachers, John K. Fairbank and Benjamin I. Schwartz, my gratitude grows warmer with the passing years and the experience they have brought. My students at Brown, undergraduate and graduate, have been a patient audience for many of the ideas presented here; I wish especially to thank Hsiung Ping-chen for her careful comments on the entire manuscript; and Kevin Fountain, Walter Montgomery, Frederic Spar, and Andrew Sommer for useful suggestions, or for drawing my attention to materials I would otherwise have missed. Abbott Gleason, Eric Widmer, and Lea E. Williams, my colleagues in the History Department at Brown, have generously given of their time, their knowledge and their encouragement. To James E. Sheridan, who suggested that I write the book and then bore with unfailing good humor the long drawn-out writing of it, I owe a debt of friendship for his insightful and candid criticism of the manuscript. Sharon Rafferty has expertly done all the typing. No author could hope for more helpful and congenial editors than I have had in Colin Jones and, latterly, George A. Rowland at The Free Press.

The Joint Committee on Contemporary China of the Social Science Research Council; the American Universities Field Staff; and Brown University have all at one time or another, and in one way or another, supported the research and the writing.

Needless to say, I alone am responsible for the views expressed here, and for the errors that remain.

Finally, for their affectionate confidence and extraordinary patience I am more grateful than I can properly express to my parents, my children Lidian and Paul, and especially my wife, to whom the book is dedicated with thanks and love.

JEROME B. GRIEDER

Providence, Rhode Island
January, 1981

Pronunciation Guide

Chinese is *not* a difficult language to pronounce correctly; it contains few sounds which are unnatural to the speaker of English. It is, rather, the systems of romanization commonly in use that make the sounds of Chinese appear exotic, and too often defeat the efforts of the uninitiated to approximate the correct pronunciation.

Following is a brief and untechnical explanation of the two systems of romanization most frequently found in English-language literature on China. The Wade–Giles system, long the standard, is the product of nineteenth-century sinological invention. It is now gradually being replaced by the *pinyin* system officially adopted by the government of the People's Republic, which is intended to become the international standard system. As I have said in the Preface, neither system is satisfactory; of the two, the Wade–Giles system is the less objectionable in my opinion, and I have used it throughout this book. In the Index, however, Chinese names and terms are cross-indexed according to both systems.

The Wade–Giles system

Vowel sounds

   a is pronounced like the *a* in f*a*ther.
   e is pronounced like the *u* in *u*p; except when it follows *i* or *y*, when it
        is pronounced like the first *e* in *e*ver.
   i is pronounced like the *e* in *e*ven; except when followed by *h*, when
        -*ih* is pronounced rather like the -*ir* in st*ir*, or the -*urr* in b*urr*.
   o is pronounced like the *o* in l*o*ft.

u is pronounced like the *u* in r*u*le.

ü is pronounced like the German umlaut *ü*, or the French *u*.

In combination, vowel sounds are always run together as diphthongs; thus *ai* = *i* in *i*ce, *ou* = *o* in *o*bey, *ao* = -*ow* in c*ow*.

When it follows *tz* or *ss*, the final *u* is hardly sounded.

Consonants

In standard (Mandarin) Chinese, -*n* and -*ng* are the only final consonants. To no real purpose, Wade–Giles introduces a final -*h*, as in *yeh* and *chieh*, which is not sounded. (Familiar names like Sun Yat-sen and Chiang Kai-shek are romanizations of non-Mandarin dialect pronunciations.)

Initial consonants present no great difficulty, so long as the following conventions are observed. The Wade–Giles system distinguishes unaspirated (or unvoiced) consonants from aspirated (or voiced) consonants by employing an apostrophe (') to indicate aspirated consonants. This yields the following pairings:

Unaspirated	*Aspirated*
ch is pronounced as the *j* in *j*aws	*ch'* is pronounced as the *ch* in *ch*aws
k is pronounced as the *g* in *g*ood	*k'* is pronounced as the *k* in *k*ind
p is pronounced as the *b* in *b*are	*p'* is pronounced as the *p* in *p*are
t is pronounced as the *d* in *d*ear	*t'* is pronounced as the *t* in *t*ear

Although technically distinguishable, *ts* and *tz* sound very much alike, and may be pronounced roughly like the -*ds* in rea*ds*. Likewise, *ts'* and *tz'* both approximate the sound of the -*ts* in ra*ts*.

hs occurs only before *i* and *ü*, and is similar in sound to *sh* which occurs before *a*, *e* and *u*.

j is pronounced like the *r* in *r*un, with just a hint of something like the French *j* mixed in.

ss is identical in sound to *s*.

The pinyin system

Vowel sounds

With respect to vowel sounds, the *pinyin* and Wade–Giles systems are similar, with the following exceptions:

Wade–Giles *u* becomes *ou* or *o* in *pinyin*. Thus, for example, *yu* becomes *you;* *lung* becomes *long*.

Wade–Giles *ü* becomes *u*, except following *l*. Thus *yü* becomes *yu;* *lü* is the same in either system.

Wade–Giles *-en* becomes *-an*, and *-ien* becomes *-ian*. Thus *yen* becomes *yan*, and *lien* becomes *lian*.

Wade–Giles *-u* and *-ih* become *i*. Thus *ssu* becomes *si*, and *shih* becomes *shi*.

Consonants

In its treatment of consonants, *pinyin* often makes more self-evident sense than does Wade–Giles. The apostrophe (') disappears; one is back again in the world of *b* and *d* and *g*, where p and t and k sound as one would expect them to sound; *j* is no longer *r*, and is assigned its own function; etc. There are, however, some formidable surprises in store for the unwary, of which the more remarkable are summarized below:

Wade–Giles	*Pinyin*
ch- as in *chi* or *chien*	*j-* as in *ji* or *jian*
ch- as in *chih* or *chung*	*zh-* as in *zhi* or *zhong*
ch'- as in *ch'i* or *ch'ing*	*q-* as in *qi* or *qing*
ch'- as in *ch'ang* or *ch'u*	*ch-* as in *chang* or *chu*
ts- as in *tsai* or *tseng*	*z* as in *zai* or *zeng*
ts'- as in *ts'ai*	*c* as in *cai*
hs- as in *hsi* or *hsueh*	*x* as in *xi* or *xue*
ss- as in *ssu*	*s* as in *si*

Chinese written characters are invariably monosyllabic. The basic unit of the written and spoken language, however, is commonly a compound of two (or more) characters, so that any system of romanization must contend with polysyllabic terms. In the Wade–Giles system, syllables are ordinarily separated by a hyphen, as in the term *t'ien-hsia*, or in the given name of an individual, which in most cases will have two syllables, as in Chang Chih-tung. *Pinyin* does not hyphenate between syllables, nor separate them; thus, for the examples used here it would give *tianxia* and Zhang Zhidong. In rare cases in which the syllable break may not be obvious, *pinyin* employs an apostrophe, as in the place-name Yan'an, which might otherwise be confused with characters pronounced *ye nan*.

For purposes of comparison, a few names and titles drawn at random from the text may be of interest. They are given below, first in the

Wade–Giles system of romanization, then as they would be romanized using the *pinyin* system.

Ch'ing   Qing [dynasty]
Ku Yen-wu   Gu Yanwu
Ch'ien Lung   Qianlong
Ssu-pu ts'ung-k'an   *Sibu congkan*
Tz'u Hsi   Cixi
Tseng Kuo-fan   Zeng Guofan
Wang T'ao   Wang Tao
Liang Ch'i-ch'ao   Liang Qichao
Hsin-min ts'ung-pao   *Xinmin congbao*
T'ung-meng hui   Tongmeng hui
Ch'en Tu-hsiu   Chen Duxiu
Hsin ch'ing-nien   *Xin qingnian*
Hu Shih   Hu Shi
Li Ta-chao   Li Dazhao

A Note on Terminology

Ages are sometimes given according to the traditional Chinese system of reckoning, or *sui*. This counted a child as one year old at birth, and added a year on the occasion of each lunar New Year thereafter. Thus the given age of a Chinese, in the old days, was never less than one, and sometimes two, years older than it would be by Western count.

The silver *tael* (abbreviated Tls.) was the standard unit of monetary value in imperial China. It was considered roughly the equivalent of one ounce, though both fineness and weight varied considerably from place to place. The standard unit of monetary exchange in day-to-day transactions was usually the copper cash.

The imperial examination system, which established gentry status and eligibility for bureaucratic appointment, was an important milestone in many of the lives touched upon in this narrative. The examinations were ordinarily held triennially, scheduled to fall in successive years. In ascending order of prestige (and, perhaps, difficulty) these were the prefectural examinations, at which the *hsiu-ts'ai* (in *pinyin: xiucai*) degree was awarded; the provincial examinations, where one might hope to enter the ranks of the "upper" gentry by winning the *chü-jen* (*juren*) degree; and, at the top, the metropolitan examinations held in Peking, where the *chin-shih* (*jinshi*) degree was awarded. In addition, "special examinations" were sometimes given for various reasons. There were also preparatory examinations for would-be candidates for the prefectural examination, and "Palace examinations" presided over the emperor himself to identify the most talented of those who had won the *chin-shih* degree. (The analogy sometimes drawn to the B.A., M.A., and Ph.D. degrees is essentially false: in content and in the style of education required for success, there was little difference among the several levels of the imperial examination system.)

The Inheritance

I go back from age to age up to the remotest antiquity, but I find no parallel to what is occurring before my eyes; as the past has ceased to throw its light upon the future, the mind of man wanders in obscurity.

—*Alexis de Tocqueville*

CHANGE IS THE GREAT THEME of modern Chinese history. Not change merely, but a vast, imponderable transformation that overwhelms any defense erected against it, overflows the channels intended to give it limit and direction, sweeps institutions and individuals before it. Chinese living in the last half of the nineteenth century or the first half of the twentieth would instinctively have understood Tocqueville's epitaph on *l'ancien régime:* and none with a more devastating sense of bewilderment than Chinese intellectuals, whether they stood as defenders of an imperiled tradition or as its critics. The crumbling of the world view that earlier generations had relied upon as certain and immutable, and the erosion of the social and political institutions that upheld the traditional order, challenged the content of inherited belief, and undermined the intellectuals' sense of vocational opportunity and social purpose. In a very personal way, then, modern Chinese intellectuals have confronted change. They have sought to deny it, to impede it; or to understand and justify it; or to shape and control it. They have been both its instruments and its victims.

Yet the enabling premise of history is that something of the past is imparted to the present: however distant and different it may be, the present carries within it something of an ineradicable past. So, although modern Chinese intellectuals have rejected much of their inheritance, they have received from it much which they did not, perhaps could not, renounce. Even detached from the foundation of intellectual confidence and vocational usefulness on which the edifice of Confucian identity rested, a sense of social obligation and purpose has remained one of the dominant motives of modern Chinese intellectual life. In the chapters that follow we will be concerned not only with what these intellectuals have thought about their common times and particular circumstances, but also, although less directly, with their effort to make for themselves, in the new order of things, a place commensurate with their inherited sense of the social responsibilities that intellectuals should bear.

New visions of the intellectuals' role are thus an important part of the history before us. But one cannot hope to comprehend the complexity and pathos of the situation in which modern Chinese intellectuals have found themselves without first perceiving the traditional order against which they reacted as a coherent and, in its own setting and terms, a compellingly persuasive system of social and intellectual values—abandoned by some reluctantly, by others enthusiastically, by none without cost.

*   *   *

We are accustomed to thinking of "traditional" China in terms of its own idealized self-image, as an essentially immutable society and culture, a harmonious moral community. We must therefore remind ourselves at the outset that these very ideals reflect a mirror image of the historical realities out of which emerged the first coherent expressions of Chinese social and political thought. In the declining age of Chou-dynasty feudalism, from the sixth century B.C., the time of Confucius, until the consolidation of a centralized imperial government under the Ch'in and Han dynasties in the third and second centuries B.C., China underwent a political and social transformation more gradual, and perhaps less dramatic, but certainly no less far-reaching in its significance and in its consequences than the revolution of recent decades. China's "traditional" political and social ideals and attitudes were, in other words, the radical prescriptions born of a time of troubles that left an indelible mark on the Chinese mind and memory.

Different thinkers responded differently to the general sense of crisis. The early philosophical Taoists rejected the very idea of government, in the same spirit in which they rejected everything else "man-made" (*wei*)—artifices intended, as they saw it, to conceal the fact that man has become separated from his spontaneous nature, his oneness with the *Tao*, the Way. At the opposite extreme, the followers of the school of law, the "Legalists" as they are conventionally known, insisted that order must be imposed without regard for the variable quality of human character, by a lawgiver who acts upon the premise that human nature is uniformly motivated by passion and self-interest and who therefore serves his own interests by making the preservation of the state his primary, and indeed his singular, concern. Somewhere between these two extreme approaches to the problem of how to achieve order out of the political and moral anarchy of the times stood a third school—that of the "scholars," the *ju*; or, as we know them, the Confucians. But Confucianism, as we shall see, though it admired moderation, was much more than an attempt to strike a moderate pose.

In speaking of imperial Chinese society or government or culture—that is, in speaking of China itself at virtually any point during the two millennia preceding the collapse of the Manchu (or, as it styled itself in Chinese, the Ch'ing, that is, the Pure) dynasty in 1911—the terms "traditional" and "Confucian" are often used interchangeably. There is excellent reason for this, despite the fact that Confucianism was only one among many schools of thought that flourished during the crisis-ridden centuries of contending states and contending philosophies that preceded the establishment of the first imperial authority at the end of the third century B.C. With its early rival, Taoism, Confucianism managed to live peaceably enough in later times: "A Confucian in office, a Taoist out of office" expressed proverbially a very real division in the Chinese personality between the busyness of bureaucratic responsibilities and the longing for a life of contemplative rustication. "A Government building, not my own home," lamented the great T'ang-dynasty poet Po Chü-i during his tenure as governor of Soochow. "A Government garden, not my own trees. But at Lo-yang I have a small house, and on Wei River I have built a thatched hut."[1] With other schools of thought, like the contemporary Legalist *realpolitik* and, much later and in very different ways, the Buddhist metaphysic that infiltrated Chinese life after the second century A.D., Confucianism remained in fundamental opposition. Yet it was Confucianism that gave enduring expression to many of the values that animated Chinese culture, the organizational principles underlying Chinese government, and the habits on which traditional social life depended. Taking to itself what it needed from its adversaries, or what it could not overcome, it became with time a richer and in some respects quite different thing from what it had once been. Still, the original concerns of Confucianism remained the dominant concerns of all later generations of scholars, teachers, statesmen, and bureaucrats; the categories of Chinese thought remained, in broad outline, Confucian; and most important, it was Confucian aspiration which enlivened intellectual life and gave it the coherence and sense of purpose which is its most remarkable aspect.

Confucianism, in its narrowest meaning, signifies the moral precepts and social visions enshrined in the ancient literary relics known as *ching*, the classic texts. These dealt primarily with ethics, ritual conduct, and the remote history of the culture—distinguishable but not, in the Confucian view, separable categories; part and parcel, rather, of a unifying

concern for questions of social governance, with ritual as its art and instrument and history as its documentary authority. Fragments of this
early literature were identified with the historical figure of Confucius
himself (551–479 B.C.), although he spoke of himself as a transmitter,
not an author. The *Analects* (*Lun-yü*), a collection of epigrams and
homilies supposedly directed at his disciples, may comprise, at least in
part, the *ipsissima verba* of the Sage. Other texts, like the *Classic of
Poetry* (*Shih ching*) and the *Classic of History* (*Shu ching*), fragments of
which date from pre-Confucian centuries, were used by him as the basis
for his own teaching, and thus incorporated into the Confucian canon.
Still others, like the texts of Mencius (c. 390–305 B.C.) and of Hsun-tzu
(c. 312–236 B.C.), were elaborations of Confucian teachings set down in
the chaotic waning centuries of the classical millennium.

By late imperial times, two thousand years later, this original corpus
had inspired an enormous accretion of derivative literature as it passed
under the sometimes careless hands of generations of copyists and the
often opinionated scrutiny of generations of editors. Though still centered
on a fairly small number of seminal texts, Confucian literature came to
comprise a vast library of commentaries, exegeses and emenda-
tions—some of such size and complexity as to constitute virtually
autonomous philosophical enterprises, as is the case with the intricate
metaphysic erected by T'ang- and Sung-dynasty "neo-Confucian"
thinkers on the foundation of the straightforward social ethic of early
Confucianism. Confucian values, moreover, came to permeate other
literary styles: historical writing, both formal and informal; belles lettres
and poetry; and even such "popular" forms as drama and the narrative
traditions which became, in the Ming and Ch'ing dynasties, the basis for
a vernacular literature.

The Confucian literary tradition was thus an inheritance with which
modern Chinese intellectuals were compelled to come to terms, not only
by its bulk, but also by the comprehensive grandeur of its intellectual
scope. They had also to come to terms with its animating concerns: its
preoccupation with social hierarchy and harmony, true kingship, and
public virtue—qualities starkly absent from the political life of those
strife-torn centuries during which Confucianism became a self-conscious
mode of thought.

There is, of course, no single and uniform "Confucian mentality."
Nor was there, in any formal sense, a Confucian creed, acceptance of
which distinguished the true believer. "I have no 'thou shall' or 'thou
shalt not'," says the Confucius of the *Analects*.[2] From the beginning,
then, the Confucian temper was at odds with the doctrinally dogmatic
and exclusive faith urged upon the Chinese by Christian evangelists inter-
mittently from the fourteenth century onward. The Italian Franciscan
monk, Andrew of Perugia, who served as bishop of the briefly flourishing
Christian community at Zayton (near modern Amoy) in the 1320s, put it

better than he knew, perhaps, when he reported to his superiors, "'Tis a fact that in this vast empire there are people of every nation under heaven, and of every sect, and all and sundry are allowed to live freely according to their creed. For they hold this opinion, or rather this erroneous view, that everyone can find salvation in his own religion. How be it we are at liberty to preach without let or hindrance."[3] This is not to say, however, that Confucianism did not ordain and establish the primacy of certain concerns, or that it set thereby no limits to the nature and purposes of human inquiry. So much so, indeed, that by the beginning of the twentieth century, reformers grounded still in Confucian belief were compelled to acknowledge the existence of a wider world of possibility. "I love Confucius," wrote Liang Ch'i-ch'ao, one of the greatest of them, "but I love the truth more."[4]

Knowledge, says Confucius in the *Analects*, means "to know man" (12:22). A commitment to humanist values is sometimes cited as evidence of the consonance between traditional Chinese and Western (Greek and/or Renaissance) perceptions of social good. Yet comparable concerns do not invariably breed similar responses. Certainly the Chinese of the late Chou period were sensitive to the general query from which all political philosophy originates—the question of why men obey, or ought to obey, a government, and to what limit. The humanistic strain in Confucianism, however, reflected assumptions intrinsic to the particular circumstances to which it was itself a response: the decline of the loosely structured feudalism of the Chou period. Questions of justice or freedom as abstract possibilities, of citizenship as a political condition, of the origins of social organization, or the genesis of political legitimacy do not figure in the Chinese traditions of political speculation in the same way, or to the same degree, that they appear in the history of Western political thought.

Confucianism assumes that social inequality, the inequality which ordains that most men will do the bidding of someone else, reflects not merely social necessity, but conformity to a natural order of things. Inequality is natural rather than artificial and imposed, first in that it takes as its model that most natural of prototypes, the patriarchal family. Though Confucians were aware that loyalty to the family and loyalty to the community or the state could be incompatible at the level of conduct, they did not discriminate (as, for example, John Locke discriminates in the *Second Treatise*) between the natural and private authority of the father and the constituted and public authority of the ruler as different *kinds* of "government." In the Confucian view, political authority required no other sanction, such as the deification of the ruler or the perpetuation of an unbroken dynastic succession, than the natural sanction which upheld the authority of the family: the moral quality intrinsic to it.

Inequality, in the Confucian view, is natural in a second and more fundamental sense as well, arising from the assumption that men are by nature endowed with different and, in respect to social function, unequal capabilities. Where one fits into the hierarchy of social and political relationships depends not only on differences of age, sex, or kinship, but also on social competence. One's place is determined by the function one is fit to perform. "There is the work of great men and there is the work of little men," said Mencius. "Therefore it is said, 'Some labor with their minds and some labor with their strength. Those who labor with their minds govern others; those who labor with their strength are governed by others.' Those who are governed by others support them; those who govern them are supported by them. This is a universal principle."[5]

In the manner of the advocate, Mencius somewhat overstates, or at least oversimplifies the case: Confucian opinion was not unambiguous on the question of the natural human endowment. Mencius himself, whose adamant discrimination between headworkers and handworkers made him the patron of the effete, long-nailed literati culture of later imperial times, was also responsible for another dictum that became an even more fundamental Confucian article of faith: Man's nature, he said, is "originally good." That is, all men possess by nature an incipient sense of right conduct; all men are capable of making moral choices, not rationally but instinctively, and are thus fit for social life. But society, in this understanding of it, is not a bargain struck to secure and promote individual interests; it is, rather, the natural and essential condition of human existence.*

To say that this is the human possibility is not to insist that it is the human reality. Confucians were not blind to the depravity of their world or to the worsening conditions of their times. Hsun-tzu, some decades after Mencius, objected to the latter's optimistic estimate of human nature, which in Hsun-tzu's view is motivated not by benign instinct, but by selfish passions. The political implications of this difference of opinion—the extent to which government must take upon itself disciplinary and coercive responsibilities—are obviously considerable. In terms of social strategy, however, the two views are not incompatible. Mencius, Hsun-tzu, and with them all later Confucians believed that men behave as their situations, their conditions of life, and their education permit. "Environment is the important thing! Environment is the important

---

* In The Concept of Man in Early China, Donald Munro argues that the distinguishing feature of early Chinese thought, Taoist as well as Confucian, is the assumption of "natural equality." It is, however, equality in this latter sense that he means, the attribution to mankind generally of the "evaluating mind" by means of which moral choice is possible. In terms of Chinese social structure—and, I believe, Confucian social theory—the importance attached to inequalities of social competence looms larger than the assumption of an abstract equality in respect to discrimination between "proper" and "improper" conduct. It is certainly true, however, that the Confucian belief in man's "aptness for society" (to which Hsun-tzu took exception) is crucial to the Confucian theory of government.

thing!" cried Hsun-tzu at the end of his discourse on the "evilness" of human nature.[6]

Confucian attention was thus from the very beginning fastened upon the real world, the world of men. Confucius' indifference to speculative conundrums is well-known: "If we do not know about life, how can we know about death?"[7] He discoursed, according to the *Analects*, not about "strange phenomena, physical exploits, natural disorders and spiritual beings," but about "culture, conduct, loyalty, and faithfulness."[8] Confucian problems were the problems of men living in society—not, to be sure, as social or vocational equals, but nevertheless in hierarchical relationships that were assumed to be ideally, and potentially, harmonious.

Confucians differed as to the sources of social harmony. Hsun-tzu, in line with his pessimistic vision of human nature, held social organization to be an artifice: the inheritance bequeathed by the singularly enlightened rulers of high antiquity whose wisdom was manifest in the rituals that must serve as the markers to later generations groping through the half-light of a degenerate age. Mencius, whose gentler opinion in this as in other respects eventually became orthodox Confucian doctrine, regarded man as instinctively social, requiring only (though too often in vain) the humane presence of a virtuous ruler, a "true king" sympathetic to human moral needs, in order to live at peace with himself and with others. Government, in the Mencian view, is the spontaneous reward of such rulership, for "the people turn in allegiance to Humanity, as surely as water flows downward or as a wild animal takes cover in the wilderness."[9]

Mencius' concern for "the people" (*min*), expressed again and again in the text that bears his name, and echoed in much later Confucian writing, more than anything else lends substance to the claim—an entirely modern claim, be it noted—that Confucianism carried within it the spirit of a genuine populism, a democratic promise.[10] It is certainly true that Mencius' admonitions to the ruler to remain ever mindful of the welfare of his people exerted an enduring ideological restraint against unscrupulous tyranny. To what extent it was also an effective political constraint is far less certain, as we shall see. Nevertheless, the injunction was there, at the very heart of Confucian doctrine: "There is a way to gain the Empire. It is to gain the people. . . . There is a way to gain the people. Gain their sympathy. . . . Share with them the accumulation of the things you wish for, and do not practice what goes against them."[11] And coupled with this came a warning as old as the most ancient records of the culture: "Heaven sees as the people see. Heaven hears as the people hear."[12] This is the classic formulation of the celebrated "Mandate of Heaven," the idea that the acquiescence of those who are governed legitimates the governing power, that rulership is, in this sense, conditional. The phrase itself calls to mind John Locke's "The people shall judge," and on this account Mencius has been given credit by some not only for entertaining democratic sentiments, but also for harboring revolutionary sympathies. The similarity, however, is deceptive. The ruler's position, as Mencius envisioned it, was not one of prerogatives definable by law or reducible to the terms of a "contract," albeit fictitious; nor would it have occured to Mencius to treat the ruler, as Locke does, as the people's "trustee or deputy," dischargeable for due cause. The ascendancy of the Confucian ruler was moral, not social: he was not elevated by the community to safeguard its own common interests but was rather, by virtue of his own moral character, the natural focal point of loyalty and source of authority.

What Confucian theory emphasized, then, was not the restless, potentially destructive competition of private interests that necessitates invocation of a public good as the price of social tranquility and continuity; but, quite to the contrary, the assumed consonance of moral instincts that makes the social community the spontaneous expression of human nature. Fundamental to this belief was a belief in the greater harmony which the social order reflects and of which it is a part. Order is pervasive: it is the essence of the *Tao*, the Way, a concept central to all schools of Chinese thought, and elastic enough to fit the particular uses to which each put it. The Way is benign—a harmonious order could not be otherwise—but without design. No purpose is ascribed to it, nor any vestige of personality. "Heaven does not speak, yet the four seasons run their course thereby, the hundred creatures, each after its kind, are born thereby. Heaven does not speak!"[13] Neither the natural nor the social order was conceived of as ordained, brought into being by the decree of some creative Power. Each was spontaneous, and both were essentially and inseparably bound together, not by the dictates of a natural law, but, as it were, in sympathetic resonance.

Confucians did not suppose that man could achieve the fullest measure of his nature without effort; and effort meant education. Learning, not revelation, was what Confucius prided himself on. "I once spent a whole day without food and a whole night without sleep, in order to meditate," he is made to say in the *Analects*. "It was no use. It is better to study."[14] Mencius, with his amiable confidence in human goodness, was not consistently certain that spontaneity and instinct required the refinement of education. "All things are complete within ourselves," he once remarked, and on another occasion he observed that "the great man is one who never loses his [originally good] child's heart."[15] From such suggestive utterances sprang, in later centuries, an introspective and meditative school of Confucianism quite different in temperament from orthodox scholasticism. Yet Mencius affirmed even more explicitly than Confucius himself the importance of the Way of the Former Kings—that is, the wisdom of the sages, enshrined in the classic texts, which (in the

Mencian metaphor) is to the building of the edifice of moral character what squares and compasses are to the carpenter in his craft. Hsun-tzu recognized the threat to textual and political authority implied by Mencius' benign view of human nature. "Suppose that man's nature was in fact intrinsically upright, reasonable, and orderly," he asked; "then what need would there be for sage kings and ritual principles?"[16] He was, as we might expect, the sternest Confucian pedagogue. "If there is no dark and dogged will, there will be no shining accomplishment," he admonished. "If there is no dull and determined effort, there will be no brilliant achievement. . . . Learning begins with recitation of the Classics and ends with the reading of the ritual texts; . . . it begins with learning to be a man of breeding, and ends with learning to be a sage. . . . Learning continues until death. . . . To pursue it is to be a man, to give it up is to become a beast."[17]

The Confucian theory of education is succinctly set forth in the opening statement of the *Doctrine of the Mean* (*Chung yung*), one of the cardinal texts: "What Nature imparts to Man is called human nature. To follow our nature is called the Way. Cultivating the Way is called education."[18] Education, in other words, is the process of becoming what one is by nature predisposed to be: it is self-cultivation and self-realization. The implication is that culture, the "breeding" of which Hsun-tzu spoke, is an essentially private—that is, personal and individual—responsibility and accomplishment. The values of culture cannot be communicated or understood in the abstract: they can only be exemplified in individual conduct. Thus it is that "the Way of the Former Kings" looms so large in the Confucian consciousness; that so much attention is lavished, in the *Analects* and in other texts, on the personal deportment of Confucius; that Hsun-tzu speaks with such reverence of the role of the teacher.

It was the function of the Confucian curriculum to establish and maintain the general standards that would prevent such individual accomplishment from becoming individualistic and idiosyncratic. To this end, the texts create an unbreakable linkage between self-cultivation and social vocation, between personal culture and social order. Confucian argument starts from, and invariably returns to, a concern for government. Human (and humane) government is the social counterpart of cosmic harmony and order, the condition which men by instinct seek, and which alone gives fullest expression to their nature. This perception is summarized with great poetic force in chapter 31 of the *Doctrine of the Mean*:

Only the perfect sage in the world has quickness of apprehension, intelligence, insight, and wisdom, which enable him to rule all men; magnanimity, generosity, benignity, and tenderness, which enable him to embrace all men; vigor, strength, firmness, and resolution, which enable him to maintain a firm hold; orderliness, seriousness, adherence to the Mean, and correctness, which enable him to be reverent; pattern, order, refinement, and penetration, which enable him to exercise discrimination. All embracing and extensive, and deep and unceasingly springing, these virtues come forth at all times. All embracing and extensive as heaven and deep and unceasingly springing as an abyss! He appears and all people respect him, speaks and all people believe him, acts and all people are pleased with him. Consequently his fame spreads overflowingly over the Middle Kingdom and extends to barbarous tribes. Wherever ships and carriages reach, wherever the labor of man penetrates, wherever the heavens overshadow and the earth sustains, wherever the sun and moon shine, and wherever frosts and dew fall, all who have blood and breath honor and love him. Therefore we say that he is a counterpart of Heaven.[19]

The idea of government is thus a very broad one, mystical in its overtones, and yet firmly grounded in the personality of the ruler on the one hand, and in the human qualities of his subjects on the other. "The superior man governs men as men, in accordance with human nature. . . ."[20]

We may summarize what has been said to this point thus: In the Confucian view of history and culture, it is the humane insight of the sage rulers of remote antiquity in which originate the forms of ritual conduct that, taken together, comprise the institutions of humane government. Government, in the broadest sense, in its turn maintains a tradition of learning in order to communicate from one generation to the next the cultural values which, absorbed through education, offer the means for perfecting individual character. Self-cultivation, however, is not viewed as a proper end in itself, but as the means by which humane government will be perpetuated. The underlying pattern is one of endless replication, not linear development. Whatever their differences, early Confucians agreed that, though the sage rulers stood at the very threshold of the history of the culture, the qualities they exemplified were by no means remote: Mencius and Hsun-tzu explicitly affirm the immanence of sageliness in humankind. Such confidence in the perfectability of human conduct did not, as we shall see, preclude the belief that, since the Golden Age of high antiquity, history was largely the record of progressive degeneration. The point to be stressed here, however, is that Confucian thought contained no concept of the fall from grace; nor did it hold forth the promise of redemption from the troubles of this world through any superhuman agency. What Hsun-tzu called "dull and determined effort" was the only redeeming hope to sustain generations of Confucian moralists.

The Confucian was a humanist and, as such, a generalist. He pursued education not for the purpose, primarily, of acquiring "knowledge," but in order to appropriate the forms of ritual conduct and literary expression—and, presumably, the values that gave meaning to such forms—which would make him the example of a cultural style. "The superior man is not an implement," said Confucius,[21] a warning taken to mean both that the superior man should not place his talent at the disposal of an unworthy ruler, and that he should prepare himself to act widely, not merely in the performance of too narrowly specialized a social or bureaucratic function. He should be no less than the living embodiment of the ideals of the culture, ideals which were themselves inconceivable apart from their exemplification in the social vocation of the superior man.

There was, in other words, no distinction drawn in the theory of Confucianism between private and public conduct. "When the Way prevails in the state," says the *Doctrine of the Mean*, "if the superior man enters public life, he does not change from what he was in private life."[22] A famous chapter from another of the seminal texts, the *Great Learning* (*Ta hsueh*), points the same moral, linking in concentric circles of argument the management of the affairs of the world at large (*t'ien-hsia*) to self-knowledge and self-discipline, and closing with this admonition: "From the Son of Heaven down to the common people, all must regard cultivation of the personal life as the root or foundation. There is never a case in which the root is in disorder and yet the branches are in order. . . ."[23]

The whole Confucian theory of government hinges upon acceptance of the notion that there is no distinction between public and private personality, and thus no tension between ruler and ruled, no differences of interest between government and governed. Only in light of such assumptions can one make sense of the Confucian vision of a government which rules without seeming to rule, and of the true king as one who occupies his rightful position "like the pole star, which remains in its place while all the lesser stars do homage to it."[24] The link forged between private education, or self-cultivation, and public vocation laid a great burden of social and moral responsibility upon the individual, while at the same time minimizing the possibility that this might lead to the assertion of self-directed individuality and thus create a sense of private interests in conflict with the public concerns of state and culture.

Viewing these ideas from the perspective of Western—or, more precisely, *modern* Western—traditions of political thought, it is tempting to conclude that what distinguished the Confucian polity is the pervasiveness of *public* power: the authority of the state, of the society, of the culture (or the Confucian amalgam of all-in-one) as against and above the autonomous authority of the individual personality. It is therefore startling to note that Chinese reformers toward the end of the nineteenth century and in the early years of the twentieth century, preoccupied with the overwhelming question of China's survival as a political order, came to almost exactly the opposite conclusion. What China most conspicuously and painfully lacked, they said, was just that sense of common identities and interests, common moral purposes, that could generate the sentiment of public loyalty, the sense of public virtue, the commitment to public responsibilities and obligations, which would ensure the survival of the nation.

What led them to this opinion was, of course, partly the threatening circumstances of a time in which it did not seem unreasonably gloomy to suppose that China might indeed cease to exist either as a political entity or as a cultural tradition; a time in which, therefore, it became paramount to reassess the connection between cultural inheritance and political identity. In part, moreover, turn-of-the-century reformist opinion was shaped by the awareness, hardly new, but very likely more keenly felt, of the great disparity between political and social ideals on the one hand, and political and social realities on the other. The imperial state in its despotic actuality was a thing far different from the moral community of Confucian imagination, bound together by the persuasive authority of virtuous rulership. In the nineteenth century, an experienced and knowledgeable Western observer—an American missionary long resident in China—depicted the workings of imperial government as it then existed in these bleak terms:

> The great leading principles by which the present administration preserves its power over the people, consist in a system of *strict surveillance* and *mutual responsibility* among all classes. . . . It is like a network extending over the whole face of society, each individual being isolated in his own mesh, but responsibly connected with all around him.
>
> The effect . . . upon the masses of the people is to imbue them with a great fear of government, both of its officers and its operations; each man considers that safety is best to be found in keeping aloof from both. This mutual surveillance and responsibility, though only partially extended throughout the multitude, necessarily undermines confidence and infuses universal distrust, while the object of complete isolation, though at the expense of justice, truth, honesty, and natural affection, is what the government strives to accomplish and actually does to a wonderful degree. The idea of government in the minds of the uneducated people is that of some ever-present terror. . . . Thus, with a state of society sometimes on the verge of insurrection, this mass of people is kept in check by the threefold cord of responsibility, fear and isolation.[25]

This description carries with it, naturally, the general values of nineteenth-century Western culture, as well as something of the particular prejudice intrinsic to the Christian evangelistic enterprise. Yet the picture it presents is sufficiently corroborated in Chinese sources to suggest that this grim image of imperial despotism is not too dramatically overdrawn. The chasm that separated the benign social vision expressed, for example, in the passage from the *Doctrine of the Mean* cited above, from the harsh realities of imperial ambition here described, had troubled the Confucian conscience long before the final crisis of Confucian self-confidence in the nineteenth and twentieth centuries. It is not our purpose to attempt to account for it here. But neither can we ignore it, insofar as the sense of identity which sustained the Confucian sense of moral purpose involved not only the intellectual tradition which we have been discussing, but also the attitude toward this tradition of those who perceived themselves as its inheritors and examplars, their view of the culture in which they participated, and of their relationship to the society which they dominated and the political order which they served.

*   *   *

Reduced to its essentials, Confucian social theory was remarkably simple and straighforward. The Mencian division of society into two primary categories—the rulers and the ruled, those who work with their minds and those who work with their hands—resulted, when translated into terms of the social strata of late imperial China, in a rather crude distinction drawn between the emperor and his officers on the one hand, and, on the other, the "commoners," the masses of the "people" (*shu min*). In fact, as we might expect, the social situation was considerably more complex. At the top stood the emperor: the sovereign power, the unchallenged source of all authority. Around him gathered the imperial establishment: the nobility, linked to the imperial line by bonds of kinship or political alliance and, in the case of the "alien" Manchu dynasty, by distinctions intended to preserve a carefully guarded ethnic identity. The bureaucracy, the emperor's officials high and low, was in theory no more than an extension of his personality, executor of his august will. By Ch'ing times, the emperor was in fact burdened by an extraordinary weight of administrative responsibility on a day-to-day basis. Yet in as far-flung and diverse an enterprise as the Chinese empire, administrative functions and, to a considerable extent, administrative initiative was necessarily portioned out to the officials in actual charge of the wide-ranging business of government. The imperial bureaucracy was thus itself a governing elite, though never independent of the emperor's policy, nor beyond the reach of his whim, nor safe from his displeasure.

It was officialdom, moreover, which constituted the link between Confucian theory and political reality. "Virtue" was imputed to the emperor, as necessity demanded. "Who but a great sage would be worthy to receive the Mandate of Heaven and become Emperor?" wrote the historian Ssu-ma Ch'ien in the first century B.C., justifying as best he could the rise to supreme power, but from the lowliest origins, of the founding emperor of the Han dynasty.[26] With the emperor's official servants it was otherwise. They were held to account: selected through rigorously competitive examinations which tested their mastery of Confucian literature and (if one accepted the crucial Confucian pedagogical premise) attested their ability to act upon the moral values which the literature articulated. It was a questionable assumption, as many Confucians themselves conceded. The examinations could and did discover a certain kind of talent, but the humanity that sanctioned the exercise of authority was much harder to discern and impossible to guarantee as a product of the examination system.

The relationship between the emperor and his officials was seldom if ever entirely trustful on either side. Without challenging the fundamentally autocratic principles of the monarchy, Confucian scholars did what they could to limit imperial ambition and to discourage the inclination of the emperor to supervise too closely the management of affairs. Tung Chung-shu, counsellor to the energetic Han Wu-ti, under whose sometimes contemptuous sponsorship Confucians began in the second century B.C. the long task of securing their privileged access to bureaucratic position, admonished the emperor to "sit on the throne of nonaction, and ride upon the perfection of his officials."[27] Wu-ti's successor expressed the impatience that such Confucian pretension more than once provoked:

> The Han have their own code, which is the code of conquerors. We are no longer living in the age of Chou, the age of government by virtue and education. The literati fail to understand the different needs of different times. They speak always of the virtues of antiquity and the evils of the present age. They impress the simple-minded, filling their ears with high-sounding and empty phrases. How is one to give positions of responsibility to men living in a utopian world and thus devoid of practical sense?[28]

The difference in temperament was enduring—but so also was the accommodation of interests between imperial master and Confucian servant. Officials might be men merely of literary taste and talent rather than paragons of social wisdom, and so fall short of the perfection ascribed to them by Tung Chung-shu; but their very mastery of the skills of literacy made them a practical necessity to the ruler, however he might scorn the woolly-headedness of their ideals and rankle at their preaching. Imperial patronage of Confucian learning was calculating and formal, but more than purely symbolic. The emperor himself was educated to a degree of proficiency in Confucian arts and to have sympathy—albeit sometimes guarded—for Confucian aims, if only for an essentially practical motive. "His training in the classical canon did not make him a philosopher," writes Harold Kahn of the great Ch'ien Lung emperor (r. 1736–1796), "but it did make him an ideologue perfectly capable of drawing upon the philosophers for the sanctions he needed to operate effectively as a king."[29] For their part, Confucian scholar-officials served imperial purposes not, at least in their own vision, as mindless agents of an arbitrary will, but as instruments of a moral cause common to master and servant alike.

The emperor, his immediate entourage, and his bureaucracy thus constituted the formal governing elite, Mencius' "rulers." Into the category of the "ruled" fell the vast majority of the Chinese people. By ancient convention, the "commoners" were further divided in accordance with the social usefulness of their vocations: the gentry (*shih*), of whom we will have more to say shortly; the peasantry (*nung*), in theory the mainstay of society, though in usual fact its victims; the artisans and craftsmen (*kung*); and last of all, the merchants (*shang*), despised in China, as in other agrarian cultures, as affluent parasites on the body of the state. Outside these comprehensive categories there remained only a small class of "mean" people—butchers, actors, isolated ethnic or cultural minorities like the boat population of Canton—so designated by virtue of the stigma of occupational or inherited status.

With the growth of an urban-centered commercial culture from the late Sung period onward, artisans and merchants, traditionally looked down upon, had in fact attained by late imperial times an economic and social importance which rendered such classical formulations anachronistic. Confucian theory, however, had not been revised to accord with social reality; and when in the nineteenth century, as in earlier ages, Confucian moralists spoke of the misfortunes of "the people," it was still, by and large, the peasant mass to which they alluded. The peasant is always there, in the fields and villages: his harvest assessed, his labor exploited to the limit; his capacity for obedience weighed; and otherwise, for the most part, neglected. An occasional poem reminds us that repeated injunctions to keep the welfare of "the people" uppermost in mind were not invariably empty exhortation. Po Chü-i wrote in the ninth century of "the strong reapers toiling on the southern hill, whose feet are burned by the hot earth they tread, whose backs are scorched by flames of the shining sky; tired they toil, caring nothing for the heat, grudging the shortness of the long summer day. A poor woman follows at the reapers' side with an infant child carried close at her breast. With her right hand she gleans the fallen grain; on her left arm a broken basket hangs. And I to-day . . . by virtue of what right have I never once tended field or tree? My government pay is three hundred tons; at the year's end I have still grain in hand."[30] Yet rarely does the peasant as a human being thus emerge from the vast Confucian literature devoted to the peasantry: frequently spoken of, sometimes spoken for, the peasant never spoke—save in the inchoate cries of rebellion. The peasantry was a mute presence, multitudinous, anonymous, inarticulate. One of the epochal events of recent history is the effort to break the impenetrable and imponderable silence of the Chinese masses—inevitably at painful cost to the heirs of the elite which, time out of mind, had given voice to the culture.

The gentry of traditional China—as it evolved, at least, from Sung

times onward—occupied a position which defied, in certain crucial
respects, the simplicity of the Mencian ruler/ruled categorization. The
gentry stood first among the classes of the "common" people, but in point
of fact their social functions placed them in an intermediary position between the governing elite and the great majority of the governed. In
Chinese sources, the terms usually translated into English as "gentry"
(shih or shen-shih) are defined as "scholars dwelling in their villages" or
some such: that is, men educated to the responsibilities of office, at least
in theory; men who had passed at least the lowest of the three levels of
the examinations. Members of the gentry constituted an acknowledged
local elite—"the respected ones of the area," as one nineteenth-century
edict put it, "respected and honored because they have read the sages'
books . . . and because their words and actions can all be models to the
villagers. . . ."[31] As such, the gentry discharged various responsibilities
of local government: the maintenance of public works (roads, waterways, bridges and dikes), support of a local peace-keeping force, upkeep
of the local Confucian shrine and support of whatever educational
facilities the locality might afford, etc. In return, gentry status bestowed
certain recognized benefits and privileges: exemption from corporal
punishment and corvée conscription, preferential treatment at the hands
of the tax collectors and in cases of litigation, and in some instances, the
payment of government stipends to aspiring scholars.*

It was the genius of the Confucian political system in this fasion to
limit the range of imperial responsibilities—and the drain on the imperial
treasury which the maintenance of a governmental structure that
penetrated into every village and hamlet would have entailed—by
delegating political functions at the local level to an elite not formally in-
tegrated into the governmental structure or supported at government expense. Thus it was that appointed officials all the way down to the level
of district magistrate could act as the agents of the central authority,
leaving it to local gentry both to implement imperial policy and, as the
need arose and opportunity presented itself, to represent local interests. It
was an arrangement, moreover, which had the entirely intentional effect
of giving the gentry, in localities scattered across the broad territories of
the empire, a greater concern for the well-being of the monarchical institution on which they depended for their status than for their own interests as a "class" or "estate."

To say that this Confucian elite was "conservative" is only to rehearse
one of the more durable clichés on which our understanding of the high
culture of old China—and, in somewhat different ways, the popular

* The whole question of the social, political and economic status of the gentry in late imperial
China is far more complex than this brief description suggests. See Frederic Wakeman, *The
Fall of Imperial China*, chapter 2, for a cogent discussion; and more specialized works by
Chang Chung-li, Hsiao Kung-ch'üan, Ho Ping-ti, Fei Hsiao-t'ung and others.

culture as well—is based. As the American philosopher John Dewey remarked in 1920 after a year-long confrontation with the Chinese predicament, "That the Chinese do not progress more systematically and rapidly because they are a conservative people is clearly repeating in other words the thing that needs to be explained."[32] Nevertheless, conscious attachment to, and replication of, the customs and judgments of earlier generations—which is the general sense of "conservatism" in popular usage—is so conspicuous an attribute of Confucian culture from first to last that the term itself is inescapable. The best we can do is to try to refine it to make it more useful.

It is worth noting, in the first place, that the manner in which "conservatism" is expressed, whether in attitude or in language, depends to a considerable degree upon the sense of the past which animates the conservative impulse: the dimensions of that past and the general perception of its relationship to the present. Thus conservatism which aims at the transmission and elucidation of inherited intellectual assumptions, the communication through time of an acknowledged "great" tradition, is a different thing from the social conservatism that is involved in the repetition of acts the authenticity of which derives from a vague awareness, or an unthinking conviction, that identical acts have "always" been performed. The latter, indeed, may not qualify as "conservatism" at all, but rather be a kind of "traditionalism," lacking the self-consciousness that distinguishes the true conservative.

In this connection, it must also be borne in mind that the environment in which "conservative" thought is expressed profoundly affects its substance. Affirmation of the continuing relevance of inherited modes of conduct and belief becomes increasingly explicit as it becomes defensive—that is, as changing circumstance calls the value of the inheritance into question. Perhaps, as Karl Mannheim suggests, conservatism as an identifiable intellectual and cultural style is in fact the product of a process of cultural disintegration, when "the simple habit of living more or less unconsciously, as though the old ways of life were still appropriate, gradually gives way to a deliberate effort to maintain them under the new conditions, and they are raised to the level of conscious reflection, of deliberate 'recollection'."[33] In China in the nineteenth and twentieth centuries, as the cultural crisis deepened and the challenge to established assumptions became ever more explicit, Confucianism became clearly conservative in the Mannheimian sense.

There is good reason, however, to regard Confucianism as a conservative mode of thought in terms of its own historical development, irrespective of the challenge of the West. As we shall see in chapter 2, Confucians had always been self-consciously, often painfully, sensitive to the fact that imperial reality mocked Confucian theory. "The adulteration of the Way" is a recurrent theme in Confucian literature; and the compulsion to return to, or to retrieve, the essential meaning of the Confucian message lies behind all the great reformations of Confucian thought: T'ang- and Sung-dynasty neo-Confucianism, the reactive emphasis on intuition identified with the Ming-dynasty scholar Wang Yang-ming, and the several styles of reformist Confucianism that dominated Ch'ing-dynasty intellectual life.

Given the vividness of the Confucian sense of the past, the place assigned to history in the classical curriculum is hardly surprising. Confucius was himself the preeminent antiquarian of his time. He believed, according to Mencius, that his permanent fame would rest upon his compilation of the *Spring and Autumn Annals* (*Ch'un-ch'iu*), the records of his native state of Lu: a sparse and cryptic chronology, the barest bones of an historical account that required extensive elaborative commentary to render it meaningful. (The two principal commentaries, the *Tso chuan* and the *Kung-yang chuan*, attained a significance of their own to which we will return in chapter 4.) From the outset, Confucians regarded history as the central authority of their beliefs, and as the principal vehicle by which these beliefs were transmitted.

The Chinese have not been alone in exploiting history as a lesson in morals, "philosophy teaching by example," in Bolingbroke's phrase. What makes the Chinese remarkable is the nature of their perception of the history that inspired them: its antiquity; their sense of an unbroken continuity of human experience reaching back from the present to the remotest past; and their certainty of the relevance of ancient values to the moral dilemmas of any age. Sober Confucian moralists often lived tormented by their conviction that the "Way" of Confucius had been corrupted by opportunistic servants of imperial enterprise. But they lived also, for the most part, secure in the belief that no cataclysmic disruption in the flow of their culture divided them from the Golden Age in which Confucian inspiration had its source.

Time, in the Chinese imagination, moved not along a line from an identifiable point of origin to a predictable culmination. Rather, the traditional Chinese time sense was cyclical: human experience turning upon itself in ponderous circles, even as cosmic events (which Chinese astronomers meticulously recorded and very early learned to predict with considerable accuracy) repeat themselves at fixed intervals. This perception of time influenced in direct and striking fashion the understanding of history. Viewed from within its own historiographic traditions, Chinese history lacked an emphatic beginning, a cosmogonic act with all the sense of metahistorical purpose and design implied thereby. It lacked also eschatological conviction, the sense of movement toward some ultimate fate, some material or moral end and justification. History was not felt, in Mircea Eliade's phrase, as "a succession of events that are irreversible, unforseeable, possessed of autonomous value," but rather as a recurrence of fixed patterns and types, variations on the theme of the "eternal return," an established inventory, *mutatis mutandis*, of familiar historical sequences (the rise and fall of dynastic fortunes) and semi-legendary archetypes (the "good first" and "bad last" ruler).[34]

By temperament, the Confucian was thus more nostalgic than hopeful. He did not look ahead to the conjectural perfection of the human condition; but backward, with a sense of loss, to the Golden Age of which, according to his belief, he possessed compelling evidence —moral if not critically historical—in the Classics. When, toward the end of the nineteenth century, the idea of progress began to make itself felt in the Chinese intellectual world—Western confidence in the orderly evolution of political institutions and cultural values, in the promise of the future—a fundamental revision of traditional assumptions was called for. Time itself became an element in the unfolding controversies of Chinese intellectual life: the sense of urgency and of optimism was the harbinger of revolutionary change.

The "fatalism" frequently attributed to the Chinese obviously draws something from this perception of history, "an ontology uncontaminated by time and becoming," in Eliade's apt language.[35] In the noblest expressions of Confucian belief one encounters the composure of minds able to contemplate the final insignificance of human experience and endeavor without giving way to despair and withdrawal. Yet Confucian scholars were too astute in their role as historians to deny that times do indeed change, and too serious in their moral commitment to foresake their social vocation. Confucius himself, and Mencius, and most emphatically Hsun-tzu, all warned against the mindless aping of the past for its own sake. One of the great problems confronting every generation of Confucian followers was that of striking the balance between enduring moral truths and changing circumstances, judging what remained relevant. The landmarks of political and moral crisis might seem familiar, but each generation traversed its own age, and each individual bore the responsibility for charting a course in accordance with the interior sense of direction bred in him by Confucian education. His life might be no more than a fragment of some far larger pattern, but in itself it had a beginning and an end, and it must be justified in terms of the Confucian ideal of engagement with the problems of a particular historical/moral situation. The Confucian thus stood squarely *in* history, seeking no understanding of what might transcend it, nor hoping for any redemption from its ultimate judgment.

Confucian reliance on history as its final authority yielded at times incongruous, even startlingly anachronistic, results. The most familiar examples of this to Westerners dated from the nineteenth century, when, confronted by the unprecedented threat of British warships prowling along the China coast in the 1840s and 1850s, the emperor's ministers upon occasion (and, one is likely to suspect, in desperation) invoked the wisdom of Yao, Shun, and Yü—the legendary founders of the culture—in their admonishments to their beleaguered monarch. The reactionary strain in Confucianism could also inspire, as we shall see in the following chapters, a "conservatism" so radical as to become subversive of the interests of the imperial Confucian establishment as it actually existed—as when, for example, early Ch'ing scholars called for a return to the "spirit" of pre-imperial feudalism, and even went so far as to identify the emperor as the greatest enemy of Confucian ideals; or again, when at the end of the nineteenth century reformers like K'ang Yu-wei rationalized in Confucian terms fundamental departures from the structure of Confucian/imperial authority.

On the whole, however, Confucian conservatism in the late nineteenth century was neither so anachronistic nor so radical. It was, essentially, a defense of the established order—a defense, that is, of the dynasty and of the interests of dynasty's Confucian servant-participants, for most of whom, as Benjamin Schwartz observes, "the essential core of the faith had now shrunk to certain basic features of Confucian individual and family morality, as well as to what might be called the basic monarchic constitution of the state."[36] This was not a "Burkean" conservatism: the view that existing institutions are the instruments, tested by time and usage, of reasonable means toward accepted ends, and must be safeguarded from impulsive and irrational change. In China by the end of the nineteenth century, few could believe with genuine conviction that the institutions of imperial monarchy could meet unchanged the reasonable needs of people or nation. In the context of late imperial Confucianism, conservatism was less a matter of trust than of habit and privilege: it meant support of the time-honored privileges of gentry status and bureaucratic service, and consequently of the imperial institution on whose patronage such privilege depended.

Intellectually and institutionally, polity and culture thus reinforced each other in a relationship that endured as long as the self-containment of the society that nourished it remained unthreatened—only so long, that is, as it was possible to maintain the view that political ascendancy and cultural ascendancy turned upon the same pivot. Sinocentricity—the cultural self-absorption of the Chinese—is another of the inescapable clichés, like "conservatism," that must be reckoned with in coming to an understanding of the traditional Chinese world view. Its commonplaceness does not render it *ipso facto* irrelevant in particular contexts. The Chinese were, and in some respects remain, singularly introverted in their cultural preoccupations, exhibiting a quality of inwardness that has obvious bearing upon the capacity to accommodate to, or even to acknowledge the desirability of, innovation. There were, for example, Jesuit priests at the Chinese court in the seventeenth and eighteenth centuries, able and more than willing to lay before the emperor and his officials the most sophisticated Western learning of the age in such fields as astronomy, geography and cartography, medicine, mathematics, and weaponry. The Chinese were at best mildly interested, at worst supremely disdainful. The K'ang Hsi emperor (r. 1661–1722), during whose long and splendid reign Jesuit influence reached its apogee and began to wane, was himself an apt audience. From his European tutors he learned, among other things, something of the rudiments of geometry, enough to recommend this new knowledge to his officials engaged in water conservancy. "I myself planted the measuring device in the ground, and got my sons and bodyguards to use their spears and stakes to mark the various distances. . . . I showed them how to calculate circumferences and assess the area of a plot of land, even if its borders were as jagged as dogs' teeth, drawing diagrams for them on the ground with an arrow." Yet Western ingenuity, not Western learning, was the real attraction. The emperor instructed one of his Jesuit advisors to construct for his amusement "a water fountain that operated in conjunction with an organ"; another "taught me to play the tune 'P'u-yen-chou' on the harpsichord." But K'ang Hsi's final verdict was devastating in its implications:

> Even though some of the Western methods are different from our own, and may even be an improvement, there is little about them that is new. The principles of mathematics all derive from the *Book of Changes* [*I-ching*, a classical text dating from pre-Confucian times], and the Western methods are Chinese in origin. . . . After all, they know only a fraction of what I know, and none of the Westerners is really conversant with Chinese literature. . . . Often one can't keep from smiling when they start off on a discussion. How can they presume to talk about the "great principles of China"?[37]

One need only contrast the Chinese attitude toward things Western and exotic with that of the Japanese during the Tokugawa shogunate (1615–1868) in order to illustrate a difference that was eventually to have profound significance. The Japanese, prohibited by stringently enforced official interdiction from intercourse with foreigners save through the licensed Dutch trading post in Nagasaki Bay, scrabbled industriously for what bits and pieces of Western learning they might thus acquire. They taught themselves Dutch in order laboriously to decipher treatises on medicine and mathematics and navigation. They explored and exploited European scientific texts translated into Chinese by the Jesuits for the benefit of their generally incurious Chinese patrons. In this fashion they contrived to put together, fragment by fragment, a partial but not inaccurate understanding of Western science long before Admiral Perry's "black ships" sailed into view in Edo Bay in the early 1850s.

The point here, however, is not to deride Chinese complacency. In

K'ang Hsi's time, such pride in culture was by no means as incongruous as it came to seem to Westerners (and to Japanese) two hundred years later. It had, as well, its positive aspect: tolerance is the other side of the coin of condescension, and for centuries one of the things that struck foreign travellers to the Middle Kingdom as remarkable was the quality of intellectual magnanimity that had so impressed Bishop Andrew in the fourteenth century, as we have seen earlier, and that continued to attract the attention and admiration of later visitors from the doctrinally sectarian West. Indeed, the whole Jesuit enterprise depended not only on Jesuit imagination, but on Chinese broadmindedness, of which K'ang Hsi himself set a notable example. Significantly, it was not until the "Rites Controversy" in the early eighteenth century that the arrogance of Papal legates sent at the behest of the Franciscan and Dominican orders to denounce the Jesuits' doctrinally conciliatory and politically elitist approach so angered the emperor that the propagation of the faith was circumscribed by imperial edict, and Christian fortunes, whatever they might have become, entered upon a fatal decline.

Still at the end of that century, Chinese self-assurance remain sufficiently secure to allow the Ch'ien Lung emperor, K'ang Hsi's grandson, to dismiss the ambassador of King George III of England with casual hauteur: "There is nothing we lack, as your principal envoy and others have themselves observed. We have never set much store on strange or ingenious objects, nor do we need any more of your country's manufactures."[38] History, as we know, would have it otherwise. Even before the end of Ch'ien Lung's reign in 1796, as corruption spread through the administration and rebellion flared across North China, the tide of confidence was beginning to ebb. In the decades that followed, the monarchy was all but overwhelmed by rebellion—the White Lotus, the Taiping, the Nien—and by the intermittent shock of foreign assault—in the "Opium War" of 1839–1842, again in the late 1850s, yet again in the 1880s and 1890s. By the end of the century, deep working changes were in train, still largely concealed by the surviving structures of Confucian institutions. Confucianism itself, however, was becoming conservative in the Mannheimian sense: no longer an implicit assumption of the reliability of established moral and social truths, but, intellectually, a matter of "conscious reflection" and "deliberate recollection"—an act of will, almost of blind faith; and, institutionally, a stubborn and ultimately panic-stricken defense of vested interests.

Li Hung-chang, the greatest of the emperor's ministers in the last quarter of the nineteenth century, and not by any measure a radical thinker, summed it up thus: "If we remain conservative, without making any change, then day by day the nation will be reduced and weakened. . . . In every foreign country nowadays, reforms are undertaken one after another, and day by day they progress, even as steam ascends.

China alone continues to preserve her traditional institutions with such dogged caution that even should she be ruined and perish, the conservatives will not regret it. Oh heaven and man! How can we understand the cause of it?"[39] Li Hung-chang expressed the foreboding of a statesman fearful for the fate of his country. More than this, he bespoke the anguish of one who sees, or feels in the depths of his being, the inevitability of change, but can neither make room for it in the traditional scheme of things, nor himself step beyond the precincts of that still hallowed tradition. It was a dilemma that overwhelmed Confucian thinkers in the final enfeebled decades of the old regime, a problem to which they found no answer that would secure the survival of their world.

Confucian Criticism

When a great multitude of men, all strangers to one another, are brought together by the concentration of a central government in one place, talents lie buried, virtues are ignored, and vices tend to remain unpunished. . . . The general effort is devoted to maintaining a government authority which its many scattered officials are forever either trying to avoid or to impose. Little enough is left over for the fostering of public well-being. . . . When a body politic is too large for its constitution, it tends to collapse under the weight of its own superstructure.

—Jean-Jacques Rousseau

CONFUCIUS AND HIS EARLY DISCIPLES idealized a world they knew, or imagined they could recall to mind. It was a world of small, culturally homogeneous principalities, socially stable, close-knit enough to render credible the idea that the ruler could be a present force, a living example to his subjects. On this vision turned the Confucian conviction that the state is a moral community, that government is a moral enterprise.

From the end of the second century B.C. onward, Confucianism in the service of the empire adjusted to very different circumstances. It owed its remarkably tenacious hold over the minds and institutions of imperial China in considerable measure to the ability and the willingness of its Han-dynasty interpreters to accommodate their tenets to the un-Confucian ambitions and appetites of an expansive imperial authority. Yet the original ideal endured if only as a rebuke to Confucian conscience or a Confucian reprimand to imperial pretension. It colored the Confucian perception of what the state should be; and thus inevitably it influenced Confucian recommendations as to the manner in which the government should respond to the crises thrust upon it—down to and including the ultimate crisis of the nineteenth century.

The nineteenth century brought together in puzzling fashion familiar evidence of moral laxity and dynastic decrepitude—administrative incompetence, loss of social morale, rebellion—with the harshly unfamiliar realities of unprecedented social pressures and, most ominously, foreign encroachment on a scale, from a direction, and with an intent quite beyond the capacity of inherited experience to comprehend. The crisis was the product of several factors, of pressures which had been building up in some instances over a span of centuries. Perhaps as early as the Sung dynasty, and certainly by the beginning of the Ch'ing, technological developments and the introduction of new crops had set in train the phenomenal population growth that put increasing strain on social theories designed to meet the requirements of a static agrarian economy. During the same period, urban commerce and culture had developed largely outside the Confucian frame of reference. These were among the indigenous ingredients of impending disaster. More easily identified (though no easier to contend with) was the foreign component: a military and political threat behind which lurked a challenge to the fundamental values on which the culture rested.

Thus confronted, it was only natural for Confucian thinkers to fall back first and instinctively upon well-tried categories of analysis and criticism, phrasing their prescriptions in the established idiom of reformist literature. Renovation was something that Confucians understood; innovation was not. Change was the irresistible challenge of the nineteenth century. The Chinese capacity to meet this challenge was conditioned by the venerable tradition of Confucian dissent and criticism to which we now turn our attention.

*   *   *

In the Confucian scheme of things, self-cultivation and self-examination were natural corollaries. Confucian scholar-officials were, or could be in individual cases and particular circumstances, deeply introspective in their appreciation of the relationship that bound them to the Confucian value system, and sharply critical of earlier interpretations of the Confucian message. Over the long centuries of its self-containment, Chinese civilization drew much of its vitality from this Confucian penchant for self-criticism, and from the seemingly inexhaustible intellectual energy that found expression in elaborations and reworkings of the fragments of original doctrine.

No social philosophy dedicated to the values of hierarchy and harmony, however, can incorporate change as a positive element within its intellectual structure. This is as true of Plato's *Republic*, or of the tripartite orders of medieval European social theory, as it is of Confucianism. Any departure from ideals held to be immutable in themselves can only be viewed as deviance, never as fulfillment. Change is an intrusion: even when the need for it has been acknowledged in the interests of practical statecraft, it remains difficult to justify. Confucian scholars were, not unnaturally, reluctant to concede the possibility of doctrinal inadequacy, to question the validity of the original Confucian insight into human nature, to cast doubt upon the authority of the past. Moreover, historiographic tradition bred in them an aversion to the very idea of institutional reforms designed to enhance the wealth and power of the state as an enterprise in its own right. The precedents for such policies were evil, bringing to mind the legendary tyranny of the Ch'in dynasty (221–206 B.C.) when, in the conventional account, Legalism triumphed and when, in consequence, punishment and reward, an impersonal law, took precedence over "righteousness and humanity." The Ch'in met a speedy end, predictably in the Confucian view. Confucius had warned against reliance on law. "Lead the people by means of governmental constraints and punishments, and though they will do their best to stay out of trouble, they will have no sense of right and wrong," he had said. "Lead them with virtue, restrain them with ritual, and they will have a sense of right and wrong and, moreover, they will become good."[1]

So strong was the Confucian commitment to the transcendent and transforming power of moral example that any effort to attach importance to the perpetuation of the dynastic establishment for its own sake was likely to provoke the darkest suspicion. The issue crops up repeatedly in the course of imperial history; the reforms undertaken or attempted by the energetic Sung-dynasty minister Wang An-shih are perhaps the most famous case in point. The Sung, sumptuously wealthy in the arts of luxury and leisure, suffered nevertheless from chronic domestic ills, economic and social, and was menaced by strong barbarian enemies to the north. Wang's reforms had to do with such diverse concerns as rural credit, the provision of horses for the imperial cavalry, and revisions in the examination system to make it more responsive to the practical requirements of bureaucratic service. Despite his avowed devotion to Confucian principles, and despite (or perhaps because of) his dedication to the strengthening of the monarchy, Wang's program was roundly denounced by many of his contemporaries. Among them was Su Shih, who is better remembered for his poetry and by his pen-name, Su Tung-p'o, than as an official, though his bureaucratic career was long and eventful. In a memorial condemning Wang's "New Laws" Su Shih expressed what can well be read as the classic Confucian position.

> What a ruler has to rely upon is only the hearts of men. Men's hearts are to the ruler what roots are to a tree, what oil is to a lamp, water to a fish, fields to a farmer, money to a merchant. . . . The preservation or loss of a nation depends upon the depth or shallowness of its virtue, not upon its strength or weakness. The length or shortness of a dynasty depends upon the stoutness or flimsiness of its social customs, not upon its richness or poverty. If its moral vir-

tue is truly deep, and its social customs truly stout, even though the country is poor and weak, its poverty and weakness will not affect its duration and existence. If its virtue is shallow and its social customs flimsy, even though the nation is rich and strong, this will not save it from coming to an early end. When a ruler knows this, he knows what is important and what is not important. Therefore the wise rulers of ancient times did not abandon virtue because the country was weak, nor did they permit social customs to suffer because the country was poor.*[2]

Such highmindedness in high places amazed and, on the whole, delighted Europeans when accounts of the Confucian monarchy began filtering westward in the seventeenth century, especially through the medium of enthusiastic Jesuit reportage. Matteo Ricci, the enterprising missionary responsible for establishing his order's privileged position at the Chinese court in the early 1600s, concluded his description of the government of "this wonderful empire" by calling attention to a fact "quite worthy of note as marking a difference from the West," to wit, "that the entire kingdom is administered by the Order of the Learned, commonly known as The Philosophers. The responsibility for orderly management of the entire realm is wholly and completely in their charge and care."[4] Thus cultivated, the European vogue for things Chinese extended beyond the *chinoiserie* that figured so conspicuously in rococo taste to embrace, in many quarters, an interest in Chinese ideas and Chinese morals. Leibniz, in a tract published in 1697 entitled *Novissima Sinica* ("the newest news of China") expressed a not uncommon view:

> The condition of affairs among ourselves seems to me to be such that, in view of the inordinate lengths to which the corruption of morals has advanced, I almost think it necessary that Chinese missionaries should be sent to us to teach us the aim and practice of natural theology, as we send missionaries to them to instruct them in revealed theology. For I believe that if a wise man were to be appointed judge—not of the beauty of goddesses, but of the goodness of peoples—he would award the golden apple to the Chinese—unless, indeed, we should outdo them in nobility by conferring on them that which is, indeed, a superhuman good—the divine gift of the Christian religion.[5]

---

* To offset the impression that Confucian statesmen were invariably humorless men, an impression hard to escape as one reads the dour rebukes they were wont to inflict upon their imperial sponsors from age to age, it may be useful to bear in mind a poem written by this same Su Tung-p'o on the occasion of his son's birth:

> *Families, when a child is born*
> *Want it to be intelligent.*
> *I, through intelligence,*
> *Having wrecked my whole life,*
> *Only hope the baby will prove*
> *Ignorant and stupid.*
> *Then he will crown a tranquil life*
> *By becoming a Cabinet Minister.*[3]

To Voltaire, writing half a century later, the fact that the Chinese had been spared "the divine gift of the Christian religion" was cause only for envious congratulation. "They have perfected Moral science, and that is the first of the sciences."[6] "We should not be fanatical about the merits of the Chinese," Voltaire cautioned in the essay on China inserted into the *Philosophical Dictionary:*

> The constitution of their empire is in fact the best in the world, the only one founded entirely on paternal power (which doesn't prevent the mandarins from caning their children); the only one in which the governor of a province is punished when he fails to win the acclamation of the people upon leaving office; the only one that has instituted prizes for virtue, while everywhere else the laws are restricted to punishing crime; the only one that has made its conquerors adopt its laws, while we are still subject to the customs of the Burgundians, the Franks, and the Goths, who subjugated us. But I must admit that the common people . . . are as rascally as ours; that they sell everything to foreigners very expensively, just as we do; that in the sciences the Chinese are still at the point we were at two hundred years ago; that they have a thousand ridiculous prejudices, as we do. . . .
>
> Let me add that their doctors cure mortal illnesses no better than ours do, and that nature cures minor ailments by herself in China, as it does here. Still four thousand years ago, when we couldn't even read, the Chinese knew all the absolutely useful things we boast about today.
>
> Once again, the religion of the men of letters of China is admirable. No superstitions, no absurd legends, none of those dogmas which insult reason and nature. . . . The simplest cult has seemed to them the best for more than forty centuries.[7]

Leibniz, Voltaire, and the considerable congregation of philosophes and physiocrats who adopted their enthusiasm for the Chinese example were of course using China to score points in an argument that had much to do with contemporary European culture and very little to do with Chinese realities. Nor was theirs the unanimous opinion, even then. Montesquieu, repelled by Chinese absolutism, wondered "what sort of virtue there can be in people who can only be ruled with the stick!"[8] Rousseau despised the Chinese for their lack of national sentiment.* Hegel, failing to discern in China any manifestation of the workings of the universal spirit, denied that the Chinese possessed a history at all. The best that Adam Smith could find to say was that "though it may perhaps stand still, [China] does not seem to go backwards."[9] The image of an immobile culture gradually became the prevailing European perception of China; the "simplest cult" came to be seen as attachment to an oppressive archaism.

A hundred years after Voltaire's time, progressive Western opinion was using China to teach a different lesson. "We have a warning example

* See the epigraph at the head of chapter 3.

in China," wrote John Stuart Mill in 1859. He was still willing to concede to the Chinese "much talent, and, in some respects, even wisdom," for which he gave credit to the influence of "a particularly good set of customs, the work, in some measure, of men to whom even the most enlightened European must accord, under certain limitations, the title of sages and philosophers." Less meticulously qualified was his admiration for "the excellence of [the Chinese] apparatus for impressing, as far as possible, the best wisdom they possess upon every mind in the community, and securing that those who have appropriated most of it shall occupy the posts of honor and power." But what Mill saw as the effect of this was far from admirable. "Surely the people who did this have discovered the secret of human progressiveness, and must have kept themselves steadily at the head of the movement of the world. On the contrary, they have become stationary—have remained so for thousands of years; and if they are ever to be farther improved, it must be by foreigners." Mill's interest in China—like Voltaire's—was merely incidental to his more immediate concern: "The modern *régime* of public opinion is, in an unorganized form, what the Chinese educational and political systems are in an organized; and unless individuality shall be able successfully to assert itself against this yoke, Europe, notwithstanding its noble antecedents and its professed Christianity, will tend to become another China."[10]

The changing European view of China, from seventeenth and eighteenth-century infatuation to nineteenth-century contempt, is instructive on several counts. It tells us, of course, something about China itself. Su Shih's idealistic admonitions may have seemed no more than a conventional piety in the eleventh century. Eight hundred years later, however, when Confucian statesmen offered virtually the same advice in virtually identical language to the harassed monarchs of the dying Ch'ing, it seemed to most Westerners, and to a growing number of Chinese as well, the expression of an anachronistic confidence, a moribund idealism. Intellectual conformity and stubborness—"the patent stagnation of the collective mind," as one observer put it[11]—these were the qualities commonly attributed to the Chinese in nineteenth-century Western accounts.

More is involved here than Confucian obduracy. Gone now were the urbane, intellectually responsive Jesuits who had reported on China from within the very citadel of the civilization and discovered there much that was worthy of respect and admiration. Nineteenth-century Western opinion was shaped by the accounts of far less sympathetic observers, geographically and culturally confined to the periphery of the empire: diplomatic emissaries rebuffed, baffled and affronted by Peking's impregnable condescension; merchants and opium runners tantalized beyond endurance by the imagined wealth of the vast market they were forbidden to enter; evangelists in the service of a jealous God and an uncompromising Faith. James Matheson, premier purveyor of opium and other useful sundries to the Chinese in the 1830s, put the view somewhat polemically when he denounced his clients as "a people characterized by a marvelous degree of imbecility, avarice, conceit and obstinacy."[12] Yet whether they came to peddle the material or the spiritual necessities of civilization, and whatever their opinion of the propriety of the opium traffic as a means to this end, Westerners who dealt with China in the nineteenth century tended more to agree than to disagree with such a description.

The values that these men brought with them to the China coast were those of a civilization itself in the process of a far-reaching and rapid transformation. In the 1750s, Voltaire could still pass lightly over the fact of China's waywardness in respect to the sciences. A hundred years later the Western lead had increased phenomenally, and no Westerner would have thought casually to dismiss the significance of this widening chasm. Traders and missionaries alike saw themselves as the representatives of a self-evidently beneficial and historically inevitable modernity: apostles of the religion not only of Christ, but also of Free Trade, Progress, and the Machine. Nor is this fundamental change in the Western perspective on China extraneous to our immediate concern; for as the century drew on, and as Western values intruded ever more forcefully upon the Chinese mind, the radical reformist literature of the Chinese themselves came to reflect certain aspects of the Western view. Among other things, the historical experience of the Confucian elite became itself an issue in the anxious passage to intellectual modernity.

*　　*　　*

Even as he called attention to the "wide influence" exercised by Confucian scholars in the administration of the Chinese monarchy, Matteo Ricci had felt compelled to concede that "the Philosophers do not govern the empire."[13] Mencius' confident claim that those who "work with their minds" constitute the natural governing class was not, in other words, descriptive so much as prescriptive. It was an attempt to authorize the intellectuals' title to a position they did not in fact occupy, in Mencius' time or later. His own life, like that of Confucius before him, was spent largely as a peripatetic and often unheeded counsellor to the kings and princelings of his day. He made his mark not as a ruler, not even as an official, but as a teacher. Under the empire Confucian scholars were incorporated into the business of the state by virtue of their monopoly of skills essential to the governing power, but not of it. They were the masters of the traditions of literacy and ritual, the educated manipulators of the symbols of value in the society and the culture. As such, their function was not to rule, but to legitimate the authority of those in whose hands the power to govern rested, and to assist them in the administration of their realm.

In medieval Europe, no less than in Confucian China, intellectual status depended primarily on the patronage bestowed in return for services rendered, services having to do principally with the administration and legitimation of secular and ecclesiastical authority. The great changes in the structure of European cultural life that began in the late medieval period and that collectively constitute the familiar history of the Renaissance gradually altered this intellectual role. The rebirth of urban life and culture made possible the removal of intellectual activity from court and cloister. The invention of printing and the diffusion of literacy gave rise to a widening intellectual community, creating the conditions prerequisite to the establishment of academic institutions and traditions less dependent than in former times on patronage by church or state. The erosion of religious unity and challenges from various quarters to received dogma gave broader scope to intellectual enterprise. A fresh enthusiasm for individual craftmanship and individual gain encouraged individualism first as a condition of livelihood and then as an abstract social value. This in turn contributed to the creation of a sense of vocational professionalism and intellectual identity founded on something more than functional competence. Nourishing this new identity were new values—the values, as we have come to think of them, of the emergent modern world: secularism and scepticism; an appreciation of the structural complexity of God's Creation (for most still thought of it as such), together with an enormous confidence in the capacity of the free-ranging and disciplined human intelligence to comprehend even the most complex and subtle relationships; and, coupled with this optimism, a sometimes ironic sensitivity to the moral ambiguity of the human condition, individual, social, or historical.

As a result of this new boldness of mind, the European intellectual class—or some significant fraction of it—came to regard itself as heir to a position derived from something other than subservience to the requirements of political authority. Such independence, it is true, remained precarious and incomplete. Most of those trained in the intellectual crafts of literacy and liturgy were employed as of old in the management of the secular and ecclesiastical bureaucracies. Indeed, the burgeoning apparatus of the state absorbed the services of a swelling army of clerks, scribes, and miscellaneous functionaries, men who felt no particular attachment to the abstract values of the intellectual vocation. Nevertheless, in the course of the sixteenth and seventeenth centuries there came into being a tradition of intellectual responsibility in which dissent from the public standards of European culture played a conspicuous part. Thus the way was paved for the arrival upon the European scene of "the party of Criticism," as Peter Gay calls the intellectuals of the Enlightenment: men living "beyond the holy circle," convinced that "since God is silent, man is his own master: he must live in a disenchanted world, submit everything to criticism, and make his own way."[14]

No party of criticism emerged in China, nor any comparable tradition of uncompromising social dissent. the Confucian literati clearly constituted an intellectual elite, capable of producing bureaucratic talent in response to the imperial demand for it, but capable also of producing scholars and even officials deeply critical of the moral effectiveness of their vocation. China experienced, moreover, in the course of the last imperial millennium, many of the same cultural and social changes that we identify in Europe as precursors of the "modern" intellectual calling. In the development of printing the Chinese were centuries ahead of the West. Paper had been in use since the first century A.D., and in the T'ang dynasty printing (from woodblocks rather than with moveable type, as befit the nature of the written language) became a common technology. By the Sung dynasty, printed books in steadily increasing number were circulating throughout the empire; by the Ch'ing, China possessed by far the largest printed literature of any of the world's cultures, and possibly a much higher rate of literacy than has generally been conceded.*

Literacy entailed in China many of the same social and cultural consequences it had in Europe. It encouraged the growth of a distinctive urban culture in the flourishing cities of central China which owed their existence to commerce rather than to the requirements of political administration. Thus the foundations were laid upon which grew the popular culture, the vernacular and theatrical literature, of the Ming and Ch'ing periods. At the same time the spread of literacy facilitated, beginning in the Sung dynasty, the establishment of private centers of intellectual activity, the academies (shu-yuan) which generated much of the serious philosophical and historical scholarship of the final imperial ages. Together with revisions in methods of tax collection and changes in the pattern of land tenure that helped to undermine the position of the older aristocratic houses after the T'ang dynasty, these transformations in the environment of cultural life were enormously important to the creation of the gentry class and to its survival over the last thousand years of the imperial epoch.

It is at this point that the comparison with Europe stops short. There is no Western parallel to the peculiar social phenomenon of the Chinese gentry class; and as much as anything else it was the requirements of gentry status that inhibited the development of private standards of dissent

---

* On the basis of the number of candidates who presented themselves for the examinations, F. W. Mote has argued persuasively that at least 10 percent of the population must have been literate by Ch'ing times; and further that this may well be a conservative estimate, given the number of literate Chinese who did not participate in the examination system and who therefore remain statistically inaccessible.[15]

in China. For while on the one hand acquisition of gentry privileges depended upon the kind of educational opportunity that the diffusion of literacy and the proliferation of academies and private clan and village schools made possible, on the other hand the exercise of these privileges continued to depend on the vocational opportunities that only imperial patronage could insure. In part, this dependence reflected ongoing social imperatives: official service, or at the very least membership in the elite class of degree-holders, remained the only path to social eminence, the only hope of improving one's position or, as not infrequently was the case with the rising class of urban merchants, the only way of transmuting wealth into social status. Over and beyond this, however, was an ideological motive: the single-minded Confucian insistence on the importance of service—service to the prince, and through him to mankind at large. Thus it was that the institutions of the Confucian monarchy were viewed, down to the very end, as the instruments of a system of public values sanctioned by the intellectual elite, which itself bore much of the responsibility for realizing these values—or for the failure to do so.

Confucian literature attests eloquently to the agony and soul-searching occasioned by the awareness that the moral purposes of Confucianism were unattained, perhaps unattainable, under the auspices of existing institutions. Seldom, however, did such disillusionment result in an attempt to transcend these institutions, much less to an abandonment of the cherished ideals of Confucian culture. There existed, of course, the Taoist (or Taoist-Buddhist) alternative of retirement from the world, a life of seclusion, of primitive rustication, sometimes of wine and idle conversation, sometimes of meditation. But renouncing public life meant the renunciation of public significance. To the serious-minded Confucian, this was the social irresponsibility of Chuang-tzu, who once, as he sat fishing by a river, turned away the princely couriers who sought him out with an offer of appointment, remarking that he preferred to remain a live turtle "dragging his tail in the mud" to becoming the dead tortoise enshrined in some royal ancestral hall. Or, even worse, this was the wild, half-mad isolation of the hermit-poet: "Cold Mountain? There is no road that goes through. . . . How can you hope to get there by aping me? Your heart and mine are not alike."[16] To believe this was to relinquish the redeeming hope of the Confucian faith that men are in their nature kindred and may therefore be led by one who sets a virtuous example.

The great source of anguish in the Confucian world, then, was the struggle that went forward within the heart of the morally and socially conscientious individual uncertain as to whether his principles would benefit a degenerate age. "Come forth when the Way prevails in the world," Confucius had counselled. "When it does not prevail, then withdraw"[17] It was left squarely up to the individual to determine which of these injunctions described his times and dictated his proper course. In making this judgment he had to weigh the possibility that history would condemn his decision to serve an unworthy ruler against the risk of incurring imperial displeasure should he decline to "come forth". If the Confucian withdrew, moreover, he repudiated not only something outside himself—the corrupt and corrupting institutions of imperial authority—but also, and even more significantly, something within himself, some part of his identity and his duty. Indeed, there was for him no duty to a transcendent abstraction—Truth, Reason, God, even Man—separable from duty to the State. With no place to make his stand outside the faith, he could at best try to preserve a sense of the distinction between the State in its widest and most humane meaning, on the one hand, and the purposes of a particular government on the other.

This is the circumstance in which we encounter the early personalities of our history proper. It begins not with the dramatic confrontation between Chinese and Western ways in the nineteenth century, but two hundred years earlier, in the decades following the establishment of Manchu rule in the seventeenth century and the inauguration of the last of the great imperial dynasties, the Ch'ing.

*   *   *

In the small city of Yü-yao in Chekiang province, not far from the much larger city of Ningpo, a Confucian scholar named Huang Tsung-hsi sat beside a rainswept window in the winter of 1663 to compose the preface to a little treatise on politics. "I am old," Huang wrote, "and I know not whether I will be able to wait, as Chi-tzu did, for an enlightened ruler to seek out my counsel. The night has scarce begun to lift; the world is plunged in darkness still: I do not choose to let my thoughts remain concealed."[18]

Huang was then in his fifties, the age at which, according to Confucius, one knows the disposition of one's fate. He had, as it turned out, another thirty years to live. He filled those years with scholarship, compiling among other things a history of Ming-dynasty Confucianism and commencing, before his death in 1695, a similar study devoted to the great Confucianists of the Sung. These works established Huang's scholarly reputation among his contemporaries; the thoughts he determined to commit to posterity in 1663, however, were not published nor widely known during his lifetime. And for good reason, inasmuch as this brief essay constituted a remarkably seditious indictment of the institutions and motives of the Confucian monarchy. But Huang was a remarkable man, one of a number of penetrating and courageous critics of the Confucian political order with whom he shared, as the Chinese proverb has it, the misfortune to live in interesting times.

Dark times, Huang called them, and he entitled his political testament "Propositions for a More Propitious Age."* At best, the times were uncertain. The Manchu dynasty had established itself twenty years earlier by right of conquest, an especially bloody conquest in the provinces of the lower Yangtze region, the wealthy and cultured Kiangnan area. In one notorious campaign the city of Yang-chou in Kiangsu, some two hundred miles north of Yü-yao, was laid waste in May, 1645, and perhaps a half a million of its inhabitants put to death. A little to the south, the population of Chiang-yin perished almost to the last soul when the city fell in October at the end of a three-month siege. Throughout the 1640s, remnants of the Ming court in flight toward the south tried futilely to rally political and military resistance to the invading force. In the 1650s, pirates loyal to the Ming cause harassed the southern coastal districts. By the 1660s the last of the Ming claimants had been hunted down and destroyed, but the political situation was still unsettled. The K'ang Hsi emperor came to the throne in 1661 a boy of seven, dominated by a regency of Manchu ministers led by Oboi, one of the great military figures of the recent conquest. The Oboi regents felt only contempt for the prosaic, palsied values of the Confucian literati upon whom K'ang Hsi's father, the Shun Chih emperor, had learned to rely. Shun Chih and his advisers, so the regents believed, had jeopardized the martial birthright of the Manchus, and they acted accordingly to advance Manchu interests at the expense of the Chinese, and to undercut Confucian administrative authority. They moved also to assert the will of the new regime over the provincial gentry, centering their hostility, not surprisingly, on the Kiangnan area, where revenue deficits and tax evasion were reportedly widespread. A number of provincially prominent scholars and gentry who protested the severity of the methods of tax collection to which frightened provincial officials resorted were found guilty of sedition and executed in Nanking in the summer of 1661; many thousands had their property confiscated and their degrees revoked. At about the same time there appeared in the bookstalls of Hangchow, the provincial capital, an unofficial history of the Ming dynasty which was found to contain occasional impolite references to the "barbarian" Manchus; in 1663 the compilers of the book, its publishers, and even some scholars who had come into possession of copies—some seventy in all—were deprived of their property and their lives.

---

* *Ming-i tai-fang lu.* This is Etienne Balazs' rendering of the title; William Theodore de Bary translates it as "A Plan for the Prince." The actual title, however, is the kind of arcane conundrum not infrequently found in Confucian literature. *Ming-i* probably refers to the thirty-sixth of the sixty-four hexagrams found in the *Book of Changes*, with the general sense of "brilliance obscured" or some such—a symbolism associated with the career of Chi-tzu, as we shall see. *Tai-fang* means "waiting to be asked for advice" or "waiting for an official visit." The character *ming*, however, is the same as that of the Ming dynasty; and *i* may mean "barbarian"—i.e., Manchu. The reader is left to draw his own conclusions as to the significance of this juxtaposition.

Huang Tsung-hsi thus had good reason to feel hard pressed. No one could have supposed that K'ang Hsi would survive the politics of this harsh regency to emerge, when he assumed the powers of government in his own right, as a great patron of Confucian learning; nor that he could weather the challenge of a long civil war—the so-called "Revolt of the Three Feudatories" (1673–1681)—to reign a full and glorious sixty years, carrying the Ch'ing, and the imperial institution itself, to the zenith of its power. It is doubtful, however, that even had Huang Tsung-hsi looked so far ahead he would have been favorably impressed by the might and magnificence of K'ang Hsi's court at its height. Indeed, imperial power and splendor were among the things that most distressed him, and with him a number of other scholars who harbored similar grievances and shared his misgivings.

In comparing his situation to that of Chi-tzu, Huang Tsung-hsi was making a carefully considered point. Chi-tzu was one of the legendary Confucian heroes, an upright minister who offered judicious counsel to a tyrannical ruler—in this case, the last king of the Shang dynasty in the twelfth century B.C.—and who was imprisoned for his pains. That was not the end of the story, however, nor its real point in Huang's view. When the victorious armies of the Chou overthrew the degenerate Shang in 1122 B.C., bringing the virtuous Wu-wang to the throne, Chi-tzu rejected all invitations to return to public life; the most that he would do was to confide privately to the king the ideals subsequently incorporated into the *Hung-fan* ("Great Plan") chapter of the *Classic of History*, one of the earliest and most poetically persuasive statements of what came eventually to be known as Confucian principles of government. For the rest, Chi-tzu remained his own man, true to the conviction that the new dynasty stood on the unrighteous foundations of usurpation.

And so it was with Huang Tsung-hsi and the men whose names are most often linked to his as loyalist supporters of the vanished Ming: Ku Yen-wu (1613–1682) and Wang Fu-chih (1619–1692). All had been degree holders under the old dynasty. Each had served one or another of the ephemeral Ming refugee regimes until the last hope of a Ming revival had evaporated. Thereafter, all remained adamant in their refusal to serve the triumphant Manchus in any capacity whatever. They were not lured into service by the special examinations, "the booby-trap examinations," as Etienne Balazs calls them, held in the 1670s expressly for the purpose of mollifying the dissident gentry of the Kiangnan area. They refused even to participate in the scholarly task of drafting the official history of the Ming, an obligation which in orthodox Confucian manner the Ch'ing had undertaken to perform on behalf of its predecessor. Huang Tsung-hsi retired to Chekiang, there to spend the last half-century of his life in private historical scholarship. Carrying with him a considerable library, Ku Yen-wu set out upon the travels that kept him on the roads of North China—visiting historical sites, paying his respects from time to time at the Ming tombs in Peking—until death overtook him at a stopping place in the remote uplands of Shansi in his sixty-ninth year. Wang Fu-chih "disappeared into the distant mountains" of his native Hunan[19] and lost himself so completely in solitude and study that he remained virtually unknown for two hundred years after his death. What brings these names together is not personal association (though Huang and Ku, at least, were aware of each other's views) nor collaborative scholarship, but a common perspective on their times.

The Ming dynasty in its decline had exhibited in exaggerated form many of the symptoms of imperial decadence: incompetence, negligence, and depravity on the part of the last emperors; the flagrant abuse of power for private ends on the part of the palace eunuchs upon whom the emperors had come increasingly to rely as a kind of personal government; demoralization and corruption spreading throughout the bureaucracy, with all the attendant administrative ills usual in such circumstances. During the Ming, moreover, the power of the autocrat had steadily increased, at the expense of traditional ministerial responsibilities, and even ministerial dignity. The public flogging of ministers in court was a not uncommon punishment for acts of *lèse majesté*, real or imagined, in late Ming times. Huang Tsung-hsi's father, a reputable scholar and imperial censor, died in a Ming prison in 1626, having incurred the enmity of the emperor's favorite eunuch, the infamous Wei Chung-hsien. A number of the elder Huang's colleagues who belonged, as he did, to the reformist faction known as the Tung-lin Party met similarly punitive deaths.

There is thus an element of paradox in the steadfast loyalty which Huang Tsung-hsi and other early Ch'ing scholars felt for the memory of what had been in fact a despicable and vicious regime. Their sentiments must be laid to more than ordinary Confucian scruple, the old belief that a worthy minister may not serve two masters. It must be laid to more, even, than their profound malaise in respect to degeneracy of Confucian institutions. Loyalty to the Ming was the expression of a deep-seated cultural reaction against the "barbarian" origins of the new dynasty. The people of Chiang-yin had closed their gates against the Manchus rather than suffer the indignity of shaving their heads and adopting the Manchu-ordained queue; Ku Yen-wu's revered stepmother, it is said, starved herself to death rather than live under these hated aliens, exacting from her son the promise not to serve even as she died. The stand taken by scholars like Huang and Ku and Wang—and others not so well remembered—was less drastic in its personal consequences, perhaps more elaborately reasoned, but in its way no less visceral.

Early Ch'ing thought thus takes its rise in a time of troubles. It is compounded in equal parts of cultural despair and moral self-righteousness—a not uncommon Confucian recipe for reformist ideas. These seventeenth-century thinkers attributed the crisis of their age primarily to distortions in the prevalent understanding of "true" Confucian principles. Their view, as David Nivison puts it, was that the Ming "had died of philosophical indigestion; its most intelligent men had wasted themselves in meaningless bickering while their world fell to pieces."[20] The great neo-Confucian systems-builders came in for their share of criticism in this regard. Ch'ing thinkers were offended by the Sung predilection for metaphysical speculation, its cultivation of a taste for endless, disputatious talk—*k'ung-yen*, "empty words." Even more vehemently, however, they repudiated the introspective school of thought that derived from the ideas of the Ming-dynasty statesman and scholar Wang Yang-ming. Wang's Confucianism pursued to its logical conclusion that aspect of Mencius' teaching which emphasized self-knowledge and the intuitive sources of moral conduct. It tended, especially in the interpretations of some of Wang's followers, to deemphasize textual authority in favor of the achievement of an "enlightenment experience" not unlike the Ch'an (Zen) Buddhist *satori* or moment of intuitive insight. "How incredibly reckless!" cried Wang Fu-chih.[21]

These early Ch'ing scholars, in sharp contrast, devoted their energies to what they regarded as "solid" or "unadorned" scholarship (*p'u-hsueh*), the meticulous excavation of facts, presented with a minimum of speculative embellishment. They relied as much as possible on Han-dynasty texts and commentaries in their effort to retrieve an understanding of the original Confucian message uncontaminated either by the pernicious influence of Buddhism or by the neo-Confucian reaction against it. From this their scholarship came to be called the school of Han Learning (*Han hsueh*). The same impulse led to their most remarkable methodological achievements, the development of techniques of philological analysis and textual criticism that would enable them to strip away from the Classics the layers of misrepresentation that had accumulated over the centuries. In their hands textual criticism (*k'ao-cheng hsueh*) attained an extraordinary degree of sophistication and refinement.

They were not satisfied, however, with a remote classicism which could too easily lead, as Huang Tsung-hsi warned, to mere pedantry. They acknowledged that in many respects Confucianism *is* what it is understood to mean in different times and circumstances—Wang Fu-chih was especially bold in articulating a theory of historical relativism—and therefore they directed much of their attention to the history of Confucianism in its relationship to imperial institutions. Huang Tsung-hsi's studies of Sung, Yuan, and Ming intellectual history, virtually the first of their kind, were examples of this interest. So, in large part, was the work for which Ku Yen-wu is best remembered, *Jih-chih lu* (roughly, "A

Record of Things Learned Day-by-Day"), a collection of the study notes, first-hand observations, and historical researches compiled in the course of his thirty years of wandering. "I never failed to clamber up to the steepest peak, to search the darkest valley, feeling out the toppled stone markers, tramping about the underbrush, cutting down the old tangled hedges and sifting through the rotten earth. Anything that was legible I made a copy of by hand, and when I came across an inscription that had not been seen by my predecessors I was so overjoyed I could not sleep." This ingratiating picture of Ku scrambling tirelessly about the ruins of his civilization (whether archeological or documentary) in search of its verifiable antiquities came to epitomize to later generations the indefatigable energy and the scrupulous regard for concrete detail characteristic of Ch'ing empiricism.

An uncompromising allegiance to the dynasty under which they had been born did not prevent these Ming loyalists from launching an extraordinarily bitter and sweeping assault on the institutions which the Ming had perpetuated. They focused their attack on the monarchy itself, the centralization of power in the imperial institution and in the person of the emperor. "The sage rulers of antiquity were impartial and public-spirited in their treatment of all men," wrote Ku Yen-wu. They had shared what was theirs to share, dividing their lands among the people. "But now the ruler considers all the territory within the four seas to be his own private domain, nor is he satisfied even so. He is suspicious of everyone. He handles all matters himself, while day by day the directives and the official documents pile higher and higher."

Huang Tsung-hsi's "Propositions" contained an even more biting denunciation of imperial despotism. He began somewhat as Hsun-tzu had—and somewhat, too, as did his European contemporaries John Locke and Thomas Hobbes—by conjuring up an image of mankind living in an original state of nature, a condition of antisocial (or at least asocial) self-sufficiency, each individual pursuing private ends, indifferent to the common good. In Huang's view, what extricated men from this unhappy situation was nothing like a "contract" arrived at out of fear or through the agency of Reason or enlightened self-interest. It was, rather, the appearance of "a man who did not think of benefit in terms of his own personal gain, but sought to benefit all under Heaven"—the advent, in other words, of the prototypical Sage Ruler, and with him the institutions and rituals of humane government: the Golden Age, the perennial Confucian "Once upon a time. . . . " The empire presented to Huang a different prospect altogether. "Those who later became princes . . . believing that since they held in their hands the power over benefit and loss, saw nothing whatever wrong in appropriating all the benefit, and leaving all the loss to others. . . . wringing the last drop of blood and marrow from the people. Thus the greatest enemy of mankind is the prince and none other than the prince. . . . It is only to be expected that the people have come to hate the prince, that they think of him as their mortal enemy, and call him a tyrant." Small wonder that Huang's essay circulated only among a circle of trustworthy friends!

Despotism breeds servility not only in the people but also, and with even more lamentable consequences, among the officials. Ku Yen-wu was outspokenly scornful of the bureaucrats who "are concerned only in moving with the utmost caution so as to stay out of trouble, and are quite unwilling to set their hand to any undertaking beneficial to the people." The moral was not, of course, to do away with the bureaucracy. Huang Tsung-hsi recognized, indeed he positively insisted upon, the emperor's need to rely upon the "hundred officers" (pai-kuan), since "in this broad realm a single man cannot rule unassisted." His defense of the ministerial role was at the same time a resounding affirmation of the age-old Confucian ideal of service:

> When we take office, it is in behalf of the empire as a whole, not in behalf of the prince alone; it is in behalf of all the people, not in behalf of a single princely house. If we take our stand in behalf of the empire and the people, then even when the Way has been lost, even when the prince would try to overawe us with a display of his majesty, we will not submit. . . .
>
> If I come to serve the prince without thought for the welfare of mankind, then I am no more than his menial servant. If on the other hand I have taken upon myself an obligation to the empire at large [t'ien-hsia], then indeed am I the prince's mentor and colleague, and only then may I be called a minister.

As the alternative to present evils, these Ch'ing critics held forth a vision of the original "feudal" Confucian commonwealth. They differed considerably, however, as to whether this ideal was to be taken literally or metaphorically. Huang Tsung-hsi, the literalist, urged that "everything be changed, until the original order is restored"—the order, that is, which had prevailed before the Ch'in unification in 221 B.C. He also argued at length, and somewhat defensively, for a "restoration" of the well-field system. The well-field (ching-t'ien) system was a kind of peasant commune, in which eight private plots were arranged symetrically around a central parcel of land which the peasants tended on behalf of the prince. The resulting pattern resembled the Chinese character meaning "a well" 井 , from which the institution drew its name. It was an arrangement attributed more by tradition than on the basis of any firm historical evidence to the age of virtuous government. Mencius had talked about it—it was by his time already only a memory—and later reformers came back again and again to the idea; even, as we shall see, an occasional twentieth-century socialist in search of indigenous sources of inspiration. Ku Yen-wu and Huang Tsung-hsi made much of it. Huang in particular was at pains to demonstrate on the basis of careful calculations that a revival of the well-field system would entail no threat to the interests of the wealthy: seventy-five percent of the arable land would satisfy the requirements of the population at large; the rich could keep the rest. "So why must there be any fuss over property limitations and equalization of land, or this needless to-do about causing the rich to suffer?" However trenchant their critique of the existing political order, these thinkers of the early Ch'ing were anything but social levelers.

Wang Fu-chih, as has been noted, developed an uncommonly (for a Confucian) relativistic theory of historical change, and was therefore keenly sensitive to the different needs of different times. He was consequently sceptical as to the usefulness of classical precedent too strictly applied. He did not repudiate the faith: "The most effective way of governing," he wrote, "is to examine the *Book of History* and temper its pronouncements with the words of Confucius." But, he cautioned,

> The crucial point is whether the ruler's heart is reverent or dissolute, his statutes too lax or too harsh. . . . The principal function of government is to make use of worthy men and promote moral instruction, and in dealing with the people to bestow on them the greatest humanity and love. . . . But when it comes to setting up detailed regulations or making up directives, then the authors of the *Book of History* or Confucius offer no guidance. . . . The ancient institutions were designed to govern the ancient world, and cannot be applied to the present day. Therefore the wise man does not try to set up detailed systems. One uses what is right for today to govern the world of today, but this does not mean that it will be right for a later day. . . . Neither the *History* nor Confucius describe feudalism [or] the well-field system. . . . Times change, conditions are different. . . . There are crises of the moment to be met in every age. . . . I have sought the source of success and failure in government, and have tried to bring my ideas into accord with the fundamental principles of the government of the sages. But when it comes to questions of particular incidents and laws, then one must follow the times and try to determine what is fitting in each case.

Ku Yen-wu occupied the middle ground. He admitted that times do indeed change and that institutions must follow suit. But to his way of thinking, this offered grounds for hope. If the ideal could be kept alive, would not the inevitable turning of history once more bring about conditions favorable to its realization? Even as feudalism had crumbled before the power of the centralized empire, so must the empire itself in time decay and be transformed. "Does this mean a return to feudalism? No, that would be impossible. But if some sage were to appear who could invest the prefectural system with the essential meaning of feudalism, then the world would attain order." What this meant, in Ku's scheme of things, was that local officials should again be invested with hereditary authority. Gone then would be the scramble for office; gone too the burdensome requirement of bureaucratic service that kept an official constantly on the move, from place to place, from one kind of responsibility to another, throughout his career. Only then could officials become in fact what they were sometimes called in the colloquial language, "father and mother officials" (fu-mu kuan), servants of the prince bound by ties of intimate and enduring affection to the people.

At the end of the Ch'ing dynasty, radical reformers eagerly adopted these seventeenth-century thinkers not for what they may seem to us, the proponents of a "feudal reaction," but as the forerunners of modernity: adversaries of the autocrat; precursors of a nationalistic reaction against alien rule; originators of a sceptical and empirical intellectual methodology. It is not hard to understand such enthusiasm, for there had been an uncommonly sharp edge to this early-Ch'ing critique of the existing order. But to see these men as the heralds of republicanism, popular sovereignty and civil liberty, of a scientific world view, of nationalism, is to claim too much—and thereby, perhaps, to make us wonder why they seem in the end to have achieved so little.

Take nationalism first. It is a term, and a political motive, that will give us a good deal of trouble as our history goes forward, one that we will have to deal with in a variety of contexts. An established axiom of Chinese history—perhaps even a fact—is that until the end of the nineteenth century, when they were compelled to confront the implications of Western (and Japanese) power and competition, the Chinese knew nothing of nationalism. In other words, it was the integrity of Confucian culture, not the survival of the Chinese state, that preoccupied them. Obviously there is more than a little truth to this view: one need only recall Su Shih's memorial to know where Confucian priorities lay. Yet it is simpler than the whole truth. Confucians were anything but indifferent to the state. It would be difficult, in fact, to conceive of Confucianism in the absence of the state, for by no other agency could the broader values of the humane social community be realized. In the secure world of traditional China, however, Confucians took the existence of the state as a political entity pretty much for granted. What they could never take for granted was the state's willingness to pursue the cultural purposes to which, as Confucians, they attached such importance. They were disposed, as a result, always to judge the legitimacy of a given political regime in terms of this latter consideration.

What occurred in the nineteenth century was a fundamental shift in emphasis. No longer able to take for granted the existence of the state itself, Confucians were forced to ask themselves some hard questions about the culture that sustained it—or that it sustained. Which was it? How did the one relate to the other? Was the essence of Chineseness the political identity now threatened, or the cultural personality which Confucians had habitually advocated and defended? The questions did not of course phrase themselves to the nineteenth-century Chinese mind in terms of such stark alternatives, nor were the answers unambiguous. In a time of self-doubt, the uncompromising boldness of thinkers like Huang Tsung-hsi and Ku Yen-wu, and especially Wang Fu-chih, carried a very natural appeal. *They* had known what it meant to be Chinese; *they* had recognized the Manchus for what they were: the conquerors of a culture, not participants in it, much less its protectors. So, two hundred years after their time, the writings of "the hermit of Hunan" were quietly published and circumspectly read by a generation to whom the Manchus had become no less an anathema than they had been to Wang and the Ming loyalists.

What Wang offered was a clear definition and an impassioned defense of the nation as a cultural community that must be preserved inviolate. This was so, he argued, because of natural and decisive differences in the human species itself. "Barbarians and Chinese are born on different soil. Their lands being different, so is the air they breathe; their climates being different, so too do they differ in their ways of life; and their customs differing, how can they not also differ in their understanding, and in their conduct?"[22] The conclusion was unequivocal: barbarians could not become Chinese. The old image of China as an ocean of civilization salting the rivers of barbarism that run into it is thus replaced by the idea of cultures divided by a fixed frontier—it needs only a little imagination to read into Wang's thought here a political as well as a cultural meaning. A frontier, of course, has two sides. Wang saw, or pretended to see, nothing wrong with being a barbarian, if one were *born* a barbarian and content to remain so. "The two lands will ignore each other, to the advantage of both. It is in accordance with the ordinances of Heaven and the dictates of human feeling that each should thus find delight only in his own ways."

In the nineteenth century, more than one Imperial Commissioner for the Management (or Suppression) of the Barbarians played variations on this theme to unresponsive audiences of assorted Westerners. It was not a debt they owed to Wang directly, but rather the expression of a defensive Chinese instinct. The problem was, of course, that Westerners refused to be cast in the role thus assigned them. They took, to be sure, considerable delight in their own ways—sufficiently to assume that the Chinese might benefit thereby. Certainly they did not think of their laws and institutions as "rude," their customs "crude," their temper "violent and savage"—Wang's terms all. To end-of-the-century rebels whose primary purpose was to rid China of the humiliation of Manchu overlordship, Wang's writings provided a rich vocabulary of cultural and racial discrimination. But the kind of "nationalism" appropriate to China's traditional relationship to her neighbors was, like so much else of the Confucian inheritance, painfully anachronistic in the crises of the nineteenth century. And neither Wang nor any of his contemporaries laid the foundation for a nationalism that went beyond this, a nationalism that would harness the energies of the people—call it self-strengthening, call it modernization, call it revolution—to the task of creating a more powerful state. Such a purpose, indeed, was not only beyond their vision, but utterly against their principles.

"One method of delivery alone remains to us," wrote Francis Bacon in *Novum Organum.* "We must lead men to the particulars themselves, and their series and order; while men on their side must force themselves for awhile to lay their notions by and to familiarize themselves with facts."[23] It is a sentiment, on the face of it, that might well have issued from the brush of Ku Yen-wu, a generation later and a world away. Ku and his *k'ao-cheng* colleagues were indefatigable in their search for facts and particulars, and endlessly patient in calling attention to them to off-set the "notions" of their time. It was Chu Hsi in the twelfth century who had raised to the status of a canonical injunction the idea that true understanding depends on "the investigation of things" (*ko-wu*) and through it "the extension of knowledge" (*chih-chih*). But for Sung and Ming thinkers, "things" still meant the underlying categories of Confucian belief. It remained for Ku Yen-wu in the seventeenth century, and other scholars who followed his lead then and later, to give substance to the idea of "investigation" through their philological and textual studies.

A good deal has been written on the "empiricism" of early Ch'ing scholarship, pro and con. Twentieth-century reformers like Liang Ch'i-ch'ao and Hu Shih, anxious to demonstrate the existence of historical affinities between China and the West, advanced extravagant claims for the scientific (or at least proto-scientific) accomplishments of the *k'ao-cheng* scholars. There were many who disagreed, however; those to whom the fact that Ku could adduce one hundred and sixty arguments in support of his case for a certain ancient pronunciation of a certain character seemed insufficient grounds on which to affirm the "scientific" instincts of seventeenth-century philologists. It is not only methodological similarities that establish a style of thought as scientific, wrote one such critic, but even more important, "a consonance of purposes."[24] In itself this is a dispute that belongs to a later stage in the evolution of Chinese self-perceptions, and we need not go into it in detail here. Certainly there was a refreshingly down-to-earth common sense underlying Ku Yen-wu's researches into the documentary sources of Confucian belief: his emphasis on intellectual originality and independence from received interpretation; his urgings that evidence must take precedence over opinion; his insistence that classical study must justify itself in terms of its relevance to present-day problems. All this bespeaks an intellectual temper strikingly in contrast to the speculative abstractness of Sung and Ming Confucianism. And indeed, to keep the cutting edge of this contrast honed always to razor sharpness was one of the principal aims of *k'ao-*

cheng scholarship. This meant, among other things, an all-engrossing preoccupation with the fundamentals of the faith: its textual authorities.

It may well be questioned whether the objectives of early Ch'ing scholarship, viewed from this perspective, were in fact consonant with the motives of empirical investigation. General curiosity is quite absent from the seventeenth-century Chinese mind; inquiry into the structure of nature or of human experience is entirely alien to it. For all Ku's intellectual energy, he is obviously not driven by Bacon's haunting vision of man's "unquiet understanding" that "cannot stop or rest, and still presses onward, but in vain."[25] Hu Shih, writing in the 1930s, drew the comparison that is to us as obvious as for him it must have been painful: "Galileo, Kepler, Boyle, Harvey, and Newton worked with the objects of nature, with stars, balls, inclining planes, telescopes, microscopes, prisms, chemicals, and numbers and astronomical tables. And their Chinese contemporaries worked with books, words, and documentary evidences. The latter created three hundred years of scientific book learning; the former created a new science and a new world."[26] In the engaging picture of Ku Yen-wu clearing away the underbrush to decipher an ancient and forgotten legend among the ruins of North China there is not, after all, much of the Baconian spirit of scientific enterprise. One is more apt to be reminded, perhaps, of Ku's fellow antiquarian and almost exact contemporary, John Aubrey, poking about among the prehistoric relics and the overgrown churchyards of his beloved Wiltshire: a small light in an obscure corner of the past, not the great illumination that could set men's feet upon the path to the future.

But this is unjust. It is to charge these seventeenth-century scholars with failing to accomplish what they never set themselves to do, or even imagined. Ku's methods were entirely purposeful, given his intent; and his intent was not, as with Bacon, the discovery of "progressive stages of certainty," but rather to achieve a greater degree of accuracy in understanding what was already certain. Joseph Levenson, who calls Ch'ing empiricism "abortive," renders the fair verdict: "What is at issue here, of course, is not ability but taste. If Chinese in modern times have been forced to wonder where science belongs in their heritage, it is not because their forebears were constitutionally unable to nurture a growing tradition of science, but because they did not care to; early Ch'ing empiricists were not aiming at science and falling short, but living out the values of their culture."[27]

So it was, too, in their political views. For all the incisive bitterness of their attack on the unrestrained exercise of imperial power, none of these early Ch'ing critics questioned the absolute authority of the ruler. What they repudiated was not the authoritarian premise but the despotic objectives of imperial rule. Following Mencius, they made the welfare of the people the first principle of government; faithful to the ancient ideal, they held the empire to be "the common possession of all men."* They were inclined to believe that these aims could better be achieved if those on whom rested more directly the burden of governing the people's lives were invested with greater authority. Their liberality of spirit did not extend beyond this to encompass in any sense a formal liberalism, however rudimentary. They envisioned no constitutional restraints on the monarchy; they did not acknowledge the legitimacy of diverse individual or social interests; they made no effort to establish a sphere of privacy from the constraints of the culture. By no stretch of the imagination can they be portrayed as incipient democrats, or even republicans. They could never have understood John Locke.

In respect at least to diagnosis they might perhaps have understood Rousseau. The problem posed by the unwieldy magnitude of political and social institutions was to them, as it was to him, profoundly disturbing. They were convinced, as he was, that "the more the social bond is stretched, the weaker does it become."[28] They believed, as he did, that the moral community could not exceed certain political and geographic limits without losing that which gives it form and value—limits surpassed, in the case of China, from the very inception of imperial rule. Their response was to invoke "the spirit of feudalism," and to distinguish (as Rousseau did also) between the moral law that creates the community and the laws which merely govern it: "legalistic muck," Huang called the dynastic codes, "unlawful laws" designed by "petty literocrats" only to safeguard, in ponderous detail, the usurped privileges of imperial power. The Confucian Sage Ruler, as they imagined him, bears some resemblance to Rousseau's Legislator, in respect both to the supreme wisdom of his endeavor and to its historical or logical primacy. "If the nation is to be governed," wrote Wang Fu-chih, "there must first be a leader who will establish the laws and institutions. . . . " He might well have finished the thought in Rousseau's own words, "in every respect an extraordinary man in the State," whose mission "has nothing in common with human empire."[29]

In a more fundamental way, however, Rousseau would have remained entirely an enigma to these Confucian thinkers. They could not have comprehended that side of him which strove to reconcile "freedom" to the claims of "sovereignty," justifying to this end the "death and destruction" of the "natural man" and submission of the individual to the General Will. In all this they would not have understood him, for these were categories quite extraneous to their minds, concerns outside the Confucian tradition of political discourse and therefore irrelevant to their

---

* "When the Way prevails, then the empire is the common possession of all men": a phrase from the opening lines of the Li-yun chapter of the Li chi (or "Record of Rituals," largely a Han-dynasty compilation of earlier ritual texts) which assumed great importance in nineteenth-century reformist thought, as we shall see.

criticism of the imperial order. Their purpose was not liberty, though for obvious reasons much that they wrote proved useful to political radicals who discovered it two hundred years later with this purpose already in mind. Their aim, as political critics and as scholars, was to illuminate the abuses that Confucianism had come to justify; this they did courageously, with uncommon vigor of mind and vividness of language. But this was not a call, premature and unheeded, for revolution.

And yet there was, for all that, a revolution in the making here, the long, often painful, ultimately unsuccessful revolution against the Confucian-imperial alliance. This was the beginning, in other words, of the attempt that was carried forward into the early years of the twentieth century to break the link forged in the Han dynasty that bound Confucian ideals to the service of imperial ambition. By establishing clearly and persuasively the idea that Confucianism had a history of its own, distinguishable from the institutions with which for centuries it had shared the edifice of Chinese civilization, these seventeenth-century thinkers prepared men's minds to consider the monarchy and the ideology as divisible entities. Never themselves doubting the authority of Confucian values, they endeavored to dissolve the damaging connection between those values and the particular forms of imperial government. Whether this could be accomplished became, in the nineteenth and twentieth centuries, the great issue on which turned the fate of Confucianism. It was not that kind of an issue in the seventeenth century, for the simple reason that, no matter how convincingly one might argue that the Confucian monarchy distorted Confucian ideals, there was then no question as to the adequacy of the imperial government as a political enterprise. Seventeenth-century political criticism thus existed, as it were, in a vacuum, unrelated to any organized movement for political reform, much less revolutionary change.

Not until the nineteenth century did the imperial system reveal the vulnerability that would call its survival into question, and pose the problem of the fate of Confucianism in an entirely new and unpromising light. In that later time, the case against both was argued, upon occasion, in terms drawn from the writings of Huang Tsung-hsi and Ku Yen-wu and Wang Fu-chih. Their own times had burdened them sufficiently; but they had been spared at least the anguish of that final doubt, and the grief of that ultimate humiliation.

The Nineteenth Century:
Rebellion and Restoration

If neither the ability of its Ministers nor the alleged wisdom of its laws, nor even the numberless multitude of its inhabitants, has been able to protect this realm against subjection by ignorant and rude barbarians, of what service have been all its wise men?

—*Jean-Jacques Rousseau*

"MANCHUS AND CHINESE ARE ONE FAMILY!" proclaimed a favorite Ch'ing-dynasty slogan. It was propaganda, of course, but propaganda that to a remarkable degree described the settlement reached by the end of the seventeenth century. The 1660s, the decade of the Oboi regency, had marked the low point in the Manchu-Chinese relationship. With the overthrow of the regency and K'ang Hsi's assumption of power in his own right in 1669, more conciliatory policies were again adopted. Throughout the life of the dynasty it remained a delicate problem of political craftsmanship to achieve a stable and effective balance of Chinese and Manchu elements within the government. Neither party was allowed to forget that ethnic as well as political lines divided them: so long as intermarriage was prohibited, any talk of Manchus and Chinese being "one family" was clearly political rhetoric, not social policy.

Nevertheless, the Manchus proved to be energetic students and enthusiastic patrons of Confucian culture, as their imperial role demanded of them. So far, indeed, had the passions of conquest receded by 1776 that the Ch'ien Lung emperor, K'ang Hsi's grandson, found it not incongruous in that year to authorize the dedication of a shrine honoring the gentry patriots who had died leading the anti-Manchu resistance in the siege of Chiang-yin in 1645. Loyalty to the principle of loyalty was regarded, after all, as loyalty to a common inheritance.

Ch'ien Lung himself was just then engaged in a stunning display of cultural fidelity, sponsoring the compilation of what was destined to become the greatest of all imperial libraries, the celebrated *Ssu-k'u ch'üan-shu* (The complete library of the four repositories). This was patronage of learning—or at least patronage of the learned—in the grand manner, involving as it did all levels of officialdom in the search for rare and ancient books, and for more than a decade employing the talents of a small army of scholars and copyists in a variety of editorial tasks. When it was finally completed the *Ssu-k'u ch'üan-shu* contained nearly thirty-five hundred individual works in seven sets of some thirty-six thousand manuscript copies each.* The Imperial Catalog compiled at the same time contained notices and critiques of over ten thousand titles, and by itself comprised two hundred volumes.

But there was another and more sinister aspect to the project. To the same edict that commanded provincial officials to submit works of local provenance to Peking—in order, as the emperor gracefully put it, "that they may flow down the river of time"—there was subjoined an additional, ominous instruction: writings discovered to be unfriendly to the Manchu house were to be "set aside to await destruction by fire."[1] Eventually this *index expurgatorius* numbered between two and three thousand items, including several of Wang Fu-chih's posthumously edited essays, Ku Yen-wu's *Jih-chih lu*, and a number of Huang Tsung-hsi's works. (The fact that *Ming-i tai-fang lu* was not among the latter suggests not that it was deemed innocuous, but that it remained even in the 1780s virtually unknown.)

So we are reminded again not only of the alien origins of the Manchus, but of the dual nature of the Chinese ruling power. Patronage of scholarship and extirpation of dissent went always hand in hand. In this regard the Ch'ing was probably not much more repressive than its predecessor, though the fault lines underlying this regime, the subterranean stresses, insured that eventual political upheaval would result in ethnic as well as regional fracture. But surveying the Ch'ing during most of its history—from, let us say, roughly the 1680s down through the 1860s or even beyond—one is more likely to be struck by the extent to which Manchu and Chinese interests appear to coalesce than by the increasingly artificial distinctions that continued to divide them. By the beginning of the nineteenth century the issue that had so exercised the Ming loyalist thinkers of the 1650s and 1660s, and that would revive once again to haunt the final decades of the dynasty's life,—the issue of Manchu "bar-

---

* The original "four repositories" were located in Peking, (one within the palace, one on the grounds of the Summer Palace outside the city), Mukden and Jehol. Three more complete copies were subsequently deposited in Yangchow, Chinkiang and Hangchow.

barism"—lay largely dormant. Manchus and Chinese shared a political culture. Manchu emperor and Chinese ministers stood together as beneficiaries and defenders of a common cultural inheritance: an inheritance imperilled by the intrusion of the West and by the threat of rebellion.

* * *

Throughout the nineteenth century the Ch'ing dynasty was on the political defensive. The century had begun inauspiciously in the shadow of imperial corruption and rebellion. The final decades of the Ch'ien Lung reign were dominated by the sinister figure of Ho-shen, a Manchu guardsman of obscure background whose ascendancy over the aging emperor was such that virtually the entire administrative apparatus fell prey to his insatiable appetites—which extended even to such exotic tastes as pearls encased in gold, a common bribe, according to one account, which Ho-shen took medicinally each morning as an aid to his powers of memory. Avarice on so grand and unguarded a scale was of course much commented upon, even occasionally condemned at considerable risk. Yet it was more symptom than cause of the rot that had begun to undermine the structure of Manchu authority. As arbitrary exactions from above grew more burdensome, local conditions became more precarious and unstable. Anti-dynastic sentiment flourished, centering sometimes around the nuclei of secret-society organizations, which in a few cases raised the tattered banner of allegiance to the long-lost Ming cause. Manchu military garrisons grown inept through a century and more of peace proved unequal to the challenge, and in some areas local disturbances swelled to the magnitude of full-scale insurrection. In 1796 the Ch'ien Lung emperor abdicated; having matched K'ang Hsi's sixty-year reign, it would have been an unfilial act to out-rule him. In that same year the White Lotus Rebellion erupted and raged uncontrollable for nearly a decade. When it was over Ch'ien Lung was dead. So was Ho-shen, by his own hand, his political machine dismantled, his fabulous wealth confiscated. It was reported that Ho-shen's private estate was richer by far than the imperial treasury, which had been sadly depleted by the enormous costs of "bandit suppression" and the misappropriation of funds by unscrupulous military commanders. The temper of the Chia Ch'ing reign (1796–1820) was one of stringency and diminished imperial self-assurance.

The White Lotus Rebellion had been a disease deep within the bowels of the empire, ravaging the central and western provinces of Honan and Hupeh, Szechwan, Shensi and Kansu, the recurrence of a chronic dynastic ailment. Simultaneously came the awareness of another affliction, an epidermal inflammation of the nerves that may have seemed at first hardly to be reckoned a serious threat to the health of the dynasty.

Foreign shipping into the city of Canton, the only port open to such trade, had increased during the Ch'ien Lung period, not dramatically, but steadily. By the 1780s and 1790s, some fifty to a hundred vessels a year, chiefly British, sailed up the broad estuary of the Pearl River to load silks, porcelains, rhubarb, and, of course, Chinese teas. For these precious cargoes they paid with British woollens, a few miscellaneous luxury items, and enormous quantities of bullion, for these were the days before Chinese addiction to Indian opium created a limitless demand for that lucrative commodity. In 1793 there arrived in China the first British envoy dispatched for the purpose of adjusting the conditions of trade more to Western advantage, or at least less to Western disadvantage. The embassy headed by Lord Macartney was viewed by the English as an entirely appropriate effort to initiate ordinary diplomatic relations, aimed hopefully at the regularization and extension of commerce. "No doubt the interchange of commodities between Nations distantly situated tends to their mutual convenience, industry and wealth," wrote George III in the confident letter which Macartney conveyed to the Chinese emperor; "as the blessings which the Great God of Heaven has conferred upon various soils and climates are thus distributed among his Creatures scattered over the surface of the Earth."[2] The Chinese saw it differently. To them the British embassy was no more than a tribute mission, albeit from an extraordinary distance, timed happily to coincide with the imperial birthday. "Now England is paying homage," wrote the old emperor complacently. "My Ancestors' merit and virtue must have reached their distant shores. Though their tribute is commonplace, my heart approves sincerely."[3]

With hindsight we may glimpse in this suggestion of cultures at cross-purposes much of the tragedy of Sino-Western relations in the nineteenth and twentieth centuries. In 1816, by which time foreign commerce had increased substantially and the introduction of opium was already beginning to affect the balance of trade, Lord Amherst, on a similar mission, met a similar rebuff. This is not the burden of the history that concerns us here. But it is important for us to recognize the extent to which the Chinese perception of their situation in the nineteenth century was shaped by the confluence of domestic and foreign crises, of familiar and unfamiliar problems. It was only natural for Ch'ing statesmen to diagnose these different problems as symptoms of a single malady, and to prescribe in austere Confucian fashion the patent moral remedies that had in the past rejuvenated dynastic fortunes. Up to a point it was a perceptive diagnosis. Foreign encroachment undoubtedly contributed to domestic instability. Conversely, the inability of the Chinese to keep their affairs in order was a principal inducement to, and justification of, escalating Western demands. But in the end it was not an effective cure. In the minds and in the careers of the generation of leaders that came to power in China in the 1850s and 1860s, the two great themes of nineteenth-century history—restoration and self-strengthening, renovation and innovation—became blurred at the level of intellectual formulation. At the level of political effect, they tended to cancel each other out.

Nineteenth-century Confucianism was by no means merely, or even primarily, a reactionary and defensive response to the challenge of Western ideas. Not until late in the century, in fact, did the Chinese perceive an intellectual dimension to the Western threat. Confucianism retained its traditional character in the nineteenth century as a varied and comprehensive complex of intellectual possibilities and vocational opportunities. The officially sanctioned interpretation remained that enshrined in Sung-dynasty commentaries, the foundation upon which preparation for the examinations was based. The essential core of conservative nineteenth-century Confucianism thus still adhered to the Sung-dynasty opinion that "only if what we call human life should come to an end could the laws of the Sage Kings ever be changed."[4] This meant that the orthodox school continued to place its greatest emphasis on self-cultivation and to regard effective government more as a moral accomplishment than as a matter of managerial competence.

Early Ch'ing thinkers, as we have seen, reacted not against the moral imperatives embodied in the "Way of the Sage Rulers," but against what they regarded as the unprofitably speculative bias of Sung and Ming scholars. In the course of the eighteenth century the tradition of philological and historical scholarship characteristic of the Han Learning had made substantial methodological advances, but at some cost. Much of the quality of moral partisanship that had enlivened early Ch'ing scholarship had been lost, giving way to a technically sophisticated pursuit of scholarship for its own sake, erudite but arid, increasingly remote from the vital issues of the time. Early Ch'ing thought remained nevertheless the principal inspiration to private scholarship, and Confucians in the late eighteenth and nineteenth centuries, responding in different ways to what they regarded as its degeneracy, were all touched by it. The T'ung-ch'eng School, so called for the city in Anhwei province that was the center of its activities, attempted to combine the Han Learning emphasis on textual authenticity with something of the moral fervor of Sung-dynasty Confucianism. T'ung-ch'eng scholars also laid great stress on the importance of a simple and straightforward prose style, taking as their models some of the great essayists of the Sung, and affecting in their own writing a formal and studied archaism. "Imitative, overly punctilious, and devoid of substance," was Liang Ch'i-ch'ao's ultimate verdict on T'ung-ch'eng scholarship,[5] but the school nevertheless enjoyed considerable repute in the nineteenth century, largely as a result of the patronage bestowed upon it by Tseng Kuo-fan, the great scholar-statesman-general of the 1850s and 1860s. It never became, however, for reasons that are perhaps obvious, a significant vehicle for reformist opinion.

Much more important in this regard were the Statecraft (*ching-shih*) writers of the nineteenth century who shared the conviction of thinkers like Ku Yen-wu and Huang Tsung-hsi that learning must justify itself in terms of practical application, and who stressed the importance of administrative competence and the acquisition of the kind of knowledge useful to the management of the bureaucratic enterprise. We will have more to say of them shortly. Finally, the "New Text" (*chin-wen*) school, exploiting in part the findings of Han Learning scholarship, attempted to derive doctrinal sanction for highly unorthodox interpretations of the "true" meaning of the Confucian legacy on the basis of a radical revision of what should be regarded as the authentic texts of Confucianism. As we shall see in the next chapter, this became in the hands of K'ang Yu-wei, its last and most formidable exponent, a rallying point for political as well as intellectual reformers in the late nineteenth century.

The school of Statecraft had as its antecedents that Confucian sub-tradition which over the centuries most closely paralleled the Legalist concern with questions of practical statesmanship and the effective functioning of administrative institutions. Its adherents accepted implicitly the moral purposes of the Confucian regime, the "Kingly Way" (*wang-tao*). What they made emphatically explicit was the connection between Confucian ends and governmental means. "In this world there is wealth and power without the kingly way. But there is no kingly way without wealth and power."[6] So wrote Wei Yuan (1794–1856) in the 1820s, in his preface to a collection of essays on problems of statecraft, the *Huang-ch'ao ching-shih wen-pien*, which quickly became enormously influential in literati circles. In the decades that followed, much of the reformist literature connected with the Self-strengthening movement, as it came to be called, was published in "statecraft collections" for which Wei's compilation served as the prototype.

It was not that Wei Yuan and other Statecraft writers thought of themselves as innovators or even as reformers. They advocated no departure from the established principles of government, nor did they envision any fundamental restructuring of its organization. They were reformers and innovators nevertheless, simply because they emphasized the importance of political competence; in the situation in which the Chinese found themselves in the nineteenth century this emphasis inevitably brought them up against problems with which no Confucian bureaucracy had previously had to concern itself. The work for which Wei Yuan is best remembered is a case in point. The *Hai-kuo t'u-chih* (An Illustrated Gazeteer of the Maritime Countries) is a general and frequently more imaginative than factual description of the alien world with which the Chinese were now compelled to contend. Wei published it in 1844, in line with the view that he had enunciated two years earlier: "To plan barbarian affairs it is necessary to know first the barbarians' conditions."[7] In itself the opinion is anything but remarkable. It is Sun-tzu, after all, the great classical strategist, who is credited with the wise advice that the key to victory is a thorough knowledge of one's enemy. As early as the second century B. C. the Han emperor, acting upon the same instinct, had dispatched one of his generals, the celebrated Chang Ch'ien, on a reconnaissance into Central Asia that took him as far west as Bactria and Ferghana in search of information concerning the barbarians who controlled the Asian heartland. The Chinese, in other words, were not historically as naive as Wei Yuan's admonition might make them appear. But in the early and middle decades of the nineteenth century they were lamentably uninformed about the world that impinged upon them, these "outer barbarians" who are, Wei warned, "as treacherous as the owls."[8]

In 1849 another Statecraft scholar and geographer, Hsu Chi-yü (1795–1873), published a far more detailed and credible description of the world. Hsu's Ying-huan chih-lueh (A Short Account of the Maritime Circuit) had not only more, and more reliable, geographical information, but also good maps and a considerable commentary on the history and political economies of the territories it surveyed. To the Chinese at mid-century it was a revelation. As Fred Drake has put it, "Hsu Chi-yü became Marco Polo, Columbus, Balboa, Tasman, Cook and Bering for many Chinese readers in the 1850s and 1860s." However, as Drake also observes, Hsu was a "vicarious explorer."[9] A native of the northern inland province of Shansi, he travelled on official appointment thoughout South China, an experience which doubtless contributed to his awareness of the newly important maritime frontier. But of the world disclosed by his geography he knew nothing at first hand, nor for several decades would a Chinese able to command the attention of his countrymen venture abroad to bring back eyewitness accounts of the West. What distinguished Hsu's work from earlier treatises like Wei Yuan's (which was itself derived from a gazeteer compiled by Lin Tse-hsü, the unfortunate imperial commissioner over whose head broke the storm of the Opium War in the early 1840s) was Hsu's willingness to incorporate into it, indeed largely to rely upon, Western works in those sections which dealt with the West. It was an American missionary in Amoy, one David Abeel, who in 1844 loaned Hsu the atlas that first provoked his interest in Western geography, and it was from other missionaries, ship captains, and consular officials that he subsequently learned much of what he came to know of the non-Chinese world.

Hsu Chi-yü was not, prehaps, a typical official of the 1840s. "He is the most inquisitive Chinese of high rank I have yet met," observed Abeel, though he conceded regretfully that Hsu's curiosity made him "far more anxious to learn the state of the kingdoms of this world, than the truths of the kingdom of heaven."[10] Hsu and his geography point up a fact of critical and increasing importance to the intellectual as well as the political history of China in the nineteenth century: the existence of the treaty ports, and within them of exotic cultural enclaves where flourished a style of life and thought distinctly alien in Chinese eyes, yet easily enough accessible to those who were disposed to go and see for themselves the manner of these unfamiliar barbarians. In the course of the nineteenth century the concessions which Macartney in 1793 and Amherst in 1816 had failed to win through diplomatic representation were wrested from the Manchus by force, or the threat of it. The treaty ports were those cities opened to foreign trade and residence by the Treaty of Nanking (1842) and later settlements. They were initially five in number, a semicircle reaching up the coast from Canton in the south to Shanghai in the north. Subsequent treaties greatly enlarged the system: by the end of the dynasty in 1911 there were some forty-eight cities designated as Customs stations, extending into the interior as far as Changsha in Hunan and Chungking in Szechwan, river ports hundreds of miles from the open ocean. In the treaty ports, subject to the legal jurisdiction of their own consuls rather than the laws of the empire, foreigners conducted business very much on terms which they themselves dictated. There they lived, insofar as local conditions allowed, in accordance with their own taste and sense of civilized convention. The economic consequences of this arrangement, the extent to which it may either have stimulated economic innovation or inhibited indigenous economic growth, are still the subject of a debate that need not detain us here. The cultural and intellectual significance of the treaty ports is less open to question. As we shall see more fully in the next chapter, they were from the very beginning the generating centers of intellectual change.

Treaty-port culture, the creation of communities largely constituted of merchants and missionaries, was a combination of commercial self-interest and evangelical zeal. On either hand the Westerners of the treaty ports were militantly confident in the propagation of their values, allied in the belief that stubborn Chinese backwardness must yield, to force if necessary, in order that the grand design both of God and of untrammelled trade might be realized. Missionary opinion, especially in the early years, tended to regard its spiritual concerns to be promoted rather than contradicted by an aggressive approach. "It is much easier loving the souls of the heathen in the abstract in America than it is in the concrete, encompassed as they are with such dirty bodies, speaking forth their foul language and vile natures," wrote S. Wells Williams in 1850.[11] Williams had arrived in Canton in 1833 on behalf of the American Board. He spent the better part of half a century in China as a missionary and diplomatic secretary. He learned the language fluently and was well travelled. He boasted a wide acquaintance in official Chinese circles. He wrote what was undoubtedly one of the most detailed and informative descriptions of the country available to the nineteenth-century readers, a work in two bulky volumes that very nearly justified its weighty title: *The Middle Kingdom: A Survey of the Geography, Government, Literature, Social Life, Arts, and History of the Chinese Empire and Its Inhabitants*. At the end of his life he returned to the United States to inaugurate instruction in Chinese language and literature at Yale. He was not, in other words, an unlearned or casual observer of the Chinese scene. Yet his condescension, by no means untypical of the attitudes of China Coast residents, remained unchallengeable. "I am sure that the Chinese need harsh measures to bring them out of their ignorance, conceit and idolatry," he wrote at the time of the treaty revision crisis of 1859–1860, which culminated with the sacking of the great Imperial Summer Palace in Peking by Western troops; "why then deplore the means used to accomplish this end so much as to blind our minds to the result which God seems to be advancing by methods whose inherent wrong He can punish at His own time."[12]

Some others, it is true, were less willing than was Williams to substitute the Last Judgment for a degree of present common sense. "It will take us some time to live it all down," wrote a fellow American missionary bleakly in 1861.[13] Sir Rutherford Alcock, H. B. M. Minister to Peking in the late 1860s and one of the staunchest advocates of the "Cooperative Policy" that ensured a few years of relative stability in Sino-Western relations during that decade, summed up the situation with grim candor: "In one way or another, however we may disguise it, our position in China has been created by force—naked, physical force."[14] Alcock was one of the few Westerners still able to perceive an element of grandeur in the historical accomplishments of the Chinese. The Confucian monarchy, he wrote in 1867,

> . . . has answered the end of all Government in a very wonderful degree. It has bound together, under one ruler, nearly a third of the human race; and under its successive dynasties they have been trained to be a peace-loving, orderly, and industrious race. . . . They have much to be proud of; much they may well be excused if they are loath to part with, at the sudden requisition of foreign powers they have not yet learned to regard as other than barbarian and inferior.[15]

But Alcock was insightful to a degree uncommon in his time; only a handful of missionaries would have agreed with him, and most of them with reservations.

Alcock was also cautious, as were a number of his diplomatic colleagues: reluctant to press the Chinese for concessions of uncertain profitability which the Western powers might subsequently find it embarrassing or difficult to defend. So, for example, the diplomats tended to discourage missionary demands that they be allowed by the Chinese government to foresake the security—and the confinement—of the treaty ports, to reside and propagate the faith in remote inland stations. The Chinese, observed Alcock in 1869, "may dislike the merchant, but the missionary they fear. . . . The one they regard as a trafficker, more or less intrusive, whose presence in the interior, with his extraterritoriality, they could well dispense with; but the other as creating an *imperium in imperio* fatal to the authority of the Emperor. And are they so far wrong in their conclusion?" The missionary response was not to deny the truth of Alcock's judgment, but to set it within the context of a larger and incontrovertible truth:

> *The very presence* of Anglo-Saxons in the East is revolutionary, and therefore we are warranted in arguing that if Christianity is to be banished because of its tendency to produce changes, the British and American Governments ought to recall every Anglo-Saxon in China. . . . If the despotic Governments of the East are to be left unimpaired, if nothing must be done which is at all likely to interfere with the ideas on which they are founded, then we have no right to bring to China the laws or the commerce of Christendom, and force the Chinese to accept them. Both are revolutionary in such countries as China and Japan. Both break up the established order of things.[16]

*   *   *

That the established order of things was breaking up in China became more and more obvious after 1850. The most dramatic evidence of this was the great rebellion that erupted in the south-central provinces at mid-century. The Taiping Rebellion, or as some writers call it, the Taiping Revolution, was one of the longest wars, and incomparably the most destructive and bloody, fought anywhere on earth in the nineteenth century—a raging inferno of insurrection that nearly razed the Confucian edifice. Like so much in the China of that day, it was touched by foreign influences; without question it shaped in fundamental ways the manner in which Chinese social, political and intellectual history evolved in its aftermath. Yet the nature of Western, and specifically missionary and Christian, influence on the development of the movement is difficult to assess, and the impact of the rebellion on the intellectual life of nineteenth-century China was largely indirect.

To Westerners who watched its progress from their coastal enclaves, what was astonishing about the Taiping rebellion was not merely its magnitude. Limited as was their access to it, they could only guess at the enormity of its geographic and social dimensions. What excited them, first with the thrill of recognition, later with the horror of betrayal, was the nature of its ideological justification. For the Taipings proclaimed themselves a Christian rebel movement—not only anti-Manchu or anti-dynasty, but anti-Confucian and dedicated to the establishment of a "Heavenly Kingdom of Great Peace" (T'ai-p'ing t'ien-kuo).

The inspiration behind this iconoclastic movement, the man who was eventually elevated to supreme rulership as the "Heavenly King" (T'ien-wang), was a failed scholar by the name of Hung Hsiu-ch'üan, a native of Hua hsien in Kwangtung province, some twenty-five miles north of Canton. Although his ancestors had settled in the hills of Kwangtung some fifteen or sixteen generations before Hung Hsiu-ch'üan's birth in 1814, the clan was still counted as one of the "guest families" (k'o-chia or Hakka), that is, as members of an ethnic and cultural minority which retained a North China dialect as the basis of its spoken language instead of the Cantonese colloquial, and which took great pride in its traditions of self-reliant industry and pugnacious independence.

Despite this parochialism, and despite frequent clashes between the highland Hakka peasants and the Cantonese lowlanders, the Hakka were not immune to the aspirations of the greater culture. As a boy, when he was not tending the family's water buffalo among the graves dotting the hillsides around his village, Hung Hsiu-ch'üan received a classical Confucian education. At the age of fourteen—this was in 1828, when Hung was sixteen sui by Chinese reckoning—he presented himself for the first time as a candidate for the prefectural (hsiu-ts'ai) degree at the great examination hall in Canton.* Success would have taken him an important step along the way toward conventional success, but he failed. For the next several years he settled into the life of many would-be scholars in similar circumstances, that of village schoolteacher. In 1836 he failed in a second attempt for the prefectural degree. On this occasion, wandering the streets of Canton outside the examination grounds, he chanced upon a foreign missionary, black-robed and bearded, preaching with the aid of a Chinese interpreter and distributing Christian literature. From them Hung received a collection of evangelistic tracts, "Good Words of Admonition to the Age" (Ch'üan-shih liang-yen), written by Liang A-fa, the first ordained convert to Protestantism and a prolific pamphleteer. At that time, with the interior still closed to them, without benefit even of the treaty ports from which to launch their crusade, Protestant missionaries put considerable faith in the efficacy of such tracts, briefer and more pointed than were the first cumbersome translations of the Bible, and able, as one English evangelist confidently put it, to "penetrate silently even to the Chamber of the Emperor. They easily put on a Chinese coat and may walk without fear through the breadth and length of the land. This we cannot do."[17]

One may well be sceptical that Christian literature in any form reached the imperial sanctum sanctorum in the 1830s. Be that as it may,

---

* The method of reckoning age in sui assigns an age of "one" at birth and adds a year on each successive lunar New Year.

in this case one of the least of the emperor's subjects packed Liang's tracts home to Hua hsien with him and, having perhaps glanced at them casually, put them upon a shelf. The following year Hung tried yet again to pass the examination, and again he failed, this time with disastrous personal consequences. He was carried home in a state of collapse and lay for some time ill and raving, possessed by a series of fantastic visions.* He saw himself carried to a high and luminous place; his internal organs were miraculously removed and replaced; thus purified, he was ushered into the presence of a patriarch whose golden beard flowed down over a long black robe. The old man showed him horrifying examples of human depravity, and then admonished him to go forth to "slay the demons," to cleanse the world of its sins. As to the means of accomplishing this, Hung was given instruction by a man of middle age whom he learned to call his "Elder Brother."

According to contemporary accounts, Hung emerged from the ordeal of his illness a changed man, filled with dignity and a sense of purpose. Yet for some time nothing came of it. The visions receded. He recovered his health sufficiently to return to teaching school. In 1843 he sat one final time for the prefectural examination, with the usual result. His failure did not provoke a recurrence of the autistic withdrawal he had suffered earlier, but he returned home bitter and rebellious. Some months later his attention was drawn to Liang A-fa's "Good Words" which had lain so long neglected—this by a cousin who had read it through and found it fascinatingly esoteric. As Hung read for himself, the full meaning of his half-forgotten visions burst upon him. The venerable sage with the golden beard was God; Hung's "Elder Brother," Jesus Christ; and Hung himself, Christ's "younger brother," the divinely ordained new messiah. Thus in a mind driven by disappointment and frustration to the very brink of derangement, the Taiping ideology took form; a chance encounter on a Canton street became an event of enormous historical consequence.

In the early days of his self-ordained ministry, perhaps even to the final despairing days of his life, Hung Hsiu-ch'üan must have possessed a personality of extraordinary force and appeal. Beginning with the conversion of a few relatives and friends, and the smashing of idols in and around his native village, Hung's "Society of God-worshippers" (*Pai huang-ti hui*) had grown by 1851 into a militant movement numbering tens of thousands of adherents. It had also fallen afoul of the authorities, and proclaimed itself in open revolt against the ruling dynasty, the "Manchu dogs" and "Tartar imps" who held the Chinese in humiliating

---

* Hung subsequently claimed that his dementia—or his period of inspiration—lasted forty days, as is generally recorded. Some scholars in recent years have tended to discount this, noting that it coincides too neatly with the duration of Christ's exile in the wilderness. Hung's illness may have lasted only a few days at most.

subjection.[18] The ensuing rebellion devastated the "ricebowl provinces" of central China and claimed uncounted millions or tens of millions of victims before it was finally beaten down in 1864. By then Hung Hsiu-ch'üan had retreated almost entirely into the dream world of his megalomania. His authority had been challenged by rivals, some of whom had discovered for themselves the advantages to be gained from private "divine revelations." Political and military leadership had passed to others, and much of the movement's early enthusiasm and momentum had vanished amid factional struggles. The rebellion failed, but it left the Chinese world greatly changed.

That social and economic conditions in nineteenth-century China were ripening for a crisis of some kind is beyond question. With each new generation, more and more peasants tried to wrest a subsistance from hardly more land, and in some cases less, than their forebears had cultivated. Pressed to the limit of survival, more and more were drifting off the land, some to the cities to work or to beg, some into the hills to join the swelling bands of brigands that pillaged the countryside. Life was becoming harder too for those who remained upon the land, a prey to exorbitant rents and arbitrary levies. It was a situation, in many places, beyond the power of the government to control or to ameliorate. The dynasty's defeat by the British in 1840–1842 had been costly not only in terms of wealth, but also in terms of its moral authority. In many hinterland areas its real authority too had all but disappeared as political and economic power passed into the hands of local gentry, merchants, and moneylenders.

The favorable balance of trade that China had enjoyed at the beginning of the century had vanished as the illicit trade in opium grew in volume and value throughout the 1830s and 1840s. Chinese silver lay in great heaps on the decks of foreign receiving ships anchored off the coast, waiting to be transferred to the holds of homeward-bound clippers that had discharged their cargoes of the drug for which it seemed the demand would forever outrun the supply. As silver drained away in this fashion, the economic consequences of the trade, like the opium itself, penetrated deeper and deeper into the interior. The common medium of exchange in the countryside was a copper currency, the famous square-holed Chinese cash. Taxes and rents, however, were computed in silver, the value of which in exchange for copper became steadily inflated. The resulting crisis spelled disaster for many, impelling them from passive endurance of misery to active revolt. It was a crisis sharply felt in those areas of Kwangsi and Kwangtung where secret society organizations coalesced in the 1840s with the nascent Taiping movement and the rebellion established its first entrenched bases.

It is thus not unreasonable to suppose that, in the circumstances in which the Chinese found themselves in the nineteenth century, rebellion was all but inevitable. The question remains, however, whether in the absence of such esoteric inspiration as that supplied by Hung Hsiu-ch'üan and his God-worshippers, rebellion would have followed the course it took, or come to the same end. In contrast to other contemporary rebel movements like the Nien, the Taiping program was in several respects explicitly revolutionary. The Taipings, for example, proclaimed the social equality of women. Footbinding was outlawed. Women were entitled to share equally in the distribution of land and wealth. They were obliged to work along side the men, even to perform military service. They were allowed to receive the same education and made eligible for appointment to the civil service if they passed the examinations. During the early years of the movement, moreover, the Taipings enacted and even enforced a rigid segregation of the sexes, prohibiting marriage for those below a certain rank.

On paper at least, Taiping economic policies constituted a comparably radical departure from the norms of the traditional culture. Land was to be shared out equally, with no one permitted to acquire more than personal need could justify. All moveable property was to be held in common, stored in state treasuries, and portioned out as individual need dictated. What the long-range social consequences of such policies might have been remains a matter for speculation, inasmuch as the policies themselves were never effectively or consistently implemented. The most the Taipings were able to accomplish, in those areas over which they exercised transient jurisdiction, was to lighten somewhat the tax burden. If it was a revolutionary movement it remained to the end a revolution in the making.

Much was written about Taiping Christianity at the time, and more has been written since in the attempt to establish the extent to which Taiping radicalism was the result of foreign, and specifically Christian, inspiration. It is generally conceded that Hung's faith was entirely the product of self-instruction, a sense of mission that came upon him with all the force of intimate personal revelation. His contacts with Western missionaries were sporadic, brief, and on the whole unedifying. In the 1850s, nevertheless, some Westerners perceived an opportunity of considerable promise in the drama unfolding in the hinterland. W. A. P. Martin, an American missionary stationed at Ningpo—and a man of whom we will hear a great deal more as we go along—wrote in 1856 of the Taipings as the "instruments of a super-human power, destined for the achievement of a glorious revolution."[19] A similarly enthusiastic appraisal came at about the same time from Thomas T. Meadows, an interpreter attached to the British consulate in Shanghai. With the Bible substituted for the Confucian Classics as the primary text in Taiping schools, Meadows found it possible to envision "a prosperous population of 360 millions of heathens . . . assiduously engaged in getting the Bible off by heart, from beginning to end. Should the thing take place, it will form a revolution as unparalleled in the world for rapidity, completeness, and extent as the Chinese people itself for its antiquity, unity and numbers."[20]

In his capacity as a British civil servant, however, Meadows was cooler in his appreciation of the degree to which Western interests might be served by giving support to the rebellion. "Except as a deeply interesting piece of contemporary history, we have nothing to do with it," he wrote to Lord Russell in 1862.[21] That was not quite the case. In that same year the Shanghai business community, Chinese and foreign, raised a force to defend the city from the threat of a Taiping assault; thereafter the Western powers, previously "neutral," sided quite unambiguously with the imperial cause. "We do not wish to revolutionize the country," observed the British minister in Peking in 1861, "for I am convinced that we are more likely to get on with a Manchoo than with a purely Chinese dynasty."[22] The treaty powers were in fact getting on well with the Manchus at that point. Having extracted from the reluctant Ch'ing in 1860 the right to establish themselves in several additional ports, including some along the lower Yangtze, it had become a decided nuisance to be prevented by the Taiping occupation of that area from exploiting these newly-won opportunities. By that time even those missionaries who had been prepared to see it as the design of God when Hung first raised the standard of rebellion were coming to the conclusion that it had instead probably been the Devil's handiwork. Issachar J. Roberts, an erratic-tempered American Baptist who had tutored Hung briefly in Canton in the 1840s and remained thereafter one of his steadiest supporters in mission circles, returned to Shanghai in 1862 from a fifteen-month stay in the Taiping capital at Nanking to denounce his former protégé as a madman and his entourage as a rabble of "coolie kings."[23]

Elements of Christian faith and discipline are nevertheless clearly evident in the regime which the Taipings established, and in the order of worship they devised. Theirs was an adamantly monotheistic creed, owing more to the stern, judgmental theology of the Old Testament than to the ideas of divine mercy and redemption found in the New Testament. Great significance was assigned to the Ten Commandments, but almost no attention was paid to the Sermon on the Mount. Neither the concept of the Trinity nor that of the Holy Spirit figure in Taiping Christianity. They did, however, accept the divinity of Christ and belief in an afterlife. A ceremony of baptism and the confession of sins was part of the rite of initiation into the Society. Regular attendance at church services was compulsory—services conducted not by a separately ordained clergy but by civil officials.

Beyond such forms, the degree of Christian influence on the spiritual substance of Taiping belief and on the policies of the Taiping government remains open to question. Western missionaries had always found it difficult in the extreme to convey any sense of the meaning of sin, the original and inescapable depravity of human nature, to a people brought up to believe on the authority of Mencius himself in the original *goodness* of human nature. The Taipings seem to have followed the path of least cultural resistance in this as in other matters of doctrinal interpretation: sin figures in Taiping scriptures essentially as a term for antisocial behavior, conduct that contradicts the requirements for maintaining the fundamental human relationships. There is more of Confucianism than of Christianity in this understanding. Even where the Taipings explicitly diverged from Confucian cultural norms, their debt to Christian alternatives remains debatable. Their attiude toward women, for example, might more sensibly be attributed to the peculiarities of Hakka culture than to Christian influences. The idea of sexual equality was hardly a principal tenet of nineteenth-century Christianity, nor is it an idea that emerges naturally from an uninstructed reading of the Scriptures. The Hakka, on the other hand, had traditionally assigned a higher social status to women than was common in Confucian culture at large, nor was it customary for Hakka girls to suffer the agonies of footbinding. And although they might be monotheists, the Taipings—at least the Taiping leaders—were anything but monogamists. Taiping polygamy was in fact a great sticking point for many missionaries who would have liked to approve of the movement. Hung Hsiu-ch'üan was reported to have acquired numerous wives (eighty-eight by one account), and his refuge during the final desperate days of the siege of Nanking was said to have been a harem well-populated with imperial concubines. Finally, it is difficult to reconcile the whole notion of sexual equality with such pronouncements as these from official Taiping texts: "Should a hen desire to herald the arrival of morning, it is one sure way of making the home miserable"; or even more ominously, "It is provided by Heaven that a hen's crowing will be followed by execution."[24]

It seems likewise improbable that Christian, or even Western, ideals of social justice underlay the radicalism of Taiping social and economic policies. While "good works" were certainly viewed as an aspect of the evangelical enterprise in China from the beginning, Christian endeavors in the middle decades of the nineteenth century were not informed by any comprehensive vision of social betterment. Missionary attention tended rather to be concentrated on concrete social disasters—famine relief, for example, in the wake of the great Yangtze floods of 1869—and on specific social ills: opium, footbinding, prostitution, gambling—moral turpitude in all the exotic guises that the ingenious Chinese could devise. Some missionaries, it is true, and some Chinese converts to the faith protested the inequalities inherent in so rigidly stratified a society. The moral they pointed, however, was not the need for a general redistribution of social privileges, but the importance of individual initiative and self-improvement. Thus even had Hung Hsiu-ch'üan been in effective communication with the more progressive missionary minds, he would hardly have found there the kind of sweeping social idealism that we find expressed, at one level, in Taiping proclamations.

A more direct source for this social vision is entirely indigenous. It is the *Li-yun* chapter of the *Li chi*, a description of the world as it will be in the age of Great Harmony (*ta-t'ung*). This was a very ancient and perennially attractive Confucian utopia, appealing alike to critics of imperial despotism in the seventeenth century and to "New Text" radicals at the end of the nineteenth, in whose theory of history it came to occupy, as we shall see, a central place. Hung Hsiu-ch'üan quoted it, word-for-word, in his "Proclamation on the Origins of Principles for the Enlightenment of the Age" (*Yuan-tao hsing-shih chao*) published in 1852. For uncertain reasons the passage was omitted from an edition of the same work issued seven years later. Perhaps the Taipings were moving away from Confucianism. More probably, as they tried to create a workable administrative order, they were moving away from the egalitarian idealism of their early days. It has troubled many historians, not least those who would like to detect in the Taiping movement the stirrings of a genuine populism, that "demotion to the status of a peasant" was stipulated in the Taiping legal code as a severe punishment to be meted out to officials found guilty of misconduct. In any case, frugality and abstinence were not conspicuous virtues of the evolving life-style of the Taiping leadership. One of the last, and perhaps apocryphal, reports we have of Hung Hsiu-ch'üan is a pitiful vignette of the "Heavenly King" trapped in his besieged capital at Nanking, distributing the jewels from his private treasury to starving troops who could buy no food for any price.

Hung Hsiu-ch'üan was a messiah *manqué*. Perhaps his greatest debt to Christian influence was the overwhelming sense of messianic righteousness that entered into him in the days of his obscurity and drove him onward through the two remarkable decades that followed. It was also the most enduring attribute of his leadership, surviving even his own death early in June, 1864. Though many had already escaped from the doomed city—it was a matter of months before the last rebel remnants were hunted down and exterminated—it is said that not one Taiping soldier surrendered to Tseng Kuo-fan's army when Nanking was finally taken in July. The slaughter was savage, and dreadfully complete.

Whether or not the Taiping Rebellion should be regarded as a Christian movement, however unorthodox, is ultimately a matter of less consequence than the extent to which the movement represented a challenge to the Confucian order and thus set itself apart from other peasant rebellions in Chinese history, a harbinger of genuine revolution. Earlier rebels had sometimes triumphed against an established dynasty, only to reconstitute, on the morrow of victory, an administrative apparatus similar in outline, and even in detail, to that of the regime they had displaced, and to reaffirm allegiance to orthodox Confucian values and assumptions. The Taipings, as we have seen, owed a debt to Confucianism. Their borrowings from Confucian sources went far beyond the idea of Great Harmony (*ta-t'ung*) that Hung Hsiu-ch'üan lifted from the *Li chi*. Their political organization was patterned largely after the forms described in the *Chou-li* (Rites of Chou), another ancient classical text. They relied heavily, perhaps by necessity, on Confucian terms to articulate their own ideas. The word *t'ien*, for example, meaning "sky" or "heaven," but with many layers of abstruse connotation in Confucian literature, is one of the primary elements in the Confucian triad of Heaven, Earth, and Man. The Taipings used the word, but read into it their own belief in an anthropomorphic Godhead, the golden-bearded patriarch of Hung's early visions: Creator, Lawgiver (this in a very concrete sense: all Taiping decrees were promulgated as commands of God), and Final Judge.

Thus the Taipings, without cutting themselves off completely from the Confucian inheritance, made it very clear that they did not consider themselves its heirs. In one of his visions Hung had witnessed the humiliation of an old man who stood with bowed head in God's presence and confessed the error of his ways. It turned out to be, of course, Confucius himself. Though they might adapt Confucian institutions and ethical injunctions to their own needs, the Taipings consistently treated Confucians as idolaters whose ancestral tablets and temples, like those of the Buddhists and the Taoists, it was their mission to destroy. It was made a capital offense to read the Confucian Classics until such time as revised editions could be published from which would be expunged all traces of superstition and idolatry. Ancestor worship was outlawed as a form of polytheism, a prohibition that struck to the very heart of the Confucian sense of the continuity through time of moral values and obligations.

It is impossible to imagine what the cultural effect of such attitudes might have been at work over a long period. Perhaps Meadows' euphoric forecast of "a revolution unparalleled in the world" would in the end have been justified, even if not in quite the form he envisioned. In the time that history allotted to the Taipings, however, their anti-Confucianism, like their Christianity, produced only negligible effect on Chinese intellectual life. More to the point were its political consequences for the rebellion itself. Other rebellions, like the Taipings, had recruited their armies from among the socially oppressed and dispossessed. Other rebellions, like the Taipings, had drawn ideological inspiration from non-Confucian sources—Taoist or Buddhist/Taoist, even Manichean folk cults, secret societies, and millennarian sects. But other rebellions, unlike the Taipings, had remained within the general framework of the values of the civilization, whether or not one chooses to call these values specifically "Confucian." Other rebellions had not transcended the traditional concept of the Mandate of Heaven. And, though they frequently began as a form of protest, more or less localized, against landlord-gentry exploitation, other rebellions had along the way reached a point at which social and political collaboration with the gentry became expedient as a means of articulating and legitimating their claims. The gentry, for their part, were open to such opportunities to the extent that their interests—which might, we must not forget, comprise moral as well as material considerations—could be served by taking advantage of them.

Not so, however, with the Taipings. Despising the Confucian elite not merely as social overlords but also as adherents to a heathen belief, the Taipings set out deliberately and militantly to repudiate what the gentry stood for both socially and culturally. In 1854, when Tseng Kuo-fan led his army into the field to launch what would become the "Ten-year Struggle" to save the imperial dynasty, it was shrewd but also entirely natural for him to address an appeal to the gentry of central China, calling upon them to rise to the defense of *their* culture, not only the Manchu ruling house. "Is this a crisis merely for the Ch'ing dynasty?" Tseng asked. No, it is rather "an unprecedented crisis in the history of Confucian moral principles. Bitterly do Confucius and Mencius weep beyond the grave. How can the educated class watch with folded hands, mere spectators, without thinking of doing something about it?"[25]

The Taiping rebellion left behind it an awesome legacy of destruction: untold millions dead in battle or by starvation and disease; the richest and most populous provinces of the empire ravaged; the traditional mechanisms for maintaining social and political order wrecked. Though it survived, the dynasty had suffered irreparable damage. The ability of the Manchus to defend their own interests had been quickly discredited in the 1850s as Manchu garrisons put up only token resistance or deserted en masse. What saved the Court in the end was its reliance on Chinese provincial militia, organized, financed, and led by officials like Tseng Kuo-fan, Tso Tsung-t'ang, and Li Hung-chang, to name only the most celebrated—men whose public loyalty lay still with the dynasty but whose political authority derived not only from imperial favor, but also from their ability to command a network of private regional loyalties. The Taiping rebellion may or may not have marked the beginning of the age of warlordism. Scholars disagree in their views on this, but there is little disagreement on the fact that the rebellion resulted in a shift in the balance of power and political initiative away from the center, and the rise to prominence of provincial interests.

Paradoxically, the effect of the Taiping rebellion on Confucian culture in the 1860s and 1870s was not to undermine traditional values, but temporarily at least to reinforce them. Elements of Taiping ideology, it is true, survived the destruction of the movement itself. Its anti-Manchu pronouncements, what various writers label its "proto-nationalism," filtered down through the medium of secret society legend to inspire revolutionaries like Sun Yat-sen a generation or two later. But the immediately conspicuous result of the rebellion was to give the Confucian intellectual order, as though in response to Tseng's challenge, a new lease on life, a fresh confidence. This respite, this Indian summer of the Confucian autumn, is what is referred to in the history of the Ch'ing dynasty as the T'ung Chih Restoration.

* * *

T'ung Chih was the reign title of the emperor who ascended to the Chinese throne in November, 1861, the eighth in the line of succession of the Ch'ing dynasty. The new emperor was a child of five (six *sui*), destined to pass the first twelve years of his fourteen-year reign dominated by a regency that included the forbidding figure of his mother, the Dowager Empress Tz'u Hsi, whose personality looms ever more darkly over the last half-century of Ch'ing history. In other respects as well, the circumstances were hardly auspicious. The tide of rebellion had not yet turned in favor of the imperial cause, but still ran at full flood through the rich Yangtze provinces; the Taipings, indeed, had just broken out of the first prolonged siege of Nanking, and things looked darker for the Manchus than they had for some time. The Hsien Feng emperor, father to the boy who now occupied the throne, had died in the summer of 1861 as near to disgrace as an emperor could come. He had fled his capital the year before as the Anglo-French expeditionary force marched toward Peking to compel Chinese compliance with the treaties of 1858. By the time Lord Elgin's troops put the torch to the great Summer Palace outside the city in October, 1860, Hsien Feng had taken refuge in Jehol, some hundred and fifty miles to the north. He never returned, nor did his empress ever forgive the foreign devils either for the humiliation inflicted upon her consort or for the destruction of the sprawling imperial pleasure dome.

It was, taken altogether, an unpromising moment. Yet the decade of the 1860s turned out to be, as we have noted, a time of political vigor and intellectual confidence, a very real if not in the end a decisive turning point in the declining fortunes of the dynasty. That this could be the case was due to a number of factors. Having imposed their will upon the Chinese in 1860, the Western powers were content to pursue a somewhat more conciliatory policy toward the Court in the years that followed, at least until the anti-foreign riots of 1870—the Tientsin Massacre—brought relations again to the breaking point. The Chinese on their part, chastened by the recent disaster and guided largely by a new generation of leaders, undertook in the 1860s a reform program designed to make the dynasty once more master of its own destiny. In areas wrested from the grip of rebellion, this meant reconstituting the traditional political and social order, oiling the rusted machinery of Confucian government. At points of contact with the foreigners, where friction generated heat, it involved the creation of institutions for which no precedents existed. In either case the aim was not what we would now call "modernization"; it was, rather, as the Chinese then called it, *chung-hsing*, or "restoration," coupled with *tzu-ch'iang*, or "self-strengthening." One detects in the China of the 1860s and 1870s nothing of the enthusiasm for modernity and Westernization as recognized political and cultural goals that plays such a conspicuous role in contemporary Japan, carrying the Japanese in the period from the 1850s to the 1870s from a rabid xenophobia to an uncritical emulation of foreign ways. "Restoration statesmen had no desire to create a new society," observes Mary Wright in her classic study of the T'ung Chih period. "They wanted to restore a society that they confidently believed had been based on immutable truth and that could therefore, with adjustments, flourish in any age."[26]

The qualification is important: "with adjustments" signified substantial innovation. A new bureau for the handling of foreign affairs, the Tsung-li yamen, was established in 1861. Though it was less than the regular Foreign Office that Westerners would have liked to see, it marked an improvement in their view over the preposterous practice of relegating all such matters to the Board of Rites in keeping with the notion that foreign nations could only be dealt with as tributary states. The Tsung-li yamen's first head was Prince Kung (1833–1898), the Hsien Feng emperor's younger brother and one of the T'ung Chih regents. It was Prince Kung, ardently antiforeign, who had been left behind in Peking in 1860 to come to terms with the British and the French. The experience had converted him. Throughout the 1860s and 1870s his was one of the steadiest voices raised in behalf of moderation, accommodation, and innovation.

In the same memorial that recommended creation of the Tsung-li yamen in 1861, Prince Kung urged the establishment of a school to provide instruction in foreign languages. "In dealing with foreign countries, it appears necessary first of all to know their nature and temperament," ran the argument. "Since we do not know their languages, there is complete misunderstanding."[27] Thus after a lapse of twenty years Wei Yuan's common-sense advice reached the point of implementation as official policy. The T'ung-wen kuan (variously translated as the Tungwen College, the Interpreters' College, and even the Imperial College) which came into being as a result was not an impressive success. Enrollment was limited initially to Manchus, and only a handful were recruited for the first courses offered in English, French, and Russian. In 1867 the institution was enlarged by the addition of a Department of Science to teach courses in mathematics and astronomy. In this case, enrollment was restricted to scholars who had passed the higher examinations, in the hope that this might lend an aura of legitimacy to the undertaking. The results were disappointing. Students remained few and often indifferent. One of the foreign instructors employed by the College complained in the late 1860s that its student body was constituted entirely of impoverished young Manchus and incompetent middle-aged literati—an unpromising collection of men on the margin of Confucian life.

By the 1870s the Tsung-li yamen had all but foresaken its stepchild. The T'ung-wen kuan survived into the early years of the twentieth century, however, when it was finally absorbed into the Imperial University established in 1898. It even prospered, in a modest way, under new leadership and assured funding after 1869. In that year W. A. P. Martin abandoned his missionary work to assume the presidency of the institution. At the same time Robert Hart, the extraordinary Irishman who served as Inspector-General of the Imperial Chinese Customs from 1863 to 1908, undertook to defray the expenses of the T'ung-wen kuan out of customs revenues. As an employee of the Chinese government, responsible to the Tsung-li yamen for the administration of what was fast becoming the most important source of imperial revenues, Hart was in a position to exert substantial influence in behalf of a variety of innovative schemes. To his mind, and to Martin's, "modernization" presented no such philosophical difficulties as troubled the literati-officials for whom they worked. The T'ung-wen kuan was clearly a step in the right direction along an inevitable road—a collaborative effort in which, as Martin phrased it, he had agreed to trim the lamps if Hart would supply the oil.

The result was a steady light, but one that did not penetrate very far into the recesses of Confucian culture. By the end of the century the T'ung-wen kuan was offering instruction in mathematics, chemistry, astronomy, physics, physiology, international law, English, French, Russian, German, and Japanese. One can read from the growing catalog of languages alone the nature of the gathering threat. Still the number of students remained small, no more than a hundred or so at any one time. Their studies did not qualify them automatically for official preferment, and graduates of the T'ung-wen kuan found the ladder to positions of eminence and influence slippery indeed, and crowded with sure-footed, old-fashioned classical scholars untainted by the odium of "Western learning." The most a member of this small band of experts in exotic languages and arts could reasonably expect was a middle-level provincial appointment in which he might or might not be called upon to deal with foreigners, or perhaps to be sent abroad for further study or to join the staff of one or another of the growing number of Chinese legations. Even in the nascent Chinese foreign service, the natural outlet for such specialists, the names of former T'ung-wen kuan students do not begin to appear with any regularity at the ministerial level until after the turn of the century, by which time Ch'ing policy had changed drastically in response to other stimuli.

The Peking T'ung-wen kuan served as the example after which several similar schools were modeled in the 1860s, largely under the auspices of provincial leaders. A T'ung-wen kuan was established in Shanghai in 1863 and in Canton a year later, both at the instigation of Li Hung-chang. On the urging of the governor of the province, Tso Tsung-t'ang, a school for Western studies was created as a part of the Foochow shipyard founded in Fukien in 1866. It was foolishness, Tso declared, to compete in a horserace mounted on a donkey. "All of us are human beings, whose intelligence and wisdom are, by nature, similar," wrote Tso in the tolerant spirit of Confucian catholicism. But, he continued, "Chinese wisdom is spent on abstract things; the foreigners' intelligence is concentrated upon concrete things. . . . Foreigners consider mechanical matters important, principles unimportant."[28] It is a theme that, with variations, echoes down the years into the twentieth century.

Among Restoration statesmen, a figure like Prince Kung was unusual. In the first place, he was a Manchu, in a movement that drew much of its driving force from Chinese officials, the great provincial governors and governors-general with their subhierarchies of semi-private administrative assistants. Secondly, and more important, Prince Kung and his Manchu colleagues had remained personally remote from the great mid-century rebellions that had shaped the careers and made the reputations of the Chinese officials who emerge as the real leaders of the Restoration and of the Self-strengthening movement in the 1860s and 1870s. It is in the lives and values of men like Tseng Kuo-fan, Li Hung-chang, Tso Tsung-t'ang, and many others that we may perceive most clearly the confluence of the ideas of renovation and innovation. In their minds such novelties as the Tsung-li yamen, the T'ung-wen kuan, the Kiangnan Arsenal at Shanghai, and the arsenal and shipyard at Foochow with their appended schools of foreign study—all these things which had not existed even in imagination a generation earlier, and which sheltered now under the general rubric of Self-strengthening—were part of a larger pattern of political initiatives which they could easily fit into a more traditional scheme of things. As restorers of the imperial regime they were fighting on familiar Confucian territory, defenders of an accepted political and cultural order, armed with well-tested weapons and buoyed up by a great confidence and esprit.

These were men still supremely confident in the rightness of their values, in great things and in small. Tseng Kuo-fan, in the very midst of the "Ten Year Struggle" against the Taipings, found time to maintain a regular correspondence with his eldest son from which it is possible to gain a sense of what was really at stake in Tseng's mind when he called upon the gentry to defend their way of life. It was a matter not merely of the sustaining principles of the culture at large, but also of the value inhering in the details of the day-to-day discipline of Confucian behavior. Thus Tseng Kuo-fan to his son:

> Since Uncle Ch'eng has moved to the new residence, you are now the lord of our old homestead. . . . My grandfather, the honorable Hsing-kang, attached great importance to the successful management of the household. First, he insisted that every member of our family should get up early in the morning. Second, the house should be washed and swept regularly to keep it clean. Third, the offering of sacrifices to the deceased ancestors should be performed in the most sincere manner. Fourth, all of our neighbors, relatives, and clan members should be well treated. . . . The honorable Hsing-kang paid constant attention to the study of books and the raising of vegetables. Recently when I wrote letters home, I often reminded you of the importance of "books, vegetables, fish, and hogs." I want you to know that when I did this I merely followed the tradition established by my grandfather. . . . As for the sacrificial ceremonies, tell your mother she should have them in mind constantly. . . . A family's fortune cannot last long if the family is not particular when offering sacrifices, no matter how prosperous it is at the moment. Remember this!
>
> . . . You have three shortcomings. Your speech is too clever and lacks clumsiness [i.e., you are likely to give an impression of insincerity]; you cannot interpret the books you read in a very profound manner; and your compositions lack ruggedness and are too prosaic. . . . Clumsiness in speech and dignity in manner will pave the way for virtue. Ruggedness and fluidity in composition will help you in your scholarship. . . .
>
> My philosophy in life can be summarized in one statement: "I will do my very best; let Heaven decide the outcome."[29]

Tseng's was the last generation that could live by this creed with confidence in the outcome that Heaven would decide. Even then confidence was draining away. The Tsung-li yamen's memorial to the throne in 1867 recommending the addition to the existing T'ung-wen kuan of a department to teach mathematics and astronomy provoked a furious response. Chief among its critics was an aging Mongol official, Wo-jen. In the Peking of the 1860s, Wo-jen was the traditionalist counterweight to innovators along the lines of Prince Kung: a staunch, unbending neo-Confucian in the most illiberal sense, *plus catholique que le pape*, appointed successively or concurrently President of the Censorate, President of the Board of Works, Tutor to the T'ung Chih Emperor, and Chancellor of the Hanlin Academy. It was by any standard an illustrious career, though Wo-jen professed to take no satisfaction from it. "He who is an official is a bitter man," he wrote; "to do the work of an official is a bitter business. He who considers official status a pleasure can never be a good official."[30] His protest against the Tsung-li yamen's proposal—protest, indeed, against the very notion that the West had anything to give or the

Chinese any need to borrow—made him for the moment the undisputed spokesman of radical conservatism. His mood was one of outrage still at the insults inflicted upon the dynasty in 1860. "How can we forget this enmity and this humiliation even for one single day?" When it came to prescribing alternatives, Wo-jen fell back upon the often-heard Confucian argument: "propriety and righteousness" are the indispensible foundation of the state, "power and plotting" of no avail. A knowledge of mathematics, wrote Wo-jen, would be "of very little use. . . . From ancient down to modern times, your slave has never heard of anyone who could use mathematics to raise the nation from a state of decline or to strengthen it in time of weakness." Besides, the foreigners could not be trusted to teach, or their students relied upon to learn, the substance of the subject. "Your slave fears that what our scholars are going to learn cannot be learnt well and yet will be perplexing, which would just fall in with [the foreigners'] plans."[31] His final appeal was to the shaken sense of Chinese self-sufficiency. If indeed it should be decided that a knowledge of mathematics is essential to the preservation of the Way, then surely somewhere in the limitless reaches of the empire it must be possible to discover a Chinese who has mastered the subject.

This final argument made it easier for the Tsung-li yamen to dismiss Wo-jen's attack as a bluff. He was invited to nominate suitable candidates, and forced to concede that there were none in his circle of acquaintance.* The Tsung-li yamen carried the day, though Wo-jen's criticisms were not without effect. Martin and others connected with the enterprise blamed him, or the kind of opinion that he articulated so vehemently, for the fact that the T'ung-wen kuan was able to attract few students of real talent or students from families of cultural pedigree. And Wo-jen, for all the virulence of his language and the archaism of his arguments, was not wrong in his instincts. He felt the sharp, thin edge of the wedge of alien influence. Under the guise of "astronomy and mathematics" a good many other things were smuggled into the curriculum of the T'ung-wen kuan over the years. On a much broader scale, the course embarked upon by the Self-strengtheners of the 1860s and 1870s brought the Chinese step by step toward a more comprehensive concern with Western "science" in the widest sense of the term, and thereby closer to the point of recognizing that divergent intellectual tra-

* Ironically, the Tsung-li yamen itself subsequently substantiated Wo-jen's claim. In 1869 Li Shan-lan was appointed to the professorship of mathematics at the T'ung-wen kuan. Li was a Chekiang scholar who had passed the *hsiu-ts'ai* examination but failed to progress further, and had devoted himself primarily to a lifelong interest in mathematics, which was by no means an exotic subject in the history of Chinese thought. In the 1840s Li published a number of his own mathematical treatises; in the 1850s he moved to Shanghai to collaborate with foreign missionaries in the translation of several texts in the fields of mathematics, astronomy, and botony. After Li's death in 1882 the professorship of mathematics at the T'ung-wen kuan was consistently held by a Chinese; some thousand of the three thousand volumes in the school's library were Chinese mathematical texts.

ditions were in competition. In the 1840s Wei Yuan had talked about the need for "ships and guns." In the 1870s Hsueh Fu-ch'eng (1838–1894), a protégé of Li Hung-chang and a forceful advocate of self-strengthening, spoke instead of China's need for Western "machinery and mathematics." The difference may seem slight, but it is in fact decisive. It is the difference between one who merely uses something and one who fully understands what it is that he is using. Feng Kuei-fen (1809–1874), another of Li's influential subordinates in the 1860s, had articulated the inexorable logic of the situation in the starkest language, issuing at the same time a passionate call to arms:

> Some say, "Suppose we buy the ships and hire the men [i.e., foreigners to operate them]." I say that this is something we cannot do. If we can manufacture them, if we can keep them in repair, if we know how to use them, then they become our weapons. If we can neither manufacture them nor repair them nor make use of them on our own, then they remain as before the weapons of others . . . We must come in the end to the realization that there is nothing at all wrong in manufacturing and maintaining and learning how to use such weapons on our own. Only then can we bring to submission the rebels within the empire, only then can we hold our heads high in the world at large, only then can we regain the strength that was ours originally, only then can we expunge the shame that has come upon us, only then can we become beyond doubt the greatest country in this wide world. . . . [32]

Feng Kuei-fen was a Soochow scholar with impeccable credentials and a reputation as one of the most incisive Statecraft writers of his day. His influence on the provincial leaders of the restoration was considerable: Li Hung-chang's memorial urging the establishment of the Shanghai T'ung-wen kuan, for example, was lifted in part word-for-word from a proposal Feng had submitted to him. In a spate of essays like the one cited here, written in a spare classical style that emphasizes the emotional impact of the message, Feng did much to popularize the idea of Self-strengthening. He it was, also, who devised the formula that made palatable the notion that the state should pursue as a primary objective the acquisition of "wealth and power." In an essay advocating the introduction of Western learning he wrote, "Would not the best of all possible stratagems be to retain the social relationships and the illustrious moral principles of China as the foundation, and to reinforce them with the techniques that the various countries [of the West] have used to attain wealth and power?"[33] In the decades that followed, this prescription was abbreviated to a symmetrically balanced eight-character slogan, "*Chung hsueh wei t'i, hsi hsueh wei yung*," or "Chinese learning for the fundamentals, Western learning for practical application." In this version it served as the justification for reformist policies down to the end of the nineteenth century.

The terms *t'i* (substance) and *yung* (function or application) go far back in the history of Chinese thought. In Buddhist literature of the T'ang period (618–906), *t'i* is used to designate the latent or potential state of a thing, while *yung* describes the realization of that potentiality. In the thought of Wang Yang-ming in the Ming dynasty, *t'i* and *yung* refer to closely linked aspects of moral character: the tranquility of the mind at rest, for example, which is at the same time the activity of the mind engaged; or, at the level of social application, *t'i* describes the substance of the state, the oneness of Heaven, Earth, and the "myriad things," while *yung* applies to the state as a universal moral force, "loving the people."[34] In traditional usage, "substance" and "function" were thus understood as coordinate aspects of a single entity.

Feng Kuei-fen and the Self-strengtheners who borrowed these familiar categories to describe the unfamiliar relationship between Chinese "essence" and Western "practice" were using the terms, so they believed, in a similar sense. Chinese "essence" was genuinely important to them. It was also, in their view, not incompatible with what had become identified in their minds as Western "application"—partly, at least, because they were able to attribute to their own civilization, in the light of their understanding of it, elements of this "alien" acomplishment. "All Western knowledge is derived from mathematics," Feng maintained,[35] but mathematics itself is a *Chinese* invention which the Westerners, true to their mechanical inclinations and preoccupations, had developed beyond the point at which the Chinese centuries ago had let it drop. What then prevents the Chinese from appropriating something to which they have a legitimate cultural claim? Advocates of Self-strengthening argued consistently that what they desired was not a departure from the Way, but a realistic and reliable means of defending it. So Hsueh Fu-ch'eng wrote in 1879, with no sense of an intrinsic anachronism:

Confronted with this situation, even Yao and Shun would not have been able to close the doors and rule the empire in isolation. . . . Some may ask: "If such a great nation as China imitates the Westerners, would it not be using barbarian ways to change China?" Not so. . . . If we really take over the Westerners' knowledge of machinery and mathematics in order to protect the Way of our sage-kings Yao and Shun, Yü and T'ang, Wen and Wu, and the Duke of Chou and Confucius [a comprehensive catalog of the patron saints of the culture], and so make the Westerners not dare to despise China, I know that if they were alive today, the sages would engage themselves in the same tasks, and their Way would also gradually be spread to the eight bounds of the earth. That is what we call using the ways of China to change the barbarians. . . . Alas! There are endless changes in the world, and so there are endless variations in the sages' way of meeting these changes. To be born in the present age but to hold fast to ancient methods, is to be like one who in the age of Shen Nung [the legendary inventor of agriculture and sometimes of fire] still ate raw meat and drank blood. . . . Such a one would say: "I am following the methods of the ancient sages."[36]

From our privileged vantage point outside the cultural milieu and the historical moment in which the Self-strengthening movement existed, it is not difficult to recognize the fragility of its logic. "Western learning," the kind of technological skills that produced "ships and guns," was the practical application of an abstract interest in the intrinsic physical order of the world and the universe. As such it was in no way an actualization of potentialities inherent in Confucian culture, which was preoccupied not with physical order but with moral order. In the hands of the Self-strengtheners the elements combined in the *t'i/yung* formula were not complementary but antithetical—a fact which Wo-jen, living his ostentatiously frugal and orthodox life in Peking, sensed more keenly than did a man like Feng Kuei-fen in Soochow. For Feng and those who followed his reformist opinion the distinction between "essence" and "application," "principles" and "practice," was an attempt, intentional or not, to limit the need for innovation to specific areas that had a direct bearing on the problem of dealing with the foreign threat, and beyond this to obscure the fact that Self-strengthening might necessitate fundamental change in respect to institutional structures and their underlying justifications."Chinese learning for the fundamentals, Western learning for practical application" was a prescription that could only result in a compartmentalization of the arts of civilization, a distinction between "belief" and "competence." For this reason it collided head-on with the irreducible core of Confucian faith.

"Restoration" signified the regeneration of the *Confucian* monarchy, reaffirmation of the principles for which it stood, refurbishment of the institutions that gave it form and effect. "Self-strengthening" meant something else. Its purpose, which remained unarticulated, was the preservation of the existing state—which, down to the end of the century, meant the Manchu ruling house—even at the expense (though Feng would never have conceded the point) of Confucian moral and vocational values. In that the perpetuation of the nation as a political entity took precedence over the integrity of the traditional culture, the Self-strengthening movement was nationalistic in its implications. The leaders of the movement did not see it in this light, or if they saw it they concealed it by wrapping the whole problem up in the *t'i/yung* formula. The result was a program, if such it may be called, of quixotic and random experimentation, conducted largely on the initiative of a few provincial officials. "Peking is the last place in China to select for the introduction of novelties," observed Robert Hart in 1873, "and the Central Government is the last authority to ask for support of any kind: local growth—and that the farther from Peking the better—is the only process of development recognized or to be relied on in this country."[37] Politically and culturally, reform remained peripheral to the abiding priorities of the Confucian order, and had little cumulative effect either on the institutions of imperial government or the traditional assumptions upon which they rested. When the accomplishments of the Self-strengthening movement were put to the test—in the Sino-French war of 1884–1885 and, precisely a decade later, in the first Sino-Japanese war—they proved woefully inadequate to the purposes which the scholars and officials of the 1860s had hoped to achieve. By the 1890s China was weaker, not stronger, than it had been a generation earlier, and the Chinese mind less confident, more divided within and against itself. Renovation had failed. That much the Chinese knew then. We know, as they could not, that revolution would follow in due course: the overthrow of the Manchus, of the monarchy, of Confucian privilege and Confucian belief. But there was still to come one final attempt to forestall the ordinance of history, one last effort, directed from the center, to create a Chinese future out of materials rescued from the Confucian past.

The Nineteenth Century: Reform

He who gives no thought to what is distant is sure to find grief close at hand.

—The Analects, XV:11

ON JUNE 13, 1898, THE KUANG HSU EMPEROR, enfeebled heir to the great legacies of K'ang Hsi and Ch'ien Lung, issued an edict: "We have received a memorial. . . recommending to our favorable notice K'ang Yu-wei (known as 'K'ang the Modern Sage and Reformer') . . . and Chang Yuan-chi . . . as being men of deep learning and exceptional abilities and progressive ideas. Let the two officers be presented to us in special audience on the 16th instant, in the Grand Council Chamber."[1] The meeting duly took place at dawn on the appointed day, the usual hour for the Son of Heaven to conduct his official business. It marked the beginning of a brief and extraordinary interlude in China's hesitant transition from ancient forms to new visions.

The Kuang Hsu emperor had come to the throne twenty-three years earlier, following the death of the profligate T'ung Chih in 1875 at the premature age of nineteen *sui*. Kuang Hsu occupied the imperial position from 1875 to 1908, longer than any other Ch'ing monarch barring the astonishing one hundred and twenty years that K'ang Hsi and Ch'ien Lung divided between them. Yet one hesitates to say that he ruled at any point during this long reign—except, perhaps, for the few short months of the summer of 1898. He lived otherwise a shadowed, melancholy life, the more so since his sympathies and instincts, from what we know of

them, were benign and by the standards of his time and station progressive, as those of his immediate predecessors certainly had not been.

Kuang Hsu was only three years old when he became the emperor of
China. His succession was prejudiced not only by the incompetence of his
age but also by the circumstances surrounding it. T'ung Chih had died
without an heir. Kuang Hsu, though much younger, was of the same
generation as the deceased emperor. In open defiance of dynastic law, he
was placed on the throne by his formidable aunt, the Dowager Empress
Tz'u Hsi, who forthwith established herself as the dominant power in the
regency proclaimed in his behalf. He never escaped the terrifying burden
of her will. Even after 1889, when the Dowager "retired" to live out her
days in the Summer Palace (rebuilt since 1860 on a lavish scale and at
enormous cost), the old woman's hold upon her unfortunate nephew did
not relax. The "Hundred Days Reform" in the summer of 1898, when
Kuang Hsu was twenty-six, was his boldest attempt to assert himself. It
ended in disaster for the reform party, and in the complete humiliation of
the emperor himself. All in all, it would be hard to find a less likely candidate to play the part of a Chinese Peter the Great, the role in which
K'ang Yu-wei endeavored to cast him.

If the emperor was a compliant and abject young man, the scholar
whom he summoned into his presence that June morning was quite the
opposite. At forty K'ang Yu-wei had already established a reputation—in
the eyes of many, a disreputable notoriety—as a political radical and exponent of the New Text persuasion. For ten years he had been submitting
memorials urging reform, and in the early 1890s he had published several
studies which turned what had been an academic controversy into the rationale for an entirely new approach to Confucian reform. We will examine his arguments in greater detail later in this chapter. Here it suf-
fices to say that by 1898 K'ang Yu-wei had emerged as the foremost
advocate of sweeping changes in the structures of Confucian government
and education, touching even upon the time-honored prerogatives of the
emperor himself. Like Hung Hsiu-ch'üan, K'ang was possessed by a messianic sense of the uniqueness of his own historical role; and though his
sources of inspiration were largely indigenous to the Confucian tradition,
in his interpretation of them he was hardly a more conventional thinker
than Hung had been.

It was to press the cause of reform that K'ang answered the imperial
summons on June 16. This was his first and only formal audience with
the emperor, though according to some reports there were frequent informal meetings in the months that followed. On this occasion K'ang
minced no words. "The prerequisites of reform," he told the emperor,
"are that all the laws and political and social systems be changed and
decided anew, before it may be called a reform."[2] This was a prescription

not for reform, but for guided revolution, a revolution from the top, with the Kuang Hsu emperor as its improbable figurehead, under the careful tutelage of "K'ang the Modern Sage and Reformer" and the band of Confucian radicals that had rallied around him.*

What was in fact accomplished over the next three months stopped far short of revolutionary change, well short even of the kind of far-reaching political and social reforms undertaken by Peter the Great and the leaders of the Meiji Restoration in Japan whom K'ang Yu-wei held up as models to be emulated. "It is not necessary to copy him in every detail," K'ang wrote to Kuang Hsu, speaking of Peter; "but if your actions are animated by a divinely inspired forcefulness, transcending the ordinary with their thunderous reverberations and dazzling brilliance . . . the marvelous speed and efficacy of such a remedy would be beyond the ability of your officials to foresee."[3] Thus sure of themselves, the reformers moved energetically ahead with their attempt to modernize the archaic Confucian administrative structure. They stripped it of many of its ancient sinecures, and abolished much of the ceremony of imperial affairs. The right to address the throne directly, traditionally reserved to officials of the higher ranks, was extended even to private subjects, presumably in the hope of generating support from reform-minded gentry. Reform of the legal system was initiated. An annual state budget was proposed. Ambitious plans were contemplated for railway construction and industrial development. Significant changes were ordered in the educational system, involving among other things the abolition of the eight-legged essay† in favor of essays on current affairs as the standard of success in the examinations. A modern school system was envisioned, to

---

* Some definitions may be to the point here. The reforms undertaken from the 1860s to the 1880s, the high tide of the Self-strengthening movement, sheltered under the general notion of "restoration" (*chung-hsing*), a domesticated Confucian term that can be traced back to the Classic of Poetry (*Shih-ching*). The reforms sponsored by Kuang Hsu and promoted by K'ang Yu-wei came to be known as "changing the laws" (*pien-fa*). This, too, is an ancient term, and not unfamiliar in Confucian history, but it derives from Legalist sources (e.g., the *Book of Lord Shang*), and thus calls to mind the traditional distinction between *li* (inherited ritual, civilized custom) and *fa* (positive law, imperial fiat). In the 1890s and 1900s, when the Chinese began to talk about "revolution" they used another old term, *ko-ming*, but gave to it an entirely new meaning. In traditional usage, *ko-ming* denotes the removal (*ko*) of the Mandate of Heaven (*ming*), and thus describes the kind of political change that had taken place many times in the course of imperial history. In its modern usage it is in effect a neologism, borrowed as were many other terms in the vocabulary of politics, economy, and technology, from the Japanese.

† This was a short, formal essay (in Ch'ing times varying in length from 450 to 600 words), divided into eight distinct and rigidly stylized sections (or "legs"). Originating in the fourteenth century as an exegetical exercise on quotations drawn from the *Four Books*, the eight-legged essay had become, long before the end of the nineteenth century, a skill essential to success in the examinations—and, not surprisingly, emptied of any creative literary or intellectual content.

teach both Western and Chinese studies. In the capital itself an Imperial University was established on premises adjacent to the Forbidden City.* An official newspaper was created to carry news of the reform program throughout the empire. A bureau for the translation of foreign books into Chinese was set up under the direction of Liang Ch'i-ch'ao, K'ang's most brilliant and influential disciple. Western learning was to be encouraged, as an edict in September put it, "to supply what we lacked for our purpose. . . . We find that Westerners are wise and far-seeing, they bring wealth to their families and comfort to their bodies; they have that which brightens the intellect and improves the person; they have even longevity at command. All these have been given them by their system of government and education."[4]

So the architects of the reform movement drew up their plans, their enthusiasm matched by a remarkable insensitivity to the vulnerability of their situation. They had incurred, inevitably, the wrath and enmity of the Dowager Empress. Implacably xenophobic, and surrounded by like-minded servants, Tz'u Hsi was the instinctive ally of those, whether Manchu or Chinese, who saw their privileges threatened by the new regime. She possessed still a shrewd and potent personality, and a talent sharpened by a lifetime of court intrigue for the kind of politics against which the reformers were ill equipped to defend themselves. They had failed to get their own men into positions of decisive authority. Some who might have aided them they had alienated. Imperial decrees were handed down only to be laid aside by cautious ministers, or to pile up unheeded in the yamen of unfriendly or confused provincial officials. Some whom the reformers had trusted in the end betrayed them. The "Hundred Days" was an audacious political offensive conducted by men who had little sense of politics. "At that time we wished to change the destiny of our country by reform," wrote K'ang's companion of that June dawn, Chang Yuan-chi, reminiscing wistfully after the lapse of half a century. "Only later did we realize that it was all only a dream."[5]

A nightmare it may well have seemed as the reaction began to marshal its forces and claim its victims in September. A scant ten days after he had issued his edict in praise of Western learning, the Kuang Hsu emperor was in disgrace, compelled ignominiously to plead ill health and to beg his aunt to govern for him. The last wretched decade of his life he spent in semi-imprisonment, an invalid by decree, totally subject to the aging empress who ruled in his name. (He was not allowed even the satisfaction of surviving her: under mysterious and probably sinister cir-

* This was virtually the only reform undertaken in 1898 that survived the reactionary coup in September. The university was closed down briefly by the Boxers two years later, but it was revived and managed to weather the successive revolutionary storms that broke upon it—and sometimes from within it—to remain China's premier institution of higher education into the present day: Peking University (Pei-ching ta-hsueh, or as it is usually abbreviated, Peita.) We will hear much more of it in chapter 6.

cumstances, he died in 1908 on the day before Tz'u Hsi herself expired.) K'ang and his party were driven into exile and in a few cases—K'ang's younger brother being one—to summary execution and martyrdom.

So ended what had been the most inventive and provocative attempt to "modernize" Confucianism by turning its values to the purposes of radical reform. So ended, too, the hope that the ancient alliance between Confucian ideals and imperial power might remain, however modified, as the focal point of authority. The coup of September, 1898, was the first in a sequence of events that led inexorably to the antiforeign paroxysm of the Boxer Rebellion in 1899 and 1900, the final desperate effort to evict the Westerners and eradicate their influence by main force. In its wake, stung by the humiliation of defeat and goaded by the rising radical temper of a new generation of political critics, the Court initiated a reform movement intended to salvage the fortunes of the dynasty at almost any cost; it made little pretense of invoking Confucian sanctions to this end.

Compared with what was soon to follow, the reforms undertaken or contemplated in 1898 do not seem impressive. In the minds of the reformers, however, far more sweeping changes loomed just beyond the political horizon. They saw China transformed into a constitutional monarchy, complete with a parliament and a political structure patterned on the democratic model of the West—all reconciled to what they held to be the enduring values of Confucianism. K'ang Yu-wei himself looked even further, to the paradise of a universal commonwealth, a genuine utopia. In his inner visions, Confucianism was stretched to the limit of private imagination, to the point, indeed, at which it ceased to have significance as a distinctive cultural identity. He was the last great Confucian theorist, in many ways an eccentric, but living proof also of the wealth of imagery and promise that Confucianism carried with it down to the end.

K'ang Yu-wei was born in 1858 in the Nanhai district of Kwangtung province, a few miles southwest of Canton. Some miles further across the flat rice fields of the Pearl River delta lay the village which several years later would be the birthplace of Sun Yat-sen, K'ang's future rival for the loyalties of China's restive intellectuals. But though they were born under the same South China sky, an unbridgeable social and cultural distance separated these two. Sun was a peasant, transmogrified by an extraordinary combination of opportunity, accident, ambition, and courage into a Westernized political radical. K'ang was born into a solid gentry family, an heir to the great culture, and he set out at an early age to become what in fact he became, in his own estimate at least: a Confucian Sage.

K'ang owed his privileged start in life in part to the exertions of a great-great-grandfather, one K'ang Hui, who in 1804 had passed the provincial (*chü-jen*) examination and thus secured for his family the respectability of upper-gentry status. The fact that K'ang Hui accomplished this when he was close to eighty years old attests to the durability of Confucian scholarly and social aspiration; the fact that the degree was conferred partly in recognition of his venerable age, a not uncommon reward for those who stayed the course as he had done, suggests one means by which such aspiration was kept alive. K'ang Yu-wei's grandfather also attained the provincial degree, and it was he who supervised the boy's education after K'ang's father died in 1868. The family tradition of scholarship inclined toward Sung neo-Confucianism rather than the kind of textual research that was the specialty of the Han Learning. In keeping with nineteenth-century temperament, however, this was a style of neo-Confucianism that stressed the importance of active moral engagement in human affairs rather than metaphysical speculation. K'ang's grandfather was reputed to be as kind as he was wise and honest; still, it is not unreasonable to imagine that the boy spent his formative years in a somewhat austere intellectual environment. This may help to account for the arrogance that distinguished him even as a youth (earning him the jibes of his schoolmates, who called him "the Sage"), and which remained a conspicuous attribute of his mature personality.

After failing in his first attempt at the provincial examination in 1876, K'ang placed himself under the tutelage of Chu Tz'u-ch'i (1807–1881), an old family friend and one of the eminent provincial scholars of the day. Like K'ang's grandfather, Chu laid great emphasis on the cultivation of moral character and the sense of social duty. He was, however, an eclectic thinker, and from him K'ang learned something of the critical methodology of the Han Learning—enough at least to react strongly against this "dry" scholarship. In 1878, when he was twenty, K'ang underwent an emotional crisis, an experience neither as intense or as eccentric as Hung Hsiu-ch'üan's fantastic visions, but no less decisive as a vocational turning point. K'ang described it thus:

> Buried as I was every day amid piles of old papers, my mind became confused, and I gradually developed a revulsion for them. Then one day I had a new idea. I thought: "Scholars like Tai Chen [1724–1777, the greatest eighteenth-century exponent of Han-hsueh scholarship], who engage in textual research, fill their homes with the works they have written, but in the end, what is the use of all this?" Thus I gave it up, and in my own heart I longed to seek a place where I might pacify my mind and determine what would be my destiny. Suddenly I abandoned my studies, discarded my books, shut my door, withdrew from my friends, and sat in contemplation, nurturing my mind. My schoolmates thought it very queer, for there had been no one who had done this before, inasmuch as the Master [Chu Tz'u-ch'i] was in favor of the personally active performance of the Confucian virtues and detested the study of Ch'an Buddhism. While I was sitting in contemplation, all of a sudden I saw that Heaven, Earth and all the myriad things were all of one substance with

myself, and in a great release of enlightenment I beheld myself a sage and laughed for joy; then suddenly I thought of the sufferings and hardships of all living things and wept in melancholy. . . . The students, observing that I sang and wept for no apparent reason, believed that I had gone mad. . . . When winter came, I took my leave of Master Chu. . . . "

In this troubled state of mind, K'ang sought refuge from the discipline of Confucian life in a mountain retreat near his home, where for several months he lived as a recluse—meditating alone, reading Taoist and Buddhist texts, occasionally breaking into bursts of song, paying no heed to his appearance. He was recalled from this untidy and unconventional existence at last by the prod of family authority: his allowance would be cut off, he was warned, unless he behaved more responsibly. But the months of soul-searching had had their effect. K'ang's sense of self-importance was now firmly fixed.

> I reflected upon the perils and hardships of the life of the people and upon how I might save them with the powers of wisdom and ability granted to me by Heaven. Out of commiseration for all living beings, and in anguish over the state of the world, I took it as my purpose to set in order all under heaven.[6]

There are elements of the perennial and universal student's complaint in K'ang's youthful repudiation of scholarship—"piles of old paper . . . what is the use of all this?" There is as well something enduringly individual. Much of his fame in later years derived from his studies of the Confucian classics and his bold reinterpretations of their meaning. But he never sought an objective or historical understanding of Confucianism. He remained to the end of his life more religious than scholarly in his disposition toward the texts, searching always for the "profound and esoteric principles" of Confucianism. The messianic dimension of K'ang's personality also emerges clearly from this early account of his spiritual crisis, asking himself how he might save the people with the powers bestowed upon him by Heaven. For the rest, it is a mixture of Buddhist pessimism and Confucian optimism, the belief that suffering is the inevitable lot of the living, coupled with the conviction that it is indeed possible for a sage "to set in order all under Heaven."

What is lacking at this point in the development of K'ang's life and thought is a sense of the means by which he might serve as Heaven's agent and an awareness of the Western presence, whether as threat or inspiration. He came first to the latter. In 1879 he paid a brief visit to Hong Kong, returning to Nanhai much impressed by the orderliness of the colony's administration. To satisfy the curiosity thus piqued, he turned to the readily accessible sources of information, including the descriptions of the Western world written by Wei Yuan and Hsu Chi-yü in the 1840s. Three years later K'ang traveled to Peking to sit for the provincial examination again. Enroute he passed through Shanghai, where he was able to observe life in the foreign settlement and to purchase more recent literature about the West and translations of Western works. He began at this point seriously to study Western institutions, to teach himself something about Western science and technology, and against the background of his earlier aspirations to weave the several threads of his imaginings into a single fabric.

We will leave him to it for a time, in order to acquaint ourselves more fully with the culture that was coming into existence along the China Coast in the later decades of the nineteenth century, and the manner in which it contributed to the perceptions and preoccupations of other reformers in the 1880s and 1890s.

* * *

By the 1880s the treaty ports had evolved remarkably from their beginnings some forty years earlier. Time had confounded Lord Palmerston's irritated first judgment of Hong Kong as "a barren island with hardly a House upon it."[7] Though still confined to the island originally ceded in 1842, to which had been added in 1860 a few square miles at the tip of the Kowloon peninsula just opposite, the colony had a population of around 130,000 in the 1880s, the vast majority Chinese. The city of Victoria spread for several miles along the narrow shoreline beneath the looming grandeur of the Peak, where already the more imposing European residences commanded a view of the splendid harbor below. "The architecture . . . in Victoria is superior to anything heretofore seen in China," commented S. Wells Williams. "The amount of money expended in buildings in this colony is enormous."[8]

At Shanghai the changes had been if anything even more striking, since there the Western settlements adjoined a much older Chinese city. Shanghai had been an important coastal port and trading center for the surrounding delta even in pre-treaty days. But it had been overshadowed commercially, politically, and culturally by the great cities of Kiangnan: Ningpo, Soochow, and especially Hangchow, the provincial capital of Chekiang, the southern terminus of the Grand Canal which for centuries carried grain north to Peking—Marco Polo's "Kinsay," reported by him in the thirteenth century to be "without doubt the finest and most splendid city in the world."[9] In the latter half of the nineteenth century, however, the Grand Canal lay useless, destroyed by decades of rebellion and inattention; Hangchow, though still a powerful and luxurious city at the head of its stately bay, backed upon a rural hinterland. It was Shanghai, at the gateway to that mighty avenue of inland trade, the Yangtze River, that commanded half the markets of China and drew foreigners inexorably to it. By the 1880s the population of the city had grown to half a million, double what it had been when the port was opened to trade. Some five thousand of these were Westerners who congregated (except for the few missionaries stalwartly manning their stations within the walls of old Shanghai) in the French Concession and the International Settlement, communities that all but engulfed the original city. There too lived a large number of Chinese, perhaps as many as 200,000 all told.

In Shanghai, even more conspicuously than in Hong Kong, there flourished the peculiar hybrid culture of the China Coast; it was a city, in Rhoads Murphey's phrase, "where two civilizations met and where neither prevailed."[10] Westerners were not entirely indifferent to their situation: the first tugboat to ply the muddy waters of the Whangpoo River, the Yangtze tributary on which Shanghai is located, was christened the "Confucius." With some notable exceptions, however, mostly among missionaries and consular officials, the Westerners who did business in Shanghai (as in the other ports) remained contemptuously ignorant of traditional Chinese civilization and its language. Thus as Western enterprise prospered there were increasing opportunities for Chinese to infiltrate the emerging economic order, however rigorously they might be excluded from participation in the governance of the foreign settlements in which they lived and worked. Out of Western condescension and Chinese entrepreneurial abilities was born the "compradore culture" of the treaty ports—the culture of the Chinese middlemen who supplied the essential skills of linguistic, financial, and cultural mediation that enabled foreigners to turn a profit—and who profited in their turn, sometimes on a very grand scale.

Feng Kuei-fen, writing in the 1860s, denounced the mongrel offspring of this marriage of convenience:

> Those who have some acquaintance with barbarian affairs nowadays are called "interpreters." They get started along this line because they are in general the type of ne'er-do-wells who loaf about the marketplaces of the city, without reputable status in their own villages, and with no other means of support. They are of low character and shallow knowledge, mean schemers disposed to nothing but making a profit. Among their skills may be reckoned only a sketchy understanding of barbarian languages, the ability to read a word here and there, barely enough to make out commodity lists and figures, and a bit of vulgar grammar. How can we expect a commitment to learning from such as these?[11]

Feng was of course anxious to press his argument for official sponsorship of a program of comprehensive instruction in Western languages and sciences that might attract even traditional gentry. In the process he did less than justice to the accomplishments of at least the more astute and enterprising treaty-port Chinese, as we shall see. But there lurked here also a genuine disdain for the cultural mutation that treaty-port life engendered, a feeling of scorn voiced again and again by later nationalist writers. Eventually the term "compradore" entered the lexicon of

Chinese revolutionary propagandists as an epithet of the bitterest contempt, the epitome of economic and cultural treason. Nevertheless, although "modern" Shanghai had come into being only in response to Western demands, it grew and flourished in considerable measure because its prosperity was profitable to an increasing number of Chinese.

This, then, was the city to which K'ang Yu-wei came as a visitor in 1882. Along the Bund, fronting the river, anchored at one end by the Shanghai Club and on the other by the spacious compound of the British Consulate, were ranged the premises of the great China Coast firms: Jardine, Matheson and Company; the Peninsular and Oriental Steam Navigation Company; Russell and Company; and a dozen more: substantial buildings, in a style waggishly called "Compradoric," faced with good English brick shipped out as ballast in the vessels that crowded the river. In their midst, incongruously, stood the Chinese temple with its colorfully tiled roofs and elaborate ornamentation that served until late in the century as the Imperial Customs House. Behind the Bund stretched the foreign settlements. The streets had once borne proper colonial names: Park Lane, Consulate Road, Mission Road; as the Chinese population increased they were renamed (whether for convenience or out of deference) variously for the cities and provinces of China, and as the opportunity presented itself, for the crowned heads and statesmen of Europe. The settlement was laid out according to no discernible design—at first the roads simply followed the intricate network of canals typical of the delta countryside, until eventually avenues took the place of waterways. But by the 1880s the streets of the foreign settlements, at least the best of them, were paved or graveled, clean and well-drained, broad enough for carriage traffic, gas-lit—electric lighting was under consideration—and policed by a mixed force of European, Chinese, and Sikh constabulary. They were lined with the imposing facades of Western shops and residences, the clubs and churches, parks and playgrounds of the foreigners whose city—or city-state—this had become. "Shanghai is the centre of our higher civilization and Christian influence for all of China," boasted a British missionary without exaggeration on the occasion of the port's Jubilee in 1893.[12] And in every commodious particular, the Shanghai of the Westerners set itself apart from what S. Wells Williams decried as "the narrow, noisome and reeking parts of the native city."[13] The contrast was not lost on K'ang Yu-wei: what he saw for himself in Hong Kong and Shanghai convinced him that these foreigners, unlike the barbarians of China's earlier acquaintance, possessed more than "useful skills;" that these were societies founded on law: and that behind the visible aspect of Western life must lie animating ideas and principles.

When K'ang Yu-wei set about the arduous task of piecing together an understanding of these ideas and principles in the early 1880s, most of the information that he had at his disposal derived directly from the motives of the Self-strengthening movement, and was intended for practical application rather than speculative consideration. The comparison with Japan's situation at about the same time is portentous. This was the decade that began with several of the energetic and still young architects of the Meiji Restoration touring Europe to study at first hand modern Western political forms and philosophy; it ended with the promulgation of the Meiji Constitution in 1889, a document heavily influenced by the monarchist views of contemporary German political theorists. It was a decade that witnessed lively discussion in the Tokyo press of such issues as the meaning of "sovereignty" and "natural rights." In the 1880s Japanese intellectuals were reading Rousseau's *Social Contract* in serial translation; one could purchase in the bookshops of Tokyo and Osaka recent translations of Disraeli's *Coningsby*, the political romances of Bulwer Lytton, the novels of Jules Verne, or the plays of Shakespeare; sympathetic accounts of Russian nihilism and terrorism were available, though they circulated at risk. By the end of the century, Chinese intellectuals would begin to reap some of the advantage of this Japanese spirit of cultural adventure. But in the 1880s, when K'ang Yu-wei turned his attention to "Western learning," he had to make do with much more meager fare.

Nevertheless, the Chinese were far from where they had been a generation earlier. In the early decades of Sino-Western contact the task of translation had fallen by default almost entirely to missionaries, with the predictable result that the bulk of Western literature translated into Chinese had been religious in content. With the advent of the Peking T'ung-wen kuan and the Kiangnan Arsenal at Shanghai this situation began to change. An end-of-the-century survey counted some six hundred translations made since 1850, roughly four hundred dealing with the natural and applied sciences, another hundred or so with Western history, geography, and social sciences.

In the latter half of the century, moreover, some of the foreigners who came to China to evangelize began to interpret their calling in terms of a more secular mission, the dissemination of the arts of Western civilization broadly construed. One such was W. A. P. Martin, whom we have already met. Attached originally to the Presbyterian mission at Ningpo, Martin soon began to chafe at the limitations imposed by the orthodox evangelical approach. His superiors on their part came to the conclusion that Martin valued the intellectual enlightenment of the Chinese more highly than their spiritual salvation. By mutual agreement he resigned eventually from the mission to become in fact as well as ambition an educator, opening up (as he hoped) "a field of influence much wider than I could find in the wayside chapels of Peking."[14] As we have seen, the T'ung-wen kuan of which he became president in 1869 was hardly a decisive force in the shaping of Chinese opinion in the nineteenth century. It was not entirely without effect, however, and Martin himself exercised considerable personal influence by earning the respect of the Chinese officials for whom he worked. Moreover, his translation of Wheaton's *Elements of International Law*, completed in the early 1860s, was instrumental in demonstrating to harassed Ch'ing "foreign affairs experts" involved in ongoing negotiations with the importunate Westerners that a knowledge of the rules of the game of international relations could be concretely advantageous.

The most prolific translator on the China Coast in the nineteenth century was an Englishman named John Fryer. Growing up as the son of an impoverished Anglican rector on the Kentish coast a few miles southwest of Dover, Fryer had been entranced by tales of China brought home by merchants and missionaries. His own career as a missionary, which began with his arrival in Hong Kong in 1861 at the age of twenty-two, was brief and unsuccessful; Fryer was soon convinced that real influence and worldly success lay elsewhere. Teaching English, first at the Peking T'ung-wen kuan, then as headmaster of the church-run Anglo-Chinese School in Shanghai, pleased him little better: "the toil of cramming knowledge into narrow skulls where there was no room for it. . . . Month after month of monotonous and wearisome labour . . . expended without any perceptible or flattering results being produced."[15] In the meantime Fryer had acquired a remarkable proficiency in Chinese, and was thus enabled to hire himself in 1868 to the Ch'ing government to take charge of the translation bureau of the recently established Kiangnan Arsenal: "an honorable and useful position as well as being respectable. . . . [It is] a powerful means for helping forward this venerable old nation and bringing it somewhat into the track of the 'March of Civilization' of which we Foreigners like generally to boast about."[16] It was, however, slow and awkward work. Collaborating with one or another of the several Chinese "writers" employed by the Arsenal, Fryer would dictate in Chinese from an English or French text, leaving it to his colleague to put the final draft into acceptably polished literary form. In the twenty-eight years he worked at the Arsenal (1868–1896) he turned out in this cumbersome fashion well over a hundred translations, chiefly related to various fields of applied technology in which Fryer had to educate himself as he went along. It makes a remarkable inventory: mathematics, manufacturing, military science, navigation, chemistry, physics, engineering, medicine, surveying, geology and meteorology, anatomy, botany, law, and political economy. Yet one can sympathize with the frustration of a student like K'ang Yu-wei as he tried to view the West through such a narrowly focused lens. "The Western works translated by Fryer all deal with such unimportant studies as military science and medicine," he complained in 1886. "Of greater importance are the books on government, for in the Western learning there are a great many new principles, none of which exist in China. It is a matter of great importance to found a bureau to translate them."[17] A dozen years later he would have his chance, but it would not be until the appearance of Yen Fu's translations of Huxley, Spencer, Montesquieu, and Mill after the turn of the century that some of the "new principles" of which K'ang spoke would gain a wide Chinese readership.

Fryer had his own frustrations. The public response to his labors, he admitted half in anger and half in sorrow, was "nothing compared with what might have been expected among such an extensive population." Of the thirty-odd translations completed by the end of the 1870s, only some 30,000 copies in all had been sold. "But," as Fryer continued, "with no regular means of communication, no postal or railway arrangements, no agencies, and no advertisements or other means of bringing them into general notice or distributing them, it is easy to understand why more have not already been disposed of."* However he might try to put a good face on the matter—"The more the Celestial mind drinks at this fountain, the greater will become its thirst for further supplies"—Fryer left China finally in 1896 a disappointed man, looking back upon his lifework there as "about as dull and unthankful a task as any foreigner could engage in."[19]

W. A. P. Martin was more sanguine by nature than Fryer and perhaps less anxious for acclaim in the opinion of the world. But he was not immune to an occasional moment of exasperation or disillusionment. On his return from home furlough in 1869 to assume his new duties at the T'ung-wen kuan, he brought with him to Peking two sets of telegraph apparatus, having himself taken lessons in their use in Philadelphia. He set the instruments up first in his own home, then in space provided in the Tsungli yamen, to introduce the "wonderful invention" to his Chinese employers. The low-ranking Confucian functionaries who witnessed the first demonstration were unimpressed. "One of them . . . observed contemptuously that 'China had been a great empire for four thousand years without the telegraph.' On being shown a few toys they were delighted,

---

* In Japan, Fukuzawa Yukichi's *Seiyō jijō* (Things Western, a general description of Western institutions and history similar in intent to Hsu Chi-yü's geography but far more comprehensive, and informed by first-hand knowledge) sold 250,000 copies after it was published in 1866, two years before the Meiji Restoration. Fukuzawa's *Gakumon-no susume* (Encouragement of Learning), a series of seventeen pamphlets published between 1872 and 1876 in praise of *jitsugaku* or "practical learning" and Western studies generally, sold an estimated 200,000 copies apiece, or an astonishing total of nearly three and a half million copies altogether in a population of perhaps forty million. "I know that no scholar or writer, no matter how great he may be, could either write or translate a book that would sell as mine did if he had not happened to hit the right time and occasion," Fukuzawa remarked. "After all, my success was not due to my ability, but it was by reason of the time I came to serve."[18] Fukuzawa was a remarkably readable writer and eloquent advocate. But Japan offered, as China did not, "the right time and occasion." (E. H. Kinmonth takes a skeptical view of the usually accepted figures in "Fukuzawa Reconsidered: *Gakumon no susume* and its audience," *Journal of Asian Studies* 37.4:677-696 (August 1978).)

spending much time in catching magnetic fish and in leading or chasing magnetic geese, chuckling all the while over the novelty of the sport. In letters they were men, in science children." The next exhibition, given for the benefit of the Tsungli yamen's senior officials, went hardly better, "the old men being almost as childlike as their clerks, only they toyed with the telegraph instead of fish and geese, sending bell signals, wrapping copper wires about their bodies, breaking or closing the circuit, and laughing heartily as they saw sparks leaping from wire to wire and setting hammers in motion." One is reminded inevitably of the Jesuits in seventeenth century Peking entertaining the courtiers of K'ang Hsi with European clocks and elaborate mechanical automata. Eventually Martin's precious telegraphic equipment was "stored as old lumber in the museum of the college." The moral to this seriocomic tale was brought home to him several years later, after the construction of the Peking-Shanghai telegraph line in 1884. As Martin recalled it,

> I fell into conversation one day with a hard-fisted peasant, who was cultivating a stony field high up on the western hills. "Why do you foreigners not take the empire?" he asked. "Do you think we could?" I inquired in return. "Certainly," he replied, pointing to a line of telegraph stretching across the plain below—"the men who made that are able to take possession of the empire." His brain had not been addled by an overdose of Chinese classics; and China is full of such men, but unhappily they are under the heel of the literati.[20]

It was to the literati, nevertheless, that these secular evangelists appealed. Even more than their orthodox missionary colleagues, who at least had pulpits to preach from or street corners where they might expound the Gospel, men like Martin and Fryer were dependent upon the written word. As Fryer observed in the days of his early enthusiasm for translation, "It gives access to the class of Chinese who form the most important part of the Nation and who can be reached in no other way."[21] And indeed, as servants of the dynasty both he and Martin were themselves literati, after a fashion: Fryer received appointment as an official of the third rank, while Martin attained promotion to the second rank of the mandarinate before he resigned the presidency of the T'ung-wen kuan in 1895.

In the Chinese scheme of things, this was a perfect instance of the ancient strategem of "using barbarians to control barbarians," following among many other precedents that set by the employment of the great Jesuit astronomers at the court of K'ang Hsi two hundred years earlier. The barbarians in question, though they sometimes felt unappreciated, did not seem to feel themselves ill-used. From their perspective the same historical precedent justified their approach to the task at hand. Like the Jesuits, they were unabashedly elitist in their search for influence. "I am after the Leaders," declared Timothy Richard late in the century; "if you get the leaders you get all the rest."[22] Richard was a Welshman who arrived in China in 1870 in behalf of the Baptist Missionary Society and soon became one of the most forceful and colorful proponents of the view that the Chinese must be approached on their own cultural terms, and at the highest level. To the consternation of missionary opinion at large he set about energetically to emulate Ricci's strategy of cultural compromise, even to the point of donning a Confucian scholar's gown, shaving his head, and adorning himself with a false queue in order to make himself acceptable to the literati. In this he succeeded, and not merely because he disguised himself to look like a Confucian. He succeeded, as did Martin and perhaps Fryer and a few others of like mind, because (and again the comparison with Jesuits is at least partially apt) an unwavering commitment to Christian faith and Western values did not extinguish their sympathy and admiration for a civilization that was neither Christian nor Western. They acknowledged Chinese cultural achievement—it was, after all, the justification for pinning their hopes on the latent capabilites of the race. "Never have a great people been more misunderstood," wrote Martin in 1868:

> They are denounced as stolid, because we are not in possession of a medium sufficiently transparent to convey our ideas to them, or transmit theirs to us; and stigmatized as barbarians, because we want the breadth to comprehend a civilization different from our own. . . . The national mind has advanced from age to age with a stately march . . . like the dawn of an arctic morning, in which the first blush of the eastern sky disappears for many hours, only to be succeeded by a brighter glow, growing brighter yet, after each interval of darkness, as the time of sunrise approaches.[23]

For all the amiability of these sentiments, there is more condescension here than may at first appear: to say that the Chinese have stood throughout their history in the gray light of a slow dawn is only a step away from calling them benighted. But that the sun would rise these men never doubted, and that is the important point. In their minds Salvation and Progress were inseparable, virtually indistinguishable, the latter a certain inducement to the former. In the nineteenth century even the least dogmatic, the most accommodating Westerner in China felt himself to be the agent not merely of a religious doctrine or a system of cultural values, but of an historical process, an epoch in the making. As the Jesuits had done, they might go to great lengths to establish the compatability of Christian and Confucian principles. Is not *jen* (human-heartedness, benevolence) simply another way of saying "Thou shalt love thy neighbor as thyself?" Is not *hsiao* (filiality) merely the Confucian version of the Christian injunction to "Hearken to thy father that begat thee, and despise not thy mother when she is old," or "Children, obey your parents in the Lord"? They might even go so far as to state flatly that "Jesus has the heart of Confucius and Mencius."[24] But—and here the Jesuits set no precedent, for the idea of progress in its nineteenth-century sense had been as alien to them as it was to the Chinese two hundred years later—these secular evangelicals would not concede for a moment that China could remain untouched by the great progressive spirit of the age, remote from the transforming forces of modernity. Implicitly, sometimes explicitly, they contradicted the unstated premise of the Self-strengthening movement. And therein lay the source of their difficulties and frustrations, the reason why, in Richard's terms, the "Leaders" of the Self-strengthening generation were so hard to "get," as Martin's dismal experience with the telegraph suggests. It was chiefly upon the younger minds, the leaders or would-be leaders of the rising generation, men like K'ang Yu-wei and Sun Yat-sen and their disciples in turn, that this enthusiasm, this assurance, this sense of historical design and purpose, would work a permanent change.

Young John Allen, whose arguments reconciling Christianity and Confucianism are cited above, was a native of Georgia who arrived in Shanghai under the auspices of the Southern Methodist Episcopal mission board in 1860—just in time to be cut off from his sources of support by the outbreak of the American Civil War. To enable himself to continue with his ministry he became a part-time teacher at the Shanghai T'ung-wen kuan, and later worked along with Fryer in the translation bureau of the Kiangnan Arsenal. He also turned to journalism, and here he broke new ground. Allen was not the first missionary-turned-journalist, but in the 1870s he was the most successful, and the most consistently progressive.

There had been a foreign press in China even in pre-treaty days. Westerners in the Canton-Macao area followed the deepening crisis of the 1830s in the pages of the weekly *Canton Press*, the rival *Canton Register*, or in the much more ambitious monthly journal, the *Chinese Repository*. The *Repository* was a mission enterprise, established by Elijah Bridgman, a Massachusetts Congregationalist who arrived in Canton in 1830. (It was to assist Bridgman in his labors that S. Wells Williams, whose opinions we have already encountered on several occasions, was trained as a printer and dispatched to Canton in 1833.) The *Repository* printed translations of imperial edicts and other government pronouncements, a good deal of inland news that filtered down to Canton, editorials on Chinese politics and Christian duty, and also serious scholarly articles, the first fruits of nineteenth-century Western sinology. Missionaries were also responsible for the earliest efforts to establish a Chinese-language periodical press, an undertaking beset by myriad difficulties. For one thing, Ch'ing policy before 1842 prohibited foreigners from learning Chinese and punished Chinese who dared to offer instruction in the language. Like the early language schools, therefore, the first foreign-run Chinese presses were located outside China, in Malacca or

Singapore or Batavia; but distribution within the Empire of the literature printed there remained inconvenient and sometimes risky. For another thing, though they might sometimes aspire to a degree of cultural breadth, the publications that came from such presses tended to be narrowly religious in content, with little value as sources of general information, much less "news."* Finally, these early periodicals reached only a tiny segment of the literate population, and in the nature of things fell largely into the hands of those whose cultural defenses against the kind of message they conveyed were all but impregnable.

With the opening of the treaty ports, the Western press advanced up the coast; the Chinese-language press was not far behind. The *China Mail* was established as a daily in Hong Kong in 1845, followed by the *Hong Kong Daily Press* in 1857. The *North-China Herald* began publishing as a weekly at Shanghai in 1850, when the foreign community of the port still claimed fewer than two hundred residents; it served for a century as the voice of British mercantile interests in China. In 1864 there issued from the same publisher the *North China Daily News*, together with a Chinese supplement, *Shanghai hsin-pao* (Shanghai News). It was as editor of this supplement that Young J. Allen made his journalistic debut. *Shanghai hsin-pao* dealt mostly in commercial and shipping news, with a small circulation confined to the Chinese merchants of the port. In 1868, therefore, Allen launched his own paper, a weekly entitled *Chiao-hui hsin-pao* (Church News). The title belied, or at least belittled, the content of the paper itself. *Chiao-hui hsin-pao* printed mission news, to be sure, including not infrequent reports of anti-missionary disturbances. It published interpretations of the Christian message like those already mentioned. But it carried also a good deal of foreign and domestic news: an account of the construction of the Suez Canal, which opened in 1869; an article on the laying of the Trans-Atlantic Cable, and another on railway construction in the United States; and such other useful material as might come to hand, including the serialization of a textbook on chemistry by the indefatigable and polymathic Dr. Martin. *Chiao-hui hsin-pao* attained a circulation of about seven hundred subscribers by the

---

* The quotation from the *Analects* which stands at the head of this chapter appeared as the motto of one such periodical, the *Tung Hsi yang k'ao* ("An examination of [the nations of] the Eastern and Western oceans"). It was published beginning in 1833, first in Canton, later in Singapore, by a Pomeranian Prussian missionary named Karl Freidrich August Gutzlaff, expressly to purge the Chinese of their "empty conceit" and to counteract their "high and exclusive notions, by making the Chinese acquainted with our arts, sciences, and principles . . . to convince [them] that they still have very much to learn."[25] Gutzlaff was a remarkable linguist, the master of several dialects, and in his way a remarkable entrepreneur. He is best remembered, whether or or not most fairly, as the missionary who, in his capacity as interpreter to several of the exploratory voyages of the opium clippers along the China Coast in the 1830s, benignly dispensed religious tracts from one side of the vessel while the crew distributed opium from the other. The *Tung Hsi yang k'ao* was a short-lived venture.

end of its first year of publication; it was sent to mission stations all along the coast and found its way even into remote inland destinations.

Chiao-hui hsin-pao prefigured what was to become Allen's most ambitious and influential journalistic venture. In 1875 he changed the name of the paper to *Wan-kuo kung-pao*, subtitled in English "The Globe Magazine." The new title served to remind Chinese readers that their ancient sense of cultural self-containment was no longer warranted. On the other hand, Allen's statement of purpose gave notice to his fellow missionaries that religious evangelism by itself was no longer a sufficient calling. *Wan-kuo kung-pao*, he wrote, was to be "Devoted to the extension of knowledge relating to Geography, History, Civilization, Politics, Religion, Science, Art, Industry, and general progress of Western countries."[26] In one way or another the paper managed to touch on all these topics, and to publish as well a substantial amount of domestic news and editorial comment on Chinese affairs. It quickly achieved a circulation of some 1800 per issue, numbering among its readers several high officials in the provincial and central governments. K'ang Yu-wei arranged to take out a subscription when he passed through Shanghai in 1882. The following year, however, when the Southern Methodists finally began remitting funds again, *Wan-kuo kung-pao* suspended publication to allow Allen to return to full-time mission work. It was revived as a monthly in 1889, with Allen again as the editor, but now under the auspices of the Society for the Diffusion of Christian and General Knowledge Among the Chinese (later less pretentiously renamed the Christian Literature Society) of which Timothy Richard served as Secretary from 1890. Throughout the 1890s *Wan-kuo kung-pao* played an important role as an outlet for reformist opinion, Chinese as well as foreign, and as a chronicle of current events. Its coverage of the Sino-Japanese War of 1894–1895, for example, was unusually well-informed, largely because Li Hung-chang made government telegraphic dispatches available to it. In 1898 it was even suggested that *Wan-kuo kung-pao* should become the official government reform organ. At that time, during Allen's absence on furlough, the paper was temporarily under the editorship of Timothy Richard, who was in close touch with several of the reform party. Nothing came of the proposal, and indeed the kind of reformist opinion that found expression in the pages of *Wan-kuo kung-pao*—broadly cosmopolitan rather than nationalistic, progressive but far from radical, and "political" only in a very general and nonpartisan sense—died with the failure of the Hundred Days. The paper itself continued publishing until shortly after Allen's death in 1907, but by that time it had long been superseded as a source of general news by the commercial Chinese press in the treaty ports, and as a purveyor of reformist opinion by the increasing number of radical reformist-cum-revolutionary polemical journals published by political activists both in China and elsewhere from their outposts in exile.

The eminence of its readership made *Wan-kuo kung-pao* perhaps the most influential Chinese-language newspaper throughout much of the last quarter of the nineteenth century. It did not have the field to itself, however, nor was it the first or in general circulation the largest Chinese paper. By the end of the 1880s Hong Kong and the treaty ports supported a number of newspapers under Chinese management. Some of these had official or semi-official backing, like the *Shih-pao* (The Times) established in Tientsin in 1886 at the instigation of Li Hung-chang. Li was by this time the Governor-General of Chihli, the metropolitan province, and concurrently Superintendant of Trade for the Northern Ports—the prepotent official of the empire and a mainstay of the Self-strengthening movement. *Shih-pao* was intended to promote the cause. It was foreign-edited, first by Alexander Michie, China correspondent for the *London Times*, and later, though only briefly, by Timothy Richard, at Li's personal invitation. In the south, Chang Chih-tung, Governor-General of Kwangtung and Kwangsi, lent his support to a similarly motivated publication, the *Kuang pao* (Canton Gazette), also established in 1886. (It was to Chang that K'ang Yu-wei submitted his plea for the creation of a translation bureau.) But reform, at least at the level of official sponsorship, was still more a matter of personality than policy; as soon as Chang Chih-tung was transferred to a different post, *Kuang pao* fell victim to political pressures and rivalries.

Other Chinese papers were launched as commercial ventures, independent either of official support or the missionary press, though in some cases foreign owned, or published as Chinese supplements by English-language papers under autonomous editorial direction. This was the case with the first Chinese papers to publish in Hong Kong, established in the 1860s. Hong Kong was also the home of the *Hsun-huan jih-pao* (Cantonese: *Tsun-wan yat-po*), founded and edited in the 1870s by Wang T'ao, a remarkable China Coast personality with whom we will deal at more appropriate length shortly. In the meantime the first commercial Chinese paper to publish in Shanghai, the *Shen-pao* (or *Shun-pao*) made its appearance in 1872.* It was British-owned until 1907, when the firm's compradore bought the paper out. From the very beginning, however, *Shen-pao* was edited and written by Chinese for a general Chinese readership. It developed a network of agencies to sell outside Shanghai, in such cities as Soochow and Hangchow; and it established a

---

* These titles present problems of translation. *Hsun-huan* means "to move in a circle, to revolve, cyclical." Roswell Britton suggests that Wang used the term to convey the idea of "the slow but sure evolution of natural law, something of the idea that the mills of the gods grind slow but exceeding fine." Paul Cohen reads it as a reflection of Wang's "deeply grounded cyclical outlook on history," with overtones suggesting "his conviction that China would come into her own again as a great country."[27] *Shen* is an old name given to the Whangpoo River; *pao*, here as elsewhere, means "to report" or "a report." *Shen-pao* is usually translated simply as "The Shanghai News" or some such. But *shen* also means "to notify, to report to a superior" and some word-play may be intended in the paper's name.

reputation for reliability in its reportage, telling bad news when there was bad news to tell, even at the risk of displeasing its audience as happened during the Sino-French War. By the mid-1890s *Shen-pao* had reached a circulation of some 15,000—well out in front of its Shanghai competitors. *Wan-kuo kung-pao*, as we have noted, was by this time publishing as a monthly, with a subscription of some 1,800 per issue.

The editorial which ran in the first issue of *Shen-pao* in April, 1872, conveys the contemporary perspective on the purpose which such publications aimed to serve:

> Today there occur many events which might be recorded but are buried and remain unknown. . . . There is no one who takes enough interest in them to record them, and so remarkable occurrences and unpretentious actions remain hidden and untold. This is exceedingly regrettable. . . . From antiquity down to the present there have been abundant works by historians and belletrists . . . but these literary treasures are all records of former ages, stories of the past. . . . When we cast about for something which records and narrates modern events in a style simple though not vulgar, and which reports current affairs concisely yet in sufficient detail so that scholars and officials as well as farmers, artisans, traders and merchants all can understand, we find nothing so suitable as the newspaper. . . . The world is very large, and its interests and affairs are myriad. The inhabitants are scattered, and can not see one another. Is there one person who can see and know thoroughly all the world's affairs? . . . Since the rise of the news press every person may know the whole world without crossing his own doorstep.* Is not this excellent?[28]

This suggests what was in fact the situation: these pioneering Chinese journalistic enterprises were not so much meeting a need as trying to create one. As with other methods of utilizing the technology of printing, the Chinese were centuries ahead of Europeans in the regular publication of edicts and other official pronouncements through the medium of a Court gazette, the *Ching-pao*, known to foreigners as the *Peking Gazette.* This was not an official publication, but privately printed in various formats and distributed by private post. It was, however, authoritative; down to the end of the nineteenth century the modern press, Chinese and foreign, depended largely on the *Peking Gazette* for "official" information on politics and policy.† In moments of local crisis, moreover, hastily printed notices might be hawked along the streets and alleys of the larger cities and towns: foreigners in Canton at the time of the opium crisis, and later in the century missionaries in isolated inland stations or even in the treaty ports themselves, were painfully familiar with the passions that such broadsides could suddenly blow to white heat among a local population. There was, however, no indigenous industry given over to the gath-

---

*A phrase from chapter 47 of the *Tao-te ching.*

†The *Peking Gazette* served unofficially, one might say, the same function that is now performed officially by the New China News Agency.

ering and publication of "news" as such. Nor was there perhaps even much of an appetite for it. Though the gentry were presumably Confucian and therefore presumably both literate and public-spirited, there is evidence to suggest that they in fact took little interest as a rule in national affairs. S. Wells Williams observed that officials were kept remarkably well informed through the medium of the *Peking Gazette.* On the other hand, the Abbé Huc, a French Lazarist who had traveled in the interior of China probably more extensively than any other foreigner in the 1840s and 1850s, tells an interesting anecdote of one attempt to provoke a political discussion among a group of local gentry drinking tea at a roadside inn. This was shortly after the death of the Tao Kuang emperor in 1851, an event which the Abbé assumed would be much on the minds of these men of opinion, especially in light of the confusion which Ch'ing succession politics generally entailed. To his consternation, every effort to launch the topic was met with stolid indifference, until, as Huc continues,

> One of these worthy Chinese, getting up from his seat, came and laid his two hands on our shoulders in a manner quite paternal and said, smiling rather ironically: "Listen to me, my friend! Why should you trouble your heart and fatigue your head by all these vain surmises? The mandarins have to attend to affairs of state; they are paid for it. Let them earn their money then. But don't let us torment ourselves by what does not concern us. We should be great fools to want to do political business for nothing." "That is very conformable to reason," cried the rest of the company, and thereupon they pointed out to us that our tea was growing cold and our pipes were out.[29]

*   *   *

Reformers at the end of the nineteenth century were thus confronted by a threefold challenge. They sought to open the minds of the Chinese to the world that lay beyond the inherited frontiers of the empire, geographic and cultural. The sought also to make the Chinese aware of their immediate world with a new kind of interest, and to weave new relationships between past and present. They sought, finally, the means of acting upon such new understanding: new modes of government, new responsibilities for the governing elite.

In the first of these endeavors Westerners had a leading part to play, as translators, teachers, general purveyors of unfamiliar modes of thought and styles of life. But at the point at which the task of reform moved from knowledge of the world at large to knowledge of the particular and private Chinese world, and from knowledge to action, at the point of cultural mediation and political organization, Westerners perforce surrendered the initiative to a new generation of Chinese reformers. Foreigners might have their preferences; they might push and prod, as they had always done and would continue to do. But the questions of

China's ultimate destiny that foreigners debated, sometimes with olympian detachment and other times with polemical fervor, were for the Chinese issues that touched the innermost springs of self. In them throbbed the sense not only of a crisis to be met, opportunities to be realized, but also of a real and dreadful peril. For them it was a slow and agonizing process of self-discovery, testing at every step the subjective sense of Chinese identity against the objective circumstances of China's uncertain place in the world. In many respects it is a process still ongoing, for although many fought shy of the term and did their best to forestall the event itself, this marks the beginning of the Chinese "revolution" as a consciously perceived possibility.

The treaty ports had a contribution to make to this process, albeit an indirect one. They served, as the occasion demanded from time to time, as sanctuaries for Chinese who found themselves beyond the pale of acceptable opinion. More important, at least in the nineteenth century, was their function in providing not only an environment conducive to the emergence of an unorthodox world view, but also career opportunities independent of the traditional Confucian ladder of scholarship and official preferment. Several of the most vehement advocates of institutional innovation, even outright Westernization, were Chinese who had established themselves in this treaty-port milieu, products of the "compradore culture" of the China Coast. Some were compradores in fact, or at least had started as such. Others were Western-educated professionals, pursuing modern careers in the context of treaty-port life. Still others were men of more traditional cultural background who for one reason or another found it congenial to live and work in the treaty ports, as journalists, educators, intellectual middlemen—"interpreters" in a much wider and more respectable sense than Feng Kuei-fen had had in mind.

Wang T'ao (1828–1897), whom we have met as the founder and editor of the *Hsun-huan jih-pao* in Hong Kong, is the preeminent example of the latter. He was born near Soochow, into a family of cultured lineage which had suffered along with the rest of the Kiangnan gentry at the time of the Manchu conquest and entered upon a long decline. Wang's father held no degree, but he was an educated man who made his living by tutoring the sons of families with bureaucratic aspirations. He naturally gave his own son a solid classical education as well, and in 1845 Wang T'ao passed the prefectural examination. That was as far as he was destined to rise in the established order; his failure in the provincial examinations in 1846 was a disappointment that rankled for a long time and probably contributed something to the critical temper of his opinions in later years.

In 1848, when his father was teaching in the city, Wang paid his first visit to Shanghai. The port was then in its infancy, but as Wang later recalled it, "I found myself all at once in a different world . . . an expanse of mist and water, and bristling through it a forest of masts. All along the bank of the river were the houses of the foreigners, which seemed to me then to tower into the sky. . . . " He visited the premises of London Mission Press and met its director, Walter H. Medhurst, who offered him a glass of port, showed him the sizeable Chinese library which the mission boasted, and entertained him with a "tune . . . on the piano which I found very charming in its own way."[30] It was a foretaste of things to come. When Wang's father died in 1849 the burden of family support descended upon him; at this juncture, Medhurst offered him a job as translator to the Mission Press which, *faut de mieux*, Wang accepted. When he moved to Shanghai that autumn he could hardly have anticipated that he would spend the rest of his life on the China Coast: in Shanghai until 1862, in Hong Kong from 1862 to 1884 (during which time he spent two and a half years in England), and in Shanghai again from 1884 until his death in 1897.

What made Wang T'ao a *rara avis*, however, was not merely the fact that he lived his life in a culturally ambiguous environment, but his ability to translate the experience into terms comprehensible to his contemporaries. His years in Shanghai in the 1850s brought him into contact with a number of the energetic and imaginative missionaries connected with the London Missionary Society (LMS) at the time: Medhurst himself, Joseph Edkins, and Alexander Wylie. Through Wylie, Wang met and became fast friends with Li Shan-lan, the mathematician who was then collaborating with Wylie on the translation of Euclid and Newton, and who was later appointed head of the department of mathematics and astronomy of the Peking T'ung-wen kuan under W. A. P. Martin: Westernization, one comes to feel, was the preoccupation of a rather small interlocking directorate in mid-nineteenth-century China, and Wang was well on his way to membership in the inner circle.

Wang probably became a convert to Christianity at some point during these years; LMS records make note of his baptism in 1854, though he never acknowledged the fact in public. It was in any case an action undertaken more out of concern for his career than for his eternal salvation. In his diary Wang mentions receiving communion from time to time and describes forays into the countryside around Shanghai to distribute Christian literature. But he also records without embarrassment frequent visits to the flourishing brothels of Shanghai and other worldly pleasures: "To feast on crabs and wine, chatting freely with the candles extinguished—is there any greater pleasure?"[31] He wore his faith lightly, in other words, nor is there any indication that Christianity per se significantly influenced his perceptions of the West. On the other hand, his missionary connections were decisive in shaping the course of his life. It was through them, first of all, that he became peripherally involved with the Taiping Rebellion when he accompanied Edkins and others to

Soochow and Nanking in the early 1860s to assess at first hand the nature of Taiping Christianity. Whether or not fairly, Wang was soon accused by the Ch'ing of harboring seditious sympathies; in 1862 he was smuggled out of Shanghai by his British friends to seek refuge in the safety of Hong Kong.

It was in Hong Kong that Wang eventually established his independent reputation as a journalist, a commentator on contemporary history, and in various ways a promoter of reformist opinions. It took him some time, however, to emerge from the chrysalis of missionary patronage. He carried with him to Hong Kong in1862 an introduction to James Legge of the LMS. Legge was a remarkable Scot, long resident in the colony, who was just then in the midst of an extraordinarily audacious and arduous labor: the translation of virtually the entire corpus of classical Confucian literature into English. Having spent a dozen years in Shanghai putting the Christian scriptures into Chinese, Wang was now enlisted as Legge's assistant in the task of rendering Chinese wisdom accessible in English. When Legge was compelled by ill health to return to Britain in 1867, Wang accompanied him. He spent nearly two and a half years abroad, continuing his collaboration with Legge at the latter's home in the rustic Scots hamlet of Dollar, visiting Edinburgh, Glasgow, and Aberdeen, touring London with Legge as his guide, and generally being made much of as something between a dignitary and a curiosity. He lectured at Oxford—where in 1876 Legge would be installed as the first occupant of the university's chair of Chinese—on the timely topic of China's relations with the West. He arrived back in Hong Kong in March, 1870, after a leisurely tour of the Continent, no longer a translator merely of languages, but an interpreter of ideas and visions, the leading cosmopolite of his generation.

In the context of late Ch'ing culture, cosmopolitanism did not signify what it had meant in earlier centuries, the cultural tolerance remarked upon by Bishop Andrew in the 1300s and by Ricci and his fellow Jesuits in the 1600s. Chinese in the late nineteenth century could not afford the luxury of such condescension. Nor did it mean what it would come to mean in the attitudes of some Chinese in the 1910s and 1920s, a sweeping repudiation of the political and cultural claims of Chinese nationalism. To the extent that the motives of the Self-strengthening movement reflected an incipient nationalism, Wang T'ao like other reformers of his time was a nationalist. Cosmopolitanism manifested itself in his thought at two levels. First and most concretely, it meant carrying forward the task embarked upon in the 1840s by writers like Wei Yuan and Hsu Chi-yü, reshaping the Chinese view of the world, fitting China into a scheme no longer dependent on the idea of the Middle Kingdom's cultural, political, and cosmic centrality. In their time, Wei and Hsu had had to start virtually from scratch; their work was perforce largely descriptive. By the 1870s and 1880s Wang was able to take a bit more for granted, to concern himself not exclusively with how the world order looked, and to examine as well the question of how it worked. His study of European history led him in turn to speculate on the interior dynamic of universal history and the ultimate confluence of cultures. Wang thus anticipated, and contributed to, a growing preoccupation on the part of Chinese intellectuals with questions of the underlying structure of historical change—preparing the way, as it were, for the reception of Yen Fu's translations of Huxley and Spencer at the turn of the century.

Given the nature of his friendships and experiences, it is hardly surprising that Wang T'ao held British institutions in high esteem. China Coast reformers in general, though they might deplore Britain's imperialist presence, nevertheless respected the political and economic system that could generate such awesome power. What is surprising, in Wang's case, is that he wrote little about Britain, for all his first-hand knowledge, and that he wrote a good deal about France, relying largely on secondary works in Japanese and on a digest of current events published serially by the Kiangnan Arsenal. Perhaps to one of his generation and outlook, the English example, however attractive, seemed too remote. "The excellence of the English system has not been achieved at a stroke or as the result of internal upheaval," wrote John Fryer in a pamphlet that was widely read by reformers in the 1880s. "It is rather the product of prudent conservatism—the promotion of everything useful and the elimination of anything harmful—which has made it possible to progress in an orderly manner toward perfection. . . . The political system of England today differs widely from that existing three centuries ago." Already by the closing decades of the nineteenth century the dilemma that would eventually confound the advocates of evolutionary reform was beginning to emerge. Fryer's assurances that "by following [the English] practice the political system of any country can attain excellence—by degrees and in an orderly way," may well have struck a responsive chord, for Wang T'ao and his colleagues were by no means revolutionaries.[32] But it cannot have been a particularly warming prospect, this notion of waiting three hundred years, given the urgency of China's peril.

Perhaps, then, Wang sensed in French experience a greater possibility to domesticate foreign example in ways useful to the Chinese present—useful, at least, in negative terms. The French Revolution offered an obvious lesson in the consequences of the abuse of autocratic power. More to the point, Wang's view of the world that now impinged on China was a grim one. He saw a world dominated by struggle, in which strength inevitably overpowers weakness—the Darwinist world, though without benefit of Darwinist theoretical justifications. In the 1870s and 1880s, France was a case in point: it was French missionary activity that had provoked the Tientsin Massacre in 1870, settled on terms humiliating to the Chinese; it was French imperial ambition that detached Annam from China, which had long regarded it as a tributary state. "France is truly a war-loving country," cried Wang T'ao. "Her kings and nobles, through the ages, have all striven for glory and victory. . . . They attack abroad and extend their frontiers at home." It is an odd conclusion to come from the hand of a chronicler of the Franco-Prussian War—but perhaps Wang had lived long enough among the English to adopt their political antipathies. The French, he wrote, "carry on the tradition of Ch'in," that is, the despotic and despised first imperial dynasty.

In the Confucian vernacular, this is a stinging rebuke. But directed against whom? The proximate target of Wang's criticism was the Japanese commentator on whose work his own history of France was based, and who professed to find French militarism—indeed, warfare generally—admirable and progressive. Perhaps, Wang suggests, Japan has "caught the disease of the French!"—and he procedes to catalog the areas where already Japanese ambition was in conflict with established Chinese interests: the Ryukyus, Formosa, Korea. Wang doubtless shared enough of the bedrock Confucian distaste for naked power to feel a genuine aversion to "the tradition of Ch'in." Yet he was himself from first to last a proponent of Self-strengthening, unmoved by the orthodox Confucian argument that moral ascendancy is the only thing that counts. The real thrust of his attack was aimed closer to home. "The scholars of Japan have eyes only for their country's imitation of the military arts of the West," he wrote. "[They] are convinced that they can become strong. They don't realize that, in fact, their strength is on the surface only, and that they are weak within."[33] Wang did not want the Chinese to be similarly misled by appearances.

For mid-century reformers, "wealth" and "power" had been terms of self-evident meaning, the equally weighted objectives of the Self-strengthening movement. Wang T'ao and other treaty-port reformers in the 1870s and 1880s began to think in different terms or, more accurately, to invest the same terms with more subtle meaning. They perceived a sequential relationship and a degree of interdependence between economic and political reform. Wealth was the means to achieve power; but without the effective and disciplined use of power, wealth itself was unattainable. Though they would not have recognized it as such, Wang and others were on the threshold of a theory of economic modernization. Wealth did not mean to them what it had traditionally meant in the context of Confucian economic theory: renovation of an essentially static economy based on agriculture and peasant labor. Nor in their minds did power mean simply the strengthening of the military capabilities of the Confucian monarchy, the enhancement of its capacity for self-defense.

They advocated the creation of modern networks of transportation and communication, the exploitation of natural resources (especially mining enterprises), and, within a still limited understanding of the economics of industrial society, the encouragement of industrial investment. Most important, they vehemently denounced the ancient Confucian prejudice against mercantilism and urged the government to stimulate private enterprise free of the constraints of official supervision.

The idea of "official supervision, merchant management" (*kuan-tu shang-pan*) was the fundamental organizational concept underlying the initial efforts made by the Ch'ing to encourage economic diversification and modernization. The aim was partly to assert the government's control over new economic enterprises and partly to underwrite the entrepreneurial risks of such undertakings. Enterprises like the China Merchant's Steam Navigation Co. (established 1872), the K'ai-p'ing Coal Mines (1877), and the Shanghai Cotton Cloth Mills (1878) went well beyond the narrowly strategic purposes of the arsenals and shipyards created in the 1860s. They remained linked, however, to the limited aims of the Self-strengthening movement as a whole. From the beginning, moreover, the distinction between "supervision" and "management" proved difficult both to define and to defend. *Kuan-tu shang-pan* enterprises were frequently exploited as a direct source of government revenue; not infrequently they were also a source of private wealth for those officials involved in the "supervisory" role as well as for the merchant managers. They were investments of uncertain profitability in the long run, which undermined their ability to attract capital or to hold their own against foreign competition.*

There is a strong element of economic nationalism in the attack directed by Wang T'ao and others against this arrangement. The British example proved to their satisfaction that commercial strength (*shang li*) and military strength (*ping li*) are essential corollaries. Therefore, ran the argument, the Chinese government should in its own interests encourage commerce by every means at its disposal rather than preying upon it. "Western governments both regulate and assist their merchants," wrote

---

* The China Merchants' Steam Navigation Co. is generally cited as the classic example of a *kuan-tu shang-pan* enterprise. it was established in 1872–1873 by Li Hung-chang, who, in his capacity as Superintendant of Trade for the Northern Ports, became the "official supervisor" of the company. The CMSNC was given by way of subsidy a virtual monopoly of government grain shipments from the Yangtze valley to the north, in addition to certain tax exemptions. With this inital advantage and a fleet of thirty-three steamers in operation in the late 1870s, the China Merchants' enjoyed a decided edge over its foreign competition in the business of coastal shipping. Yet by the early 1890s the company had fallen on hard times, as a result partly of official rake-offs on the grain shipments, partly of the misappropriation of funds for private investment in real estate and other traditional modes of investment, and partly of the ability of more heavily capitalized foreign shipping firms to underbid it. By the mid-1890s shipping companies owned by the British firms of Jardine, Matheson & Co. and Butterfield & Swire had overtaken and surpassed the China Merchants' in their share of both coastal and river shipping.

Wang to Li Hung-chang. "Consequently, the profits [of the merchants] are immense, and the revenues [of the government] are ample." Wang foresaw, moreover, that as Chinese economic power increased, so inevitably would foreign domination of Chinese markets decline. Not long after his return from England, Wang outlined a thesis that is, as Paul Cohen puts it, remarkably "proto-Leninist." If Britain could be deprived of the profits of the China market, Wang declared, the consequences for the domestic British economy would be a catastrophic depression and mass unemployment; England "might snap like a mad dog and struggle like a hemmed-in beast," but the sun would set upon the British Empire. Twenty years later Wang was still confident that if the proper authorities would take the appropriate initiatives, "within a decade or so many Western merchants would have their profits snatched away from them by Chinese."[34]

In the thinking of late nineteenth-century reformers, economic development was but one aspect of a more far-reaching mobilization of resources—in Wang's words, a policy of "reliance on the collective energy and intelligence" of the people.[35] "The real strength of England lies in the fact that there is a sympathetic understanding between the governing and the governed," wrote Wang in the early 1880s, "a close relationship between the ruler and the people."[36] By then this was becoming a common theme in reformist circles. In 1886, two years after he settled again in Shanghai, Wang was appointed director of the Shanghai Polytechnic Institute and Reading Room. The Institute had been one of John Fryer's schemes for popularizing scientific learning among the literati, an aim in which it achieved at best only a modest success. More successful was the essay contest that the Institute sponsored to encourage Chinese scholars to express themselves on timely issues. One of the topics set for this purpose—itself more a statement of belief than a question—captures nicely the temper of progressive political opinion in the waning decades of the century:

> Nowadays there is a complaint that "those in power hold aloof, far away, from the common people; hence the latter find it impossible to bring their wants to their Sovereign's personal notice." In view of this state of affairs, it has often been mooted that China should inaugurate a Parliament, for the purpose of bringing the people into closer relationship with the Throne. . . .[37]

The first man to make this "often mooted" proposal was probably Cheng Kuan-ying, the most interesting of the compradores-turned-reformers. He was born in Kwangtung, probably in 1842, the year in which the Treaty of Nanking was signed. Having studied for the civil examinations as a youth, and like so many others touched upon in this history having failed to win distinction in this traditional manner, Cheng moved to Shanghai in his late teens and began to work his way up in the

commercial world of that already thriving port. He studied English for a
time with John Fryer—one doubts that his was one of the "narrow skulls"
without room for the kind of knowledge Fryer was anxious to impart—and by the 1860s was employed as a compradore to the great
British firms of Dent & Co. and, subsequently, Butterfield & Swire. By
that time also, though still very young, he was beginning to make a name
for himself as an essayist and expert on "foreign matters" (*yang-wu*). A
collection of his essays was published in 1862, entitled *Ch'iu-shih chieh-
yao;* the title goes clumsily into English, but an adequate rendering might
be "What Is to Be Done?" A decade later a revised and enlarged edition
appeared under the title *I-yen*, literally "Easy Words," but more probably meaning something like "Obvious Advice." In 1893 came the version
of Cheng's proposals in the form in which they received their widest circulation. *Sheng-shih wei-yen,* or "Words of Warning to a Prosperous
Age," went through several revisions in the 1890s and had a considerable
influence on the reformers of that decade.

By then Cheng had become an entrepreneur in his own right, involved in the management of several of Li Hung-chang's pet Self-
strengthening *kuan-tu shang-pan* enterprises: the Shanghai Cotton Cloth
Mill, the K'ai-p'ing Coal Mines, the Hanyang Iron Foundry, the Imperial
Telegraph Administration, various shipping and railroad projects, and a
number of private investments as well. He had become a wealthy man,
with better reason than many to view his time as a "prosperous age." In
fact, however, there is a scornful irony in Cheng's choice of a title. The
terrible humiliations of the mid- and late-1890s lay still ahead, but
China's loss of Annam to the French in 1884–1885 was a fresh wound,
and tensions with Japan over the Korean question were already mounting
ominously. In this situation Cheng launched his defense of "foreign"
learning on a bitter note:

> Those who have a reputation as purists these days, and who regard themselves
> as upright men, haughtily refuse to discuss foreign matters, and condemn those
> who advocate seeking Western learning as offenders against the sacred prin-
> ciples of the tradition and as a disgrace to the scholarly class. Bah! In Burma
> today, in Annam, how are the mighty fallen! The virtuous have thrown
> themselves into the sea in despair; those without virtue live out their shameless
> and dishonored lives. Of what use to such times and to the urgent concerns of
> men is the conventional fidelity of conventional people to conventional prin-
> ciples?* Foreign matters nowadays are timely matters. If we would seek a cure

* This is a cumbersome translation of a four-character phrase from *Lun-yü* 14:18. It illustrates the propensity of classical Chinese to expand on contact with any other language;
also, and more to the point, it suggests the degree of cryptographic expertise taken for granted
by a writer like Cheng, who was not called "the scholarly compradore" without reason. The
passage in the *Analects* concerns Kuan Chung, who served as minister to Duke Huan of Ch'i
in the seventh century B.C., and to whom are credited many wise and good administrative in-

to the disease of the age we must prescribe for the symptoms. If your prince or your father lay critically ill would you, as a loyal minister or a filial son, do whatever you could to seek out and master the arts of medicine, or would you, neither seeking nor studying it, disparage medical knowledge as unreliable, and swearing an oath to be buried with the body, sit by to watch death come? May we not then get on with it, wasting no more words in argument as to whether we should or should not discuss Western learning?[38]

These sentiments fit easily enough into the general framework of Self-strengthening ideas. The only remarkable thing about them, as the impatience of Cheng's tone suggests, is that such a labored justification should still be the necessary preface to reform proposals in the 1890s. He was anxious to "get on with it," to move beyond the attitudes of the 1860s. Immersed as he was in the implementation of *kuan-tu shang-pan* undertakings of one kind or another, he was at the same time an audacious critic of the rationalizations of the Self-strengthening movement. If China sought more than the superficial appearances of "wealth and power," much more radical measures were called for.

This is the context within which Cheng's advocacy of parliamentary government must be understood. When it was first enunciated in the 1870s it was unprecedented. By the 1890s others had taken up the idea. Nevertheless the argument, as Cheng restated it in his *Words of Warning*, deserves our attenetion, since for at least a generation, down to the 1911 revolution and even beyond, the case for "popular sovereignty" would be argued most often in the terms in which Cheng casts it here, emphasizing the causal connection between parliamentary forms of government and national power.

The welfare of the nation depends upon human talent. The moral quality of the talent available to it depends upon the method of selection. If we leave it to one man to make the selection, partiality may result. If the people as a whole make the selection, then the difficulty of discovering excellence rests with public opinion at large. . . . The monarch does not bear the burdensome duty alone, nor are the people perversely inclined to live an irresponsible existence. Ruler and people are in harmony, each trustful of the affectionate regard of the other. There is a universal truth, and a universal justice; though the world is wide, and the people a numberless multitude, still what is sweet is sweet to all, and what is bitter is a bitterness shared by all. As we pass from our present misfortune to future well-being, high and low are of one heart, ruler and people of one body. How then can enemies and calamities from abroad still have

---

novations. Confucius here defends Kuan Chung against the charge of infidelity—his brother had been murdered by Duke Huan before Kuan Chung took office—with the comment "Would you require from him the small fidelity of common men and common women, who would commit suicide in a stream or a ditch, and no one knowing anything about them?" Cheng Kuan-ying has only to employ the phrase "a ditches-and-drains fidelity" (*kou-tu chih liang*) to summon up—in his classically educated reader!—the substance of the whole argument, and behind it Kuan Chung's reputation as a man who could cope with the problems of his age resourcefully.

power over us, to insult and shame us? . . . If we desire to institute a general and impartial system of law [*kung-fa*], nothing is more important to this end than expanding the authority of the state. To achieve this, nothing is more important than winning the people's minds and hearts. To achieve this, nothing is more important than understanding the sentiments of the masses; and to accomplish this, nothing is more important than establishing a parliament. If China is content to remain poor and weak, indifferent to national wealth and power, then it must resign itself to the fact that it can never become a great nation in the world. But if, on the other hand, China desires peace within its borders and an end to foreign encroachment, if we would govern well, and cherish the people, and under an all-embracing and impartial law preserve forever an increasing prosperity and tranquility, then we must begin with the establishment of a parliament.[39]

Wang T'ao spent his life on the China Coast for reasons of occupational opportunity and political necessity. Cheng Kuan-ying made his living there. More than either, Ho Kai (Ho Ch'i, 1859–1914) was a product of the nineteenth-century treaty-port culture, quintessentially a "Westernized" Chinese. He was a second-generation Christian, the son of a Hong Kong merchant and sometime preacher for the LMS, and received an education that was almost entirely Western, first in Hong Kong, and subsequently at Aberdeen University, St. Thomas' Medical and Surgical College in London, and Lincoln's Inn. Having acquired degrees in both medicine and law, membership in the Royal College of Surgeons, and an English wife in the bargain, Ho easily became the colony's most eminent Chinese resident after his return to Hong Kong in 1882. He was a barrister by profession, but he also taught at the College of Medicine for Chinese, which he had been instrumental in helping to establish; with the estate left to him by his wife he founded the Alice Memorial Hospital, named in her memory and administered by the LMS; he served for nearly a quarter of a century as an Unofficial Member of the Legislative Council of the colony. It was a distinguished career, and it brought Ho appropriate honors: not the Single-eyed Peacock Feather which the Son of Heaven was wont to bestow upon public-spirited subjects of his realm, but designation as a Companion of the Order of St. Michael and St. George in 1892, and twenty years later a knighthood. The energy that Ho Kai devoted to the welfare of Hong Kong's Chinese population was thus acknowledged with rewards that weighed heavier in Westminster than within the precincts of the Forbidden City; but his concerns were not limited to the life of the Crown Colony. As a friend and correspondent of men like Wang T'ao and Cheng Kuan-ying, Ho was as concerned as they with the broader issues of China's political transformation. In 1894 he published a collection of essays entitled *Hsin cheng lun-i* (A Discussion of Political Reform), in collaboration with a classical scholar whose job it was to put Ho's ideas into acceptably polished literary Chinese—an art to which Ho himself, for all his accomplishments, had not been educated. His discussion of parliamentary government was long and intricate, including detailed suggestions for the transformation of the gentry into local representative bodies. His justification for such innovations reads in part as follows:

> Surveying the world at large, from antiquity down to the present time the only forms of government have been monarchy [*chung-chu*], democracy [*min-chu*], and joint rule by monarch and people [*chun min kung chu*]. How can we explain the essential principle according to which a government may be carried out by both monarch and people? Government is something which belongs to the people, and is conducted on their behalf by the monarch; it is not a possession of the monarch, managed on his behalf by the people. Since government belongs to the people, the sovereign power [*chu*] also belongs to the people. But the people, fearful that they cannot protect their own lives, look to the monarch to protect them; fearful that they cannot safeguard their own property, they beg the monarch to safeguard it for them. The people themselves fully understand the kinds of laws and regulations which are necessary to accomplish these ends; they fear only that, left to themselves, they will be unable to implement them. Therefore they elevate one man as the supreme power [*chu*], and thus democracy *is* monarchy, and monarchy *is* democracy. Mencius said, "He who has the confidence of the peasantry may become the Son of Heaven." . . . Thus if the king would extend his sway, if he would expand the dignity of the realm, then he must hold elections in order to achieve a sense of the people's sentiments, and institute a parliament in order to display fairness. Then if the nation endures ten thousand years, the monarch enjoys a position that endures ten thousand years. There is no better reason than this for winning the people.[40]

These political reformers of the 1880s and 1890s shared a commitment to what we may legitimately call "republicanism." It is a republicanism better understood in a traditional Confucian sense, however, than as a debt owed to Western political theory. Their belief in the primacy of the people reaffirms the Mencian conviction that "The people are most to be valued [in the state]. . . . The prince the least of all." It is significant to note, however, that when Ho Kai invokes Mencius' wisdom he quotes not this statement, but the shrewd bit of political advice that immediately follows it: shifting the emphasis, as it were, from the populist premise to the monarchist conclusion. There is, indeed, a Machiavellian (or, in the Chinese context, a Legalist) motive running throughout these arguments. Popular forms are justified ultimately by the ruler's self-interest, which in turn is identical with the interests of the state. As Ho Kai put it, "Nowadays the ruler alone cannot establish the state; it is established by the people. The ruler alone cannot bring prosperity to the state; it is the people who make the state prosperous. Therefore he who would be a ruler must take it as his duty to protect the people, in order that they will establish the state for him; he must make it his responsibility to bring prosperity to the people, in order that they will make the state prosper for him."[41]

Taken together, these reform proposals seem progressive in the context of the late nineteenth-century crisis, the first stirrings of what would become in the next generation a full-scale revolutionary movement. But these men were not revolutionaries any more than they were democrats. It was not their purpose to shift the locus of sovereign authority from monarch to people, as witness Ho Kai's ambiguous use of the term *chu* in the passage cited above. They did not call for the creation of a politically active and responsible "new people," as would more radical reformers after the turn of the century, nor had they abandoned the tradition of Confucian paternalism. "The government above should exercise its power to change customs and mores," wrote Wang T'ao in one of his *Hsun-huan jih-pao* editorials, "while the people below should be gradually absorbed into the new environment and adjusted to it without their knowing it."[42] Parliamentary forms would achieve a somewhat greater degree of political participation, especially by the local gentry, but they were admired more as a means of strengthening the bond between ruler and ruled than as a means of "opening up" the political process to a diversity of interests.

Viewed in this light, it is evident that these late-Ch'ing reformers shared much in common with early-Ch'ing critics of Confucian despotism—as much, perhaps, as with the political radicals who were to follow them. They addressed themselves to the same problem that had so profoundly distressed Huang Tsung-hsi and Ku Yen-wu: the great chasm that separated the prince from his people. Even their recommendations sound similar; the parliamentary institutions they advocated, for all the strangeness of the terms, embodied in new guise a familiar prescription: what Frederic Wakeman calls the idea of "gentry home rule."[43] And they believed, even as Huang and Ku had believed before them, that their ideals were true to ancient principles which could once again animate the Confucian polity. The theme of a return to the ways of the ancients (*fu ku*) runs throughout this reformist literature. In his history of France, Wang T'ao ends his account of the National Assembly with the observation that "the institutions established in China during the Three dynasties and before had this very same spirit. Each time that I get to this point in my study of European history, unfailingly my gaze is drawn far back to the age of the Yellow Emperor, Shen Nung, Shun, and Yü, and I sigh over how close [the Europeans] are to the ancients."[44] Even Ho Kai, the most Westernized among them, spoke in these terms. "Only if we can return to the ancients can we accomplish what the times require of us," he wrote in 1894. "The greater is our desire to respond to the times, the more must we think of returning to the ways of the ancients."[45] Ch'en Chih (d. 1899), a reform-minded Kiangsi *chin-shih* and middle-level official in the central government, put the sentiment eloquently in the preface he wrote for Cheng Kuan-ying's *Words of Warning* in 1894, at the same time expressing unequivocally the profound distrust with which these "Westernizers" viewed the West.

> Those who are obedient to the ordinances of Heaven [*t'ien*] survive; those who defy them perish. If one does not accept what Heaven profers, then one must suffer the consequences. The virtuous know this, the degenerate do not; the young and able-bodied know this, the aged and enfeebled do not; the far-seeing know this, those of little insight do not. I despise the Westerners; I think back upon the Ancient Way. If the proper forms are lost, then we should seek even in the wilderness, selecting what is good and following it, and thus gradually returning to the life-giving regulations of our own Yü, Hsia, Shang and Chou dynasties. . . . Therefore I say, China's contact with the Westerners is an act of Heaven, an opportunity granted us by Heaven to return to the past, the starting point from which we may achieve a regeneration of politics* and a great unification.[46]

It would be foolish to suppose that these thinkers believed that a "return to the ancients" was in fact possible. We find here no talk of "the spirit of feudalism," no thought of reviving the well-field system. Their sense of the relevance of antiquity to the problems of their own age sprang partly from their idealization of a political community in which authority was purposeful and pervasive without being at the same time oppressive. Partly, too, it reflected their faith in the old Confucian vision of a sage ruler—an enlightened autocrat we might better call him in these circumstances—who could in actual fact "set in order all under heaven." But as the events of 1898 were to demonstrate, the Confucian system as it existed could not produce a ruler wise and potent enough to rescue China from its time of troubles.

*   *   *

K'ang Yu-wei and his disciples were disposed to magnify the historical originality of his role by representing his reformist ideas as unprecedented and *sui generis*. As we have seen, however, there were numerous elements in the intellectual environment of the 1880s and 1890s that doubtless contributed to his understanding of the "modern" world. His radical interpretations of Confucianism were likewise drawn from an existing tradition of scholarship, the so-called New Text (*chin wen*) school—to such an extent, indeed, that K'ang was accused by some of his contemporaries of plagiarism. Nevertheless, it is beyond dispute

---

* The term here translated "regeneration" is *wei-hsin*. It is the same compound used, in its Japanese reading, to designate the Meiji "restoration" (*Meiji ishin*) carrying connotations of much more fundamental changes than are implied by the term *chung-hsing*, "restoration," as in *T'ung Chih chung-hsing*. Classical Chinese allusions refer back to the early Chou period, when Chou Wen-wang received the mandate and instituted his singularly sagacious reign.

that K'ang's ultimate vision was uniquely his own, the product of an individual and in many respects eccentric mind.

In 1883, after his return from Peking and Shanghai, K'ang retired for a time into a life of scholarship and writing. He lived sometimes with friends in Canton city, sometimes in the countryside villa built by a granduncle who had pursued a modestly distinguished official career. The House of Calm and Contentment, as it was called, was a pleasant place in K'ang's recollection of it, with his uncle's library facing the main house across a pond, the whole set amidst an ornamental garden where a grove of ancient junipers sheltered a secluded pavilion. This tranquilly traditional setting contrasted sharply with K'ang's restless mood. Having failed again in the examinations, he determined to have nothing more to do with the conventional Confucian struggle for recognition. Family pressure made it a resolution impossible for him to keep. In 1893 he finally passed the provincial examinations in Canton, and in Peking two years later, on the eve of his emergence into national notoriety, he attained the *chin-shih* degree. In the interval, however, a great deal had happened to give form and direction to his thought.

In Canton in the 1880s K'ang plunged into a rigorous course of self-instruction, reading among other things the collected statutes and edicts of the Ch'ing, Huang Tsung-hsi's histories of Sung, Yuan, and Ming Confucianism, the writings of Chu Hsi, and (from what sources other than the *Wan-kuo kung-pao* it is difficult to determine) a mixed bag of Western scientific topics "such as acoustics, optics, chemistry, electricity, and mechanics, as well as histories and travelogues."[47] He carried within him still the sense of prophetic messianism which had come upon him several years earlier, the visionary quality that was to make him a compelling teacher and a difficult leader of men.

> My thoughts wandered far into the mystery and infinity of space and time. I gathered the deep and more abstruse statements in the classics and in other philosophic works, examined hidden meanings in Confucianism and Buddhism, studied new ideas developed in China and in the West, traced the evolution of man and nature, compared the tenets of various religions, pored over maps of the world, reviewed the present and the past in order to see the pattern of the future. . . . The purpose of my creation was to save the masses of living things . . . even if instead of going to the Pure Land I had to come to this unclean world to save them; and even if instead of being an emperor or a king, I became a common scholar in order to save them. . . . Thus every day the salvation of society was my aim in life, and for this aim I would sacrifice myself.[48]

It was probably in the mid-1880s that K'ang first sketched out in preliminary fashion the vision that was elaborated upon several years later in *Ta-t'ung shu* (The Book of the Great Community, as Hsiao Kung-ch'üan translates the title.) During these years he wrote several works which prefigure the striking departures that K'ang would make from established Confucian social theory when he drafted his utopian scheme.* He advocated, for example, complete sexual equality, the freedom of men and women to select mates and to change them at will, the raising of children in public institutions at public expense to liberate them from the constraints of filial obligation. As authority for these remarkable proposals K'ang posited "universal laws" (e.g., man is by right his own master) founded on "principles of truth" (e.g., men are born good, but corrupted by evil custom) which he claimed to have derived from the application of Euclidian geometric axioms to the realm of social relationships. The effort very nearly finished him: in 1885 he suffered from a long illness from which he recovered only by dosing hinself with Western medicines after Chinese doctors had given him up. K'ang's self-image as a "survivor" with an ordained mission to perform was reinforced by the experience, as it would be again in the aftermath of the Hundred Days.

To say that K'ang was already a "radical" in the 1880s is not to say that he had abandoned Confucianism. Though his speculations ultimately carried him far beyond the boundaries of Confucian social structures, he never escaped the gravitational pull of the Confucian conviction that society, however it is structured, exists ideally to enable men to live a "benevolent" life. Indeed, the "pattern of the future" which he sought he discovered eventually imbedded deep in the Confucian past; and in New Text Confucianism he found as well the theory of historical progress that would enable him to lead men toward it.

The New Text school was far from new. The origins of the dispute between proponents of the "new" and "old" texts lay in the remotest period of the imperial past. In 213 B.C., Ch'in Shih Huang-ti, the First Emperor, had ordered the destruction of the literature of the contending schools of the late Chou period, taking the Legalist view that private opinion was a divisive influence that could only be subversive to the unity of the state he had created. As a result, the Confucian texts which circulated in the Former Han period (206 B.C.–9 A.D.) were reconstructions pieced together largely from memory, and committed to writing in the "New-style script" (*chin wen*) of the time. Toward the end of the Former Han, however, unfamiliar versions of many of the classical texts ap-

---

* E.g., *Shih-li kung fa* (Substantial Truths and Universal Laws and *K'ang-tzu nei wai p'ien* (A Treatise on the Inner and Outer Worlds of Master K'ang). It is difficult to arrive at a clear understanding of the evolution of K'ang's ideas, partly because he was less than meticulous in recording his debts to others, and partly because some of his major writings are hard to pin down as to date of composition. Motivated perhaps by the desire to make his thought appear more consistent in its development than it was, K'ang sometimes attributed to earlier stages in his intellectual development works and/or ideas that were in fact of later date. The preface to *Li-yun chu* (The Li-yun Annotated), for example, is dated 1884, but the work itself was probably not written until 1902.

peared, written in the "Old-sytle script" (*ku wen*) of the pre-imperial age. These texts, it was claimed, had been hidden away to save them from the bonfires of the Ch'in and only recently unearthed—some from within the walls of Confucius' old home. Among the champions of the *ku wen* texts was Liu Hsin (46 B.C.–23 A.D.), an eminent scholar of the time who served as minister of state to Wang Mang, the Han official who usurped the imperial power and established a short-lived interregnum, the so-called Hsin dynasty, which divided the Former and Later Han epochs. During the first and second centuries both *chin wen* and *ku wen* versions had their followings, but in the course of time the latter gained the ascendancy. The great scholar Cheng Hsuan (127–200) borrowed from both, but he gave greater credence to the *ku wen* texts. Under the influence of his syncretic commentaries, which were regarded as definitive until they were displaced by the commentaries of Chu Hsi in the thirteenth and fourteenth centuries, the *chin wen/ku wen* controversy gradually lost its edge. For the next millennium and a half when Confucians lamented the corruption of the Way, as they were prone to do, it was not usually the authenticity of the textual tradition that they questioned, but their predecessors' interpretations of that tradition.

From the seventeenth century onward, however, scholars with increasingly sophisticated methodologies of textual and philological criticism at their disposal turned to the texts with fresh questions in mind. Their aim, as we have seen in chapter 2, was not to discredit Confucian premises but to ascertain the verifiable basis of Confucian belief. One of the first and greatest of these Ch'ing critics, following in the footsteps of Ku Yen-wu, was Yen Jo-chü (1636–1704). Yen devoted thirty years to a study of the *Shu ching* (Book of Documents, Classic of History), a *ku wen* text purportedly recovered from Confucius' house, and was able to prove conclusively that it was a late forgery. As other scholars followed Yen's example, the cumulative effect of their efforts was to demonstrate beyond reasonable doubt that the classical canon was, in many of its parts, hardly more than a patchwork of spurious fragments. That such findings did not suffice to dislodge the traditionally accepted texts from their privileged position as the officially authorized versions of Confucian wisdom is testimony to the extent to which state Confucianism had become by late imperial times a matter of academic habit and orthodox faith rather than intellectual conviction. Nevertheless in the nineteenth century the opportunity existed, for those who were inclined to exploit it, to approach the inherited textual tradition sceptically, without abandoning the belief that somewhere in the Confucian legacy one might find answers to the perennial problems of the human condition. Several of the Statecraft essayists of the 1830s and 1840s were *chin wen* adherents. It remained for K'ang Yu-wei however, to transform what had been largely a scholastic debate into a rationale for political reform.

One of the most important results of New Text scholarship, and its principal contribution to K'ang's reformist thinking, was the rehabilitation of the *Kung-yang Commentary* (*Kung-yang chuan*) on the *Spring and Autumn Annals* (*Ch'un-ch'iu*). The *Annals,* as we have noted in chapter 1, were the chronicles of the small feudal state of Lu for the period 772–481 B.C.* Tradition has it that the work was compiled by Confucius himself; he was a man of Lu, and died, according to the conventional dating, in 479 B.C., two years after the *Annals* cease. We know, on the testimony of Mencius, that Confucius laid great store by the *Annals* as the text which would insure the perpetuation of his name and his teachings. But this confidence was itself something of a riddle to later Confucians, in that the *Annals* consist only of very brief and apparently random notations unconnected by narrative and barren of context. Whatever guidance to right conduct the work might contain—and it was early assumed that this must be its purpose—required a key of some kind to unlock it. Several commentaries came into existence in response to this need, the most important being the *Kung-yang chuan*, a *chin wen* text, and the *Tso chuan*, a *ku wen* text. Both purported to be explanations of the hidden meanings of the *Annals* based on oral elucidation of the text by Confucius to his disciples, and both bear the names of their alleged authors—claims which have been equally discounted by modern critical scholarship. (*Chuan* simply means "commentary.") Both the *Tso chuan* and the *Kung-yang chuan* set the fragmentary chronicle contained in the *Annals* into a context intended to render its lessons comprehensible, but they approach the task rather differently. The *Tso chuan,* which is the bulkiest of the so-called "thirteen Classics," is essentially an exercise in historiography which creates for the reader a fuller account within which to fit the incidents recorded in the *Annals.* Sometimes it points the moral explicitly; more often it lets the narrative speak for itself, with a vividness that makes the *Tso chuan* a landmark in the development of Chinese historical literature. When *chin wen* critics turned their attention to the *Tso chuan* in the eighteenth and nineteenth centuries, the very merit of the text as history undermined, in their view, its authenticity as a commentary on the *Annals.* The *chin wen* verdict was that the *Tso chuan* had been originally an historical compilation covering roughly the same period as that treated in the *Annals,* but quite independent of the latter; and further, that it had been edited and rearranged by Liu Hsin to give it the appearance of a commentary, intentionally to obscure the "true" meaning of the *Annals* beneath a wealth of distracting detail while at the same time drawing attention away from the *Kung-yang chuan.*

The *Kung-yang chuan* differs from the *Tso chuan* both in style and in approach. It is not indifferent to the matter of historical context, but it is

---

* The *Ch'un-ch'iu* is arranged chronologically according to the reigns of the rulers of Lu, but it contains many references to the affairs of other states of the period.

more concerned with the "esoteric meaning" of the *Annals* and with the general moral injunctions that may be extracted from the historical incidents it contains. An example may help to illustrate the problems inherent in the *Annals* and the nature of the solutions proposed by the *Tso* and *Kung-yang* commentaries; it may also serve to explain the popularity of the latter among nineteenth-century reformers.

In the *Annals*, among the entries for the eleventh year of Duke Huan (700 B.C.) we find the following unadorned statement: "In the ninth month, the people of Sung seized Chi the younger of [the state of] Cheng." The *Tso chuan* provides a bit of background. It describes in some detail the intrigues of Duke Chuang of the state of Sung to advance the fortunes of the son of a Sung woman married to the recently deceased ruler of the neighboring state of Cheng. To this end the younger Chi, identified as a favorite of the late Duke of Cheng and one of his ministers, is captured by Sung and forced on pain of death to establish the Sung claimant in place of the rightful heir. The *Kung-yang chuan* takes the tale further, and uses it to convey a general maxim. It identifies the luckless Chi as the chief minister of Cheng, and it places him squarely between the rock and the hard place: he must decide whether to connive in the overthrow of the designated heir or subject his state to the threat of a Sung invasion and probable extinction. He chooses the former course as the lesser of two evils. Cheng will survive, and in time perhaps he will be able to bring about the return of the rightful ruler. It is a praiseworthy decision, in the view of the *Kung-yang chuan*. "What virtue was there in Chi the younger? He is to be considered as knowing how to act according to circumstances. . . . What is meant by acting according to the exigency of circumstances? It means acting against ordinary standards of right conduct in order to secure a [greater] good. Only the present threat of death or devastation can justify such a course, and it has a Way of its own. One may act according to the exigencies of circumstances when the result injures only oneself; one may not so act to the injury of others. To kill another in order to save oneself, to ruin another in order to preserve oneself—this is not the conduct of the superior man [*chün-tzu*]."[49]

The *Kung-yang* elaboration upon the cryptic statement of the *Annals* echoes Confucius' condemnation of the futility of "the conventional fidelity of conventional people to conventional principles" which we have encountered already as an aspect of Cheng Kuan-ying's reform proposals. It also emphasizes the importance of acting as the needs of the times dictate, a favorite theme with nineteenth-century Statecraft writers. Such altruistic moral relativism was appealing for obvious reasons to late Ch'ing reformers who strained against the shackles of immobile orthodoxy, impatient for an opportunity to seize the political initiative, anxious to act "according to the exigency of circumstances," and full of rebellious self-confidence. Such a man was K'ang Yu-wei.

Ironically, the scholar to whom is generally accorded the credit for confirming K'ang in his *chin-wen* enthusiasm fits this description hardly at all. Liao P'ing (1852–1932) was a Szechwanese literatus who spent most of his long life at a self-imposed distance from the intellectual and political controversies of the time, a timid man embarrassed and not a little frightened by the boldness of his ideas. His career illustrates the capacity for compartmentalization inherent in late Confucian intellectual life. Struggling up from a background of economic stringency, if not actual poverty, Liao was regarded as a precociously brilliant student. He proved it in the accepted fashion, becoming a *chü-jen* in 1879 and a *chin-shih* in 1881. He thereupon set to work on a study intended to prove that the scholarly tradition he had mastered with such success for the examinations was radically flawed, based on ancient forgeries which distorted the true significance of Confucius' historic role. It was this work which K'ang Yu-wei evidently saw, in some form, when Liao visited Canton briefly in the late 1880s. Although the charge of plagiarism was never formally brought, Liao subsequently claimed that K'ang had stolen from him the ideas that made him famous, a verdict confirmed by a number of Liao's contemporaries and several later scholars who have looked into the matter. We need not put K'ang into the dock here, however; as Joseph Levenson has observed, it was K'ang, not Liao, "who assumed the risks, and made history."[50] Liao for his part returned to Szechwan. He stood conspicuously apart from the reformers of 1898 who were animated by K'ang's inspired visions. Like K'ang, he lived on uncomfortably into the post-Confucian age, and died in obscurity, neglected and still aggrieved.

In the decade 1888–1898 K'ang devoted less time to the abstruse and mystical musings that had preoccupied him in the early 1880s and applied himself instead to "practical" scholarship and politics. In 1888 he submitted his first reform memorial to the Kuang Hsu emperor. It was framed against the backdrop of China's defeat in the Sino-French war, but the immediate provocation was a landslide that occurred near one of the imperial tombs—an ill omen in a curiously antique sense. Like most of the memorials that K'ang would submit over the next several years, this one was intercepted by cautious or unfriendly ministers and never reached the emperor's attention. K'ang forged ahead undaunted, laying the theoretical foundations for the reform program and becoming involved in various kinds of direct political activity. In 1891 he published the first book which called general attention to his ideas (or Liao P'ing's), *Hsin hsueh wei ching k'ao* (An Examination of the Forged Classics of the Hsin [Dynasty] Learning). This was essentially a restatement, albeit a singularly forceful one, of views already in general circulation among nineteenth-century *chin wen* scholars. Its central thesis was that Liu Hsin had fabricated the *ku wen* texts which later generations of scholars had come to revere as genuine, intentionally to discredit the authentic *chin wen* versions.

The *Forged Classics* stirred considerable controversy, and sufficient condemnation to cause the Court to ban it in 1894. This did not prevent K'ang from winning the *chin-shih* degree the following year, however. His presence in Peking coincided with the signing of the Treaty of Shimonoseki, which concluded the Sino-Japanese War on terms highly demeaning to China and commensurately unpopular with reform-minded Chinese scholars. K'ang was not the only one who saw it as the last nail in the coffin of the Self-strengthening policies of the 1870s and 1880s. He exploited the occasion to organize a "mass" protest: a memorial signed by some twelve hundred of the assembled degree candidates demanding (without effect) that the Court should reject Japan's conditions. During the months he spent in Peking K'ang also submitted several memorials of his own, only one of which reached its intended recipient. The Kuang Hsu emperor had been favorably impressed, K'ang learned, but he was powerless to act—more so than K'ang was able to acknowledge, then or later. It was at this time, however, that K'ang made the acquaintance of Weng T'ung-ho, the Imperial Tutor, whose support later proved instrumental in his rise to power in the winter of 1897–1898. On the eve of the inauguration of the Hundred Days, Weng reversed himself and repudiated K'ang as "unpredictable," but by then the reform movement had already attained sufficient momentum to carry it forward through the summer.

Before K'ang left Peking in the autumn of 1895 he helped to establish the "Society for the Study of National Strength" (*Ch'iang hsueh hui*), an organization which generated a good deal of official and semi-official interest, and even some guarded support. This and similar "study groups" that were springing up throughout China in the 1890s had a political significance to which we will return in the next chapter. Here we need only note that by the time K'ang traveled south again late in 1895 he was probably justified in regarding himself as the most celebrated advocate of "Confucian" reform. As such he attracted followers to Canton, where he established a school, the "Thatched Hut Among Ten Thousand Trees" (*Wan-mu ts'ao t'ang*), within the precincts of the Confucian Temple and set about devising a curriculum of study suited to the needs of the times. "K'ang did not lightly impart his knowledge to others," recalled Liang Ch'i-ch'ao, the greatest of the disciples who attached themselves to K'ang at this time, and intellectually the most restless. "Because he was so anxious to be erudite and different, he often went so far as to suppress or distort evidence, thereby committing a serious crime for the scientist. . . . As a man, K'ang was totally subjective in myriads of things. His self-confidence was extremely strong, and he maintained it very stubbornly. As for objective facts, he either ignored them completely or insisted on remolding them to his own views. . . . It is precisely because of this that he was able to found a school of thought and rise to fame with it for a time, and it was precisely for the same reason that he was unable to lay a strong and solid foundation for it."[51]

This reminiscent evaluation, made from the perspective of the 1920s, provides a remarkable insight into K'ang's personality, but it misstates the nature of his purpose. For all his interest in "scientific" knowledge, however randomly acquired, K'ang was not even in the broadest sense a scientist any more than he was a disinterested historian. He was an evangelist, and his second major work, published in 1897, made this very clear. K'ung-tzu kai-chih k'ao (Confucius as a Reformer) portrays Confucius as an innovator who had created out of his own genius the institutional models which he advocated. He had attributed these inventions to an ancient and sacrosanct tradition, K'ang argued, only to lend them the authority necessary to win acceptance. Behind this image looms the Confucius of Han-dynasty chin wen belief, closely identified with the thought of Tung Chung-shu and other Han interpreters who had used the esoteric passages of the Kung-yang chuan to substantiate their vision of Confucius as a transcendant Sage, no mere transmitter of ancient learning as he had claimed to be, but a prophet in his own right, an "uncrowned king" (su-wang). Around this figure a considerable apochryphal literature had accumulated that endowed the Sage with an aura of magical significance and millennarian promise. "Sages are not born for nothing," says a Han-dynasty text; "they must institute something, in order to reveal the mind of Heaven. Thus Confucius . . . instituted laws for the world." Why should men so believe? The text is full of portents and miracles, mysterious legends and supernatural transformations—like the small red bird which flew down one day when Confucius was lecturing on the Classics and transformed itself into a piece of yellow jade on which was inscribed: "Confucius, holding [Heaven's] Mandate to act, has created these governmental institutions in accordance with the laws."[52]

The attraction of the vision of Confucius as a reformer, and thus as a legitimator of reform, is obvious. Another idea which K'ang found adumbrated in the Kung-yang traditions of the Han period proved similarly useful. This was the notion of the Three Ages (san shih) of Confucian history. Han writers had used the concept to distinguish eras within the period covered by the Annals according to Confucius' proximity in time to the events he was recording; or, later, to schematize the spreading universality of the Confucian order from antiquity down to the (Confucian) present. K'ang's generalization of this idea transformed it into a comprehensive and progressive theory of historical growth. The language in which he expounded the concept suggests, moreover, that magic and mystery were far from repugnant to his own temperament. The Han apocrypha, for example, made much of the tale that Confucius had been conceived while his mother dreamed of consorting with a "Black Emperor."* This is K'ang's point of departure in the following passage:

> Heaven, having pity for the many afflictions suffered by the men who live on this great earth, [caused] the Black Emperor to send down his semen so as to create a being who would rescue the people from their troubles—a being of divine intelligence, who would be a sage-king, a teacher for his age, a bulwark for all men, and a religious leader for the whole world. Born as he was in the Age of Disorder, he proceeded, on the basis of this disorder, to establish the pattern of the Three Ages, progressing with increasing refinement until they arrived at Universal Peace.[53]

In combination with other elements perhaps already present in his thinking in the 1890s but not fully elaborated until after 1898, the idea of the Three Ages became a crucial part of K'ang Yu-wei's ultimate "utopianism." In the more limited and concrete context of the reform movement itself, however, the function of this idea was simply to underscore, and to provide justification for, a view that K'ang shared in common with other New Text advocates and with reformers generally: the conviction that political action must be appropriate to the needs of a given time. Confucius had recognized this truth, and acted upon it with transcendent wisdom. "The [spirit of the] regulations of Confucius is that they must be employed according to the proper period," wrote K'ang. "The present time . . . is the Age of Approaching Peace. It is therefore necessary to promulgate the doctrines of self-rule and independence, and implement parliamentary and constitutional rule. For if the laws are not transformed, great disorder will result."[54]

This was the message K'ang conveyed to the Kuang Hsu emperor in June, 1898, with the disastrous consequences sketched at the beginning of this chapter. The summer of 1898 witnessed a brief convergence of reformist visions, bringing K'ang Yu-wei into the emperor's presence to advocate much the same political program toward which treaty-port thinkers like Wang T'ao, Cheng Kuan-ying, and Ho Kai had been working their way since the 1870s. None of these names appear in K'ang's autobiographical account; his habitual disinclination to acknowledge his intellectual debts makes it difficult to reckon how much he may have owed to them directly, or to the influence of the China Coast culture in general. We do know that Ch'en Chih, whose preface to Cheng's *Sheng-shih wei-yen* has been cited above, collaborated with K'ang in establish-

---

* Han cosmology, as developed by Tung Chung-shu and his followers, involved a complex system of attributions, correspondences, and sequences, far too cumbersome to describe in detail here. These had to do with the five elements (earth, wood, metal, fire, water), the five colors (yellow, green, white, red, black), the five points of the compass (including "center"), the five viscera, etc. The color attributed to the Chou Dynasty was red; since black is next in sequence, the appearance of a "Black Emperor" was taken to mean that Confucius' birth signified that the Chou mandate was exhausted.

ing the Ch'iang hsueh hui in 1895. We know, too, that Timothy Richard was interested in the enterprise, and was in close touch with Liang Ch'i-ch'ao in the years immediately preceding the reform movement. Several of Richard's exhortations to reform were among the books which K'ang called to the emperor's attention in 1898. K'ang himself corresponded with Richard sporadically after 1895, and some scholars have concluded that he was significantly influenced by the Welshman's progressive opinions—a judgment that rests, in the absence of corroborating documentary evidence, on the general consonance of their views, especially in the area of economic reform.

However we account for it, the fact remains that in 1898 there existed a general consensus among spokesmen for reform. Like the treaty-port reformers whom we have already considered, K'ang Yu-wei urged the inauguration of parliamentary forms and constitutional monarchy primarily as a means of strengthening the polity by bridging the chasm that separated ruler from ruled. He was no more a populist or a democrat than they, nor did he envision a transfer of sovereign power from monarch to people. What distressed him, and accounted in his mind for China's weakness, was the autocratic isolation of the imperial institution. "One ruler and a few high ministers govern the country," he wrote in the preface to a historical sketch of the French Revolution which he submitted to the emperor in the summer of 1898. "How can the country not be weak? For it is the nature of things that the many are better than the few . . . nor can the private interests [of the ruler] override the common interests [of the people]." So much for diagnosis. K'ang's prescription has a similarly familiar ring. "The secret of the strength of Japan and the Western countries lies solely in their adoption of constitutional government and the convening of parliaments," he argued in 1898. After describing the tripartite division of legislative, judicial, and executive functions common to "constitutional" regimes, K'ang concluded with the assurance that "the ruler stands above them all. A constitution is enacted, which binds the ruler and all others alike. The ruler's person is inviolable; he can do no wrong, since administrative responsibilities are shouldered by the government. In this way the sovereign and the people are welded together into one body politic. How can the nation not be strong?"[55] This argument is entirely consonant with the advocacy of parliamentary government articulated by Cheng Kuan-ying and Ho Kai. K'ang may well have been inspired also by the example of the Meiji Constitution promulgated in 1889, which exalted imperial sovereignty and stressed the mystical unity of ruler and people in very similar terms.

In one important respect, however, K'ang's intellectual position in 1898 differed from that of the "Westernized" treaty-port reformers. Although his program claimed as its rationale a far more elaborate apparatus of classical scholarship than theirs, he was paradoxically freer than they of the constraints of the tradition. When they invoked the "essence" or the "spirit" of Chinese culture to legitimate present policies, they relied upon the symbolism of a legendary antiquity, a past to which they urged a "return." K'ang's allegiance to the *Kung-yang* persuasion liberated him from such anachronistic antiquarianism. For him the "spirit" of Confucianism was embodied in the injunction to move with the times, not against them, to create new institutions appropriate to changing circumstances, even as the Sage had done. The shades of Yao, Shun, and Yü did not haunt him. But the paradox is compounded by an irony. By the logic of his belief that reform must meet the needs of a given historical moment, K'ang was trapped into an inflexible advocacy of what, as he saw it, "the times" demanded. This was the age of "Approaching Peace," in which only the forms of constitutional monarchy could be deemed appropriate and effective. So K'ang argued in 1898, and so he maintained through all the years to come. Consequently he opposed with unflagging energy and with all the resources at his disposal the aims of the revolutionary movement that gathered force after the failure of the Hundred Days. "The course of my life has zigzagged strangely," he remarked soon after his arrival in Tokyo, his first refuge in exile, "and at each turn I have emerged alive so that I am still unscathed. Perhaps my life is preserved for a purpose: perhaps China will not fall, and our great enterprise will go on."[56] But it was not to be.

With the disaster of 1898 K'ang Yu-wei became, like Huang Tsung-hsi two hundred and fifty years before him, a loyal minister cast adrift in the world. His house in Tokyo was styled Ming-i ko, "The Hall of Brightness Obscured." There, on the first day of the New Year of 1899, he gathered a few of his friends and surviving disciples around him to perform a sombre ceremony:

> *The rising sun at early dawn shines on the*
> *northern door.*
> *From afar, beyond the sea, I perform the court*
> *ceremonial. . . .*
> *Last year with measured steps I walked through the*
> *guards of the imperial throne.*
> *This morning I bustle into my worn-out court robes.*
> *An absconded official, I look out toward the west*
> *with a broken heart.*[57]

*   *   *

That was a bleak moment. But it was not the end of the road: K'ang Yu-wei still had a far way to go, and he was not a man to be easily discouraged. As long as the Kuang Hsu emperor lived, K'ang strove to promote his reinstatement as China's rightful ruler. To this end, with the assistance of Liang Ch'i-ch'ao and other supporters, he established in 1899 the Pao-huang hui (Society for the Protection of the Emperor).

Throughout the prerevolutionary decade K'ang traveled tirelessly in search of funds and support for its activities. Twice he crossed the Pacific, six times the Atlantic. One might find him wherever there were overseas Chinese communities to organize in behalf of his cause, wherever there was money to be begged or useful contact to be made—or, not infrequently, simply interesting sights to be seen, for K'ang had been an enthusiastic tourist ever since as a boy he had tramped through the hills of Kwangtung with his grandfather visiting its celebrated scenic spots. So now his wanderings carried him from Darjeeling to Denver; from Luxor to London to Lapland; from Penang to Pocatello, Idaho; from Yokohama to the Yucatán Peninsula. The Pao-huang hui established newspapers, publishing houses, and schools. To finance its expanding enterprises K'ang speculated, for awhile quite profitably, in Mexican real estate and other investments. Along the way he became a personage. Foreign ministers and heads of state granted him interviews. Hotels where he stayed flew from their staffs the dragon flag of the Imperial Ch'ing. (The Empress Dowager had in the meantime placed a handsome price on K'ang's head, a compliment which K'ang repaid by busily and ineffectually plotting her assassination.) His fiftieth birthday, in 1907, was the occasion for a gala celebration with friends and admirers, held at the Waldorf Astoria where K'ang was stopping in New York. As a retreat from this life of hectic celebrity K'ang purchased a small island off the coast of Sweden, but he was able to spend precious little time there.

Yet one wonders whether at heart this indefatigable traveler ever really left home. He dressed always in proper Confucian attire—the scholar's skullcap, long gown, and embroidered jacket. He spoke no language but Chinese, and had always to be accompanied by an interpreter-secretary, among them a Chinese-American girl whom he took as concubine in 1907. Most important, even as he fretted about problems of land development in Mexico and rice brokerage in Malaya, struggling always to meet the demands from his lieutenants for more and more money, a part of K'ang's mind pondered still the Confucian truths to which, he believed, he held the key.

During his years of exile, the bulk of K'ang's writings consisted of political tracts and exhortations, travelogues, and endless collections of poetry. In 1901 and 1902, however, which he spent mostly in Penang and Darjeeling enjoying the protective hospitality of British colonial officials, he devoted himself energetically to classical studies. In the course of these two years he produced annotated versions of the "Four Books" (i.e., the Analects, the Mencius, the Great Learning, and the Doctrine of the Mean). It was in 1902, moreover, that K'ang completed the works on which rest his reputation as a utopian thinker, the Li-yun chu (An annotated version of the Li-yun chapter of the Li chi), and Ta-t'ung shu (The Book of the Great Community).

The history of these works is difficult to trace. Both incorporate some of the radically egalitarian social ideas that were foreshadowed in K'ang's writings of the early 1880s. K'ang claimed to have "completed" *Ta-t'ung shu* at about that time, and the preface to *Li-yun chu* is dated 1884. Scholars who have studied the texts closely, however, have concluded on the basis of internal evidence that neither could have been written, at least in the form in which they became known, before 1902. Only fragments of *Ta-t'ung shu* were published during K'ang's lifetime; not until 1935, eight years after his death, was the work published in its entirety. K'ang had warned Liang Ch'i-ch'ao in 1896 that the world was not ready for such ideas—and he was right.

The *Li-yun* is a short chapter from the *Li chi*, or "Record of Rites," a compilation of late Chou and early Han ritual texts dating from the first century B.C. The *Li chi* deals with a wide range of subjects, taking as its unifying concern the significance of the ritual practices ascribed to the earlier Chou period and the ritual conduct of Confucius himself. The *Great Learning (Ta hsueh)* and the *Doctrine of the Mean (Chung yung)* are also chapters from the *Li chi*, elevated to canonical status by Chu Hsi in the twelfth century. The *Li-yun* chapter (translatable, rather awkwardly, as "The Evolution of the Rites") was not accorded such honor. As we have seen, however, it frequently served as a source of inspiration for social idealists, largely because it enshrines the following passage:

> When the Great Way prevailed, all under heaven was held to be the common possession of all men. The virtuous and able were selected [as rulers]. A man's word was his bond. The people cultivated amiable relationships. They cherished the parents of others as they cherished their own parents, and the children of others as their own children. The aged were provided for until their time came. For the able-bodied there was work to do. The young were educated. Widows, orphans, the childless and the infirm were succored. Each man had his share of the work, every woman her own hearth. The people could not bear to leave the wealth of the earth uncultivated, but they did not strive to store up wealth for themselves alone. Not to devote their full strength to their work was hateful to them, but they did not labor for themselves alone. Thus scheming for private gain could not arise, thievery and brigandage were unknown, and gates remained without locks. This was the Great Community *(ta-t'ung)*.

This is the *locus classicus* of this perennially attractive social vision. But, as the *Li-yun* goes on to point out, the real world is very different. "Now the Great Way is obscured," and men live under conditions contrary in every particular to those of the age of universal harmony. Therefore virtue must be inculcated, and men must learn to abide by the prescriptions of inherited ritual. In this age of "Minor Peace" *(hsiao-k'ang)* the duty of the ruler is to emulate the example set by the

Duke of Chou and his sagacious predecessors who immersed themselves in the study of ritual in order to make clear to the people the boundaries of right conduct. In other words, men fashion structures of moral discipline only when the moral instinct is no longer a sufficient guide to action. Such a verdict finds close parallels in the Taoist critique of Confucian dependence on forms, which contends that men give names only to virtues that they no longer possess.

The *Li chi* was, of course, a part of the classical corpus, and K'ang may well have been familiar with the *Li-yun* "utopia" even before the 1880s. But it was not until sometime around the turn of the century that he linked this idea with the notion of historical progress which he had derived from the *Kung-yang* doctrine of the "Three Ages" and thus arrived at his own distinctive interpretation of the significance of *ta-t'ung*. The *Li-yun* vision of a community of strifeless abundance serves as a starting point, and at least in spirit as the ultimate destination toward which K'ang would lead mankind.

Translated into English, the passage quoted above acquires a temporal aspect which is not explicit in the original text, uncomplicated as it is by tense. The *Li-yun* commonwealth has generally been attributed, by translators and by Chinese commentators alike, to the "Golden Age" of remote antiquity, in keeping with the nostalgic temper of Confucian thought, the assumption that moral simplicity can be achieved only under the conditions of material and social simplicity which prevailed "once upon a time." The yearning for a primitive uncomplication of life pervades Mencius' idealization of the well-field system and all later variations on this theme. Similar visions animate the anarchic, egalitarian idealism of Taoist parable and legend. Even rebel movements which owed an ideological debt to the millennarianism of Buddhist, Manichean, or, in the case of the Taipings, Christian doctrines tended to articulate their moral purposes in terms of the retrieval of a long-lost spontaneous virtue. K'ang Yu-wei would have none of this. The appeal of his utopia does not depend upon nostalgia or the idealization of primitivism. K'ang borrowed from the *Li-yun* tradition hardly more than the key term, *ta-t'ung*, and something of the notion of an unacquisitive, noncompetitive, industrious, and harmonious social order. The substance he gave to this idea, however, departed fundamentally from the models provided in his own culture, and his utopia was located not in a past which becomes more remote with each passing day, but in the future toward which each dawn brings men closer. We must therefore set *Ta-t'ung shu* into the larger context of modern utopian literature which seeks to describe, as George Kateb puts it, "perfection at the happy ending of world history . . . a world permanently without strife, poverty, constraint, stultifying labor, irrational authority, sensual deprivation," a life made gracious by the "consonance of men and their environment."[58]

It is a long book, and an elaborate one, but at the expense of much engaging detail its central argument may be summarized quite briefly. K'ang begins by asserting (in good Mencian form, one would be inclined to suppose) that men are by nature compassionate. He then contradicts himself by expounding an adamantly materialist theory of human psychology and motivation. The universal and immutable law of life is that men seek pleasure and avoid pain. There is nothing whatever spiritual about this: by "pleasure" K'ang means the satisfaction of human desires, the physical, even carnal, urges of nature. Pain is desire unsatisfied. The notion that life is synonymous with suffering echoes enduring Buddhist influences on K'ang's thought. It is distinctly un-Confucian. But K'ang rejects the Buddhist contention that suffering can be overcome only by escape from the world of men and of feeling, the extinguishing of desire, *nirvana.* He insists, rather, that life must be restructured. This he views as a matter of "abolishing the boundaries" (*ch'ü chieh*)—the categories which imprison humankind in affliction, whether they be "boundaries" of human contrivance (national allegiance, social class) or those which originate in natural differences (sex, race). How this will come to pass remains unclear, though much of *Ta-t'ung shu* is devoted to detailed descriptions of the progressive stages through which the world will pass on the road to utopia. From these it is evident at least that K'ang did not envision violence or struggle as the necessary agent of change. He was a determinist, as we have seen, believing that the conditions of a given epoch prepare the way for the next, and believing too that men must act in ways appropriate to the age in which they find themselves.

It is probable that sometime in the late 1890s K'ang's sense of historical direction was reinforced by an acquaintance, albeit superficial, with Darwinist hypotheses. Yen Fu's translation of T. H. Huxley's "Evolution and Ethics" was completed in 1896, and Liang Ch'i-ch'ao was privileged to read it in manuscript. The extent to which K'ang may have been influenced by it, directly or via Liang's account, remains conjectural. K'ang's determinism in any case conveys no sense of dialectical inevitability. It is rather a religious conviction, a faith based on the revelations which he had derived from the "profound and esoteric" doctrines of *Kung-yang* Confucianism.

A resumé of several of the more radical proposals put forward in *Ta-t'ung shu* will suffice to suggest something of the mood of K'ang's utopianism. In the Age of the Great Community, he writes, the family will have been abolished, its social maintenance functions (childrearing, education, care for the ill and aged) assumed by public institutions. "Marriage" will remain, but only as a voluntary, short, and fixed-term relationship. Homosexuality will be socially as acceptable as heterosexuality. Women will have achieved absolute equality in social, economic, and political status. Upon marriage the woman will retain her own family name rather than assuming that of her husband's family—he will be, after all, only a temporary mate. Nation-states will of course have disappeared. Instead, the world will be divided into one hundred degrees of longitude and latitude, creating a gridwork of "degree territories"— 5,238 of them comprising the habitable land area of the globe by K'ang's account—which will form the basis of regional government. Governmental responsibility at this level will be concerned primarily with the administration of public social, educational, and economic institutions, uniform in organization throughout the world, under the general supervision of a representative world government with both administrative and legislative functions. All occupations will have become public. Communities will be organized on the basis of occupational groupings rather than such natural affliliations as kinship or lineage. These residential-work communities will constitute the basic unit of local self-government.

These proposals, especially those that have to do with the reform of social, economic, and political relationships and institutions at the local level, have prompted some scholars to speculate that K'ang Yu-wei exerted at least as decisive an influence on the Maoist social revolution as did Karl Marx. Mao Tse-tung himself tells us that K'ang was one of the reformist heroes of his boyhood, long before he had become either a revolutionary or a Communist. In his later writings, Mao occasionally refers to K'ang as a failed utopian—a man who saw into the future but lacked the means to transform the present. There are unquestionably some engaging resemblances between K'ang's visions and Maoist revolutionary practice: the notion of semi-autonomous local community-governments, for example, in which the productive (i.e., economic), social, and political identities of the members are fused into a single creative personality. Do we see here the prototype of the new "Maoist man"? Are the People's Communes an attempt, however disguised, to realize K'ang's Great Community? Is Marxism, as has been argued, no more than the means that Mao has used to attain K'ang Yu-wei's utopian ends?

It seems, on balance, improbable on a variety of counts. Mao's language is often derived from traditional sources, and to the extent that he was himself a utopian thinker—which is a puzzling question in its own right—he drew on Chinese as well as Western inspiration. There is thus a natural congruence of images and modes of expression underlying Mao's explicit (and infrequent) references to K'ang's *ta-t'ung*. It is clear from Mao's writings that he partakes of a broad tradition of socialist idealism that comprises within it, among other things, elements of humanistic Marxism. We might more reasonably explain the People's Communes as a Maoist solution to the problem of alienation than as an effort to animate K'ang's vision of *ta-t'ung*. There are, moreover, telling differences in respect to the ends in question. As Maoism has evolved, conflict, contradictions, and struggle have been transformed from means into ends in themselves: class against class, masses against Party, Party cadre against Party leadership, "Red" against "expert," and, fundamentally, Man against Nature. Nothing could be further from the Great Community of K'ang's imaginings, free from the struggle for physical survival, for social recognition, for political identity. The spirit of his utopia is a selfless hedonism, not a dedicated altruism.

Like other utopian writers, K'ang ornamented his picture of the land of nowhere with much inviting detail—not, as with Fourier, oceans of lemonade, anti-beasts and anti-insects, but rather a Jules Verne-like paradise of technological delights. He foresaw the development of telecommunications to provide, among other things, the means for instantaneous and universal suffrage. He imagined huge airborne hotels fitted out with every luxury. In the communal dining halls of his residential-work units, meals will be served by robots or will appear on tables rising from beneath the floors, to the accompaniment of music and three-dimensional moving pictures. On humane grounds, vegetarianism will be universal—K'ang regretted that the vegetable kingdom must be excluded from the generally prevalent spirit of benevolence if human life is to survive. Only the liquid essences of food will be consumed, which together with daily physical examinations will prolong life expectancy to several hundred years. The incurably ill, however, will be released from suffering by electrocution. In order to distinguish themselves as far as possible from bestial forms of life, human beings will shave all the hair from their bodies and perfume themselves liberally. Toilet facilities will be sweetly scented, with piped-in music and automatic flushing mechanisms, in order that people may take best advantage of life's most serene and private moments.

And so on. There are flashes of prescience in *Ta-t'ung shu*, and enough that is sufficiently eccentric to suggest to the sceptical reader that one is dealing here not with the product of a mind that has perceived a higher reality, but rather with a mind to which reality has become irrelevant. But like other utopian works, *Ta-t'ung shu* cannot be read merely for its description of the world toward which it points the way; it must be read as a protest against the world which exists. It is an indictment of Confucian society, in the first instance, but also of human society at large. In his discussion of sexual roles, for example K'ang takes as his starting point the subservient status of women in Chinese society, their exploitation as domestic slaves or as sexual playthings. But this is a criticism that can easily be generalized: K'ang condemns with equal vigor the Chinese practice of footbinding and the Western practice of corsetting.

The most significant aspect of K'ang's *Ta-t'ung shu* is what remains after all the constraints on human happiness have been abolished. It is here that the profoundly anti-Confucian temper of K'ang's radicalism is most striking—and that the lingering attraction of certain Confucian assumptions is most evident. In the boundaryless world of the Great Community nothing survives of Confucian social and political institutions, the structures of "imperial" Confucianism. This in itself is not remarkable. K'ang was not the first to distinguish between *official* Confucianism and *true* Confucianism, as we have seen. But K'ang goes further than earlier critics had done, to eliminate much that might be considered essential to the spirit of true Confucianism itself. The whole thrust of his argument contradicted the Confucian belief in natural differentiation and, as its counterpart, Confucian insistence on social hierarchy. K'ang thus struck at the very foundation of the traditional concept of social justice and political order.*

That K'ang could make such a radical departure was due in part to his economic expectations. Confucian social theory presupposes an environment of material scarcity. The austere, ritual-laden Confucian pursuit of moral discipline provides the constraints that will enable men to survive in such a world—to live, hopefully, in harmony, or at least each with a clear understanding of his place and his just due. K'ang on the contrary postulates an economy of abundance, and the possibility of gratifying not only the basic wants of life, but all human desires. In his view the limits which Confucianism (in common with other social theories) imposes upon appetites and consumption are themselves the source of deprivation and suffering—present necessities, perhaps, but anachronisms in the future of the Great Community. K'ang's absolute faith in material progress, his romantic and uncritical exaltation of technology, his willingness to make desire rather than necessity the proper standard of human conduct—all these justifications of self-gratification go hand in hand with his neglect of inculcated virtue as a prerequisite to social harmony. He regards the human capacity to make moral choices as a natural acquisition, just as is the knowledge that knives cut or that fire burns. Moral conduct is not a discipline to be imposed from without or refined to higher levels of discrimination by education. Thus K'ang undermines the whole edifice of Confucian self-cultivation as well as the formal structure of the Confucian curriculum.

Yet virtue is there, at the very foundation of K'ang's own utopia. It is the quality that he calls *jen*: human-heartedness, spontaneous fellow-feeling, the instinctive sympathy of one human being for another, the

---

* Some "traditional" tendencies remain nonetheless. For example, K'ang places a high social value on education and academic attainment. In the Great Community students who fail their course of study will lose their right to public support. They will be compelled to seek menial jobs on their own; since all occupational functions are publicly administered it remains unclear how this will be accomplished. Those who are unable to find employment will be condemned to lives at hard labor in public poorhouses, supported by the community, but in effect deprived of their status as members of it.

compassionate nature that insures mankind's ability to live in accordance with standards of right conduct even in the absence of structures of moral discipline. K'ang does not see this as a distinctly Confucian or uniquely Chinese value: *jen* is merely the Chinese term which describes an attribute common to all mankind in any age. The idea is clearly Confucian-inspired, however, resonant with echoes of the Mencian suggestion that the moral order is "complete" within the self. K'ang Yu-wei's elevation of this belief in the essential goodness of human nature to the level of a universal truth foreshadows the efforts of later thinkers to identify the spiritual heart of Confucian faith and to rescue it from the wreckage of Confucian institutions.

In another way as well K'ang's universalistic utopia anticipates the intellectual disposition of some who came after. Only in the expectation of a world in which *all* cultural identity had been lost was K'ang able to forsake Confucian forms. When Westerners had ceased to be Western, Chinese could cease being Chinese. And this will come to pass only in the Age of the Great Community—not "once upon a time," but an equally fictitious "sometime."

So K'ang Yu-wei, the most visionary of Chinese thinkers, lived out his life in the most orthodox Confucian fashion, the prisoner of his own age of "Approaching Peace," a cultural loyalist to the end. The death of the Kuang Hsu emperor in 1908 and the demise of the dynasty itself four years later deprived him of the political cause for which he had struggled throughout his years of exile. The Republic to which he returned in 1913 seemed to him out of its time: a great destructive force without the power to create values or institutions which would replace those it had overthrown. He spent his declining years tilting at windmills: when China's most persuasive intellectual spokesmen were proclaiming the bankruptcy of the Confucian tradition, K'ang promoted Confucianism as a state religion; long after the Manchus had vanished utterly from the stage of Chinese history, K'ang lent his waning influence to evanescent schemes for the return of the dynasty to power. His utopia, finally, was reduced to a private dream-world. In the last chapter of *Ta-t'ung shu* K'ang had speculated on the disappearance of the ultimate "boundary" that constrains human happiness—the sense of a distinct *human* identity that binds mankind to life and to life's inevitable companion, death. With old age upon him, he gave himself over increasingly to musings on the "extragalactic heavens," where freed from the burden of life one might "wander among the stars." He had long been interested in astronomy as the meeting ground of science and mystery. Three years before his death he established, somewhat to the embarrassment of old friends and disciples, an "Academy of Celestial Peregrination," and for it provided a textbook, "Lectures on the Heavens" (*Chu-t'ien chiang*). We do not take leave of K'ang Yu-wei. It is he who takes leave of us.

My thoughts are in the Extragalactic Heavens
  Where are found countless star clusters:
With green light or purple flames each glows and shines,
  Rolling clouds, glittering and scintillating,
  illuminate the Universe.
In our Heavens of the Silvery Stream are two hundred
  millions Suns—
  Forming merely a part of the Starry Orbit . . .
The ancestor of our Sun does not rule these
  Extragalactic Heavens,
  Azure and boundless . . .
I look up and sigh—hoping to roam with the Immortals.[59]

*   *   *

In November 1883 Robert Hart, the Inspector General of the Imperial Maritime Customs, received a telegram from the Customs commissioner at Canton. The fact that it had come to hand in Peking hardly more than twenty-four hours after it had been dispatched from Canton, across a distance that imperial couriers only a few years earlier had needed a month to cover riding at top speed, was enough to encourage Hart. "This shows some progress does it not?" he wrote to his London agent. "The introduction of these novelties, steam, electricity, etc., although put on rather like patches on a rotten exterior will in time be followed by their working their way down centrewards, and, once arrived there will acquire a new life, and, like yeast, will work outwards again, changing the nature of the mass and producing the great and grand China of the future."[60] It was a confidence shared by many, as we have seen, Chinese as well as foreigners; a cautious hope not uncharacteristic of reformist opinion of the 1870s and 1880s. But down to the end of the century, *yang-wu*—things Western, or modern, or untraditional, however we may choose to call them—remained hardly more than patches applied to the visible surface of Chinese life; even as the treaty ports themselves, linked by tenuous filaments of trade and intercourse with the vast interior, remained worlds unto themselves, closer to each other and to Singapore, Calcutta, London, Boston, or New York than to Peking or Hangchow.

In his perceptive study of the intellectual life of these decades, Paul Cohen distinguishes between reformers of the "littoral" and those of the "hinterland." Among the former are Wang T'ao, Cheng Kuan-ying, Ho Kai and several others who were active in the ambivalent culture of the "Hong Kong-Shanghai corridor"; in the ranks of the latter we find such figures as Feng Kuei-fen and Hsueh Fu-ch'eng, scholar-bureaucrats rooted in the Confucian culture of Peking and the provincial capitals. To the littoral reformers Cohen ascribes the function of innovation, both institutional and intellectual. The validation of change was accomplished, or at least attempted, by hinterland reformers in the service of the great mandarins like Li Hung-chang and Chang Chih-tung on whom depended the fate of the dynasty. "This two-phase process assumes the form of a succession of littoral assaults upon the hinterland, followed in each instance by hinterland attempts to legitimize the assaults through Sinicization."[61] This is a strikingly graphic representation of the phenomenon we have been examining in this chapter. It describes aptly the sense of a distance that is more than merely geographic or political or cultural dividing the anomalous foreign enclaves along the coast from the walled bastions of traditional civilization in the interior.

The boundary between "modernity" and "traditionalism," however, was more than a frontier that one might step across somewhere along the hundred-mile journey from Shanghai to Hangchow. It was a division also within the minds, the hearts, and the lives of individuals. Wang T'ao the cosmopolitan commentator on European history remained always, in some part of his being, Wang T'ao the failed Soochow degree candidate. In Ho Kai, the eminently successful Westernized professional man, there lingered still the flickering vision of a legendary Confucian commonwealth. K'ang Yu-wei, the preeminent nineteenth-century "hinterland" reformer, sure to the very end of the wisdom of Confucian insight, saw in his furthest flights of fancy a world transformed beyond recognition. Such cultural or psychological disjunction is difficult to fathom. Joseph Levenson has measured it in terms of the conflict between "history" and "value": recognition, on the one hand, of objective historical circumstance as a compelling inducement to the abandonment of the past, in perpetual and often destructive tension with a residual allegiance to the values of the traditional culture as the only source from which to derive the assurance of a continuing identity.[62]

Nevertheless, for all the bitterness of their condemnation of the ineptness of China's rulers, the anachronism of imperial institutions, the sterility of Confucian pedagogy, reform-minded Chinese intellectuals down to the end of the nineteenth century were still able to draw their sense of vocation, of public purpose and private worth, largely from within the inherited tradition. Like other reformers before them, they perceived an ominous distance separating the emperor from his people, the ruler from the ruled. They did not seek, as remedy, to deny the distinction, to cast the emperor down or raise the masses up. They remained convinced of the virtue of paternalistic leadership, if it be wise; and of the wisdom of relying on a conscientious minority, if it be virtuous. They tried to bridge the gap by instilling in that minority a broader vision and a braver voice. Although an unfamiliar vocabulary lent an aura of daring strangeness to their prescriptions, until the debacle of 1898 the great preoccupation of Chinese reformers remained what it had always been over the long centuries of Confucian supremacy: the problem of right rulership. This they still saw partly as a matter of the integrity of the imperial position, and partly—the more important part—as a question of ministerial competence. On either hand it had become, by the late 1890s, difficult to sustain the earlier sense of confidence. In the gloomy aftermath of the Sino-Japanese War, Robert Hart's assessment of China's prospects was a good deal grimmer than it had been a dozen years before.

> There must be a dynastic cataclysm before wholesome reform can operate, and now the *Chinese people* begin to smart under the suffering and disgrace brought on the country by incompetent rulers—to which result, however, purely Chinese mandarins, quite as much as Manchus, contributed their full share—and the great *Li* [Hung-chang] perhaps more than any other by the outwardly perfect, but *inwardly rotten* condition of the partial reforms he led the state to believe in, and pay for, as progress![63]

The Reform Movement of 1898 was not the dynastic cataclysm of which Hart spoke. It was rather a desperate and disastrous attempt to vindicate reformist premises—dazzling as a rocketburst against a darkening sky that leaves the night blacker than before. After the Hundred Days, Chinese intellectuals lost whatever hope might have remained to them that reform could come from on high, bestowed as a gift upon a grateful people. For all the eloquence of K'ang Yu-wei's exhortations to the hapless Kuang Hsu, there would be no Meiji Restoration for China. In the decades that followed, the reformers' preoccupation with the problem of enlightened rulership gave way increasingly to the revolutionaries' efforts to generate in the people at large a capacity for responsible citizenship—the effort to create not simply a new government, but a new people. Along the way, Chinese intellectuals began to define a new vocation for themselves. What they learned abroad reinforced the sense of their own importance bred by the culture which had nourished their forefathers from generation to generation. But that tradition made no place for them in the role to which they now aspired, standing on the threshold of China's revolutionary century, as the agents of politics and the creators of culture. The Confucian age was over.

The Revolution of 1911: Intellectuals as Political Entrepreneurs

Exiles feed on empty dreams of hope. . . .

—*Aeschylus,* Agamemnon

THE EDICT THAT SUMMONED K'ANG YU-WEI to his fateful audience with the Kuang Hsu emperor in June, 1898, also commanded the Tsung-li yamen to seek out one Liang Ch'i-ch'ao, a Kwangtung *chü-jen,* and report his whereabouts to the Throne. This may have been the first time that the Ch'ing court took official notice of Liang; it was by no means the last. As K'ang's protégé, and a celebrated publicist already in his own right, Liang was active in the events of the ensuing summer. With K'ang he paid the price of exile. In Japan Liang soon emerged as the principal propagandist of the reform party established to promote the cause of constitutional monarchy. He remained a monarchist, and therefore nominally a supporter of the Manchus, until the very eve of the revolution which toppled the dynasty in 1911. The disciple's sense of fidelity to his master was a weighty obligation in the literati culture from which both K'ang and Liang had sprung; less and less, however, did they share a common vision.

Exile put K'ang on the defensive intellectually, while for Liang these were years of far-ranging exploration through unfamiliar cultural and historical terrain. He traveled, as Philip Huang succinctly puts it, "with little intellectual baggage and no fixed itinerary,"[1] describing to an enraptured readership each new vista that opened out before him. Liang contributed at least as much as did the self-proclaimed revolutionaries to the radical education of the generation which came of age in the aftermath of the Hundred Days. "Liang Ch'i-ch'ao is the great statesman of our revolution," wrote one of the schoolboys of those prerevolutionary years shortly after Liang's return from exile in 1913. "His greatness lies in his having renovated our intellectual world. Whatever our countrymen have learned of racial spirit [min-tsu ssu-hsiang chu-i] and of the affairs of the world at large over the past fifteen years is entirely to Mr. Liang's credit. . . . Without his pen, how could Sun Yat-sen . . . have achieved such quick success?"[2]

It was Sun Yat-sen, however, who symbolized the brief triumph of the republican revolution in 1911-1912; and to Westerners at least his had long been the more familiar name. Sun moved easily in the turn-of-the-century culture of imperialism, comfortable in an environment he could not condone. Peasant-born, educated for the most part in mission schools, he spoke English fluently and wrote indifferent Chinese classical prose. He was a Western-trained medical doctor, a profession without opportunity in the Chinese interior of the late nineteenth century. He was, moreover, a baptized Christian, though it was a faith he claimed when the occasion required more from political than from spiritual motives. Sun was, in other words, a product of the China Coast culture. Unlike Ho Kai or Cheng Kuan-ying or Wang T'ao, however, he never made a career for himself in the treaty ports. He spent the prerevolutionary years in exile—the penalty in his case for involvement in an abortive insurrection in Canton in 1895 that was blamed by the outraged Ch'ing on the subversive influence of Chinese Christians.

Thereafter Sun traveled with a price on his head, drumming up support from overseas Chinese in North America, Europe, and Southeast Asia for his first revolutionary organization, the Hsing Chung hui (Revive China Society). In 1896 he was kidnapped by agents of the Chinese Legation in London and held incommunicado for several days while preparations were made to smuggle him back to China where beheading was the most hospitable welcome he might expect. Only the intervention of British friends, the London press, and, somewhat tardily, the Foreign Office rescued Sun from this distressing prospect. He emerged as something of an international celebrity to resume his revolutionary activity more confident than ever of the righteousness of his mission. When K'ang Yu-wei and Liang Ch'i-ch'ao arrived in Japan in 1898, Sun was already ensconced in Yokohama, in touch with other Chinese radicals and with the coterie of Japanese pan-Asianists who for reasons of their own were to contribute substantial moral and financial support to the Chinese revolutionary movement over the next decade.

At the turn of the century the revolutionary movement had yet to assume organizational identity. Sun was only one of the many who advocated the anti-Manchu cause. Others were more prolific writers than he, or more eloquent, at least on paper; others were capable of a subtler logic and more rigorous argument. But Sun possessed some quality of character and personality—a presence which the dour, almost drab photographs that survive quite fail to capture—that made him a compelling spokesman for a political change that many promoted. He was a man of persuasive sincerity, contagious enthusiasm, and an honesty of belief seldom challenged, even when his leadership of the revolutionary movement was disputed. He devoted himself tirelessly to the revolutionary cause, begging money, weapons, allies, conspiring in plots which either failed to materialize or ended in disastrous confusion. It was hardly a triumphant record, but in spite of it Sun became—for reasons that may forever remain elusive—the dominant revolutionary personality, the center of gravity, as it were, around which revolved a constellation of intellectual activists and politicized students who sought an end to Manchu overlordship and to the Confucian monarchy itself.

Thirteen years separated the collapse of the Hundred Day Reforms in September, 1898, from the insurrection in Wuchang in October, 1911, that signaled the beginning of the end for the Ch'ing dynasty. The history of Chinese radicalism during those years has most often been told in terms of the rivalry between reformers and revolutionaries in exile, bidding for the allegiance of a disparate constituency. There were, of course, fundamental and abiding disagreements between those who advocated the amendment of existing institutions and those who demanded their immediate destruction. It might be well to emphasize at the outset, however, not what divided "reformers" from "revolutionaries," but what they had in common. Despite their differences, they were alike animated by the spirit of political entrepreneurship, a commitment to political activism as the intellectual's appropriate vocation. Sustained by their belief in the primary importance of a transformation of political values and institutions as a means to liberate the civic spirit of the "new people," the intellectual radicals of the prerevolutionary decade shared certain attitudes and expectations that set them apart both from their immediate predecessors, the reformers of the late nineteenth century, and from those who were to follow, heirs to the failed promises of the 1911 Revolution.

The voluntary association of men of like opinion to promote a course of political action, and the affirmation of private standards of belief as justification for it, were ominous contraventions of the norms of responsible Confucian conduct. In the traditional view, from which even the more imaginative reformers of the nineteenth century had not entirely escaped, partisanship was regarded as subversive of the moral and political integrity of the state and the culture. Chinese intellectuals after the turn of the century inhabited a different world; theirs was a time when "for every moral decision there were available at least two standards, and for every cosmic and social happening at least two explanations."[3] Uncertainty did not unman them or turn them into sceptics. They were by temperament enthusiasts and therefore optimists. The desire to act implied the need to choose a course of action, and they took sides. Partisanism divided them on many issues, but it was itself an attribute of their common radicalism.

Whether monarchists or republicans, moreover, these men shared a vocabulary and, in several respects, a similar sense of the present crisis and similar visions of the future. They were at one in their concern for the survival of the Chinese state. Though they differed on the question of whether the nation should be entrusted to the auspices of a Western/ Japanese style constitutional monarchy or a republican form of government, they were alike convinced that political change was the first order of business; and, further, that China must be rebuilt on the solid foundation of a politically aware and responsible citizenry. The theme of a "new people"(hsin min) is a recurrent motif in the polemical literature of these years, reformist and revolutionary. With a confidence that later events did little to justify, the politically minded intellectuals of the prerevolutionary decade cherished the expectation that the transformation of political forms and the opportunity for political action would generate broader changes in social and cultural values that would sustain the new political order.

The frustration of these hopes in the aftermath of 1911 offered a lesson that the next generation took to heart. Many of China's intellectual spokesmen in the May Fourth period—that is, roughly, the decade from 1915 to 1925—disavowed the activist, entrepreneurial role that prerevolutionary radicals had tried to play. They cast themselves instead as what we may call political amateurs, taking the view that while politics (at least in its broader sense) is an appropriate avocation for men of public spirit, it cannot be regarded as the intellectuals' proper vocation. Progressive political change, they argued, can only be insured as the result of prior changes in social and cultural values which are the intellectuals' natural concern. In chapter 6 we will explore the implications of this shift in emphasis at greater length.

In the prerevolutionary decade the case for radical change, whatever its immediate political aims, was easier and safer to argue outside of China than within it, an advantage that the exiled advocates of both monarchist and republican persuasions exploited to the full. They proselytized with considerable success among communities of overseas Chinese, especially among the wealthy merchants of the Straits settlements, the Dutch East Indies, and what had now become French

Indo-China. These were, in many cases, the descendants of Chinese who had emigrated for primarily economic reasons several generations earlier. But they still thought of China as the cultural homeland, and their circumstances as partially acculturated aliens in non-Chinese surroundings, enhanced by an instinctive clannishness, made them quickly receptive to the idea of a revival of Chinese fortunes. K'ang Yu-wei on behalf of the Pao huang hui and Sun Yat-sen and other agents of the evolving revolutionary movement were energetic in their efforts to secure overseas Chinese funds to underwrite the costs of their competitive political enterprises.

It was the students, however, in China and abroad, who constituted the most vocal and adventuresome following for radical causes. Contentious and difficult to organize, they were nevertheless activists by inclination and natural patriots. The reformers of earlier years had addressed themselves primarily to the literati—the established intellectual elite, the acknowledged men of opinion. Turn-of-the-century propagandists were not indifferent to the importance of such support, but they appealed not only to the traditionally educated. From this time forward an emphasis on the special responsibilities of youth becomes an increasingly significant element in radical literature. Without this new audience to share the urgent sense of crisis and impending disaster, the intellectuals who gave voice to the aspirations of those years could hardly have attained the influence that is attributable to them.

*   *   *

Swift and drastic changes were overtaking the Chinese in the first decade of the twentieth century. China's defeat by Japan in 1895 had provoked an ominous quickening of imperial interest in the "Chinese question," and there ensued a frenzied competition to wrest railroad and mining concessions from the stricken Manchu government. This was the era when talk of "spheres of influence," of "slicing the Chinese melon," was heard in London, Paris, Berlin, St. Petersburg, Washington, Tokyo—and nowhere with greater satisfaction than in the Western clubs of Shanghai and Peking. The attempted reforms of 1898 were undertaken against this background. In May of that year, even as K'ang and his party awaited their opportunity, Lord Salisbury, the British Prime Minister, summarized imperialist assumptions with cool irony:

For one reason or another—from the necessities of politics or under the pretext of philanthropy—the living nations will gradually encroach upon the territory of the dying. . . . It is not to be supposed that any one nation of the living nations will be allowed to have the profitable monopoly of curing or cutting up these unfortunate patients, and the controversy is as to who shall have the privilege of doing so, and in what measure. . . . It is a period which will tax our resolution, our tenacity and imperial instincts, to the utmost.

A few weeks later the Colonial Secretary, Joseph Chamberlain, put the issue even more pointedly: "It is not a question of a single port in China—that is a very small matter. It is not a question of a single province; it is a question of the whole fate of the Chinese Empire."[4]

Contemplating the situation from quite a different vantage point, the Chinese were ready to agree that the fate of the Empire hung in the balance. The Court's instinctive reaction to the combined threat posed by Westernizing reformers within and Western imperialists without was the blind and fearful rage vented in the Boxer Rebellion in 1899-1900. The outcome was calamitous, as the more prescient mandarins had known it must be. To one of these, the aged and ailing Li Hung-chang, fell the melancholy duty of signing the Protocol of 1901, the instrument of the dynasty's ultimate humiliation. It stipulated death or banishment for several high officials, demotion or dismissal for numerous lesser offenders. A subtler punishment was meted out to the miscreant gentry in some forty-five districts in North China where antiforeign incidents had taken place and where, in retribution, the examinations were to be suspended for five years. The Legation Quarter in Peking, where under the very walls of the Imperial City the foreign community had withstood the summer-long seige of 1900, was henceforth to be closed to Chinese residents and garrisoned by foreign troops, as was the access route from the coast to the capital. A punitive indemnity amounting to Tls. 450 million (or just under $334 million) was imposed, at four percent interest per annum—this staggering sum to be secured by turning over to foreigners the principal sources of revenue that still remained to the central government: the maritime customs, the native customs, and the salt gabelle. Lord Salisbury's disquisition on the living nations and the dying nations perhaps struck his listeners in the Albert Hall as a pleasant metahistorical excursion. But it would have rung true to a Chinese audience after the turn of the century—and they knew for whom the bell tolled.

Even the Empress Dowager was chastened, or at least thoroughly frightened. For the second time in her life she had been driven from the imperial capital by the arrival of foreign troops. She had been a young woman when she had accompanied the Hsien Feng emperor in his flight to Jehol in 1860, the years of power still before her. But the aging empress who escaped from Peking in August, 1900, disguised in the blue cotton costume of a North China peasant and concealed in a common donkey cart, clung to a discredited authority. With the unfortunate Kuang Hsu in tow she sought refuge in Sian, whence there issued in the course of 1901 the first of a series of edicts in the emperor's name intended, at least according to the letter, to launch the dynasty finally on the road toward progressive change. In the view of the Court's contemporary critics, and almost unanimously of historians who have since reviewed the record, these imperial concessions came probably too late, and offered in any case too little in the way of substantive reform to rescue a regime already destitute of both wealth and honor. Nevertheless the Ch'ing reform movement provided, as it were, a counterpoint to the rising radical clamor during the last decade of the dynasty's life. By what it tried to accomplish no less than by what it refused even to contemplate, the Court helped to shape the fate which eventually overtook it.

The Ch'ing reforms touched upon a range of subjects: the commercial and penal law, political administration especially in the area of foreign affairs, and military modernization. From the outset, education was a major concern of dynastic reformers. The edict that inaugurated the search for new policies in 1901 laid to rest—or so it seemed—the notion of Western skills that could be appropriated without damage to a Chinese "essence." "In recent years the study of Western methods has been limited to languages and technical skills—the superficial aspects of Western arts, not the underlying sources of Western knowledge."[5] This imperial request for counsel elicited a flood of proposals from the progressive officials of the realm, prominent among them several of the great governors-general: Chang Chih-tung in Hunan/Hupeh; Liu K'un-i in Kiangsu/Kiangsi/Anhwei; Yuan Shih-k'ai in Shangtung and then, after the death of Li Hung-chang, in Chihli. The archaic eight-legged essay style, abolished and revived in 1898, was finally abandoned in favor of examinations that rewarded more timely competence. The creation of a new school system was sanctioned, though neither the funds to support it nor the teachers to staff it were readily available. It was assumed that as the "new schools" flourished, the traditional curriculum would gradually lose its following, and that the Confucian examination system itself would in time wither away. Elaborate provisions were drafted to integrate students with modern educations into the time-honored categories of the Confucian academic hierarchy as *hsiu-ts'ai*, *chü-jen* or *chin-shih*. The dilemma, however, could not be resolved by word play. By the older generation, including even many of the official sponsors of educational reform, Western learning was still regarded as a utilitarian adjunct, essential but inferior. As long as Confucian learning retained its prestige and traditional opportunities for honor and advancement existed, the new system remained at a competitive disadvantage. Finally in 1905, officials stunned by the implications of Japan's victory over Russia acknowledged the inexorable logic of the situation. Yuan Shih-k'ai put it bluntly in the memorial that brought the issue to a head, late in August.

A moment's time is worth a thousand pieces of gold. Human talent is not something that can be created overnight. . . . Will the strong neighbors lying in wait at our frontiers grant us the necessary respite? In recent years the foreigners have looked askance at our policy of renovation [*wei-hsin*], and have urged us to reform [*pien-fa*]. They have distrusted our obstinate adherence to old customs, and ridiculed our indecision. They doubt our sincerity, and hold us always in contempt. . . . If we wish to save the situation, we must start by establishing more schools; and if we wish to establish more schools, we must first abolish the examinations.[6]

And so it came to pass. The edict of September 2, 1905, which effected the demise of the Confucian examination system admonished the gentry to devote their energies to the task of spreading "modern" education to the people. But the act itself severed the last traditional link between the monarchy and its principal social constituency, and made starkly evident the divergence of interests between the imperial institution and the gentry class. From this time forward, gentry interests were increasingly defined in terms of local wealth and power in confrontation with the wealth and power of the central government. In its way, then, the abolition of the examination system was as dramatic and decisive a turning point in the decline of the Confucian system as was the destruction of the dynasty in 1911.

In part to meet the urgent need for qualified teachers to staff the new schools, the central government and various provincial officials began in 1901 to encourage students to seek the kind of training abroad that they could not acquire in China. A handful had preceded them. Yung Wing (Jung Hung, 1828–1912), the Cantonese protégé of American missionaries from whom he had received his early education, had graduated from Yale in the class of 1854. He subsequently played a peripheral role in the Self-strengthening movement, notably as one of the sponsors of the Chinese Educational Mission, an enterprise which for a time enjoyed the backing of Li Hung-chang. Under its auspices, and the disapproving supervision of a stringently conservative Confucian director of studies, a hundred or so youngsters were educated in the United States between 1872 and 1881. It was in the late 1870s, too, that Yen Fu was dispatched to England to study naval science, an opportunity which led eventually, albeit indirectly, to his epoch-making translations of Adam Smith, J. S. Mill, T. H. Huxley, and Herbert Spencer. Such cases, however, had been conspicuous by their rarity. Not until the very end of the century did Chinese students begin to travel abroad in any numbers, and only after the Boxer Rebellion did the academic emigration begin in earnest.

Many of the intellectuals whom we will encounter as this story goes forward participated in this diaspora, as did many of the men who later emerged as the political and military elite of the Republican period. The "returned students" (liu hsueh-sheng) played, indeed, an inordinantly prominent role in the history of China in the first half of the twentieth century. It is easier, however, to identify individuals whose lives were in one way or another touched by the experience of overseas study than it is to describe in terms of social and economic background, or even size, the group to which they belonged. With the sparse and scattered information at our disposal, the best we can do is to try to suggest something of the nature of the phenomenon.

A few hundred Chinese students found their way to Europe and the United States in the prerevolutionary decade, among them a number who figured influentially in the intellectual life of China in the teens and twenties, as we shall see. In the period with which we are here concerned, however, it is Japan which commands our attention, for Japan was by far the most common destination of young Chinese who set out in search of a "modern" education abroad between 1900 and 1912. The reasons are not hard to find. The disgrace of the reform party in 1898 had not tarnished the luster of the Japanese example, even in the eyes of the Court. It was easy and relatively inexpensive to reach Japan, and cheaper to live there than in North America or Europe. Cultural differences, though startling, were probably less overwhelming in Japan than in the West. The language, at least in its written form, was more easily learned than English, French, or German; a knowledge of Japanese, moreover, gave access not only to the rich and varied literature of the Meiji period, but also to a wealth of translations of Western works unavailable in Chinese. The Japanese had the advantage of an appreciable headstart in their absorption of Western ideas. As early as the 1870s they had begun to argue their own future course in terms drawn somewhat randomly from the writings of Rousseau, Montesquieu, Bluntschli, Darwin and Spencer, Edward Bellamy, Henry George, and Samuel Smiles; the literary tastes of Meiji intellectuals had been enlarged by acquaintance with the novels of Bulwer-Lytton, Disraeli, Dumas, Hugo, Dostoievski and Turgenev, the poetry of Shakespeare and Byron, Goethe and Heine. In other words, the Japanese entered the twentieth century with a well-informed command of the intellectual resources of the nineteenth: apt and enthusiastic purveyors of "modern" culture, with a keen and sometimes arrogant sense of their peculiar status as its agent in Asia.

For the same reasons that made it attractive to students, Chinese radicals had discovered in Japan an environment congenial to their purposes. Nor was the Ch'ing government blind to the fact that by subsidizing Chinese students in Japan it was helping to create an audience for the constitutionalists and revolutionaries who were its sworn enemies. An Inspectorate of Chinese Students, under the jurisdiction of the legation in Tokyo, did what it could to keep track of the students' activities, and the Chinese minister periodically requested the intervention of the Japanese government to discipline student factions that had become too stridently anti-Manchu. For their part, the students were sensitive to the ambiguity of their situation. It was, of course, Japan's astonishing success in extricating itself from the disadvantages of unequal status vis-à-vis the Western powers that recommended Japan to the Chinese as a model to be emulated. Yet by the time Chinese students began to arrive in Tokyo, Japan was already a member in good standing of the imperialist club. Memories of the 1894–1895 war, when Japanese propaganda had mercilessly mocked the pigtailed, pumpkin-headed Chinaman, were still vivid and hurtful. "On to Peking," a ditty popular in Japan at the time, expressed an attitude more durable than the chauvinism of the war years:

> *China was wise of old*
> *China is wise no more:*
> *Back into darkness has rolled*
> *For all her sages and lore.*
>
> *She may boast as the Kingdom of Heaven*
> *But her barbarous heart is of hell:*
> *What light to the East shall be given*
> *Till our wisdom her darkness dispel?*[7]

Of the several nationalities that comprised the legation garrison in Peking after 1901, the Japanese force was the largest—and of all the foreign troops on Chinese soil, the Japanese were to prove in the end the most intractable and the most difficult to evict. From time to time contigents of Chinese students would pack up and return to China, incensed by the policies of the Japanese government, or to protest its acquiescence to Ch'ing diplomatic pressure aimed against the student movement. Some students were deported; several commited suicide or made the attempt; a few seem to have shuttled back and forth between Tokyo and Shanghai with fair regularity.

The number of students in Japan thus fluctuated as the barometer of Sino-Japanese relations rose and fell, but the general tendency was upward—and in the early years of the century dramatically so.[8] From a handful in 1897, the number increased to around a hundred in 1898, the year of the abortive reforms. By the winter of 1902–1903 the effect of post-Boxer Ch'ing policy was becoming evident. Seven hundred and sixty-three students are listed in the official census undertaken by the Inspectorate of Students in early 1903, and that was only the beginning. By 1904–1906 the tide was at full flood—an increase attributable in part to Japan's triumph over Russia and to the abolition of the examination system. One estimate puts the figure for these years at around eight thousand annually. After 1906 the numbers decreased somewhat, to roughly four thousand in 1908 and 1909, and a mere fifteen hundred or so in 1912. By then, however, more than thirty-five thousand Chinese had studied in Japan.

The 1903 census is sufficiently informative to permit some generalizations concerning the Chinese student population in Japan at that time. They were young, as we might expect, averaging in their mid-twenties, though students as young as six and as old as forty-five were listed. Over a

third were, or had been, cadets at Seijo gakkō, where candidates for admission to the Japanese military academy were prepared.* Nearly half
were enrolled in schools established expressly to meet the needs of
Chinese students seeking intensive, short-term instruction in such oppor-
tune specializations as physics and chemistry, teacher training, and
police administration. Of these the most popular were the Kōbun gakuin
and the Dōbun shoin, both established in 1902, the latter under the
auspices of Japanese Pan-Asianists who for their own reasons saw fit to
promote Chinese progressivism. Relatively few Chinese students were
enrolled in Tokyo Imperial University or in such prestigious private
universities as Waseda; a considerable number were scattered among a
score of technical institutes and academies.

A number of students were identified in the 1903 census not by province of origin, but by inherited status, as members of the Imperial
Household, or as Bannermen. Of the latter, twenty-six in all, seventeen
were Manchus, seven belonged to the Chinese Banners, and two were
Mongols. For the rest, students from seventeen of the eighteen provinces
of China Proper and from the Manchurian province of Feng-t'ien (present-day Liaoning) were listed; only the sparsely populated province of
Kansu, in the remote northwest, was not represented. The geographic
distribution was far from even, however. Nearly two-thirds of the
students listed came from the five provinces of the lower and middle
Yangtze region, with Kiangsu and Chekiang together accounting for
more than a third of the total. An additional twenty percent of the total
was claimed by the southern coastal provinces of Kwangtung and
Fukien. In other words, close to eighty percent of the students surveyed
in 1903 came from only seven provinces in south and central China,
while the north was badly underrepresented, with only the metropolitan
province of Chihli ranking among the top ten.

Well over half of these students were paying their own expenses. Provincial funds were the principal source of support for the remainder,
though a hundred or so were financed in one way or another by the central government, and the Bannermen (all of whom were enrolled in the
short course in police administration offered by Kōbun gakuin) were
funded by Peking municipal revenues. Two students from Chekiang were
supported by local subscription, as promising examination candidates
had been upon occasion in former times.

We cannot assume that this sketch depicts in accurate detail the situation that prevailed generally throughout the prerevolutionary decade; it

---

* The first Chinese cadets were admitted to Seijo gakkō in 1898, at request of Chang Chih-
tung. Until 1903, both government-sponsored and privately funded students were admitted
to the school. In that year, as student radicalism became increasingly a problem, Ch'ing officials asserted the authority to limit Chinese enrollment to students nominated by (and
presumably loyal to) the dynasty.

does, however, suggest some reasonable conjectures concerning the Chinese student population in Japan soon after the turn of the century. In the first place it appears that, imperial edicts urging the Chinese to probe "the sources of Western knowledge" notwithstanding, most students who went to Japan were anxious to acquire the rudiments of a technical or professional education in the shortest possible time. It has been estimated that less than ten percent of the more than thirty-five thousand students who received some schooling in Japan during these years actually completed a formal course of study. Many of those who did, moreover, were enrolled in six- or eight-month courses at institutions that catered to their particular requirements, and were thus to some degree insulated from the mainstream of Japanese secondary or higher education. Relatively few, in other words, were as deeply immersed in, or as responsive to, late-Meiji intellectual life as were their mentors, men like Liang Ch'i-ch'ao or, on the revolutionary side, Chang Ping-lin, Wang Ching-wei, or Chu Chih-hsin. It is also true, if contemporary accounts are to be relied upon, that many students were as interested in the leisure arts of modern civilization, like ballroom dancing, as they were in more professional studies. Nevertheless we may fairly suppose that, however brief and superficial the experience was in many cases, most of the young men (and the very few young women) who returned to China from an academic sojourn in Japan saw their country and its problems in a new light.

The preponderance of students from the lower Yangtze region and the maritime littoral suggests the influence of the China Coast culture as an incentive to overseas study, and perhaps a connection between the treaty port/compradore economy and the ability to meet the costs of a foreign education. On the other hand, great private wealth does not seem to have been a prerequisite for study in Japan: the costs were relatively low, and personal accounts attest to the fact that many students scraped along on a bare minimum.*

Nevertheless, whether rich or poor, most of the students who went abroad in the prerevolutionary years claimed the kind of social background that would have made them, in an earlier generation, likely aspirants to official preferment through the examination system. There is little evidence that the "returned students" represented a hitherto submerged social group whose rise to intellectual opportunity and social status is comparable, for example, to the emergence of the *raznochintsy* in nineteenth-century Russia, or the "men of talent" (*shishi*) in

---

* Y. C. Wang estimates that it cost the Chinese government less *per capita* annually in 1909–1910 to educate students in Japan than in one of the three existing Chinese institutions of higher education (Peking University, Peiyang University, and Shansi University), and only a fraction of what it cost in Europe or the U.S. See *Chinese Intellectuals and the West*, p. 517, table 15.

nineteenth-century Japan. What we *do* perceive here, perhaps, is evidence of a shift in the social/intellectual center of gravity. The disproportionate representation of the Yantze provinces among overseas students may be attributable to several factors: the cultural and economic influence of the China Coast culture, as already suggested; the proud tradition of academic attainment characteristic of the Kiangnan gentry for centuries past; the fact that the governors-general of several of these provinces were among the more forward-looking officials of the time. It contrasts strikingly with the situation that prevailed under the quota system which governed access to gentry status under the traditional examination system. The quotas for the metropolitan province of Chihli, for example, were consistently inflated in relation to the province's share of the total population, while in the crowded Yangtze provinces the quotas were generally almost exactly proportional to the population as a whole. Putting these facts together, one is led to conjecture that a fair number of ambitious young men from south-central China whose prospects under the examination system were less than promising in terms of numbers alone began, after 1901, to elect the untraditional alternative; or, to put it another way, that even before the abolition of the examination system, the constraints which it perpetuated were crumbling as education began to respond to what we might call "free market" conditions.

The Japanese provided more than book learning to their Asian protégés after the turn of the century. Japan was also a school of manners, where the Chinese might aquire the social habits befitting civilized citizens of the modern world. As Liang Ch'i-ch'ao put it, "When one arrives in Hong Kong or Shanghai from the interior, one's horizon suddenly changes: the interior seems rustic, vulgar and of little account. When one reaches Japan, one's perspective changes again: it is Hong Kong and Shanghai that seem backward and commonplace."[9] Almost from the moment that Commodore Perry's squadron invaded their seclusion in the 1850s, the Japanese had reacted with a sense of cultural embarrassment inconceivable among nineteenth-century Chinese. "Don't let the foreigners laugh at you!" was a slogan characteristic of Meiji attitudes—attitudes that now began to infect the immigrant student population. Chinese students disembarking in Yokohama or Kobe or Nagasaki hastily cut off the queues that were the mark of political and cultural outlandishness; or, if their intended stay was short, coiled the shameful pigtails atop their heads to be hidden under their caps. They found themselves often ridiculed as uncouth bumpkins who stuffed their mouths with food as they walked, blew their noses between their fingers without recourse to handkerchiefs, and affected a strange mixture of Chinese and Japanese attire. Their vade mecum was a pamphlet entitled "Essential Admonitions Concerning the Deportment of Overseas

Students" (*Liu-hsueh-sheng tzu-chih yao-hsun*) which was full of sound and perhaps occasionally necessary advice:

> Walk to the left side of the road. If you meet a friend on the street, do not call loudly to him or stand long in conversation; it is better, after speaking briefly, to bow and go on your way. You must not spit, or relieve yourself, just anywhere. Be sure to observe the Entrance and Exit signs when sightseeing, and keep your voice down. Be solemn in your manner with servant girls; do not be flippant, or fool around. If the tramcar is crowded, yield your seat to old people, children or women. In the public bath, get into the tub as soon as you have washed your lower half. When your roommate is writing a letter or studying, don't peek. Don't rummage through the books on someone else's desk, or the things in someone else's drawers. Keep your clothes clean. Do not go naked, even in summer . . . . "[10]

Thus did Japan discharge, in modern coin, a cultural debt owed to China since the T'ang dynasty. In part, of course, repayment was made in more negotiable currency. Though the Japanese came late to the competition, by the first decade of the new century translations into Chinese of Japanese works, or retranslations of Japanese renderings of Western literature, substantially outnumbered those from Western languages. Between 1896 and 1912 some five hundred Japanese titles were translated; of 533 translations from all languages made in the period 1901–1904, more than sixty percent were from Japanese. Something of a highpoint in this enterprise was reached in 1903 with the publication of an ambitiously conceived "Everyman's Encyclopedia" (*P'u-t'ung pai-k'o ch'üan-shu*), based on the textbooks then in use in the Japanese middle schools. Fifty of its one hundred volumes were devoted to the natural sciences and various industrial and commercial subjects; history, geography, law, and government accounted for another thirty-six titles; only half a dozen dealt with philosophy or religion, and only one with literature—a history, needless to say, of Japanese literature. These summary figures probably do not include the considerable number of textbooks intended specifically for Chinese consumption or translations that ran serially in the Chinese periodical press both in Japan and at home.

This brings us to one final aspect of Japan's impact on the emerging culture of China after the turn of the century; that is, the Japanese contribution to the creation of a modern vocabulary in almost every area of contemporary Chinese concern. The Chinese language is by nature resistant to the incorporation of phonetic borrowings. Sinified English, for example, is inhibitingly awkward: such terms as *te-mo-k'o-la-hsi* for "democracy" or *sai-en-ssu* for "science" enjoyed only a transient popularity. They retained a distinctly exotic flavor, and gave way easily to Japanese terms based not on phonetic rendering but on Chinese characters: *min-chu* (Japanese *minshu*, "the people as the basis") and *k'o-hsueh* (Japanese *kagaku*, "the study of things in orders and series").

The latter is an example of Japanese inventiveness, a neologism that conveys an idea indigenous to neither the Chinese nor the Japanese intellectual traditions. In other cases the Japanese lifted terms of very ancient usage from their original contexts and adapted them to quite untraditional applications, in which form the Chinese reappropriated them: *min-chu* or *minshu* ("democracy") is one example; *ko-ming* or *kakumei* ("revolution") is another. A comprehensive inventory of these linguistic borrowings would run to hundreds of items, and would include much of the basic vocabulary of modern civilization: "government," "politics," "socialism," "capitalism," "communism," "proletariat," "bourgeoisie," "intelligentsia," and a host of other terms. It has been said that the Chinese language changed more drastically in the first several decades of the twentieth century than in all the centuries of dynastic imperialism from Han through Ch'ing. To this change, and to the equally remarkable change in the Chinese world view which it reflects, the Japanese contributed greatly.

The Chinese thus learned much from the Japanese during these years: something of the mores of the greater world; something of science, both natural and social; something of history and of politics; and, if only as spectators, something of the *feeling* of progress, purpose, and self-assurance. Both by inference and from the message constantly dinned into their ears by radical propagandists, they learned the meaning and importance of nationalism. The lesson that most took home with them is perhaps best epitomized in the lines of "The Song of Diplomacy," a bit of doggerel popular in Japan in the 1880s:

> *There is a Law of Nations, it is true,*
> *But when the moment comes, remember,*
> *The Strong eat up the Weak.* [11]

*   *   *

Notions of the struggle for existence, the survival of the fit, and the inexorably gloomy fate of the unfit became the common language of political and intellectual discourse among Chinese reformers in the early years of the twentieth century. For this, too, the Japanese could claim a share of the credit. Herbert Spencer enjoyed a wide popularity among Japanese liberals, beginning in the 1870s. By the end of the century more than thirty translations of his works were available, including a six-volume rendering of *Social Statics*. (Spencer himself, sought out by Japanese disciples, was adamantly unsympathetic to the liberal reading given to his message; he reportedly approved of the absolutist principles enshrined in the Meiji Constitution of 1889.) The theory of evolution had even been rendered into five- and seven-syllable "new style" poetry by a Japanese enthusiast in the 1880s:

The characteristics the parents possess
Are transmitted by heredity to the children;
The fit go on flourishing,
The unfit perish.
In the present world all that exists:
Bellflowers, pampas grass, the wild valerian,
Plum blossoms and cherry blossoms, clover
and peonies . . . .
And butterflies that alight on the grapeflower leaves,
Song thrushes that warble among the trees . . .

                And even man,
Called the soul of all creation,
His present body and his talents too,
If traced back to their source have all
Little by little, with each generation,
Improved . . .

With an acuteness of vision
Unmatched through all history,
The ones who determined this was so
Were Aristotle, Newton, and one
Neither better nor worse than they in ability,
Mr. Darwin, whose discovery it was,
And, no inferior to him, Spencer,
Who developed the same principles.[12]

Whatever its deficiencies as poetry, this fashionable dithyramb summarized clearly enough the prevailing popular understanding of Darwinism. Neither the Japanese nor the Chinese, however, concerned themselves unduly with the application of evolutionary theory to plum blossoms and butterflies; or even as a key to the understanding of individual human experience. It was for them a revelation of the essential nature of the relationships among human beings in the aggregate, a means to the understanding of national character, and the direction in which history was tending.

By the end of the nineteenth century the Confucian conviction that history can be understood in terms of human moral purpose had been discredited. Even K'ang Yu-wei's bold attempt to link the idea of progress to the achievement of a Confucianized moral destination seemed unpersuasive in the context of China's situation after 1898. By 1902 Liang Ch'i-ch'ao had abandoned K'ang's doctrine of the "Three Ages," and fallen instead under the influence of the writings of Katō Hiroyuki, a Japanese writer who expounded in the social-evolutionary idiom a militant theory of "the rights of the strong" (*kyōken*). For the Japanese the idea carried with it, by the turn of the century, the promise of dominion in Asia. For the Chinese, it posed the question of national survival in stark and uncompromising terms.

Although the Chinese gained some part of their familiarity with Social Darwinism from Liang's writings and from those of other radicals in exile, it was Yen Fu's translations of T. H. Huxley's "Evolution and Ethics" (1898) and Herbert Spencer's *A Study of Sociology* (1903) that fixed Darwinist terms in the Chinese mind as primary categories of explanation. In intellectual disposition and political temperament, Yen belongs to the group that I have labeled "political amateurs," and we will encounter him again in chapter 6. But no account of the intellectual history of the prerevolutionary decade would be complete without a brief description of Yen's contribution to it.

Yen Fu was born late in 1853 or early in 1854 in Fukien province, a hundred miles or so west of the port of Foochow, into a family of modest but well-established gentry status. Yen's father was a respected practitioner of traditional medicine, and enough of a scholar to launch the boy along the way toward a solid classical education before his death in 1866. That event and the economic hardships that ensued forced Yen Fu into a very different pattern of development. He became, in his early teens, a scholarship student at the recently established Naval Academy attached to the Foochow Shipyard, where he pursued a course of study which included English, mathematics, physics, chemistry, and astronomy in addition to naval science. He excelled in these subjects just as, evidently, he had earlier excelled in his study of the philosophers of the Han and the Sung. Yen' appreciation of the literary culture of Confucian China remained with him throughout his life; with it he coupled what was for that time an extraordinarily well-informed command of "Western learning." In 1877 he was sent to England to study naval science first at Portsmouth and then at the Greenwich Naval College. It was during the months he spent there that he gained his familiarity with the recent and contemporary literature of British political economy and social theory, and aquired at first hand a sense of the temperament of Western life.

The career upon which Yen Fu embarked after his return to China in 1879 lived up neither to his attainments nor to his expectations. His outspokenness quickly earned him the distrust of such patrons of the Self-strengthening movement as Li Hung-chang, who used his talents sparingly. He failed repeatedly, moreover, in his attempts to gain a position of greater responsibility through the traditional examination system. Finally, in the mid-1890's, he began to write, and then to translate, on his own. With the publication of 1898 of *T'ien-yen lun* (On Evolution), Yen's reputation was made.

T'ien-yen lun is an annotated rendering of T. H. Huxley's 1893 Romanes Lectures on the relationship of ethics to evolutionary theory. As

Benjamin Schwartz observes in his magesterial study of Yen Fu's thought, it is a work more revealing of the translator's preoccupations than of the author's intentions. Huxley's aim in *Evolution and Ethics* had been to rescue Darwinism from the amoralism of Herbert Spencer's evolutionary scheme of Man-in-Nature. The result was an argument which pitted "ethical nature" against "cosmic nature" in a secular struggle whose outcome Huxley foresaw with, at best, guarded optimism:

> Ethical nature may count upon having to reckon with a tenacious and powerful enemy as long as the world lasts. But, on the other hand, I see no limit to the extent to which intelligence and will, guided by sound principles of investigation, and organized in common effort, may modify the conditions of existence, for a period longer than that now covered by history.[13]

A few of those who read Yen's translation may have gleaned from it something of this confidence; Hu Shih, for example, who like so many others of his generation encountered *T'ien-yen lun* in the course of a prerevolutionary education, managed to remain a pretty cheerful evolutionist to the end. But this was rather despite than because of Yen Fu, who omitted ethics not only from his title, but also from the substance of his interpretation of Huxley's essay. He had been a confirmed Spencerian ever since the early 1880s, when he had read *The Principles of Sociology* for the first time. His interlinear elucidations of Huxley's text were a forceful defense of the Spencerian vision of a Nature indifferent to human moral purpose or intervention, and of Man as but one subject of the cosmic process—a process no more malign than benign, but remorseless. Following Huxley, Yen translated a stanza from Alexander Pope's "Essay on Man:"

> All nature is but art, unknown to thee;
> All chance, direction, which thou canst
>   not see;
> All discord, harmony not understood;
> All partial evil, universal good . . .
>
> One truth is clear, Whatever is, is right.

There was for Yen, however, no such urge as there had been for Huxley, even in his agnosticism, to "vindicate the ways of God to man." Pope's clear truth emerged from Yen's translation altered in sense as well as language: "One principle is now abundantly clear, that there is in creation no intrinsic flaw."[14]

What purpose was there in telling this to the Chinese, distressingly situated as they were in the early years of the twentieth century? Yen Fu was not insensible to the deterministic implications of Spencer's ideas, but neither was he daunted by them, nor particularly faithful to them. *T'ien-yen lun* was intended, we might say, as a silver spike driven through the heart of the unquiet spirit of Confucian moral historiography. But it was also Yen's statement of the terms in which the Chinese must strive to understand the world at large and China's place in it. China is not merely the passive victim of a history beyond human understanding. History, however, must be understood as the record not of moral accomplishment, but of physical and cultural struggle. China reflects the character of its people and their culture. The moral was unambiguous and adamant: that character must change. Struggle, compete—and (perhaps) survive. Yield to the ancient sense of diffident condescension—and (inevitably) perish. In Yen Fu's mind, wealth and power are no longer merely the armor of the state; they are its very essence.

T'ien-yen lun, as Benjamin Schwartz remarks, was "the first serious attempt since the Jesuits to present contemporary Western thought to the literati, and to demonstrate the high seriousness of this thought"; as such, "it was bound to create a sensation."[15] And so it did. Yen approached his task fully cognizant of the cultural differences that any translation must overcome, and himself not a little awed by the profundity of the ideas with which he contended. In this as in all his translations, he addressed himself deliberately to the literati, employing a style as spare, as cryptically subtle, as carefully balanced as a classical text—to which, indeed, some of his readers compared it. Nevertheless he won a wild popularity among the younger generation. His thoughtful rendering of such specialized terms as "evolution" (*t'ien-yen*), "the struggle for survival" (*ching-ts'un*), and "natural selection" (*t'ien-tse*) conveyed a sense of concise authenticity. More than one schoolboy of those years borrowed his *nom de plume*—or *nom de guerre*—from Yen Fu. In English the effect can only be ludicrous: Yang Ching-ts'un, for example, becomes Struggle-for-survival Yang; Wang T'ien-tse must be called Natural-selection Wang. In the circumstances of that time, however, such names sounded both modern and appropriately stalwart.

The first edition of *T'ien-yen lun*, printed from woodblocks, had been published in 1898. In 1905 the Commercial Press in Shanghai brought out a much larger edition. The year 1905 was also a landmark that encompassed the Japanese victory over Russia; the abolition of the examination system; an abortive revolt in the Yangtze area; and, in radical intellectual circles in Tokyo and Shanghai, faintly echoing news of revolutionary upheaval in St. Petersburg. The moment was ripe for Yen's message; thereafter, as Hu Shih recalled, evolutionism "spread like wildfire, igniting the imaginations and strengthening the resolve of innumerable youngsters. . . . Only a few could understand the import of Huxley's contributions to the history of thought and of science. What they could understand was the significance of a formula like 'the survival of the fittest' [*yu-sheng lieh-pai*] in application to international relations.

Such terms . . . became the journalistic jargon of the day, catch phrases on the lips of ardent young patriots."[16] In some respects, perhaps, Yen Fu very soon found himself preaching to the converted.

* * *

From the reminiscences of Hu Shih and others who knew the city then, one gathers the impression that by the first decade of the new century Shanghai had become a hotbed of radicalism, swarming with "ardent young patriots" and seething with sedition. The impression is probably more accurate than not, though it is difficult to substantiate with specific detail. A number of personalities stand out, and several particularly dramatic incidents, around which to piece together a description of the political and intellectual disposition of what Westerners somewhat patronizingly called "Young China" in the waning years of the dynasty.

As we have observed already, imperial edicts authorizing the creation of a modern school system were of little consequence in the absence of textbooks, teachers, and adequate funds. What was achieved along this line was largely the result of initiatives taken by provincial officials, private sponsors, or in some cases the students (or would-be students) themselves. The Pei-yang College in Tientsin and the Nan-yang College in Shanghai, established in 1895 and 1896 respectively under the aegis of Sheng Hsuan-huai, are notable examples of what could be accomplished with official backing even before the turn of the century. Sheng Hsuan-huai (1844–1916) was China's premier *kuan-tu shang-pan* entrepreneur in the 1890s and the early 1900s, enjoying the patronage successively of Li Hung-chang and Chang Chih-tung. The schools in Tientsin and Shanghai were founded as technical institutes, intended to serve as feeders for Sheng's various enterprises: the Hanyang Iron Works, the Hua-sheng Spinning and Weaving Company (formerly the Shanghai Cotton Cloth Mill), the Imperial Railway Administration and others. They were also the agency through which a number of students reached Japan in the early days. Nan-yang served, moreover, as an academic *pied-à-terre* for several of the senior generation of radicals-in-the-making, including some whom we will meet shortly.

"New schools" established under private auspices, sometimes as money-making ventures, sometimes in the spirit of social philanthropy, proliferated at an astonishing rate in Shanghai and the other ports in the first decade of the new century. Many were short-lived. All were small, catering as best they could to the demands of a shifting and sometimes shiftless student population. Any school was "new" that offered rudimentary instruction in Western history, natural science, mathematics, and a foreign language, in addition to more traditional courses in Chinese literature and history. Frequently a Westerner or two from the local foreign community might be enlisted to serve, at least part-time, on the faculty. What is remarkable is that in many cases students who received their introduction to "Western learning" in this catch-as-catch-can academic environment went on to distinguish themselves in their later studies at the great universities of Europe and the United States. Against formidable odds, some brilliant young minds were given shape and direction during these prerevolutionary years.

Political activism, if not outright revolutionary conspiracy, was unquestionably the principal extracurricular activity of most of these young men and women—for there were, in fact, a few young women caught up in the new education and the rising tide of radicalism. The line between academic and political education was impossible to draw in most instances, as the histories of two of the more celebrated educational experiments of those years will serve to illustrate. One of these was the Chung-kuo kung-hsueh (China National Institute), established in 1906 by students who had returned to Shanghai from Tokyo in protest against stringent regulations imposed by the Japanese government at the end of 1905 to curb Chinese student activities. Once home again, their manners proved more than even the worldly-wise Shanghailanders could comfortably accommodate: with clipped hair, dressed out in Western style, or clad in kimono and clattering about in wooden *geta*, they made themselves conspicuous objects of public suspicion. No less startling was the constitution of the school they established. They called it the China *National* Institute (*kung-hsueh*) to emphasize its difference from the many schools which restricted enrollment to a parochial clientele. Students from thirteen provinces constituted the first class, and the medium of instruction was the national language (*p'u-t'ung hua* or *kuan-hua*, what we commonly call Mandarin) rather than the local Shanghai dialect as was ordinarily the case. The China National Institute was organized along the lines of an academic democracy, its administration elected by and responsible to the students, who also participated in the formulation of curricular policy and even in instruction. It is hardly surprising that the school encountered political and financial difficulties almost at once. In April, 1906, the secretary of the student organization, a young Hunanese named Yao Hung-yeh, became so despondent that he threw himself into the Whangpoo River. The apologia he left behind is eloquent testimony to the fevered passions of the time:

> I die in the cause of the China National Institute. . . . I pray that after my death my comrades give no more thought to me, but concern themselves only with the China National Institute. I pray that my four hundred million countrymen will be able to sympathize with one such as I, ignorant and uneducated, without talent and lacking in courage, as I confront my death: let the exalted employ their power, the wealthy give of their wealth, the learned

bestow their knowledge and insight, that by their combined efforts our China National Institute may be supported and sustained.[17]

The most obdurate opposition could not resist the example of such high moral purpose and self-sacrifice: the necessary support was forthcoming, though at some cost to the radical principles of the students. The China National Institute survived, on the campus to which it was later moved in Woosung on the outskirts of Shanghai, until the second Sino-Japanese War—the oldest Chinese-founded private institution of higher education in the country.

The school that had served as a model for the students who established the China National Institute in 1906 had enjoyed a much briefer and an even stormier history. The Patriotic Academy (Ai-kuo hsueh-she) had been established in 1902 and had survived for less than a year. In this short time, however, it had played a role of special importance to the development of the revolutionary movement. The Patriotic Academy brought together, and elevated to prominence, several personalities whose influence was felt long after the school itself fell victim to the forces of political repression; and it was intimately linked with the great radical *cause célèbre* of the prerevolutionary decade, the so-called "*Su-pao* case" in 1903.

The Patriotic Academy was the offspring of the Chinese Educational Association (Chung-kuo chiao-yü hui), created in 1902 nominally to promote the publication of modern textbooks and similar progressive enterprises. The moving spirit behind the association was Ts'ai Yuan-p'ei (1868–1940), a literatus with an interesting background and an even more intriguing future. Born in Shaohsing prefecture, Chekiang province, in 1868, into a once prosperous merchant family, Ts'ai had distinguished himself at an early age as a classical scholar. He won the *chin-shih* degree in 1890 at the precocious age of twenty-two; four years later he attained the pinnacle of Confucian aspiration by being appointed a Compiler of the Hanlin Academy. Then came the Sino-Japanese War, which for Ts'ai as for many others marked a major intellectual and political turning point. He became a promoter of "Western learning," first in Peking and then, after the failure of the 1898 reforms (in which he was not much involved), as the principal of the Sino-Western School (Chung-Hsi hsueh-t'ang) in his native Shaohsing. In 1901 he arrived in Shanghai to join the faculty of Nan-yang College, where he encountered Wu Chih-hui.

Like Ts'ai, Wu Chih-hui (1864–1953) was a classical scholar of considerable accomplishment. The scion of a decrepit Kiangsu gentry family, he had passed the *chü-jen* examination in 1891, but failed to rise further through the examination system. In the late 1890s he taught Chinese at Pei-yang College in Tientsin, and came briefly within the orbit of the K'ang-Liang reformist circle. By the summer of 1898, however, Wu had moved south to Nan-yang College. The events of that year, and the Boxer disaster two years later, brought him to an outspokenly antiauthoritarian position: side with the people in any dispute with the monarchy, was his motto; side with the students in any dispute with their teachers; side with the younger generation in any dispute with the older generation. Such opinions were a trifle advanced for turn-of-the-century Shanghai. Wu was encouraged to pursue his studies in Japan, where he arrived in the spring of 1901. The experience did little to settle his disposition, and in 1902, at the request of the Chinese minister in Tokyo, the Japanese deported him. Wu protested by attempting to commit suicide while en route to Kobe. He was finally escorted back to Shanghai in the protective custody of Ts'ai Yuan-p'ei, who had been on holiday in Japan. Shortly thereafter the Chinese Educational Association came into existence. Not surprisingly, its purposes were not as innocuous as the name suggested.

The principal of Nan-yang College in 1902 when Ts'ai and Wu returned to Shanghai was Chang Yuan-chi (1866–1959)—the same Chang Yuan-chi who, only four years earlier, had accompanied K'ang Yu-wei to his dawn audience with the Kuang Hsu emperor. Chang, too, was a well-accredited Confucian, a *chin-shih* of 1892 (and thus a "classmate" of Ts'ai), and a man of progressive opinions who encouraged the students to read Yen Fu's translations and the radical literature smuggled into Shanghai from Japan. Such instruction was not unanimously favored by the Nan-yang faculty, nor did it meet the approval of the school's official sponsors. In the autumn Chang was dismissed from his post, a conservative administration was installed, and student unrest ripened into active revolt.* In November a number of students withdrew to establish the Patriotic Academy, under the general auspices of the Chinese Educational Association, with Ts'ai Yuan-p'ei serving as the school's principal and Wu Chih-hui as a member of the faculty.

* Chang Yuan-chi went on to a distinguished and influential career with the Commercial Press, one of China's earliest and eventually its largest modern publishing house. His first job was as director of the Press's Compilation and Translation Department, which earned enormous profits from the publication of textbooks, many translated from the Japanese. In 1904 Chang established and served as the first editor of *Tung-fang tsa-chih* ("The Eastern Miscellany"), published monthly by the Commercial Press as a magazine of general news and commentary and documentary record; moderate in its political position, *Tung-fang tsa-chih* soon became one of China's most widely read and trusted outlets for liberal opinion, and the most durable: it survived the vicissitudes of the warlord period, the ideological pressures of the Nanking era, the hardships of the Sino-Japanese War, and the civil war of the late 1940s, ceasing publication finally in 1949.

Chang Yuan-chi was named general manager of the Commercial Press in 1920, and ten years later became chairman of the Press's board of directors. In these positions, he was instrumental in the compilation and publication of several landmarks in the history of modern scholarship in the 1920s and 1930s: the *Ssu-up ts'ung-k'an*, a great compendium of classical literature; the *Po-na* edition of the twenty-four dynastic histories; and a collection of rare books included in the *Ssu-k'u ch'üan-shu*. He remained a political progressive to the end of his long life, an adamant critic of the Nationalist regime in its final years, and twice elected to the National People's Congress in the 1950s—a remarkable end to a life that had begun when the T'ung Chih "Restoration" was at its height.

From its inception the Patriotic Academy was as much a political as an educational enterprise. The students, as Mary Rankin characterizes them in her study of Shanghai radicalism, "wanted to control their own affairs, discuss current policies and 'advanced theories,' display their patriotism, hold meetings, and do a little studying in between."[18] Military drill was a regular part of the curriculum. The students frequently gathered on the grounds of a nearby estate known as "Chang's Garden," where they discussed the political issues of the day; before long they were receiving academic credit for these "debates." Ts'ai Yuan-p'ei, it is said, included instruction in the manufacture of bombs as part of the chemistry course he taught—a memorable revolutionary vingette, or at least a worthy revolutionary legend. Clearly, the mood of the times was changing.

A few Shanghai publishing houses and bookstores donated textbooks to the Patriotic Academy, and some progressive individuals provided funds, but like similar ventures the new school was financially hard-pressed. In 1903, therefore, the students and faculty worked out an arrangement with the *Su-pao* (The Kiangsu Gazette), Shanghai's leading radical newspaper in 1902–1903, to contribute articles in return for a monthly subsidy. In May of that year Chang Shih-chao, a student at the academy, became the *Su-pao's* editor, and within a few weeks the "*Su-pao* case" burst upon the Shanghai intellectual world. For the Patriotic Academy it marked the beginning of a quick demise. For the revolutionary movement as a whole, however, it was one of the events that marked the emergence of a clearer distinction between the fervent but vague radicalism of the past and a firmly articulated antimonarchist revolutionary ideology.

The *Su-pao* case directly involved two personalities connected with the Patriotic Academy. Chang Ping-lin (1868–1936), a classical scholar of enormous erudition and idiosyncratic opinions, already celebrated for his outspokenly anti-Manchu views, had joined the faculty in March 1903. Shortly thereafter a young Szechwanese named Tsou Jung (1885–1905) enrolled in the Academy. Tsou had been a student at Dōbun shoin in Tokyo during the preceding winter, until his activities brought him to the unfavorable attention of the Ch'ing Inspectorate of Students. He had fled Japan one step ahead of the officials sent to deport him, and arrived in Shanghai carrying with him the manuscript of a brief anti-Manchu tract which he had written as a school exercise in the course of his Japanese sojourn. With a laudatory preface by Chang Ping-lin, Tsou's *Ko-ming chün* (The Revolutionary Army) was published in May and took the country by storm.

> To sweep away the despotism of these thousands of years, to cast off the servile nature bred in us over these thousands of years, to exterminate the five million and more hairy and hornèd Manchus, to expunge the pain and anguish of our

two hundred and sixty year humiliation, to cleanse the great land of China. . . . this most exalted and incomparable aim is Revolution! How imposing a thing is revolution! How magnificent a thing is revolution! . . .

Unjust! Unjust! The most grievous injustice in China today is to endure as our ruler these untameably wild nomads, this contemptible race of contemptible Manchus. For us, getting ahead in the world means crawling to them, cringing and fawning, bowing and kowtowing—drunk with delight, it would seem, to be their subjects; shameless, insensible to our own plight. Ah, my countrymen, you have no sense of mastery! Ah, my countrymen, you have no sense of national character! Ah, my countrymen, you have no sense of racial character! Ah, my countrymen, you have no sense of independence![19]

In June, *Su-pao* reprinted Chang's preface to *The Revolutionary Army*, together with several enthusiastic reviews, and a number of other inflammatory anti-Manchu essays. It also published Chang's "Open Letter in Refutation of K'ang Yu-wei's Views on Revolution," a vituperative diatribe against the Manchus and a scornful denunciation of the constitutionalists' stubborn hope that the Ch'ing would, or could, serve as the agency of genuine reforms. For the Kuang Hsu emperor, whom K'ang still held in affectionate esteem, Chang had nothing but ridicule: "Tsai-t'ien is a low comedy character who can't tell the difference between beans and wheat!"[20] The insult was rude enough in itself; but to refer thus to the emperor by his personal name—Tsai-t'ien—was an outrageous contravention of rigid customary taboo, an act of *lèse majesté* that figured prominently in the charges soon brought against Chang.

All this was too much for the authorities. Pressed by the Shanghai taotai and by incensed provincial officials, the Shanghai Municipal Council, the governing body of the International Settlement, closed down both the *Su-pao* and the Patriotic Academy. The warrants issued for the arrest of Ts'ai Yuan-p'ei and Wu Chih-hui were useless: by prudent coincidence, both had left the city. Wu departed shortly for Europe, not to return until after the revolution in 1912. Ts'ai soon reappeared in Shanghai. In 1904 he was named president of the Restoration Society (Kuang-fu hui), a revolutionary organization comprised largely of young radicals from his native province of Chekiang. When the Restoration Society was absorbed into the Revolutionary Alliance (T'ung-meng hui), Sun Yat-sen's Tokyo-based party, Ts'ai became the secretary of the Shanghai branch. His affiliation with these organizations seems to have been more nominal than substantive, however; eventually Ts'ai too embarked on his European *Wanderjahre*, becoming in his middle age a student of philosophy and psychology at Leipzig. We will hear more of him anon.

Tsou Jung and Chang Ping-lin were, of course, the principals in the *Su-pao* case. Once assured that they would not be extradited to Chinese jurisdiction, but tried in the Shanghai Mixed Court, they surrendered to

Settlement police. After a lengthy trial they were convicted of sedition. The Chinese judges urged life imprisonment for both, but public opinion, Chinese and foreign, was generally sympathetic, and the final sentences were kinder: two years for Tsou, three for Chang, to include the year that had passed since their arrest. Unfortunately, Tsou Jung's constitution proved less sturdy than his rhetoric. In prison he sickened and died, a martyr to his cause at the age of twenty. But he had made his point, and his reputation. Despite the best efforts of the government, *The Revolutionary Army* continued to circulate widely. It was reprinted in Hong Kong, Yokohama, and Singapore, and several times in China; it was laboriously hand-copied by candlelight in school dormitories in the dead of night; it was smuggled, upon occasion, through the foreign postal service. Tsou Jung's niche in the annals of the revolution was secure.

Chang Ping-lin survived the rigors of imprisonment, occupying his time with scholarship and poetry. On his release in 1906 he was escorted in triumph to Tokyo by a delegation dispatched for the purpose by the Revolutionary Alliance, and there installed as one of the new party's luminaries. Thither we must return with him at this point, to examine in greater detail the issues that animated the ongoing political and intellectual life of the exile community.

* * *

As Chang Ping-lin observed, Tsou Jung's *The Revolutionary Army* was something that even peddlers and butchers could understand. Neither in logic nor in language was it a subtle argument. Its appeal lay not in any pretension to originality, but in the directness of its address and the eloquence with which it organized the clichés of the moment: the invocation of the liberating spirit of revolution; the virulent attack on the Manchus, coupled with a detailed indictment of their tyranny; the rehearsal of Darwinist assumptions; the ardent appeal to the historical greatness of the Hans; the affirmation that freedom and equality are the natural human condition; the importance attached to civic education in preparing the people to assume their proper political responsibilities. All these were familiar themes in the polemical literature of the radical emigré community in Japan—and at the time when Tsou was there, in the winter of 1902–1903, this was the message preached not only by the self-styled revolutionaries, but also by the reformers who advocated the inauguration of a constitutional monarchy.

Monarchism proved in the end a losing cause. But Liang Ch'i-ch'ao, its principal spokesman, was indisputably the dominant intellectual figure, the great broker of ideas, throughout much of the prerevolutionary decade, exercising an influence that went far beyond the advocacy of a particular political program. Inexhaustibly energetic and insatiably inquisitive, Liang was the first and greatest transmitter of late-Meiji intellectual concerns to a Chinese readership. He had plunged into the study of Japanese while still on board the Japanese gunboat that smuggled him out of Tientsin in the autumn of 1898; it was the only foreign language he mastered, despite a life-long effort to gain command of English or French, but he put it to excellent use. Essays flowed from his brush in endless profusion, written in a style distinctively his own and singularly forceful. As he himself observed, no sooner had a subject caught his attention than he would begin to expound upon it. So we find him writing about the unification of Italy and the partition of Poland, the colonial subjugation of Annam and Korea, and the history of ancient Sparta. He composed biographical introductions to a host of Western philosophers, political theorists, and patriots, among them Descartes, Spinoza, Hobbes, and Rousseau; Cromwell, Cavour, Mazzini, and Kossuth. He held forth at length on the qualities of mind and character which his countrymen must learn if they hoped to survive in the new age that was upon them. Looking back upon these years of youthful enthusiasm from the disenchanted decade of the 1920s, Liang faulted himself for having been intellectually self-indulgent, superficial, and inconsistent. K'ang Yu-wei had too many fixed ideas, Liang remarked, while he himself had too few. Yet of the many writers who championed the radical cause in the early years of the new century, Liang Ch'i-ch'ao stands out as perhaps the most ingratiating, a man of engaging candor and attractive warmth in his personality and in his opinions. He judged his own role with considerable insight: he was, he said, a rebel who contributed mightily to the overthrow of the established order, only to be overwhelmed by the forces which shaped the new age—"the Ch'en She of the new intellectual world."[*][21]

There was nothing in Liang's family background or his childhood to suggest the nature of the role he would play. He was born, in February 1873, in the Hsin-hui district of Kwangtung province, not far from K'ang Yu-wei's native Nan-hai, and closer still to the district of Hsiang-shan where, seven years earlier, Sun Yat-sen had been born. Liang's was a genteel family. Generations of peasants had produced, in his grandfather, a scholar. Liang's father too attained the *hsiu-ts'ai* degree, and earned his living as the village schoolteacher. Like almost every Chinese who ever made a name for himself, Liang Ch'i-ch'ao was reputed to have been an astonishingly precocious child. In his case the claim is evidently

---

[*] Ch'en She is credited with having first raised the banner of revolt against the tyrannical Ch'in dynasty in 209 B.C. "When Ch'in rule failed," wrote Ssu-ma Ch'ien, "Ch'en She marched forth. The lords sprang to revolt like a great wind rising, like clouds that cover the sky, until the house of Ch'in at last crumbled. All the world took its cue from Ch'en She's rebellion." (translated by Burton Watson: *Records of the Grand Historian of China*, vol. 1, p. 19.) The comparison is not entirely flattering to Liang: Ch'en She's eventual failure is attributed by Ssu-ma Ch'ien to the distrust or indifference which he inspired in his onetime followers.

substantial: he became a *hsiu-ts'ai* at the age of eleven, and only five years later, in 1889, he passed the provincial examinations to obtain the *chü-jen* degree. In the early 1890s he tried several times, unsuccessfully, to win the *chin-shih* degree in the metropolitan examinations—but by that time his perspectives were already changing. In the spring of 1890, returning via Shanghai from his first visit to Peking, Liang became acquainted with Hsu Chi-yü's geography—by then some forty years out of date—and with several of the translations turned out at the Kiangnan Arsenal. "Then for the first time I learned of the five continents and their various countries," recalled this exemplary product of the orthodox Confucian educational regimen. "I coveted these books, and could not resist buying them."[22]

Only a few years earlier, and in much the same stumbling manner, K'ang Yu-wei had discovered the world. It was in the summer of 1890 that Liang was introduced to K'ang in Canton. In later times he was able to assess his teacher's eccentricities and shortcomings with considerable detachment, but that first encounter, when Liang was only seventeen, left him thunderstruck—feeling, he recalled, as though he had been beaten about the head and doused with cold water. Forthwith he renounced his allegiance to the Han Learning which until then had preoccupied him, and proclaimed himself K'ang's disciple.

This meant, among other things, adherence to the New Text persuasion. Liang accepted the fundamentals of K'ang's interpretation of Confucianism as a rationale for reform, but without the fervent religious enthusiasm of his master. Liang's real contribution to the reform movement of the 1890s lay in the area of political organization and propaganda, not philosophical and textual disputation. He had a hand in drafting the memorial submitted by K'ang on behalf of the assembled degree candidates in 1895, protesting the terms of the Treaty of Shimonoseki. He was active in the organization of the Ch'iang hsueh hui. In 1896–1897 he edited the Shanghai *Shih-wu pao*, the reformers' major propaganda organ. In the winter of 1897–1898 he taught at the Shih-wu hsueh-t'ang (Current Affairs Academy) in Changsha, patronized by Hunan's progressive governor, Ch'en Pao-chen. These involvements naturally brought him into contact with many of the most innovative and interesting men of the time: T'an Ssu-t'ung, who would sacrifice his life for the reform movement in 1898; Chang Chih-tung's protégé Wang K'ang-nien, who managed the *Shih-wu pao;* Huang Tsun-hsien (1848–1905), a diplomat who had served in Tokyo, San Francisco, London, and Singapore, and who was the preeminent Japan expert of his generation; Timothy Richard, busily diffusing the message of salvation through progress; Yen Fu, who let Liang read the manuscript of *T'ien-yen lun.* By the time Liang received the imperial summons in the summer of 1898, he was widely acquainted in reformist circles, an apt choice to undertake the duties assigned to him as head of the ill-fated government translation bureau.

Liang Ch'i-ch'ao was only twenty-five when he fled to Japan in the autumn of 1898. He was forty when he returned again to China. In the course of the intervening fifteen years he made several excursions to rally support for the Pao huang hui, including a tour of North America in 1903 that proved to be a turning point in his political and intellectual development. Most of this time, however, he spent in Japan—studying, teaching, organizing, debating, and writing, writing, writing. Within weeks of his arrival Liang launched his first political journal, the *Ch'ing-i pao* (Journal of Disinterested Criticism, to borrow Chang Hao's translation of the title), its costs largely underwritten by the Chinese merchants of Yokohama, with Liang serving as editor and principal contributor. It was not intended, Liang insisted, to promote a narrowly partisan point of view. Its aims, as he set them forth, were to disseminate knowledge (*che-li*), especially foreign ideas; to unmask the decadence and corruption of Court politics; and to impress upon its readers the inescapable laws of international relations: that struggle is the price of survival, and that only the fit may hope to endure. Beyond this, Liang wrote, "*Ch'ing-i pao* takes as its paramount aim the promotion of popular rights [*min ch'üan*]. . . . The seas may dry up, rocks may split and crumble, but our party [*tang*] will not cease its labors until this principle is universal throughout our country."[23]

The Ch'ing Court recognized the challenge, and tried to deal with it. Chang Chih-tung demanded that *Ch'ing-i pao* be suppressed soon after the journal made its first appearance. A year later, in February, 1900, even as the Boxer movement spread through the northern provinces, the Emperor endorsed (at the Dowager's behest, of course—and one wonders with what private emotions) an edict bitterly condemning his erstwhile mentors as "utterly depraved" and "intractably rebellious." "Indeed, it makes the hair stand straight up in anger!" The considerable sum of Tls. 100,000 silver was offered as a reward for K'ang and Liang, dead or alive. (Alternatively, appointment to brevet rank might be conferred "without regard to the usual formalities"—revealing testimony to the cash value of elite status.) The reformers' writings were ordered burned and banned; those caught in possession of such subversive literature were to be summarily and severely punished.[24]

The interdiction had little effect. Liang retained his liberty, and *Ch'ing-i pao* continued to publish, and to circulate widely in Japan and China, until a fire in the Yokohama printing works brought it to an end in December, 1901. Less than two months later Liang embarked on what was to become an even more memorable venture. Early in February, 1902, the first fortnightly issue of *Hsin-min ts'ung-pao* (The New People's Miscellany) was published in Yokohama. For the next five years it served as the principal outlet for reformist opinion in the increasingly heated debate with the revolutionary party.

In the early years of his exile, from the time of his arrival in Japan in 1898 until his return from the United States in 1903, Liang was in a "radical" frame of mind, outspokenly hostile to the Manchus and critical even of the monarchical institution. During this time his views were often closer in temper to those of the enemies of the imperial regime than to those of the emperor's self-proclaimed defender, K'ang Yu-wei. K'ang's initial stay in Japan had been brief. The reform party claimed a number of influential Japanese patrons; nevertheless, in the spring of 1899 the Japanese government, bowing to Ch'ing demands, advised K'ang to leave—at the same time covertly providing him with funds for the journey and assuring him that nothing would be done to hinder the promotion of the reformist cause.

Liang Ch'i-ch'ao, who remained in Japan, was of course the principal beneficiary of this liberality. In the months that followed the relationship between master and disciple was strained almost to the breaking point as Liang intensified his attack on the abuses perpetrated by the despotic institutions of Confucian imperialism. With K'ang at a safe distance, and with a good deal of Japanese encouragement, tentative negotiations were undertaken to bring the anti-dynasts together in a united movement. Nothing came of it in the end: political differences, personal jealousies, and an irreducible cultural gap divided the major protagonists. K'ang regarded Sun Yat-sen as "unlettered"; in Sun's view, K'ang was "a rotten worthless Confucian."[25] From afar, K'ang brought to bear upon Liang all the authority of his position as Teacher; and Liang, though his confidence in K'ang's philosophical convictions was rapidly waning, accepted nevertheless his obligations as a Follower.

Liang wrote so much, and on such a diversity of subjects, that no resumé can do more than partial justice to the full range of his ideas. Certain recurrent themes, however, suggest the nature of his central concerns at this time: freedom, and its opposite, the slavish nature bred by centuries of subjection to autocracy; individualism, and the countervailing claims of society or the community (ch'ün); progress, struggle, and the dreadful peril of remaining bound to traditional norms and attitudes. Encompassing all of these was Liang's dedication to nationalism, and to the creation of a politically responsive and responsible citizenry—a "new people" (hsin min) that would make the nation a vital and enduring reality. Liang knew that "China" existed as an historical fact, however prejudiced its future; he knew the "Chinese state" existed as a political entity, however anachronistic its institutions. Why, then, did not China exist as a nation? And how could the Chinese nation be created de novo, without at the same time destroying the very things—historical memory, cultural identity, the inherited sense of political unity—that justified

China's claim to nationhood? Liang had no clear or consistent answers to these vastly troubling questions. But he put the questions themselves with greater force than did any other writer of his time; and in his search for answers he did much to shape the categories of explanation, and to create the vocabulary, in which his countrymen would perceive and articulate the issues of China's survival for at least a generation.

Until his trip to the New World in 1903, Liang was largely preoccupied with the question of China's failure to develop the sense of national identity and purpose that would enable it to compete successfully in the struggle for survival. The answer, he thought, must reside in the character of the people, deformed by the institutions that had governed their lives since time immemorial. "The first stage in the evolution of society is tribalism [*pu min*], not nationalism [*kuo min*]. When the people of a tribe become the people of a nation, this is the step from barbarism to civilization. Wherein lies the difference between tribe and nation? When a community is divided into clans which govern themselves according to their own customs, we call this tribalism. When the idea of nationalism is abroad, and the people themselves constitute their own government, we call them citizens [*kuo min*]. The history of the world has never witnessed the existence of a nation without citizens."[26] Why, then, had not the Chinese taken the step from barbarism to civilization? Because "autocracy wears away the character of the people like the steady drip of water. Nature endows Man with rights; with the ability to exercise these rights; with the capacity to protect these rights. If the people are left to govern themselves in freedom, then the ability of the community to govern itself must steadily improve. . . . But treat them as slaves, guard against them as against thieves and brigands, and the people will act as slaves, as thieves and brigands; given the opportunity to shirk, or to turn a profit, even at the expense of family and business, they will seize it. . . . The reason that China does not progress in self-government [*ch'ün-chih pu chin*] is because the people have no regard for the common good; they have no regard for the common good because they have lived as slaves and thieves; they have lived as slaves and thieves because tyrants have made the empire their private domain and property, and have made slaves and thieves of my people."[27]

When he wrote the essays from which these excerpts are drawn, a series entitled "On the New People" (*Hsin min shuo*), which began in the first issue of *Hsin-min ts'ung-pao*, Liang was untroubled by doubts as to the native political instinct of the Chinese people or the relevance of his political ideals to China's condition. "'Give me Liberty or give me Death'—these words expressed the basis on which the peoples of Europe and America established their nations in the 18th and 19th centuries. Is this great principle of freedom applicable to China at the present time? I say: Freedom is a universal principle [*kung li*], and a human necessity, useful and appropriate in any circumstances."[28] What then was to be done? First, the people must be educated to perceive the predatory nature of existing institutions. "Those who would be citizens must look upon the autocracy as the common enemy of the people."[29] More important still, the people must be educated to undertake their proper responsibilities, as individuals and as members of the greater political community. Aristotle was right: Man is a political animal. But Darwin and Spencer were right, too: natural faculties atrophy from disuse.

Therefore the Chinese people must learn to exercise their political talents individually. For "a nation's citizenry is made up of individuals, and a nation's sovereignty consists in the aggregation of the rights of individuals. If therefore we want our people to think and to feel and to act as citizens, this cannot be accomplished if we ignore the thoughts, feelings and actions of the individuals who constitute the parts of the whole. That nation is strong whose people are strong; that nation is weak, whose people are weak. . . . "[30] What was called for was a new sense of self-respect (tzu-tsun) and public morality (kung te), and a new spirit of daring. "There is no resting place in the world: if you don't forge ahead, you fall behind. Life has its joys and its afflictions; if you won't risk difficulties, then you fall into danger. As I survey the international scene today, no country is falling behind faster, or stands in greater peril, than our China—and I am greatly afraid. There is more than one reason why the peoples of Europe are stronger than the Chinese; but of special importance among them is the fact that Europeans are rich in the spirit of taking risks in order to forge ahead." This particular exhortation ended—a bit anticlimactically—with a verse, printed in the original English:

> Never look behind, boys,
>   When you're on the way;
> Time enough for that, boys,
>   On some future day.
> Though the way be long, boys,
>   Face it with a will;
> Never stop to look behind
>   When climbing up a hill . . .
> Success is at the top, boys,
>   Waiting there until
> Patient, plodding, plucky boys
>   Have mounted up the hill.[31]

From the outset, however, Liang's concern for the reshaping of individual character was justified by a concern for the creation of a sense of membership in the political community as a whole. Individualism was not a sufficient end, or even a social good, in and of itself; it was the essential means to larger ends—nationalistic ends. So Liang wrote in 1900:

> Those who entertain no idea of self-benefit [*li chi*] must inevitably abandon their rights, abdicate their responsibilities, and ultimately lose their independence. . . . In the West there is a saying to the effect that Heaven helps him who helps himself. No calamity in life is greater than the failure to help oneself, hoping only that help will be forthcoming from others. . . . But no man can survive alone in the world, and for this reason the community comes into existence. Living within the community, among one's fellows, it is of course impossible to live completely to oneself, paying no heed to the question of whether something beneficial to oneself may harm others. . . . Thus those best able to benefit themselves must first be of benefit to the community. From this will follow benefit to themselves.[32]

Set against the background of a social ethic which, from the time of Mencius, had warned against the consequences of "selfishness," such commonplaces of Victorian social philosophy conveyed to Liang's Chinese readers a much more startling message than we can read out of them.

Liang Ch'i-ch'ao's early confidence in the ability of the Chinese to bear the burden of self-motivated progress diminished with the passage of time and the accumulation of frustrations. He held to the view that national character is determined by individual character, and on this count he remained bitterly critical of the abuse of civic talent by the Chinese autocracy. But increasingly the question of how to save China without resorting to methods that would in all likelihood destroy it came to preoccupy him; and less and less was he able to believe that the sense of civic responsibility essential to China's survival would manifest itself as a result merely of the destruction of autocratic restraints. Any such simplistic and drastic "solution" to China's problems, Liang came to feel, invited only disaster: political disintegration, a new tyranny proclaimed in the name of "democracy," and a final and decisive imperialist assault upon the defenseless remnants of the Chinese state.

The American tour that Liang undertook on behalf of the Pao huang hui confirmed his disenchantment with the revolutionary approach to China's predicament. He left Japan in February, 1903, bound for Vancouver. He spent two months in Canada and five in the United States. His itinerary was arranged to bring him into touch with as many as possible of the Chinese who had emigrated to the New World—more than 100,000 by the turn of the century, living in the congested, busy Chinatowns of New York and San Francisco—the Chinese laundrymen, restaurateurs, and houseboys of American legend; or those scattered in isolated railroad and mining towns, scavengers of the profligate wealth of the raw western hinterland. Thus Liang traveled from coast to coast and back again; from Vancouver to Ottawa to Boston and New

York; as far south as New Orleans; up through the midwestern heartland, and again across the Rockies. He was a superb tourist: sharp-eyed, strong-legged, quick to register impressions of people and places, open to amazement but sufficiently self-assured not to be unnerved (though often appalled) by the rush and clamor of American life. His account of the journey is crammed with facts and figures: immigration statistics, annual corporate revenues, expenditures on naval armaments, public and private welfare expenditures in New York City. But it is also full of shrewd observations and deftly sketched land- and city-scapes. Liang was horrified by the airless stench of New York's tenement districts, the streets crowded with ragged people listless in the summer's heat; wretched worlds unto themselves, for "the tramlines do not penetrate these quarters, and even carriages are few." The seductive springtime fragrances and the calculated symmetry of the nation's capital, on the other hand, enchanted him; and the mountains of Montana moved him to song. It amused him that Americans would lavish money on a tomb for Ulysses S. Grant, having allowed the former president to die in poverty. It astonished him that Americans would safeguard a wilderness in the very heart of New York City: "The rents that might be earned from Central Park, were it turned over to commercial development, would amount to three or four times the annual revenues of the Chinese government!" The great public libraries, full of books and crowded with silent readers, impressed him greatly. This was indeed a mythically wealthy, varied, and strange land.

Liang was welcomed as something of a celebrity, if not quite as a dignitary. Newspapers heralded his passage: "Dream of Big Republic Thrills All Chinatown. Leong Kai Cheu Rouses Latent Patriotism of Meek Mongolians. . . . Oriental Marc Antony Tells Chinamen How they Have Only Been Slaves. . . . " "Big Chinaman Comes . . . to Lecture to Local Celestials." So read the headlines, from Boston to Walla Walla.[33] J. P. Morgan granted him an audience; Liang was speechless with awe. John Hay, the Secretary of State, listened attentively for two hours to his account of recent political developments in China; Liang was gratified. President Theodore Roosevelt received him at the White House and suggested that if he intended to promote civic virtue among Chinese he could not do better than to begin with the Chinese in Chinatown; Liang was silent. He was, in fact, already coming to the same sobering conclusion. The habits of his countrymen, viewed in this unfamiliar setting, did not encourage him. True, he had encountered a promising few studying at Harvard, Columbia, Berkeley, and elsewhere. But on the whole his contacts with "local Celestials" had been distressing. He was by no means blind to the racial discrimination that limited the range of opportunity for his compatriots in America, especially those who lived cut off from any sizeable community of Chinese. But on the other hand, Liang acknowledged that no Chinese in China lived in an environment as congenial to the nurturing of civic responsibility as did the Chinese populations of Boston, New York, or San Francisco. By contemporary Chinese standards these were prosperous and well-favored communities. Their inhabitants were educated, or at least literate; there were newspapers—six Chinese-language papers were published in San Francisco at that time—and considerable opportunity for political organization and self-expression. Yet the Chinatown Chinese remained parochial in their concerns, divided and exploited by political gangs, clannish rather than public spirited, slaves to tradition rather than progressive, dedicated to the pursuit of selfish gain and indifferent to the larger welfare of the community. On the evidence he himself presented, Liang could no longer contend that the Chinese were "natural" citizens, held back only by autocratic repression. As he prepared to embark for Japan in October— he sailed, by a pleasant irony, aboard the Canadian Pacific liner *Empress of China*—Liang offered this pessimistic summary of his findings:

> Freedom, constitutionalism, republicanism: these are but the general terms which describe majority rule. But China's majority, the great, the vast majority of Chinese, are as I have described them here. Were we now to resort to rule by this majority, it would be the same as committing national suicide. Freedom, constitutionalism, republicanism—this would be like wearing summer garb in winter, or furs in summer: beautiful, to be sure, but unsuitable. No more am I dizzy with vain imaginings; no longer will I tell a tale of pretty dreams. In a word, the Chinese people must for now accept authoritarian rule; they cannot enjoy freedom. . . . Those born in the thundering tempests of today, forged and molded by iron and fire—*they* will be my citizens, twenty or thirty, nay, fifty years hence. *Then* we will give them Rousseau to read, and speak to them of Washington.[34]

This was the mood in which Liang returned to Yokohama, persuaded that the cherished ideals of earlier years must be abandoned. "I do not mind criticizing myself of yesterday with myself of today," he wrote. His farewell to "myself of yesterday" was nevertheless a cry of heartfelt pain:

> Woe is me! Republicanism! For ten years I have been drunk on it, I have dreamed of it, I have sung its praises. . . . Now I must take leave of it . . . Republicanism! Republicanism! I love thee, but not as much as I love my fatherland, nor as much as I love freedom. As fate would have it, you do not point the way to fatherland and freedom for us. As human nature dictates, our fatherland and our freedom would be sacrificed in your hands. Alas! Republicanism! Republicanism! I cannot bear again to defile thy sweet name, lest those who talk of politics should have still more reason to revile thee. Some will ask, Is it then that you now favor constitutional monarchy? Not so, say I. For indeed, my thought has regressed, so that even I cannot comprehend the change. I return from America to dream of Russia.[35]

These sentiments were set forth in an essay entitled "The Theories of the Great Political Scholar Bluntschli," published in *Hsin-min ts'ung-pao* a few months after Liang settled again in Japan. Johann Kaspar Bluntschli (1808–1881) had been, in point of fact, a not very notable Swiss-German professor of jurisprudence at Munich and Heidelberg, whose exposition of the theory of the "organic" state and monarchical authority had earned him the esteem of Japanese interested in promoting similar ideas in the 1870s and 1880s. Katō Hiroyuki, from whom Liang borrowed much of his understanding of Darwinist theory, had translated a portion of Bluntschli's *Allgemeines Staatsrecht* in the early 1870s, and Katō's influence on Liang is doubtless in evidence here. Certainly Liang had come to share Katō's view that it would be madness to entrust the future of the nation to an uneducated and irresponsible mass, prone to dereliction of civic duty and an easy prey to demagoguery. Like Katō, Liang had come to believe that progressive change—the prerequisite to national survival itself—could only be achieved under the guidance of a tutelary autocrat. For all the vehemence, and the evident sincerity, of his earlier attack on the autocracy, Liang had never burned his bridges to monarchism. In 1902, in the same essay in which he had admonished his readers to look upon the autocrat as the great enemy of the people, he had cautioned them also to discriminate between an irresponsible autocracy and a responsible monarchy. It was a distinction to which he returned, in somewhat different terms and much more elaborate form, in a long essay "On Enlightened Autocracy" that ran serially in several issues of *Hsin-min ts'ung-pao* early in 1906.

Liang stated his argument bluntly: for China, it is not a question of preference, but of necessity. Autocracy (*chuan-chih*) is the form of government best suited to certain times and circumstances: the circumstances of a new nation, or one just delivered from barbarian despotism*; of a nation recovering from great destruction, or one in which government has been weak and ineffective; of a nation whose people are uneducated, whose area is extensive, whose population is ethnically diverse. Measured by any or all of these standards, China requires autocratic government. Autocracy, however, assumes many forms, of which monarchy is only one; history also records both aristocratic and popular autocracies. It is not, then, by its composition that the merits of autocracy should be soley judged, but also—and far more important—by its level of competence, and by the spirit which animates it,

* What Liang meant by "barbarian" despotism, in this case, was not the Manchus. The distinction he drew was between the kind of autocratic rule exemplified, on one extreme, by the unprincipled and self-gratifying government of Louis XIV; and, on the other extreme, by the far-sighted statesmanship of Frederick the Great. Throughout the essay, Liang uses the term *chuan-chih* in a variety of contexts; he seems to mean by it, in the final analysis, any government which is not modified by the participation of representative institutions in the decision-making process.

its underlying motives. Like any form of government, autocracy can be evil; a "popular" autocracy, Liang maintained, was likely to be the worst possible. But a government dedicated to the achievement of national strength, organized to administer an impartial justice, and conscientiously mindful of the needs and feelings of the people, should not be rejected simply because it is "autocratic." What Liang advocated was just such a government, an "enlightened" (*k'ai-ming*) autocracy. Without it, he warned, China must abandon even the hope of survival in the fiercely competitive century into which it had entered.

So Liang rejected the idea of a constitutionally limited monarchy, and renounced, for the time being, the ideal of popular rights (*min ch'üan*) to which a few years earlier he had declared himself imperishably devoted. Constitutionalism, he reasoned, must encompass parliamentary rule. But how can a parliament mediate the interests of a people too politically immature to articulate their own interests, or even to recognize them? In any case, parliamentary politics as practiced in the West really meant cabinet politics, and cabinet politics came down to party politics, and party politics eventuated in the dictatorship of the party leadership. In the prospect of such partisanism Liang saw no promise of the kind of unity of purpose and dedication to the common good that, he believed, was essential to China's salvation.

Liang had, indeed, "regressed." The Russia that inspired him was not the Russia of revolutionary idealism and anarchist self-sacrifice that had briefly aroused his admiration in the earliest years of his exile; still less the blindly reactionary autocratic regime that would excite his contempt in 1905. It was the Russia of Peter the Great of which he dreamed again, as he had during the Hundred Days. His aim was not to justify the status quo, or to ingratiate himself with the Manchus. The Kuang Hsu emperor was not the "enlightened autocrat" of Liang's hypothesis: 1898 had taught that lesson all too painfully. Indeed, Liang's argument was vulnerable to the criticism that, however persuasively he might put the case in favor of an enlightened autocrat, no likely candidate to play the role existed in fact. His detractors were thus able to denounce him as both reactionary and impractical. But such criticism missed Liang's point. His advocacy of enlightened autocracy was at the same time an argument against easy acceptance of the idea of popular sovereignty as a sufficient end in itself; and, even more pointedly, against the idea of a "democratic" revolution as the infallible remedy to the sickness of the age. "China today is in fact an autocratic monarchy. Nothing short of a revolution could transform it into a constitutional republic. But revolution cannot bring that republic into being. On the contrary, its only result would be the creation of a new tyranny."[36] The only fruits of revolution would be demagoguery and the chaos of mob rule, and this could not meet the crisis of the times. Instead, Liang argued, existing in-

stitutions must be invested with new purposes. "What China most conspicuously lacks today, and stands in most urgent need of, is an organic
unity and a forceful ordering of priorities. Why? Because a tribal people
[pu min] must be forged into a united citizenry [kuo min] before we can
begin to speak of the welfare and happiness of the citizens."[37] Liang had
used the same terms earlier. But then he had been willing to entrust the
step from tribalism to citizenship, from barbarism to civilization, to the
untutored instinct of the people. Now he was convinced that such a fundamental transformation could go forward only under the guiding hand
of a benign tutelary power.

Thus the issue was joined. By 1905 any hope that Chinese radicals
might make common cause against a common enemy had vanished. The
revolutionary movement, dedicated to means and to ends which Liang
had now explicitly rejected, attained greater organizational coherence
than it had previously enjoyed with the establishment of the T'ung-meng
hui—the Revolutionary Alliance—in August 1905. It also gained a
stronger voice, with the launching a few months later of the Min pao
(The People's Report) to serve as an outlet for revolutionary opinion. The
revolutionaries, no less than Liang, put the creation of a Chinese nation
at the top of their list of priorities. But the nationalism of the Revolutionary Alliance was aimed at the accomplishment of a single overriding
purpose: the liberation of the Han people from subjection to the alien
Manchu dynasty.

*   *   *

Anti-Manchuism was far from a new element in Chinese thought, as
we have seen; nor was it, at the turn of the century, a reliable measure to
distinguish revolutionaries from reformers. Radicals in the 1890s and the
early 1900s had at their disposal a considerable corpus of seventeenth-
century "Ming loyalist" literature which they mined with energy and
skill. Huang Tsung-hsi's Ming-i tai-fang lu was a staple item in the
radical propaganda of those years, as was Wang Fu-chih's Huang shu
(The Yellow Book), a violent attack on the Manchus and an impassioned
invocation of the greatness of the descendants of the Yellow Emperor. A
horrifying eyewitness account of the destruction of the city of Yangchow
and its population by the Manchus in 1645 was widely circulated. Anti-
dynastic rebel movements, especially the proto-nationalism of the Taipings, were recalled with admiration. The general temper of "progressive" opinion was antiauthoritarian, antimonarchical, and—at least by
implication—anti-Manchu.

The publication of Tsou Jung's The Revolutionary Army in 1903 contributed, as we have seen, to the emergence of a sharper distinction between revolutionary and reformist points of view. It is symptomatic of
the times that one of the great figures in Tsou's pantheon of revolutionary

heroes was T'an Ssu-t'ung, who had offered himself as a martyr to the cause of reform in 1898. T'an Ssu-t'ung (1865–1898) was a well-born Hunanese, the misunderstood son of a conservatively conventional bureaucrat. The younger T'an was neither conservative nor conventional. In the 1890s, while his father was serving as the governor of Hupeh province, T'an Ssu-t'ung became an active member of the reformist group that congregated in the neighboring province of Hunan at the invitation of its forward-looking governor, Ch'en Pao-chen. He was a close friend and collaborater of Liang Ch'i-ch'ao, through whom he came under the influence of K'ang Yu-wei's ideas. The work for which T'an is best remembered, *Jen hsueh* (The Study of Humane Affection), is a visionary synthesis of Confucian, Buddhist, and Christian ideals that comprises variations on several themes enunciated by K'ang: an attack on the tyranny of traditional social relationships; a celebration of the miracles of technological progress; and the dream of a utopian future, an age of "great harmony." But *Jen hsueh* also contains sweeping denunciations of the despotism of imperial institutions and the injustice of Chinese subjection to barbarian rule:

> The idea that the empire belongs to the ruler, that he has it, as we might say, in his pocket, is not of recent origin; it has been with us for several thousand years. But . . . the evils perpetrated by the [barbarian dynasties] Liao, Chin, Yuan and Ch'ing surpass the despotism of anything that had gone before. Theirs is a poor and dusty land; theirs a people who stink like the sheep they tend; their hearts the hearts of animals; their customs the customs of the yurt. Supreme in their talent for savage cruelty and stealthy murder, one day they invade our heartland, steal our children, plunder our treasure. Our land is trampled beneath the hooves of their horses, and laid waste.[38]

In September 1898 T'an refused to flee from the fate that he knew must overtake him. "In no country have great reforms been accomplished without the shedding of blood," Liang recalls him saying. "Until now, China has not heard of blood being shed in the cause of reform, and therefore the country does not progress. Let it begin with Ssu-t'ung."[39] Together with K'ang Yu-wei's brother and a few others, T'an was arrested and summarily executed. Liang carried the manuscript of *Jen hsueh* with him to Japan, where it was published posthumously in *Ch'ing-i pao*. Little wonder that Tsou Jung was impressed.

A sense of racial identity fed by ancient cultural pride and by the inculcation of Darwinist imperatives was thus the first fruit of nationalism in China. Anti-Manchuism was not the only issue preoccupying the minds of revolutionaries in the first decade of the twentieth century, but it tended increasingly to permeate the ongoing political debate between revolutionaries and reformers. Thus the question of Chinese sovereignty was argued not primarily in terms of Chinese rights vs. Western imperialism, but in terms of Han subservience to Manchu overlordship. The question of political participation was argued not only by weighing the relative merits of democracy vs. enlightened despotism as political systems, but also in terms of the Manchus' willingness to initiate, or even to tolerate, a significant liberalization of the political process. The question of "wealth and power"—that is, the administration of a program of economic modernization—was addressed in terms of whether it would profit the Chinese people or serve only as a prop to sustain the eroding power of the alien conquerors. In his study of prerevolutionary intellectual trends, Michael Gasster has speculated that the revolutionary movement might have been better prepared to confront the enormous tasks of reconstruction that awaited it on the morrow of 1911 had not so much of its energy and its intellectual resources been expended, in the prerevolutionary years, in the effort to develop an anti-Manchu rationale to dispute the claims of the constitutional monarchists. The fact that the Manchus vanished quickly and completely in the wake of the 1911 revolution—not only as a political force, but also as an ethnic or cultural community of any significance—lends credence to the view that anti-Manchuism was, if not a bogus issue, at least inflated beyond proportion to its true importance. Yet given the nature of the Confucian monarchy, its ideology and its traditions, it is not hard to understand why the general problem of political change should have been inextricably linked with the specific issue of Manchu dominance.

It was, of course, effective propaganda to depict the Manchus as T'an Ssu-t'ung did, and Tsou Jung, and many other writers including, upon occasion, Liang Ch'i-ch'ao: as barbaric nomads, filthy and stinking, dressed in animal skins and governed by crude tribal custom. This did not, however, accord very well with the political or cultural realities of the situation. Grievous as may have been their shortcomings as custodians and defenders of the Confucian monarchy, the Manchus certainly were not savages. Yet the attempt to argue the case against them in more elaborately reasoned terms of essential biological differences between Han and Manchu was not without its difficulties, as is illustrated by Chang Ping-lin's exposition of his own brand of nationalist-racist theories.

Chan Ping-lin was born in Chekiang in 1868, into a family of well-established scholarly traditions. At an early age he developed an enthusiasm for the Han Learning, and a concommitant interest in the protest literature of the late Ming and early Ch'ing periods. Thus estranged from the existing regime, Chang eschewed the examinations and devoted himself in his twenties to historical and philological scholarship as a student at one of the celebrated classical academies of Hangchow. He was provoked into a more activist political role by the shock of the Sino-Japanese war in the mid-nineties, and became an early member of K'ang

Yu-wei's Ch'iang hsueh hui. This brought him into contact with Liang Ch'i-ch'ao, with whom he collaborated for a time on the Shanghai *Shih-wu pao*. Chang's unabashedly anti-Manchu sentiments were already well known, however, and as an "Old Text" adherent he was divided also on doctrinal grounds from K'ang's reformist coterie. He was nevertheless among the intended victims of the purges that began in September, 1898. For the next several years he moved around a good deal, taking refuge briefly in Taiwan, teaching for awhile in a mission-run school in Soochow, and twice traveling to Japan where, finally and bitterly, his connection with the K'ang-Liang party was severed. Even before the *Su-pao* case brought him to prominence in 1903 Chang had already enunciated his principles of racial struggle in a short work entitled *Ch'iu shu* (translatable, if at all, as "A Testament to Persecution"), written in 1902. Upon his triumphal arrival in Tokyo in 1906, Chang became the editor of *Min pao*, a position which afforded him ample opportunity to enlarge on the racial theories which were his principal contribution to the revolutionary cause.

Chang Ping-lin's racial nationalism was based on evolutionary ideas that he derived partly from the writings of Wang Fu-chih and partly from Herbert Spencer, some of whose essays Chang had helped to translate in the late 1890s. From Wang, Chang appropriated the concept of an evolving sense of group identity corresponding with the differentiation of species and cultures. Wang's "evolutionism" was historical and cultural rather than biological in its categories, and moral rather than physiological in its motives. It constituted nevertheless a startling departure from orthodox Confucian theory, and Chang found it not incompatible with Spencer's concepts of differentiation-from-unity and complexity-from-simplicity. Chang also borrowed from Wang Fu-chih the conviction that the Han Chinese claim as their common progenitor—metaphorical if not literal—the Yellow Emperor, legendary predecessor of Yao, Shun, and Yü. Spencer provided the generally progressive framework within which to set these several notions, and to display the historical evidence which Chang assiduously marshaled to prove his case against the Manchu conquerors.

Chang's justification for affirming a distinctive Han indentity was the belief that cultural differences reflect underlying racial differences. The idea of cultural assimilation is a chimera, he proclaimed. Manchus remain Manchus, however hard they may try—however well they may even succeed—to conceal the fact beneath a veneer of Sinified culture. Following a number of contemporary Japanese writers, Chang further distinguished between "civilized" and "barbaric" races. He included in the former category both the white and the yellow races, which shared similar histories of victimization at the hands of a predatory barbarian neighbors. But the "yellow race" is obviously a much more comprehensive category than that of the "Han people," whose spokesman Chang was. On what grounds is it possible to discriminate against elements of the former without at the same time condemning the latter? Chang conceded that culture—that is, the attainment of a level of civilization that differentiates a given people within the encompassing ethnic environment—does in fact establish the identity of a people (*chung-tsu*) within the larger category of the race as a whole (*min-tsu*). But it is not enough, Chang insisted, simply to ascribe cultural identity. True to his evolutionary principles, he contended that a distinctive culture comes into existence through adaptation, and that it can be maintained over time only through use. The existence of a culture means little unless it is confirmed by an awareness, on the part of those who participate in it, of the identity thus created. The community which the culture delineates can only be sustained by a continuing cultural consciousness. Thus the Chinese are "descendents of the Yellow Emperor" not merely, or even necessarily, in a strictly biological sense, but as active communicants in an ongoing culture.

It is possible, in other words, for the Chinese to lose their "Chineseness," a point Chang illustrated with historical examples of Han frontier outposts which had with time lapsed into "barbarism." But if this is possible, is not the obverse then also possible? Might not non-Han peoples be acculturated if they subscribe to the values of the Han? This was, of course, the crucial question insofar as the issue of the Chinese-Manchu relationship was concerned. Chang avoided such a damaging concession by asserting that self-rule is the essential requirement of cultural identity. It was, to be sure, an argument that cut two ways. So long as the Han culture remained politically subservient to aliens, this must be taken as evidence that the Han people lack the spark of national consciousness and have therefore not fully realized their racial-cultural identity. But on the other hand, while the Manchus might become "Sinified," the very fact that they continued to impose themselves as rulers upon the subject Han gave the lie to their cultural pretensions and branded them as unregenerate barbarian overlords.

Chang Ping-lin's nationalism was thus racial in its categories, but cultural and political in its objectives and justifications. It is the community's awareness of the common culture that imparts the sense of nationhood, Chang asserted, and self-rule that confirms its existence. The original premise—that culture is itself determined by racial characteristics—was thus muted, but not entirely abandoned: it remained a useful argument to justify rejection of those aspects of China's traditional culture to which Chang was opposed. Since "Chineseness" takes precedence (historical and/or logical) over "Confucianism," fidelity to Han culture does not require uncritical acceptance of the political and intellectual traditions of the imperial order. In common with his revolutionary colleagues, for example, Chang regarded the Confucian monarchy as an oppressive bureaucratic despotism. Yet he remained a cultural nationalist, unable in the final analysis to distinguish between the Han as a biologically or racially distinct community and the Han as heirs to a cultural legacy that was, at least in the broadest sense, Confucian. Chang's sense of history was vivid and affectionate; his deepest instincts were conservative.

> What sets mankind apart from the birds and the beasts is precisely the sense of past and future. If it is said that the sense of the past should be swept away, then men will also be cut off from a sense of the future, and know only the passing moment. What use, then, to bemoan the misfortunes of a thousand years, or to busy oneself with plans for the improvement of society?[40]

It is worth noting that these sentiments were addressed to a small group of Chinese anarchists (among them Chang's old colleague at the Patriotic Academy, Wu Chih-hui) who were promoting the adoption of Esperanto, "the new international language," in the pages of *Hsin shih-chi* (The New Century), published in Paris. This was the point at which Chang Ping-lin the revolutionary encountered Chang Ping-lin the Han Learning scholar and philologist. The Chinese language, in Chang's view, is the distilled essence of Han culture. It is a living link to the past when China, no less than Greece and India, emerged as one of the great seminal civilizations, and it remains the most important factor contributing to a sense of continuous cultural identity. Chang therefore accorded the classical language a reverential respect, and he took a kind of private delight in exploiting its arcane peculiarities to the utmost. Even in essays written to serve the polemical purposes of the revolutionary movement, Chang's style was enshrouded in an aura of high scholarship and frequently marked by an almost impenetrable erudition. "I could not even punctuate the sentences let alone understand them," recalled one of the students* who read Chang's *Min-pao* essays; "and the same was true of many young people in those days. . . . I liked this paper, not because of [Chang's] old-fashioned and difficult prose style or his dissertations on Buddhist philosophy and 'bilateral evolution,' but because of his campaigns against Liang Ch'i-ch'ao who was for retaining the monarchy. . . . He really put up a gallant and inspiring fight."[41]

Chang Ping-lin has been described as an "ethnically nativist" thinker whose ideas "logically led to a more tribalized image of the future, in which the values Chinese treasured could only comfort and strengthen a special, parochial community."[42] As a theorist of race and nation, Chang was the spokesman of the Han community at large. As a scholar, however, he spoke for, and to, the elite community of the classically

---

* The student was Lu Hsun, who later became the first and probably the greatest master of vernacular style.

cultured. The vehemence of his anti-Manchu opinions and his scholarly prestige reinforced each other to make him inevitably a leading revolutionary figure. Racial nationalism (*min-tsu chu-i*) was probably the most politically significant of Sun Yat-sen's "Three Principles" in the pre-revolutionary years, and Chang was certainly among its most subtle and eloquent proponents. He was, however, frequently at odds with his colleagues in the Revolutionary Alliance. The parochialism noted above contrasted sharply with the general temper of "progressive" opinion, which held nationalism to be the means whereby China would enter the *marche générale* of history. More important still, Chang was bitterly hostile to all forms of political authority. He had no confidence in the efficacy of government as a redemptive agency; in him there ran the corrosive scepticism of the Taoist critic of Confucian moral-political activism. Thus he rejected not only the central premise of Confucian statecraft, but also the political idealism that inspired and animated revolutionaries and reformers alike. In an essay caustically entitled "On the Four Varieties of Humbug," written in 1908, Chang stated his case in these terms:

> What the ancients regarded as sacred and unopposable, they called "fate." What modern man regards as sacred and unopposable, he calls "universal principles" [*kung li*], or "progress," or "materialism," or "nature." . . .
>
> Man is not born for the sake of the world, or society, or the nation; or bound by any reciprocal relationships to others. Originally, therefore, he owes nothing to society, or to the state, or to other men. Such obligations come later: a man must first owe something to another, before he has anything to repay. . . .
>
> That no harm be done to another is the only constraint governing the conduct of man in society. To go further than this, to hope that the multitude will display virtue, is an unrealistic hope. The advocates of nationalism expect the people to "do their duty"; even such skills as medicine and engineering are regarded as a form of service to the state. This is no more than the residue of feudal custom. . . .
>
> If I labor wholeheartedly for the benefit of others, seeking neither emolument nor reward, this is because of a love that lies within me, not dictated by some law outside myself . . . . One should not be condemned for acts which harm oneself but not others; nor for acts which are beneficial to oneself but not to others. Only an act which results in injury to others may be condemned. This is called transcendent impartiality [*ch'i wu*]; it is quite a different thing from universal principles [*kung li*].*

* *Ch'i wu* is a term with strong Taoist connotations. *Ch'-i wu lun*, translated by Burton Watson as "Discussion of making all things equal," is the title of the second chapter of the *Chuang Tzu*. (See Burton Watson, trans.: *The Complete Works of Chuang Tzu*, N. Y., Columbia University Press, 1968.) In this context, "things" refers not to material possessions or social position, but to fundamental epistemological distinctions; this is the chapter that ends with the famous parable in which Chuang Tzu dreams that he is a butterfly, and upon waking wonders whether he may not be in reality a butterfly dreaming that it is Chuang Tzu. It

Half the countries of Europe are founded on religion, and not far removed from feudalism. Those [Europeans] who claim profound insight into the human mind and heart contend that man is born for society, not for himself; that he should contribute all he possesses, his full talent and strength, to the community as a whole. Originating as a political and religious injunction, this has come to be regarded as customary; and since it is customary, it has been confused with what is natural to human motives.[43]

This blend of the ideas of J. S. Mill, Hsun-tzu, and the philosophical Taoists could hardly be read as a call to revolutionary self-sacrifice. It is not surprising that even before 1911 Chang Ping-lin had acrimoniously parted company with many of his erstwhile comrades. He acknowledged the revolution when it came: the end of the dynasty had long been his aim, and the coincidental demise of the monarchy did not unsettle him as it did K'ang Yu-wei. With the eviction of the Manchus, however, Chang believed that the revolution had accomplished as much as could be expected of it. He did not welcome the Republic. Though all government was suspect, in his view, none was more contemptible than "representative" democracy. By 1918, after several humiliating forays into the jungle of postrevolutionary politics, Chang had retired completely from public life, to devote his last years to scholarship. He managed to preserve his integrity, never becoming a servant of political reaction. Until his death in 1936, however, he remained a staunch cultural conservative, nurturing and defending with all the enormous resources of his scholarship and his pen the Chinese "national essence" (*kuo ts'ui*) against the ever more insistent claims of a generation of "Westernizers."

* * *

Chang Ping-lin, then, was a powerful but not entirely a representative spokesman for the revolutionary cause. We may doubt, indeed, whether the movement had a "representative" spokesman, so diverse, so frequently cacophonous were the voices raised in its behalf. The overthrow of the Manchus was the political aim, on the one extreme, of tradition-bound and semi-literate secret society elements, some of whom still proclaimed allegiance to the Ming dynasty; and, on the other extreme, of a handful of social revolutionaries and undoctrinaire anarchists whose political philosophies were as diffuse as they were radical. Within the catholic ranks of the Revolutionary Alliance were some who favored the creation of a strong centralized government, and others who favored no government at all; anti-imperialists or xenophobic nationalists and cosmopolitan Westernizers; provincial gentry leaders and bandit chiefs. All were committed to a change of regime. But there was little common

---

is this frame of mind which Chang Ping-lin here contrasts with *kung li*, meaning the Western disposition (echoed by Liang Ch'i-ch'ao and by many of Chang's revolutionary comrades-in-arms) to think and speak in terms of absolute moral-social imperatives.

ground for them to occupy once this purpose had been accomplished. The full history of the revolution of 1911 in all the complexity and diversity of its social components and political motives has yet to be impartially written. The ideas that animated it—or we might better say, its published purposes—are more easily perceived through the pages of the revolutionary press.

Of the many revolutionary periodicals that came and went in the decade before 1911, none was more important in respect to the stature of its contributors or the influence of their opinions than *Min pao*, the official organ of the Revolutionary Alliance. The first issue of *Min pao* was published in Tokyo in November, 1905—or, as it announced in large type, in the 4,603rd year since the founding of China (*Chung-kuo k'ai kuo*). That event was dated from the reign of the Yellow Emperor, whose idealized portrait (a bearded face, proud, stern, and pensive) appeared as the frontispiece of the new journal under the legend: "The world's first nationalist hero." Rousseau and Washington came next, "the world's first democrat" and "the world's first founder of republican government" respectively; and finally Mo-tzu, "the world's first advocate of equality and universal love." As time went on, the illustrations in successive issues of *Min pao* were less benign, featuring conspicuously a mixed bag of terrorist assassins and their victims, before and after. But nationalism or racialism, republicanism and/or democracy, and dedication to humanitarian ends—even if achieved by terrorist means—remained the characteristic aims of the Revolutionary Alliance, and of *Min pao*. The party's published platform comprised six planks tacked to the skeleton of Sun Yat-sen's "Three Principles of the People": (1) to overthrow the present evil government (in the appended English version, "evil" became "autocratic"); (2) to establish a republican political structure; (3) to preserve genuine world peace; (4) to nationalize the land; (5) to promote amity between the Chinese and Japanese peoples; and (6) to seek international support for the Chinese revolutionary enterprise.* A further purpose of *Min pao*, unstated but by no means unimportant, was to provide the revolutionary movement with a weapon to press its attack against the reformist case so eloquently argued by Liang Ch'i-ch'ao in his rival publication. Many of the articles published in *Min pao* were written explicitly "in refutation of the recent views of *Hsin-min ts'ung-pao*" on this or that issue of current contention.

Sun Yat-sen's contribution to the development of the revolutionary message preached by *Min pao* is difficult to assess. He was thirty-nine

---

* "*Chung-kuo chih ko-hsin shih-yeh,*" literally, "the task of renovating China." To the end of his life, Sun hoped for more generous and sympathetic assistance to his cause than was forthcoming from the Western powers. The hope seems sometimes at odds with the anti-imperialism that figured ever more emphatically in Nationalist ideology in Sun's later years; but anti-imperialism itself was at least in part a result of Sun's repeated disappointments.

years old in August, 1905, when he was elected Tsung-li, or director, of the newly-organized Revolutionary Alliance in Tokyo. By whatever means he achieved this eminence—and Sun's most fair-minded biographers have not found it easy to explain—it was not by the force of intellect and ideas. Alone of the personalities on whom this history has touched, Sun was the offspring of a family not only without scholarly traditions, but also, apparently, without scholarly aspirations.

Born in November, 1866, in the village of Choy-hung in the Pearl river delta north of Macao, Sun received only a rudimentary traditional education before being shipped off, at the age of twelve, to live with an older brother who had established himself as a merchant in Hawaii. From that time forward his mind was shaped by Western rather than Chinese educational experiences. He graduated from Iolani College, an Anglican mission school, in 1882. After a brief and evidently miserable visit to his native village, he continued his education at Queen's College in Hong Kong. In 1886 he embarked on the study of medicine, first at Paak Tsai Hospital School in Canton, the oldest mission hospital in China, and then at the Alice Memorial Hospital established by Ho Kai in Hong Kong. By 1892 Sun had become a certified surgeon and physician, and a baptized Christian. He found himself unable to launch a satisfactory private practice in Macao or Canton, however, and in 1894 when he traveled north to Tientsin to offer his services to the great Li Hungchang, he was met with indifference. This rebuff, coupled with China's defeat by Japan in 1895, may have been what turned him irrevocably against the imperial regime. In any event, within the next twelve months Sun had established his first "revolutionary" organization, the Hsing Chung hui (Revive China Society), among overseas Chinese in Honolulu, and was deeply involved in the Canton conspiracy that condemned him to exile.

Sun was preeminently an astute manipulator of political aspirations, not a theoretician. Harold Schiffrin characterizes his ascendancy within the revolutionary movement as the result of "entrepreneurial leadership in the sense that the leader provides no original ideas, only the means for achieving what everyone feels is required."[44] Sun was not, to be sure, entirely without ideas. His "Three Principles of the People" (*San min chu-i*), first enunciated in 1905, comprised the essence of progressive opinion at that moment: racial nationalism (*min-tsu chu-i*), democracy (*min-chu chu-i*), and finally, as it is sometimes rendered, socialism (*min-sheng chu-i*). A part of Sun's genius lay in his ability to deliver such optimistic generalities with persuasive conviction. The task of exposition, elaboration, and disputation he preferred to leave to others.

Nevertheless, as the party's leader Sun contributed a brief dedication which appeared in the first issue of *Min pao*. "In any group there exists an especially qualified minority, those most capable of planning in accordance with the needs of the group, to assure the progress of the group as a whole. . . . This is the pioneering mission of our *Min pao*, to insure that the ideals of the most progressive theories may enter men's minds and become common knowledge. . . . "[45] This was Sun's only offering to the new undertaking; there is even some uncertainty as to whether he wrote the statement to which he signed his name. Be that as it may, the notion of a "revolutionary vanguard" hinted at here was to figure importantly in the later history of Sun's party.

Chang Ping-lin served as editor of *Min pao*, with brief intervals, from soon after his arrival in Tokyo in July 1906 until the journal was suppressed by the Japanese authorities in the autumn of 1908. A number of men younger than he, and perhaps basically more in sympathy with the republican visions of the movement, had charge of the enterprise before Chang's arrival on the scene, and they continued to share the responsibility for expounding the revolutionary message in the years that followed. Sung Chiao-jen (1882–1913) and Ch'en T'ien-hua (1875–1905) were both central figures in the contingent of Hunanese student radicals that formed an important component in the Revolutionary Alliance. Sung, who had arrived in Japan at the end of 1904, edited a short-lived publication called "Twentieth-Century China" (*Erh-shih shih-chi chih Chih-na*), the precursor of *Min pao*. He remained a regular contributor of commentary on the passing scene to the new magazine, though his principal responsibilities in connection with the Revolutionary Alliance lay in the area of organization. Ch'en T'ien-hua, on the other hand, was primarily a propagandist, a reformer turned revolutionary—a tormented man whose brief affiliation with the Alliance ended on a tragic note. He had been sent to Japan on provincial scholarship in the spring of 1903, and promptly enrolled in the Kōbun gakuin to study Japanese. Politics, however, quickly took precedence over education. "From the moment he arrived in Japan," Ch'en's roommate recalled, "he concentrated his energies so completely on the business of patriotic propaganda that after six months he still could not speak even a word of Japanese."[46]

In the circumstances it was an understandable preoccupation. The Chinese student community was just then in a particularly militant mood, awash in a tide of nationalist reaction against the threat of Russian advances in Manchuria. The patriotic effort to organize a student volunteer corps was viewed with dismay by the Ch'ing, especially after the students turned out in some force for small-arms drill. In response to Chinese diplomatic representations, the "Student Army" was eventually disbanded by the Japanese government, with predictable consequences: radical sentiment hardened, and the revolutionary movement gained many converts. One of these was Ch'en T'ien-hua; before the year was out he had returned to Hunan and was actively engaged in revolutionary conspiracy and polemics. "The Harsh Awakening" (*Meng-hui-t'ou*), the first of the tracts on which his fame rests, was written in the months that followed. The second, "A Tocsin for the Age" (*Ching-shih-chung*), was composed after Ch'en returned to Tokyo toward the end of 1904. Both were inflammatory and quickly banned; both were widely circulated in Japan and China and were wildly popular.

"A Tocsin for the Age" is remarkable for its style; unlike the general run of polemical literature, revolutionary and reformist, it is written in a fluent vernacular that closely reproduces the nuances of the colloquial language. It is remarkable, too, for the violence of its anti-foreignism:

> Kill! Kill! Kill! People nowadays all say that China is very weak, that it has few weapons, and therefore how can it wage war upon the foreigners? They have a point. And if the foreigners had not come to carve up our China, we certainly would not stir up trouble unprovoked, aping the Boxers. But now they disregard whatever we may say, and without any justification they come to carve us to pieces. . . . Rather than allowing ourselves to be cut to pieces all unawares, it would be better to put a price on our dismemberment by killing a few of them. As the saying has it, a dog driven to the wall will turn and attack. Do you mean to tell me that four hundred million men are less than a dog at bay? If the foreign soldiers do not come, then there's an end to it. If they do, then I make bold to exhort every man to screw up his courage, and to have no fear of them. Students, lay aside your brushes. Tillers of the soil, put down your spades and your hoes. Merchants, close up shop. Craftsmen, put away your tools. Sharpen your knives, all of you; look to your ammunition. . . . Kill the foreign devils [*yang-kuei-tzu*]; kill the traitors who have gone over to the foreigners, the compradores and Christian converts [*erh-mao-tzu*]. If the Manchus help the foreigners to kill us, then we will first exterminate the Manchus. If thievish officials help the foreigners to kill us, then we will first exterminate the thievish officials. . . . My beloved countrymen! Advance—Kill! Advance—Kill! Advance—Kill! Kill! Kill! Kill those who have been our enemy from generation to generation. Kill our great enemy from without. Kill the traitors who have sold out to the foreigners. Kill! Kill! Kill![47]

Western imperialism hung like a pall over the minds of China's early revolutionary nationalists. For the most part, however, writers for the Revolutionary Alliance treated imperialism as a sinister presence in the background, an evil brought upon China by the weakness and venality of the Ch'ing government. Rescue China from the Manchus, they argued, and its subjection to foreign oppressors would thereby be ended. Ch'en T'ien-hua was one of the few who put anti-imperialism ahead of anti-Manchuism, or who gave such impassioned expression to anti-Western sentiments.

Despite differences in temperament and emphasis between himself and other revolutionary spokesmen, Ch'en joined the Revolutionary Alliance in the summer of 1905 and contributed several essays to the first issue of *Min pao* when it appeared in November. The Chinese student community was again in turmoil, as a result of restrictions imposed by the Japanese government on student political activity, and the increasingly critical, even derogatory, treatment accorded to Chinese students in the Tokyo press. By year's end some two thousand students had returned to China in angry protest—this was the crisis, it may be recalled, that led among other things to the establishment of the China National Institute in Shanghai early in 1906. Ch'en T'ien-hua's protest assumed a different form, and had in fact a different motive. Early in December, 1905, he drowned himself in Edo Bay. The second issue of *Min pao* published his photograph: a square, strong countenance framed by hair cut long in imitation of the Taiping rebels. It also published his final warning to the age.

> Alas, my countrymen—who among you sees China as it truly is today? China today has lost its sovereignty; its rights have vanished. Pessimism is universal; optimists no longer exist. If there remains a single thread of hope, it is that the number of students abroad increases day by day. Gradually the grip of custom will relax; progress will be steady; all will be moved by patriotic sentiment to devote themselves to their studies in order to save the fatherland. Ten or twenty years from now, things must take a turn for the better. But as I survey my fellow students today, while it is certainly true that their numbers have increased, still there are not a few faults that can be pointed out. . . . Their aim is to seek their own fortunes, not to shoulder their responsibilities."[48]

Ch'en's suicide was a despairing admonition, a private sacrifice intended to stand as a public rebuke.

Ch'en T'ien-hua's gloomy assessment notwithstanding, there were still optimists to be found in the ranks of the Revolutionary Alliance. Foremost among those upon whom fell the burden of expounding the hopeful message of the revolution in the pages of *Min pao* was a trio of Cantonese student radicals: Hu Han-min (1879–1936), Wang Ching-wei (1883–1944), and Chu Chih-hsin (1885–1920). All were the sons of minor bureaucratic functionaries—*mu-yu*, or private secretaries in the employ of appointed officials. All had received conventional classical educations, constrained by the poverty that was their common lot. All had arrived in Japan on government scholarship. And all were among the founding members of the Revolutionary Alliance in 1905. They shared a timely antipathy to the Manchus and a scornful distrust of the aims of the constitutional monarchists. Collectively, however, Hu, Wang, and Chu were the most eloquent spokesmen for those idealistic aspects of revolutionary ideology that went beyond the immediate aim of the destruction of the dynasty: republicanism, confidence in the ability of the people to assume unfamiliar political responsibilities, and a concern for the social consequences of political change.

These were the concerns addressed by the second and third of Sun's "Three principles," *min-chu chu-i* and *min-sheng chu-i*. Neither term is unambiguous. *Min-chu* means, literally, "the people as the basis"; *min-sheng* may be rendered "the welfare of the people," or as it is more often found in Sun's own writings, "the people's livelihood." Both ideas have classical connotations reminiscent of Mencius. Closer at hand, both have antecedents in the protest literature of the seventeenth century and in the Statecraft collections of the nineteenth century. The notion that "the people are the basis" may be used to justify allegiance to republican principles and/or to democratic political processes—or to neither, as in the case of traditional Confucian reformers. A commitment to republicanism was explicitly empasized in the propaganda of the Revolutionary Alliance; democracy remained an implied promise of the revolution, though its institutions were never described in terms of specific processes and responsibilities. The revolutionaries were far more anxious to assert the collective rights of the Chinese people against the claims of the Manchu autocrat than they were to affirm the right of the individual either to participate in the political process or to seek protection from it. "What we demand is the freedom of the collectivity [*tsung-t'i*], not the freedom of the individual," wrote Ch'en T'ien-hua in the inaugural issue of *Min pao*. "If we construe republicanism in terms of the freedom of the individual, then indeed we will go far astray. Under a republic, the majority decides, and it cannot but infringe upon the freedom of the minority."[49] Wang Ching-wei put the same idea more positively: "What is the citizenry [*kuo min*]?" he asked. "It is that constituency which creates the state, united in freedom, equality and universal affection. This is the spirit which informs the fundamental law of the state [*kuo-fa*], which is simply the general will of the citizenry. . . . Oh, may my people be transformed by nationalism from a race into the citizens of a nation!"[50]

In an essay published in the third issue of *Min pao* in April, 1906, intended partly by way of rebuttal to Liang Ch'i-ch'ao's advocacy of enlightened autocracy, Hu Han-min enlarged upon the revolutionaries' "six great principles." His discussion of republicanism summarizes as aptly as any single example of revolutionary propaganda the political assumptions and expectations of the movement, and deserves to be quoted at some length.

> It is generally acknowledged that destruction without construction is senseless. Nor is construction something that can be postponed: preparation must precede action. This is a point on which we differ with the anarchists. We believe that the present level of citizenship of the Chinese people renders anarchism infeasible. The longstanding prerogatives of the alien government must be destroyed. At the same time, the autocratic system of government which has endured for thousands of years must be restructured [*kai-tsao*]. Only then can we preserve the race in the struggle for survival.
>
> That autocracy is unsuited to the present age is beyond dispute. . . . In the twentieth century, the first concern of those who wish to establish a new

political order must be the destruction of autocracy, root and branch. There have been successive changes of regime [ko-ming] in China in the past. None have in the end proved effective, because it has not been possible to alter the basic political structure. . . . If the aliens are expelled, but those who replace them—albeit of the same race as the people—maintain the autocratic structure as of old, this cannot fail to disappoint the heartfelt desires of the people.*

According to accepted theories of government, republicanism stands at the opposite pole from autocracy. Broadly speaking, there are three categories of republicanism: aristocracy, absolute democracy, and constitutional democracy. Constitutional democracy differs not only from aristocracy, but also very greatly from absolute democracy. Conventional people nowadays insist that there are no democratic customs in the history of our race, and alas! on these grounds they discourage our young patriots. Not only are they ignorant of the study of government; they are moreover incompetent to discuss history. Of the problems experienced by the several nations which have established constitutions, none is more difficult than the struggle of the common people against both the monarchy and the aristocracy. The establishment of constitutional rule and the extension of democratic government was uniquely easy in America because at the time of independence there were only the common people. And this is indeed one of the peculiar features of our own political history, since in our country the aristocracy vanished at the time of the Ch'in and the Han dynasties. (The only exeptions, unimportant in themselves, are the ranks of nobility maintained under the Mongol and Manchu dynasties in accordance with their alien systems.) Thus we have only to strike down the Manchus in order to destroy inequality among us. (Even the United States still has economic classes, whereas none exist in China.) In comparison to the experience of others, the establishment of a constitutional regime will be, for us, a simple and easy matter.

But now we hear from the most up-to-date legal scholar [i.e., Liang Ch'i-ch'ao] who tells us that before a constitution can be enacted there must first be a period of enlightened autocracy. The "enlightened autocrat" takes the cultivation of democracy as his aim and democratic methods as his means, to train his people and instill in them the character of citizens of a constitutional regime. . . . But as far as China is concerned, enlightened autocracy prevailed long ago, at the height of the Han and T'ang dynasties; nor was its influence entirely eradicated even by the disorders consequent upon subjugation to alien rule. Those who cite history as evidence that out people cannot implement a republican form of government or enact a constitution know not whereof they speak. . . .

There must be a revolution, before we can talk of establishing a constitution. and on the morrow of the revolution, we must strive for the fairest and best political system. . . . Absolutism, whether monarchical or democratic, is unprincipled and inegalitarian. Constitutional monarchy preserves the distinction between those who govern and those who are governed, and from the sentiments which attach to this distinction, classes arise. It is otherwise with con-

* Hu uses the the historical example of the Ming dynasty, which evicted the barbarian Yuan, (that is, the Mongols), in the fourteenth century only to establish its own despotic rule in their stead. It seems reasonable to assume that Hu's intention is to point a present moral.

stitutional democracy, under which equality prevails. Because the nationalist-racial and democratic ideology of our Han people is already fully developed, we will be able to drive the Manchus out and to establish our own state. This being accomplished, it is unthinkable that in light of the general disposition of our social ideals we should turn away from an egalitarian system, to retain instead the old distinction between ruler and ruled.[51]

This extract tells us a good deal about the style and substance of revolutionary thinking, and reveals some durable characteristics of the ideology that the revolutionaries developed to rationalize their hopes. It suggests, in the first place, the extent to which Chinese radicals in the early twentieth century were able and anxious to relate their own aspirations to what they understood of the historical experiences of other states and peoples. With the possible exception of Chang Ping-lin, in whose vision the anti-Manchu revolution had a significance more narrowly racial and cultural, the *Min pao* writers were inclined to view their enterprise as a product of the age: an event both appropriate and inevitable, thrusting China at long last into the stream of universal history; the act that would assert China's claim to a place in the modern world and attest China's ability to survive there.

The revolutionaries insisted, nevertheless, that the manner of this modern transformation must be affected by the uniqueness of China's tradition. They magnified the importance of the spirit of liberality which they perceived as an aspect of the traditional political culture and likewise the distorting influence of the long centuries of autocratic imperialism. China, they asserted, suffered from none of the inherent conflicts of social privilege and interest which had fueled the revolutionary movements of the West. The one great division they acknowledged and emphasized was a familiar one: the distinction between ruler and ruled, between the governing elite and the governed masses. This they attributed, however, not to the legacy of traditional political theory which linked hierarchy to harmony, but rather to the perpetuation of the autocracy. They distinguished, at least nominally, between autocracy and alien rule. But in fact they tended to treat the autocracy as hardly more than a prop to Manchu dominance. By this logic, to which the revolutionaries adhered with remarkable consistency, it was made to appear that once the Manchus were gone, all else must follow in the natural course of things. History, and what Wang Ching-wei called "the spirit of China's moral law,"[52] pointed to the same confident conclusion: the accomplishment of the great destructive aim of the revolution would of itself assure the realization of its positive purposes, the establishment of republicanism and democracy—ideals which seem not only related, but virtually synonymous, in the writings of revolutionary spokesmen. Released from the constraints which had smothered their political nature, the Chinese would claim their rightful inheritance; and since the tradition offered republican precedents, so must it also guarantee the realization of democratic aspirations. "When it comes to the establishment of a democratic constitution," wrote Wang Ching-wei, "our citizens possess their own distinctive spirit. We need not frantically seek to emulate England, France, or America. This, indeed, is neither possible nor necessary. As to the general spirit [of constitutional democracy], history attests to the fact that we possess whatever it is that constitutional states share in common. It is not a question of whether we possess what England, France or America possess; it is a question, rather, of the degree of refinement."[53]

This was precisely the kind of sweeping affirmation of China's political competence that Liang Ch'i-ch'ao found unconvincing in the absence of carefully considered corroborative evidence and a well-thought-out program to attain the desired ends. In truth, the *Min pao* writers paid scant attention to what must happen in the aftermath of the revolutionary victory they so confidently forecast. The best guidelines available in this connection were the sketchy generalizations set forth in the "Manifesto of the Military Government" (*Chün cheng-fu hsuan-yen*) promulgated by the Revolutionary Alliance in 1905. This called first for a period of military dictatorship under the control of the "righteous armies" (*i shih*) of the revolution. This would be the destructive stage of the revolution, sweeping into oblivion all impediments to progress, great or small: oppressive government, corrupt officials, avaricious underlings, inhumane punishments, burdensome tax levies, the shameful queue, opium addiction, footbinding, and geomancy. After three years the period of "provisional constitutionalism" would begin, at which point the management of local affairs would be entrusted to elected local (i.e., district or *hsien*) governments still under the general supervision of the revolutionary military government. The final phase would begin six years later with the promulgation of a permanent constitution that would make provision for the election of a president and a parliament and the creation of the necessary administrative apparatus. But who would be responsible for drafting the constitution, and under what conditions? Who would comprise the electorate, and what would be the basis for representation in parliament? What would be the relationship between the executive and legislative powers of the government? How would local interests and responsibilities be balanced against those of the new central government? Such perplexing questions were neither asked nor answered. Instead, the Manifesto ended with an exhortation to civic duty: "May our citizens progress in an orderly fashion, cultivating within themselves the capacity for freedom and equality, for this indeed is the foundation of our Chinese Republic."[54] Platitudes were doubtless expedient, intended as they were to unite a fractious and inherently unstable revolutionary alliance. But when Sun's party came finally to power twenty years later—transmogrified in the interval into the Kuomintang—an inherited unconcern for the details of a workable democratic system contributed lamentable qualities to the political character of the Nationalist government.

Liang Ch'i-ch'ao and the Revolutionary Alliance spokesmen were not as distantly divided on certain issues as their adversary relationship might make it appear. Hu Han-min and his colleagues reproached Liang for disparaging the political instincts of the Chinese people by insisting on the need for a period of enlightened autocracy; yet from the beginning they themselves incorporated into their long-range strategy the idea of a tutelary stage in the revolutionary process. The difference came down, then, to the question of the appropriate auspices, given China's circumstances, and the necessary means. The revolutionary position was clearly stated by Ch'en T'ien-hua. Japan might well set an inspiring example of how a nation could achieve wealth and power, Ch'en conceded. But in respect to the underlying theory of the state, Japan offered no model for the Chinese to follow. The accomplishments of the Meiji Restoration had sprung from the reassertion of imperial authority made possible by the overthrow of the Tokugawa Shogunate. But, Ch'en continued:

> Our royal house [*wang shih*] disappeared more than two hundred years ago. Our present government is in the same category as the Tokugawa line. Japan would not be where it is today had not the shogunate been overthrown. China cannot be revived unless the Manchus are thrown out. It is for this reason that we do not wish to emulate Japan's constitutional monarchy, but must rather advocate constitutional democracy, which is appropriate to China's particular situation. Indeed, if China rejects democratization, is there any alternative strategy that will enable it to achieve independence? I assure you that there is not. To try to sell the notion that we should put our trust in the Manchu government would be irresponsibly to follow the course of least resistance, and we will not hear of it. Therefore we acknowledge only this principle: if we wish to save China, we must promote popular rights and establish democracy. The way to begin is to prepare for popular rights and democracy by means of enlightened autocracy [*k'ai-ming chuan-chih*]. And the first step is revolution.[55]

Liang Ch'i-ch'ao would have read this statement with mixed feelings. He believed that the anti-Manchu issue had been exaggerated by the revolutionaries. There were Manchus sympathetic to the reformist cause—notably Tuan-fang (1861–1911), the governor of Hupeh (1901–1904) and Hunan (1904–1905), governor-general of Liang-Kiang (1906–1909), and a member of the Imperial Commission dispatched in 1906 to investigate Western constitutional systems. Liang was willing, and indeed anxious, to cultivate such support. But at heart he had little affection for, or confidence in, the Court. Popular rights remained

Liang's aim, albeit in a more distant future than he had once hoped might be the case. He would certainly have been gratified by Ch'en's espousal of the idea of enlightened autocracy. "Revolution" was the bone that stuck in Liang's throat. He was convinced that revolution opened no path to China's future; he saw it at best as a hazardous detour that must lead to social disintegration and, in all probability, to the kind of political disaster that would invite imperialist intervention. He challenged the revolutionaries to prove that it would be otherwise.

For their part, the *Min pao* writers were awed by the political accomplishments of Western revolutions, and desperately anxious that China should take its place in the universal history of human progress. But they too were distressed by what they feared might be the social consequences of the enormous transformation they contemplated; and they were as concerned as Liang was that China be spared the necessity of retracing, step by bloody step, the history of European social upheaval. Hu Han-min's disquisition on republicanism, cited above, suggests the characteristic attitude of the revolutionaries toward their projected enterprise—what we might call its prophylactic motive. The revolution they envisioned was to be the timely stroke that would simultaneously accomplish its necessary political purpose—the destruction of the autocracy and the expulsion of the Manchus—while insuring the intergrity of China's social inheritance by preventing the polarization of wealth and privilege that had brought the West to the brink of social dissolution. Just as the democratic inclination imbedded in the inherited culture would facilitate the political transition to republicanism, so too, they believed, China would benefit at this critical turning point in its history from an indigenous tradition of socialist idealism. This view was clearly enunciated in an early issue of *Min pao*, in an essay entitled "Socialism and the Future of China's Political Revolution." The author was Feng Tzu-yu, a revolutionary organizer whose association with Sun Yat-sen can be traced back to the founding of the Hsing Chung hui in 1895.* "The sources of socialism in China," wrote Feng, "antedate the civilizations of ancient Greece and Rome: *viz.*, the well-field system of the Three Dynasties."

---

* Feng Tzu-yu (1881–1958) was born in Yokohama, the son of a printer and stationer prominent and politically active in the local Chinese community. When the Yokohama branch of the Hsing Chung hui was founded in 1895 Feng Tzu-yu was enrolled, at the age of fourteen, as its youngest member. He was educated in Japan, and was active in both party and student politics over the next decade. After the establishment of the Revolutionary Alliance, Feng served as its principal organizer and fund-raiser successively in Hong Kong, Vancouver, and San Francisco. His involvement in revolutionary politics continued into the early Republican period, though his importance diminished as the bitterness of his opposition to reorientation of party policies increased. After the reorganization of the Kuomintang and its merger with the Chinese Communist Party in the early 1920s, Feng ceased to play an active role. He is now best remembered as the author of a reminiscent history of the early years of the revolutionary movement, and several accounts of the role of overseas Chinese in its development—subjects of which he had unique first-hand knowledge.

Though he conceded that the well-field system had embodied "only a hint of the idea of egalitarianism, by no means adequately encompassing the whole substance of socialism," Feng insisted that "after the Three Dynasties there were always some who tried to implement this ideal." In this he was at least partially correct; as we saw in chapter 2, the well-field system (whether or not it ever existed in fact) had represented to Mencius and to such later thinkers as Huang Tsung-hsi and Ku Yen-wu the essence of an equitable relationship between the prince and his people. The examples that Feng adduced to substantiate his claim were, significantly enough, all "outsiders" from the perspectives of conventional Confucian historiography: Wang Mang, the Han-dynasty usurper of imperial authority who had attempted to revive Chou institutions; Wang An-shih, whose eleventh-century reforms were resoundingly condemned by his Sung contemporaries; and, closer at hand, the Taiping rebels. Feng asserted, on the basis of this evidence, that "the Chinese created socialism several thousand years ago." He then ascended to an even more grandiose proposition:

> Surveying the various nations of the world, we see that the only one which has not yet suffered deeply the evils of capitalism is our China. This being so, the only one which can give practical application to socialism, and thereby serve as a model for other nations, is our China. As we gaze down from the heights of the K'un-lun Mountains upon the place that China occupies in this wide world, we see that among the peoples of the earth the Chinese are indeed in a uniquely advantageous position. Great is China! Splendid is the Chinese people! We have only to kindle the flame of socialism in our fatherland for it to spread abroad to mankind at large.[56]

It became an axiom of revolutionary ideology in the decade before 1911 that China had thus been twice blest by history: it claimed as its native inheritance a tradition of social idealism, yet it remained untroubled by the crisis in economic relationships that had generated class struggle in the modern West. These assumptions were widely shared by the radicals of those years; and, albeit expressed in different terms, a belief in China's social distinctness continued to influence the development of revolutionary thought in later decades.

The *Min pao* writers knew a good deal about contemporary Western socialism—a knowledge acquired, as was Liang Ch'i-ch'ao's, largely through the medium of Japanese translations and a personal acquaintance with Japanese socialists. Chu Chih-hsin came close to being a doctrinaire socialist, even a proto-Marxist. His translation of selections from the *Communist Manifesto*, published in the second issue of *Min pao* together with brief biographical introductions to Marx and Engels, was the first into Chinese. Revolutionary Alliance thinkers knew enough, certainly, to recognize the consonance between their own political aspirations and the social and economic ideals of socialism. They knew enough, too, to realize that the historical assumptions characteristic of European socialism rendered it in many respects irrelevant to China. Chu Chih-hsin was an emphatic advocate of social revolution. Yet even Chu chose to stress what set China apart from the West. "There is, certainly, a distinction between rich and poor in China today; but the distance that separates them is not very great. We could make no more serious mistake, however, than to argue that since inequality is not as pronounced in China as it is in Europe and America, there is therefore no justification for social revolution. Those who are in the right in this matter know that if we press ahead with the social revolution, aiming to forestall inequalities before they become great, then its objectives will be easily achieved. . . . But if we wait . . . then though it may become easy to see the need for social revolution, to achieve it will become difficult."[57]

At the level of specific policy proposals the "socialist" component of the revolutionary program was confined to the question of land. It was perhaps almost a matter of instinctive reflex for Chinese reformers to fasten upon the idea of a land tax as the basis for their economic program—the traditional Chinese state had always had to grapple with the problem of how to translate the wealth of agriculture most effectively (and in theory most equitably) into government revenues. Sun Yat-sen had espoused the notion of "the equalization of property rights" (p'ing-chün ti-ch'üan) early in his career. He considered himself a follower of Henry George, whose single-tax doctrine he had encountered when it was at the height of its popularity in England in the 1890s. George also enjoyed a considerable vogue among Japanese socialists at the turn of the century, thereby exercising a wider influence on Chinese radicals. The central premise of the single-tax theory was that appropriation by the state of the unearned increment of land value would suffice to meet the needs of the state without recourse to other revenue-producing mechanisms. The idea was appealing for obvious reasons to men who preferred to regard socialism as a preventative rather than a remedial measure, and the benefits that China might expect to derive from the single tax were expounded at length in Min pao in 1906 and 1907.

Yet for all the attention they devoted to the land question, these early Chinese socialists were not particularly sensitive to the problems of the traditional economy, nor were they much interested in what appears to us so clearly, in retrospect, the looming issue of China's social revolution: a settlement of the historic grievances of the peasantry. George's economic theory, with its emphasis on the rising value of land as an increasingly scarce commodity, was clearly better suited to Chinese realities at the turn of the century than was the Marxist preoccupation with the capitalist mode of production and the revolutionary role of the proletariat. Its dynamics, however, were those of an urbanizing economy, with little relevance either to the entrenched social inequities or to the developmental problems of a fragmented agrarian economy that was both technologically and institutionally stagnant. One suspects that when Sun Yat-sen held forth on the virtues of the single tax, his vision was informed more by his familiarity with the West, or with Hong Kong and Shanghai, than by memories of the village life he had left so far behind him.

What Sun and his followers took from George in any case was not an economic philosophy; it was, rather, something of his moral confidence, and the mechanism of the single tax. George had opposed the idea of nationalization. The purpose of the single tax was to encourage the rational exploitation of economic resources by private enterprise. To his way of thinking, "confiscation of rent" was by no means synonymous with confiscation of private property, nor was it a rationalization for massive governmental intervention in the economy. The published program of the Revolutionary Alliance, however, called forthrightly for "nationalization of the land" (*t'u-ti kuo-yu*). Writers for the *Min pao* did not explore the implications of a possible discrepancy between this idea and Sun's earlier slogan of "equalization of property rights"—both were accepted simply as being suggestive of the movement's commitment to the ideal of social justice. In his exposition of the "Six Great Principles" of the Revolutionary Alliance, Hu Han-min incorporated certain Georgean postulates into his argument. He embraced the notion, for example, that land is by natural right no more alienable for purposes of turning a private profit than is sunlight or the air men breathe. Hu's conclusion was that the land itself, not merely any unearned increment on its value, must belong to the community at large. This was an idea for which, as Hu pointed out, Chinese precedent existed.

> The great affliction of the civilized world at present is the existence not of political classes, but of economic classes. Socialism has arisen in response to this. Its theories are diverse, but all take as their basis the levelling [*p'ing*] of economic classes. The major division within socialism is between communism [*kung-ch'an chu-i*] and state socialism [*kuo-ch'an chu-i*]. Nationalization of the land is one aspect of state socialism. The only countries in the world which can implement state socialism are constitutional democracies, in which the executive authority rests with the state, while the state's sovereign authority is vested in an assembly of the people's representatives. This insures that the feelings of society as a whole are reflected at the top, and the state can accordingly plan for the welfare and happiness of the citizens. . . . State socialism cannot be put fully into practice in our country at its present stage of development. But in respect to the nationalization of the land, we may perceive a model for this in the well-field system of the Three Dynasties. On the basis of an inherited racial disposition, therefore, this should not be difficult to implement in a time of great political transformation.[55]

Liang Ch'i-ch'ao strenuously disputed the wisdom of this commitment. He was prepared, he said, to acknowledge socialism as "a lofty and pure principle." He went further, to express the hope that "the spirit of state socialism" would characterize the period of autocratic tutelage, "in order to forestall the eventual calamity of a social revolution." What Liang meant by state socialism was a strategy of economic development comparable to what he had found in Japan: nationalization of crucial industries, and government initiatives to underwrite the entepreneurial risks of innovation in other economic areas. But nationalization of the land, in his view, meant social revolution *now*—and to provoke the fever in order to prevent the disease seemed to him a dubious logic. Liang was motivated in part by political considerations; the reformist party drew much of its support from gentry sources—though it remains unclear to what extent the interests of the landlord "class" may have overlapped with "gentry status" in the first decade of the twentieth century. By birth and breeding, of course, Liang was sensitive to the values of traditional gentry elitism, however bitter his resentment of the constraints that the traditional culture imposed on the development of the values of citizenship. Perhaps most important, Liang was by temperament a moderate, deeply discomfitted by the specter of social violence which he accused the revolutionaries of seeking to summon forth. "For men of wild ambition to advocate social extremism simultaneously with political and racial revolution—this, I say, is only a means of stirring up beggars and ne'er-do-wells." The real issue, as Liang saw it, was one of means, not ends. "The socialism of reasonable discourse is certainly not the same thing as the unfettered emotionalism of social revolution. Socialist objectives may be achieved by other means than the incitement of the people to social revolution. . . . To carry out nationalization of the land during the revolutionary period will only condemn the nation to extinction."[59] Socialism, in other words, must be subordinated to, and placed in the service of, nationalism.

The bristling charges and countercharges of this ongoing debate tend to obscure a fundamental consonance of purposes which Liang shared with the spokesmen of the Revolutionary Alliance: their common commitment to the attainment of "wealth and power." It is not to disparage the humane impulse that animated these early revolutionary thinkers to observe that they were as interested in economic development (or "modernization") as they were in social justice. They resisted Liang's implicit suggestion that they might be forced, as he had been, to choose between these objectives. Indeed, one of the great attractions of George's single-tax concept was the cheerful conviction that it would generate, with a minimum of administrative supervision or economic dislocation, more than adequate revenues to underwrite the costs of economic growth. But, Liang asked, how large in fact would be the revenues raised by the single tax? Were landowners to be compensated for property of which they had been deprived by the state? If so, at what cost, and where would the money come from? Would the economic condition of the peasantry actually improve as a result, or would the peasantry in the end bear an inordinate share of the burden of economic modernization? How large a national debt could China incur without recourse to massive borrowing from foreign sources? If nationalization replaced the free market in land, how would land "value" be determined for purposes of establishing the tax base? Who, ultimately, would bear the responsibility for the allocation of resources, the setting of priorities, the overall management of industrial and commercial development?

The task of responding to this relentless critique fell largely to Chu Chih-hsin and Hu Han-min. We have remarked that in the exposition of their political program the *Min pao* writers favored general propositions at the expense of careful consideration of the details of the future political order. In justice to them, we must add that in defense of their economic proposals, Chu and Hu redressed the balance to a considerable extent. They produced, indeed, an elaborate series of speculations and conjectures, full of ten- and twelve-digit estimates of expected revenues and expenditures, reinforced by hypotheses concerning the rate at which the population would become urbanized, and the speed with which China might overtake Japan, or even Europe, in its econmic growth. Yet they successfully turned aside Liang's effort to wrest from them an answer to the more fundamental question: were they social revolutionaries or social reformers? They wanted to be both. They desired the results of revolution, but they were unwilling to pay the cost. They rejected the idea that China presented a revolutionary situation, and thus they persisted in the belief that their ends could be achieved by essentially reformist means.

On both sides it was a dispute that seems, in retrospect, not without substance, but without particular consequence. It did little to define or clarify the underlying problems of China's social and economic condition that remained for another generation to analyze and solve. As Martin Bernal suggests in his painstakingly thorough reconstruction of the debate, this early polemic on social policies bequeathed to that later generation an awareness of socialist doctrines that made the eventual appropriation of socialism more natural than it might otherwise have been. But in its own time, and in its own terms, it did not establish the necessity for social revolution as an adjunct to the political revolution which remained first and foremost the objective of *Min pao* propagandists.

To the extent that historical evidence tended to support his view that revolution is a process whose social and political consequences are difficult to foresee or to control, the natural advantage perhaps belonged to Liang Ch'i-ch'ao. Yet in the end it was he who first retired from the contest, dejected if not defeated. "The normal social roles of realism and idealism are reversed in the acute phases of a revolution," Crane Brinton once observed. "We are here in a land fabulous but real, where the wisdom and common sense of the moderate are not wisdom and common sense, but folly."[60] Something of this mood pervaded Chinese radical circles during the last years of the dynasty. Liang's role as a nay-sayer placed him at a competitive disadvantage against the optimistic enthusiasm of his opponents, whose belief that the best outcome was not only probable but inevitable gave to their preaching a persuasive self-assurance. The issue ultimately came down, as Bernal rightly observes, to a difference of opinion concerning human nature. Liang's reluctance to put his trust in populist socialism reflected his lack of confidence in popular politics, his unwillingness to place responsibility for government in the hands of an uneducated people.

There were those who shared his misgivings on this score—but by and large they were not to be found among the radical Chinese student population of Tokyo or Shanghai. Among this erstwhile constituency, Liang's reputation as a spokesman for progressivism was on the decline. Fully cognizant of the political risk, he had publicly disapproved of the tactics to which the students resorted in their confrontation with the Japanese authorities in 1905. In 1906 and 1907, publication of *Hsin-min ts'ung-pao* became erratic and infrequent, with predictable results: Liang complained that the readers were disgruntled; circulation was falling off; financial problems were becoming so acute that he feared the "independence" of the enterprise might be compromised. In any case, said Liang, he had lost heart: he no longer had the strength to wage single-handed combat against "that partisan paper."[61] In the spring of 1907 the offices of *Hsin-min ts'ung-pao* were damaged by a fire. In July, the journal ceased publication. Liang had lost much of his audience, but in the meantime other opportunities had presented themselves, and a new challenge had come to engage his energies.

In September 1906 the Ch'ing Court accepted, at least in name and on paper, the idea of "a constitutional polity in which the supreme authority shall be vested in the crown, but all questions of government shall be considered by a popular assembly."[62] Two years later, not long before the deaths of the Kuaug Hsu emperor and the Empress Dowager, a nine-year period of preparation for constitutional rule was inaugurated, to encompass a careful census of the eventual electorate, the creation of local and provincial assemblies, the establishment of a modern judicial system, and a widespread campaign of civic education. A constitution, and the election of a national parliament, were promised for 1916—by which time, according to the official estimate, a literacy rate of one in twenty would have been achieved. Liang Ch'i-ch'ao and the constitutional monarchists thus saw their program preempted, in large part, by a government that remained obdurately hostile to the reformers who had advocated such policies since 1898. Now, rather than urging upon the Ch'ing a course which it had no intention of adopting, Liang found himself burdened by the equally thankless task of demanding that the Court abide by and enlarge upon commitments it had made. Increasingly he turned his attention away from the restless students in Tokyo, in an effort to influence the opinions and gain the support of gentry reformers in China who espoused the constitutional movement because it offered the hope of a degree of political significance at least at the provincial level. In 1907 a new organization was established to promote the cause, the Society for the Dissemination of Political Information (Cheng-wen she) with K'ang Yu-wei as its nominal president, Liang Ch'i-ch'ao as the animating genius behind the scenes, and a membership that included a number of prominent and progressive gentry leaders. In October the public meeting held in Tokyo to launch the new enterprise turned into a rout for the reform party, effectively marking the end of Liang's career as the political mentor of the younger generation. Boistrous radicals seized the platform; when he tried to speak, Liang was shouted down with cries of "Fool! Fool!" Significantly, the headquarters of the Society was transferred shortly thereafter to Shanghai, a more congenial setting despite the fact that Liang himself remained *persona non grata* in the city.

The declining fortunes of the reformist party did not signify a corresponding prosperity for the Revolutionary Alliance. The shift in Ch'ing policies after 1906 introduced an element of ambiguity into the political situation that took its toll on support for the revolutionary cause, and tended to shift the arena of political struggle onto new ground, closer to home. The Alliance had been from the beginning a fragile coalition of disparate components, threatening always to fly apart. The first and nearly fatal intraparty dispute erupted early in 1907, over the compelling issue of an appropriate design for the party's flag.* At about the same time the Japanese government at last acceded to Ch'ing demands that it cease giving aid and comfort to the revolutionaries. Some thirty student members of the Revolutionary Alliance were deported, and Sun Yat-sen himself was requested to leave the country. He departed for Southeast Asia in March, accompanied by Hu Han-min and Wang Ching-wei; Chu Chih-hsin returned to China. The Japanese government softened the blow, as it had for K'ang Yu-wei several years earlier, with a generous subsidy. Sun also received substantial funds from private Japanese supporters. He left Chang Ping-lin in Tokyo, with two thousand yen of this

---

* One faction, comprising chiefly the Hunanese contigent led by Huang Hsing, wanted the standard to carry the character *ching*, as in *ching-t'ien* (well-field), to represent the party's social ideals. Sun Yat-sen thought this too anachronistic and erudite, and held out successfully for the red banner with its white sun on a blue field that became familiar in later years as the flag of the Nationalist government.

newly acquired wealth to meet the publishing costs of *Min-pao*. The discovery that Sun had quietly appropriated a much larger sum to finance his own operations created a major scandal within the organization, and sparked the first of a bitter series of challenges to Sun's leadership. We are suddenly presented with a picture quite different from that of the selfless revolutionary. "Sun Yat-sen has never been sincere, open, modest or frank with others," complained Sung Chiao-jen. "His way of handling things is almost dictatorial and intransigent to an unbearable degree." Chang Ping-lin banished Sun's portrait from the offices of *Min pao*, denounced him as a traitor, and demanded his immediate removal from his party posts.[63] In its last year, *Min pao* served increasingly as an outlet for the quasi-anarchist opinions of Chang and others. By the time the Japanese police closed the paper down in the autumn of 1908, the Revolutionary Alliance itself had, in Sun's estimate, ceased to exist as a purposeful revolutionary organization. From 1907 to 1911 whatever momentum the revolutionary movement managed to sustain came largely in the field: a ragged series of disorganized and uncoordinated uprisings in South China; random terrorist actions in Peking, Shanghai, and eleswhere. The insurrection which broke out unexpectedly in Wuchang and Hankow in October, 1911, and which burgeoned in the following months into *the* Chinese Revolution, was less the culmination of these efforts, or a vindication of the revolutionaries' beliefs, than a fortuitous sequence of events that coincided briefly and deceptively with their anti-dynastic aspirations.

*   *   *

"The yeast of change—whether it be the desire for progress the returned students and traders bring back, or jealousy of Japan's success—is at work and more or less fermentation is perceptible all over the country." So wrote Sir Robert Hart to his London agent in 1907. As he approached the end of a career that spanned more than half a century, Hart surveyed China's situation with the astuteness and the caution bred by long familiarity with Peking politics. "Some difficulties are sure to crop up, and there will be a parting of the ways and taking up of sides, and of underhand doings of foes, rivals, and competitors, which, sooner or later, will make Peking a very important diplomatic centre and China a very troublesome quantity to deal with. . . . Around us . . . on all sides there is unrest and anxiety and the materials for a conflagration are accumulating: nobody can say what will happen and the disappearance of either Empress Dowager or Emperor will fix the mine. Some folks are awfully pessimistic and the outside appearance of quiet and progress are said to be but additional reasons for expecting a possible worst. . . . China is going in for new methods, new measures, and new men. . . ."[64] Other observers, hardly less seasoned than Hart, were more optimistic. "The state of things today presents a great contrast to what it was when I arrived here," wrote an American missionary in 1905, looking back across more than forty years in China. "Then everything was dead and stagnant; now all is life and motion . . . [with] promise of great things in the near future." At about the same time a Western journalist well acquainted with the country remarked, "For the first time in history the Chinese have discovered a common ground of union which has appealed to men of all classes and trades, of all religions, and all sections of the community. Unconsciously the Chinese have welded themselves into a nation."[65]

These are foreign views, of course; and more to the point, the views of men who sensed the profound changes that were taking place in the political and intellectual worlds of those Chinese for whom the abstractions of political and social theory possessed compelling force. It is doubtful that a traveler through the Chinese countryside would have gained a similar impression. Peasant life remained much as it had been in living memory: bearable at best, at worst insupportable, the balance always precarious. Droughts, floods, plagues, and pestilences—and famine, the inseparable companion of all—continued to be recorded as annual calamities somewhere within the domain of the Son of Heaven. In the villages, change only tested further the peasants' ability to endure; its measure was the relentless crowding of more and more human lives upon the land, the slow crumbling of dikes, the gradual silting up of canals, the creeping horror of social violence—the accumulating costs of neglect by an impoverished, preoccupied, and indifferent government. In 1906–1907 the wealthy Yangtze provinces were ravaged by a devastating visitation of flood and famine. Even while the revolutionaries squabbled over flags and funds in Tokyo, and Liang Ch'i-ch'ao tried to rally his constitutionalist forces; while in Peking Sir Robert Hart pondered the consequences of the emperor's demise, and across the world in New York City K'ang Yu-wei celebrated his fiftieth birthday surrounded by friends and well-wishers—in March and April of 1907 an epidemic of rice riots swept through the villages and towns of Chekiang, Kiangsu, and Anhwei, eventually engulfing even the great cities of Hangchow and Shanghai.

When one tries to bring these images into focus as aspects of the same picture, one is forced to the conclusion that, as substantial as were their accomplishments as civic educators in the years between 1898 and 1911, the radical intellectuals, whether revolutionary or reformist in political persuasion, had failed in the effort to create a Chinese nation: a failure confirmed by the collapse of radical hopes in the aftermath of 1911. This is not to gainsay the importance of nationalism as a political motive during these years; it is to suggest, however, that there is a telling difference between the awareness of nationalism as a value and the creation of a community which can give expression to that value. Nationalism, it has been said, is a state of mind that corresponds to a political fact.[66] For the Chinese whose ideas and activities have been chronicled in this chapter, the state of mind was real enough. The political fact, however, the political community, remained for them an intellectual construct, an hypothesis defined in accordance with whatever the individual held to be the paramount constituency of "nationhood." For Liang Ch'i-ch'ao it was "the new people," a term that expressed equally a commandment and an invocation. For the revolutionaries—for Tsou Jung or Chang Ping-lin, at least—it was "the Han people," the statement of an ethnic, cultural, and political claim. For other revolutionary writers it was a category at once more general and vaguer, "the citizenry," or simply "the people." "The revolutionary party is the party of the people," wrote Wang Ching-wei in 1910. "It stands with the common people [p'ing-min], sharing their feelings, sharing their concerns, sharing the same sufferings which afflict them. . . . The ideal of revolution is not a thing within the power of party men to create; it arises out of the sufferings visited upon the common people."[67] Yet even here one senses that Wang is speaking of, not to, the likes of those hunger-driven peasants and townsmen who looted the riceshops of central China in the dreadful spring of 1907.

The image of a self-reliant people responsive to the challenges and the opportunities of history, animated by a unifying sense of its own political and cultural identity, able and anxious to assume the responsibilities of citizenship: these several overlapping visions became part of the political mythology of the prerevolutionary decade. It was a mythology that appealed to, and in part described, the young audience of activists whose education both in and out of school was informed by these ideas. But it was a work of invention, or of autobiographical fiction, not a political program. As time went on, as one failure followed upon another and the sense of collective purpose became harder to sustain, these values were translated to the level of individual conduct, and the idea of revolutionary heroism came increasingly to capture the radical imagination.

Anarchism, nihilism, and terrorism were themes discussed in Chinese radical literature from the turn of the century onward. Even Liang Ch'i-ch'ao had been impressed, initially, by what he read in Japanese accounts of the Russian nihilist movement. His enthusiasm soon waned, but the mystique of the "hero" exercised a more enduring hold upon some other minds. "If he succeeds, myriads will burn incense in his honor," wrote Chiang Fang-chen* in 1903. "If he fails, his grave will be

---

* Chiang Fang-chen (1882–1938) was one of the first and most brilliant Chinese students of military science in Japan, graduating from the military academy in 1905 at the top of his class. (The Japanese, humiliated by having to confer the highest honor—the gift of a sword by the emperor himself—upon a foreigner, thenceforth segregated Chinese students at the academy.) Chiang was originally one of Liang Ch'i-ch'ao's protégés, but he soon gravitated toward the revolutionary movement. He became, in his later years, a military advisor to Chiang Kai-shek.

overgrown with brush, and the autumn crickets will chirp there."[68] The suicides of Ch'en T'ien-hua in Tokyo at the end of 1905, of Yao Hung-yeh in Shanghai a few months later, and numerous similar tragedies, suggest both the rising level of violence and the growing introversion of radical thought. The second issue of *Min pao* carried the portrait of Sophia Perovskaya, a leader of the terrorist People's Will, which had been responsible for the assassination of Tsar Alexander II in 1881. The third issue displayed photographs of Michael Bakunin, identified as "the founder of anarchist and universal revolution," and of Wu Yueh, a young Anhwei radical who had died in 1905 in the single-handed attempt to assassinate the members of the imperial commission sent abroad to study Western constitutional systems. Chang Ping-lin, Wu Chih-hui, and Ts'ai Yuan-p'ei were all attracted to anarchist ideas, albeit of an idiosyncratic and undoctrinaire sort. The Restoration Society (Kuang-fu hui), in which Ts'ai was active for a time in 1904 and 1905, served as a rallying ground for extremists from Chekiang, Kiangsu, and Anhwei. By 1907 a cult of terrorism had taken form. In March, Wang Ching-wei inserted into one of his attacks on Liang Ch'i-ch'ao and the constitutionalists some favorable observations on terrorism as a revolutionary tactic. "Assassination can assist the revolution, but not take its place, since assassination can only get rid of one or two elements of the organization, it cannot destroy the organization itself." Nevertheless, wrote Wang, "I do not disparage terrorism [*an-sha chu-i*]. In the period before the revolutionary army has taken the field, acts of terror can shred the meat of those public enemies, as a warning to the lawbreakers—how can this be anything but good?[69] In April 1907 *Min pao* published a lengthy supplement entitled *T'ien t'ao* ("Heaven's Justice"), vengefully anti-Manchu in tone. Wu Yueh's picture appeared again—the portrait of a studious young man staidly dressed in the attire of a Confucian gentleman—and with it a posthumous selection of his writings, including an essay entitled "The Time of Assassins" (*An-sha shih-tai*):

> If we look westward toward Europe, or to Japan in the East, we see that their revolutions grew from the seeds planted by assassination. . . . For us, comrades, this is a season for assassins; another time will bring the age of revolution for our Han people. If we would reap that harvest, we must plant its causes today. . . . Life must triumph over death; only then is it possible to live. Death must triumph over life; only then is it possible to die. . . . This is called knowing fate; this is called heroism.[70]

Wu served the ornamental needs of *Min pao* one final time, a few months later—a grisly photograph of the failed assassin disemboweled by his own bomb, his shattered corpse held dangling from the hands of gendarmes on the Peking railway platform where the commissioners had been about to entrain.

Wu Yueh was a member of the Restoration Society, as were several young radicals whose activities, in the summer of 1907, brought the tide of terrorism to a brief crest before government reaction temporarily suppressed the movement. On July 6 the Manchu governor of Anhwei was fatally shot by one Hsu Hsi-lin, a member of the Restoration Society who had infiltrated the provincial bureaucracy and was serving as director of the new-style police academy in Anking. Hsu was apprehended without difficulty and summarily executed; his "revolutionary" support had consisted, improbably, of only a handful of police cadets. The crackdown that followed, however, uncovered a fairly extensive terrorist organization poised for action. Among its principals was Ch'iu Chin, Hsu Hsi-lin's cousin, a leader of the Restoration Society and concurrently provincial director of the Revolutionary Alliance in Chekiang, and surely one of the most intriguing personalities cast up by the rising wave of radicalism. Ch'iu was a woman, a fact in itself both unusual and suggestive. Even as a youngster, the daughter of a prosperous and indulgent Chekiang family, she had displayed considerable originality, priding herself on her swordsmanship, her ability to ride, and her head for wine. Her marriage, to a conventionally ambitious bureaucrat, was inevitably a disaster. In 1903, in her late twenties, she abandoned her family to become a student in Japan. There she plunged headlong into student politics and bohemianism, dressed sometimes *à la japonnaise* and carrying a samurai's short sword, sometimes in the costume of a Western man-about-town, complete with cap and walking stick. Ch'iu joined the Revolutionary Alliance when it was founded in August, 1905, and at the end of that year she was among the student protestors who returned to China. She spent the next two years engaged in feminist education and revolutionary conspiracy, mostly in Chekiang. There she was tracked down, a few days after Hsu Hsi-lin's execution, and accorded the martyr's death to which, one suspects, she had aspired. Ch'iu Chin was beheaded at Shaohsing on July 15. "Great men in the world should consort with spiritual beings," she had written; "For how can the scum of the earth be worthy company for them!"[71]

Ch'iu Chin's radicalism was one of style and personality as well as politics. She would probably have been considered an eccentric even by the standards of contemporary student culture, yet the place she earned in the growing pantheon of revolutionary heroes was well deserved. A picture of her grave appeared as the frontispiece of the penultimate issue of *Min pao*, clandestinely published by Wang Ching-wei in Tokyo in February, 1910. Wang had by this time all but abandoned hope for the victory of "the revolutionary armies"—the small, disorganized, and heterogeneous forces that had been defeated and dispersed in one disastrous insurrectionary attempt after another since 1907—and was himself preparing to adopt the course of revolutionary self-sacrifice. He made his way secretly to Peking, where with a few confederates he planned to assassinate Ts'ai Feng, regent for the child-emperor Hsuan T'ung, in early April. The plot was discovered, and the conspirators taken into custody two weeks later. Wang seized the opportunity of his trial to broadcast his revolutionary message, but he was denied the privilege of final martyrdom. Whether because the Court was becoming more enlightened, or susceptible to the kind of example Wang had set, or whether because (as seems probable) it was becoming more cautious in its dealings with its enemies, Wang was sentenced only to life imprisonment. He regained his liberty eighteen months later, in the aftermath of the October Revolution.

In the meantime the Ch'ing moved reluctantly to implement its program of sponsored reform. Elections were held in 1909 for the purpose of creating provincial assemblies. The electorate was miniscule, averaging less than one half of one percent of the total population; the franchise, moreover, was defined in such a way as to give clear preference to the old-style gentry—that is, the holders of degrees conferred under the now defunct examination system. Not surprisingly, provincial gentry interests overwhelmingly dominated the assemblies. In 1910 the Court grudgingly invited a National Assembly to convene, specifically as a deliberative and advisory body, without legislative power or any political jurisdiction. Half its members were appointed by the Court, the other half by the provincial assemblies. Again, gentry opinion predominated. National politics, in the last year of the dynasty, became a contest of wills between the Court and the deliberative bodies it had allowed to come into existence. It seemed an unequal contest, given the negligible authority of the latter. By the summer of 1911, reformist expectations had all but vanished—but so had the vitality and resilience of the imperial institution.

On April 27, 1911, at Canton, the revolutionaries staged what proved to be the penultimate insurrectionary attempt. Sun Yat-sen was in Canada, raising money, but several of the leaders of the Revolutionary Alliance were involved: Huang Hsing, the principal figure in the Hunan contingent, was in overall command; Chu Chih-hsin served as his chief of staff; Sung Chiao-jen and Hu Han-min arrived on the night boat from Hong Kong too late to take part. The coup failed, disastrously: the plot had been betrayed to the Canton garrison commander, who was suitably prepared, and in the confusion revolutionary forces fired on each other with bloody results. The Canton uprising bequeathed to the history of the revolution the celebrated legend of the "Seventy-two Martyrs"—casualties were in fact considerably higher—but it gave little encouragement to those who hoped for a revolutionary victory. Liang Ch'i-ch'ao, reading the news reports in Tokyo, was moved to reflect somberly on the accomplishments of exile:

Our party has steadfastly opposed revolutionary insurrection, because throughout history revolution is a thing of ill omen. Any country that has undergone a great revolution must endure a period of ten years, or even several decades, before its spirit and vitality can be restored. Our country even now is ravaged by a dreadful wasting disease. How can a withered tree withstand the buffeting of wind and rain, the cruel grasp of frost and snow? . . .

But the revolutionary party argues that the fate of our five-thousand-year-old nation, and the fate of our four hundred million people, rests in the hands of the present government—and ask, what hope now remains for the present government? With each day that it survives, our vitality is dissipated by another small measure. Now whether one succumbs to a wasting disease, or whether one dies from a dose of poison, death is death, and what's to choose between? And though a strong purgative may kill the patient, upon occasion it may cure the disease instead. If one has the courage to take it, then a life may be saved out of the multitudes of death. Surely this is preferable to sitting quietly, waiting for death to come.

In this vein they rebuke those who oppose the revolution—and the latter have no answer to give. . . . If the revolutionaries in China today have not been able to prove their case, still less have the opponents of revolution been able to prove theirs.[27]

Liang could not know that within six months China's history would pass irretrievably beyond the reach of the revolutionary activists, the civic educators, the intellectual radicals whose efforts to shape the course of events prompted this gloomy appraisal. The Republic that emerged out of the tangled contests of 1911–1912 did not confirm the reformers' darkest misgivings, but still less did it vindicate the high hopes of the revolutionaries. Nevertheless, the standards against which the Republic was to be judged and found wanting in the years to follow were, by and large, the standards of purposeful and progressive government affirmed, though not effected, by the prerevolutionary generation—whether at home or abroad, a generation of exiles.

The New Culture Movement: Intellectuals as Political Amateurs

I take those things are to be held possible which may be done by some persons, though not by everyone; and which may be done by many, though not by any one; and which may be done in succession of ages, though not within the hourglass of one man's life; and which may be done by public designation, though not by private endeavor.

—Francis Bacon:
Advancement of Learning

ON A WINTER DAY IN 1905 A CHINESE STUDENT, a slight young man in his middle twenties, sat with his Japanese classmates in a microbiology course at Sendai Medical College. The lecturer had finished early, and as was his patriotic habit took up the slack time by showing lantern slides of the Russo-Japanese War. On this occasion, among the pictures of victorious Japanese troops in the field, there was one of a Manchurian Chinese: a spy for the Russians, it was said, under sentence of death, who stood with bound hands, surrounded by a crowd of Chinese onlookers—impassive spectators of the monitory fate of the central figure who awaited the executioner's sword upon his neck.

Chou Shu-jen had come to Sendai in order to escape the hectic and, as he thought it, dissolute life of the Chinese student community in Tokyo; he was, in fact, the only Chinese student enrolled in this coastal city two hundred miles north of the capital. He had elected to study medicine partly in deference to the times—it was the kind of useful specialization popular with his generation—and partly in remembrance of his father's long and painful death, in 1896, under the grotesquely inept care of practitioners of traditional medicine. But the stark photographic image of that circle of stolidly apathetic witnesses to the death of a compatriot etched itself on Chou Shu-jen's mind. "After this film I felt that medical science was not so important after all," he recalled. "The people of a weak and backward country, however strong and healthy they may be, can only serve to be made examples of, or to witness such futile spectacles. . . . The most important thing was to change their spirit, and . . . at that time I felt that literature was the best means to this end. . . ." When Chou returned to Tokyo a few weeks later he announced his change of plans to a friend in blunter language: " 'I've decided to study literature. How can China's idiots, her rotten idiots, ever be cured by medical science?' We looked at each other and exchanged a grim smile, for the twin categories of 'idiots' and 'rotten idiots' had long been stock phrases in our everyday conversation."[1]

Chou Shu-jen would indeed make his mark as a writer and critic. Known to the world under the pen name of Lu Hsun, he became in the late teens and twenties China's most celebrated man of letters, the author of short stories that describe with anger, compassionate ridicule, and deep sympathy the anguish of lives trapped in the wreckage of a crumbling culture. His youthful conversion from medicine to literature—from a science that treats physical infirmity to an art that assesses the significance of spiritual impairment—may for our purposes exemplify a more general trend among Chinese intellectuals in the bitter aftermath of the 1911 Revolution. The "political entrepreneurs" discussed in the last chapter had diagnosed a political ailment, and prescribed what they regarded as the necessary purgative. The "political amateurs" whose opinions shaped the mood of the New Culture movement perceived a systemic resistance to the remedies that had been attempted, a cultural rejection of the political innovations ushered in by the revolution. They sought to establish cultural and social conditions to nourish the qualities of individual and collective character which might, in time, mend the disease. The shift in emphasis was slight, but for a time decisive. As we have seen, intellectual radicals in the prerevolutionary decade were hardly indifferent to the cultural aspect of the political cure they hoped to effect, but they tended to take it pretty much for granted. New Culture intellectuals, for their part, were much concerned with the eventual political consequences of their endeavors. They had, however, all but abandoned the idea that the patient could be restored to health by a process of political experimentation.

The earlier generation of reformers and revolutionaries had attributed China's vulnerability to the survival of an anachronistic despotism which they identified with the Confucian monarchy and the Manchu ruling house. Although the political debate of the prerevolutionary decade was conducted in terms that reflected a new and progressive political consciousness, radical thought before 1911 must still be understood, at least in part, within the terms of an inherited context: the old Confucian problem of creating and sustaining a harmonious relationship between ruler and ruled.

The disappearance of the Manchus in 1912 and the calamitous disappointment of republican expectations in the years immediately following offered persuasive evidence that the theoretical disputes of earlier years had somehow missed the major point. New Culture intellectuals generally accepted their predecessors' view of the *ancien régime* as an oppressive political order that had endured only at the cost of suppressing the vital intellectual and social energies of the people. They tended, however, to regard this as an inevitable result of a fundamentally repressive culture, and therefore to emphasize the primary importance of liberation from the intellectual and social constraints perpetuated by the traditional culture. They fell out among themselves in respect to the appropriate strategies of social reconstruction and its political implications. But they agreed on the need for a reappraisal of the relationship between culture and social values. They shared, for a time at least, a commitment to the idea that intellectual and social change must take precedence over political reform if political institutions are to be invested with genuine purpose.

The New Culture period may, for our purposes, be taken to encompass the dozen years or so between 1915, when China stood at the brink of political partition and warlordism, and 1927, when the country was at least nominally reunited under the flag of a national government which claimed for itself the revolutionary inheritance of earlier times. By 1915, the failure of the republican revolution to achieve its intended purposes was manifest. Yuan Shih-k'ai had exploited his command of a superior military force, an advantage compounded by the disarray within the ranks of the revolutionaries, to seize control of the newborn Republic in 1912. In return for vague assurances, Sun Yat-sen relinquished the presidential office into Yuan's keeping. The capital was moved from Nanking, in the Yangtze provinces where the revolutionaries enjoyed their greatest support, to Peking, where Yuan's position was virtually unassailable. Thereafter, republican forms were observed, if at all, in name only. The revolutionaries' attempt to reassert parliamentary authority in 1913—the so-called "Second Revolution"—was bloodily suppressed, and Sung Chiao-jen, the revolutionaries' parliamentary leader, was assassinated. Sun retired again into exile in Tokyo, while in Peking Yuan contrived to have himself designated President for Life. Toward the end of 1915 he launched a campaign to restore the imperial forms of government and to become himself the founding emperor of a new dynasty. Republicans were outraged; but a far more important factor contributing to the eventual frustration of Yuan's imperial design was the jealousy of rival militarists and aspirant successors.

Within a year of Yuan Shih-k'ai's death in 1916, the anarchy of warlordism was loosed upon China. Even the tenuous control that his government had exercised vanished as the country disintegrated into a jigsaw puzzle of regional domains under the control of military "governors" (tu-chün), some commanding all or part of the territory and wealth of several provinces, others no more than impoverished local satrapies. Contemporary accounts offer appalling evidence of the rising level of social violence, proportional to the eroding capacity of any government to assert itself for long in an environment so charged with conspiracy, greed, treachery, and violence. In 1917, for example—a bad year, but no worse than others—a report from Shantung noted "a recrudescence of highway robbery all over the province." That year in Shensi, "bands of t'u-fei [local brigands] roamed through the province, plundering and looting." In Szechwan, "there was scarcely a place unaffected by military operations." Hunan province was "from the beginning of the year . . . in a state of unrest and under martial law." Northern Anhwei was reportedly "in a state of anarchy." Chekiang experienced "a temporary declaration of independence, local disturbance, and rebellion of troops, with the usual looting which accompanies these outbreaks." In Yunnan, "outlaws, who were mostly disbanded soldiers, made inland travel extremely unsafe." Throughout the country, natural catastrophes compounded these man-made disasters. Summer floods ruined the rice crop in Hunan; large areas in Chihli, Honan, and Shantung were laid waste by a combination of drought and flood; in the northwest, pneumonic plague was reported to have reached epidemic proportions.[2]

So year by year China sank into "that condition which is called Warre; and such a warre, as is of every man, against every man. . . . In such condition, there is no place for Industry; because the fruit thereof is uncertain; . . . no Arts; no Letters; no Society; and which is worst of all, continuall fear, and danger of violent death; And the life of man, solitary, poore, nasty, brutish, and short."[3] Hobbes' terrifying metaphor cannot, of course, be applied literally. Civilization did not perish in China in the warlord era. Those who were concerned for its survival will engage most of our attention in the pages that follow. But we would do well to remember, as this narrative goes forward, that we are dealing with the minority for whom the life of opinion and argument was not only important, but possible; those for whom the abstraction "China" possessed both a political and a cultural significance; while the lives of most Chinese were governed not by moral or aesthetic judgment, or by intellectual preference, or by political conviction, but by ingrained social habit and grim physical necessity. That this had always been so, in China as in other human communities, does not diminish the importance of the distinction. New Culture intellectuals, by the very nature of their enterprise, put a great distance between themselves and the masses of the Chinese people. At the same time they sensed, perhaps more keenly than had the reformers of an earlier generation, the implications of the distance that separated their world from its surrounding social and cultural environment, an awareness that in itself contributed something to their understanding of the promise of the New Culture they sought to create.

* * *

The New Culture movement cannot conveniently be defined by a point of origin and a *terminus ad quem* that establish its historical context—as is the case, for example, with the period that began with the attempted reforms of 1898 and culminated in the 1911 Revolution. It does, however, boast a striking centerpiece: the celebrated May Fourth Movement in 1919. This began, more or less spontaneously, and without any disciplined ideological commitment, as an angry outburst of nationalist sentiment directed against the government of the day in Peking, and against the peacemakers then assembled in Paris. The Western powers, with whom the Chinese government had allied itself in 1917, displayed at the peace table a remarkable indifference to the justice of Chinese claims for the return to Chinese jurisdiction of concessions in Shantung originally ceded to Germany by the vanished Ch'ing, and subsequently appropriated by the Japanese as their major contribution to the Allied cause in World War I. The May Fourth demonstrations were provoked by the humiliating news from Paris that Japan's title to these possessions had been confirmed. Thousands of students and a few professors poured into the streets of Peking, first of all, and then the cities of the Yangtze. Anti-Japanese boycotts were organized: stevadors refused to unload Japanese cargo, and merchants to offer Japanese goods for sale—at least in Shanghai and Tientsin. The government was brought down. The Chinese delegation at Versailles, subjected to unprecedented expressions of popular outrage, refused to sign the treaty that legitimized Japan's easily acquired privileges. In China, especially among Chinese students and intellectuals, the events of May and June, 1919, generated an enduring sense of patriotic mobilization that found numerous outlets in the months and years to follow. Not without justification, historians interested in the evolution of Chinese radicalism trace the origins of the social revolution to which, eventually, the Chinese Communist Party laid claim, to the emergence of a politically significant popular protest in the May Fourth period. The movement did not encompass any sustained attempt to reach out into the villages or to arouse the peasants' sense of political responsibility. But May Fourth intellectuals launched a frontal assault upon traditional standards of social authority that foreshadowed the eventual rebuilding of the revolutionary movement on the foundation of an ideology that drew much of its energy from an iconoclastic social doctrine and strategy: the notion of "mass" culture and "mass" mobilization.

It is true that the preoccupation with the relationship between culture and state encouraged, among some intellectuals in the teens and twenties, a reaffirmation of allegiance to "native" values. Despite the disappearance of Confucian political institutions and pedagogical traditions, Confucian assumptions concerning human nature and the good society still claimed the loyalty of some. The Chinese, moreover, were quick to sense the implications of growing Western self-doubt in the aftermath of World War I. The consequent development of what we may call a "neo-traditionalist" reaction against "Westernization" or "modernization" is one of the themes we will explore in this chapter.

Nevertheless, the characteristic mood of the New Culture era was critical of the social and intellectual tradition, and adamantly iconoclastic. "The East has decided to go back to school, and has put Western lesson-books in its satchel," wrote a British observer in 1913, in a retrospective appraisal of the temper of progressive Chinese opinion since the turn of the century that captures something of the irony of the situation prevailing on the morrow of the revolution.

> Is China about to cast to the winds all her own inherited culture, and does she, in the eagerness of her haste to emulate the material achievements of Western States, intend to tear up the roots of her ancient civilisation so as to make room for the novelties imported from Europe and America? . . . Anxious to adopt the whole material equipments [sic] of Western civilisation, from battleships to fountain-pens . . . [the Chinese] are showing signs of an indiscriminate distrust of the wisdom of their national sages, the graces of their national literature, even the glories of their national art.
>
> It is a bewildering phenomenon that just when China was ceasing to appear grotesque to Western eyes she began to appear grotesque to the eyes of many of her own sons. . . . We long tried our best to persuade them that their philosophy was absurd, their art puerile, their religion Satanic, their poetry uninspired, their ethics barbarous, their conventions upside-down; and now, when we are more than half conscious of our own errors of judgment, they are putting us to confusion by insisting that we were almost wholly right.[4]

The writer was Reginald Johnston, then serving as magistrate of the British Leased Territory of Weihaiwei in Shantung. Johnston was a self-conscious connoisseur of China's traditional high culture, whose greatest claim to fame was his appointment, in 1919, to serve as English tutor to the deposed Manchu emperor, "Henry" P'u-yi. He was also enough of an imperialist to exaggerate both the impact of Western opinion on Chinese self-perceptions and the usefulness of Western intervention as a means of rescuing China's past from China's present.* The legacy of Western con-

---

* To the latter end, Johnston proposed his own quixotic scheme: the establishment of "A League of the Sacred Hills," under the supervision of "a small group of lovers of art and literature in England and China." The headquarters of the League would be situated on the slopes of T'ai-shan in Shantung, the most revered of China's sacred mountains, and the site upon occasion of extraordinary imperial sacrifices. More exactly, it would be located within the precincts of Ling-yen ssu, the Monastery of the Divine Cliff, a once-flourishing Buddhist temple now derelict and populated only by "a few dejected monks"—who, presumably, would be invited to pursue salvation eleswhere. Refurbished, and furnished with a well-

tempt for things Chinese doubtless contributed to the temper of New Culture iconoclasm. So, too, however, did the kind of patronage bestowed by foreigners like Johnston upon the elite culture of a social tradition that many Chinese intellectuals had come to despise.

A more significant motive underlying the assumptions of the New Culture intellectuals was the lingering influence of Darwinian premises which, virtually without exception, they had been educated to accept as axiomatic truths in the early years of the century. The Darwinist slogans that had so neatly expressed the prerevolutionary estimate of China's predicament no longer sufficed, in many cases, to satisfy the intellectual demands of a generation more discerning of the substance and the subtleties of modern culture. But the sense of imminent peril remained as strong as it had been. Nationalism, broadly construed as a concern for the survival of the Chinese political and social community, remained after 1911 as important a motive as it had been in the years leading up to the revolution, though it was no longer interpreted exclusively as an ethnic claim, or conceived of simply in terms of the introduction of "modern" political institutions. Whether "conservative" or "radical," nationalism in the New Culture era manifested itself as a concern for the invisible foundations of the social order, a problem of cultural identity at the level of both individual and collective self-consciousness.

For all the violence of the rhetoric, therefore, the cultural rebels of the teens and twenties were not the indiscriminate wreckers that observers like Reginald Johnston viewed with such misgiving. We might better think of them—as they would have preferred to think of themselves—as apprentice architects, heirs to the ruins of a civilization that had collapsed upon itself, its moral foundations undermined, its social and political superstructure brittle with rot. Before a sound and habitable structure could be erected to take its place, parts of the old edifice remained to be demolished. But even as they pulled down the tottering remnants of the old culture, New Culture intellectuals searched through the debris for whatever they might salvage to serve as structural support or appropriate ornamentation. For though much that was new and foreign would go into its design and fabric, their aim was to build not simply a new nation, but a new China.

*   *   *

chosen library, Ling-yen ssu would provide comfortable lodging at a safe distance alike from the dusty tumult and malarial miasmas of the lowlands—but, Johnston was quick to point out, within easy reach of the Poshan station on the new Tientsin-Pukow Railway. There an international congregation of savants—residents, as it were, of a Sung-dynasty landscape painting brought miraculously to life—would labor to sustain "what is highest and noblest" of the traditional culture.

On an extended visit to China a few years later, Bertrand Russell observed shrewdly that "the old beauty no longer has any vitality, and . . . it can only be preserved by treating the whole country as a museum." And Joseph Levenson, writing in the 1960s, treated eloquently the implications of a culture "preserved, embalmed, deprived of life in a glass case. . . ."[5]

This was the first Chinese generation to count among its intellectual, political, and professional elite a substantial number who knew the West at first hand and were prepared to contend with it on its own terms. Statistics remain random and sketchy for the period after 1911, as they are for the prerevolutionary years.[6] Clearly, however, Japan maintained its attractiveness as a destination for Chinese students despite the inter- mittant crises in the Sino-Japanese relationship from 1914 onward. In that year there were an estimated five thousand Chinese students in Japan; a decade later, as anti-imperialism became more and more the motive of student activism, the number had shrunk to around a thou- sand. Even before the 1911 Revolution, however, and in greater numbers thereafter, some Chinese students moved on from Japan to universities in Europe or the United States, joining there the small but growing number who had gone directly from the "modern" schools of the China Coast to further study in the West. Of these, the United States claimed a steadily increasing share. Between 1905 and 1915 the Chinese student population in the United States rose from just over one hundred to around one thou- sand, roughly the level at which it remained during the following decade. A survey of students embarking for the West in the period 1921–1925 lists a total of 1,189, of whom 934 (78.5 percent) were bound for the United States; Germany (127), France (89) and England (29) together accounted for only 245 (20.6 percent). The fact that Europe was struggling through the postwar recovery cannot entirely account for this disparity. Living expenses on the Continent were reportedly well within the means of students on Chinese government stipends, and the fare to London or Marsailles on the P. & O. or the Messageries Maritimes was more than met by the travel allowance of Ch$500. Political considera- tions may have been a more influential factor. In the eyes of patriotic students of the 1920s, Great Britain vied with Japan as the principal im- perialist aggressor. But among Chinese educated in the treaty ports, English was far more common than either French or German as a foreign language.* The United States thus enjoyed an advantage that was materially enhanced by the inducements offered to encourage study there. American influence was paramount throughout the system of mission-supported educational institutions; and by the mid-twenties there were some 3,500 students enrolled in Christian colleges, more than

---

* Some idea of the motives that sometimes impelled young Chinese into the study of English, and the fact that despite its popularity it was not always a language expertly taught, is sug- gested by (among other examples that might be cited) the publication in Shanghai in the 1930s of a do-it-yourself text entitled *Correctly English in Hundred Days*, under the imprint of the Correctly English Society. "This book," states the Preface, "is prepared for the Chinese young man who wishes to served for the foreign firms. It divided nearly hundred and ninety pages. It contains full of ordinary speak and write language. This book is clearly, easily to the Chinese young man or scholar. If it is quite understood, that will be satisfaction." Feng Kuei- fen might have been amused.

25,000 in Christian middle-schools, and perhaps a quarter of a million in mission-affiliated primary schools. In some cases, American mission boards defrayed at least a part of the costs of foreign study for students who had risen through this system. Furthermore, a larger percentage of those bound for study in the United States received Chinese government support than did those who pursued their studies in Europe. In the period 1921–1925, for example, well over half of the Chinese students in the United States benefited from such subsidies, while only about 22 percent of those studying in England, France, and Germany were so supported.

For obvious reasons, provincial expenditures to underwrite the cost of overseas study declined drastically during the warlord era, though the "central" government continued to set provincial quotas after 1911 as it had in the final years of the dynasty. The most generous and reliable source of government support for students in the United States was the Boxer Indemnity fund, established in 1908 by Congressional action which authorized President Roosevelt to lop more than US$10 million off the United States' original share of the Boxer Indemnity imposed in 1901, with the stipulation that the sum remitted be used to endow educational programs. Forty-seven Boxer Indemnity students arrived in the United States in 1909 in the first "class." Two years later, Tsing Hua College was established in Peking, supported by Indemnity funds, as a preparatory school for students who aspired to continued education in the United States. Tsing Hua was under the jurisdiction of the Ministry of Foreign Affairs, and its administration was predominantly Chinese; but its curriculum and most of its faculty were American. Until the reorganization of the educational system effected by the Nanking government in 1929, all Tsing Hua graduates were assured the opportunity for further study in the United States. Initially the period of grant was for seven years, intended to encompass both undergraduate and graduate education. By the 1920s, however, Tsing Hua students were deemed adequately prepared to transfer into American institutions at more advanced levels, and the period of tenure of Indemnity scholarships was accordingly reduced to five, and ultimately to four years. Not surprisingly, Tsing Hua graduates made up the great majority of the 1,268 Indemnity students in the United States between 1909 and 1929—though this figure also includes over one hundred graduates from other institutions and a number of women, for though there were women on the Tsing Hua faculty, the college remained an all-male institution. However they were recruited, the numerical preponderance of students from the Lower Yangtze and littoral provinces, noted in connection with the prerevolutionary period, continued to characterize the overseas student population throughout the Republican era, with Kiangsu, Chekiang, and Kwangtung particularly favored.

Boxer Indemnity students were conspicuously better off financially

than were their compatriots on "regular" government stipends. Their
travel and living expenses, as well as their academic fees, were paid in
full, and liberally. But it would be incorrect to label this privileged group
a minority, at least in respect to Chinese students in the United States. Of
the nearly five hundred who arrived in the United States on government
stipend between 1921 and 1925, for example, more than three-quarters
were Indemnity scholars.

The Ch'ing government had stipulated in 1909 that 80 percent of the
Indemnity students must specialize in various fields of scientific or
technological study. Although this regulation was not subsequently enforced, in the period 1909–1929 a preponderance of Indemnity scholars
did pursue their degrees in engineering, in assorted scientific disciplines,
in medicine, or in agriculture; roughly a quarter studied social science,
with economics accounting for the largest share of these; something over
10 percent studied business administration; and another 10 percent was
divided fairly evenly between the humanities and education. Chinese
students, in other words, gravitated toward areas of specialization that
were regarded as "useful"—and, we may conjecture, areas where the
sense of cultural confrontation would be least acute. *

Influence is difficult to measure. The available biographical studies
confirm the reasonable assumption that the experience of study abroad
greatly affected the values and the careers of many Chinese who rose to
prominence in the Republican period. The nature of that influence,
however, can only be assessed by looking at individuals individually.
Generalizations are even less feasible when it comes to evaluating the impact that these "returned students" had upon their own students or upon
a Chinese audience at large. Most of the established spokesmen for progressive opinion in the New Culture era—Ts'ai Yuan-p'ei, Ch'en Tu-hsiu,
Li Ta-chao, Hu Shih, Chiang Meng-lin, Ting Wen-chiang, Ch'ien
Hsuan-t'ung, Lu Hsun, to name only the most celebrated—were intellectually mature men with considerable Japanese and/or Western schooling
behind them. The men who emerged as "student" organizers and
publicists in 1918 and 1919—Fu Ssu-nien, Lo Chia-lun, and Ku Chieh-
kang at Peking University; Lo Lung-chi and Wen I-to at Tsing Hua;
Chou En-lai at Nankai University; Mao Tse-tung in Hunan—were
students in fact, or recent graduates, for many of whom (though not for
all) the experience of foreign study lay still ahead. Yet the disparity in age

---

* Full remission of the U.S. portion of the Boxer Indemnity was made in 1924, the remitted
funds used largely to support the activities of the China Foundation for the Promotion of
Education and Culture, administered by a Sino-American board of directors. In the 1920s
other countries began to follow the U.S. lead: Great Britain in 1922, Japan in 1923, and
France in 1925 announced plans to remit their share of the Boxer debt still outstanding, for
benign though sometimes ill-defined purposes. The government of the U.S.S.R., in keeping
with its policy of repudiating imperialist concessions granted to the Tsarist regime which it
had overthrown, likewise remitted the Russian portion of the Boxer Indemnity.

was not on the whole very great. Ts'ai Yuan-p'ei, who celebrated his fifty-first birthday in January, 1919, was the "grand old man" of the New Culture radicals in more than a purely symbolic sense. Ch'en Tu-hsiu turned forty that year; Lu Hsun was thirty-eight. Li Ta-chao, at thirty, was only four years older than the Hunanese normal school graduate whom he befriended in the winter of 1918, Mao Tse-tung. Hu Shih was an *enfant prodigue* of twenty-eight, a scant four or five years older than his favorite students at Peita, Fu Ssu-nien and Ku Chieh-kang.

The difference—and there *is* a difference—must thus be reckoned not only in terms of age, but in terms of experience; and not only foreign experience, but the experiences of youth. We are suddenly brought face to face here with the phenomenon of historical acceleration—the rapidity with which the world of Chinese intellectuals was changing. Ts'ai Yuan-p'ei had attained the still coveted *chin-shih* degree in 1890 at the age of twenty-two; before he became a revolutionary he had been a Hanlin scholar. Ch'en Tu-hsiu suffered successfully through the *hsiu-ts'ai* examination in 1896, when he was seventeen; Lu Hsun, at the same age, made a half-hearted stab at it in 1898. For those born in the late 1880s and the early 1890s, a classical education had already lost much of its vocational purpose and pedagogical rationale. They were old enough, however, to be involved as adolescents in the political and intellectual ferment of the prerevolutionary years when the dynasty was still a force, or at least a problem, to be reckoned with. But by the 1910s "Confucian" China had already become an abstraction: something to be described, analyzed, and understood, if only the better to attack it; but no longer something that could be experienced or reacted to as a coherent system of intellectual and moral values or political institutions. Even as they were being educated to shape the future of their country, the students of the late teens and twenties were being educated to interpret the meaning of its past. In both its aspects this was a task undertaken in many cases by teachers and writers whose ideas, methodologies, and perspectives were informed by foreign standards.

Many of the men and women who returned to China with degrees from American and European universities in the teens and twenties themselves became teachers, most often in the still small number of public and private institutions of higher education. Y. C. Wang reckons that in 1925 nearly a third of the American-educated returned students were teaching at the college or university level, in all fields; 15 percent were in the employ of the central or provincial governments, and another 15 percent were involved in the modern sector of the economy—the "treaty port sector"—as bankers, merchants or industrialists; only a little over 3 percent were "professionals," chiefly physicians and lawyers.[7] Foreign influence was also brought to bear directly by a procession of prestigious visitors, of whom the most notable were John Dewey and Bertrand Russell. Russell's impact was considerable, but his time in China was briefer than Dewey's, and marred by illness and by political contentiousness. Dewey's visit was an intellectual event of some magnitude and duration.

Intending only a brief stay, Dewey arrived in China literally on the eve of the May Fourth demonstrations in 1919; he remained, as it turned out, for a two-year tour in the course of which he lectured widely and attracted an enormous amount of attention. Several of his former students or self-proclaimed disciples were already active in China. Kuo Ping-wen (Ed.D., Columbia, 1914) was president of Nanking Higher Normal School, which became, in 1921, National Southeastern (Tung-nan) University. Chiang Meng-lin (Ph.D., Columbia, 1917) was editor of *Hsin chiao-yü* (The New Education), and acting chancellor of Peking National University in the summer of 1919. Hu Shih (Ph.D., Columbia, 1917) taught Chinese and Western philosophy at Peking University, and served as dean of the College of Arts. T'ao Hsing-chih (Ph.D., Columbia, 1917) was chairman of the Department of Education at Tung-nan, and Chiang Meng-lin's successor as editor of *The New Education*. Chang Po-ling, founder and president of Nankai University in Tientsin, held no Columbia degree, but he had been a student at Teachers College.

Dewey thus passed from one friendly audience to another, lecturing not only on education or academic philosophy, but on broad issues of social and political reconstruction—lectures that were translated and published, in the newspapers and journals of the day and in book form, almost as soon as they were uttered. The lecture series delivered in Peking during Dewey's first winter in China, with Hu Shih serving as platform interpreter, appeared as a 500-page book, with 100,000 copies in print in 1921; by 1924 it had gone through sixteen printings. *The China Weekly Review*, American owned and edited, observed with understandable smugness in 1920, "It may be guessed that by means of the spoken and the written, or printed, word Professor Dewey has said his say to several hundred thousand Chinese." Understandable too, against this background, is the consternation expressed by a British journalist, commenting on the occasion of Tsing Hua's tenth anniversary celebration in 1921:

> Educated under the American system, constantly reminded of the happy associations of their school days through the influential alumni organization, aware that they owe their scholarships to American justice, and saturated with American sentiment by five to eight years' residence in the country, they will look to the United States solely for cooperation in the troublesome years to come. *Why should we not share an influence that we formerly monopolized and that is now slipping away from us?*" [8]

In the course of the 1920s, when to the perennial student demand for "relevance" was joined an increasingly ideological and activist nationalism, a different and darker aspect of the picture began to emerge. Anti-imperialism spawned, among other things, a demand for the return of "educational rights." It was a demand aimed primarily at the mission-supported educational enterprise, but with broader implications. Study in the United States did not inevitably produce students "saturated with American sentiment." Young Chinese sometimes returned embittered by the racial prejudice they had witnessed or to which, in some instances, they had been subjected; disenchanted by the realization that Americans at home did not practice what Americans abroad preached; or persuaded that Americans, with a self-confidence born of ignorance and indifference, were the true provincials. "For a Chinese young man with a mind of his own to stay in America, the feeling he experiences defies description," wrote one Tsing Hua graduate to his family at home in 1923. "I am not a man without a country. We have a history and a culture of five thousand years, what of us is inferior to the Americans? Should we say that because we cannot manufacture guns and cannons for manslaughter therefore we are not as honorable and praiseworthy as they are?"[9] For their part, students who remained in China sometimes challenged both the purpose and the perspective of their education:

> The educators love to say: "The aim of education is to save the country." We [would] like to ask, how? . . . Why [seek] a university education? The answer is to get a diploma. Why [get] a diploma? The answer is to become a middleschool teacher. Thus men revolve around education, generation after generation. Can such a merry-go-round save the country?
> The university teachers teach American politics, American economy, American commerce, American railways, American this, American that. They praise the United States the same way old scholars praised the sages Yao, Shun [and] Yü.[10]

When, thirty years later, the newly-established government of the People's Republic indicted virtually a whole intellectual generation for its servile "worship America" mentality, it fanned into flame a resentment that had been smouldering in some minds for a long, long time.

*   *   *

China's acknowledged educational and intellectual metropolis in the teens and twenties was Peking, with its cluster of celebrated universities and colleges: the National Peking University, the National Normal University, Tsing Hua, Yenching, Peking Union Medical College, and a scattering of smaller schools. Between 1909 and 1922, the number of institutions of higher education in Peking had risen from ten to forty, and the student population had increased from 2,115 to 15,440; the city accounted for 30 percent of China's colleges and universities, and for over

40 percent of its college students.* Of these several institutions, the National Peking University (Kuo-li Pei-ching ta-hsueh, or as it is invariably abbreviated, Peita) was incontestably the most renowned, bringing together on its faculty a remarkable assemblage of radical intellectual leaders, and more than once serving as the storm center of the student movement that played an increasingly important role in the political and intellectual history of the New Culture era.

The Imperial University (Ching-shih ta-hsueh-t'ang) had been established in June, 1898, in the confident early days of the Reform Movement, to serve, in the language of the enabling edict, "as a first example of our aims."[12] It was located on a site just east of the walls of the Forbidden City, in that quarter of the capital known as Ma shen miao (The Temple of the God of Horses), and not far from the offices of the Tsungli yamen, which bore primary responsibility for its maintenance. The university was modeled on the still surviving T'ung-wen kuan; and W. A. P. Martin, having resigned as president of the latter in 1895, was appointed in 1898 to serve as dean of the Department of Western Studies in the new institution. Virtually alone of the innovations of the Hundred Days, the imperial university weathered the ensuing reaction only to be shut down by the Boxers during the months that they held Peking in thrall. When it reopened in 1902 it absorbed what was left of the old T'ung-wen kuan into its School of Foreign Language (I-hsueh kuan). Throughout its early history the university thus harked back to the motives and attitudes of the Self-strengthening era, and gave little intimation of what it would become in the teens and twenties.

On the eve of the 1911 Revolution, the institution removed to "a large, ugly foreign building of red brick" constructed for its use, adjacent to its original premises in Ma shen miao which were converted to serve as dormitories.[13] (There it would remain until the Japanese occupation of Peking in 1937; and there it would return in 1946 from exile in the southwest. Shortly after the establishment of the People's Republic in 1949, Peita was moved to the far more scenic campus of the recently disestablished Yenching University on the outskirts of the city.) But it continued to offer more courses in the Department of Classical Studies (ching-hsueh k'o) than in the Department of Polytechnics (kung k'o), more even than in the Departments of Natural Science (ko-chih k'o) and Agriculture (nung k'o) combined.† Graduates were awarded the chin-

---

* In 1918–1919 Hopei (Chihli), with 610,916 students enrolled in schools at all levels (including public, private and mission) accounted for 11.5 percent of the national school population of 5,320,364. Kiangsu (408,618) and Chekiang (368,494) together claimed 14.5 percent.[11]

† The Department of Classical Studies offered separate courses in each of the Thirteen Classics (excepting the Hsiao ching and the Erh-ya), and a course in Sung-dynasty Confucianism (li-hsueh). The Department of Polytechnics offered instruction in civil engineering, electrical engineering, machine design, shipbuilding, arms manufacture, munitions, in-

shih degree, and received appointment as Hanlin scholars at varying ranks according to their class standing. They might then pursue their studies under the informal tutelage of selected members of the university faculty, as fellows of the "Academy of Sciences" (T'ung-ju yuan) or be appointed to the rank of expectant officials at the provincial level.[14]

This was the institution created to serve, during the final years of the dynasty, as both capstone and example to the modern educational system. As we have noted earlier, the system took shape only very slowly: according to one estimate, primary school enrollments in 1909 stood at just under 1.5 million nationwide.[15] In any case, the university did not fulfill its exemplary function with particular distinction. So disreputable, in fact, were both academic and personal standards that the institution was derisively known as "The Gamblers' Den," and its faculty and students were collectively labeled "The Brothel Brigade." The 1911 Revolution brought a new name, but no immediate improvement in the situation, though initially the prospects may have seemed auspicious. During his brief tenure as provisional president of the new Republic, Sun Yat-sen appointed Ts'ai Yuan-p'ei to the post of minister of education; a few months later, Yuan Shih-k'ai appointed Yen Fu to the chancellorship of the university. Although they diverged fundamentally in their political sympathies, both were men of honorable reputation, but neither lasted in office more than a few months. Between 1912 and 1916 the enrollment at Peita nearly doubled in size, from 818 to 1,503 students. In spirit, however, the university seems to have remained what it had been from the beginning: a training school for would-be bureaucrats and a haven for academic idlers. Not until Ts'ai Yuan-p'ei was prevailed upon to assume the chancellorship in 1916 did Peita's renaissance begin. Then within a year or two it became an institution endowed with an almost legendary renown.

Since his departure for Europe in 1907, Ts'ai Yuan-p'ei had lived the peripatetic and sometimes indigent existence of an itinerant emigré scholar. He spent a year in Berlin, learning German and supporting himself, through the good offices of Chang Yuan-chi, by doing translations for the Commercial Press. He then moved on to Leipzig, where he plunged for three years into the study of aesthetics, experimental psychology, ethnology, and philosophy. Throughout these years he maintained his ties with the revolutionary movement, and within a month of

---

dustrial chemistry, metalurgy and mining, and architecture. Courses in the Department of Natural Science included mathematics, astronomy, physics, chemistry, botony and zoology, and geology; those offered by the Department of Agriculture included agriculture, forestry, agricultural chemistry, and veterinary medicine. The university also comprised Departments of Law and Administration, with two courses; History and Philology, which taught courses in Chinese and world history and geography, as well as Chinese, English, French, German, Russian and Japanese literature; the Department of Medicine, which offered one course in medicine and one in pharmaceutics; among the three courses offered in the Department of Commerce was one—inevitably—in Customs administration.

the Wuchang uprising he was home again in China. The following summer, however, after his unsuccessful stint as minister of education, he returned to Leipzig. He hastened back to China again in 1913, hoping for the victory of the "Second Revolution" against Yuan Shih-k'ai. With its failure he once more sought refuge in Europe, where he remained until the autumn of 1916, writing philosophical treatises and collaborating with Wu Chih-hui and others to promote the fortunes of a work-study program to bring Chinese students to France.

Ts'ai's decision to accept the chancellorship of Peita at the end of 1916 was received with scepticism by his longtime revolutionary colleagues. Although Yuan Shih-k'ai was dead, Peking was still regarded as hostile territory; many believed, moreover, that the university itself was beyond redemption. In Ts'ai's view, however, education was one thing, politics another. He immediately made it clear that he expected more and better things of Peita students than had been demanded of them in the past. "You who come here to study should have a firm purpose in mind," he admonished them in his inaugural address in January, 1917. "In order to know whether or not your aim is appropriate, you must first understand the nature of the university. . . . A university is a place dedicated to the pursuit of scholarship. Outsiders like to point to the decadence of this school. Those who study here, they say, think only about official appointment, or getting rich. . . . Now there is no shortage of special schools in Peking for those whose aim is to secure a bureaucratic appointment, or to make money . . . and they have no business coming to this university. Your aim in coming here should be to seek learning."[16] A few months later Ts'ai established on the Peita campus an organization called "The Society for the Promotion of Moral Rectitude" (Chin-te hui).* Its membership was divided into three categories according to their appetite for abstinence: the first promised not to gamble, or to consort with prostitutes, or to take concubines; the next higher pledged in addition to refuse official appointment and not to serve in parliament; the most resolute rejected tobacco, alcohol, and meat. "There is a saying common among men nowadays, that the West honors public virtue [kung te], while the East honors private virtue [ssu te]," Ts'ai wrote at the time; "and further, that if one discharges one's public duty, then one's private behavior is of no concern. This is wrong. I am one part of society, and if that part is rotten, then the whole must be affected."[17]

We may detect, in these sentiments, faint echoes of Confucian puritanism, or of the kind of socially responsible "individualism" popular at the turn of the century. As we shall see in a moment, a more unconven-

---

* Named and modeled after a similar organization founded in 1912 by Wu Chih-hui, Li Shih-tseng, Wang Ching-wei and several other quasi-anarchists, most of them old friends of Ts'ai's. Ts'ai himself, then serving as Minister of Education, became a member. At about the same time he was also the founder of an organization similarly highminded but more straightforwardly named: the "Six Don'ts Society" (Liu pu hui).

tional and more important aspect of Ts'ai's vision of Peita's character explicitly contradicted the notion that public duty and private conduct are
inseparably linked. Nevertheless, in the cynical and blasé environment of
the mid-teens such stalwart moralism struck a responsive chord: astonishingly, the Chin-te hui soon claimed a membership of nearly a thousand,
or roughly half of the Peita student body.

Had he stopped at this, however, Ts'ai's influence at Peita would very
likely have been only transitory, and the university's impact on contemporary intellectual life only marginal. Ts'ai's real accomplishment at
Peita went far beyond the reformation of student character. He brought
with him to the chancellorship a clear and forceful idea of what a genuinely great university should be, and what it must represent to the society at large. Although he acknowledged China's urgent and continuing
need for what he had once called "utilitarian" education, at Peita he
stressed the primary importance of creative scholarship and pure
research. He emphasized the central educational role of the arts and
sciences, and he tried, by various administrative measures, to discourage
the inclination of students to pursue narrowly professional courses of
study. Despite his best efforts, more students continued to enroll in the
College of Law (reorganized to comprise the departments of government,
law, and commerce, with 947 students in 1919) than in the College of
Arts (Chinese, English, French, philosophy, and history, with 756
students in 1919) or the College of Sciences (physics, chemistry, mathematics, and geology, with 496 students in 1919). The philosophy in accordance with which Ts'ai governed the university, however, set standards
of liberality that made Peita a symbol of progressivism. "In my capacity
at the University I am guided by two principles," he wrote in 1919, in
response to strident and well-publicized criticism of his administration:*

> In respect to intellectual theories, I adhere to the example of universities the
> world over in upholding the principle of "freedom of thought" and in pro-
> moting inclusiveness and toleration [*chien-jung ping-pao chu-i*]. . . . No mat-
> ter what school of thought a man may belong to, if what he says is judicious,
> and if he has reason to uphold his views, if his opinions have not fallen by the
> way in the process of natural selection, then even if there be disagreements, all
> may expound without hindrance. . . .
>
> As for the faculty, scholarship is the primary consideration, so long as, in
> discharging their academic responsibilities, they do not contravene the princi-
> ple set forth above. They have complete freedom in what they say or do outside
> the school; this institution does not seek to interfere, nor can it take any respon-

---

* The critic was Lin Shu (1852–1924), the celebrated translator of Western fiction into
classical Chinese. Working with the collaboration of intermediaries—Lin himself could read
no foreign language—he produced stylistically elegant versions of the works of a staggering
number of Western writers, ranging from Dumas *fils* and Balzac to Dickens, Scott, Defoe
and Swift, from Shakespeare, Homer and Tolstoy to H. Rider Haggard and A. Conan Doyle.
Lin remained, however, adamantly opposed to the New Culture movement in its every
aspect.

sibility. . . . Between the public and the private realm there is a natural distinction."[18]

Ts'ai thus set a policy well designed to attract to Peita a lively-minded faculty. Much of his genius and his reputation as an educator lay in his ability to recruit men of uncommon character and diverse opinions to the university; and the measure of his commitment to the goals he had enunciated was his willingness to stand up for his faculty, even when he disagreed with individual members on intellectual or political issues, or when—as he ruefully conceded was sometimes the case—their personal standards of conduct would have disqualified them from membership in the Chin-te hui.

There were cultural conservatives and political traditionalists on the Peita faculty in the New Culture era, notably Liu Shih-p'ei, an important figure in the "National Essence" party of which we will have more to say shortly, and Ku Hung-ming (1857–1928), a remarkable cultural hybrid who brought to Peita the tastes and opinions of aristocratic Toryism. Born in the Straits and educated at the University of Edinburgh (M.A., 1877) and on the Continent, upon his return to Asia Ku donned the Confucian scholar's gown, adopted the queue, and eventually joined the staff of the puissant viceroy Chang Chih-tung, in whose service he remained for many years as secretary-interpreter. In the 1890s and the early 1900s he was a vehement anti-imperialist and a bitter critic of the moral pretentiousness of Western missionaries; for reasons doubtless related, but more dubious, he was also an ardent admirer of the Dowager Empress and the Boxers. "The Empress-Dowager, Prince Tuan and his Boxer lads are not the enemies, but the real true friends of Europeans, and the true European civilization that has been trying to realise itself since the last Great Boxer rising in Paris in '89 [1789?!] [They] have risen against the real enemies of Europe, of the world and of true civilization,—the sneak and the cad who have just entered into partnership to cheat, swindle, bully, murder and rob the world and finally to destroy all civilization in the world." Ku embellished his essays, many of which were published in the English-language press of the China Coast and Japan, with quotations from Heine, Goethe, Ruskin, Arnold, Carlyle, Emerson, Zola, Beranger, Flaubert, Voltaire—as well as Confucius and Mencius—each in his own language, each considerately translated, when appropriate, for the convenience of his less cosmopolitan readers. He was probably the only Chinese of his (or any) generation able to express his views in the guise of a passable Scots ballad ("Then each Boxer lad who loves fighting and fun/Let him follow the bonnets of bonnie Prince Tuan. . . .")[19] To this peculiarly urbane xenophobe has been attributed, finally, the argument that concubinage is justifiable on the same principle that requires a teapot to be accompanied by more than a single teacup. At Peita in the late teens, Ku Hung-ming gave instruction in

Latin. When he died in 1928, his queue still proudly in place, Hu Shih remarked that for all the differences that had divided them, Ku's bearing had always been such as to merit the epithet to which he most aspired: he had been a *chün-tzu*, a Confucian gentleman.

Ts'ai Yuan-p'ei could thus justifiably insist that under his stewardship Peita sheltered a varied intellectual community. Unquestionably, however, the university's preeminence in the New Culture era is directly attributable to the purveyors of progressive opinion who congregated there: aggressive, self-confident, articulate, and enthusiastic advocates of the values of modernity.

* * *

One of Ts'ai Yuan-p'ei's first acts after assuming his new responsibilities in 1917 was to appoint Ch'en Tu-hsiu to occupy the vacant deanship of the College of Arts. Ch'en's affiliation with Peita was to last scarcely more than two years; he was arrested and jailed in the aftermath of the May Fourth demonstrations, and on his release in the autumn of 1919 he returned to Shanghai. Brief as it was, however, Ch'en's presence in Peking was significant, not only because of his opinions—it was during these years that he moved from progressivism to political radicalism—but also because he provided the first voice, as we might say, for Peita's growing community of cultural rebels. Ch'en brought with him to Peking the magazine he had founded two years earlier in Shanghai: *Hsin ch'ing-nien* (The New Youth), which by 1917 had become China's leading forum of cultural debate.

Ch'en Tu-hsiu was himself a rebel in both thought and temperament. He was born in October, 1879, in Huaining district in southwestern Anhwei province, into a modestly prosperous gentry family. His father died a few months later, and Ch'en's early education was taken in hand by his paternal grandfather, whom he recalled as a viciously ill-tempered, neurotically fastidious old man, an opium addict, and a harsh taskmaster. "Old Whitebeard" died when Ch'en Tu-hsiu was only eight—but not before the boy's distrust of the character bred by the traditional society was already well established. Thereafter he passed under the tutelage of a number of teachers, the last of them his older brother, an amiable and not very demanding pedagogue. Nevertheless the young Ch'en applied himself, perhaps less out of respect for the intellectual tradition he was expected to master than from motives which he later described with a touch of stylized sentimentality: "My mother's tears drove me to study very diligently. . . . [They] certainly had more authority than my grandfather's stick."[20]

In 1896 Ch'en passed the prefectural examination with high distinction. The essay that won him this honor was an intentionally incoherent pastiche of classical nonsequiturs that quite overawed the befuddled and bookish examiner; its successful reception only enhanced Ch'en's contempt for the traditional curriculum. A year later he took his first trip away from home, to sit reluctantly for the *chü-jen* examination in Nanking. Throughout this nine-day ordeal the several hundred candidates were confined virtually as prisoners in their airless scholars' cells that afforded space neither to stand erect or to lie down, row upon row sweltering and stinking in the late-summer heat. Ch'en failed, perhaps because in these grotesque surroundings his mind strayed from the task at hand:

> From the strange circumstances in which the candidates found themselves my thoughts ran on to speculate on the misfortunes that might befall my country and my people when these creatures achieved their aim in life; and this in turn prompted me to think that the whole "great ceremonial" for selecting men of talent was in fact simply a gathering together, every few years, of bears and monkeys to stage an animal show. Then I thought to myself that probably every one of our national institutions was flawed to the same degree, and I concluded that what men like Liang Ch'i-ch'ao were saying in the *Shih-wu pao* made good sense. . . . An hour or two of such musings determined the course of my activities over the next decade and more. Such was the unexpected benefit that I derived from the provincial examination to which originally I had been so loathe to submit![21]

Not long after this, Ch'en plunged into a career as a radical publicist, though he remained for nearly twenty years a rather obscure (or anonymous) one. He traveled several times to Japan and studied briefly at Kōbun gakuin.* He was in touch with the revolutionary movement, but he did not join it, purportedly because he objected to its narrowly racist brand of nationalism. His sympathies, however, were clearly with the revolutionaries. Among the friends of these years was Chang Shih-chao, whom we have already met in his capacity as the editor of *Su-pao* at the time of its celebrity in 1903. Ch'en collaborated with Chang, among others, in the publication of several reformist journals, both in Shanghai and in his native Anhwei, written for the most part in the vernacular language in the hope of attracting a popular readership. Some time later Ch'en also contributed to Chang's *Chia-yin tsa-chih* (The Tiger Magazine), established in 1914 as an outlet for moderate-liberal opposition to Yuan Shih-k'ai, and prudently published in Tokyo. The first issue of Ch'en's own *Ch'ing-nien tsa-chih* (Youth Magazine) was published in Shanghai in September, 1915. From the beginning it bore the French

---

* Some biographers contend that Ch'en also studied in France at some point in the period 1907–1910. Others insist, for apparently better reason, that he did not, and that his well-known admiration for French civilization was acquired at second hand. It is an intriguing comment on the reticence of the subject (and also perhaps on the state of the art) that a fact of such significance concerning the life of a major figure in China's modern history should somehow have slipped through the cracks of historiography to vanish into the realm of conjecture. The question is fully addressed by Chih Yü-ju in *Ch'en Tu-hsiu nien-p'u* (Hong Kong, 1974), pp. 16-17.

subtitle *La Jeunesse;* in September 1916 the name was changed to that by which it is remembered: a name that invoked the spirit of the age—*Hsin ch'ing-nien* (The New Youth). With its appearance, the days of Ch'en's obscurity were over.

By 1915 Shanghai was the center of what may fairly be called a popular modern press. Predictably, the tone was frequently light: "Leisure Time" (*Hsiao-ch'ien ti tsa-chih*), "Humorous Times" (*Hua-chi shih-pao*), "Orioles and Flowers" (*Ying hua tsa-chih*), and "The Comic Magazine" (*Hsiao-lin tsa-chih*) were among the periodicals that issued monthly from the city's presses. *The New Youth* was not, however, the only magazine of the time to address itself with a sense of high seriousness to issues of substance. *Tung-fang tsa-chih,* established in 1904 under the auspices of the Commercial Press, continued to publish throughout the hectic decades that followed. Chang Shih-chao's *Tiger Magazine* was soon suppressed by the Japanese government in response to representations made by the government of Yuan Shih-k'ai; but early in 1915 its role as a vehicle for "liberal" reformist opinion was at least partially filled by a new publication, *Ta Chung-hua* (Great China), which numbered among its contributors such eminences as Liang Ch'i-ch'ao and Yen Fu. There were also, by this time, a number of scholarly or semi-scholarly journals in existence, like the monthly *K'o-hsueh* (Science), which advertised itself as the publication of "returned students from the United States actively engaged in scientific research," and recommended itself "to all who wish to save the country through learning."[22]

The New Youth nevertheless quickly established a special place for itself, catching the imagination of young Chinese intelectuals as no magazine had done since, perhaps, Liang Ch'i-ch'ao's *Hsin-min tsung-pao* in its earliest days. The editorial with which Ch'en launched the new venture was ringingly addressed to this intended audience:

> Among the Chinese, it is a compliment to say, "Despite his youth, he carries himself with the gravity of age." "Keep young while growing old," is a bit of advice Englishmen or Americans are likely to offer. This expression of the racial difference between East and West has far-reaching implications. Youth is like the coming of spring, the first light of dawn, plants in the bud, the sharp blade fresh from the stone: life's most precious time. Youth in society is comparable to fresh and vital cells in the human body, the new replacing the old. . . . If society follows the natural way of new replacing old, then it will flourish. But if old and decaying elements predominate, then society must perish.[23]

Ch'en's "Appeal to Youth" contained several specific admonitions. Be independent of spirit, not servile. Be progressive, not conservative. Assert yourself, do not be self-abnegating in your manner. Be cosmopolitan, not parochial, in your outlook. In your thinking, be pragmatic and scientific, not abstruse and intuitive. This was not a new message; indeed, during the first year or so of its existence, *The New Youth* took up the task of cultural enlightenment pretty much where Liang had left it a decade earlier. Nor was it a message presented, at least at first, with much discrimination in regard to sources. An early reader of *The New Youth* confronted a large and crowded canvas, a mélange of individual styles and tastes. Ch'en himself favored a vivid palette and broad, bold strokes: the greatness of French culture; the fundamental differences between East and West; the history of modern civilization. But he was also a skillful miniaturist, producing biographies, for example, of "two great contemporary scientists," Ilya Mechnikov (1845–1916), a Russian-born biologist, and Wilhelm Ostwald (1853–1932), a German chemist. Ma Chün-wu, an old revolutionary and the Japanese-educated translator of *The Origin of Species*, contributed a detailed academic portrait of the German evolutionist Ernst Haeckel (1834–1919). Kao I-han, who held a degree in political science from Meiji University, published subtle discussions of the meaning of republican citizenship and the distinction between freedom and liberty.

The general tone of the magazine, however, was strong on exhortation and short on analysis. There were lengthy excerpts from a tract entitled *The True Citizen* (by W. F. Marwick and W. A. Smith), prefaced by appropriate "Memory Gems": "The child is father of the man," and "Whatever is worth doing at all, is worth doing well," and "No one can cheat you out of ultimate success but yourself," and "Genius is nothing but labor and diligence." "America" and "La Marseillaise" were presented as exemplary patriotic hymns. Benjamin Franklin's autobiographical account of his youth was translated at length, and its author elevated as "a suitable model for youth in his spirit of energetic, tireless, courageous self-advancement." Oscar Wilde's *An Ideal Husband* ran serially, offered as "a description of English political and social life and character;" Wilde was introduced, rather oddly, as "a great writer of the contemporary naturalist school in European literature." Interest in "the woman question," destined to become one of the great social issues of the May Fourth period, was adumbrated by Ch'en's translation of *Thoughts on Women* by Max O'Rell,* including such wise witicisms as "Men who always praise women do not know them well; men who always speak ill of them do not know them at all." To accompany an enthusiastic description of the organization, the Boy Scout Law was reprinted and translated in full: the "patient, plodding, plucky boys" apostrophized by Liang Ch'i-ch'ao a dozen years earlier were now introduced to the catechism of obedience, loyalty, courtesy, thrift, and friendliness, and admonished to smile and whistle in the face of all adversity.

To be sure, some more substantial items were on display in this jumble sale of edifying remnants. There was, for example, an exerpt from T.

---

* Pseudonym of Paul Blouet (1848–1903), a minor French-English journalist and lecturer.

H. Huxley's *Lay Sermons*, "On the Advisableness of Improving Natural Knowledge," rather more comprehensibly retitled in its Chinese translation as "The Scientific Spirit in Modern Thought." There was Edmund Burke, speaking on "The Spirit of Liberty in the American Colonies." The abiding impression, however, is one of randomness; and one is reminded again how rapidly, and with how little opportunity for speculative consideration, the Chinese were compelled to sort through an unfamiliar inventory of ideas and ideals for what seemed useful to the end that Ch'en and his colleagues had in mind. "This is a time of mortal peril," wrote Ch'en in 1916. "The agencies of our extinction may be the strong enemy without and the tyrant within. But the cause of our extinction is the conduct and character of our people. Our ultimate salvation must be sought through reform of the conduct and character of our people."[24]

By 1917 the circulation of *The New Youth* had increased from the thousand or so copies published each month in 1915 to an estimated 15,000 to 16,000 copies per issue. Along the way the magazine had become virtually the house organ of the liberal Peita intelligentsia. Early in 1918 an editorial committee was created, numbering among its members Ch'en Tu-hsiu, Ch'ien Hsuan-t'ung, Hu Shih, Li Ta-chao, and, somewhat later, Kao I-han. From time to time the editor of the month would devote his issue to a particular topic. Hu Shih, for example, put together a special "Ibsen number" in June, 1918, and in April, 1919, welcomed John Dewey to China with an issue devoted to Experimentalism. By portentous coincidence this was followed, in May, 1919, by an issue edited by Li Ta-chao and given over to Marxism and Bolshevism. For the most part, however, *The New Youth* remained a general review of radical opinion until 1920, when, once again under Ch'en Tu-hsiu's exclusive control, it became China's first major Marxist journal. From the history of *The New Youth* and the ideas of several of its early contributors one may, as it were, read the larger history of China's intellectual search in the New Culture era, and the gradual transition from cultural to social and political radicalism, to which we will turn our full attention in chapter 7.

In an essay entitled "The Revolutionary Forecast for 1917," published in January of that year, Kao I-han brought Ch'en Tu-hsiu's concern for "reform of the conduct and character of our people" into sharper focus:

> At the present time we must strive with all our strength to eradicate two fallacies bequeathed to us by our tradition of autocratic theory. In the area of politics, we must expose the idea of "government by virtuous men" for what it truly is. In the area of education we must destroy the fixed idea that Confucianism is the root of self-cultivation. The revolution of earlier years was a revolution in forms; now the revolution must be one of the spirit. Our people already know full well how to carry out a revolution in political institutions;

they do not yet know how to carry out a revolution in political spirit and educational principles.[25]

Broadly construed, these became the principal objectives pursued by the *New Youth* group in the years 1917–1919, when the magazine had its widest and least partisan appeal, and by Chinese liberals consistently thereafter. Kao's first point translated into an effort to depersonalize politics; in other words, to revise the traditional opinion that viewed culture as a product of personal moral government, and in its place to establish the idea that government is merely an instrument of the culture at large, reflecting the civic values of the community. An obliquely stated corollary to this was the desire to legitimate a new relationship between intellectuals, as the agents of culture, and the state. To this end Kao's second point was, in the minds of many New Culture intellectuals, in matter of fact a prior necessity. To discredit the explicit categories of Confucian belief and the implicit assumptions of the Confucian social theory was the requisite first step toward the creation of a new and vital social and political order. But New Culture radicalism went further, as we shall see, to the daring and truly revolutionary attempt to replace Confucianism's all-embracing moral dogmatism with an inclusive, pragmatic, and liberal scepticism as the basis for nurturing human character and regulating human behavior.

*   *   *

In laying siege to the traditional culture, New Culture intellectuals had at their disposal a novel and potent weapon aimed against the very citadel of the old high culture. The issue of *The New Youth* that carried Kao I-han's revolutionary prognosis for 1917 also published Hu Shih's first major contribution to the magazine, an essay entitled "Tentative Suggestions for the Improvement of Literature." This was the opening salvo of what was soon to become an all-out assault on the classical language, its literature, and the social and pedagogical traditions it had nourished through the centuries. As we have already noted, Confucianism was not a creed into which the neophyte was initiated by a confession of faith. It was, rather, a curriculum of moral education, aimed at propagating certain social and political norms. As such, it was also an elaborate, highly developed and durable system for monopolizing the social and political benefits derived by a minority from the mastery of the essential skills of literacy. A challenge to the agency by means of which this monopoly had been perpetuated—the classical written language, the literary conventions that disciplined its use, the literature that embodied the aesthetic and moral values of Confucian taste—was at the same time a challenge to the principle of elitism (social *and* moral) that constituted one of the chief supports of the Confucian order. Nothing could have symbolized more dramatically the determination of the New Culture intellectuals to break the hold of the past upon the mind of the present. "We have men but no voices, and how lonely that is!" wrote Lu Hsun in 1927. "Can men be silent? No, not unless they are dead, or—to put it more politely—when they are dumb. To restore speech to this China which has been silent for centuries is not an easy matter. It is like ordering a dead man to live again. Though I know nothing of religion, I fancy this approximates to what believers call a 'miracle'."[26]

The modest title of Hu Shih's essay thus understated the significance of the movement that it set in train. A certain diffidence, and with it a stubborn self-assurance, were enduring qualities of Hu's personality. His steady confidence in the fitness of the values he espoused and expounded, and his unflaggingly optimistic faith in the progressive ends of historical change, were for Hu not merely the expression of intellectual convictions firmly held, but the product of a gratifying and reassuring personal history. In many respects he was the preeminent example of the successful "new-style" intellectual: a young man who had triumphed over the social adversity of his early years, and who had survived without evident injury the psychological shock of China's cultural and political collapse, to emerge as one of the stellar luminaries of the New Culture generation, an articulate, prolific, and often persuasive advocate of its ideals.

Hu Shih was born in Shanghai, where his father held a minor bureaucratic appointment, in December, 1891. His youth, however, was spent far from the cosmopolitan excitement of China's greatest treaty port, in the family's native village in the highlands of southern Anhwei province, where his mother resided after his father's death in 1895. The circumstances of Hu's upbringing were not auspicious, but neither were they uncommon or strikingly less promising than those of many of his contemporaries. The family's genteel pretensions were no guard against a demeaning poverty and the ever-present threat of creditors at the gate. One of Hu's older half-brothers died a lingering consumptive death; another was hopelessly addicted to gambling and opium. Over this tense and unhappy household Hu's mother—the third wife of a man already old, taken in marriage as what the Chinese called with colloquial candor a "room-filler," and a widow at the age of twenty-three—exercised as best she could her titular matriarchal authority. For Hu Shih there were long hours of study under the dull instruction of inept teachers in the clan school; there was the unremitting pressure to succeed, brought to bear by the almost illiterate woman whom he recalled as a paragon of maternal virtue and self-sacrifice; and there was the gnawing uncertainty as to what constituted "success" in the changing intellectual and social environment of turn-of-the-century China. On the latter question Hu accepted the opinion of his invalid half-brother, who had traveled to the cities of the Yangtze. He therefore eschewed mastery of the eight-legged essay style, turned his back on the examinations, and in 1904, at the age of thirteen, set out with his brother for Shanghai in search of a "modern" education.

Hu's vivid reminiscent account of the six years he spent in Shanghai conveys a lively sense of the excitement of exposure to unorthodox ideas and lifestyles, the burgeoning awareness of new definitions of social and political responsibility, and the personal frustrations that often characterized student life in the prerevolutionary decade. He attended several "modern" schools, including the China National Institute, whose history was summarized in chapter 5. He read, with avid attention, Tsou Jung's *The Revolutionary Army*, Liang Ch'i-ch'ao's disquisitions on the character of the new citizen, and Yen Fu's translations of Huxley, Spencer, Mill, and Montesquieu. He became actively involved, typically for that time, in student politics and propaganda. But he remained, perhaps untypically, on the periphery of the revolutionary movement, and dubious of its aims. The sense of national crisis and impending disaster, the ambitions aroused as ancient prejudices were cast off, and the lack of meaningful personal opportunity, combined to drive Hu, like many of his fellow students, to the edge of the despairing and dissipated life of a superfluous intellectual. He took himself in hand, finally, to cram for the Boxer Indemnity examinations—a last resort in which, against his expectations, he was successful. He arrived in the United States in the autumn of 1910, one of the seventy members of the second Indemnity "class."

Deferring to the popular view that Chinese students must acquire "useful" knowledge, Hu enrolled initially in the College of Agriculture at Cornell University. His aptitudes and his real interests, however, lay elsewhere, and in 1912 he transferred to the College of Liberal Arts, where he majored in philosophy and literature. He was an industrious, brilliant student, and inevitably a stunning success despite the somewhat random nature of his preparation. During his years at Ithaca he garnered prizes in English literature, scholarships in philosophy, and membership in Phi Beta Kappa. He also played an active role in the affairs of the Cornell Cosmopolitan Club, one of the larger American affiliates of the Fédération Internationale des Etudiants. In the heyday of Wilsonian idealism this was an organization that enjoyed an enthusiastic following on American campuses, embracing as it did the principles of pacifism and internationalism against the horrifying background of the European conflagration. The sentiment emblazoned on the standard of the Cosmopolitan Club became for Hu a life-long article of faith: "Above All Nations is Humanity." In his mind thereafter cosmopolitanism was no mere intellectual affectation, but an ingrained and genuine habit of feeling and temperament. Of all the leaders of the May Fourth generation, Hu was perhaps the least sympathetic to, or comprehending of, the claims of political nationalism.

From Cornell, Hu moved on to Columbia in 1915 to take his Ph.D. under the tutelage of John Dewey. As we have seen, he was by no means Dewey's only Chinese disciple; but after his return to China in 1917 he was probably the most celebrated and widely read popularizer of what he chose to call "experimentalism." He was not by nature a philosopher, however; Dewey's influence upon him seems to have been chiefly to confirm a predisposition to believe that philosophy must justify itself in terms of common sense, not abstruse theory. The conviction that the most reliable guide to responsible action is a well-developed critical intelligence; the belief that individual choices informed by the capacity to think clearly about the consequences of one's actions will not contradict the requirements of social purpose and coherence, but contribute to social progress; the belief that a confident and methodical scepticism is a surer spur to understanding than is dogmatic enthusiasm—these several tenets of the message that Hu returned to China to preach were not a revelation born of his American experience. They originated, rather, in his own thinking, inspired initially by the tradition of Confucian religious scepticism to which he had been exposed as a boy, by the vigor and candor of Liang Ch'i-ch'ao's writings, and by Yen Fu's renderings of Huxley and Mill. Revolutionary radicalism was not the single and inevitable product of the kind of civic education to which Hu and his generation were exposed during the prerevolutionary decade. Seven years in the United States gave Hu a more spacious vision of the world, and a firmer faith in the universality of human nature, than he might otherwise have gained. They imparted to him a remarkable intellectual self-confidence. But they did not fundamentally alter the inclination of his beliefs.

Yet Hu Shih returned to China more profoundly moved by the experience of foreign study than were many of his contemporaries. What he witnessed abroad gave him the confidence to believe that it is possible for a society to live according to the principles of the faith he espoused—an optimistic faith in human reasonableness. "In this land," he wrote years later, "there seemed to be nothing which could not be achieved by human intelligence and effort."[27] In the New Culture era this was a faith quite in keeping with the mood of the times. In later years it came to many to seem incongruous, against the background of China's deepening political and social crisis. Hu's diffidence, his distrust of passion, appeared then as evidence of indifference; his self-assurance was seen as arrogance; his distaste for doctrinaire political nationalism served to estrange him from his audience. No example, perhaps, illustrates more clearly the fragility of New Culture expectations than the biography of this returned student *sans pareil*.

The idea of a vernacular written language—*pai-hua* or "simple speech"—was not new in 1917. As we have noted, many of the leaders of the May Fourth generation, including several who later opposed the vernacular movement, had been involved in their student days in the publication of newspapers intended for a "popular" readership and written in the vernacular. Various schemes for the romanization of the written language had been devised and debated. Esperanto even claimed a small but articulate following. Against this background the proposals that Hu Shih set forth in his "Tentative Suggestions"—written, it is interesting to note, in careful classical style—seem something less than a revolutionary manifesto. If you must say something, he urged, say something of substance. Don't pattern your style on antique models. Write clearly. Don't pretend to emotions you don't genuinely feel. Rid your style of archaisms. Avoid classical allusions. Don't rely on literary devices and clichés. Don't shun colloquialisms (su-tzu su-hua).

Where Hu broke new ground was in his insistence, throughout the ensuing polemic, that the vernacular language must take the place of the classical literary language rather than serving merely as an adjunct to it. Pai-hua, he argued, must be regarded as more than an expedient means to the end of communicating with the semi-literate and educating the illiterate. Education itself is meaningless unless it takes place within the context of a culture. Therefore pai-hua must become the national language, with a literature of its own. The foundations of this literature already existed, Hu maintained, buried beneath the debris of the traditional culture. The vernacular novels of the Ming and Ch'ing periods, the informal lyrics of some of China's greatest poets, the popular dramatic literature that had developed since the Yuan dynasty, even the lay sermons of Chu Hsi and other Confucian thinkers, provided both testimony to the evolutionary history of China's literary forms and suitable models to inspire forms better suited to a new time. "Pai-hua literature is the orthodox literature of China, the only literature China has possessed in the past thousand years," Hu insisted. "All that is not pai-hua literature is unworthy to rank as literature of the first class. . . . A thousand years of pai-hua literature has sown the seeds of the literary revolution. . . . Henceforth Chinese literature will have left behind the old road of blind and natural change, and will travel instead upon the new road of conscious creativity. . . . I hope that we who advocate the literary revolution will exert our energies constructively, so that within the next thirty to fifty years we may create for China a new and vital Chinese literature."[28]

Hu Shih was not unaware of, nor was he unsympathetic to, the social implications of his proposals. Unless the vernacular language becomes the universal language of the new culture, he warned, the result will be "to divide society into two classes: on the one side, 'we,' the gentry; and on the other side, 'they,' the common people, the masses."[29] Others were more disposed than he, however, to exploit the vernacular movement as an instrument of social destruction. With characteristic flamboyance,

Ch'en Tu-hsiu quickly translated Hu's "tentative suggestions" into the call for a "literary revolution," a sweeping challenge to the social and cultural assumptions of the traditional order.

> The destiny of the literary revolution has only just begun to unfold. The pioneer who first raised the banner of revolt is my friend Hu Shih. I defy the enmity of academic circles throughout the country to answer my friend's call to rally to the standard of "The army of the literary revolution," upon which are inscribed its three great aims: to overthrow the ornamental, self-serving literature of the aristocracy and to create a straight-forward and direct literature of the people [*kuo-min wen-hsueh*]; to overthrow the putrid, over-elaborate classical literature and to create a fresh and honest literature of realism; to overthrow the abstruse and obscurantist literature of reclusive scholars, and to create a lucid and popular social literature. . . . A common failing of these three [traditional] styles of literature* is that they do not touch upon issues of cosmic significance, or of human life, or of society. There is a cause-and-effect relationship between this literature and the character of our people—self-satisfied, boastful, full of empty conceits, bigotted. If now we would reform our political life [*cheng chih*], we *must* reform the literature that shapes the spirit of those who dominate public affairs.[30]

Another early and eloquent recruit to the ranks of this "revolutionary army" was Ch'ien Hsuan-t'ung (1887–1939), the scion of a scholarly Chekiang gentry family. His father had held appointment to that most Confucian of offices, the Board of Rites; an elder brother was one of the dynasty's more experienced diplomats and had served, in the last years of the old regime, as supervisor of Chinese students in Japan. Ch'ien Hsuan-t'ung himself was a student at Waseda University from 1906 to 1910. In Japan he attached himself to the group of young radicals that congregated around Chang Ping-lin, enthralled as much by Chang's esoteric erudition as by his proto-anarchist politics. A brilliantly apt student of classical literature and philology—the subjects he was appointed to teach at Peita in 1915—Ch'ien became by conviction a cultural radical, one of the most adamant of the self-proclaimed iconoclasts of the teens and twenties: "The Doubter of Antiquity" (I-ku), as he was wont to style himself. In the literary revolution he perceived not only the social implications that Ch'en Tu-hsiu emphasized, but also the key to intellectual liberation:

> In several earlier essays [he wrote to Ch'en in 1918], you, Sir, have strongly urged that Confucianism be discarded, and argued for a reform of moral principles, taking the view that if a fundamental solution to the problem of moral principles is not achieved, then the signboard of the Republic will not long remain in place. . . . Hsuan-t'ung regards your proposal as the only means to

---

* The distinction among three different traditional genres to which Ch'en here alludes is clearer in the original than it can be in translation.

save China at the present time; and I would carry it a step further: if we wish to destroy Confucianism, we must get rid of the Chinese language [*Han wen*]; if we wish to eradicate the childish, uncivilized and reactionary thought prevalent among our people, we must first dispose of the Chinese language. . . . In regard to its application to modern learning, it contains no terms to describe new ideas, new facts, new things; in regard to its past history, it has served, to the virtual exclusion of anything else, as the repository for Confucian morality and Taoist superstition. Such a language is utterly unsuited to this new era, to the twentieth century.

Once more I boldly repeat my manifesto: the destruction of Confucian learning and Taoist religion is the fundamental solution if China is not to perish and if the Chinese people are to become a civilized people of the twentieth century; and the eradication of the Chinese language, which has been the repository of Confucian theories and Taoist superstitions, is the necessary means to this end.[31]

What was to be done? Romanization, in Ch'ien's view, was an awkward and unsatisfying alternative. He advocated instead the adoption of Esperanto. As for the vast corpus of China's traditional literature, "the only thing to do is to pack it away on a high shelf."

The latter recommendation was carried to its inevitable extreme by another sometime Esperanto enthusiast, the jovial old anarchist Wu Chih-hui—"China's Voltaire," in whose mind *écrasez l'infâme* and *épater le bourgeois* were inextricably mingled and equally pleasurable motives. "The old books are worthless trash," he wrote in 1924, on the fifth anniversary of the May Fourth incident. "To keep them out of the hands of students, they should be disposed of in the latrine."[32]

*   *   *

There were, of course, those who felt otherwise. To those whose sense of personality was deeply rooted in the rich traditions of the classical literary culture, it seemed, not unreasonably, that the end of a world was at hand. "We acknowledge that Latin cannot be done away with," wrote Lin Shu. "By the same logic, it is unsuitable to discard the works of Ssu-ma Ch'ien, Pan Ku, Han Yü, and Liu Tsung-yuan.* This I know, though I cannot expound the reason for it—and such, indeed, is the chronic infirmity that besets those of us who love the ancient ways. . . . My generation is old, and cannot right the wrongs of the matter. But a hundred years from now, will there be anyone left to argue our case?"[33] Yen Fu, China's other great first-generation translator, was similarly opposed to the use of the vernacular, at least as a medium of the high culture. "Principles that are subtle to begin with certainly cannot be expressed in a language that lacks eloquence," he once wrote, defending the difficult and archaic style of his own renderings. True to his convictions, however, Yen left the resolution of the issue to forces beyond the power of human

---

* Historians and essayists of the Han and T'ang dynasties, all celebrated classical stylists.

advocacy: evolution, he said, would determine the outcome. "In a revolutionary period innumerable theories arise. When they gain general circulation, the fit will survive and the unfit perish. Though there be a thousand Ch'en Tu-hsius, ten thousand Hu Shihs and Ch'ien Hsuan-t'ungs, they cannot expect to impose their opinions indefinitely. . . . And those who dispute them, like Lin Shu and his kind, are no less ridiculous."[34]

Lin Shu and Yen Fu were speaking as literati. New Culture iconoclasts easily dismissed such protests as the thin echo of voices from the past, "cast iron proof" of the poverty of the classicists' cause, as Hu Shih observed of Lin's querulous lament. Whatever their ultimate influence on their audiences, neither Lin nor Yen had any affiliation with the radical political movements of earlier years. Before the collapse of the dynasty, however, as we have seen in the case of Chang Ping-lin, revolutionary politics and cultural nationalism had not infrequently been combined in a single subversive personality. Chang himself did not play a leading role in the polemic on the new literature, but several of his erstwhile colleagues and disciples entered the lists on both sides. Ch'ien Hsuan-t'ung and Lu Hsun were notable apostates from the "nativist" faith. Of those who carried forward the traditionalist implications of Chang's racial and cultural nationalism, one of the more energetic and erratic was Liu Shih-p'ei.

Liu Shih-p'ei (1884–1919) was the last of a distinguished family of scholars from Yangchow whose consecutive careers as teachers, editors, and commentators spanned the final century of the Confucian age. From these illustrious forebears Liu inherited a profound interest in classical studies, a remarkable erudition, and the burden of upholding the family's scholarly reputation. This entailed, among other things, the compilation of a commentary on the *Spring and Autumn Annals,* an enterprise bequeathed as a legacy from generation to generation since the time of Liu's great-grandfather. It also meant an intimate familiarity with the ideas of the seventeenth-century Ming loyalists, and especially with the writings of Wang Fu-chih, whose collected works had first been edited by Liu's grandfather and published under the auspices of the Kiangnan Printing Office in the 1860s.

Liu Shih-p'ei passed the provincial examination in 1902, at the age of eighteen. The next year, having failed in the *chin-shih* examination, he became active in revolutionary politics in Shanghai. Together with Ts'ai Yuan-p'ei, Chang Shih-chao, and others, he was involved in the publication of a succession of short-lived radical papers that tried to take the place of the recently suppressed *Su-pao.* Under his newly-acquired *nom de guerre,* Liu Kuang-han (Kuang-han meaning roughly "the recovery by the Han race of its rightful inheritance") he became a radical publicist in his own right, the author of such revolutionary tracts as "On Expulsion" (*Jang shu,* preface dated 1903) and "The Spirit of the Social Contract in China" (*Chung-kuo min-yueh ching-i,* preface dated 1904). The first of these, as the title suggests, was an anti-Manchu manifesto approximating in argument Chang Ping-lin's exposition of the evolutionary connection between race and culture. The second was an attempt to extrapolate from the archaic social myths of pre-classical China a presentiment of Rousseau's "natural" community and thus to affirm the existence of a "democratic" inclination manifest in the earliest social institutions of the Chinese race.

Not surprisingly, Liu became in due course a member of both the Restoration Society and the Revolutionary Alliance. Nor is it surprising that he was one of the founders of, and a prolific contributor to, a journal entitled *The National Essence (Kuo-ts'ui hsueh-pao),* established in 1905 as an outlet for more scholarly celebrations of China's cultural traditions than were commonly published in the revolutionary press of the day. Liu carried these several political and intellectual concerns with him to Japan in 1907, in response to Chang Ping-lin's invitation to join the staff of *Min pao.* In Tokyo he became for a time an enthusiastic spokesman for the anarcho-communist ideas that were then gaining popularity among student radicals in exile. Then in 1909, from motives that have remained open to conjecture, Liu turned traitor to the revolutionary cause—and, it is generally believed, betrayed several of his former comrades to the Ch'ing authorities in the process. He returned to China to enter the service of Tuan-fang, the great Manchu official on whose staff he remained until Tuan-fang was murdered by mutinous troops in November, 1911. In the early years of the Republic Liu added insult to infamy, in the eyes of the republicans, by supporting Yuan Shih-k'ai's autocratic aspirations: he was one of the principal sponsors of the organization established to stimulate (or simulate) a "popular demand" for Yuan's reestablishment of the imperial institution.

Throughout these years of shifting political allegiances, Liu remained true at least to his commitment to the high culture and scholarly traditions of old China. He remained, too, after his own fashion, an intellectual and political radical, invoking the antique spirit of his race both as a rebuke and as an inspiration to his people, in somewhat the same way that the Ming loyalists had done in their time. Such was his reputation as a classical scholar that Ts'ai Yuan-p'ei, faithful to the principle that scholarship and politics are separate categories, appointed Liu to the Peita faculty in 1917. Two years later he died of tuberculosis at the age of thirty-five. In the final months of his life he published the last of several successors to *The National Essence,* this one entitled *The National Heritage (Kuo-ku tsa-chih),* in the pages of which the vernacular movement was denounced as an act of cultural vandalism no less barbaric than Ch'in Shih-huang-ti's infamous "burning of the books" in 213 B.C.

In Liu Shih-p'ei, traditional political radicalism and modern political reaction were linked. Chang Shih-chao, the revolutionary student editor of *Su-pao* in 1903, presents us in the May Fourth era with a less ambiguous example of what we are accustomed to regard as "conservative" opinion. For Chang, the political radicalism of the *Su-pao* period had receded under the influence of several years spent reading political economy at the University of Edinburgh, absorbing the ideas of Mill, Bagehot, and Hobhouse in an environment more congenial to their understanding than Shanghai or Tokyo could provide. He returned to China after the 1911 Revolution imbued with a cautious confidence in constitutionalism and the rule of law, and dared on these grounds to denounce Yuan Shih-k'ai's monarchical pretensions in the pages of *The Tiger Magazine* in 1914. But the vulnerability of republican institutions to the manipulations of ambitious warlords and unprincipled politicians persuaded Chang that China was not yet ready for representative democracy. He came finally to believe, moreover, that industrialization may be, for an agricultural society, too high a price to pay for "modernity." In the 1920s Chang emerged as an outspoken critic of the cultural and social consequences, as he envisioned them, of the vernacular movement. His own prose style was esteemed for its terse elegance; his rise from Hunanese peasant origins lent credibility to his revival of the egalitarian mythology of the Confucian educational order:

> Mr. Hu [Shih] says that society must not be divided into two classes. . . . It is commonly held today that the written language belongs to the aristocracy, and that it must be vernacularized in order to make it accessible to the common people. Now in my village, when I was young, the herd boys and the woodcutters' sons all enjoyed the opportunity to enter the village school at the appropriate time. The *Thousand-character Classic*, the *Four Books*, and the *Anthology of T'ang Poetry* kindled their enthusiasm. They entered the district school. They became gentry [*t'uan-shen*]. Many were renowned as "the good scholars of the village." My own humble family had been farmers for generations. My grandfather was the first to study, and to seek to make a name for himself in the examinations, in order to pass this tradition down to his sons and grandsons. Anyone who knows anything about our natonal character knows that in our country it is possible to accomplish by one's own effort whatever one sets one's mind upon, whether one is highborn or the lowest of the low. The notion that the written language creates a barrier that limits men's abilities is something never heard before.

Chang insisted that, contrary to the claims of "modern" educationalists, it is the new-style education that is "exclusive," irrelevant at the level of village life either to vocational competence or social status, and therefore attracting—or accepting—far fewer students than had matriculated under the old system. "Today's schools have created a kind of aristocratic education, but this has nothing whatever to do with the dispute between the classical and the vernacular languages."[35]

Chang Shih-chao evoked, in idealized form, a remembered way of life. A more pertinent critique of the vernacular movement, phrased in terms of the contemporary culture that May Fourth radicals aspired to emulate, was published in the pages of *Hsueh heng* (The Critical Review), a monthly journal of literature and literary criticism established in January, 1922. Mei Kuang-ti (1890–1945) and Wu Mi (1894–   ), its principal sponsors, were members of the English faculty at Tung-nan university in Nanking, and were themselves very much products of the new age. Both had been students at Tsing Hua, and in the course of their subsequent studies in the United States both had come under the influence of Irving Babbitt, Harvard's contentious and controversial professor of French literature. Neither racial or cultural ethnicity, nor a nostalgic affection for "Chineseness," played much part in their thinking. They were "modern" intellectuals by education and taste, well able to substantiate the cosmopolitan claims published (in English) as the purposes of *The Critical Review:* "to study, elucidate, and systematize the Chinese learning with critical method and scholarly equipment," and "to introduce and to assimilate what is best and most important in the literature, philosophy, art, etc., of the West, presenting Western Civilization in its entirety and most salutary aspects."[36]

To these ends, *The Critical Review* published literary criticism, poetry, short stories, and translations of Western authors from Aristotle to Voltaire to Arnold to Babbitt himself. If this was less than "Western Civilization in its entirety," neither could it be dismissed as a last-ditch defense of Confucian culture in its stereotypical modes. "Who does not recognize the need to create a new culture?" asked Mei Kuang-ti. The age of China's splendid and unchallenged cultural isolation is over and done with; now, for the first time, the Chinese must look abroad for inspiration, "borrowing the strengths of others to make good our own shortcomings—an opportunity unprecedented in the several millennia of our history, that should be a matter for delight and gratification to our people." This critique of the New Culture was not intended to reassert traditional Chinese parochialism and cultural exclusivism. It was the expression, rather, of resistance to the encroachment of the universal phenomenon of modernity, echoing Babbitt's critique of contemporary realist and naturalist literature, and affirming his conviction that the individual's cultural personality must not be compelled to conform to mass values and tastes or sacrificed to the realization of collective social ends.

Babbitt's inspiration was classical. The neo-humanists' hero was not Man created in God's image, nor yet Man as a creature of primitive Nature, but Man as an autonomous moral actor. Culture, Babbitt insisted, must not debase human character by reducing it to a naturalistic commonality, or at the other extreme by encouraging undisciplined individualism, the arrogant anarchy of romanticism, in art or in politics. It is not difficult to understand why a doctrine that exalted human moral uniqueness should appeal to the minds of young men educated, if only indirectly, to a Confucian faith in the moral corrigibility of human character and the "natural" human disposition to act in accordance with essentially moral instincts. Interestingly enough, among the things that attracted other Chinese students to Columbia to study under John Dewey at about this time were ideas that resonated in somewhat similar fashion with notions inherited from the Confucian past: an implicit confidence in human moral capability and a corresponding emphasis on education; a belief in the importance of the cultural and social environment that establishes the context of human choice and action; a concern for social and historical coherence.

But Dewey conceived of "the good" and "the true" as terms of relative meaning subject always to the "proof" of the results achieved in application, and subservient, in the final analysis, to the necessities of individual and social survival. It has been remarked that the main thrust of Dewey's philosophy is aptly epitomized in the title of one of his own early works: *The Influence of Darwin on Philosophy*. Babbitt, on the other hand, excluded evolutionary necessity from consideration. He despised technology and intellectual specialization—the survival skills of modernity. He defined moral value in terms of more or less fixed classical forms and aesthetic norms, and he deplored as degenerate the emphasis of contemporary literary culture on social realism, romantic egoism, subjectivism, and spontaneity.

Neo-humanism was readily translated by Wu Mi and Mei Kuang-ti into an attack on the pretensions of China's new intellectuals." The inaugural editorial of *The Critical Review*, signed by Mei, was a sweeping denunciation of the rationale of the New Culture movement. It was also a scathing indictment of its leaders, whose talent for self-advertisement and skill in misleading a growing rabble of followers forced Mei to assume a responsibility from which, he insisted, he derived no pleasure: "I must tear the masks from their faces, and reveal them for what they truly are."

It was not a flattering portrait. China's "modern" intellectuals, Mei wrote, are not thinkers, but sophists; not creators, but copyists; not scholars, but celebrity-seekers; not educators, but politicians. "They toady to the young with theories new and marvelous, affirming their own prejudices and opinions as established fact, espousing whatever is fashionable or expedient, and remaining utterly indifferent to imperishable truth." They foist off on a naive and susceptible audience ideas already outmoded and repudiated in the West. Even as they deride the Chinese for "following the ancients," they themselves copy slavishly

from the West, exhibiting in their own work as little creativity as did the
most pedantic masters of the discarded eight-legged essay style. They
rush into print with half-informed opinions on every subject under the
sun, establishing magazines, attracting a following, writing congratula-
tory prefaces for each other's books. They pander shamelessly to the
demands of their juvenile constituents for "student autonomy" and "open
academic administration." In sum, "To speak to them of scholarly standards or conscience is like preaching ethics to a merchant or chastity to a
whore."

An element of cultural pride still shows through. "Our culture being
what it is, it must carry within it the inextinguishable spark of greatness,"
Mei wrote. "We are not like the island peoples of the Phillippines or
Hawaii, or the American blacks, who, having no culture of their own to
speak of, must borrow culture from others." As Mei himself conceded, his
representation of the "true" scholar was an idealized description of the
Confucian man of letters, a veritable *chün-tzu:* sincere, true to his purpose, unswayed by the demands of academic or worldly fashion.
"Scholars seek truth for its own sake, and value what they know to be
true, not merely conventional wisdom. They prize what they have
themselves accomplished, not the rewards that life may bestow upon
them. They labor diligently all their lives long, holding fast to what they
have gained, and not casually publishing the results of their learning.
They must think a thing through before they will say a word; they must
ponder a matter until it is entirely clear, and only then will they commit
their thoughts to paper." So much for the glib and garrulous purveyors of
the New Culture.[37]

Beneath this virulent prose we may detect a slight but important shift
from the position occupied by cultural nativists like Chang Ping-lin and
Liu Shih-p'ei, or conservatives like Chang Shih-chao. For Mei Kuang-ti
the preservation of a Chinese "essence" was a matter not merely of native
forms, but of the universal relationship between cultural form and
human character. He valued the standards of classical Chinese literary
culture (not only the classical language) not as an inheritance sacrosanct
by virtue of its Chineseness, but as the indigenous expression of values of
universal significance: intellectual self-discipline and aesthetic restraint,
the integrity of the creative spirit. *The Critical Review* criticized not
what was *foreign* in the New Culture, but what was, or pretended to be,
modern. It thus foreshadowed a broader "neo"-traditionalist critique of
the material and spiritual consequences of China's modernization. Before
turning our attention to this dispute, however, we must look more closely
at certain aspects of the New Culture itself.

*   *   *

We have spoken thus far of the New Culture intellectuals as a group,
and of their common educational programs and journalistic enterprises as

a movement. It would be well at this point to stress the caution with which such generalizations must be interpreted. Just as the revolutionary movement in the period 1898–1911 had encompassed a diverse constituency whose agreement on a particular political objective engendered little agreement on either means or ends, so the New Culture movement was the undertaking of intellectuals who shared an antipathy to the "old culture," but who differed among themselves as to how broadly this should be construed, and the appropriate means to its transformation. For a few years, roughly the period from 1915 to 1920, there was a degree of unity within their ranks. Then, from the early 1920s onward, the growing appeal of social and political ideologies, together with the revival of revolutionary organizations, brought about a division between what we may call, for convenience, the moderate and the radical factions of the movement. The sun at noon is the sun declining, observed the ancient master of paradox Hui Shih: some historians have argued that the May Fourth incident, with its manifold political and ideological repercussions, marked not the beginning, but the beginning of the end, of the New Culture experience—and more broadly, of the era of intellectual experimentation and "enlightenment" that had begun a generation earlier.

Despite the hardening of ideological commitments after 1920, however, and the increasingly politicized context of intellectual discourse, the New Culture phenomenon cannot be dismissed merely as an interlude, either epilogue or prologue. It created an environment congenial to innovative thinking and the popularization of novel political and social ideas. It restored much of the self-confidence and self-respect that Chinese intellectuals had lost in the disillusioning early years of the Republic. Thus on the one hand, it prepared the way for increasingly programmatic responses in the continuing quest for purpose and direction. On the other hand, however, the values of unhampered inquiry and self-expression, of pragmatic judgment and reasonable expectations, all central to what we might call the New Culture mentality, established with enduring effect the criteria by which many Chinese intellectuals continued critically to assess the legitimacy of later regimes, down to and even beyond the great turning point of 1949.

"How can we Chinese feel at ease in this new world which at first sight appears to be so much at variance with what we have long regarded as our own civilization?" asked Hu Shih in 1917 as he returned home to take up the task for which he had been preparing himself during his years in America. "How can we best assimilate modern civilization in such a manner as to make it congenial and congruous and continuous with the civilization of our own making?"[38] Many Chinese intellectuals—many, even, of Hu's destined critics and adversaries—would have agreed with the issue so stated. Even for those who cherished the memory of a bygone time, it was no longer a question of returning to the forms and institutions of the dead past. Only a handful had followed K'ang Yu-wei's lead, to support a short-lived and inept restoration of the Manchus in July, 1917. For most Chinese intellectuals in the late teens and early twenties, as for Hu himself, the question was one of maintaining, or creating, a sense of continuity between past and present that would make China's survival meaningful.

As Laurence Schneider has pointed out in his studies of intellectuals of the "national essence" persuasion, the concern for continuity was frequently expressed as a demand for the persistence, in varying combination, of the literary forms, the aesthetic norms, and the moral pedagogy that together comprised the content of China's inherited elite culture. Less evident, but in many cases no less important, was a concern for the persistence of the intellectuals' traditional vocation, as spokesmen of the state-and-culture and, therefore, men of public significance.

The New Culture was subversive of such claims, not merely because it attacked Confucian institutions and values, but also because of the intellectual and social role its advocates endeavored to exemplify. They were not the first to espouse individualism as a social value; that distinction belongs, as we have seen, to Liang Ch'i-ch'ao, Yen Fu, and the early revolutionary polemicists. New Culture intellectuals were, however, the first to affirm the *primary* importance of individualistic styles of thought and conduct as expressions of private conscience. They were by no means indifferent to the interests of the community. But, as we have noted, they tended to define the community in terms of its cultural personality rather than its political identity, giving precedence to qualities of mind and character that reinforced the independence of the individual from the group, and of intellectuals from the state. The "slavishness" they denounced as an attribute of traditional Chinese society was nowhere more apparent, in their view, than in the relationship of servile dependency that had bound the Confucian scholar to the uses and the whim of imperial power.

In the New Culture generation, then, we encounter for the first time what we may properly call a Chinese intelligentsia: an intellectual community of self-consciously critical and self-critical "men of the opposition," whose demand for a hearing arises from the conviction that private opinion, private character, and private tastes possess civic significance and deserve public attention.

If the New Culture movement had an ideology of its own, this can only be described by a term as ambiguous and contentious as "liberalism." It is a troublesome term, carrying with it diverse political and historical connotations peculiar to its use in Western contexts, but lacking substantive connotations in the history of Chinese political theory or institutions. The institutions central to the existence of a "liberal" political system were unknown to the Chinese, either in practice or as aspects of the Confucian tradition of speculative discourse. Nowhere in the enormous political literature of Confucianism does one find precedents for the ideas of government limited by the rule of law; of inalienable popular rights defined and protected by constitutional compact; of the representation of popular opinion or popular interests in the legislative process. Nor is it possible to discover, even in the "liberality" of Mencius' Confucianism, any precedent for the notion of liberty or freedom as a political and social condition.

There was, literally, no word for it in the inherited vocabulary. "Freedom" or "liberty" was rendered into Chinese around the turn of the century by the term *tzu-yu*—one of the many words borrowed in the nineteenth century by the Japanese from ancient Chinese sources to accommodate modern uses, and eventually reappropriated by the Chinese, though in this case without particular conviction. In its original Chinese settings, *tzu-yu* conveyed an idea strongly colored by Taoist-Buddhist notions of "free-and-easy-do-what-you-will-ism"—a style of conduct roundly condemned by Confucians as socially reprehensible. Even Liang Ch'i-ch'ao complained that the term carried with it connotations of reckless or licentious behavior. Yen Fu disagreed: *tzu-yu*, he insisted, means whatever one intends it to mean in context. He struggled valiantly with the problem in his translation of J. S. Mill's *On Liberty*; the best he could do, however, was to suggest the use of unfamiliar homophonous characters that might deceive the reader's eye and misdirect his sense of association. When the translation was published, in 1903, Yen abandoned his original title, "On *tzu-yu*" (*Tzu-yu lun*), and called the work instead "On the Boundaries of the Rights of Society and the Individual" (*Ch'ün chi ch'üan chieh lun*), a change that reflected not only terminological difficulties, but also Yen's understanding of the gist of Mill's treatise.

Liberal-minded Chinese in the teens and twenties thus did not commonly call themselves "liberals," or speak as the advocates of a "liberal" program. For our purposes, nevertheless, liberalism remains the most appropriate designation to describe their general undertaking, both in its essential aims and in its political implications. New Culture liberals sought to establish, as standards that would encompass the whole of society, the values essential to the cultural activity and the life style of an enlightened, critical, and self-critical intellectual elite. This endeavor entailed certain political propositions, framed in slightly different language in manifestos published from time to time in the late teens and early twenties. These liberal manifestos invariably centered on similar, and predictable, demands: that freedom of speech, press, assembly, and belief be guaranteed by right; that the government be responsive and responsible to public opinion, as expressed through parliamentary institutions; that the executive respect the independence of the legislative power, and be governed by laws not ordained by itself; and, most fundamental of all, that the polity be constitutionally legitimate—that is, governed in accordance with the values affirmed by a broad political and social consensus.*

As witnesses to the tragedy of the stillborn Republic, however, New Culture liberals were convinced that even the most carefully designed and progressive institutions would not, on paper, accomplish the necessary ends of reform. Their emphasis, therefore, was less on the institutional aspect of a liberal settlement, and more on the inculcation of attitudes toward the self and the community that would, in time, invest appropriate institutions with enduring vitality. They demanded for others—and from others the willingness to exercise—the freedom that they themselves exemplified: what José Ortega y Gasset has called "Liberty of spirit . . . intellectual power . . . measured by its capacity to dissociate ideas traditionally inseparable."[40] Hence their insistence, at one level, that Chinese culture, as represented in popular traditions of literary and artistic self-expression, and Confucian culture, as represented in the despised Classical canon, are distinguishable and radically different traditions. Hence, too, their insistence on the importance of distinguishing between the political order and the moral order, between public culture and private culture, and, in terms of more mundane admonition, between custom and intelligence as rationalizations of conduct.

Hu Shih was among the most widely read proselytizers of this "new attitude"—an attitude, he wrote in 1919, that "acknowledges only true or false, good or bad, fit or unfit, and is not concerned with the attempt to reconcile past and present, or Chinese and foreign, components." As Hu defined it,

> The critical attitude can be summarized as the application to all things of a fresh judgment as to whether or not they are good [hao yü pu-hao]. . . . We must ask, "Do the institutions and customs inherited from the past retain in the present any value to justify their existence? Do the sage precepts bequeathed to us by antiquity still hold true in the present? Must something be right because it is generally held to be so by all and sundry, as is the case with the standard of conduct and the beliefs commonly and unthinkingly sanctioned by society as a whole? If others behave in a certain fashion, must I also? Can it be that there is no other way of acting that is better than this, more reasonable, more

* The two most widely circulated examples were the "Manifesto of the Struggle for Freedom," and "Our Political Proposals." The first, published in August 1920, was signed by Hu Shih, Chiang Monlin, Li Ta-chao, Kao I-han, T'ao Meng-ho, Chang Wei-tz'u and Wang Cheng. It denounced the "pseudo-republicanism of the last nine years," and called for "a genuine republicanism . . . initiated by the people," which could only be achieved by encouraging "an atmosphere wherein a genuine spirit of free thought and free criticism can be nurtured." "Our Political Proposals" was published in May 1922 by the same signatories, joined in this case by Ts'ai Yuan-p'ei, Ting Wen-chiang, T'ao Hsing-chih, Liang Shu-ming and several others. It demanded the creation of a "government by good men," and urged progressive Chinese, regardless of ideological differences, to unite under this broad banner.[39]

beneficial?" . . . Whenever you do something without asking yourself, "Why am I doing this?"—that is meaningless life. . . . The "why" of life makes it meaningful.[41]

Hu Shih was preaching here in his accustomed (and at that time still comfortable) role as the preeminent popularizer of American pragmatism. Pragmatism in several of its guises—as a formal philosophy, as a critique of philosophy or a philosophy of philosophy, or as an epistemology—held no particular fascination for Hu, nor, for that matter, for most other Chinese disciples of the Sage of Morningside Heights. Dewey as an educational theorist was one thing; in the reshaping of the Chinese curriculum, his influence was truly and widely felt. But Dewey as an academic philosopher was less easily assimilable, and less useful. Dewey's validation of the philosophical enterprise in terms of its concrete application to practical ends was addressed to problems too deeply imbedded in the history of Western philosophical disputation to appeal generally to an audience that was not a party to the dispute. On the other hand, Hu Shih and other New Culture liberals certainly recognized the relevance to their own message of Dewey's insistence that "morality"—socially necessary and therefore socially sanctioned behavior—is not a fixed standard, arbitrary and absolute, but a standard that evolves from age to age through the fluid interaction of social need and human nature. The New Culture understanding of human nature, however, owed less to the subtleties of Dewey's social psychology than it did to a kind of old-fashioned rationalism: a compound of Confucian scepticism, Mencian faith in man's moral corrigibility, an Enlightenment confidence in the invincible authority of Reason, and a nineteenth-century respect for intellectual order and common sense—all bound together by a commitment to education as the enabling experience. Hu never tired of saying that pragmatism, or experimentalism as he preferred to call it, is "only a methodology"—a way to think about life, not what to think of it. That such a methodology could be useful in the struggle for liberation from the orthodoxies of the past was self-evident to Hu and to his audience. As we shall see, it was a position calculated also to challenge the authority of orthodoxies strange and novel.

However untraditional his questions and his answers, the focus of Hu Shih's scholarly interest remained in a certain sense traditional: the history of Chinese thought and literature—the history, in sum, of Chinese humanism. For him, and for students upon whom his influence is most conspicuous (one thinks of Ku Chieh-kang, of Yü P'ing-po, of Fu Ssu-nien, of Wu Han), libraries and archives rather than laboratories or experiment stations provided the appropriate opportunities for demonstrating the usefulness of the "scientific method." In Hu's exposition of it, this came down to a formula that enjoined an energetic search for new data; scrupulous regard for objectivity in its interpretation; sensitivity to the evolutionary or diachronic dimensions of the problem in hand; an awareness of the larger implications of one's conclusions, and a constant willingness to revise them in light of new information.

Hu's first major scholarly publication, the first volume of a general history of Chinese philosophy that remained unfinished, exemplified his approach. It took as its organizational scheme the methodologies of early Chinese thinkers rather than the traditionally accepted "Hundred Schools"; it traced the emergence of Chinese thought to the social and political chaos of the late Chou period; and it began the history not with the legendary culture figures of high antiquity, but with Lao Tzu and Confucius. "Before I began lecturing on Chinese philosophy at Peita in 1917," Hu later recalled, "it was regarded as essential to launch into the topic by talking about Fu Hsi, Shen Nung, The Yellow Emperor, and Yao and Shun. According to Ku Chieh-kang's notes, when in my first day's lecture I talked about Lao Tzu and Confucius, I very nearly provoked a student demonstration in the classroom!" Hu's studies in the history of Chinese vernacular literature, in which he attempted to establish the authorship and motives of the great novels of the Ming and Ch'ing dynasties, were likewise intended to demonstrate "the intellectual method of Huxley and Dewey given practical application. My textual examinations of these novels . . . are simply 'profound and clear' examples to teach people how to think."[42] With his talent for popularization, Hu reduced the scientific method to an easily remembered ten-word slogan: "Be bold in framing hypotheses, be meticulous in seeking proofs."

Hu Shih was not by education a scientist, any more than he was by intellectual disposition a speculative philosopher. Others who shared his enthusiasm for the scientific method were better equipped than he to speak of it intimately. Among the first generation of modern Chinese scientists, none was more eminent or a more able representative of science as a discipline than Ting Wen-chiang (V. K. Ting, 1887–1936). The classically educated son of a Kiangsu gentry family, Ting had joined the academic emigration to Japan shortly after the turn of the century. He spent a year and a half in Tokyo before embarking for Europe at the invitation of Wu Chih-hui, who wrote from Edinburgh in glowing terms of the excellence and the modest cost of a genuine Western education. The expense far exceeded Wu's cheerful estimates, forcing Ting to live in straitened circumstances during most of his seven years in Great Britain. He was an apt student, however, and when he returned to China in 1911 he held the Sc.B. degree from Glasgow University in both geology and zoology, and boasted as well a certain amount of premedical education. He had also acquired a substantial first-hand acquaintance with European life in the course of several extended tours of the Continent. In the unsettled early years of the Republic, Ting quickly established his reputation as an energetic field surveyor, principally in the remote and mountainous provinces of the southwest. In 1916 he was appointed to be the first director of the China Geological Survey. For Ting Wen-chiang the "scientific attitude" was thus more than a conventional metaphor for "the progressive view of things." Science, he wrote in the 1920s,

> . . . is the best instrument available for education, because the daily search for truth, the constant desire to banish preconceptions, not only gives the student of science an ability to seek truth, but moreover inspires in him a sincere love of truth. No matter what he may encounter, he can always proceed to analyse and examine it with detachment and candor, seeking simplicity out of complexity, and order out of confusion, using reason to discipline his thinking and thus increasing his intellectual powers, using experience to guide his intuition, and thus enlivening his intuitive powers.[43]

The zeal for science as "a way of knowing, not a set of things known"[44] remained one of the more durable components in the New Culture consensus. The idea of science, however, did not appear *ex nihilo* in China in the 1910s. In this as in other respects, the New Culture was an elaboration of themes already present in turn-of-the-century reformist thought. It was Liang Ch'i-ch'ao and Yen Fu who had been responsible for popularizing, among the generation that was coming of age intellectually in the prerevolutionary decade, the conviction that human experience and aspiration must be understood within the governing context of evolutionary theory. It was Liang and Yen who thus laid the foundation for what D. W. Y. Kwok has called "scientism" as the new orthodoxy: "that view which places all reality within a natural order and deems all aspects of this order, be they biological, social physical, or psychological, to be knowable only by the methods of science."[45] Although their intellectual beneficiaries generally acknowledged the debt, neither Yen nor Liang was unreservedly esteemed by the New Culture generation. Indeed, before the end of their lives (Yen died in 1921, Liang in 1929) both had retreated from the materialist implications of the "scientific" world view. But a belief in the existence of an understandable design beneath the surface of human experience, and the sense of historical dynamism, mechanism, and purpose that has animated Chinese political and social idealism in the twentieth century, owes much to the persuasive and confident evolutionary progressivism preached by Yen Fu and Liang Ch'i-ch'ao.

The enormous popularity of Social Darwinism in China in the early years of the century has been remarked upon in chapter 5. The possible reasons for that popularity, however, deserve further comment. Why should a doctrine that, as Richard Hofstadter put it, "walked hand in hand" with conservatism in the United States in the late nineteenth century, and "brought with it a paralysis of the will to reform," have enthralled reform-minded young Chinese to such a degree? Of what practical or spiritual use to them was a philosophy whose temper was epitomized in Edward L. Youmans' rejoinder to Henry George's query as to what he proposed to *do* about problems of political corruption and social inequity: "Nothing!" said Youmans. "You and I can do nothing at all. It's all a matter of evolution. We can only wait for evolution. Perhaps in four or five thousand years evolution may have carried men beyond this state of things." What comfort could Chinese who strained to seize control of their own destiny draw from the inspiration behind Youmans' placid assurance that "the spirit of civilization . . . is pacific, constructive, controlled by reason, and slowly ameliorating and progressive. Coercive and violent measures which aim at great and sudden advantages are sure to prove illusory."[46]

The Chinese, to be sure, did not receive their introduction to Spencer and Darwin in the first instance through the mediation of American interpretations. Yen Fu read and reacted to the seminal texts in the original. Liang Ch'i-ch'ao and other early radicals relied initially on such sources as *Wan-kuo kung-pao* and later and more significantly on Japanese translations and interpretations. A distinctively American mode of evolutionism made its influence widely felt in China only with the growing popularity of Pragmatism in the New Culture era, and by that time both the message and the context in which it was understood had changed markedly.

Early Chinese enthusiasm for evolutionism doubtless derived, nevertheless, from sentiments akin to those communicated by Edward Youmans to Spencer himself: "What we want are ideas—large, organizing ideas."[47] Evolutionary theories helped the Chinese to wrest some meaning, however grim, from their recent experience, as discredited Confucian historiography no longer could. We may speculate further that it was perhaps psychologically less burdensome to share with the human race at large the prospect of an almost unbearably slow progress than it was to accept the verdict of moral delinquency that was the characteristic Confucian response to political and cultural disaster. Spencerian determinism held out at least the hope of a future, albeit a future toward which mankind inched its way as insensibly and ponderously as a glacier approaches the sea.

Neither Yen nor Liang, moreover, allowed themselves to be deflected from their immediate purposes by the deterministic implications of Spencerian evolutionism. As Benjamin Schwartz has shown, Yen used Spencer (as he used Huxley, Mill, Montesquieu, and the other Western sources of his inspiration) to argue a case quite in keeping with the reformist temper of the time, and on the whole encouraging. No less than for his politically more engagé and radical contemporaries, for Yen the wealth and power of the state remained the primary objective. Evolutionism, by justifying the historical function of conflict and competition, helped to explain China's predicament. It also provided a key to the liberation of the social and political energies of the Chinese, holding forth the promise that they could become what they were not, nor perhaps had ever been: a civic community able to sustain the responsibilities of nationhood. Spencer and Mill notwithstanding, there was an emphatic element of voluntarism and collective purpose in Yen's message, and in Liang's.

"One is not deceived by the ancients or cowed by those in authority," wrote Yen Fu in 1903.[48] Such general scepticism in regard to received doctrine was a part of the inheritance claimed by New Culture iconoclasts impartially from revolutionaries and reformers alike. But the liberals of the late teens and twenties were in a more specific sense the designated heirs of Liang Ch'i-ch'ao and Yen Fu. Liang and Yen were gradualists, who conceived of social and political change not as the rapid and decisive sequence of events awaited with such impatience by the revolutionaries, but as a slow and unpredictable process. As good evolutionists, they distrusted the notion that history could be abruptly diverted, to flow in unaccustomed directions.

This sense of the necessary continuity of historical experience became, in the next generation, a conspicuous aspect of New Culture liberalism, but with a significant shift in emphasis. Political institutions and capabilities, insisted the New Culture radicals, are the derivative products of a cultural environment. But for Liang and Yen, as for other turn-of-the-century reformers and revolutionaries, the problem that bulked largest was still the problem of political leadership, or right rulership, a problem which, as they viewed it, could only be solved within the framework of China's cultural limitations. The revolutionaries called for political tutelage; Liang invoked an enlightened autocrat; Yen imagined the advent of a modern Sage, who would "labor tirelessly to promote whatever will advance the talents, virtue and strength" of the people, and thus "acknowledge their capacity for freedom to the fullest."[49]

With whatever misgivings, Liang Ch'i-ch'ao resigned himself to life under the Republic, and accommodated his opinions to the changing world of the 1910s. Yen Fu could not; his tacit support of Yuan Shih-k'ai's monarchical ambitions diminished his reputation in the eyes of those who had been educated by his translations of Mill and Montesquieu, even as the scheme itself finally discredited the claim that the 1911 Revolution had resolved the issue of China's political future. As the New Culture movement gathered momentum, Yen Fu retired to spend his final years in cheerless seclusion, pondering the truth that he had spent so many years expounding: "There is no escape from the laws of the struggle for existence and natural selection. . . . In the struggle between the superior and inferior, one side must die."[50]

It was a homily that the New Culture generation had learned by heart. It proved, however, a hard lesson to live by at full strength. By the late teens many Chinese intellectuals were abandoning the gospel of Social Darwinism, repelled in some cases by its dehumanization of history, in others by its indifference to the possibility of purposeful intervention in the course of events. The somewhat gentler evolutionism of Kropotkin's "mutual aid" anarchism attracted a considerable following, though for many (Mao Tse-tung is a prominent example) this was no more than a stopping-off place. As we shall see in chapter 7, it was at this time that Marxism first began to receive serious attention. This was partly because the dialectic offered, as many came to think, a convincing analysis of the social and economic forces that were impelling China's history forward: partly it was because Marxism made place for a program of radical action: a way to change the world, not merely to understand it. For intellectuals whose sympathies lay at the opposite pole of the political and cultural spectrum of opinion, the subjective evolutionism expounded most persuasively in Henri Bergson's philosophy of *élan vital* justified a reaffirmation of the significance of moral self-consciousness and unique historical experience.

Chinese liberals, however, tended on the whole to remain faithful to the tenets of Social Darwinist theory. They rejected the idea of moral/political *dirigisme* as Yen and Liang had formulated it, as they rejected also the revolutionaries' insistence on the need for "Party tutelage." But they remained confident of what we might call "intellectual evolution"—the belief that if ideas are allowed to circulate freely the result must be the survival of the "fittest": the ideas best suited to insure China's gradual revival and transformation. They retained also the evolutionary view of time as a controlling factor in the organic processes of social and cultural change. In the topical essays of Hu Shih, Ts'ai Yuan-p'ei, Chiang Monlin, Ting Wen-chiang, and other Western-educated intellectuals in the late teens and twenties we find, in curious combination, a lively sense of the urgency of the present crisis and the need for resolute action, together with a stubborn conviction that the pace of change cannot be unduly hastened. Again and again after May Fourth, China's activist student patriots were counseled by their academic mentors to contemplate unflinchingly the prospect of decades, or even generations, of slow civic maturation; students were urged in the meanwhile to pursue singlemindedly their primary responsibility, which was to study.

For reasons not difficult to fathom, this was an attitude that soon brought the liberals into open confrontation with the restless younger generation. In his capacity as acting chancellor of Peita during Ts'ai Yuan-p'ei's brief retirement in the summer of 1919, Chiang Monlin told the students bluntly to get their priorities straight.*

* Distressed alike by what he regarded as the students' excesses and by the harshness of the government's reaction—and seeking, perhaps, to forestall a move to fire him—Ts'ai "re-

Now the youth who are involved in the movement for national salvation protest against one thing today, and something else tomorrow. Truly, as the ancients have it, "It is a pity to spend one's life with needle and thread, mending other people's wornout garments." This is not a way of getting at the fundamental issues. If we really want to save the country, we must first devise plans for cultural advancement. What good does it do to spend every day patching up what is already ragged and threadbare?[51]

Your patriotic motives in the recent demonstrations are to be highly commended. But if you keep on doing this your valuable time will be wasted and the existence of the institution where you drink at the fountain of wisdom will be endangered. A new nation is not made in one day. . . . The demonstrations are trifles in comparison with the work you have to do in classrooms, in the library, in laboratories, and in seminars. . . . [52]

Ts'ai Yuan-p'ei addressed himself to the student body in similar terms when he returned to Peita in September. And on the first anniversary of the May Fourth incident, after a winter of sporadic campus unrest, Chiang Monlin joined with Hu Shih to publish yet another appeal to the students. Their protests were favorably compared to similar movements in prerevolutionary Russia and Germany, and, closer to home, to the student protests of the 1890s and the 1900s: natural manifestations in a time "when the government is evil and corrupt, and the people possess no institutional means to put the situation to rights." But, cautioned Chiang and Hu, "We must remember that this sort of movement is extraordinary—inevitable in an abnormal society, but also extremely wasteful and unfortunate." The long-term effects would be disastrous, they warned. Students would learn to rely exclusively on group action, forgetting that "there is much that the individual by himself can do." Truancy would become a habit indulged in for its own sake. Intellectual irresponsibility, the fashion of following the crowd, would flourish. Students must study, Chiang and Hu insisted, not only to master what they have set out to learn, but also to set an example of personal self-cultivation and civic self-discipline.[53]

Such admonitions set the tone of the relationship between New Culture liberals and the emerging student movement. There was more to it, however, than sober professorial reaction against the disorders of 1919–1920. On Hu Shih's part it was the expression of a position that he had argued during his own student days in the United States. *Let us be calm,"* he had urged in 1915, at the height of the Sino-Japanese crisis of that year which had inflamed the passions of Chinese students abroad.

---

signed" the chancellorship on May 9 and sought refuge in Hangchow, where, as Chiang Monlin observed, "he lived . . . surrounded by gentle hills [on the shores of the historic West Lake], enjoying nature as a traditional scholar of the old days." (*Tides from the West*, p. 123.) It was, indeed, a very old-fashioned form of remonstrance, invoking the moral authority of the *chün-tzu* who "withdraws when the Way does not prevail." Ts'ai resumed his duties at Peita in September; but this was not the last time he would resort to this Confucian mode of protest.

"Let us DO OUR DUTY which is TO STUDY. Let us not be carried away by the turmoil of the newspaper from our serious mission. Let us apply ourselves seriously, calmly, undisturbedly and unshakenly to our studies, and PREPARE OURSELVES to uplift our father-land, if she [sic] survives this crisis—as I am sure she will,—or to resurrect her from the dead, if it needs be!"[54]

Behind this moderate advice lay convictions that Hu never abandoned. Much of the temper of the Chinese liberalism of the twenties and thirties was already in evidence in Hu's confidences to his American friends in the teens. "I have come to hold that there is no shortcut to political decency and efficiency," he wrote to one of these. "Good government cannot be secured without certain necessary prerequisites. . . . I do not condemn revolutions, because I believe that they are necessary stages in the process of evolution. But I do not favor premature revolutions, because they are usually wasteful and therefore unfruitful. . . . Personally I prefer to build from the bottom up. . . . My personal attitude is: 'Come what may, let us educate the people. Let us lay the foundation for our future generations to build upon.' This is necessarily a very slow process, and mankind is impatient! But, so far as I can see, this slow process is the only process."[55] Twenty years later, when China faced a far graver threat of Japanese aggression in the bitter days after the Manchurian Incident, Hu still optimistically urged patience and the long view. "Our final victory is beyond the shadow of a doubt! . . . In the long life of a nation, of what importance are four or five, or forty or fifty, years?" "We must not be pessimistic. Look! In the very midst of our silent endurance of this suffering, a new people [and] nation has gradually taken form."[56]

This sense of history seems baffling, in retrospect, knowing as we do how rapidly the rush of events was to overwhelm such sanguine expectations that time was on the side of a program of slow enlightenment. To an increasing number of Chinese, indeed, it came to appear unrealistic; some even saw it as treacherously designed to thwart men of stalwart purpose. Throughout the 1920s and 1930s, as we shall discover, the New Culture liberals fought a losing battle to retain the attention and respect that they had commanded in the period 1915–1920. But in those early years, gradualism was an attitude generally characteristic of New Culture radicalism. It was an essential corollary to the pervasive enthusiasm for the "scientific attitude," the slow accumulation of "facts" on which to base an objective description of the realities of Chinese life as a first step toward the solution of China's problems. Even Ch'en Tu-hsiu—impetuous, an activist by nature—initially conceded the necessity of this piecemeal approach. "To elucidate the truth by means of science means weighing one fact against another," he wrote in his "Appeal to Youth" in 1915. "The pace is certainly slow, in comparison to what can be accomplished by leaps of the imagination or by dogmatic assertion. But progress is firmly grounded."[57]

It was Hu Shih who gave the classic formulation to this gradualist, particularist strategy. The "new thought," as Hu epitomized it, had four primary aims: to identify, and then to analyse, specific problems; to broaden the analytical frame of reference by importing foreign ideas and theories; to authenticate and "systematize" (*cheng-li*) what should be regarded as genuinely a part of the Chinese tradition; and by these several means, gradually to reconstruct "civilization" (*wen-ming*). "Civilization is not created wholesale," he cautioned in 1919.

> It is created bit by bit and drop by drop. Progress cannot be achieved all at one go, of an evening; it is achieved bit by bit and drop by drop. Nowadays men are fond of talking about "liberation and reconstruction." They must realize that liberation does not mean liberation at the level of vague generalities, nor does reconstruction mean reconstruction at the level of vague generalities. Liberation means liberation from this or that institution, from this or that belief, for this or that individual—it is liberation bit by bit and drop by drop. Reconstruction means the reconstruction of this or that institution, of this or that idea, of this or that individual—it is reconstruction bit by bit and drop by drop.
>
> The betterment of the world is not impossible; nor is it something we can catch sight of merely by putting our hands in our sleeves and raising our eyes. The betterment of the world is attainable, but it requires each of us to set to work with all our strength. The more effort we put into it, the sooner will the world improve. The world is built little by little, a bit at a time. And even this depends entirely upon the energetic contributions of you and me and the other fellow.[58]

Hu Shih's outpouring of essays on "the significance of the new thought" in 1919 and 1920 coincided with, and echoed, John Dewey's lectures to Chinese audiences. Dewey, even more than Hu, set forth the liberal strategy in terms that brought it down to the level of concrete daily concerns. "Here in China a number of people have asked me, 'Where should we start in reforming our society?' " he observed in his second lecture on social and political philosophy at Peita in the autumn of 1919.

> My answer is that we must start by reforming the component institutions of the society. Families, schools, local governments, the central government—all these must be reformed, but they must be reformed by the people who constitute them, working as individuals—in collaboration with other individuals, of course, but still as individuals, each accepting his own responsibility. Any claim of the total reconstruction of a society is almost certain to be misleading. The institutions which make up the society are not "right" or "wrong," but each is susceptible to some degree of improvement. Social progress is neither an accident nor a miracle; it is the sum of efforts made by individuals whose actions are guided by intelligence.

We do not always know how to start in dealing with human problems; and when we do get started, we make mistakes, whether or no. . . . If we approach our problems one by one, and seek to solve them individually rather than by rule, we will still make mistakes; but we will not make nearly so many, nor such serious ones.

I imagine that most of you in the audience today are students; and as students, you must be peculiarly aware of the truth of what I have been saying. You know from your experience that the accomplishment of a series of small tasks results eventually in significant achievement. . . . If each of us does his duty and faithfully performs the various small tasks which confront him, the final result can be the reformation which all of us desire. But if we focus our attention on this reformation alone, losing sight of myriads of minor undertakings of which we are capable, I fear that little—more probably, nothing—will be accomplished.[59]

To friends and critics alike it was obvious that New Culture liberals had more in mind than simply the introduction of a new curriculum, a new written language, new scholarly methodologies, new bits and pieces of exotic knowledge, new "facts." Their underlying motive was to popularize, by exhortation and example, new modes of conduct, a new personality type—to create, in fact, a "new people." But whereas earlier reformers had emphasized the creation of a new citizen, able to assume the responsibilities and to discharge the obligations of participation in a political community, New Culture reformers stressed the importance of the cultural and intellectual dimensions of the new personality they hoped to nurture. They tried to inculcate the kind of critical consciousness (*tzu-chueh*), the openness to the significance of individual experience (*chueh-wu*), that would enable the Chinese to function as members of a community defined not so much by political allegiance as by common social expectations and shared standards of intellectual integrity, responsibility, and tolerance. They sought, in other words, to generate by means of critical analysis and "scientific" education, under what we might well call laboratory conditions, the kind of consensus that a few other societies—the societies that New Culture liberals most esteemed—had achieved through generations and centuries of social experience and political evolution.

This was a vision as chimerical, in its own way, as had been the dreams of a sudden political breakthrough cherished by prerevolutionary republicans. It proved as vulnerable to the contingencies of history, and even more vulnerable in the polarized political environment of the 1920s to attack from both right and left. We will return in the next chapter to a consideration of the revolutionaries' critique of New Culture liberalism, and ideological alternatives to it. At this point, however, we must turn our attention to the challenge that came from the cultural (and eventually from the political) right: the conservative or neo-traditional attempt to discredit the notion that the "scientific attitude" provides a desirable, or even a feasible, substitute for moral education.

* * *

"As I have grown older and observed the seven years of republican government in China and the four years of bloody war in Europe—a war such as the world has never known—I have come to feel that Western progress during the last three hundred years has only led to selfishness, slaughter, corruption, and shamelessness. . . . This is not my opinion alone. Many thinking people in the West have gradually come to feel this way."[60] In this brief observation, addressed to an old friend and disciple in 1918, Yen Fu enunciated several of the themes that came to dominate neo-traditionalist thinking in the 1920s: disillusionment with republican institutions; horror of the war that had engulfed Western civilization; realization of the fact that Westerners were themselves disconcerted and full of doubts; and a growing conviction that the goal of "wealth and power" carried with it ominous social and moral corollaries. Yen did not live to take part in the dispute that sputtered and flared throughout the 1920s and 1930s between the critics of science—which came more and more to mean "Westernization" in general—and its defenders; this correspondence, in fact, was published posthumously in the pages of *The Critical Review* in 1922 and 1923, when the battle lines were already drawn. If credit can be assigned, it was Liang Ch'i-ch'ao who drafted the neo-traditionalists' plan of attack, at least in general terms.

In 1919 Liang headed an unofficial delegation of Chinese observers to the Paris Conference. This was his first (and only) trip to Europe, and his longest sojourn in the West. With Paris as his *pied à terre* he traveled extensively on the Continent and in England, assuming once again his familiar role as reporter and indefatigable tourist: Stratford-on-Avon; a Buckingham Palace garden party; the mills of Manchester; Bastille Day in Paris; sunrise in the Swiss Alps. It was a hectic tour, and in that war-scarred setting often uncomfortable and ultimately disheartening. Liang's trip to the New World in 1903 had convinced him that China still had a long way to go; his trip to the Old World persuaded him that the West had gone too far. He returned to China in 1920 despairing of the fate of the civilization that had once inspired his awe and admiration.

Liang Ch'i-ch'ao's "Impressions of Travels in Europe" sketched a distressing picture of material impoverishment and spiritual depletion. No longer able to sustain its faith in rationalism and progress, morally vanquished, fearfully contemplating the approach of an inevitable social upheaval, postwar Europe lived, as Liang put it, "beneath the leaden skies of autumn." "It is no longer a question of how moral standards should change [in response to the times], but of whether any moral standard can survive." Liang found reason to hope that Western moral aspiration was beginning to turn in promising directions. He cited, for example, the popularity of Kropotkin's doctrine of cooperative, non-violent socialism, and the antimaterialist, idealistic philosophies of Henri Bergson and Rudolph Eucken. The West, Liang suggested, could thus be seen to be groping its way toward a wisdom that—however imperfectly it had been realized under the imperial political system—had remained paramount in the Confucian cultural order: the congruance of moral value and social practice, "consistency in ideal and practical application." So, after a century of Western evangelism, religious and secular, it was now time for the Chinese to repay the debt—or to turn the tables. "Our beloved youth! Attention! Forward march! On the far shore of the great ocean millions of people are bewailing the bankruptcy of material civilization and crying out most piteously for help, waiting for us to come to their salvation!"[61]

Liang's dismay at what he had witnessed in Europe was evident and genuine; but so, too, was the hint of self-congratulation that his critics were quick to detect and to deplore. Other observers, however, whose "Westernizing" sympathies were less open to ambiguous interpretation, generally corroborated Liang's findings even if they disagreed with his conclusions. Ting Wen-chiang, for example, who had traveled with Liang's party for several months in 1919, drew a different moral from the same dismal evidence. "If indeed European culture is bankrupt—and at present time this is not the case—the responsibility cannot by any means be assigned to science. . . . The principal cause is the war, and those who must bear responsibility for the war are the politicians and the educators, the majority of whom are still unscientific. Their mentality much resembles that of our own Chang Chih-tung; metaphysics [*hsuan-hsueh*] as the basis, and science for practical application." European barbarism, Ting insisted, demonstrated only that the benign and dispassionate values of "the scientific world view" had not yet infiltrated European popular culture.[62]

A somewhat different appraisal came from T'ao Meng-ho (1887–1960), Sc.B., University of London, a professor of sociology and government at Peita, and one of the staunchest of the New Culture liberal coterie. T'ao, like Liang Ch'i-ch'ao, was appalled by the material degradation and intellectual malaise he found in Europe in 1919, and profoundly disquieted by the looming threat of social revolution, a force against which, he prophesied, no Western government could hope to prevail. But T'ao foresaw no Chinese missionary movement bringing spiritual comfort to the troubled West. On the contrary, he predicted that the future of world civilization depended on the energy and resources that Westerners themselves could bring to the solution of the social and political problems that confronted them. The evils of untrammeled competition must be minimized, T'ao argued, by an ever greater concentration of productive power; but at the same time, control of production must become "public" and "democratic" (*min-chih ti kung-yu*) in order to undermine the monopoly of economic power by a handful of great industrialists. A "public" economy, T'ao insisted, is not synonymous with a nationalized economy, which would result only in the bureaucratization of management, not in the democratization of economic life. He was far from confident that such a drastic change could be effected in Europe without recourse to revolutionary means, by which he meant (as liberals increasingly tended to mean) a strategy of class violence. What was certain, he wrote, was that the Chinese must learn as never before the meaning of self-reliance, for in the future Westerners would be fully preoccupied with the problems of their own survival.[63]

It is significant that at the moment when Marxism was beginning to attract an audience among Chinese intellectuals, the Marxist description of Western materialist (or capitalist) society thus received confirmation from a variety of Chinese witnesses, many of whom were by no means Marxist in their sympathies. Whether as a result of historical coincidence or historical inevitability, this image of a culture on the brink of economic collapse and social disintegration reinforced the appeal of Marxism as an anti-imperialist weapon in China's struggle against the West, with consequences that we will examine more closely in chapter 7.

Liang Ch'i-ch'ao protested subsequently that he had been misunderstood. His purpose, he insisted, had not been to disparage science, properly defined and applied. In calling science "bankrupt" he had only been reporting what he had heard from the Europeans themselves. His point, and theirs, was merely to suggest that the nineteenth-century dream of the "omnipotence of science" (*k'o-hsueh chih wan-neng*) had vastly exaggerated the relevance of the scientific approach to the solution of problems of social welfare and moral education. Liang's "Impressions" did, in fact, affirm a commitment to his own style of progressivism. Allegiance to the Chinese tradition, he wrote, must be based on a thorough and "scientific" reappraisal of that tradition. He urged China's youth to rededicate themselves to individualism: in his own words, "*chin hsing*"—to realize one's full potential. Only thus, Liang warned, can the dangers of "German-style nationalism" be averted, the forcing of individual character into a uniform mold, thereby diminishing the variety and vitality of society as a whole.

This was a sentiment quite in harmony with New Culture values. It is, however, revealing of Liang's position that he chose to drive the point home not with a quotation from John Dewey, or even John Stuart Mill, but with a phrase from *The Doctrine of the Mean:* "Only the most sincere can fully realize their nature." The *Doctrine of the Mean* is among the most persuasive expositions of the Confucian belief in a natural inclination toward social feeling, epitomized in the statement that "the humane is human" (jen che jen yeh). In the Confucian lexicon, moreover, "sincerity" (ch'eng) is a term burdened with connotations of righteousness, moral insight, perseverence, and integrity. "To think how to be sincere is the way of man. He who is sincere is one who hits upon what is right without effort and apprehends without thinking. He is naturally and easily in harmony with the Way. Such a man is a sage. He who tries to be sincere is one who chooses the good and holds fast to it."[64] So it is written in The Doctrine of the Mean—and most of Liang's readers would unerringly have supplied the classical context to which he alluded. Very subtly, Liang was inviting his audience to reconsider the tenets of a native faith, an inherited confidence in the reliability of moral intuition.

It was one of Liang's longtime and loyal followers who threw down the gauntlet that provoked the 1923 debate on "science and the philosophy of life."[*] Chang Chun-mai (1886–   ), the son of a well-to-do Kiangsu family, had proclaimed himself Liang's disciple during his student days at Waseda University in Tokyo, at a time when Liang's influence in Chinese student circles in Japan was waning. Chang had joined the Society for the Dissemination of Political Information, Laing's constitutionalist "party," in 1907, thus embarking on a life-long history of illicit and generally ineffectual political affiliations. He remained Liang's friend and political ally as long as the older man lived, serving the cause as a journalist and lecturer. In Japan he had studied law and political economy; in 1913 he traveled for the first time to Europe, to study philosophy at the University of Berlin. He returned to China, and to the hazards and frustrations of warlord politics, in 1916. It was only natural for Chang to accompany Liang to Europe in 1919, and there he remained until 1922, for the most part under the tutelage of Rudolph Eucken at Jena. From Eucken, and from his reading of the works of Henri Bergson and Hans Driesch, Chang acquired a fluent and sympathetic command of the idiom of the contemporary irrationalist and introspective critique of materialism and positivism. It is a critique that may not have seemed alien to one educated as Chang had been in his early years in the Chinese understanding of the organic unity of human and cosmic nature. "The duty of philosophy," Bergson had written in Creative Evolution, "should be . . . to examine the living without any reservation as to practical utility, by freeing itself from forms and habits that are strictly intellectual. Its own special object is to speculate, that is to say, to see; its attitude toward the living should not be that of science, which aims only at action, and which, being able to act only by means of inert matter, presents to itself the rest of reality in this single

---

[*] "Philosophy of life" is the usual translation for jen-sheng-kuan, a term which has no really satisfactory English equivalent. The German Weltanshauung or the Russian mirovozzrenie perhaps come closer to conveying the full sense of the Chinese: whatever concerns one's understanding of and attitude toward the human experience.

respect. . . . In renouncing the factitious unity which the understanding imposes on nature from outside, we shall perhaps find its true, inward and living unity."[85]

It was an admonishment very like this in tone that Chang Chun-mai conveyed to an audience of Tsing Hua students early in 1923, soon after his return to China. You must be wary, he told them, of the expectations bred by your education. Not all of life's questions can be reduced to the clear-cut formulae of science. The scientific method is analytical and governed by the laws of reason; its usefulness is in fact limited to improving our understanding of relationships that can be viewed objectively, solving problems that by definition have little to do with human relationships. The philosophy of life (*jen-sheng-kuan*) differs point by point: it is subjective; it is the result of direct experience; it synthesizes, rather than analyzing; it posits free will and individual uniqueness, not determinism and uniformity. Most important (and here Chang's debt to both Eucken and Mencius was especially evident), *jen-sheng-kuan* takes account of the fact that human motives cannot be understood only in terms of physical or material necessity and rational calculation; there remains a moral dimension to human character, a sense of "ought," "a necessary tendency toward the good . . . marvelous and unfathomable." Finally Chang got down to the nub of his argument. "The controversy throughout our country in recent times over the New Culture, and the direction of cultural change, is not extraneous to [the kinds of problems dealt with by] the philosophy of life. We have our culture. The West has western culture. How are we to select what is beneficial from the West, and get rid of what is harmful? This process of selection depends entirely on the point of view."[66]

Ting Wen-chiang was the first to respond to Chang's challenge. Ting charged him with having willfully misrepresented the dominant assumptions of contemporary Western scientific philosophy, which Ting identified as "sceptical idealsim" and attributed impartially to Charles Darwin, T. H. Huxley, William James, Ernst Mach, Karl Pearson, and John Dewey. Theirs is an idealist philosophy, Ting wrote, because it holds that sense data are comprehended in conceptual relationships only by the mind; it remains sceptical because it concedes the possibility of a reality beyond the reach of the senses, and hence unknowable. To Ting's satisfaction, the search for demonstrably verifiable knowledge—i.e., "truth"—is thus reconciled with the mystery of what must remain speculative. But this does not justify, he insisted, the reliance on subjectivism, intuition, and idiosyncracy that Chang Chun-mai would license. "The aim of science is to eradicate the subjective prejudices of the individual . . . and to discover truths that can be generally acknowledged. The scientific method is to weigh the truth or error of facts, meticulously to categorize true facts, and then to discern their order and relationship, and to devise a simple, clear way of expressing this. Thus the authority [wan-neng], the universality, the pervasiveness of science derive not from its materials, but from its methodology. Einstein on the theory of relativity, James on psychology, Liang Ch'i-ch'ao on Chinese historiography, and Hu Shih on *The Dream of the Red Chamber**—all these qualify as science."[67]

The ensuing dispute was inky, occasionally ill-tempered, and in the nature of things inconclusive. Ting chastised Chang for the generality and vagueness of his original theses; more neutral observers complained that neither side defined its terms, and that the issues remained elusive. The ever lengthier rejoinders and rebuttals published by the principals did little to redress this grievance, nor did the entry of other contestants into the lists. Liang Ch'i-ch'ao came to the support of Chang Chun-mai, albeit without either much enthusiasm or much effect. A more systematic and thoughtful critique of Ting Wen-chiang's position was offered by Chang Tung-sun (1886–). The two Changs were old friends and, in the years that followed, close political allies. Chang Tung-sun was perhaps the more serious philosopher, lacking Chang Chun-mai's first-hand acquaintance with Europe (his only foreign education had been an interlude in Japan before 1911), but possessing a subtle and well-informed familiarity with the categories of contemporary Western intellectual discourse, and a considerable speculative originality. Chang took Ting to task for his simplistic reduction of science to a descriptive and taxonomic enterprise, a mere methodology of ordering data. How could science so understood account for Einstein's theory of relativity? Chang asked. He argued, in rebuttal, that the universal laws of science are not, as Ting would have it, simple explanations that encompass the largest possible number of "facts." Science generates formulae that do, indeed, derive from a specific content or body of facts, but that have wider implications and applications. Science is more than a methodology; it is a process in which the organizing mind derives insights that transcend the logic of the organization itself. Chang left open to further debate the question of whether, or how, the existing cultural environment may influence or even determine the nature of such insights.

It was, in Chang Tung-sun's view, a fatuous "debate" in any case. Ting Wen-chiang, he observed, was not really using "science" to attack "metaphysics": he was merely rehearsing the familiar New Culture arguments against superstition and in favor of scholarly objectivity and industry. Several of Ting's allies, on the other hand, faulted him for leaving the "unknowable" as an escape for subjectivism, and for not going far

---

* Chinese historical thought and writing was one of Liang's abiding interests, and the subject of a good deal of his late scholarship and some of his most widely known academic lectures. Hu Shih's textual studies of the great eighteenth-century novel *Hung lou meng* (The Dream of the Red Chamber), in collaboration with Ku Chieh-kang and Yü P'ing-po, were among the first and most celebrated examples of the use of new critical methodologies

enough in the direction of a materialist scientific world view. Wu Chih-hui, sixty years old now, and recently returned from his final European sojourn, weighed in with a meandering apologia proclaiming an adamantly mechanistic-materialist "personal faith" that impartially blended Darwinist concepts of an evolutionary natural order and Taoist notions of spontaneous cosmic generation and transformation. Hu Shih, never further from science as a discipline than at this moment, insisted on reading Wu's whimsical disquisition as the final word in the dispute, and lavished praise on this courageous old campaigner who "with a brush stroke banishes God, obliterates the spirit, and punctures the old myth that 'Man is sublime among the creatures of the earth'."[68]

Despite the looseness of the arguments, the "science and the philosophy of life" debate possessed a degree of definition and coherence. A selection of the essays written in the months following Chang Chun-mai's Tsing Hua speech were published at the end of 1923 in a two-volume collection, with prefaces contributed by Ch'en Tu-hsiu and Hu Shih. Ch'en was by this time a confirmed Marxist, and the Secretary-General of the fledgling Chinese Communist Party—a transformation to which we will give our full attention in chapter 7. Although they disagreed as to the proper understanding of "material causes," both Ch'en and Hu from their divergent perspectives supported the "materialist" point of view and were partisans of the cause of science. The fact that it was they who were privileged to summarize the lessons learned from the debate reflected the prevalent opinion that the "scientists" had won the battle.

But a wider war still raged. The science vs. metaphysics controversy was part of an even more diffuse argument over the nature and significance of fundamental differences between Eastern (or Chinese) and Western cultures—an issue familiar since the late nineteenth century, and one that worked its way, translated into a new idiom, into the revolutionary and counterrevolutionry ideologies of the 1920s and 1930s. For obvious reasons it was an issue of crucial importance in the minds of New Culture liberals, Western-educated themselves and self-consciously cosmopolitan. Even as he conceded that history favored his opponents, Chang Chun-mai touched a raw nerve in the course of the 1923 polemic:

> The fundamental principles upon which our nation is founded are quietism, as opposed to [Western] activism; spiritual satisfaction, as opposed to the striving for material advantage; a self-sufficient agrarianism, as opposed to profit-seeking mercantilism; and a morally transforming sense of brotherhood, rather than racial segregation. . . . A nation founded on agriculture lacks a knowledge of the industrial arts, [but] it is likewise without material demands; thus, though it exists over a long period of time, it can still maintain a standard of poverty but equality, scarcity but peace [*kua erh chun, p'ing erh an*]. But how will it be hereafter? . . . It is abundantly clear who are the strong and who the weak, who the fit and who the unfit, in today's world. . . . In the

future, a condition of prosperity without equality, wealth without peace, will probably prevail.[69]

The social ideal of equalized poverty was phrased here in language borrowed from the *Analects:* "Those who bear the responsibilities of governing a state or a household are not concerned that there is little, but by inequality; they are not grieved by poverty, but by strife." (*Lun yü* 16.10) The sentiment was basic to the Confucian political economy, and the phrase itself was often used by Chang and other neo-traditionalists to designate an alternative to Self-strengthening, while affirming China's spiritual superiority to the West.

In the early 1920s this neo-traditionalist or "Sinophile" position was given its most elaborate expression by Liang Shu-ming (1893-   ), one of the more remarkable personalities to figure in twentieth-century China's social and intellectual history. As a descendant in the twenty-third generation of a scholarly family that, despite the vicissitudes of politics, had maintained its cultural integrity and breeding since the thirteenth century, Liang was heir to an aristocratic tradition in the truest sense in which the term can be applied in China. His grandfather had died fighting against nineteenth-century rebels in Shansi; his father, Liang Chi, a concubine's son but the only heir, was raised and educated in Peking, in a household in thrall alike to poverty and to strenuous moral and academic expectations. Liang Chi became in time a stalwart Self-strengthener, a supporter of K'ang Yu-wei's contemplated reforms, and a reformer in his own right. His official career, in the waning years of the dynasty, was inconspicuous and ill-rewarded, but honorable; at home he set an example sharply at odds with that of the sterotypical Confucian patriarch by encouraging his children to pursue unorthodox educations and to cultivate the sense of intellectual independence and self-reliance that Liang Shu-ming, the second son, exhibited to an extraordinary degree throughout his life.

Not surprisingly, Liang Shu-ming's early education in Peking brought him into contact and sympathy with radical reformers and, eventually, with the revolutionary movement. An estrangement grew between father and son as Liang Shu-ming became actively involved in revolutionary politics and journalism in Nanking in 1911 and 1912. Liang Chi, a constitutional monarchist with little confidence in republicanism, hated from the first the moral laxness and political cynicism that disfigured China's postrevolutionary new order. Liang Shu-ming, too, was soon disenchanted, but his reaction did nothing to heal the breach with his father. He retired from the world of public events, to immerse himself in the doctrines and discipline of Buddhism—a cure no less distressing, from Liang Chi's point of view, than had been his son's earlier revolutionary fever. From this seclusion Liang Shu-ming emerged, in 1916, spiritually replenished and filled with a sense of messianic self-confidence and intimations of sageliness. When Ts'ai Yuan-p'ei, whom he had encountered during his earlier incarnation as a revolutionary journalist, invited him to join the Peita faculty to teach courses in Indian philosophy, Liang accepted.

That was in 1917, when Liang Shu-ming was twenty-four. About a year later, early on a November morning in 1918, Liang Chi drowned himself in one of Peking's ornamental lakes, on the shore of which he had for some years inhabited a rustic scholar's refuge from the confusions of the world. It was an act long contemplated—a sacrifice "in behalf of the Ch'ing dynasty," as Liang put it in his final "Warning to the Age." The suicide created a considerable commotion in intellectual circles, eliciting comment—defensive, patronizing, or sympathetic as the case may be—from many of the sponsors of the New Culture, which, as some believed, had driven Liang to this drastic protest. Liang's death had in fact little to do with fealty to the Manchu house itself: he had died not in the cause of any particular ideal, monarchical or otherwise, but of idealism itself: to manifest "the rectitude and righteousness that may rescue our national customs from degeneracy," as he had also written.[70]

The impact of this tragedy on Liang Shu-ming was understandably traumatic. He became, literally, a convert to the Confucian faith in which his father had died. For the first time he read carefully the classical sources of Liang Chi's beliefs. He abandoned Buddhist celibacy to take a wife, in obedience to the Mencian injunction that the failure to procreate is the most heinous act of filial impiety; eventually he sired two sons. More to the point of our present inquiry, he began over the next several years to synthesize the disparate elements of his own intellectual experience. The first result of this exercise was a series of lectures, published in 1922 under the title *The Cultures of East and West and Their Philosophies*.

It is a visionary work, ingenious in its theoretical structure and sometimes extravagant in its philosophical assumptions. Liang began by bluntly posing the question "Can China survive?" He rejected at the outset the feasibility of cultural compromise. "Taking the best of East and West," the approach popularized by cultural cosmopolites like Hu Shih, Liang dismissed as an attempt to obscure fundamental and ineradicable cultural differences. To be China, China must be Chinese. Liang had been sufficiently schooled in the curriculum of his generation, however, to take evolutionism to heart. The survival of "China," therefore, had somehow to be fitted into an evolutionary framework. To this end, Liang put forward an elaborate argument to demonstrate that culture—the aggregate human response to environment—is divisible essentially into three types or categories. Each of these reflects a different subjective consciousness or "Will," each plays a necessary historical role, and all are linked, ideally, in a continuous, progressive, and universal historical pattern. The first "stage," typically Western, is the aggressive, confident attempt to subdue the natural environment in order to meet the material requirements of human survival. In the second stage, typically Chinese, mankind turns from problems of physical survival to a concern for the social ethic that will insure the survival of the community and the culture. Finally, in the "Indian" stage, an introspective preoccupation with human spirituality becomes the dominant concern.

According to this scheme of things, Western superiority and Chinese vulnerability are both explicable in terms of relative development along a single evolutionary continuum. The Chinese, Liang reasoned, having turned too early from the first to the second road, had created and then been condemned to endure a culture of material insufficiency that easily fell victim to Western military, economic, and intellectual aggression. But now, Liang continued, the West had traveled the first road to the point of self-destruction and cultural and spiritual exhaustion. Impelled by its instinct for survival, it was turning spontaneously to the "Chinese way." What Liang meant, philosophically, by the "Chinese way" has been characterized by his biographer, Guy Alitto, as "left-wing Wang Yang-ming Confucianism":[71] active involvement, intellectual and social, in the problems of the human condition, reliance on intuition rather than knowledge (whether textual or scientific) as a guide to moral action, and insistence that moral principles be justified in terms of their application to concrete social relationships.

To substantiate his claim that such was indeed the tendency of Western intellectual development, Liang marshaled corroborative evidence culled from diverse contemporary Western sources. Kropotkin and Eucken came naturally to mind. So did Bergsonian Vitalism, with its emphasis on instinctive, nonrational responses to experience. Liang also called some more surprising witnesses to the stand in his defense, notably John Dewey and Bertrand Russell, the Western wisemen most likely to be familiar to his audience in 1921–1922. There was, of course, a fundamental incompatability, of which Liang was by no means unaware, between the kind of intuitive moral insight that he regarded as paramount and Dewey's definition of "true" knowledge as "systematic knowledge, knowledge that has been systematized by the arrangement of natural phenomena through human action. . . . Those ideas which can be empirically verified and which produce predicted results." Liang saw American pragmatism, viewed in this light, as the "culmination" of the Western approach to life. But at the same time—indeed, in the same lecture, almost with the same breath—Dewey had expressed a distrust of abstract philosophical speculation quite in keeping with Liang's own attitude. There is, moreover, a definite affinity between Wang Yang-ming's "pragmatic" doctrine of the unity of knowledge and action (chih *hsing ho-i*) and Dewey's admonition that "there can be no true knowledge without doing. . . . We cannot expect to gain true knowledge without acting upon our ideas."[72] In one of his Peita lectures, Dewey himself deplored the Western preoccupation with the study of nature to the exclusion of other concerns, especially human affairs (*jen shih*). True, he felt that Eastern philosophies had gone too far in the other direction, and voiced his hope for a reconciliation of these extremes. Liang for his part was content to observe, "Now, for a fact, Western philosophy is turning its attention to the fundamental problems of human affairs."

Bertrand Russell presented Liang also with the need to be judiciously selective. He introduced Russell as "an old-fashioned rationalist whose philosophy has not been influenced by evolutionary theory."[73] But Russell came to China in a mood of anguished pessimism over the recent course of European history and outspokenly sceptical of the values of industrial culture. He arrived, moreover, bitterly disillusioned by his glimpse of revolutionary socialism as practiced in the Soviet Union, and in the course of his Chinese visit he developed a romantic affection for certain aspects of traditional Chinese culture not uncongenial to Liang Shu-ming's prejudices. "I went to teach," Russell wrote; "but every day that I stayed I thought less of what I had to teach them and more of what I had to learn from them." And he continued:

> Those who value wisdom or beauty, or even the simple enjoyment of life, will find more of these things in China than in the distracted and turbulent West. . . . Confucianism . . . assumes people fundamentally at peace with the world, wanting only instruction as to how to live, not encouragement to live at all. . . . The distinctive merit of our civilization, I should say, is the scientific method; the distinctive merit of the Chinese a just conception of the ends of life. It is these two that one must hope to see gradually uniting. . . . I wish I could hope that China, in return for our scientific method, may give us something of her large tolerance and comtemplative peace of mind.[74]

"A just conception of the ends of life" was precisely what Liang Shu-ming regarded as the essential and redeeming genius of the "Chinese way."

> The Chinese are on the whole tolerant both of Nature and of Man, exhibiting no trace of the combative attitude of the West. Therefore ancient institutions have never been improved. . . . For thousands of years we have been unable to free ourselves from the tyranny of the powers that stand over us, or to develop our individual or our social natures. In this aspect of our lives, we fall far short of the West. Yet from another perspective, what seems our failure is in fact our triumph. . . . Before they could affirm naturally-endowed rights, Westerners had to possess the concept of the Self. Only then could the sense of individuality develop. But among these individuals the lines of demarcation must be very clearly drawn: you must speak immediately of rights and obligations, of legal relationships, of who is accountable to whom—even in respect to

the relationship between father and son, or husband and wife. Such a life is indeed unreasonable [*pu ho-li*], such a life is indeed too bitter. The Chinese attitude is contrary to this. Westerners rely on the intellect; Chinese rely on intuition and emotion. Westerners have the Self; Chinese do not want the Self. . . . Because the spiritual ideal of Confucianism was never realized, there existed [in traditional China] only a few ancient ceremonial regulations, lifeless precepts that created a tomb-like oppression and caused no little suffering. Yet within the family, and in society at large, it was everywhere possible to achieve a kind of satisfaction—not of a cold, indifferent, hostile and calculating kind, but of a kind to nourish human life. Surely this is a great excellence, and a great triumph![75]

The Cultures of East and West encompassed all of the major premises of neo-traditionalist thinking. Of these perhaps the most basic was the division of the human personality into "inner" and "outer" spheres, or spiritual and physical aspects—a polarity with its origins deep in the Confucian and neo-Confucian understanding of human nature. Liang reacted with characteristic neo-traditionalist dismay to the denial of this distinction at the level of social relationships. Even the most progressive and benign Western political cultures respond to the need for social control by creating a network of formal, impersonal, legalistic relationships which perpetuate the idea that human beings can relate to each other only on the basis of calculated interest. The antithesis of such an assessment of the human potential was the neo-traditionalist vision of the community bound together in a common morality, a feeling of "humankindness"—and the familiar concept of *jen*, which remained for Liang the throbbing heart of Confucianism.

It is hardly surprising that critics and admirers alike read Liang's lectures as an effort to revive traditional values against the claims of the modernizers. Liang was disconsolate. To be dismissed as an "obstacle" to the New Culture movement "makes me feel very sad. I do not feel that I oppose their movement! I applaud and encourage their efforts!" [76] Indeed, Liang did urge the necessity of many of the changes that New Culture enthusiasts were endeavoring to supervise. And in so doing, he found himself impaled on the horns of a familiar dilemma. He had begun by adamantly rejecting cultural synthesis, repudiating the notion that the substance of a civilization, its collective cultural personality, is somehow distinct from the functional applications of human insight, whether intellectual or intuitive. He had specifically denounced as illogical the old nineteenth-century *t'i-yung* formula. But he came, in the end, to a position that struck some of his readers as virtually identical. To secure its own salvation, Liang proclaimed, the West must turn now to the "Chinese way." But China on its part, and for equally compelling reason, must pursue the "Western way." It is our great good fortune, Liang wrote, that Eucken and Bergson have stayed at home, while Dewey and Russell have come among us.

The urgent necessity that now confronts us is to end the domestic strife that
divides us, to allow for the firm establishment of individual rights to life and
property. . . . The sprit [of science and democracy] is entirely appropriate to
our circumstances—we can only acknowledge this unconditionally and
without reservations. Therefore I have urged that we "totally accept" Westernization. The present exigency is how to accommodate the spirit [of science and
democracy], for otherwise we will never be worthy to speak of human
character or true learning. Look closely at the nature of our recent sufferings
and you will know that I do not put the matter extravagantly.

But Liang qualified his endorsement of Westernization—and thereby
disqualified himself as its legitimate spokesman in the eyes of its principal
patrons—by calling not only for "total acceptance" of science and
democracy, but also for "a fundamental rectification of [Western] excesses," and "a critical reaffirmation of the original Chinese attitude."
For, he insisted finally, "in essence the future civilization of the world
will be a renaissance of Chinese civilization," exalting "the pulse and
flow of instinct and moral impulse" in order to nourish "a psychology of
happiness and tranquility" that will enable men to live "a vital and joyful
life . . . a humane life . . . a Confucian life."[77]
It was a stern kind of joy, if one may judge by Liang's example. The
austerity of his life syle and the unbending gravity of his manner became
in time so well known that his rare displays of public joviality were
deemed newsworthy. Yet even his severest critics could not dismiss Liang
simply as a conservative, or a cultural nativist, or even as a traditionalist.
Unlike Chang Shih-chao, or Liu Shih-p'ei, or the *Critical Review* writers,
Liang was not enmeshed in the web of memory, or wedded to the
perpetuation of particular cultural forms. His vision of the future was
hardly less utopian than K'ang Yu-wei's *ta-t'ung*: a transcendent univer-
salization of Confucian values, linked to a differently conceived but
comparably idiosyncratic evolutionary scheme. Liang's ideas were more
firmly grounded in what he identified as Confucian categories than is the
case with K'ang's "Great Community." He even went so far as to suggest
that in the world's "Chinese" future, Confucian rites and music would
replace laws as the means of maintaining social discipline. Unlike K'ang,
whose fancies were richly ornamented with technological wonders, and
whose utopia was designed to satisfy the whole range of human appetites,
Liang reaffirmed a social ideal still within the Confucian tradition of
self-discipline and self-cultivation, moral restraint and material constraint. And unlike K'ang, who in the end puttered happily off into the
boundless realms of Celestial Perigrination, Liang Shu-ming remained
true to the inspiration of Wang Yang-ming's "muscular Confucianism,"
and kept his feet firmly planted on the ground of Confucian social concern. In the mid-1920s he abandoned academia to devote his energies
throughout much of the rest of his long life to the starkly concrete pro-

blems of China's peasants; we will encounter him again, in his role as a leader of the rural reconstruction movements of the 1920s and 1930s.

It is in their self-images, and in the authority that each invoked, that K'ang and Liang seem most alike. Each saw himself as a Sage, a self-ordained transmitter of the Way, the instrument chosen by History, or Fate, to reveal ancient and essential truths to the present world—truths not of the mind, but of the heart. This was not a sense of vocation likely to appeal to the leaders of the New Culture movement, however sincerely Liang might protest that he sympathized with their efforts. New Culture liberals on the whole treated *The Cultures of East and West* with hardly more respect than they might have felt for K'ang's *Ta t'ung shu*. Ts'ai Yuan-p'ei tacked a hasty comment on it to the end of a survey of recent philosophical trends. Liang had raised some significant philosophical questions, Ts'ai conceded; but he cautioned that Liang's conclusions were only "the thoughts of a single individual at a given moment," and he suggested that philosophy is one thing, and culture quite another.[78] Hu Shih gave the book a full review, largely devoted to the logical difficulties inherent in Liang's argument. He pointed out (quite rightly) that although Liang attached great importance to environment and evolutionary development, he had failed to explain in evolutionary terms the radical differences he attributed to Western, Chinese, and Indian civilizations or cultural modes. This provided Hu with an opportunity to deliver a lecture of his own. All human communities have evolved in response to the conditions imposed upon them by environment, he insisted. Whether a culture or a race appears in the light of history as victor or victim cannot be attributed to the influence of a distinctive cultural personality that itself determines the outcome of evolution. It must be construed, rather, as the ultimate measure of a culture's success or failure in meeting the challenge of survival.

The issue touched upon here was in fact a matter of crucial concern to the New Culture intellectuals. For them to concede the possibility of a fundamental psychological disparity between Westerners and Chinese would have been, in effect, to discredit their belief in the universal significance of the "scientific attitude," and thus to cast into doubt their confidence in China's inherent capacity to transform itself into a modern civilization. It required an argument less ambiguous than Liang's, and more threatening to the momentum of the New Culture movement, to wrest such a damaging concession from Hu and his allies. From the mid-1920s onward, such a threat was posed by the ascendancy of political nationalism under the aegis of the Kuomintang, and its adoption of culturally reactionary policies in forms that were by no means ambiguous. This alliance between the modernizing state and "traditional" social values was not formally published until the inauguration of the so-called "New Life Movement" in the 1930s. The conservative disposition of the Kuomintang was already foreshadowed, however, by the time the party came to power in the period 1926-1928, in its pronouncements on social and educational policies and in its sponsorship of traditional moral teachings and archaic cultural symbolism.

Responding to this challenge on behalf of the interests of the New Culture movement, Hu Shih accepted the traditionalists' characterization of the Chinese as a people content to endure poverty and to accept without resistance the suffering that had been theirs in abundance—a fatalistic race, immune to the inspiration of "Divine discontent" which, even as a student, Hu had greatly admired as a facet of the Western personality. But he ridiculed as pernicious nonsense the traditionalists' effort to wrest a moral victory out of the jaws of material disaster by attributing to the Chinese a spiritual supremacy over the decadent West. On the contrary, a civilization which "cannot liberate itself from subjection to the physical environment, which cannot, by the use of human reason and intelligence, temper the environment and improve the human condition—this is the civilization of a lazy and retarded race, truly a materialistic civilization. Such a civilization can only restrain mankind's spiritual demands, it can never satisfy them. . . . The quest for knowledge is a naturally-endowed spiritual demand of human life. The ancient civilizations of the East not only did not attempt to satisfy this demand, but on the contrary often sought to keep it in check. . . . Here, truly, is a fundamental difference between the cultures of East and West: on the one hand, unthinking blindness to one's own interest, and on the other, an endless search for truth."[79]

Such opinions earned for New Culture liberals in general a reputation as "total Westernizers." It was an epithet intended critically, a rebuke to men estranged from their own culture and, more broadly, alienated from their own society—a new mandarinate, an academic aristocracy that lived in protective urban intellectual enclaves and remained self-consciously insulated from the social and cultural realities of the great mass of the Chinese people. Whether New Culture intellectuals were in fact more isolated from their surroundings than has commonly been the fate of the cosmopolitan (and metropolitan) intelligentsia in other societies remains a matter for later comment. The point to be stressed here is that the notion of "total Westernization" (*ch'üan-pan Hsi-hua*) did not figure in the vocabulary of New Culture enthusiasts in the late teens and early twenties. They spoke then as the advocates of cosmopolitanism: not an imported culture, but an open and fluid culture, appropriate to the age. It was the increasingly obdurate ideological resistance to the purposes of the New Culture movement that, in the course of time, made "total Westernization" an issue; even then, "complete cosmopolitanization" (*ch'ung-fen-ti shih-chieh-hua*) remained the preferable motive in the minds of Hu Shih and like-minded thinkers. "Pitiful and despairing old revolutionary party!" Hu wrote in the autumn of 1934, shortly after the Nanking government's revival, with considerable pomp and ceremony, of Confucius' "birthday" as a national holiday. "You wanted a revolution, but now that the revolution has achieved these twenty years of unprecedented progress, you disown it. What progress there has been in the last two decades is not a gift from Confucius, but the result of a common revolutionary struggle, the result of a common acceptance of the new civilization of a new world. Our only hope lies in moving forward."[80]

Cultural innovation is not an easy process to program, Hu admitted. He admitted, too, that no standard of value—not even the "scientific attitude"—provides an entirely reliable or predictable strategy for cultural change. The resistance to innovation of particular aspects of a culture will depend upon their intrinsic utilitarian value. But, he warned, to promote "conservatism" *per se* is neither necessary nor wise, for in the final analysis any kind of cultural change will inevitably be limited by the conservatism inherent in any culture. "At the present time our only possible course is the complete acceptance of the civilization of the new world. If we who are destined to be leaders speak emptily of compromise and selectivity, the result can only be the cherishing of useless remnants and the preservation of our shortcomings." So, Hu urged, China must "accept without prejudice the scientific-industrial world culture and the spiritual civilization that underlies it. . . . There is no doubt that the eventual product must be, as a matter of course, a culture established on a Chinese foundation."[81] Or, as he had put it nearly twenty years earlier, "congenial and congruous and continuous with the civilization of our own making."

Despite Hu's disclaimer, New Culture liberals did of course propose a strategy of cultural transformation that they regarded as "scientifically" reliable: particularism and gradualism. As educators they sought to inculcate a problem-solving habit of mind that would define solutions in terms of problems that are specific and concrete rather than general and theoretical. As shapers of human character they endeavored to encourage a nature patient enough to draw sufficient comfort from the incremental benefits accruing over a long period of time from discrete reforms. Implicit in this strategy was the assumption that a society, or a culture, can be dismantled piece by piece, its components scrutinized to determine whether they remain useful or must be discarded, and then the whole slowly reassembled, piece by piece, purposefully and peacefully altered in social form and intellectual substance. "It is always reason that guides and directs," wrote Hu Shih in 1935.[82]

This, we may say, was the irreducible core of liberal commitment. It was anathema alike to the liberals' critics on the cultural right and the political left. Traditionalists and neo-traditionalists, from a perspective in which the Confucian vision of the moral community coincided with and found confirmation in certain Western images, conceived of society as a vital organism which cannot be dismembered—however razor sharp the edge of reason—without lethal consequences to the life force that animates it. Political radicals—those on the left, at least—did not share this view of society as a living entity to which moral personality may be attributed. Like the liberals, they expounded a "scientific" understanding of social relationships and mechanisms, and they espoused with equal enthusiasm a program of social engineering. Society in their view, however, comprises an integral whole, a complex of reciprocating social forces and interlocking socioeconomic relationships: a closed system, in which the modification of any component necessitates the modification of every other component. They dismissed as impractical, therefore, or as deliberately disarming, the liberals' strategy of trying to concentrate on the solution of specific problems in isolation from the social and material context that renders them significant. What China needs, they argued, is not selective, inevitably slow, and apparently random "solutions," but an all-embracing, sweeping "fundamental" solution—a revolutionary solution.

The inclination toward greater comprehensiveness was characteristic of the kind of ideological thinking that, as we shall see in the next chapter, contended seriously in the twenties and thirties for the attention of the audience that New Culture liberals had commanded in the late teens. It challenged not only the strategic premises of New Culture liberalism, but also the values of reasonable scepticism and ordered, sequential change, basic elements in the liberal outlook. And it called into question the New Culture vision of the role that intellectuals should play, by right and obligation, as critical educators and as educated critics.

* * *

"Imagine a house, made of iron, windowless, indestructible. Sound asleep within are many people soon to die of suffocation. But since they will enter death from the darkness of sleep, they will not feel its agony. Now you begin to shout the alarm, and a few of the lighter sleepers are warned to wakefulness. This unfortunate minority must thus confront the anguish of an approaching fate they cannot escape. Can you really forgive yourself for that?"

"But, since a few *have* been aroused, you can't say for a certainty that there is no hope of destroying the iron house."

Right . . .

The stark metaphor is Lu Hsun's. So, too, is the bleak mood, and behind it the shadowed memory of the photograph glimpsed so many years earlier: the dulled, dumb faces in the crowd, asleep to human feeling. By the winter of 1922, when he wrote this preface to his first collection of short stories, *A Call to Arms*, Lu Hsun had achieved recognition as a principal architect of the New Literature. Although he had fulfilled his youthful vow to minister to his people with the cathartic of literary imagination, he remained unsure of the significance of his vocation. "To raise one's voice among the living and to receive no response, neither support nor opposition—to be as in a trackless desert with no help at hand—how melancholy a thing this is! . . . For my part, I no longer feel an urgent need to speak out. But probably because I haven't been able to forget the misery of my own loneliness, I still raise a shout from time to time to give heart to those bold-spirited ones who hasten forward in loneliness, to encourage them to press onward."[83]

Estrangement from hope, and an unceasing struggle against the isolation of despair, pervade Lu Hsun's short stories written in the New Culture era and the polemical "miscellaneous essays" (tsa-wen) that became his weapon in the last decade of his life. It is, perhaps, this mood that gives to his writing the power that carries it beyond its particular time and place, to implicate a wider audience in the human tragedy that Lu Hsun records and comments upon. Under his hand, the personal and parochial experiences of a life spent among the ruins of China's traditional society are transformed into statements of universal human meaning and importance.

Lu Hsun, or Chou Shu-jen (1881–1936), was born in Shaohsing, a few miles southeast of Hangchow across the rich, water-laced Chekiang coastal plain. It was a city renowned for the shrewdness of its sons as self-schooled clerks and lawyers, and for the potency of the rice wine bearing its name, the celebrated Shaohsing chiu. Whether for either or both of these reasons, Shaohsing is well represented in the annals of the revolution: such luminaries as Ch'iu Chin and Ts'ai Yuan-p'ei claimed it as their native place; Chiang Monlin, among others, studied at its Sino-Western Academy (Chung-Hsi hsueh-t'ang) in the 1890s. Lu Hsun's Shaohsing upbringing followed a not uncommon pattern: a classical education to begin with, declining family resources, and the resort to Western learning. The circumstances of Lu Hsun's youth, however, were perhaps less ordinary than this familiar outline suggests; in any event, they scarred him for life. His was a sprawling family, its generations and branches crowded together within the derelict courtyards of the ancestral Great House. The patriarch of this helter-skelter establishment was Lu Hsun's grandfather, a scholar of sufficient attainment to have won the chin-shih degree and that most honorable of Confucian nominations, appointment as a Hanlin compiler in Peking. The advantages that accrued to the family as a result of this great distinction were disastrously offset in 1893 when Grandfather Chou was convicted of attempting, on behalf of various collateral relatives, to bribe the head examiner dispatched to preside over the Chekiang provincial examinations. At ruinous cost the family contrived to buy successive reprieves from the beheading to which the old man was condemned; from his Hangchow jail cell he continued to manage family affairs *in absentia*, overseeing the collapsing fortunes of a remarkable assemblage of disappointed scholars, opium addicts, contentious womenfolk, and profligate offspring, the assorted social debris of China's failing culture. As Lu Hsun's biographer, William Lyell, has put it, the home environment "was at once interesting (as a madhouse is interesting) and gloomy (as a madhouse is gloomy). It was an ambience characterized by failure and lack of human fulfillment. Everywhere one looked there were shattered lives. . . . "[84]

Lu Hsun's father, strong neither in physique nor in character, hastened his own death in 1896 through an intemperate fondness for wine and opium. Two years later Lu Hsun left Shaohsing for Nanking, where he enrolled first in the Naval Academy attached to the Kiangnan Arsenal and then in the School of Mines and Railroads, from which he graduated in the winter of 1901–1902. The latter institution boasted its own coal mine and its own power plant—though as Lu Hsun noted, with a characteristically sharp eye for ironic detail, the mine yielded only sufficient coal to enable the generators to produce the power needed to keep the pumps running that prevented the mine from flooding. So much for the accomplishments of the Self-strengthening movement at the turn of the century. Early in 1902, disillusioned and with few prospects, Lu Hsun left for Tokyo and Sendai, where we encountered him at the beginning of this chapter.

The seven years Lu Hsun spent in Japan brought him little sense of fulfillment. After his conversion from medicine to literature he tried his hand at writing, in an archaic style influenced by Chang Ping-lin, on questions of philosophy and the social role of poets and literary critics. He also made a start as a translator, an avocation he pursued with energy and skill to the end of his life, showing from the first a predilection for Russian, East European, and Balkan writers—the literature of "oppressed peoples," put into Chinese from Japanese or German translations. Ambitious publishing schemes came to naught, however, and in 1909 Lu Hsun returned to China with scarcely more sense of purpose or accomplishment than he had left it. The next decade he spent virtually in retirement from the causes of the day, first as a schoolteacher in Shaohsing, then, through the good offices of Ts'ai Yuan-p'ei, as a bureaucrat in the Ministry of Education in Peking. The only outlets for his creative energy during these years of frustration were epigraphy and scholarly researches in the history of Chinese literature. Not until 1918 did he turn again to writing, in response to importunate invitations from Ch'ien Hsuan-t'ung, an old friend from student days in Tokyo, to contribute something to *The New Youth*. The publication in its pages of his first short story, "A Madman's Diary," in May 1918 elevated Lu Hsun forthwith to fame as a member of the New Culture elite. With the appearance of his longest fictional work, "The True Story of Ah Q" (*Ah Q cheng chuan*), a novella published serially in the Peking *Ch'en-pao* in the winter of 1921–1922, he quickly achieved celebrity as an internationally recognized literary figure.

In style, mood, and texture, as well as length, these are very different stories, but the point they make is similar: in China, reality can only be revealed to us by the deranged or the deluded. Derangement, the madman's paranoia, imprisons him in the dreadful conviction that he is condemned to be killed and eaten by his elder brother. Lu Hsun enunciates here a terrible metaphor to which, with variations, he frequently returned in his later writing: the cannibalism of the traditional culture and society.

> Since antiquity, I seem to recall, cannibalism has been common. But I'm not clear about it. I tried leafing through my History. But this History is without chronology; on every page are scrawled the words "Benevolence, Righteousness, Morality." Tossing and turning, I could not sleep, and so I read closely half the night—and then I began to make out words between the lines. The whole book is written with the two words, "Eat men!" . . .
>
> How can I, with this family history of four thousand years of cannibalism—even though I was at first ignorant of it, and only now understand it—how can I look real men in the eye?
>
> Are there still children who have not eaten men?
>
> Save the children. . . . [85]

Delusion is represented by Ah Q, a simple-minded village vagrant, a man literally without a name or a place, despised and derided by his fellows: archetypically the eternal victim, shrewd only in his aptitude for transforming the insults and defeats of his existence into imaginary but self-gratifying "spiritual victories." In the end Ah Q is executed by a "revolutionary" firing squad—like the anonymous figure in the photograph, surrounded by a crowd indifferent to anything but the promised spectacle, the befuddled victim of a fate over which no "spiritual victory" is possible, of mindless violence that will change nothing. "Ah Q-ism" soon worked its way into the intellectual vocabulary of the 1920s as a bitterly vivid characterization of China's social and psychological disabilities.

Satire was Lu Hsun's principal weapon in the campaign to purge "China's rotten idiots" of their physical and spiritual infirmities. His was an angry art, mocking the stubborn survival of ancient prejudices and superstitions, but mocking, too, the pretensions of self-styled "modern" men. Lu Hsun hated his world, but with a hatred born of love and sympathy for its victims. The defiant enemy of superstition, he was himself haunted by the spectres of memory; his short stories and reminiscent essays are crowded with the ghosts of his childhood and youth, by the failed dreams of his generation. In a story written in 1924, the principal character puts the point directly. Once ambitious and full of hopeful dreams for China, he has become a cultural derelict. "Oh, yes," he tells the narrator, "I still remember the times we went together down to the City God's Temple, to tweak the gods' whiskers. And the times we argued the whole day through over ways to reform China—and even came to blows. But now I am as you find me: I get along, catch as catch can." This turns out to mean that he scrapes by as an underpaid private tutor of the Confucian classics, the traditional niche of academic cast-offs.

"Do you mean to say that what you're teaching is 'Confucius said . . . ' and 'As it is written in the Odes . . .'?" I asked in astonishment.
"Of course. Did you think I was teaching them the ABCs? . . . I don't even teach them mathematics. Well, it isn't that I won't teach it—it's that they don't want it taught. . . . Their old man wants them to study this sort of thing. They're no kin of mine, so what's the difference? What does such foolishness matter, anyway? The important thing is to take things as they come. . . . "
"Do you make enough to live on?" I inquired, getting ready to leave.
"Yes. Well, twenty dollars a month—I don't get along all that well."
"So, then, what about the future?"
"The future? I don't know. Look, now: has even one of the things we imagined, back then, come out as we'd hoped? Now I don't know anything—even about tomorrow, even about a minute from now. . . . "[86]

For Lu Hsun, hope was always an act of will, defying the mounting evidence that would justify despair. His dark vision, and the bitterness of an anger frequently disguised by a talent for ironic understatement, estranged him from the self-confident, urbanely dispassionate "inner circle" of the New Culture elite. "The high command in those days was opposed to negativism," he recalled of the years when his first stories were published in *The New Youth*. "And as for me, I certainly did not want to infect with the bitterness of my loneliness youngsters who were still dreaming the sweet dreams that I had dreamed when I was young."[87]

Temperamentally, then, Lu Hsun remained from the first an outsider; eventually he was to become a strenuous critic of the New Culture personality. But even in the early years, he was not alone in perceiving that a kind of cultural no-man's-land divided the New Culture intellectuals from the people whose interests, ultimately, they hoped to promote. Peking's academic intelligentsia, or the "modern" intellectuals and professionals of the Treaty Ports, or in many cases even the radical students whose enthusiasm fueled the protest movements of the 1920s, had left the past behind them. But it was otherwise in the myriad villages of the hinterland, or in the narrow, noisome alleyways of innumerable provincial towns, or even in the swarming backstreets of the great cities. There no boundary existed between past and present. There, where law could not break the tyranny of custom, young girls still suffered the agony of foot-binding. There clan elders still presided over the erection of ceremonial arches to honor chaste widowhood, and there from time to time betrothed child-brides starved themselves in traditional mourning of the death of a husband-to-be. There, occasionally, a rebellious daughter would hang herself rather than submit to the indignities and abuses of an arranged marriage. There, to borrow the macabre imagery of Lu Hsun's "Medicine," a consumptive child might still be fed a lump of steamed bread soaked in the fresh blood of a decapitated criminal, in the desperate hope of a saving miracle.

New Culture intellectuals were not blind to the chasm that opened before them. Chiang Monlin, for example—American-educated, one of John Dewey's prominent disciples, well situated as a spokesman for the academic establishment, and as we have seen by no means a rabble-rouser—even Chiang Monlin could see the problem, and in his capacity as editor of *The New Education* he stated it bluntly:

> If the only result of the New Culture movement is to enhance the authority of some fragment of the intellectual class, then the people as a whole will receive no benefit from it.
>
> Social progress is not something that a few intellectuals can accomplish on their own. It can be achieved only when the great mass of the peasantry has made progress. If a minority within the society discusses culture day in and day out, while the great majority remains ignorant even of the fact that the earth is round, if society is thus divided into two worlds which cannot communicate with each other, how can society progress!
>
> Since the eighteenth century, social progress has originated with the lower classes. Once the common people at the bottom have seized the initiative, the aristocracy at the top has found it impossible to keep its balance. . . . You intellectuals: you have been our social elite, and when in the future the peasants start to move, you will lose your footing.[88]

New Culture intellectuals addressed this problem of "two worlds" in two ways. In the first place, as we have seen, they persistently affirmed the general relevance of the values of intellectual individuality and social pluralism upon which the success of their own efforts depended—reviving in modern form, one is inclined to suggest, the ancient Confucian notion that human character is amenable to unlimited improvement. Secondly, again with an emphasis that is reminiscent of Confucian precedent, they stressed the singular importance of education as a means of character development. We cannot dismiss these faint but harmonious resonances with the past: they help us to understand why it was that, for all the vigor of their anti-traditionalism, New Culture radicals still instinctively felt themselves at home, architects of a modern *Chinese* solution to China's problems. Undergirding this confidence in human educability, however, was a very untraditional vision of the ultimate social purpose to be served. "A self-governing society and a republican nation require only that the individual have the right to choose freely, and furthermore that he bear the responsibility for his own conduct and actions," wrote Hu Shih in his introduction to the special "Ibsen number" of *The New Youth* in 1918. "Otherwise he certainly does not possess the ability to create his own independent character."[89] No Confucian would have comprehended the pluralistic social values advocated here; nor would he have understood the programs advanced by educational reformers in the late teens and twenties as means to the attainment of such ends.

In the latter regard, several things happened between 1917 and 1922 that seemed to justify a cautious optimism that the approach to social reform through cultural initiatives was indeed proving effective. The use of the vernacular spread rapidly in the public press, aided by an extraordinary proliferation of progressive periodicals at the time of the May Fourth movement. In 1920 the Ministry of Education ordered the adoption of *pai-hua* in all grade-school texts. Confirmed Deweyites seized control of commanding positions at the major normal universities (Southeastern University in Nanking and Peking Higher Norman University), as well as at Peita and other nationally important institutions. In 1922 a comprehensive educational reform was published, drafted with the participation of both John Dewey and his Columbia colleague Paul Monroe, and establishing a curriculum based on a distinctively progressive (and American) philosophy of education. The aims toward which Chinese education was henceforth to be directed were defined very much in New Culture terms: flexibility in adapting educational objectives to evolving social conditions and values; promotion of democratic attitudes and habits as a part of the educational experience; encouragement of individuality; dedication to the ideal of "education for life"; awareness that universal education must at the same time comprehend the needs of students of divergent economic backgrounds and social circumstances. At the same time the school system was reorganized by the introduction of a 6-3-3 curriculum, with an additional three years of university education for those who were not diverted into vocational training midway through their secondary-school careers. It was further stipulated that examinations were to be administered course by course, or subject by subject—a small point, seemingly, but with large implications: now, once and for all, was laid to rest the traditional idea that both academic achievement and social status should be confirmed through the mechanism of a single comprehensive examination which certified not only academic performance but also, at least in theory, the attainment of uniform moral norms.

Intellectuals, however, could only propose; it was the gods of warlordism who disposed. "The difficulties in the way of a practical extension and regeneration of Chinese education are all but insuperable," observed John Dewey gloomily in 1922, a few months after his return to the United States, viewing in retrospect the aspirations and frustrations of his Chinese friends. "Discussion often ends in an impasse: no political reform of China without education; but no development of schools as long as military men and corrupt officials divert funds and oppose schools from motives of self-interest. Here are the materials of a tragedy of the first magnitude."[90] Support of educational reform by the Ministry of Education in Peking was hardly effective, given the Ministry's limited jurisdiction and its inability to command sufficient funds even to pay professorial salaries, which with distressing frequency were in arrears. Reformers looked more hopefully for backing to organizations like the Kiangsu Provincial Education Association (Kiangsu sheng chiao-yü hui) and the National Association for Vocational Education (Chung-hua chih-yeh chiao-yü she), which came together in 1919, along with Tung-nan and Peita, to form the Society for the Promotion of the New Education (Hsin chiao-yü kung-chin she), with *The New Education* as its official organ. In 1922 the Society was in turn absorbed into the newly established National Association for the Advancement of Education (Chung-hua chiao-yü kai-chin she), comprising all educational associations that had no affiliation with the "central" government. T'ao Hsing-chih, another product of Columbia's Teachers College, took over the editorship of *The New Education* from Chiang Monlin, and served concurrently as director-general of the Association. Under its auspices a procession of American educationalists were active in China in the early 1920s, conducting surveys and submitting recommendations in such areas as science instruction and the standardization of testing. But measured against the need for large-scale and steady support and funding, such comings and goings, however purposeful in intent, seemed inconsequential in effect. Chiang Monlin was close to despair when, at the end of 1922, he wrote, "We who are involved in education have felt recently that the light of day is fading quickly."

> We used to think that politics was no good, and that the way to improve politics was to set to work in education, to nourish human talent. In these last years politics has become even more contentious, with the result that education has suffered unprecedented blows both economically and psychologically. Evidence has accumulated to prove that education is not only economically bankrupt, but spiritually bankrupt as well. So the blind faith of a few years back, the notion that "One should talk only about education, and not about politics," has gradually been discredited. . . .
>
> The academies [*shu-yuan*] of former times did, after all, possess a certain academic character of their own. But with changing circumstances and changing times, the old academies have all vanished. The schools now, however, are like a general store that is neither Chinese nor Western—what kind of

academic character do they possess? Our schools now . . . resemble the new-fangled Western chairs sold in the marketplace: not as comfortable as foreign chairs, nor yet as sturdy as old-fashioned armchairs. It's like trying to draw a tiger, and coming up with the picture of a dog—and yet we still say that in such schools we can nurture human talent.

Alas! What is the use of high-sounding talk and grand theorizing? Even the inadequate and deformed schools we have won't last the year. There is no money. What kind of preparations can be made, without money? What will the students have to read? What opportunities will the teachers have to improve their own knowledge, not to speak of advancing scholarship?

Politics is rotten—but how can we *not* talk politics? Yet if we talk politics, how can we educators escape the havoc wrought by the politicians, or their enmity, or their attempts to exploit us? Take it back a step: even if we don't talk politics, must we not still stand up for a certain moral standard [*kung tao*]? And if we do, then surely we will be given a hard time by the general run of people who care not a whit for any moral standard.[91]

Impoverishment and neglect were bitter and crippling problems for New Culture reformers, undermining the integrity of the educational mechanisms upon which they relied to generate a new social personality. Chiang Monlin's *cri de coeur* hints at another problem, however, even more disabling in the long run: the sense that the new education is somehow an anomalous innovation, possessing neither traditions nor a character of its own. On the part of many Chinese intellectuals in the 1920s there was a growing conviction that the values of New Culture liberalism were not, in fact, generalizable. In the eyes of its critics, the vaunted "new education" created only an intellectual elite divided in personal taste and style of life, and even more important, in vocational competence and social expectations, from the masses whose welfare they were supposed to promote. Chang Shih-chao expressed something of this sentiment when he denounced the new schools as a breeding ground for a "new-style aristocracy." Liang Shu-ming made the point more cogently, and with a turn of a phrase reminiscent of Feng Kuei-fen's derisive criticism of the "interpreters" of the 1860s:

Once a child from the countryside goes to a higher primary school in the city, he can no longer live the old, simple life. He cannot eat the old food, wear the old clothes, drink the tea, or smoke the tobacco. He looks down on everything and has no patientce with it. But, as for the knowledge and ability that a rural family needs, he has not a whit! Instead he has some half-baked, irrelevant, scientific knowledge in English, physics, and chemistry. He cannot actually do farm work; instead he can play ball and do [Western] calisthenics and has developed the habit of lazy loafing.[92]

Liang's response was characteristically vigorous and personal. From the mid-twenties onward he plunged into rural reconstruction work at the village level, in Kwangtung, Honan and, most notably, Shantung, hoping to reanimate Confucian modes of social organization and education as a means to restore the linkages between the concrete experiences of daily living and the abstractions of social ideology. Other intellectuals, too, were turning to the countryside at this time, with a differently inspired but similarly urgent desire to shape a social ideology that would draw upon the energies of the masses in order to meet their needs, while once again rendering morally coherent the relationship between leaders and led. In this very broad sense, China's problems in the 1920s and 1930s were increasingly perceived as problems of politics and of a governing ideology. To these we will turn our attention in the next chapter.

Writing for an American audience in the spring of 1920, John Dewey aptly epitomized the spirit of the movement of which for the past year he had been a sympathetic observer and occasional mentor.

> In politics, Young China aims at the institution of government by and of law . . . But it realizes that political development is mainly indirect; that it comes in consequence of the growth of science, industry and commerce, and of the new human relations and responsibilities they produce; that it springs from education, from the enlightenment of the people, and from special training in the knowledge and technical skill required in the administration of a modern state.

New Culture liberals would have found nothing to quarrel with here. But Dewey detected—or, as an outsider, felt more at liberty to disclose—an aspect of the situation that his Chinese admirers tended to overlook, or to ignore. "One realizes," he concluded, "how the delicate and multifarious business of the modern state is dependent upon knowledge and habits of mind that have grown up slowly and that are now counted upon as a matter of course."[93]

This was, indeed, the liberal dilemma, and the dilemma of the New Culture movement at large. Its strategies of social and intellectual transformation were predicated on the assumption of conditions that made possible the achievement of desired ends through peaceful, gradual, piecemeal reforms—conditions that could not be "counted upon as a matter of course" in the China of their time. Many factors contributed to the changing temper of Chinese ideas and politics in the twenties and thirties: rising levels of social violence and civic neglect, and the emergence of militant political ideologies and new techniques of political mobilization as the revolution entered upon its culminating phase. No less important was the spreading conviction, even within the ranks of the New Culture enthusiasts themselves, that liberal expectations were too dependent on social, political, and economic forces over which the liberals exercised no control, and to which they often seemed strangely indifferent.

Beyond this there lay an even more fundamentally damaging doubt. The New Culture movement was born in the confidence that, individually and collectively, human beings are ultimately the masters of their own destiny; that history's design, however slowly it may manifest itself, can only be progressive and benign. Few Chinese could sustain such confidence through the discordant, strife-torn, bloody decades that led their country into war and revolution.

7

The Claims of Ideology

A rising of the masses is not made, gentlemen the judges. It makes itself of its own accord. It is the result of social relations and conditions and not of a scheme drawn up on paper. A popular insurrection cannot be staged. It can only be foreseen.

          —Leon Trotsky, at his trial in 1906

THE FIRST ISSUE OF *The New Youth*, published in September, 1915, bore on its cover the portrait of Andrew Carnegie. Inside the magazine, ten pages were devoted to a biographical sketch of this exemplar of what it means to have "struggled and triumphed over adversity," enumerating both Carnegie's fabulous investments and his lavish philanthropies, digesting his preachments of the gospel of wealth, praising his upright industriousness, and lauding with equal warmth his high moral principles and his shrewd insight into the psychology of material success.

The sources of Carnegie's achievements are, first of all, his ability to use men [*yung jen*], and secondly, his managerial skill. Next must be reckoned his robust spirit and his patience in the face of adversity. He has said, "Any man of business who accomplishes great things relies in large measure on the ability to draw upon the strength of others." Therefore Carnegie treats his workers as a kind father would treat his children, and his workers serve him as filial sons would serve a loving parent. . . . His ideals are high, his spirit vigorous. How can our people, impoverished idlers chancing everything to luck in their fools' paradise, fail to acknowledge the aspect of true humanity when confronted by this old man.[1]

"No calamity in life is greater than the failure to help oneself," Liang Ch'i-ch'ao had admonished, way back in 1900; a generation later this remained an unshaken tenet of progressive belief. Carnegie was thus a timely hero to the Chinese in 1915. But no less timely—and thus strikingly suggestive of the manner in which the times were changing—were the sentiments expressed by Ch'en Tu-hsiu just five years later, on the fifth anniversary of *The New Youth's* first appearance. "To begin with the facts," he wrote, "we must clearly understand that in every country in the world the most unjust and grievous thing is simply this: that the small minority of indolent consumers, that is, the capitalist class, by means of such agencies as the state, the government, and the laws, oppresses as less than cattle, horses or machines the suffering majority, which is the productive laboring class. The only way to eradicate this injustice and this suffering is for the oppressed producers, the laboring class, itself to create a new power, itself to stand where the state stands. . . ."[2]

It is noteworthy that the essay in which Ch'en voiced this opinion was entitled "Talking Politics." By 1920, as we have observed in chapter 6, whatever agreement had united New Culture intellectuals in the late teens was breaking down; already in evidence were the stresses that would, within a brief few years, become deep fissures of disagreement, misunderstanding, and distrust. The problem of politics provides one key to an understanding of this process of fracture. It was, at one level, a question of "talking politics"—a question, that is, of whether or not it is profitable, or even proper, for intellectuals to involve themselves in political debate and activity. At another level it reflected, as we shall see, a fundamental disagreement over the very meaning of "politics" and the relationship between public responsibility and private culture.

A more obvious perspective on the disintegration of the New Culture consensus sees it as the result of intellectual radicalization, a process ongoing throughout the period from 1915 onward, impelling men like Ch'en Tu-hsiu and Li Ta-chao eventually beyond the charmed circle of New Culture assumptions and expectations. It was, in part, a change of mind; but it was also a growing awareness of the implications of differences that had existed from the beginning between "moderate" or "liberal" and "radical" spokesmen of the movement, differences thrown into sharper relief as the content of radicalism changed in the late teens in response to the introduction of diverse and provocative new ideological components.

We may detect something of this inner dynamic in the reminiscences of those who came of age intellectually during these unsettling years, imbued (as one 1918 graduate of Hunan Normal College recalled it) with "vague passions about 'nineteenth-century democracy,' Utopianism and old-fashioned liberalism," and struggling, against the tradition of elitist intellectualism, to make sense of the "curious mixture of ideas of liberalism, democratic reformism, and Utopian Socialism" that they found represented in the pages of *The New Youth* and other progressive journals.

> I started out as a student [he says], and in school developed the habits of a student. It did not seem proper for me to do even a little bit of hard work such as carrying my own baggage, in front of a whole crowd of students who were unable to shoulder a load or pick up a heavy weight. At that time I felt that the only clean people in the world were the intellectuals. . . . After the revolution when I joined in with the workers, peasants, and soldiers, I gradually came to know them thoroughly, and they too gradually came to know me. . . . Only then did I basically outgrow those bourgeois and petty-bourgeois sentiments which the bourgeois school had taught me. [I came to feel] that the intellectuals not only were in spirit unclean in many places, but their bodies too were unclean. The cleanest ones were still the workers and peasants—even taking into account that their hands were black and their feet covered with cow dung, they were still cleaner than the bourgeoisie, big and small. This then is what is meant by outgrowing one's sentiments and changing from one class to another. If our intellectual and art workers who have come from the ranks of the intelligentsia would make their own works welcomed by the masses, they must transform and completely reconstruct their own thought and feelings. . . .
>
> The last problem is one of study. I mean by this the study of Marxism-Leninism and of society. . . .[3]

It is Mao Tse-tung who speaks here, in the first instance genially recalling his intellectual apprenticeship for Edgar Snow's benefit, in a Yenan cave in 1936; in the second, at the Yenan Forum on Literature and Art in the spring of 1942, using that same experience as a means of instructing the intellectuals in their revolutionary duty. One hesitates to characterize a figure of such looming, almost surrealistic historical reputation as having been somehow "typical" of his time and generation; nor is it wise to suppose that Mao, even in his more informal moments, ever publicized his recollections without having a point to make. It is nevertheless true that the experience touched upon here, the transition from high-minded but fuzzy progressivism to a comprehensive ideological commitment, was by no means uncommon among Chinese intellectuals from 1920 onward.

It is not Mao himself who will concern us in the narrative that follows, nor will we treat "Mao's China" except in passing, and summarily. We will have a good deal to say about the particular insights and prejudices of Marxist-Leninist ideology as it worked its way into the discourse of Chinese intellectuals in the aftermath of the May Fourth movement, and we will try to assess Chinese revisions of this revolutionary ideology. By way of preliminaries, however, we will offer a description of the phenomenon of ideological thinking itself, and we will be concerned throughout with the manner in which ideology as a style of thought challenged the assumptions of New Culture liberals and affected the condition of Chinese intellectuals. We will see that revolutionary ideology contradicted, in several respects, the message that progressive intellectuals had been preaching since the closing years of the nineteenth century, and that it reaffirmed, if only obliquely, assumptions that seem in some ways strikingly "traditional." We will examine the devolution of New Culture ideas in an intellectual and political environment that was increasingly polarized, and the way in which the meaning of those ideas changed in response to China's changing circumstances. We will also see that the very idea of revolutionary change could not have flourished in China as it did, and perhaps still does, had it not been for the radical transformation of the Chinese view of the world, and of history, and of their own place, that had taken place since the turn of the century.

New Culture liberals were described in the preceding chapter as the advocates of cultural values essential to their own survival—the values, that is to say, of an enlightened and progressive intellectual elite—as being both relevant and essential to the welfare of society at large. Social revolutionary ideology, as it manifested itself in China from about 1920 onward, was in several respects antithetical to this view. New Culture intellectuals insisted on the social relevance of elite values; revolutionaries regarded intellectual elitism with suspision, and postulated the values of (or imputed to) "the masses" as those which must encompass all of society. New Culture intellectuals were not indifferent to social issues; they were, however, on the whole unsympathetic to a strategy of social change based on the idea of fundamental class antagonisms and conflict, choosing instead to emphasize qualities of individual character that they assumed to be universal. Social revolutionaries, on the other hand, seized upon the existence of social and economic inequalities as a justification for, and as a means to, the organization of an ideologically committed constituency—again, "the masses," or at least the Party of the masses. New Culture liberals affirmed the intellectuals' role as the responsible strategists of social and cultural change; under the revolutionary dispensation, intellectuals were regarded—not without distrust—as necessary collaborators in the great undertakings of social and cultural transformation. But they were deprived of the authority of design. They became, like other men, laborers: skilled artisans who could render services essential to the construction of the new order, but who were no longer entitled to think of themselves as its architects.

As the Chinese revolution moved toward its climactic episodes in the 1930s and 1940s, weaving together social idealism and social oppression, nationalist pride, anti-imperialist resentment, and civic exhaustion into the intricate and bloody design of general insurgency, intellectuals of the New Culture generation, or those schooled in its values, found their status challenged and the social and cultural functions to which they aspired dismissed as irrelevant or denounced as treasonable. Enthusiasm replaced scepticism as the touchstone of intellectual responsibility, and the question of the intellectuals' proper vocation was posed in uncompromising and unprecedentedly painful terms.

*   *   *

"Men are open to ideological discipline only at certain moments in history," writes Michael Walzer in his study of the confluence of political radicalism and religious enthusiasm in the course of the Puritan revolution in sixteenth and seventeenth century England. "Most often, they are immune, safe from whatever it is that inspires self-discipline and activism, disdainful of all enthusiasm. The crisis of modernization might be defined as the moment when old immunities are suddenly cancelled, old patterns of passivity and acquiescence overthrown."[4]

Whatever their political or cultural allegiances, Chinese intellectuals with few exceptions attained this point of "cancelled immunities" sometimes in the course of the first two decades of the twentieth century. The progress of the Chinese social revolution might be viewed as the process by which a comparable experience penetrated into the larger society of urban and rural Chinese life. In the revolutionary idiom this is what has been meant by "liberation"—liberation from the bonds of "feudalism" and the indignities of imperialism. For Chinese peasants, or for Chinese coolies, "liberation" was not so much a matter of intellectual persuasion as it was the slow and painful creation of a new sense of social identity in the immediate context of relationships within the family, the village, on the land, or in the workshop. It was not an experience readily comprehended within the vocabulary of New Culture admonitions and exhortations. Social revolution ran counter to the intellectualism of New Culture values; yet, as we shall see, it drew much of its ideological energy from the same sources that animated the New Culture endeavor. Before we turn our attention to the particular characteristics of Maoist Marxism as an ideological strategy, therefore, we must first examine briefly the general characteristics of ideological thinking as an intellectual style.

Common to all ideologies, whatever peculiarities may serve to distinguish them, is the general assumption that the question of identity cannot be answered by looking at the individual as an individual, but only by looking at the individual as a member of some larger collectivity. "Man is dissolved away into his social circumstances," as Bernard Crick puts it.[5] In other words, ideological thinking denies the possibility of absolute individual personality, and insists that "personal" identity, properly understood, is neither more nor less than a representation of collective personality. What the individual is, or thinks, or does, derives according to this view not from any quality of singularity or uniqueness attributable to the individual, but from the wider categories that shape the identity of the collective, whether it be race, class, culture, political or religious affiliation, or some compound of these.

A corollary to this is the assumption that a true understanding of the world—its social organization, its economic motives, its political structures, its historical purposes or direction—cannot be achieved by generalizing on the basis of individual experience, but must be framed in terms of the categories that define collective identity. From this essential perception follow several of the intellectual or psychological commitments that distinguish the ideological style of thought. The primary significance ascribed to comprehensive categories creates the need to categorize, that is, to fit all particular cases into those larger classes which will render them understandable. Thus, in the words of Edward Shils, ideological thinkers "aspire and pretend to systematic completeness."[6] Historically, the ideological mode of thought flourishes in periods when the processes of social and political disintegration or change have reached a critical stage, when a sense of crisis has become general, and when customary responses—indeed, even traditional questions—no longer suffice to provide a sense of direction, purpose, or security. Ideology, as Shils remarks, "is the product of the need for an intellectually imposed order on the world."

On the one hand, then, the ideological mode of thought embodies a sweeping critique of existing structures of social and political governance, existing rationalizations of human motives, and existing explanations of human experience. But ideology goes beyond this, to provide (again citing Shils) "an attendant vision of a positive alternative to the existing pattern of society and its culture and an intellectual capacity to articulate that vision as part of the cosmic order . . . placing at its very center certain cosmically, ethically fundamental propositions." Ideology thus inspires in its adherents "the belief that they are in possession of and in contact with what is ultimately right and true."

More than anything else, perhaps, it is this quality of cosmic comprehensiveness, the self-assurance of the "true believer," that distinguishes ideological thinking from more moderate—or "liberal"—intellectual responses to the challenge of historical crisis. The moral authority derived from the sense of being in touch with ultimate truth, and the confidence in the explanatory force of categorical attributions, combine to encourage insistence upon historical, moral, and intellectual imperatives that, in turn, breed the enthusiasm, the dogmatic assertion of one's own Right versus another's Error, that makes the ideological persuasion exclusive and total. A distrust of established authority, whether political, social, ecclesiastical, or moral, is a part of the ideological critique of existing structures. Yet in their very nature, ideologies are doctrines of governance, concerned with the issue of fundamental authority. It is also in the nature of ideologies that this sense of governance tends to be polarized: the Saved *vs.* the Damned, Exploited *vs.* Exploiters, We *vs.* They in one or another of the manifold forms that the belief in superiority or victimization can produce.

To suggest that the character of their own political and cultural traditions has in some ways predisposed the Chinese to respond ideologically to their situation in the twentieth century is not simply to confirm the stale cliché that a people ultimately achieves the government it deserves. Still less is it to agree with the disreputable opinion offered by a Western savant, that for the Chinese "the almost compulsive need for ideologies is far more significant than the content of any one of their ideologies. No other people in history have had as great a need to dress up their politics in formal ideological trappings."[7] There are, as we shall discover, durable assumptions at the foundation of Chinese ideologies, ancient or modern; and it is true that in certain important respects traditional Confucianism approximated an ideological style of thought. Especially in the neo-Confucian interpretation that gained the ascendancy from the fourteenth century onward, Confucianism affirmed the primary importance of comprehensive social and metaphysical categories as a means to understand the world and act upon it. In the attempt to impose order upon the chaotic fragmentation of earlier traditions, neo-Confucianism as an intellectual system aspired to explanatory completeness. It carried within it a strong sense of "we" and "they"—ruler *vs.* ruled, emperor *vs.* minister, the superior man *vs.* the inferior man, those who can understand *vs.* those who must be made to conform, civilized *vs.* barbarian. And, finally, it embodied a critique of existing rationalizations of political and moral authority, a spirit of criticism that, however attenuated, remained always an aspect of Confucianism's "interior" personality.

There is, however, a final aspect of the ideological style of thought that finds no precedent in the Confucian tradition. Ideological comprehensiveness has, as its temporal dimension, a strong belief that men move *through* history toward some unique historical destination, a millennial *terminus ad quem*—a chiliastic fervor epitomized by Shils as an "obsession with futurity." As we have seen, Chinese traditions of social idealism possessed their own millennarian visions that found modern expression in the utopianism of such thinkers as Hung Hsiu-ch'üan and K'ang Yu-wei. But utopianism is essentially ahistorical, offering an alternative whose authenticity derives more from its moral than from its temporal relationship to the age which it condemns. The linear sense of history, on the other hand, is one of the central components of what we are here describing as ideological thought—the decisive difference, as Marx saw it, between "utopian" and "scientific" socialism. Had it not been, then, for the intervention of reformminded, progressive evolutionists like Liang Ch'i-ch'ao, Yen Fu, Hu Shih, and several other luminaries of the New Culture generation, and the fundamental revision of the Chinese sense of history that their ideas inspired, revolutionary ideology could hardly have played the role it has in China's modern metamorphosis.

"The transformation of the Rights of Man into the rights of the Sans-coulottes," observed Hannah Arendt, "was the turning point not only of the French Revolution but of all revolutions that were to follow."[8] It is this that marks the most conspicuous difference in temper, in organization, and in objectives, between the revolutionary movement that culminated in 1911–1912 and the revolutionary movements that took form in the course of the 1920s, and over the next three decades dominated China's social and political history. The 1911 Revolution had triumphed (or failed) without benefit of "mass" support. The leaders of the Revolutionary Alliance had been well aware that their new order would require a popular constituency; they were evidently convinced, however, that the very act of revolution would itself generate the kind of popular support necessary to their success. The social discontents that were randomly exploited for "revolutionary" purposes in pre-1911 uprisings tended to be localized, disorganized, and apolitical in any programmatic sense. Nor, indeed, could it have been otherwise. A revolution *for* the masses was one thing; a revolution *of* the masses meant social revolution—and social revolution, as we have seen, was not on the agenda of the 1911 revolutionaries.

By the 1920s the revolutionary vision had grown to encompass social purposes and, as time went on, strategies of social mobilization. The quickening pace of civic disintegration was, of course, one important reason for this, but not the only one. New Culture intellectuals were more perceptive than their predecessors had been of the links between social conditions on the one hand, and cultural values and political relationships on the other. The coincidental introduction into China of Marxism-Leninism, to which we will turn shortly, imparted to this maturing social awareness an organizing structure and a discipline, new categories of analysis, and an eloquent vocabulary of protest. At the same time the revitalization of earlier revolutionary energies and organization created the opportunity for purposeful opposition to the political abuses and near anarchy of warlordism.

In the rapidly changing circumstances of the 1920s and 1930s it was often difficult to preserve a balance, or even to distinguish, between the social and the political motives of the evolving revolutionary movement. How, and to what extent, was social exploitation related to political, economic, and cultural oppression? In what ways did the struggle against foreign economic and cultural influence, or military aggression, reinforce or contradict the demands of "modernization"—that is, the struggle against the past? How, in the language of the time and the cause, was imperialism related to feudalism?

In the mid-1920s these insurrectionary motives converged under the terms of an uneasy but temporarily effective alliance between the fledgling Chinese Communist Party (CCP) and the reviving Nationalist Party (Kuomintang, or KMT) of Sun Yat-sen. The CCP, established in 1921 by a dozen enthusiastic converts to the gospel of Marxism-Leninism, operated throughout the first decade of its existence in compliance with the dictates of the Third International (Communist)—the Comintern—which ordained, among other things, a policy of collaboration with Sun's resurrected revolutionary party. In his declining years, an embittered Dr. Sun basked in the warmth of Comintern approval of his increasingly strident anti-imperialist sentiments, and his party reaped the benefits of Comintern (and Soviet) subsidization of what was doctrinally sanctified as the KMT's "bourgeois nationalist" aspirations. The Northern Expedition of 1926–1928, which at least nominally reunited China under Nationalist control, was in its early phases a cooperative undertaking. But in April, 1927, two years after Sun's death and a year and a half before the formal establishment of the new government at Nanking, Chiang Kai-shek and the right wing of the KMT turned decisively against their erstwhile Communist allies, and against the social aims of the revolutionary movement. One reason for this, perhaps, was the fact that the KMT's claim to legitimacy rested on its links to an earlier and more narrowly defined revolutionary tradition. A more important reason, however, must be sought in the social composition of the Nationalist party-and-government itself, its membership increasingly representative of those whose interests were to defend, not to overturn, the established social order. From the brushfire encounters of the late 1920s to the all-consuming inferno of the late 1940s, China's civil war was at the same time an ongoing social revolution.

On the ultimately triumphant side, the strategies and principles of this revolution were shaped by the ideology formed, from the late 1920s onward, through the interaction of Marxist-Leninist theory and the revolutionary experiences of the Chinese Communists themselves. In the content of "Maoism"—the convenient cognomen of China's distinctive brand of latter-day Marxism—we may identify ideas that originated in the restless intellectualism of the May Fourth era. The revolutionary phenomenon itself, however, promoted the spread of an ideological style of thought fundamentally hostile to the pluralistic scepticism that New Culture intellectuals endeavored to encouage. The May Fourth Movement, broadly considered, may indeed have marked the beginning of China's *real* revolution, as Communist historians persistently maintain, meaning by this the emergence of a historically necessary alliance of revolutionary social classes. Viewed in retrospect, however, it is difficult not to see the New Culture decade as the final phase in a process of intellectual disestablishment that had been under way since the closing decades of the nineteenth century, marking the end of an interlude when Chinese intellectuals stood, as we might say, between orthodoxies.

* * *

In April, 1917, Ch'en Tu-hsiu commented editorially in *The New Youth* on the revolution that a few weeks earlier had toppled the Russian autocracy from power. He was primarily concerned with the effect that events in Russia might have on the course of the European war and on the eventual peace-making. Characteristically, however, he cast these considerations into the broader context of mankind's moral progress. "The causes and the consequences of this European war are certainly complex. Of great importance, in this connection, is the question of the relative strength of monarchism versus democracy, of aggression versus humanism. . . . The Russian Revolution did not merely overthrow the Russian imperial house; it overthrew also the principles of monarchism and aggression."[9]

Ch'en's observations were, of course, inspired by the coup that had resulted in the establishment of the moderate-liberal Provisional Government in Petrogard; in April the triumph of Bolshevism still lay far beyond the horizons of expectation. As for Ch'en himself, fully three years would pass before his "conversion" to Marxism-Leninism would be accomplished. In due course the principles of "scientific socialism"—that is, Marxism in its philosophical dimension—together with the Leninist theory of imperialism and Bolshevik principles of revolutionary organization, would exercise a profound influence on Ch'en and other Chinese intellectuals. Historians still debate the relative importance of these several contributions to the genesis of an organized Communist movement in China. There is little disagreement, however, that the very fact of a revolutionary victory in Russia, a humanitarian triumph that stood in startling contrast to their own recent disappointments and to the spectacle of European self-destruction, created among Chinese intellectuals a sense of anticipation, and a hope that the ideals which the Chinese revolution had failed to realize might now find historical vindication.

Credit for the early popularization of Marxism-Leninism in China is commonly assigned to two members of the Peita inner circle in the late teens, Ch'en Tu-hsiu and Li Ta-chao. Ch'en we have already met; with Li we will become acquainted shortly. They were men of quite different character and temperament: the one pugnacious, sharp-tongued, and bitter, the other affable, cooperative, and gentle-minded. They came to their faith in the world revolution from different directions, and although their paths ran parallel, they pursued their cause to different destinations. Ch'en Tu-hsiu, older by ten years, was in point of time a slightly later convert to Marxism-Leninism. He became, however, the first conspicuous Chinese Communist personality, the Party's first designated leader, one of the first victims of its early political disasters, and its first great renegade—though in his own mind never untrue to the ideals that had originally seized his imagination. Li Ta-chao's role was less prominent, though his labors on behalf of the Party in its early days were far from negligible, and in the end he paid the ultimate price for his beliefs. He is best remembered, and justly so, as an interpreter of Marxist theory in the light of Chinese circumstances and aspirations, who left an enduring impression on the evolution (or devolution) of Communist theory in China.

In order better to understand the nature of the ideals that sustained Ch'en through a troubled life and the significance of Li's reworking of Marxist premises, it may be useful at this point to review the principal theses of the Marxist-Leninist argument—bearing in mind that the following summary does scant justice to the subtleties and ambiguities that make Marxism a rich, provocative, and sometimes puzzling body of ideas. The tenets of classical Marxism expound economic (or materialist) determinism; a theory of class conflict; proletarianism; and internationalism. Human motives are interpreted as the expression of a collective consciousness shaped by material factors, or more specifically, by the relationship of economic/social classes to the mode of production that is dominant in any given historical period. The engine of history is the inevitable struggle between, on the one hand, the class which controls the means of production and therefore profits from the distribution of wealth in the general context of an economy of scarcity; and, on the other hand, the class whose labor creates economic value—that is, wealth—but whose share of this wealth is dictated in accordance with the self-interest of the exploiting class. In the modern West, which was the primary source of Marx's information and always the focus of his concern, the phenomenon of class struggle takes the form of a confrontation between the capitalist-industrialist bourgeoisie and the proletariat. The values of the bourgeoisie infuse every aspect of contemporary public and private culture: all social and political institutions, all formal and informal codes of behavior, all standards of moral, aesthetic, or ethical judgment are instruments by means of which the bourgeoisie establishes or confirms its own self-image and perpetuates its authority. On the other hand, by reason of the singular organizational demands of the industrial mode of production, the proletariat is a laboring class alienated as never before in history, not only from control over the conditions under which it labors, but also from the final product of that labor and therefore from any realization of its own humanity.

This situation, however, is neither fixed nor stable. The ineluctable dynamic inherent in economic/social antagonisms—the dialectic—generates change and insures the emergence of new antithetical relationships. So, in response to economic conditions over which it has in fact no ultimate control, and in pursuit of its own survival, the capitalist-industrialist class is becoming ever smaller in aggregate numbers, its wealth and its power more and more concentrated, while on the other side the proletarian class is growing always larger and more destitute as it approaches its moment of destiny. The time is at hand, Marx believed, or soon must be, when the proletariat will spontaneously achieve an understanding of its interests as a class, and rise up to overwhelm the bourgeoisie and to seize control of the industrial mode of production. And what will matter then will be the common interest and identity that unites proletarians the world over, not the anachronistic bourgeois distinctions that divide them along nationalistic lines, as British workingmen or French workingmen or German workingmen. In the bold language of the *Communist Manifesto*, "The working men have no Fatherland."

The inevitable triumph of the proletariat will not mark simply the beginning of a new stage in the ongoing history of class struggle, the ascendancy of a new exploiting class which will in time generate its own social antithesis. It will signal, rather, the end of history so conceived, the end of the ages-old war between masters and slaves that has thus far constituted the record of human progress. This millennarian expectation was justified, in Marx's argument, by the nature of industrialism itself, at once the most brutally dehumanizing and the most fantastically efficient mode of production ever known. Now, for the first time, productive capabilities have transcended the necessity for limitations such as those imposed by all traditional economic systems. Once the productive class, the proletariat, has itself assumed control of the means of production, for the first time the problem of how to justify and enforce the unequal distribution of scarce resources will give way to the happier problem of how to administer the equitable distribution of abundance; in Engels' phrase, ". . . the government of persons is replaced by the administration of things." Then all the mechanisms devised by human ingenuity under the prod of social necessity to compel and coerce adherence to the belief in social and political inequality—the state, its laws, theological religion and ecclesiastic discipline, the appeal to custom—must vanish from the face of the earth. Then, indeed, will human beings achieve their true humanity, possessing a genuine *self*-consciousness.

It is not difficult to imagine why this vision should appeal to Chinese intellectuals. Marxism promised the benefits of modernity without the social injustices of which the Chinese had become increasingly apprehensive. It offered as the certain destination of history a "Westernized" utopia, while at the same time providing an informed and highly critical analysis of the political and moral infrastructure of existing Western values. It purported to argue its case scientifically, revealing laws which explain social dynamics in terms as precise and irrefutable as those which describe physical phenomena. Yet beneath this unimpassioned exposition of the workings of the social order, the spirit of Marxism is one of passionate humanism.

But it is also easy to understand why Chinese reformers and radicals should have paid only cursory attention to Marxism when it first came to their attention. "We develop new principles for the world out of the world's own principles," Marx once remarked.[10] And indeed, much of the force of his argument derives from the uses to which Marx put materials already present in the European mind. But for the Chinese there was no shock of recognition: the principles of Marx's world were not theirs. Marxism's theory of progress and eventual accomplishment is dependent on a social history which the Chinese had no reason to regard as relevant to their own experience, and on the assumption of fundamental social antagonisms which they were at pains to discount, at least in application to China. If industrialism creates the economic conditions necessary to insure the eventual transcendance of social inequality, this offers at best a remote hope to a people still burdened by a vast agrarian, pre-industrial economy. If the agent of historical redemption is the industrial proletariat, what comfort can be drawn from that fact by men living in a society in which, even in the cities, fragmented small-scale craft guilds remained the overwhelmingly predominant mode of "industrial" organization? Finally and decisively, proletarian internationalism ran directly counter to the reformers' desire to generate among the Chinese people at large an untraditional sense of civic responsibility and national identity.

These difficulties were overcome, to a certain extent, by Lenin's amendment of classical Marxism, the effect being to render it more congenial to situations that do not conform to Western European conditions. The most generally important Leninist innovation is the theory of the revolutionary Party as a "vanguard" made up of individuals committed to revolution as a profession, an organization not *necessarily* proletarian in respect to the social origins of its members, which assumes the responsibility for summoning the proletariat to the performance of its revolutionary duty. The rigid determinism inherent (as some at least insist) in classical Marxism is thus relaxed to a degree. The possiblity of proletarian revolution is no longer entirely dependent on the natural or spontaneous—and unpredictable—maturing of the proletariat's consciousness of its predicament, its capabilities, and its mission. The way is thus opened for the creation of a revolutionary elite to bear the burden of instigating the revolutionary transformation; at the same time, a first step is taken away from the notion that proletarianism is essentially the state of mind of the proletariat itself, and it becomes instead a revolutionary attitude least hypothetically independent of class origins.

The idea of the Party as a revolutionary vanguard was Lenin's response to a number of factors: the repressive conditions under which radicals tried to operate in late imperial Russia; the country's political and economic backwardness, and the insignificance of the Russian proletariat in either economic or social terms; and the fear that, left to itself, the working class would never move beyond what Lenin contemptuously called "trade-union consciousness." Lenin never maintained, however, that a proletarian revolution could succeed in Russia except in the larger context of a general proletarian uprising in the industrialized West. Marx had implied, if not promised, the imminence of such an event, but in the generation since Marx's death the chains of capitalist nationalism had bound Europe ever tighter: the Second International had foundered on the rocks of patriotism when even Socialist deputies joined their bourgeois colleagues to vote in favor of war credits in their respective national assemblies in the awful summer of 1914. Lenin, still in exile, addressed this unhappy state of affairs in his 1916 pamphlet entitled "Imperialism, The Highest Stage of Capitalism," a polemical elaboration of ideas hinted at by Marx himself and later developed further by other socialist thinkers. European capitalism, Lenin argued, instead of collapsing under its own weight, has bought time by incorporating the rest of the world into its economic system through the mechanisms of imperialist expansion and exploitation, which Lenin identified as the central issues of the war. Therefore, in order to hasten the demise of capitalism in those countries where industrialism is most highly developed, the system must be stripped of the colonial dependencies which provide the resources, the markets, and the opportunities for the investment of finance capital, that prolong its life. Paradoxically, then, the cause of proletarian internationalism must be advanced by promoting anti-imperialist nationalism in the non-European world, even at the expense of establishing temporary alliances with the native bourgeois or proto-bourgeois classes whose nationalistic consciousness is more highly developed, or more susceptible to stimulation, than is the case with the nascent working class.

These ideas, originally set forth during the last years of Lenin's prerevolutionary exile as an exercise in theory, laid the basis for Soviet and Comintern policies toward Asia in general, and China in particular, during the 1920s, providing the requisite ideological justification for the alliance between Sun Yat-sen's "bourgeois-nationalist" Kuomintang and the Chinese Communists. Students of the subject disagree among themselves, however, as to the extent to which the still small number of Chinese who were actively committed to Communism in 1921, when the Party was founded, were in fact familiar with or decisively influenced by Leninism. The first Comintern agents dispatched to survey the revolutionary scene in China arrived in 1920, and duly made contact with Li Ta-chao in Peking and Ch'en Tu-hsiu in Shanghai. Their chief effort in those early days, however, was to try to turn a few scattered groups of interested intellectuals into effective political organizations. The Leninist theory of nationalist colonial wars in support of European proletarian internationalism, though already much in evidence in the proceedings of various congresses of the international Communist movement, did not begin firmly to dictate Comintern policies in China until 1922. Nor was the issue thereby resolved: both within China and outside it, it has remained a lively and by no means entirely academic question whether China's social transformation is best understood as an indigenous phenomenon with a primarily nationalistic significance, or is only comprehensible as an aspect of worldwide socialist revolution.

In any event, it was the actions of the newly-created Soviet government that contributed more than any theoretical formulations to the burgeoning Chinese interest in Marxist socialism. Within a few months of the Bolshevik seizure of power in 1917, G. Chicherin, the People's Commissar for Foreign Affairs, proclaimed the government's intention to renounce the privileges and indemnities wrested from China by the fallen Tsarist regime. In July, 1919, a similar declaration was made by L. Karakhan, the Deputy Commissinar, committing Soviet military forces to the noble task of "bringing to the [Chinese] peoples liberation from the yoke of the foreign bayonnet, from the yoke of foreign gold." To this end it offered, among other concessions, to restore to China "without compensation" the Chinese Eastern Railway, a spur of the Trans-Siberian that bisected Manchuria in order to abbreviate the journey from Chita to Vladivostok. These overtures, however intended, were inexpensive gestures at a time when the Soviet government exercised no authority in Eastern Siberia: by 1919 the Red Army had established only a small and vulnerable revolutionary perimeter on the Asian side of the Urals. Karakhan was bestowing gifts not then in his power to give, and their luster was tarnished, after the Soviets established their jurisdiction in Russian Asia, by the prolonged controversy that ensued over the precise terms of the deed.[11]

In 1919, nevertheless, coming as it did within weeks of the betrayal of Chinese expectations at Versailles (a coincidence by no means absent from Russian calculations) the Karakhan Manifesto created an immediate and lingering impression of friendliness toward the revolutionary Russian regime on the part of Chinese intellectuals. In 1922, when Adolph Joffe arrived in Peking as the first representative of the Soviet government (as distinct from the Comintern, at least nominally) in China, Ts'ai Yuan-p'ei was moved to welcome him, on the occasion of a banquet given at Peita in his honor, in language perhaps a bit warmer than etiquette alone required:

The Chinese revolution was a political one. Now it is tending towards the direction of a social revolution. Russia furnishes a good example to China, which thinks it advisable to learn the lessons of the Russian revolution, which started also as a political movement but later assumed the nature of a social revolution. Please accept the hearty welcome of the pupil to the teachers.[12]

Lenin took a more cautious view of the extent to which Russian experience provided a useful model for Asian Communists to emulate. Russia was, he conceded, "the most backward country in Europe"—but still, it is European, and therefore, if only peripherally, a part of the world that Marx had described. "The Russian Bolsheviks have succeeded in making a breach in the old imperialism . . . which the British, French or German proletariat will consolidate," he said. But, he continued, "You, the representatives of the working masses of the East, have before you an even bigger and newer task. . . ."

You now face a task which has not confronted communists anywhere in the world until now: relying on general communist theory and practice, you must adapt yourselves to specific conditions of a sort not met with in European countries; you must learn to apply that theory and practice to a situation in which peasants form the bulk of the population, and in which the object is to struggle against medieval survivals, not against capitalism.[13]

It is not too great a simplification to suggest that in China, Ch'en Tu-hsiu and Li Ta-chao each seized upon a different part of this challenge: Ch'en throwing himself into the "struggle against medieval survivals," Li pondering the revolutionary future of China's numberless and anonymous peasantry.

*   *   *

In a generation when iconoclasm flourished among Chinese intellectuals, Ch'en Tu-hsiu was the iconoclast *par excellence*, an uncompromising and uncommonly virulent critic of the Chinese past, and of the shibboleths of contemporary "progressive" discourse. Others more temperate than he, like Hu Shih, made at least an effort to discriminate between Confucian and non-Confucian elements in China's traditional culture, and to distinguish between the sterile pedagogy of orthodox Confucianism and other more vital subtraditions of criticism and self-expression within the whole. For Ch'en, however, a simpler working hypothesis was sufficient: everything "traditional" in China has been corrupted by the influence of Confucianism, "a formless instrument that unifies and controls our spirit"[14]; everything Confucian is evil and hateful; therefore the Chinese tradition in all its parts is corrupt, evil, hateful and unworthy: unfit, and not fitting the Chinese to survive. "Far rather would I see our country's past culture vanish, than to see our race, now and in the future, unfit to survive in the world, and doomed to extinction," Ch'en wrote in his "Appeal to Youth." "The Babylonians are dead and gone; of what use to them now is their civilization?"[15] A year later, in the aftermath of Yuan Shih-k'ai's attempted imperial restoration, Ch'en responded with characteristic vehemence and a hint of sarcasm to the proposal that Confucianism be elevated to the status of China's official state religion:

> If we still believe that Chinese laws and Confucian morals are sufficient in order to organize our nation, to regulate our society, and to insure our survival in the competitive modern world, then not only may we dispense with the Republic and the constitution, but moreover we should regard as meddlesome interference, as mistakes, these ten years and more of reform and bloody revolution, the establishment of a National Assembly, reforms of the legal code, and indeed everything that is new in politics and in education. By all means, put an end to such things, call a halt, preserve our old ways, lest our resources and our talents be wasted.
>
> But if, perchance, one is not comfortable or content with this notion of where one's duty lies, if one still desires to create a Western-style new nation, a Western-style new society, in order to insure survival in the modern world, then the fundamental issue remains the essential prerequisite of importing the foundations of Western-style societies and nations—that is to say, the new belief in equality and human rights.
>
> We must be fully aware of the fact—and bravely resolved to act upon our awareness—that Confucianism is antithetical to the new society, the new nation, the new faith. Otherwise the result can only be a stalemate, an impasse.[16]

Survival, then, was Ch'en's first concern—a priority by no means strange for a reformer whose political awakening had been influenced by the evolutionist exhortations of Liang Ch'i-ch'ao and others at the turn of the century. But, in Ch'en's mind, the survival of what? He tirelessly proclaimed his indifference to the fate of Chinese (read Confucian) culture; but he was no less contemptuous, in these years, in his denunciation of nationalistic aims. Like other spokesmen of the New Culture, Ch'en was self-consciously cosmopolitan, an attitude he urged upon his youthful audience. "Do not be parochial," he had warned in 1915, for "the man who builds his cart behind locked gates may find, when the gates are opened, that the cart will not fit the track."[17] But where others were internationalists or supranationalists, Ch'en was vigorously an *anti*-nationalist, in sharp contrast, for example, to Hu Shih's Olympian condescension. "We hope there is a patriotism founded on something better than prejudice," Hu wrote in his student diary in the summer of 1914, copying Carlyle; "that our country may be dear to us, without injury to our philosophy. . . ."[18] Ch'en Tu-hsiu, in an essay called "Patriotism and Consciousness of Self" written at almost exactly the same time, looked at the issue from the bottom up—the perspective, one may surmise, of a proto-revolutionary. "Some people argue that the nation, even if loathsome, is better than no nation at all," he wrote, with the proponents of autocracy doubtless in mind. "But I say that the ruthless exploitation of the people—the situation in which we find ourselves—is more marked under a loathsome nation than when no nation exists at all. . . . Those who wish passionately to preserve even a despicable nation would, in fact, protect a despicable government."[19] Four years later, in a celebrated essay calling for "The Destruction of Idols," Ch'en summed up his case in these terms:

> What is the nation? If one heeds the explanations offered up by scholars of government, one becomes more confused the more they try to explicate. I will put the matter bluntly: the nation is also a kind of idol. A nation is merely a piece of territory within which one, or several, peoples have come together, and to which they have arbitrarily afixed a name. If you take away the people, then only the territory remains; where then is the nation? . . . We can see, then, that the nation is nothing but a deceptive idol, with no genuine powers intrinsic to it. . . .
>
> Destroy! Destroy the idols! Destroy the empty images! Our belief must maintain the true and the reasonable as its standard. The unreasonable beliefs that have been bequeathed to us, the vanities and deceptions of religion, politics, and ethics, we must consider as idols that must be destroyed! IF SUCH EMPTY IDOLS ARE NOT DESTROYED, THEN THE REAL TRUTHS OF THE UNIVERSE AND THE PROFOUNDEST BELIEFS OF OUR INNER HEARTS WILL NEVER BE AT ONE.[20]

Was Ch'en then a populist? The question begs an easy answer. He was undoubtedly a democrat and a republican, in the sense that had been read into these terms by reformers since the turn of the century. He believed, as they did, that the state exists for the people, its only justification residing in its ability to respond to the needs of the people; he believed that the kind of loyalty to authority on which Confucians had placed a premium should not be confused with genuine patriotism. On these points Ch'en was explicit, and consistent. But "the people" as an abstraction was one thing, and the people in their physical reality quite another. To the idealized "new youth" of his visions he offered a portrait of the Chinese that even the most contemptuous nineteenth-century Western missionary could not have improved upon:

> That we Chinese meet with insult wherever we set foot is not entirely because the nation is moribund. It is also because of unclean customs, not least our filthy and despicable plaited hair and our traditional attire. . . . The country has no established system of public hygiene. Hawking and spitting are not prohibited; excrement and weeds clog the streets. Dirty and unwashed, [the Chinese] stink worse than Western cattle, dogs and horses. . . . Stand on a streetcorner and watch the passersby: not one in a hundred dresses tidily; only unkempt hair and grimey faces meet the eye. The filth is overpowering. . . . The unschooled retain a little natural hardiness, but as for the general run of pedants [*shu-suan-tzu*] . . . heads thrust foolishly forward on crooked necks,

backs hunched, waists bent, shoulders slumped, faces sallow and gaunt: neither their senses nor their bodies are strong or keen or useful.[21]

These are hardly the sentiments of a man who esteems "the people" as the guardians of a popular culture that serves as the repository of inherited folk wisdom, or displays evidence of an instinctive socialist impulse. Such confidence in the popular character is generally absent from the ethos of the New Culture intelligentsia—with the enormously important exception of Li Ta-chao, as we shall see. What one might call "radical populism," a sympathy on the part of intellectuals for the people or an intellectual movement "to the people" in any way comparable in motive or expectations to the Russian *narodnik* movement of the 1860s and 1870s, does not figure prominently in the early history of Chinese revolutionary socialism. Chinese radicals, even the early Chinese Communists (as Mao Tse-tung's reminiscences remind us), were Chinese intellectuals, in background and disposition. One of the delicate tasks that confronted the Comintern advisors who arrived in China in 1920 and 1921 was to try to persuade scattered clusters of cerebral *soi-disant* Marxists to engage in purposeful contacts with the "revolutionary classes," the great unwashed. Even after the revolutionary role of the peasantry had been acknowledged, at the level of strategic formulations, the question of the relationship between "popular culture" and "mass revolutionary culture" remained an uneasy and contentious issue. Ch'en Tu-hsiu, for one, never developed the common touch. His style was down to earth, laced wth traditional aphorisms, and often blunt to the point of rudeness—but what he wrote was intended for a literate and sophisticated readership. His perspectives changed fundamentally in the course of 1919 and 1920, but his aspirations remained still very much within the elitist tradition of New Culture reformism.

Ch'en Tu-hsiu has been described as "above all a Westernizer, who turned to Communism as the most efficient method for modernizing Chinese society."[22] Like other New Culture intellectuals, he was still struggling in the late teens with the dilemma that had disconcerted Chinese radicals since the turn of the century. China must be able to compete if it is to survive: it must become modern. To achieve this, foreign example suggested that political authority must be given over into the hands of the people—which for China meant a people manifestly unprepared in terms of social custom and civic experience to assume so awesome a responsibility. To Liang Ch'i-ch'ao and the anti-dynasts, political tutelage had seemed the only answer, under the auspices of an enlightened autocrat, on the one hand, or of a self-sacrificing revolutionary leadership on the other. Ch'en and other New Culture intellectuals called instead for the nurturing of a new personal and social culture through education as the best means of establishing durable foundations for a self-governing civic community. But it was a slow, vulnerable, and uncertain progress—and, earlier than some, Ch'en's confidence in the outcome broke.

Ch'en Tu-hsiu's writings do not provide us with the kind of expository analyses that Li Ta-chao furnished in his early essays on Bolshevism and Marxism, which might allow us to follow Ch'en's path toward his new faith closely. We must judge as best we can, knowing something of his ideas, his temper, and his experiences in 1919 and 1920, what moved him in the direction he took. In May and June of 1919 he was actively involved in the May Fourth disturbances. While Hu Shih and Chiang Monlin counseled patient moderation, and Ts'ai Yuan-p'ei retreated in dignified protest to the West Lake, Ch'en Tu-hsiu threw himself into the battle: he was not a patient man, nor one to stand upon his dignity. In mid-June he was arrested, charged with distributing inflammatory handbills in support of the students who had been mistreated and jailed at the time of the May demonstrations. He spent the summer in prison, suspended as it were between his past and his future. "World civilizations have their origins in two places," he wrote; "the study, and the prison. . . . The only true civilization is the civilization born in these two places."[23] In September he was released—paroled, according to Hu Shih, "in the traditional manner," that is, through the intercession of fellow provincials from Anhwei. Officially on leave of absence, he continued to draw his Peita salary for the few months that he remained in Peking, but his association with the university was effectively at an end.

He was not yet a confirmed Marxist, however, or even a comitted revolutionary. Until the end of that momentous year the *New Youth* consensus held together. In the December issue a statement of editorial policy reaffirmed the magazine's dedication to familiar aims:

> If we would promote social progress, we must destroy the prejudiced faith in "unalterable principles" and "thus it has always been. . . ." We must resolve to abandon these old notions, on the one hand, and on the other, to combine whatever wisdom past and present may have to offer, together with our own ideas, and thus to create new concepts in politics, ethics and economics, establishing a new spirit and responding to a new social environment.
>
> The new age and the new society to which we aspire is open and honest, progressive, affirmative, free, equitable, constructive, beautiful and good, peaceful; a society of mutual affection and assistance, in which there is joy in labor. Its aim is the happiness and prosperity of the society as a whole. We hope for the gradual disappearance and ultimate extinction of every vestige of whatever is counterfeit, conservative, negative, constraining, socially divisive [*chieh-chi-ti*], conformist, deformed and evil, aggressive; all evidence of exploitation and contention, idleness and melancholy, and whatever promotes the interests only of the minority. . . .[24]

That the manifesto's sponsors should find it expedient to express themselves at this level of high-minded and meaningless generalization suggests, perhaps, the extent to which the *New Youth* group was already divided by internal discord. That they were provoked to speak out, and able to do so with any semblance of harmony, was probably due to the influence of John Dewey, whose lectures on social and political philosophy had engaged the attention of the Peking intelligentsia throughout the autumn of 1919. Dewey's ideas were clearly reflected in the manifesto's bill of particulars: democracy signifies not simply institutions, but a participatory style of political life; government is an instrument, not an end; the scientific attitude must replace blind faith. Indeed, the December issue of *The New Youth* might well have carried a dedication to Dewey. It included the first installment of Kao I-han's transcription of the lectures referred to above, together with Hu Shih's unabashedly Dewey-esque appraisal of "The Signficance of the New Thought." Ch'en Tu-hsiu contributed a long essay entitled "The Foundations for the Realization of Democracy," in retrospect his final tribute to the long-cherished ideals of liberal democracy. In it Ch'en reaffirmed his confidence in the efficacy of bit-by-bit reforms that dealt with particular, concrete problems. He dwelt, as Dewey had, on the importance of encouraging political reform from the bottom up, relying in the first instance on what one might regard as the "natural" sources of political understanding and experience, self-government at the village level and through the craft guilds.

Within a few months, however, Ch'en had left Peking for Shanghai, taking *The New Youth* with him. In the course of 1920 Ch'en became a Communist, and *The New Youth* became the first major Marxist journal published in China. Ch'en threw himself into organizational and propaganda activities: as a founder of the Socialist Youth League (Chung-kuo she-hui ch'ing-nien-t'uan); as publisher of *The Worker* (Lao-tung-che), intended to carry the Communist message to a proletarian audience; and as one of the Comintern's principal contacts in South China. In December he accepted the invitation of the "revolutionary" Cantonese warlord Ch'en Chiung-ming, to become director of the Education Department of the Kwangtung Provincial Government. When in July, 1921, a dozen delegates convened in Shanghai to bring the scattered fragments of Communist organization together into a national party, Ch'en Tu-hsiu was unanimously elected, in absentia, to serve as the first Secretary of the Central Committee of the newborn Chinese Communist Party.

Although Ch'en's intellectual progress during these months is sketchily documented, the essay on the implementation of democracy, written when he stood on the threshold of his new commitment, suggests something of the motives that inspired him. The republican revolution had failed utterly, he wrote. "No one nowadays finds those beautiful words 'political democracy' any longer appealing." For this failure he discovered several reasons. Only a short time had passed since the revolution. The armies of the nominal Republic had been from the beginning under the command of militarists, not "citizens." Most important has been the failure in understanding. "We once regarded the establishment of a republic as too easy a matter, and therefore cut short the time required for the propagation of democratic ideas before the revolution." Moreover, the prevailing understanding of the meaning of democracy had been fundamentally flawed.

> No one has yet paid full attention to the question of China's social and economic democracy. . . . Partisans of the Progressive Party [Liang Ch'i-ch'ao's political coterie] and of the Nationalist Party, the defenders of the Republic, have not understood the true nature of democracy; they have assumed that the government is all-powerful, and therefore they have devoted all their attention to the question of the constitution, and the National Assembly, and the cabinet, to the problems of water conservancy and communications at the national level. Whereas no one has inquired into the fundamentals of democracy—that is, self-government, and the cooperative actions of the people themselves. . . . Even the minority which advocates local self-government, though it eschews the superstitious faith in the central government, still puts an unreasonable emphasis on large-scale provincial and district self-government. In fact, self-government of this kind is no more than a matter of dividing authority between local and national governments, a problem of delimiting administrative and bureaucratic jurisdictions: it is still bureaucratism [*kuan-chih*] as of old, a different thing entirely from the establishment of a true democracy, the direct and genuine self-government by the people as a corporate whole.[25]

Under John Dewey's transitory spell, Ch'en was writing here as what we might call a "radical" liberal. Dewey's definition of the problem—the view that "democracy" means a way of communal life rather than a system of institutions—remained relevant in Ch'en's thinking virtually to the end of his life. But Marxism-Leninism soon came to offer, in his view, a more satisfying solution to it than did the particularistic approach advocated by Deweyite liberals. Instead of the political education of the people in terms of the obligations of citizenship as these had been propagated by the radicals of the revolutionary era, and instead of the cultural and social reformation of the people to enable them to assume the responsibilities of autonomous indivduality, as the New Culture reformers insisted, might not the solution to China's civic problems lie in quite another direction? Might not the people enter upon the stage of history as protagonists in a drama quite different from that envisioned by the proponents of liberal-democratic reformism, if one were to accept the postulates of revolutionary socialism? If one were to consider the people not as an amorphous multitude, nor yet as numberless particular individuals, but rather in terms of their objective collective identity—that

is, in the aggregate categories of socioeconomic classes—then the people
become naturally and necessarily the agents of progress. For progress is
no more than a name for the phenomenon of class conflict, which is the
mainspring of history's mechanism. If, then, the assumptions of Marxist
class analysis can be applied to the Chinese people, the whole issue of
their political capability will assume a different complexion: indubitably
exploited, the masses—"the suffering majority," "the oppressed producers"—are by the same logic just as evidently the bearers of history's
purpose.

It is, of course, a big "if." Over the years much ink and some blood
has spilled in the course of successive efforts to fit Chinese social realities
to the procrustean bed of Marxist class analysis. It was not a problem that
seems greatly to have exercised Ch'en Tu-hsiu, however, at least until
such time as it became a part of the ongoing ideological dispute provoked
by the Comintern's assessment of revolutionary social forces in China. It
came naturally to him to think in terms of antithetical social categories,
as we have seen, for example, in his earliest pronouncements on the
significance of the literary revolution. Whether or not his reasoning
followed along the lines suggested above, sometime in 1920 Ch'en took,
as it were, a leap of faith, embracing without a backward look the
assumptions and the vocabulary that we found him expounding with
such conviction at the beginning of this chapter.

In one important way Marxism-Leninism eased what was very likely
a painful sense of predicament for Ch'en. He was an anti-nationalist at a
time when most of the youthful audience he hoped to capture was ardently nationalistic in temperament. From 1920 onward, however, anti-
imperialism became for Ch'en a surrogate for nationalism; or, to put it in
other words, the struggle against Western and Japanese encroachment
allowed him to accept a nationalistic sense of purpose. This change in attitude was strikingly documented in Ch'en's changing view of the
historical significance of the Boxers. In a controversial 1918 essay on the
von Ketteler monument—the memorial erected, at German insistence, to
mark the spot where the German Minister had been murdered by Boxer
braves in the summer of 1900—Ch'en excused the vengefulness of the
Boxer settlement as the lamentable but inevitable consequence of Chinese
backwardness. "The Boxers were the crystalization of every social
superstition and depravity. . . . There are now two great roads in the
world: one is the bright road of science and atheism that leads toward republicanism; the other, the dark road of superstitution and theism that
leads toward autocracy. If our people do not wish for a revival of the
Boxers, if they would not again contemplate the erection of such
shameful memorials as the hateful von Ketteler Monument, which of
these roads, when all is said and done, should we take?"[26] By 1924 Ch'en
had revised this opinion markedly. Unquestionably, the Boxers had been

"barbarous," "backward," and "superstitutious." But now Ch'en was ready to hail the Boxer Rebellion as "the great and tragic prologue to the history of the Chinese national revolution," possessing "an importance no less than that of the revolution of 1911." To think otherwise is to "see only the xenophobia of the Boxers, but to ignore the causes of the appearance of the Boxers' xenophobia—the fact that, since the Opium War, all of China has had to suffer the bloody stench of oppression by foreign soldiers, diplomats and missionaries. . . . If those who participated in the Boxer movement constitute a minority among our people, then those who participated in the revolution of 1911 and the May 4th movement were also a minority among the people. . . . It is fortunate that there was a minority of barbaric Boxers to save part of the reputation of the Chinese people!"[27]

One wonders whether Ch'en followed the thought through, in his own mind, to its obvious conclusion. The Communist Party was itself "a minority among the people"—"scientific" and "progressive," to be sure, not "superstitious" and "depraved". But like the Boxers, it was the movement of a self-constituted minority which articulated and brought to the point of action the general sentiment of the whole people; each, in its own context, is the instrument of the same great historical protest.

Having discovered in Marxism a rationale for the socialist modernization of Chinese society, and in the CCP the appropriate instrument through which to achieve this end, Ch'en Tu-hsiu was ill-disposed to contend patiently with the kind of ideological and political wrangling that resulted from the alliance with the KMT. Collaboration with the forces of "bourgeois nationalism" was not, in his view, a timely concession to political realities, as it was advertised, but rather a backward step. He regarded Comintern policy in the mid-1920s as tending to divide the Communists from the genuine source of revolutionary energy, the proletariat—a term that Ch'en interpreted broadly, but still within the limits of Marxist orthodoxy. Nor did he concede that China must pass through a stage of bourgeois revolution before the conditions would be ripe for transition to the final socialist revolutionary phase; in this regard, as Benjamin Schwartz has put it, he was a "proto-Trotskyite" well before Trotskyism emerged as a distinctive school of Marxist commentary. In his capacity as the Party's leader, then, it was his fate to preside over the implementation of policies which proved, in the end, even more disastrous than he had perhaps foreseen. It was his personal misfortune to be held finally responsible for this failure, denounced as an "opportunist", and relieved of his Party posts in the summer of 1927.

The final break came two years later, with a turn of events which suggests that irony is the essence of history. The Nationalists had by this time achieved their aim of encompassing all of China under their flag. Although the new government was doing its utmost to smother the social revolution kindled in the course of its rise to power, it remained committed to the anti-imperialist purposes of earlier times. In July, 1929, therefore, Chiang Kai-shek moved to expel Russian influence from Manchuria by, among other actions, armed seizure of the Chinese Eastern Railway, still under Soviet control a decade after the Karakhan Manifesto. Obedient as always to the dictates of the Comintern, the CCP denounced this as an attack on the Soviet Union, eliciting from Ch'en Tu-hsiu a letter inquiring acidly whether the Party wished to convey the impression that it placed Russian interests above Chinese. An acrimonious exchange of views, touching on a number of policy disagreements, lasted into the autumn and resulted in November in Ch'en's expulsion from the Party, indicted for having failed fully to repent the error of "his" earlier policies.

In vain did Ch'en protest that his judges were the real "opportunists." "How can this have come to pass. . . ? I, who have spent most of my life struggling against the evil forces in society, how could I be willing to commit such unprincipled, unscrupulous, base acts? . . . I wish as before to work hand in hand to serve the proletariat with any comrade in the Party who is not a diehard follower of Stalinist (international or Chinese) opportunism!"[28] For a few years, living in the relative security of the International Concession in Shanghai, Ch'en in fact contrived to lead a fissiparous self-proclaimed Trotskyite "Left Opposition" to the CCP Central Committee and the Comintern. Then in 1932 he was arrested, extradited to Nanking, and put on trial for sedition. At this point a few of the allies from an earlier time rallied around. His legal defense was undertaken—without Ch'en's approval—by his old friend Chang Shih-chao, by this time a prominent and successful Shanghai lawyer. Fu Ssu-nien, who had been a student at Peita in Ch'en's day and latterly a professor of history there, published a scrupulously liberal protest: "The government, which bears the responsibility for maintaining law and order, cannot casually exercise leniency; but neither does the Kuomintang have the right, at a time when the forces of reaction are growing ever stronger, to put to death this firey, long-tailed comet of the Chinese revolution!"[29]

In the event, Ch'en was sentenced not to death, but to prison. And his prison became his study. Disavowing any further interest in politics, and resolutely rejecting the KMT's importunate invitations to settle some old scores with his erstwhile comrades, he devoted himself to scholarly research in epigraphy and the ancient forms of the written language. Paroled at the beginning of the Sino-Japanese War in 1937, he spent his last years living a secluded life in Szechwan—no longer politically active, no longer politically important, but still preoccupied with the questions to which he had given so much of himself over the years. He concluded, toward the end, that "not every time and circumstance can generate revolutionary conditions. It is the height of folly to take a reactionary

situation and, by playing with words, to try to turn it into a revolutionary situation. . . . The experience of the last ten years [in the Soviet
Union as well as in the imperialist West] does not permit us to exaggerate
the strength of world-wide proletarianism . . . or fatuously to proclaim
that 'the knell has sounded for capitalism'." But although he could no
longer sustain the confident expectation of an imminent revolutionary
victory, and although revolutionary victory itself appeared a more ambiguous achievement than had once seemed possible, Ch'en's fundamental faith in humanity's progressive destiny still burned strong. "From the
time that mankind first devised political organization, and until such
time as government shall wither away—in every age from that of Greece
and Rome down to the present and into the future—democracy is the
great standard under which that class that comprises the majority of the
people has always opposed the special privileges of the minority."[30]

"Shih-chih [Hu Shih] has called me a life-long oppositionist," Ch'en
remarked little more than a year before his death; "and so indeed it has
been with me—not because I wished it so, but because in the circumstances I had no choice."[31] Ch'en was, in fact, always at the barricades,
hurling his opinions down upon the heads of one enemy or another: the
pedagogues of his youth; the monarchists, before and after 1911; Confucianists, whether as supporters of the tradition of gentry intellectualism,
learning and literature, or as defenders of a superstitious faith in the adequacy of inherited custom; uncritical apologists for either East or West;
imperialists, and nationalists who preached the state as its own justification; political hypocrites, whether disguised as tepid liberals or as
ideological opportunists. His beliefs were consistent and, essentially, simple: he believed in "democracy" and in "science." What such belief
signified, however, in the changing contexts of Ch'en's times, is best
revealed as a reflection of what he opposed in the course of an embattled
and, one may suppose, a lonely life. His was a nature, it seems, in which
sympathy was dominated by an enduring sense of injury and outrage.

* * *

Li Ta-chao, Ch'en's colleague at Peita and his collaborator—indeed,
his forerunner—in the popularization of Marxism-Leninism among
Chinese intellectuals, was a man of quite different humor: an amiable
enthusiast, firm of purpose and gentle of manner, a courteous revolutionary. "Modern civilization is cooperative civilization," he wrote in the
same April, 1917, issue of *The New Youth* in which Ch'en first saluted
the Russian revolutionary victory. "The aristocracy cooperates with the
common people, the capitalists cooperate with the workers, and the
landlords with their tenants. . . . Modern society is the society of reconciliation."[32] Unlikely opinions, one may think, to come from the hand of
China's first prominent convert to the Marxist doctrine of class struggle.

Some of his friends at Peita, notably Ch'en Tu-hsiu and Ch'ien Hsuan-t'ung, found Li's ideas at this time lamentably conservative, especially his expressed hope that the fashionable enthusiasm for the vitality of youth—which he shared—should not utterly discredit the traditional view that wisdom comes with age.

By the time Li announced his conversion to Marxism, some eighteen months later, the vision of an age of cooperative reconciliation had receded, at least at the level of rhetoric, giving way to the "we vs. they" language of the new ideological persuasion. "The victory of Bolshevism," he proclaimed, is "a mighty rolling tide . . . beyond the power of the present capitalist government to forestall or to stop, for the mass movement of the twentieth century combines the whole of mankind into one great mass. . . . In the course of such a world mass movement, all those dregs of history which can impede the progress of the new movement—emperors, nobles, warlords, bureaucrats, militarists, capitalists and the like—will certainly be destroyed as though struck by a thunderbolt. . . . Henceforth all that one sees around him will be the triumphant banner of Bolshevism, and all that one hears will be Bolshevism's song of victory." Yet Li's underlying inspiration had altered less, perhaps, than this militant declaration makes it at first appear. His immediate purpose in "The Victory of Bolshevism" was to comment on the imminent defeat of German militarism—a victory, Li insisted, that could not properly be credited to the battlefield. He saw it rather as evidence of the collective progress of humanity, and it was here, rather than on the phenomenon of class struggle that in the Marxist view impels history forward, that Li's attention tended always to remain. The triumph over Germany, he proclaimed, is "the victory of humanitarianism, of pacifism; it is the victory of justice and liberty; it is the victory of democracy; it is the victory of socialism; it is the victory of Bolshevism; it is the victory of the red flag; it is the victory of the working class of the world; it is the victory of the twentieth century's new tide. . . . The bell is rung for humanitarianism! The dawn of freedom has arrived!"[33]

Li Ta-chao was born late in 1888 in Lo-t'ing hsien, Chihli province, some hundred miles east of Tientsin and only a little farther from Peking. The only child of peasant parents, he was orphaned in infancy and raised by his grandparents in what would eventually come to be classified as a typically "middle-peasant household" of small-scale landlordism and moderate prosperity. He recalled it as a lonely childhood, but it was also, apparently, unshadowed by the kind of petty domestic tyranny that left Ch'en Tu-hsiu, in comparable circumstances, embittered for life. Li began his education in the village school, submitting to the classical curriculum before moving on, as did so many of his generation, to pursue a more timely course of "Western studies." In Li's case this meant enrolling, at the age of eighteen, as a student of political economy in the Peiyang College of Law and Political Science (Peiyang fa-cheng chuan-men hsueh-hsiao) in Tientsin. There he remained for seven years, witnessing from this vantage point the death throes of the dynasty and the unpromising birth of the Chinese Republic. His own opinions on questions of politics and society were, at this time, indistinguishable from those of any other reform-minded young progressive committed to the potentially incompatible aims of popular welfare and national "wealth and power." Among the revolutionaries, Li admired Sun Yat-sen and Sung Chiao-jen; in his personal friendships, however, he was closer to several of the gentry-constitutionalists who favored Liang Ch'i-ch'ao and, in 1912 and 1913, supported Liang's newly-established Progressive Party (Chin-pu tang). Appalled by the alternative prospect of total political disintegration, Li for a time tolerated Yuan Shih-k'ai's incipient autocracy, until the assassination of Sung Chiao-jen in March, 1913, and the republican rout that followed, changed his mind.

In September, 1913, Li Ta-chao left Tientsin for Tokyo. He had the financial backing of T'ang Hua-lung (1874–1918), a Progressive Party spokesman and Speaker of the hard-pressed National Assembly in 1913–1914—and perhaps more to the point, himself a native of Hopei (Chihli). For three years, as republican fortunes plunged toward their nadir, Li pursued his study of political economy and English at Waseda University. Except for a six-month trip to the Soviet Union in 1924 this was his only trip abroad, and in fact his longest absence from North China. In Japan he met Chang Shih-chao, then in his liberal anti-Yuan phase. It was in Chang's *Tiger Magazine* that Li first began to publish his opinions for the benefit of a general readership; as in numerous other cases, foreign study provided both the opportunity and the confidence to speak out. It also provided the provocation: coinciding with the crisis generated by the Japanese seizure of Tsingtao and the Twenty-one Demands, the years in Japan gave a lastingly anti-foreign edge to Li's nationalism.

Li Ta-chao returned to Peking in 1916, however, without to all appearances having undergone a fundamental change in outlook. His first employment after his return was secretary to T'ang Hua-lung and editor of one of the Progressive Party's journals. These connections did not last long. Yuan Shih-k'ai's death in June, 1916, provoked a scramble among the "parliamentarians" of the day to align themselves with one or another of the emerging militarist factions, a spectacle of unbridled political opportunism from which Li retreated in disgust. By mid-1917 he had severed his connections with the parliamentary movement. In January, 1918, he joined the editorial committee of *The New Youth;* the following month he accepted Ts'ai Yuan-p'ei's invitation to become Librarian at Peita, where two years later he was concurrently appointed to teach law and government. Li's affiliation with the university, begun when he was twenty-nine years old, lasted throughout the final years of his life, until shortly before his execution in April, 1927, at the age of thirty-eight.

As this sketch suggests, "the father of Chinese Communism" achieved his destiny only by degrees. Yet within a year of his arrival at Peita, Li had publicly embraced the ideals of the October Revolution, and organized the first of the Marxist study groups that eventually became the nucleus of the Chinese Communist Party. Even as students took to the streets in May, 1919, by fortuitous coincidence Li published the first installment of a lengthy two-part exposition, "My Marxist Views." Although he did not play a leading role in the organizational meetings that preceded the founding of the CCP in 1921 nor in the higher echelons of the Party organization thereafter, he was from the beginning a central figure in the activities of the Party in North China. He was also (unlike Ch'en Tu-hsiu) a willing supporter of the alliance with the Nationalist Party ordained by the Comintern in 1922; in 1923 he was the first CCP member to become concurrently a member of Sun's party; and he was the only Communist member of the presidium of the reorganized KMT when that party held its first national congress in Canton early in 1924. In that same year he served as the leader of the Chinese delegation in attendance at the Fifth Congress of the Comintern, convened in Moscow in June. Li's commitment to his new beliefs was thus no mere matter of intellectual speculation.

For the Chinese Communist movement the years from 1925 to 1927 were a time of great activity, rising hopes, and, finally, ideological confusion and almost total organizational ruin. The struggle for control of the revolutionary movement after the death of Sun Yat-sen in March, 1925, was complicated by the beginning of the Northern Expedition, the long-awaited offensive against warlordism launched in the summer of 1926. The CCP grew rapidly in size and influence as Nationalist armies marched northward from their stronghold in Kwangtung toward the rich Yangtze provinces, armed with Soviet weapons, advised by Comintern agents, and preceded by Communist cadres whose mission it was to organize the peasants and workers into a social revolutionary base. To some who watched this steadily encroaching tide, it was an ancient dread come true. "It must be considered greatly to their credit if they can root out the multifarious evils done by the warlords," wrote Liang Ch'i-ch'ao anxiously in January, 1927. "We wanted to do so, but we couldn't manage it; so if the task is accomplished by others, we can only approve. But does the light shine on the road ahead? By no means. They have muddled matters by stirring up the labor movement and by giving political power to the scum of society, which in turn has smashed the rice bowls of those workers who mind their own business and look out for themselves. . . . All the South now belongs to the workers, while intellectuals are indiscriminately branded 'counter-revolutionaries.' But these so-called workers are really only a filthy refuse of unemployed vagabonds."[34]

Meanwhile the northern warlords fought bitterly among themselves, and expended what energy remained to harass the revolutionary organizations within their territories. In Peking, Li Ta-chao was forced into hiding and driven finally to seek refuge in the Soviet Embassy. Eventually even this sanctuary failed him, when in April, 1927, Chang Tso-lin, the pro-Japanese warlord then in control of the city, ordered his troops into the Russian compound. Documents were seized as evidence of Comintern subversion and espionage, and Li, with several other refugees, was arrested. Three weeks later he was executed by strangulation—not the first martyr to his cause, but the most famous, and the most widely mourned. Had he survived until the Nationalist armies finally reached Peking a year later, his fate might have been less savagely traditional, but it would likely have been no kinder. Even as Li awaited death in Peking in 1927, in Shanghai Chiang Kai-shek turned against his Communist collaborators and inaugurated the vengeful White Terror that, in the space of a few months, reduced the CCP to a shattered remnant of what it had become, and drove the survivors underground.

Li Ta-chao thus died at the moment when the Chinese Communist movement was effectively cut off from its orthodox Marxist—that is, urban-proletarian—bases, and increasingly from Comintern intervention in its development. Slowly, but it seems in retrospect in accordance with an inevitable logic, the center of Communist activity shifted after 1927 away from the urban centers and into the hinterland, the social universe of the peasantry, where it was compelled to devise survival techniques that would draw more heavily on indigenous revolutionary resources. It would far exceed the scope of this discussion to trace in detail the genesis of revolutionary strategies designed to mobilize the vast social energies latent in the Chinese countryside: a slow process, erratic, fraught with political rivalries and ideological disputes that more than once brought the Party to the brink of extermination or self-destruction, and successful only after two decades of harsh experience, experimentation, and considerable refinement in respect to both social analysis and political techniques. The point to be emphasized here is the manner in which Li Ta-chao's understanding of Marxism anticipated the evolution of Chinese revolutionary theory, a translation hardly begun when Li met his death at the hands of Chang Tso-lin's executioners in the spring of 1927.

Li Ta-chao's influence on the May Fourth "student" generation is well attested, and it went beyond those who eventually followed him into the Marxist camp. At Peita he encouraged numerous student activists and a wide range of student activities. He served, for example, as faculty advisor for *Hsin-ch'ao* (The Renaissance), edited by Fu Ssu-nien, Lo Chia-lun, and other later famous students at the university, and one of the more important of the many publications that came into being in the New Culture era. Li enjoyed, and deserved, a reputation as a friend who could be counted upon for advice, support, and sympathy, regardless of differences in political or ideological persuasion. This quality of principled amiability moved him, even after the establishment of the Communist Party and his own irrevocable commitment to it, to ally himself from time to time with his old liberal colleagues in their published demands for "good government." To the end of his life Li remained on terms of respectful friendship with Hu Shih, despite the fact that he had disagreed fundamentally and publicly with Hu's approach to the solution of China's problems as early as 1919.

Among those who encountered Li at a critical moment in their own development, Mao Tse-tung is in retrospect preeminent. Twenty-five years old, a recent graduate of the Hunan Normal College in Changsha, Mao made his first trip to Peking in the summer of 1918, accompanying a group of Hunanese students some of whom were bound for study in France. At this time neither a Marxist nor even a confirmed revolutionary, Mao was drawn to Peking because it was so conspicuously the storm center of intellectual rebellion in those years. He was frustrated, however, in his efforts to make contact with the preoccupied and, as he recalled them, self-absorbed leaders of the New Culture movement, who "had no time" for an unknown young provincial speaking the broad dialect of his native Hunan. The humiliation rankled at the time, and may well have helped to shape Mao's later attitude toward intellectuals in general, which was never more than sceptically tolerant. Ch'en Tu-hsiu and Li Ta-chao were well-remembered exceptions. Mao's debt to Ch'en was perhaps greater: "he had influenced me more than anyone else," Mao remarked to Edgar Snow, a decade after Ch'en's political disgrace. Precisely what that influence had been remained unspecified, as did also the nature of Mao's debt to Li. But Li at least gave him a job, as an assistant assigned to register the sometimes famous names of readers in the Peita library periodicals room—thus enabling Mao to eke out a meager existence during the several uncomfortable months that he remained in the ancient capital.

The episode looms larger in Party hagiography than it probably did at the time, in Li's eyes or even in Mao's. Nor was Mao's the only hand to shape the clay of later revolutionary experience into the vessels of Communist theoretical rationalization. The fact remains, however, that what came to be called "Maoism" reflected, in a number of its fundamental premises, ideas set forth or hinted at by Li Ta-chao in the late teens and twenties. In February, 1927, two months before Li's execution in Peking, Mao submitted to the Party leadership the findings of a recent month-long walking tour through the Hunanese countryside—the famous "Report on the Peasant Situation in Hunan," long and properly regarded as one of the earliest authentic expressions of Maoism. It began with a bold prediction: "Within a short time, hundreds of millions of peasants will rise in Central, South, and North China, with the fury of a hurricane; no power, however strong, can restrain them. They will break all the shackles that bind them and rush towards the road of liberation. *All imperialists, warlords, corrupt officials, and bad gentry will meet their doom at the hands of the peasants.* All revolutionary parties and comrades will be judged by them. *Are we to get in front of them and lead them . . . ?*" Mao's "Report" also contained the portentous statement (prudently omitted from later versions as being too heretical) that "Giving credit where credit is due, if we allot ten points to the accomplishments of the democratic revolution, then the achievements of the urban dwellers and the military units rate only three points, while the remaining seven points should go to the peasants in their rural revolution." [35]

The vindication of this judgment, twenty years later, has lent to Mao's 1927 "Report" the sanctity of prophetic utterance. In fact, Hunan had been the target of intensive organizational efforts in the months preceding, with the result that Peasant Associations and other proto-revolutionary infrastructures were uncommonly strong in areas within the province. It remains still a matter of scholarly dispute whether rural conditions generally had yet deteriorated to the revolutionary flashpoint to which the ensuing decades of civil war, foreign invasion, and ungovernable political corruption would bring them. Nevertheless, whether he glimpsed the future or simply seized the present, in thus assigning primary importance to the villages, Mao was indeed working toward a distinctive Chinese revolutionary strategy—and, mindfully or not, preparing to turn to political uses insights that were fundamental to Li Ta-chao's vision of China's revolutionary destiny.

Although Mao's "Report on the Peasant Situation in Hunan" was not without its visionary aspects, it was primarily a position paper, concerned with the tactics of social mobilization at the village level. It was, one might say, an attempt to shape a positive answer to his own challenge by analyzing rural class structure in terms of its intrinsic injustices, and then suggesting how these antagonisms might be transformed into revolutionary energy. By 1927 these were issues already under active discussion within the Communist movement. In the following years, throughout the Kiangsi and Yenan soviet periods, the question of how most effectively to turn the villages of China into social battlefields remained always at the forefront of Party concern. Among a population living generally at the subsistence level, when in many instances the measurement of social disparity was not between conspicuous wealth and evident destitution, but a much more subtle distinction among gradations of deprivation, it was not easy to recognize the natural allies of revolution or to identify its natural enemies. Mao was not the first to turn his attention to the peasantry, nor were his assessments of the situation invariably correct in terms of political results. But he was a patient tactician.

Such tactical considerations were not Li Ta-chao's principal concern, though in some of his later essays he did address, in passing, the problem of social dynamics in the countryside. It went against his grain, however, to think of the village divided against itself; it was rather a community unto itself, in his abiding view: uncorrupt in its essential nature, but appallingly vulnerable to corruption from abroad, by the political, economic, and cultural forces that impinged upon it. In Li's characterization of the Chinese village one may sense much of the ambivalence and contradiction that has troubled the relationship between China's modern intellectuals and her peasant masses in recent decades.

> Youth! Hasten now to the village! Go to work when the sun rises; rest when the sun sets. Till the fields for your food; dig wells for your water. The old men, the women, the children, who have spent their lives upon the land—they are the comrades of your heart. By kitchen fires, in the shadow of the hoe, harking to the mingled sounds of chickens and dogs—only there can you order your lives and achieve your destiny![36]

So reads the peroration of Li's remarkable short essay "Youth and the Village," published in February, 1919. The village, Li says, is a place of "*human* activity" (*jen ti huo-tung*), full of happiness, full of brightness, where the air is pure, and where the spirit may be purified. All this is by way of contrast to city life: dark, oppressive, degrading, stifling, "a devil's life" of physical idleness, hectic sycophancy, and cultural vagrancy. "Return then to the village," he admonishes. "Simplify your lives a bit. It matters not whether you labor with your mind or with your muscle; whether you plant vegetables, or plow the fields, or teach in the primary school. For eight hours a day, work at something useful to others as well as to yourself; for the rest, go out and do something for the betterment of the village, to improve the livelihood of the villagers—thus on the one hand laboring yourself, and on the other, in amiable conversation with your comrades in labor, discussing the principles by which life can be made better."[37]

In his study of Li Ta-chao's thought, Maurice Meisner calls this "probably the most faithful expression of the spirit of early Russian Populism to be found in modern Chinese intellectual history."[38] Li was himself quite conscious of the Populist precedent. He invoked it, however, more as a source of moral inspiration than as a model for the Chinese to follow. Conditions in China today, he said, bear little resemblance to Russian conditions in the nineteenth century, beyond the indisputable fact that in both cases "peasants constitute the vast majority of the working class." He was aware, perhaps, that in a number of respects Russian Populism had rested on different premises from his own "to the village" doctrine.

Before they awoke to the unpromising realities of the situation and turned, in their frustration, to terrorism, the Russian Populists had approached the village confident that their intervention would spark an almost immediate revolutionary conflagration. Li Ta-chao entertained no such sanguine expectations. The mission of China's "constitutional youth," as he rather awkwardly addressed them, was to teach the villagers how to organize defensively against predators within and without, and how to recognize those common interests which, eventually, they would have an opportunity to promote by parliamentary means: in short, to "prepare a fertile soil" in which to "plant democracy." In Russian Populism, moreover, there was a strong element of anti-modernism; for many of the intellectuals who made their way to the countryside in the 1860s, "going to the people" meant a return to a kind of idealized pre-industrial social and economic primitivism (and therefore earned the contempt of Karl Marx). Li Ta-chao, it is true, hoped that by making the village the pivot of the process of modernization China might avoid the worst abuses of the capitalist stage of development. His intention, however, was not to retrieve the past, but to ease the transition to the future: "enlightenment," "development," and "progress" were the watchwords of his call for rural action.

Finally, the Russian Populists perceived (or imagined) in the traditional Russian village evidence of an indigenous peasant socialism, institutionally centered in the peasant commune which in prefeudal times had exercised considerable autonomy in matters of land distribution and the levying of taxes. Their purpose was to awaken the socialist instincts dormant (as they insisted) in the peasants' inherited nature. Li Ta-chao ascribed no such instincts to China's peasantry, nor did he ransack the distant reaches of China's history in search of socialist prototypes. Other radicals and self-styled socialists since the turn of the century, and still in the 1920s, discoursed at length in this connection on the significance of the *ching-t'ien* system, speculations almost entirely absent from Li Ta-chao's writings on the peasant question. His confidence in the social and historical importance of the village did not depend on an idealization of peasant traditions—or, for that matter, upon an idealization of the existing rural situation. Despite the romantic overtones of "Youth and the Village," Li's view was on the whole a realistic one. He depicted the village not as a haven of social innocence, but as a hell of social victimization: the peasants are ignorant and condemned by their ignorance to suffer without recourse the multifarious abuses visited upon them by militarists, bureaucrats, "bad gentry," and local bullies.

What, then, was the substance of Li's "populism"? It must be viewed, at least in part, as the contemporary expression of an alternative style of social idealism that runs throughout Confucian traditions of criticism, and is especially prominent in Statecraft literature from the seventeenth century onward—a protest against the social and cultural consequences of urbanization. In the Confucian age both adherents to and critics of orthodoxy had held the social and cultural foundation of the state to be an idealized community in which gentry and commoners—intellectuals and peasants—shared a sense of place. Confucian social theory did not accommodate the phenomenon of urban development, ongoing since the Sung and Ming dynasties. For centuries, Confucians had worried about the increasing distance dividing city from countryside, in terms of social expectations, economic motives, and cultural values. The intrusion of the West and the extraordinary apparition of the treaty ports did not initiate this process, though undoubtedly it enhanced the disquieting sense of disjunction. Equally important, if not more so, the spread of social unrest and rebellion in the nineteenth century and the relentless march and countermarch of private armies in the twentieth accelerated the desertion of the villages by those who sought not only the economic opportunities but also the security that cities, and even the larger provincial towns, could provide.

It was, then, a familiar concern that Li Ta-chao echoed in 1919, from his new perspective and with a fresh urgency. His admonition to "return" to the fundamental honesty and the natural humanism of village life was at the same time a warning against the intellectual irresponsibility, the social corruption, and the vocational parasitism bred by city life. "In China today the city and the village have become separate entities, very nearly two different worlds," he wrote in September, in an essay entitled "'Young China' and 'The Youth Movement'." "The problems spawned by city life, the culture that emanates from it, are utterly unrelated to the lives of the villagers, while village life is of no consequence to city dwellers who have no conception of it whatever."[39]

The problem, as Li analysed it in 1919, was one of communications and communication. Improved technology could provide a solution to the former; the latter was a far more difficult and troubling matter. In Li's thoughts on how to bridge the chasm between two worlds, his debt to Populist inspiration and his essential modernism came together. He did not advocate a return to rural parochialism, to the kind of social, economic, and moral autonomy that had appealed to Confucian reformers and that, a few years later, Liang Shu-ming would try to revive in his experimental communities of Confucian faith in Shantung. Li stressed instead the political transformation of the village, a process in which he saw a crucially important role to be played by Young China's intellectuals:

> Only let us turn our footsteps toward the villages of the hinterland. There, in contact with pure and beautiful Nature, in that deep, rich soil, the seeds of a spiritual transformation will naturally germinate and flourish. The peasants, daily in touch with the natural world, have in the nature of things become disciples of humanism [jen-tao chu-i ti hsin-t'u]. In a life of labor shared with them, not only will it be possible invisibly to spread our influence among them,

but moreover the instruments of culture produced in the cities—publications and the like—must flood into the back-country in the footsteps of our youth. We should emulate Mr. Tolstoy: in the off-season, come to the cities to write; when the season is at its busiest, work in the fields. Only thus will the atmosphere of culture merge with the smoke of kitchen fires in tree-shaded villages, transforming those ancient villages sunk in rustic quietude into alive and active new villages. The great coming-together of these new villages—*that* is our "Young China."[40]

In Li's later writings, "Young China" was often rendered as "our young revolutionary comrades" or the like, but the vision remained the same. It is a vision only superficially similar to the notion of political and cultural tutelage current in reformist thinking since the turn of the century. For Li the tutelary agency is neither an enlightened autocrat, nor an omniscient revolutionary party, nor yet a system of educational institutions. It is virtually a whole generation which, as with the members of a religious order, finds its self-fulfillment in self-abnegation. "You, youth of the villages who have achieved self-awareness; you, teachers in rural primary schools; you, intellectuals: all, indeed, who have gone to the countryside to participate in the peasant movement . . . millions of peasants, on the brink of extinction and suffering the torments of the damned, wait with the greatest eagerness for you to lead them from this pit of suffering onto the bright road."[41] There is thus an important change in the temper of Li's call to duty, and in its implications. The relationship he describes between "Youth" and "the Village" is more symbiotic than paternalistic. Antaeus-like, "Young China" will be invincible only so long as it keeps its feet planted firmly on the nourishing earth of China's vast countryside. This is a conviction that penetrates to the core of Chinese Communist strategy in the course of the 1930s and 1940s, and an important source of inspiration in the evolution of the populist mythology of Maoism. It has been, moreover, from time to time a consideration in policy-making, most conspicuously during the tumultuous years of the Cultural Revolution of the 1960s. Whatever may have been the immediate political and disciplinary motives behind the massive campaign to "rusticate the intellectuals" (*hsia fang*), and however coercive its implementation, its theoretical justification may well have had its origins in Li Ta-chao's benign vision of intellectuals and peasants working side by side in progressive collaboration.

Unlike Ch'en Tu-hsiu and other New Culture cosmopolites, Li Ta-chao was instinctively, even viscerally, a nationalist, and that in a strict sense of the term. The nation, he contended, is not merely an efficient means for achieving collective political or social ends. It is the highest expression of the universal human aspiration to a transcendent identity. "The significance of consciousness of self [*tzu-chueh*] lies in promoting the spirit which manifests itself in the establishment of a state," he wrote in 1915, taking explicit exception to Ch'en Tu-hsiu's denigration of nationalistic sentiments.

> It lies in seeking a state worthy of being loved, and in loving it. One ought not to repudiate one's nation because it is unworthy of being loved. Still less is it fitting, by reason of the fact that our people have never enjoyed the benefits of a state worthy of their love, recklessly to classify ourselves together with those who possess no state, as being incapable of establishing a state worthy of love. . . . Bad government brings suffering to the people, like unto the ravages of wild beasts—a lamentable situation, in truth, and one from which it is quite appropriate to try to escape. But to argue that the condition of the victims of such a regime is more pitiable than that of a people which has lost its state, is to be led by blind emotion into pessimistic exaggeration. Such a condition is only a passing thing, not a calamity comparable to the loss of the state, which cannot be recovered through all eternity.[42]

This was an awkward position from which to move in the direction of Marxist antinationalism and proletarian internationalism. For a time in 1918 and 1919, in the first flush of the rapture that "the victory of Bolshevism" inspired, Li adopted a supranational stance. "The morality we demand today is a morality suited to a life in which all men are of one body, all the world one society," he wrote at the end of 1919. "The clannishness [chia-tsu chu-i] and nationalism of former times, born of the age of clan economies or national economies, certainly cannot survive in the age of a world economy. Not only should they be done away with; they must be done away with."[43] The conviction that China's revolution is an integral part of the world's socialist future has never been supplanted. But early in 1920 Li supplemented it with an interpretation of anti-imperialism that in time strongly influenced the Chinese Communists' perception of the context in which their revolutionary struggle is being waged.

For Ch'en Tu-hsiu, who began with a contrary prejudice, anti-imperialism rendered nationalism palatable by making it the servant of internationalism. For Li, anti-imperialism eased the implications of internationalism by allowing him to magnify nationalism to the point at which it merged with a world-wide revolutionary confrontation. China, he declared, is a "proletarian nation." Oppressed not by indigenous capitalism, but by imperialism, "our whole people have gradually been transformed into a world proletarian class, living in conditions of great suffering and insecurity." In these circumstances, the revolutionary liberation of the exploited class can no longer be anticipated in classical Marxist terms. "The proletariat that comes into being in a country suffering the social oppression of the capitalist system still retains the opportunity to seize and use the capitalist mode of production. But a world proletarian class brought into existence by world-wide capitalism is denied the opportunity to exploit the capitalist mode of production." The oppressed masses lack, moreover, the social cohesion that would enable them to function as a class. "Some remain, to become soldiers, or brigands; some flee abroad, to become coolie laborers, constantly on the move, selling their strength on the cheap, objects of the contempt with which people view the working class." The difference, as Li summed it up, penetrates to the very foundations of Marxist explanations of social and historical change. "The economic transformation which has taken place in Europe and America has come as the natural response to indigenous conditions. The economic changes which have taken place in China are the result of oppression by an alien power, and therefore the sufferings of the Chinese people have been more painful, and their sacrifices greater."[44]

To this analysis Li subsequently appended a racial (or racist) interpolation. The present struggle, he said in 1924, must be understood not simply as a confrontation between capitalists and proletarians—the imperialists and the imperialized—but also as the first phase of a coming struggle between the white and the colored races of the world. By justifying their economic motives through an appeal to "the civilizing mission," Westerners have introduced cultural issues into the situation, making it inevitable that "in the future racial struggles will break out, and . . . will merge with the 'class struggle'! . . . It can be foreseen, on the basis of the numerical comparison [of the racial composition of the world's population] . . . that the coloured races will be victorious. . . . The new meaning of nationalism is closely related to the racial question. . . . We must all advance courageously with all our force, we must once again appear on the stage of the nations to display our national characteristics, we must once again . . . clearly manifest our national spirit!"[45] By 1924, nationalism had clearly won the unequal struggle for Li's mind and heart.

When one synthesizes these several aspects of Li Ta-chao's thought as it developed in the last decade of his life, one may discern at least in embryonic form the shape of the distinctive revolutionary ideology that emerged in China in the 1920s and 1930s, and sense something of the logic that supported it. Li's assertion that China is a "proletarian nation" was advanced, obviously, without strict regard for the orthodox Marxist-Leninist understanding of the meaning of "proletarianism" and the historical role that the proletariat was destined to play. Whether or not by conscious intent, Li was taking an important step toward the liberation of Chinese Communist theory from rigid conformity to the categories of Marxist class analysis.* Nationalism remains the primary

---

* Li was not the only Communist to come early to this analysis. "In my opinion," wrote one ardent young Communist in 1921, "all of China is a proletarian country. (The large scale and middle-size producers are very few in number, while there are very many genuine proletarians; and semi-proletarians—that is, middle-class families—come next in number.) The

motive: the preservation of the Chinese state, and the revival of Chinese national spirit. But since China is both a "proletarian nation" and a nation of villages, the revolution must encompass both a struggle against foreign oppression—the "proletarian" struggle against "world capitalism"—and the transformation of the culture and social structure of the village.

Li Ta-chao, China's first Marxist, fittingly provides us with the earliest evidence of a tendency that characterized the ongoing development of Chinese Communist ideology, that is, the disposition of Marx's Chinese disciples to dissolve the categories that give Marxism its analytical force in application to Western conditions into larger abstractions that render the Marxist concept of social struggle relevant to China's peculiar situation. In China, social revolution meant the politicization of the masses, the implementation of a strategy of class struggle in the countryside, and, finally, reliance on the "mind of the people" as one of the components in policy making—what in due course would come to be called the Mass Line. In China, therefore, "proletarianism" no longer designated the consciousness of a specific socioeconomic class shaped by a particular, objective historical experience. It became, rather, a metaphor, having little to do with the character that Marx had originally ascribed to the proletariat, or even with "*class* consciousness" at all. It came to signify a subjective condition, the collective determination of the oppressed to overthrow the oppressor, a state of mind virtually synonymous with revolutionary will power.

No question is more perplexing to the student of Marxism than that of the relationship between historical conditions and conscious human effort to change those conditions. And on no point have the Chinese amended Marxism with more startling effect. The logic of Marxist materialist determinism, carried to its extreme, suggests that prerevolutionary history moves in response to social forces against which human intervention is impossible—forces more predictable, perhaps, but no more governable than those which drive the clouds across the sky. In this as in other respects, it is the revolutionary transformation—"the seizing of the means of production by society," bringing to an end "the mastery of the product over the producer"—that marks "the ascent of man from the kingdom of necessity to the kingdom of freedom," as Engels put it in *Socialism: Utopian and Scientific* (1880). By "the kingdom of necessity"

Chinese capitalist class, then, is the capitalist class of the five Great Powers, to which the small minority of native Chinese militarists, financiers and capitalists is a mere appendage. The class war in China, therefore, is an international class war."[46] The writer was Ts'ai Ho-sen, one of Mao Tse-tung's Hunanese school fellows, his roommate in Peking in 1918, and when this letter to Ch'en Tu-hsiu was written, a student in France. Ts'ai was executed by the KMT in 1931.

Engels meant "the whole sphere of the conditions of life which environ men, and which have hitherto ruled man" by means of "the laws of his own social action, hitherto standing face to face with man as laws of nature foreign to and dominating him." Entering "the kingdom of freedom," man enters a world which "now comes under the dominion and control of man, who for the first time becomes the real, conscious lord of nature because he has now become master of his own social organization . . . [which] hitherto confronting him as a necessity imposed by nature and history, now becomes the result of his own free action. . . . Only from that time will man himself, more and more consciously, make his own history. . . ." A decade later, Engels retreated from this position, but only a careful step or two. "We make our history ourselves," he wrote to Joseph Bloch in 1890, "but, in the first place, under very definite assumptions and conditions. Among these the economic ones are ultimately decisive."[47]

Historical determinism offers a paradox and an unwelcome restraint to men anxious to meet Marx's challenge to change the world, not merely to understand it. The desire to shape history rather than patiently to submit to its terms was one of the motives behind Lenin's doctrine of the Party "vanguard" of professional revolutionaries, one of the rocks of jagged controversy on which the Russian Social Democrats broke apart into Bolshevik and Menshevik factions at the portentous Brussels-to-London Congress in 1903. The opportunity of the moment, it has often been said, took precedence in Lenin's thinking over considerations of abstract ideology; the same may be said with equal truth of Mao Tse-tung and other emergent leaders of the Chinese Communist movement in the 1920s and 1930s—and, perhaps, of any effective leadership. Theory, however, influences the perception of opportunity, establishing the frame of reference within which to arrange the evidence gained from experience. In the ideology of Maoist Marxism, the implications of historical determinism have been understood largely in terms of Li Ta-chao's activist and, therefore, unorthodox interpretation.

Clemenceau once remarked that he could invariably identify anything written by the great French socialist Jean Jaurès because all the verbs were in the future tense; of Li Ta-chao it might be said in the same spirit that he should always read in the present tense. His activist instincts were as deeply rooted in his character as were his nationalist sentiments, and just as difficult to accommodate within the confines of received doctrine. It was to him inconceivable that the power of human will should be held hostage to historical necessity, or that the present moment with all its possibilities should be sacrificed to a future sometime, however great its promise. As a result he treated Engels' "kingdom of freedom," in effect, as if it were of two parts or divided into two stages, the one concerned with freedom *from,* the other with freedom *to.* Freedom from economic, social, and political oppression was the goal of revolutionary liberation, which Li conceded lies still in an indeterminate future. But the freedom to act toward this end, with conscious intent and premeditated purpose, Li ascribed to the present, and assigned as a duty to all right-thinking men.

"I believe that the most precious thing in the world is 'now,' and the easiest thing to lose is also 'now'." So Li wrote in 1918, in an essay appropriately entitled "Now." Here, and in an earlier essay called "Spring," published a few months after his return from Japan in 1916, he preached his faith in the potency of the present with an almost religious fervor, an air of metahistorical mystery. His text in both cases was a quotation from Emerson: "If you love eternity, you should love the present. Yesterday is gone beyond recall; tomorrow is not yet a reality. The only certainty within our grasp is today. One today is worth two tomorrows." We cannot return to the past [*fu-ku*], Li wrote, because the past does not exist: the only past we know is interred in the present. Likewise the only thing we can know of the future lies in the hopes of the present. Therefore,

> We who live in this age cannot despise the present, dwelling only on the past, or dreaming only of the future, and thus letting slip the opportunities for present endeavor. Nor can we be satisfied with the present, to the extent that we do not exert ourselves now to plan for the future. The proper thing to do is to seize hold of the present, in order to create the future. Whether its consequences are for good or evil, what is done now will never vanish. Therefore the cardinal duty of human life is to move in concert with the progressive course of reality, in order to create a great good for posterity, in order to contribute to the happiness of that eternal "self," enlarging oneself through space and time until one attains the point at which "the universe is I, and I am the universe."[48]

The revelation of Marxism which was soon to break upon him did not overwhelm this conviction. On the contrary, Li's sense of the precious urgency of the moment profoundly affected the uses to which he put his new-found faith.

In an essay on "The Value of the Materialist Concept of History in Modern Historiography," published in *The New Youth* in December, 1920, Li addressed the problem of historical determinism squarely, and summarily dismissed the idea that it might contradict his own activist inclinations. "Some men," he charged, "have misconstrued the materialist concept of history to mean that social progress depends entirely on natural changes in the material sphere, permitting no action on man's part, except to await the coming of the new order. Consequently, critics of the materialist concept of history have seized upon this theme, and say that such fatalism [*ting-ming jen-sheng-kuan*] is an evil influence. This is a great and particular fallacy: in point of fact, the influence of the

materialist concept of history on human life is quite the opposite."
Hitherto, Li argued, the historian's sole function has been to sanctify the
authority of the ruling class and glorify its achievements; man himself has
been "an abandoned boat adrift on the boundless wild ocean, without a
sail, or oars, or a compass." History so conceived inevitably breeds
fatalism and passivity, for it "always reverts to the idea that fate is a
divine weapon, compelling the reader to acknowledge that however difficult his circumstances, it is all a matter of destiny. The only comfort he
can seek from present suffering is in prayer, and in hope for the future."

It is the materialist concept of history, Li insisted, that inspires
courage and determination, largely because it treats the conditions of life
as most men know it, assigning primary significance to social and
economic circumstances. Li's description of materialist historiography
makes it virtually synonymous with the methlogies of modern critical
scholarship generally advocated by New Culture intellectuals: disinterested in motive, its purpose being "to train the scholar's powers of
judgment and to teach him discrimination in the evaluation of facts,"
and its success depending upon "whether the facts are true, and whether
they are appropriately explained." This was an exemplary New Culture
injunction, and Li's conclusion, despite its emphasis on collective rather
than individual action, was more in keeping with the mood of New
Culture reformism than it was a summons to a revolutionary *guerre à
outrance:*

> Now for the first time man sees that the world in which he lives is in a process
> of constant change and flux; now for the first time man sees that all these
> changes are the result of the practical application of new knowledge, the
> result, that is, of the inventions and discoveries made by men just as ordinary
> as he is himself. This idea imbues him with great hope and courage. Now for
> the first time man sees that progress is only possible through unity, and the
> planning of the group, and therefore he becomes aware, for the first time, of
> his own power and his position in society, and from this awareness he derives a
> new attitude. Formerly he was merely a passive, negative animal, patiently
> submitting to the manipulation of others. Now he has become animated and
> positive. He wants to know the facts of life, and their significance, and
> wherein lies the opportunity for progress. He wants to put his shoulder to the
> wheel of life, to push and pull it forward. With this attitude he can become his
> own man, and only thus, with head held high, finding satisfaction in his own
> life, he can become of use to society. . . .
>
> Viewed in this light, the old historical method and the new historical
> method are utterly opposed to each other. One teaches that the causes of social
> conditions reside outside society itself. . . . The other seeks and finds in the
> nature of mankind the strength to guide and promote the improvement of
> social conditions. One offers timid impotence as a philosophy of life; the other,
> a philosophy of life that is enthusiastic and full of confidence in one's own
> capabilities! This is because one attributes all social activity and change to the

will of Heaven, while the other attributes all social activity and change to human creativity. . . .[49]

Materialism is presented in somewhat more orthodox terms in an essay Li wrote in 1919 and published in *The Renaissance*, entitled "Material Change and Moral Change." Here he expounded the accepted Marxist view that ethical codes are rooted in material circumstances and evolve in response to changing material demands. Standards of social morality are a necessity of social survival and therefore reflect the relative values of the society at a given moment, not an absolute standard of right and wrong. They are a part of what Li called the "spiritual superstructure," comprising "such things as ideas, principles, philosophy, religion, ethics, and law." Up to this point what Li was saying was hardly distinctive: Hu Shih and other "pragmatists" insisted no less vehemently on the relativity of moral standards and on the evolutionary history of customary sanctions. Li's Marxism showed itself in his assertion that, while the spiritual superstructure reflects the "material base," the material base itself cannot be directly influenced by elements of the spiritual superstructure; in other words, material conditions shape ideas, but ideas cannot change material conditions. This was, perhaps, the most emphatic and sympathetic statement of the Marxist premise yet published in China, and Li's exposition had the advantage as well, by way of illustration, of an entertaining anthropological excursion into such curiosities as the religion of the New Guinean tribe that believes itself descended from the cocoanut palm and the custom of certain Central African natives to borrow courage on the eve of battle by devouring their fathers, thus also sparing them the possible humiliation of being taken prisoner. These and similar examples were displayed as evidence that moral primitivism is the inevitable result of material necessity—and, even more important, to throw into bold relief the very different character of modern man. Here Li's debt to Marxism is suddenly canceled, and he strikes the note that he was to sound again a year later in his essay on historical materialism: the past is behind us, he says, with all its superstitious constraints upon human creative freedom: man is now fully conscious. It is worth noting that Li advances this claim on behalf of mankind generally—not the intellectuals alone, but also the working class, whose understanding comes only from the experience of labor:

Because they work every day in factories, every day serving nature, every day using nature, [the workers] have come to understand nature. Nature no longer exercises over them the authority of the mysterious or the inexplicable. They also understand the nature of human society: they know that the present capitalist system is the sole cause of their suffering; they know that present-day laws are the laws of the capitalist class; that politics is the politics of a class; that society is the society of a class. Their understanding of the true nature of society is, I venture to say, better-grounded and clearer than is that of the general run of gentry scholars. The sun has risen; man no longer makes his way by lantern light.

The idea that the workingman discovers himself through labor, even under present conditions, suggests that the concept of alienation did not penetrate very deep into Li's understanding of Marxism. What makes "Material Change and Moral Change" a truly remarkable essay, however, is not only this conclusion, but the premise from which Li launches his argument. Among "the world's own principles" that Marx had accepted was the conviction that self-interest, expressed in terms of class interests, is the dominant motive in human behavior, at least in its prerevolutionary phase. Li, on the contrary, begins this essay with an affirmation of his belief in the existence of a universal, instinctive, and spontaneous moral sense.

> That moral sense [*tao-te-hsin*] exists is a perfectly clear and uncontrovertible fact. All the various matters we encounter elicit naturally an authoritative voice in our hearts which tells us whether a thing is good or evil. . . . If we are guided by this authoritative voice, such moral values as "loyalty," "uprightness," and "justice" can all find their expression in us. If we do not follow it, then we are reproached by our consciences. If we commit an evil act, even if no one else knows of it, we ourselves feel shame and remorse, simply because in our hearts the demands of duty make themselves heard. This spontaneity and natural authority are the unique characteristics of the moral sense. Natural science, law, politics, religion, philosophy—all these are subjects that must be studied in order to know them; they are not possessed of a natural authority. Only the moral sense exhibits this natural authority.[50]

As we observed earlier, Li Ta-chao was not as concerned as some other early socialist were to try to demonstrate that the peasants possess a "natural" inclination to socialism. But here he makes a much broader and less doctrinaire affirmation: *all* men are apt for society. All men are capable of conducting themselves in accordance with moral judgments made on the authority of a reliable instinct to distinguish right from wrong, judgments that have nothing to do with experience, intellectual understanding, rational calculation, or particular material circumstances. Thus, in the context of an exposition of Marxist materialism, Li reasserted the most important argument of Confucian moral idealism. "All things are complete in me," Mencius had said, meaning that the human heart is morally autonomous. With similar meaning, and equal conviction, Li Ta-chao might have summed up his beliefs with a paraphrase: "The new order is complete in me—and in all men."

When full account is taken of Li Ta-chao's reservations and amendments, implicit or explicit, one may be moved to inquire whether his credentials as a Marxist should be allowed to go unchallenged. One is tempted to say that for Li, Marxism was more an inspiration than a discipline. Many of his "Marxist views" fit comfortably enough into the mold of New Culture reformism. Others, perhaps unconsciously, echo inherited themes and beliefs. On the other hand, while the fact that he considered himself a Marxist cannot be regarded as decisive, neither can it be dismissed as irrelevant. Clearly, Li felt that more than a label was involved; that Marxism, as he understood it, offered a distinctive and promising approach to China's problems.

We may perhaps best understand this conviction if we understand that, in the political and intellectual environment of China in the teens and twenties, what Marxism meant in general was, in a way, more important than what it meant specifically. It meant revolution—not in the sense in which the events of 1911–1912 had constituted a "revolution," nor in the sense in which the Nationalists laid claim to a "revolutionary" mission, but in a much more uncompromising way. And Li was a revolutionary, at once more thorough-going than his predecessors, and with fewer misgivings than his contemporaries entertained as to the consequences of the revolutionary enterprise. He did not believe that history is blind, or indifferent to human purpose. Neither did he believe that history can be guided by intellectual power alone. He believed (and on these points his Marxism was firmly grounded) that history is driven forward by the dynamic force generated in the process of social struggle, and further, that the conditions are now prepared for a final confrontation between the privileged minority and the great masses of the oppressed. That this signified, in China, a peasant mass still far from conscious of its own political interests did not deter him, any more than did the fact that, by his own admission, China's experience departed fundamentally from the economic history on which Marx had based his prediction that the industrial proletariat will achieve the class consciousness it must have in order to fulfill its revolutionary destiny. In the terms of his dispute with Hu Shih in 1919, to which we will turn our attention in the following chapter, Li insisted that China's problems demanded a "fundamental solution"—not a remedy, but a resolution. And, the need being evident, Li's faith convinced him further that the possibility of meeting that need must also exist, in the revolutionary collaboration of the intellectuals with the masses. "This is the epoch of the common people of the world," he wrote in 1920. "We should recognize our own power, and hasten to unite, so that in pressing our demands upon life, we may create a new history of the common people of the world."[51]

Li Ta-chao was a radical democrat. Others had approached this ground, surveyed it, and retreated finally from the precipice of unconditional reliance on "the people"—whose condition they pitied, whose welfare they sought to promote, whose energies they wanted to harness, but whose stolid, incurious ignorance of any world beyond the inherited horizon baffled and repelled them. Li's true legacy to the movement to which his early enthusiasm gave momentum was less a doctrine than it was a gift of vision: the ability to see the world of peasants and villages not merely as the eventual beneficiary of liberation conferred upon it, but as the place where the struggle for liberation must begin.

The Dilemmas of Modernity: Intellectuals as the Victims of Politics

China's ancients said, "He who works with his mind rules; he who labors with his strength is ruled." Now we would turn this proposition around, and say, "He who labors with his strength rules; he who works with his mind is ruled."

—Ch'en Tu-hsiu,
"The Awakening of the
Working Man," May 1, 1920

In the Chinese democratic revolutionary movement, it was the intellectuals who were the first to awaken. . . . But the intellectuals will accomplish nothing if they fail to integrate themselves with the workers and the peasants.

—Mao Tse-tung,
"The May Fourth Movement,"
May, 1939

WHILE CH'EN TU-HSIU SAT IN A PEKING JAIL in the summer of 1919, and Ts'ai Yuan-p'ei "perfected his virtue in solitude" among the scenic beauty of West Lake, while students debated and organized and demonstrated, Li Ta-chao and Hu Shih confronted each other in their famous debate on "problems and theories," or "problems and isms" (*wen-t'i yü chu-i*).

Their forum was a small and short-lived journal of political criticism called *The Weekly Critic (Mei-chou p'ing-lun)*, established late in 1918 by several contributors to *The New Youth* (Ch'en and Li among them) who had grown impatient with the older magazine's scrupulously apolitical editorial policy. Hu Shih was away from Peking at the time, attending to family affairs in Anhwei following his mother's death in November—an occasion he exploited to demonstrate publicly his contempt for the funeral customs which, traditionally, a filial son was bound to observe. His friends in Peking, in the meantime, seized the opportunity of his absence to establish an outlet for the kind of political discussion that Hu had consistently maintained was not properly the business of New Culture educators.

Hu was an influential advocate of the view that intellectuals should renounce political entanglements, verbal or otherwise. He was not the first to adopt this position, however, or the only one to uphold it. "Party politics" and "bureaucratism" were anathema to turn-of-the-century reformers and revolutionaries alike, and to their New Culture heirs. Before and after 1911, the quasi-anarchist societies promoted by Wu Chih-hui, Ts'ai Yuan-p'ei, and others had commonly included as a part of their discipline a prohibition against political activity or government service, even to the point of forbidding their adherents to stand for parliamentary election. So also, for that matter, did the articles of the Society for the Promotion of Moral Rectitude that Ts'ai established at Peita in 1916.

To most early readers of *The New Youth*, then, Ch'en Tu-hsiu's initial insistence that the magazine would take "the education of youth as its mission, in anticipation of a fundamental awakening of our people" seemed both appropriate and praiseworthy.[1] Ch'en abjured the "superstitious faith in the omnipotence of politics" which in the past "has inflicted uncounted evils upon society. . . . Not to put too fine a point on it, politics is an enormous obstacle to the progress of the group [*ch'un*]. . . . Nor is the cultivation of youth a cause well served by talking politics." At the same time, however, Ch'en sensed early-on the dilemma that would generate dissension within the New Culture elite and lead eventually to its dissolution. "The basis of social progress lies in education and industry, not in politics," he conceded. "But there can be no room for progress in education and industry until a certain level of political progress has been achieved. . . . When it comes to the great policies which affect the fate of the nation, its very survival, then how can we bear to remain silent? . . . To be broadly learned but unable to put one's learning to use, to be cold-bloodedly indifferent to the realities of life—that is the style of China's old-fashioned pedants, not of our new youth of the twentieth century."[2]

Hu Shih launched the "problems and isms" exchange with an essay published in mid-July, soon after he had assumed editorial responsibilities for *The Weekly Critic* in place of the imprisoned Ch'en Tu-hsiu.

The ensuing "debate" comprised rejoinders from Li Ta-chao and, at the other end of the spectrum of opinion, Lan Kung-wu, one of Liang Ch'i-ch'ao's party, together with an elaboration of Hu's original statement. The title of Hu's first essay summed up its avowedly pragmatic thesis and, indeed, the gist of his whole argument: "Study more about specific problems, and talk less about general theories." It was a warning, in language already familiar to Hu's accustomed audience, against what he regarded as the pernicious infatuation with "isms": abstract representations of what had once been "concrete proposals addressed to the problems of a given moment." In the real world, Hu insisted, "there is no abstraction that can fully comprehend the concrete proposals of a particular person or party. . . . Today the great danger is a fondness for theories on paper, and a refusal to engage in the factual examination of what, in the final analysis, constitutes China's present social need."[3]

True to his particularist principles, Hu would speak of "problems" only in discrete and specific terms—interconnected, to be sure, and thus allowing reasonable expectation of a cumulative effect as "solutions" are achieved, one by one; but essentially identifiable as distinct objects of "scientific" investigation, figuratively or literally. Thus the working conditions of Peking's rickshaw coolies, the customs and prejudices that perpetuated the social abuse of women, standards and systems of public health, elementary and secondary school textbooks and curricula, scholarly issues having to do with the interpretation of China's historical and literary inheritance—in Hu's mind, all these were "problems" of comparable significance. Their solution was not to be sought in a single act, or a single understanding, but through the patient pursuit of an investigation that must require specialized knowledge in order to bring it to a practically useful conclusion. In Hu's scheme of things, then, primary responsibility rested with the individual investigator or scholar, the expert.

Li Ta-chao expressed himself in complete agreement with the view that intellectuals should address themselves to "real" problems and refrain from the complacent discussion of intellectually gratifying but practically useless theoretical issues. But behind Hu's broadside attack on "isms" Li rightly detected a criticism of Marxism in particular, which he moved quickly to turn aside. His rejoinder was phrased in conciliatory language, and began with a verbal gesture in the direction of Hu's "instrumentalism." Li's emphasis on the importance of the collective recognition of problems, however, and on collective action to solve them, cast into sharp relief the underlying issues that divided them. "I do not feel that 'problems' and 'isms' can be completely divorced one from the other," he began. And he continued:

> The solution to any social problem must depend upon the concerted actions of the social majority. If we wish to solve a problem, therefore, we must first devise the means to insure that it *is* a problem, in the eyes of this

> majority . . . and that this majority which will collectively discover the solution to this or that social problem is first inclined toward a common ideal, an ism, against which to test the degree to which they are satisfied or dissatisfied with the conditions of their own lives. (Call it a kind of instrument.) Only those actual conditions concerning which there exists a collective sense of dissatisfaction can, one by one, become social problems for which there is hope of a solution.[4]

In thus rejecting the primary role assigned by Hu Shih to the individual, Li also rejected, by implication, individualism as a primary social good. Speaking still in terms of friendship and respect, he expressed what would become in later years, and from other voices, an often contemptuous condemnation of the elitist irrelevance of the liberal approach. "However industriously you investigate your problems, the great majority in society will feel no sense of involvement in them," he cautioned. "There can never be any hope of solving such problems, nor can their investigation ever influence reality."

Li's confidence in the effectiveness of collective social consciousness, coupled with his conviction that the concrete opportunities of the moment must not be subordinated to an imagined future—the "thirty or fifty years hence" that the moderates spoke of so easily—gave him both a sense of urgency and a firm faith in the possibility of achieving a "fundamental solution." Any less comprehensive strategy, he suggested, must arise from a misconception of China's true condition. China is not "a well-organized and vital society," he wrote, but "a disorganized and moribund society, its faculties already impaired. . . . In such circumstances, I venture to say, there must first be a fundamental resolution before there can be any hope of solving specific problems one at a time." Li anchored this argument to the bedrock of Marxist materialism. The "problems" that Hu had identified, he insisted, are problems of superstructure; in each case, the foundation is the economic infrastructure. "The solution of the economic problem is the fundamental solution. As soon as [*i-tan*] the economic problem has been solved, then whatever problems there may remain concerning politics, the legal system, the family system, the liberation of women or the liberation of the laboring man, can all find their solution." The Russian example came naturally to mind: "Before the overthrow of the Romanovs and the reorganization of the economy, no solution to any problem was feasible. Now, all problems have been solved."

Li brought his thoughts on the issue of "problems and isms" to a conclusion with an eloquent reaffirmation of his own activist philosophy which was, at the same time, a cogent statement of the dilemma of his own party, soon to become his own Party:

> If you take only the first premise of this historical-materialist theory, that is, only the belief that economic change is natural and unavoidable; and if you utterly disregard its second premise—that is, the theory of class struggle—and

make no attempt to apply this theory as a means of uniting the workingmen into a real movement, then, I venture to suggest, the economic revolution will never be realized; or, if it can still come to pass, then who can say after how long a time? Many Marxist socialists have been deceived by this theory. Every day they are down there among the masses, spreading the glad tidings of the inevitable coming of collectivism—with the result that, save to wait upon the event, they have made no plans at all. This, indeed, is one of the causes of the crisis that has overtaken socialist parties throughout the world at present. We must recognize that the only right course to follow is to seize the opportunities that the moment offers, to move with existing circumstances, from which we may derive the means to work toward a fundamental solution; and that, before we can reach a fundamental solution, there is still a considerable amount of preparatory work to be done.

With this, Li Ta-chao had had his say on the "problems and isms" issue; much of the remainder of his life and his writings was devoted to one or another aspect of the "preparatory work" of which he spoke with such urgency. With Hu Shih it was otherwise: a proper understanding of pragmatic theory was itself the purpose he promoted. He pursued his attack against "isms" through two further installments in the summer of 1919, and returned to it from time to time in the years that followed. A decade after the debate had subsided—a year and a half after Li Ta-chao's execution in Peking—Hu offered his own definition of China's "fundamental problems," writing now to oppose the "revolutionary solutions" proposed by the recently established Nationalist government in Nanking. "Which road should we follow?" he asked: the revolutionary road, or the road that leads by a different route to the same destination? If by "revolution" one means an isolated episode of violent change, culminating in what pretends to be a final and fundamental solution, then, Hu still insisted, it would be better to count oneself a counter-revolutionary. But in fact, revolution should signify simply a stage within a longer and larger evolutionary process, a stage during which conscious intellectual direction supervenes in place of unguided evolutionary forces. Thus to justify an appeal to violence in the name of a revolution that fabricates imaginary enemies in order to sustain its cause is, in whatever circumstances, wasteful and wrongheaded.

Our real enemies are poverty, disease, ignorance, greed and disorder. . . . Not such as can be overthrown by the resort to violence. The true revolutionary struggle against these five enemies has only one course to follow: clearly to recognize our enemies, clearly to recognize our problems, and then to bring together the best talents and intellects that the country has to offer, to adopt without reservation the scientific knowledge and methodologies of the world at large, and then step by step to implement conscious reforms, under conscious leadership, thus little by little reaping the benefits of uninterrupted reform. . . .

This fundamental attitude and approach is not the same thing as relying on natural evolution; nor is it a blind resort to violent revolution, or a revolution of sloganeering and rhetoric. It is simply to achieve uninterrupted reform through conscious effort.[5]

The liberal program, far-sighted in its confidence in the authority of reasonable intelligence, myopic in its indifference to social analysis, was perhaps never more aptly summarized than in these lines.

Surveying the "problems and isms" debate from Li Ta-chao's perspective, Maurice Meisner has suggested that it may be understood in terms of what Max Weber called "the ethic of ultimate ends" versus "the ethic of responsibility." Hu Shih, upholding the ethic of ultimate ends, urged that the individual remain true first and last to himself, to his own ideals, regardless of the consequences measured in terms of social effectiveness or the lack of it. Li Ta-chao, exemplifying the ethic of responsibility, asserted that means must be subordinated to ends, if the ends in view promote the betterment of the social condition. Confronted by the moral ambiguity inherent in the choices open to them, in other words, the one elected to preserve the purity of his principles, while the other acknowledged the need for action and accepted the risks involved.[6]

The liberal academics and modern professionals who constituted Hu Shih's natural audience did, indeed, place a high value on their "uncommitted" (*wu-tang wu-p'ai*) position. It was an attitude at once prudent and principled, self-indulgent and self-assured. They preferred their self-styled role as "disinterested critics" to involvement in the sordid intrigues of politics as practiced by the warlords or, on a larger scale, by the Nationalists, or to the very real hazards of placing themselves in radical opposition to the powers of the day. But it was not merely a matter of fastidiousness or a lack of courage. The liberal view reflected the attempt to distinguish more clearly than the Confucian tradition had done, or than the emerging revolutionary ideology was disposed to do, between the public and the private dimensions of the individual's identity. It thus had much to do with the liberal definition of the proper meaning of civic responsibility, to which we will turn our attention shortly. Hu Shih's disagreement with Li Ta-chao, moreover, went beyond the choice of a personal ethic, to touch upon the fundamental question of human nature itself.

Liberalism has commonly been identified with the effort, largely a product of North Atlantic political and cultural history since the seventeenth century, to enlarge the sphere of individual responsibility by broadening the range of intellectual opportunity and autonomy. But at heart, the liberal view of human nature is not an exalted one. The best that liberals expect is that, if human beings are allowed to consult their individual interests in the light of reasonable expectations of their fulfillment, the judgments that result will be conducive to the preservation of a social community whose members acknowledge that the protection of their own freedom of mind and action enjoins a respect for the exercise of the same freedom by others. Institutionally, the liberal enterprise may be seen as an attempt to minimize the community's reliance on a benign assessment of human motives in order to achieve the degree of public justice necessary to insure social cohension and continuity: a government of laws *vs.* a government of men; Hobbes and Locke, in their different fashions, *vs.* Rousseau; and, at one level, Marx *vs.* Bakunin.

Hu Shih proudly called himself an optimist, and took on the whole the cheerful view. But his estimate of uninformed human nature was not always sanguine. He did not share the confidence that justified Li Ta-chao's belief in the promise of present opportunity. It was not Li, however, but Lan Kung-wu who elicited the most forthright statement of this view in the course of the "problems and isms" debate. Stepping forth as a defender of the "spiritual" claims of human nature, Lan argued that general theories—"isms"—express, among other things, the need to transcend the concrete and the rational, and to manifest the "mystical nature" (*shen-mi-hsing*) that is inherent in mankind at large. Hu Shih's rejoinder was brusque, and uncommonly revealing of the elitist prejudices that undergirded liberal optimism—and, it may be, eventually helped to undermine the liberals' cause:

> Speaking frankly, what Mr. Lan calls "the mystical nature" is simply human folly [*yü-mei-hsing*]. Foolish and ignorant, mankind is easily led. . . . History is full of wiley and hypocritical politicians who, recognizing only too clearly that men possess this depraved nature [*lieh-ken-hsing*], habitually resort to overblown abstractions in order to deceive the great majority into taking their part in the struggle for power or profit, and to be sacrificed on their behalf. . . . Mankind has already suffered the ill effects of this depraved nature long enough! We who are scholars by vocation, we whose lives are devoted to shaping public opinion, should take pity on mankind's infirmities; we should destroy its superstitious faith in abstractions, and make it impossible for mankind again to be so deceived. . . . [7]

* * *

In style and substance, the problems and isms debate was an argument born of its time, expressing a modern sensitivity to the complexity of the processes of social growth and change, and new visions of the ends that should be pursued. But the underlying issue was one with which the Chinese had been contending since the policy debates of the 1860s and 1870s; an issue that would continue to command some part of their attention throughout the thirty years that separated the May Fourth summer of 1919 from the revolutionary victory of 1949, and that would intrude upon public life with even greater urgency during the decades that have elapsed since that epochal event.

It is the problem, simply stated, of whether the business of government is best managed by "insiders," who live with an interior sense of the problems with which they are dealing, or by "outsiders," whose understanding derives from observation, analysis, and the calculated application of specialized knowledge and techniques. It is the difference between those, on the one hand, whose perception of what must be done is animated by a passionate subjectivism, and whose knowledge is in the final analysis a matter of belief or of ideological persuasion; and, on the other hand, those whose claim to competence derives from their ability (whether real or assumed) to remain dispassionately objective, submitting all problems to critical examination, and relying finally not on belief but on expertise, the authority of rational calculation and intellectual technique. This is not to imply that "insiders" are indifferent to the importance of technique, or that "outsiders" are uncommitted to any purpose larger than the problem at hand. The difference is one of emphasis, affecting the intellectual's perception of the character of his own role and shaping the strategies that will be adopted in order to enlist a wider following.

The inculcation of belief requires methods of education (or indoctrination) designed to stimulate (or to simulate) a sense of participatory responsiveness to a general situation. In contrast to the kind of problem-centered and individual-oriented education espoused by New Culture liberals, it aims at the cultivation of a sense of subjective involvement in the social condition—a replication of experience of the kind that Li Ta-chao assumed must result from "Young China's" sympathetic intercourse with village life. In this as in other respects, Li anticipated the ideological style that came in time to characterize the Chinese Communist movement. His insistence that the masses must be educated to an awareness of social problems as a prerequisite to the discovery of appropriate solutions reflected, perhaps, a cognizance on his part of the Leninist notion of the Party as the agency through which "proletarian consciousness" is instilled in the working class. Of greater importance to the subsequent development of Maoist theory and practice, however, is the manner in which this perception foreshadows the dynamic of the strategy of the Mass Line—that is, the idea that "educating the people" and "learning from the people" are inseparable dimensions of the same dialectical process. It is here, at what is in some respects its most radical affirmation of populism, that Chinese Communist ideology responds most obviously to the gravitational attraction of traditional precedent, or to that style of inherited social idealism which took to heart the Mencian dictum that "Heaven sees as the people see, Heaven hears as the people hear," and which preserved, consequently, a due regard for the "minds and hearts" of the people.

The comparison must be qualified forthwith. By no stretch of the imagination is it possible to read "proletarian revolution" into, or out of, the

Confucian legacy. Communist theory asserts, as Confucianism never did, that the process of teaching-and-learning is one of progressive movement, in constantly changing circumstances, across a predictable sequence of historical points. Communist theory ordains, and Communist social strategy is designed to generate, class struggle as an essential aspect of this process, and of the business of government as a whole—a startling and profoundly significant departure from the Confucian ideal of a frictionless, noiseless, harmonious social order. The Confucian elite was the self-conscious bearer of the high culture; and, when in office, the instrument (at least in theory) exclusively of imperial interests. The Communist Party, as the bearer of proletarian consciousness and the catalyst which activates the masses, exercises a broader range of functions while at the same time preserving the authority of the center, or of the Revolution.

It may be argued that, however diverse the means, the management of government always and everywhere comes down to the attempt to balance competitive political interests one against another in such a way as to maintain the existing regime in power. In China under the old regime, the aim was to perpetuate the mandate of an hereditary ruling house while preserving a social equilibrium that would insure the elite status of a non-hereditary ruling class. The Confucian official had to balance the demands of the imperial government which he served against the ability, or the willingness, of the jurisdiction over which he presided to respond to these demands. He had to balance the need to intervene in local affairs against the political risks of ineffective intrusion. He had further to preserve a fragile and conditional acceptance of imperial authority against the idealistic notion that he represented or exemplified absolute authority within a shared vision of the moral community. In the People's Republic, the aims are those of a modernizing revolutionary society in which political authority derives from the presumption of popular sovereignty, while political power, the power to decide matters of high policy, rests with a government against whose decisions no appeal is sanctioned, and over whose actions no effective institutional checks exist. For the Chinese Communist Party in power, from the land-reform campaigns of the late 1940s and early 1950s down through, and perhaps beyond, the Great Proletarian Cultural Revolution of the 1960s and early 1970s, the problem of political equilibrium has been in large part the problem of balancing mass spontaneity against the need for ideological discipline; the mobilization of popular support against the insistent demand for effective and coherent organizational structures; the risk of unleashing unpredictable or ungovernable mass action against the threat of institutional self-aggrandizement and inflexibility.

Thus, while both Confucian China and Communist China may accurately be described as essentially authoritarian regimes, comparisons at the level of institutional structure and behavior frequently reveal resemblances that, on closer scrutiny, turn out to be secondary rather than primary. There is, however, a primary congruance between the old regime and the new, in the fact that the state, whether Confucian or Socialist, is conceived of ideally as a community of faith. Common to each is the conviction that the human personality is communal rather than individual; in each, therefore, government assumes the character of a moral enterprise, in what it does and in what it urges men to do or to become, each in accordance with its own definition of the social good. In each, moreover, the authority of government is exercised—at least in theory—by example and persuasion rather than by coercion. In each, in the final analysis, the responsibilities of leadership are seen as being best exercised by the "virtuous"—that is, those who possess moral insight, those sensitized through ideological training to perceive the human element, the social element, in any problem that may be encountered, and to address themselves idealistically to practicalities. In terms of their underlying assumptions, then, both are governments by men, not governments of law: governments by men educated to assess their opportunities for acting upon the world in the categories of the reigning ideology.

This characteristic of the evolving sense of revolutionary identity was clearly expressed in the words of a Party pamphlet written in 1939, its purpose being to convey to new recruits an image of the ideal Party member:

> Revolution is a stupendous and trying undertaking and the conditions of the Chinese revolution . . . are particularly complex and kaleidoscopic; the reason why the C[ommunist] P[arty] is able to control, under changing and complex circumstances, the great revolutionary movement and guide it towards victory is because it possess a revolutionary ideology. Accordingly, a CP member must understand this revolutionary ideology; then he can find a way out of highly complex situations; he can work out his course in the ever-changing [revolutionary] movement, and can carry out his revolutionary assignments successfully. Unless he does so, he will lose his way and direction in the midst of his complicated and ever-changing revolutionary environment. . . . Thus every CP member must learn through work whenever and wherever possible, elevate his political and cultural level, increase his revolutionary knowledge, and deepen his political vision.[8]

It was thus not incongruous for Liu Shao-ch'i, in his famous lectures at Yenan in the summer of 1939, to describe the task of "being (or becoming) a good Communist" in terms of the traditional discipline of self-examination, self-criticism, and self-cultivation, an exhortation that drew without apology on Confucian moral precepts,* and the point driven home with a quotation from the writings of a Sung-dynasty Con-

---

* *How To Be a Good Communist* is the usual translation of the title of Liu's "Lun Kung-ch'an-tang-yuan ti hsiu-yang," a more literal rendering of which would be "On the Self-Cultivation of a Member of the Communist Party." In these lectures, Liu quoted the Confucian *Analects* four times, Mencius twice, the *Doctrine of the Mean* and the *Classic of Poetry* each once; Mao Tse-tung was quoted six times; Marx and Engels, Lenin, and Stalin, five times each. Only one of the classical quotations is distinctly pejorative in context.

fucian reformer who had written, "The scholar should be the first to become concerned with the world's troubles and the last to rejoice in its happiness."[9]

* * *

"I think that perhaps my nerves are cracking," wrote Lu Hsun in 1925. "Otherwise it is too frightening. . . . I feel that everything must be done over. . . . "[10] It was a feeling shared by an increasing number of Chinese writers and intellectuals as the self-confidence born of the May Fourth experience ebbed away. By the late 1920s, Chinese Communism had begun to develop a cultural personality—a penumbra of literary and academic sympathies and commitments. Communist historians in general, and some disinterested historians of Chinese radicalism, portray the two decades following the "Second Revolution" of 1925–1927 as a time when intellectuals fled *en masse* from the side of "reaction" to the side of "liberation": the critical turning point in this as in every other great revolutionary movement when the *ancien régime* is deserted by those of thoughtful sense and generous spirit.

Lu Hsun himself stands as a case in point—and Lu Hsun alone makes a powerful case. He left Peking in the summer of 1926, numbed with horror by the cynicism and the mindless bloodletting of warlord government. First-hand acquaintance with the revolutionary movement then gathering strength in the south only increased his despair: there he witnessed not the expected struggle of the young against the old, but the dreadful spectacle of the young murdering the young. In the autumn of 1927 Lu Hsun took refuge in Shanghai where, nine years later, he died and was accorded, against both his own wish and the wishes of the Nanking government, a titan's funeral. By then he had long been acknowledged, at home and abroad, as China's leading radical intellectual, active in the sponsorship of such organizations as the League of Leftwing Writers and the China League for Civil Rights in the early 1930s, a bitter critic of the Nationalists' revolution who satirized its pretensions and condemned its brutalities.

But, as he himself once observed, Lu Hsun's pen was not for sale. He might believe in the proletariat, but he could not believe in proletarianization. His sympathy for the young and vulnerable, the powerless, the exploited and oppressed, did not engender an enthusiasm for ideological categorization or make him amenable to ideological discipline. He died timely: had he survived, he must surely have been warned, as were a number of his protégés among the writers assembled at Yenan in 1942, to "transform and completely reconstruct [his] own thought and feelings," as Mao Tse-tung pointedly phrased it. One wonders with what effect. One wonders, too, with what humor he would have accepted his posthumous reputation. "On the cultural front," Mao intoned in 1940, Lu Hsun was "the bravest and most correct, the firmest, the most loyal and the most ardent national hero, a hero without parallel in our history."[11]

In the course of the 1930s, under the deepening threat of Japanese aggression, and harassed by a government which seemed more concerned to silence its critics within than to confront the enemy without, many Chinese students, a fair number of academicians, and many of the country's most persuasive and popular literary talents drifted toward the Left, like Lu Hsun finding it difficult to acknowledge a danger on that quarter. The polarization of intellectual and cultural life that began then continued, and gathered momentum, throughout the years of war and civil strife that followed. But the erosion of confidence in the Nationalist government was not matched, step by step, by a corresponding growth of confidence in the revolutionary alternative posed by the Communists. Against the vision of intellectuals as the servants of ideology, whether in its vestigial traditional manifestations or its emerging modern forms, the New Culture liberals and their descendants in the second and third generations—the "political amateurs," the "outsiders"—waged a long and losing battle. Within the lifespan of the original May Fourth generation, history outran argument. The question of whether it is proper or productive for intellectuals to talk politics lost whatever point it may originally have had when the very right to do so was denied, with lesser or greater effect, under the dictatorships that governed China from the 1920s onward. Insistence that the intellectual vocation carries with it the privilege to be heard lost its meaning when intellectuals could no longer claim the right to express private opinions. The attempt to limit the exercise of state power by constitutional means turned upon itself when such phrases as "except in accordance with the law" or "as provided for in the Constitution" became themselves weapons in the arsenal of state power.

A losing battle, then—but never entirely lost. Even when a government fabricates the constitutional rules under which it operates it must concede, if only tacitly, that its claim to universal competence is necessarily limited by the complexity of the responsibilities it has assumed. Even a government which distrusts the elitist implications of the intellectual vocation and resists the intellectuals' claim to autonomy must make use of their skills and make place for some exercise of independence on their part: if not "freedom of speech and opinion," then at least some encouragement to preserve and perpetuate intellectual skills. In the circumstances which prevailed in China, the defeat of liberalism as a philosophy of government, or as an accepted set of norms governing the transaction of public business, is less remarkable in retrospect than is the stubborn persistence of intellectual professionalism and, as a corollary, of liberal scepticism as a style of political criticism directed against the ideological enthusiasm of unequivocally illiberal regimes.

Many of the prominent and articulate liberal intellectuals of the 1930s and 1940s were educators in a more or less formal sense: teachers and writers, journalists and publishers—and, not infrequently, all at once. Others belonged to the emerging "class" of modern professionals—doctors or lawyers, technicians and engineers, bankers, a few military men, and a larger number of civil servants in such fields as public health, transportation and communications, mining, trade and finance, and the Customs. All took as a matter of course the kind of education that a generation or two earlier had still been viewed with distrust by some and by others as glamorously exotic. Virtually all had studied in the West or in Japan or had at least been the students of Western-trained teachers. On many, directly or indirectly, the influence of Anglo-American political, social, and educational ideas and ideals had been considerable. Many had appropriated, without evident self-consciousness, a Westernized (or "modern") lifestyle. With few exceptions they were urbanites: to some, the rural hinterland was a distant—and unromanticized—childhood memory; to others it had become, physically and spiritually, a *terra incognita*. They were, in short, the self-aware progeny of China's uncertain pursuit of modernization—its advocates, its beneficiaries, and its dependents.

This, then, was the audience that Hu Shih addressed as those "whose lives are devoted to the shaping of public opinion." It was a more diffuse group than the handful of Peking intellectuals who had risen to prominence in the late teens in the pages of *The New Youth* and the lecture halls of Peita. Nor was it a constituency in any way formally organized to promote a fixed program based on a carefully articulated philosophy. Those who sought a public forum, however, found it with little difficulty. There were the great newspapers, with their weekly literary and cultural supplements, notably the two firmly independent Tientsin papers, the *Ta-kung pao* ("L'Impartial") and the *I-shih pao*. There were such durable journals of general interest as *The Eastern Miscellany*, still published by the Commercial Press.

There were also the small but widely read liberal journals that came and went in these decades when the cost of publication was low enough to be largely underwritten by the contributors themselves—"the golden age of independent journalism," as Hu Shih wistfully recalled it. In 1922 Hu and Ting Wen-chiang established *The Endeavor* (*Nu-li chou-pao*), which for a year or so took up the moderate message that was no longer welcome in the pages of *The New Youth*, now a Communist Party organ. In the mid-twenties a group of Peking and Shanghai university professors came together to publish *The Contemporary Review* (*Hsien-tai p'ing-lun*), more concerned with cultural and scholarly issues than with politics, but identifiably liberal in outlook. Several of the same sponsors were involved in the publication of *The Crescent* (*Hsin yueh*), which first appeared in 1928 as a literary review, but soon enlarged its range to accommodate the interests of a number of political writers who thought of themselves as Fabian socialists. Some of the most cogent criticism of the Nanking government ever written appeared in its pages, along with lengthy debates with left-wing writers on the subject of proletarian culture in general, and proletarian literature in particular.

In 1932, after the demise of *The Crescent,* Hu Shih and several of his friends established *The Independent Critic (Tu-li p'ing-lun)* in Peking, which survived as the most forthright liberal journal of the 1930s until the war with Japan swept discussion of political alternatives into oblivion. In the early 1940s dissent surfaced again, expressed chiefly in such publications as *The Democratic Weekly (Min-chu chou-k'an)*, the official organ of the Democratic League, a pathetically vulnerable political opposition to the Nationalists. In the postwar years, before the country sank into the final convulsions of civil war, periodicals like *The Observer (Kuan-ch'a)* provided an uncertain outlet for increasingly desperate liberal criticism.

China's moderates thus seldom lacked a voice, despite the obstacles placed in their way from time to time by the Nationalist government: censorship before or after publication; denial of access to the postal service; the suppression of objectionable publications; occasionally, the judicial or physical intimidation of individual writers. Worse was to come. The liberals were never more clearly defined, as a group, than when in the early 1950s the newly-established government of the People's Republic marshaled its impressive propaganda apparatus in a nationwide campaign to denounce and defame these "old-style [*sic!*] intellectuals"—the "cultural compradores" who, according to the indictment read against one after another, had tried to divert China's youth from its revolutionary duty and destiny by holding up before it the doctrine of intellectual individualism, the vision of personal fame and fulfillment, the deadly "returned students' dream."

In retrospect, then, the Chinese Communists did not take at face value the liberals' view of themselves as disinterested critics occupying a position outside of, or above, the political struggle. And in this the Communists' assessment, however partisan its motive, was essentially astute. The New Culture liberals were at heart political men. However genuine, however vehemently expressed, was their scepticism of the pretensions of the regimes under which they lived, they were by no means sceptical of the need for government. They insisted merely that it must be a government properly constituted to promote the interests of the community as a whole, and to respect their own vocational values—aims which they regarded as entirely congruous. Their demand that the government be constitutionally empowered, that it act only within the bounds of well-defined legal procedures, and that it commit itself vigorously and in good faith to the extension and protection of civil liberties, was a demand intended to limit the evident powers of government. The attempt to limit also its arrogation of an all-encompassing moral authority was more difficult to reduce to specific injunctions. It took the form of repeated exhortations against the notion that the state is rightfully the embodiment of abstract values, be they those of Confucian virtue-in-office, or of militant nationalism, or of class-sponsored social revolution.

Government, the liberals argued, is no more than an agency through which individuals of talent are recruited and given the opportunity to exercise their expertise in the interests of society at large. "Government is a most difficult and important art," wrote Hu Shih in 1929. "Knowledge and action must go side by side. . . . Could anything be more difficult than to administer a country as vast as this if we rely on men who possess no knowledge of the modern world? . . . It is essential to call upon the advice of eminent experts, and to utilize modern knowledge. 'Action is easy' can serve as a prescription only to poorly educated militarists and politicians."[12]

The target of Hu's displeasure here was the ideology of the government recently established in Nanking, its legacy from Sun Yat-sen. The notion that "knowledge is difficult, action is easy" had been Sun's final rationalization for the failures of the early Republic—failures not in conception or design, which might call into question the authority of Sun's vision, but failures in execution, the fault not of the leader, but of the followers. Sun divided the revolutionary party into three categories: "fore-knowers," "after-knowers," and "doers"—with himself, one suspects, in his own mind the singular example of the first of these, the party rank and file relegated to the last, and the masses excluded entirely. It was a theory ready-made to enhance the authority of the Party over the people, and of the Party leadership over the organization as a whole, proclivities which Sun's introduction to the fundamentals of Leninist party theory would do much to reinforce in the early 1920s. By 1929, with Sun himself only a sanctified memory, the Nationalists were content to define "knowledge" simply as unquestioning loyalty to "the all-embracing ideology of our Party" and "the precious teachings of the Tsung-li [i.e., the Leader, an honorary title posthumously reserved to Sun Yat-sen]."[13]

The liberals' rejection of this sweeping ideological claim carried with it an important corollary. The liberals regarded themselves not merely as intellectuals or as members of the "intelligentsia"—a term that gained popularity without precision in the 1920s and 1930s—but also as professionals, that is, as disciplined practitioners of particular intellectual skills and specializations that justified their sense of civic significance. Time and again they castigated the Nanking regime for its failure energetically to recruit, or systematically to employ, "human talent" (jen ts'ai). The term possessed a venerable Confucian pedigree, but it was used now in an un-Confucian meaning, of which professionalism was very much a part. A government of men may be served by generalists; but a government by law, a government of instrumental institutions, requires the services of specialists, of experts. The liberals' sense of social competence and responsibility was formed, on the one hand, by the conviction that each individual should bring to bear upon society whatever skill, aptitude, and interest most fully expresses his individuality; on the other hand, just as the government must recognize limitations upon its powers, so must individuals accept the fact that talent is inevitably limited in its range. "A modern man may not necessarily know more than did his medieval counterpart," observed T. F. Tsiang, the American-educated chairman of the Tsing Hua history department in the early 1930s. "But a truly modern man understands what he knows, and can therefore afford to express his opinions about it. As for what he does not know, he should keep his mouth shut."[14]

"Between the public and the private realm there is a natural distinction," Ts'ai Yuan-p'ei asserted in 1919, defending the values of the new thought against its critics. Set against the traditions of a political culture which had never made room for private culture in public life, any more than the emerging revolutionary ideologies of the 1920s and 1930s were inclined to do, this commonplace distinction constituted a startling challenge. Unlike their Confucian predecessors, whose vocation was the moral art of government, and unlike their radical contemporaries whose vocation was the moral cause of revolution, the liberals persisted in the view that their civic status was not to be determined or valued exclusively, or even primarily, in terms of its public dimension. They thought of themselves not as public men, but as private individuals with a legitimate claim to be invited to influence public life.

The reformers of the early years of the century, and many of the spokesmen of the New Culture in the late teens and twenties, took the whole phenomenon of social, cultural, and political modernity as their study, and were unembarrassed in offering their opinions across an astonishing range of issues. By the late 1920s and the 1930s, however, there was a growing number of intellectual specialists educated to survey China's predicament more narrowly from the perspectives of particular disciplines: as sociologists, economists, anthropologists, critical historians, and students of law and of political theory. Of the latter, one of the most consistent and articulate advocates of liberal doctrines in general, and of the cause of expertise in government in particular, was Lo Lung-chi (1896–1965), who must for our purposes typify the omnium-gatherum.

Born into a family of gentry antecedents in Kiangsi in 1896, Lo Lung-chi was educated at home in the traditional curriculum until he was sixteen. A year after the 1911 Revolution, however, he went north, to enroll in one of the first classes at Tsing Hua, an important first step toward Western study. He remained in Peking for nine years, throughout the period during which the ancient capital became the center of the new thought. He played an active role in student politics and journalism at the time of the May Fourth excitements, and by the time he arrived in the United States on a Boxer Indemnity scholarship in 1921, though only in his mid-twenties he was already a well-established member of the rising generation of "modern" intellectuals. Having received his B.A. and M.A. degrees from the University of Wisconsin, he embarked in 1925 on a more significant intellectual adventure: two years of graduate study at the London School of Economics. There he became much interested in the liberal socialism of the Fabians, and fell especially under the influence of Harold Laski, newly appointed to the professorship of political science. In 1927 Lo returned to the United States to complete his Ph.D. at Columbia with a dissertation on the British parliamentary system. Thus certified, he arrived back in China in 1928, where he taught political science at Kuang-hua University and soon joined the group of Anglo-American-educated academics who had come together to publish *The Crescent*. Lo was one of those responsible for turning the magazine into a political review, and for its Fabianesque tone; his own reputation as an incisive political critic spread rapidly.

Laski's *A Grammar of Politics*, published shortly before Lo's arrival at the L.S.E., offered a philosophy of government whose imprint is clearly evident in Lo's contributions to *The Crescent*. * "A working theory of the State," Laski maintained, "must . . . be conceived in administrative terms." Critics of government, he insisted, should "concentrate attention less on the problems of power than on the problems of administration. . . . For so long as we deal with the concept of an intangible State, so long shall we miss the central fact that what is truly important is the relationships of those who act as its agents. It is the things they do and fail to do, the process in which their actions are embodied, that constitute the reality of political discussion." The proper functioning of the civil service, and especially of that small minority within it which is "engaged in genuinely creative work"—that is, decision-making and the shaping of policy—were of particular concern to him. He held forth at length upon the need for the executive power at every level of government to rely upon the advice of men with "special competence," and he argued forcefully for the establishment of "a much more organic connection than there is now between the public service and the universities," for only in the universities, he asserted, can political problems, problems of administration and execution, be "rationalized into their abstract forms."[15]

This was Lo Lung-chi's perspective on the political situation to which

---

* *A Grammar of Politics* was translated into Chinese by Chang Chün-mai in the late 1920s.

he returned in 1928—a situation in some respects even less promising than that he remembered from his Tsing Hua student days. The warlords had been concerned with power, and sometimes merciless in dealing with whatever seemed to threaten it. But on the whole they were indifferent to ideas. "Intellectually China has the advantage of a weak and corrupt government," John Dewey observed in 1921. "The uniform attitude of the educated class toward their government . . . is critical."[16] That attitude, or the level of expectation, had changed to a degree with the advent in 1928 of a government pledged to modernization. But so, too, had the ideological commitment of the government, which proved in the end the more decisive change. Lo Lung-chi remarked bitterly in 1929 that he had been freer as a foreigner abroad to criticize the governments of the United States or Great Britain than he was as a citizen of the renascent Chinese Republic to call into question the fundamental premises of Nationalist policy or ideology. "It is considered 'rebellious' to discuss a constitution, and 'a cover for nefarious plotting' to discuss human rights. We are labelled 'petty-minded' if we vent our dissatisfactions. We seek national salvation, in the absence of a nation to save; we wish to be patriotic, without a nation to love."[17]

Such frustrations did not deter Lo. His contributions to *The Crescent* and his editorials in the Tientsin *I-shih pao*, which he joined in 1931, encompassed the whole range of liberal concerns: civil liberties; the Nationalists' habit of flouting established legal procedures when it suited their convenience; the whole concept of "tutelage government" and "government by men." He was critical also of Marxist theory, deriding the expectation that the state would "wither away" on the morrow of the revolution, and the belief that the revolutionary act would fundamentally alter human nature by transmuting selfishness into altruism. But the Chinese Communists themselves were at this time a besieged rebel force, confined to their highland strongholds in southern Kiangsi or, later, in the impoverished hinterland of the northwest, virtually unknown, and impossible to assess as an administrative system. Accepting Laski's view that a political critic should concentrate his analysis on what the government in power does and fails to do, Lo directed his heaviest fire against the Nanking regime. His most trenchant criticism was often phrased in terms appropriated directly from Laski, arguing the case against the "intangible State," and demanding the delegation of decision-making and administrative authority to a carefully selected and well-qualified bureaucracy.

A political system, wrote Lo, must be established on the principles of "entrusted power" (*jen-min wei-t'o ti chih-ch'üan*) and "expert service" (*chuan-chia chih-shih ti hsing-cheng*). The English translations are his own; for the latter, a more accurate rendering would be "administration by knowledgeable experts," a point Lo emphasized repeatedly in his indictment of the Nationalist government. Undeniably, there were "knowledgeable experts" in the ranks of Nanking's bureaucracy, some retained from earlier regimes, some recruited. In this respect the Nationalists had established a more modern and efficient government than those it had replaced, and somewhat less distrustful in its attitude toward "experts" than its revolutionary successor would prove to be. But considerations of Party loyalty, of political affiliations within the Party, and of personal relationships remained paramount in recruitment and advancement. The Examination Yuan, one of the five branches of the central government in accordance with Sun Yat-sen's innovative scheme, designed to provide a modern counterpart to the old imperial examination system, never functioned effectively. "Become an official and get rich" (sheng-kuan fa-ts'ai), the derisive apothegm directed against imperial bureaucracies over the centuries, was now used against Nanking. "The impulse of the Revolution is dead," wrote an American observer in 1934. "The revolutionary zealots now nestle in the comfort of public office and concern themselves less with their public responsibilities and the welfare and progress of their country and people, and more with their personal fortunes and jealousies."[18]

Against this unseemly reality, Lo Lung-chi set the liberal view of the state as "an instrument for the realization of the aims of the people as a whole." "The way we see it," he wrote in 1930,

> . . . the state is an organization comparable to a commercial company. In the case of such a company, if it operates under a legally constituted board of directors and employs the services of expert executives, its growth is assured. In the twentieth century, the state is just like this. The legislative organ is the company's board of directors, and the executive organ is its administration charged with the responsibilities of management. If the legislative organ commands the political authority entrusted to it, and if the executive organ employs men of specialized talent, then most of the problems that arise with respect to the political institutions of the state will be *ipso facto* resolved.[19]

The metaphor is distressingly mundane, but it expressed aptly enough a growing sense of frustration with what Hu Shih had called Nanking's "slap-dash" administrative style. The Nationalist regime, however, though willing to prolong indefinitely the so-called "educative period"— that is, the period of political tutelage, which meant in effect one-party dictatorship—was by no means willing itself to be lectured to. In November, 1930, Lo Lung-chi was arrested in Shanghai and briefly imprisoned. Several months later Nationalist gendarmes raided the Peking offices of *The Crescent*, arrested several staff members, and confiscated upwards of a thousand copies of a recent issue in which Lo had published a scathing indictment of the theory and practice of party tutelage. Soon thereafter, *The Crescent* ceased publication altogether.

The demand for an opening-up of government to allow intellectuals to participate in public life on their own enlightened terms was thus reduced to an appeal for administrative efficiency—a "liberal" appeal only to the extent that its sponsors were themselves committed to the liberalization of political opportunity. Lo Lung-chi's personal faith was firmly enough anchored in liberal assumptions, but his case against the Nationalists was explicitly elitist, and by implication antidemocratic. It rested on the distinction between ability and authority: the ability of the "expert executives," exercised under the authority of the legislative "board of directors." In this respect it bore an uncanny resemblance to one of the central premises of the ideology that Lo and his fellow liberals so warmly detested, the incubus of Sun Yat-senism. In his rambling descriptions of the state that would emerge from his revolutionary dream, Sun, too, had distinguished between political authority (*ch'üan*) and political ability (*neng*). The people, he was fond of saying, might have a clear idea of where they wanted to go, and direct the driver accordingly; but the people did not know how to drive the car. Sun bequeathed to his followers no adequate notion as to how the destination chosen by the people was to be communicated to the government, which sat in the driver's seat, and which possessed the only road map.

The 1930s was not a prosperous decade for democratic liberalism in the world at large. The "crisis of democracy" manifested itself differently in Italy, in Germany, in Poland, in Spain, in Japan—but it was a general crisis. In China, these were years when the cloud of war spread darkly over the political landscape: the prospect of war with Japan, despite Nanking's unpopular efforts to forestall it, and the reality of civil strife, not only between the Nationalists and the Communists, but within the Nationalist regime itself in the form of sometimes bloody factional struggles. In these desperate circumstances, it came to seem to many that the creation of a government effectively in command of the nation's resources, human and material, must become the first priority, whatever its principles.

In the 1930s this sentiment found expression in a discussion of "democracy vs. dictatorship" in the pages of *The Eastern Miscellany, The Independent Critic*, and other progressive non-Party journals. "We need a government with centralized powers that can produce the best talent that is efficient and competent," wrote one contributor; a government, in the words of another, that is able to "sweep away yesterday's planless, unorganized, anarchic conditions, and implant social, economic, and political controls that are organized and planned."[20] Or, as a third bluntly put it, "What China needs is a capable and principled dictatorship."[21] Though for obvious reasons the Nanking government was quick to try to exploit such views, these were not the words of Nationalist hacks. They were the opinions, rather, of American-educated "modern men"—two of the three professors of government at leading universities, who had earlier been bitterly critical of Nanking, and who would again find themselves in opposition. Indeed, those who argued in favor of dictatorship in the 1930s were more interested in reforming the Nationalist government than in supporting it, but in a direction quite different from that which had been urged a few years earlier.

Ting Wen-chiang, whom we have met as an eloquent advocate of science in the 1923 debates, was equally eloquent a decade later in his attack on both Nanking's ramshackle dictatorship and on its liberal critics. China's real choice, he wrote, lies not between democracy and dictatorship, but between "old-style" and "new-style" dictatorship. He meant by the latter a leadership that puts national interests above the interests of party or class, that fully understands and appreciates the nature and requirements of the modern state, and that is willing to delegate administrative authority to "experts." "In China at the present time, such a dictatorship is not yet possible," Ting conceded. "But we must strive to make it possible at the earliest moment. A first step in this endeavor is to abandon our advocacy of democracy. . . . The only hope is for the intelligentsia to unite in the task of transforming our present old-style dictatorship into a new-style dictatorship."[22]

Behind the general frustration with Nanking's pretensions and incompetence lay a deeper sense of unease in some minds, a growing belief that by committing themselves to Western ideals of liberal democracy, Chinese progressives since the turn of the century had espoused fundamentally anachronistic theories and institutions. Some regarded the democratic-liberal tradition as already outmoded: "China's current situation absolutely does not allow us time for old-fashioned Western thought. We should immediately abandon superstitions about democracy."[23] Others now saw China as hopelessly behind the West, permanently outside the stream of what had once been thought of as "universal" history, with little expectation of ever achieving self-generating modernity. T. F. Tsiang, the historian, framed his opinion that "the only transitional method is one-man dictatorship" in the context of a carefully constructed historical argument:

> The political history of every country may be divided into two stages, the first being the creation of the state, the second, the use of the state to promote the general welfare. We have yet to accomplish the first of these. . . .
>
> Western governments are frequently criticized as governments of the capitalist class for the exploitation of the workers. Whatever the truth of this, it would at least mean that in the West there are governments which plan for the welfare of a class. We have not attained even this. Out government concerns itself only with the welfare of an individual and his friends and relations. Eight or nine out of every ten so-called revolutionaries are frustrated politicians or ambitious militarists. . . .

> China today is like England before the Tudors, France before the Bourbons, Russia before the Romanovs. We are capable at present only of civil war, not of genuine revolution.

Tsiang and like-minded thinkers stood on the same bleak shore of doubt where Liang Ch'i-ch'ao had stood in 1903 to bid farewell to freedom. But Tsiang's despair struck even deeper. "I do not demand that this government be enlightened," he wrote, for enlightenment is too abstract a quality to make it the criterion of political legitimacy. "The more enlightened, the better—but I demand only that the central government be able to preserve domestic peace and tranquility."[24]

A few voices were raised in democracy's defense, Hu Shih's the most famous among them. His rejoinder to his friends who had abandoned the liberal cause was argued in predictable terms, but it touched, indirectly, on issues that went beyond the question of a form of government appropriate to the times and China's needs, from which we may gain, in retrospect, a sense of the formidable difficulties that confronted those who would translate liberal doctrine into a Chinese idiom.

In the 1920s, no one had been more adamant than Hu in calling for "a government with a plan"; none had been more anxious than he to dissociate liberalism from the laissez-faire principles of classical liberal thought. Now, however, he constructed his case against "new-style dictatorship" around a proposal for what he called "government by non-action" (*wu-wei cheng-chih*). The idea has its origins in the primordial epoch of Chinese thought. Each of the principal "schools" of early Chinese political thought interpreted in its own manner the paradoxical notion that "through non-action, nothing is left undone" (*wu-wei erh wu pu-wei*). This is the Confucian sage ruler who governs by moral force and himself remains fixed, in the metaphor of the *Analects*, like the polestar, while the constellations turn about it. This is the Legalist ruler who sits motionless and remote, like a great spider at the center of his web of administrative regulations. This is the Taoist who survives in an uncertain and perilous world by mastering the discipline of non-striving compliance with the Way. In practical terms, if one can imagine such a doctrine transformed into policy, *wu-wei* government was credited for stabilizing an empire vastly enlarged but nearly exhausted by the vigorous expansionist reign of Han Wu-ti in the second and first centuries B.C.—a precedent Hu Shih was pleased to cite. Contrary to the claims of the Nationalists, he said, and to the views of those who contended that China's survival depended on a ruthlessly efficient one-man rule, what the country really needed was a relaxation of government demands—the demands, at least, of a government whose appetite overreaches its resources, and whose exactions return no benefit to the people, but only increase the already intolerable burden borne by them.

It was, one may suppose, a painful concession for Hu to admit that

China and the West could, after all, hardly be measured by the same standards: thus far he agreed with T. F. Tsiang. "We are only poor children, how can we dream of imitating the great show of a rich family?" Therefore, as he wrote in 1933, "What China needs now is certainly not the positivist, activist political philosophy current in Europe and America since the nineteenth century. What is needed now is a political philosophy that advocates non-action. When the philosophers of antiquity preached non-action, they did not intend that men should refrain from all activity, but merely to warn against blind and wild action: to urge men to examine the situation in which they found themselves with open eyes, in order to determine, in light of objective material conditions, whether any action is feasible."[25]

Many of Hu's readers greeted this suggestion as, at best, an example of academic whimsey. Hu good-humoredly insisted that it was by no means to be dismissed as "a bad joke": his purpose was to point up the absurdity of such superficial evidence of "progress" as motor roads laid out across what had been productive crop land, for the exclusive use of military transport. It serves our purposes, moreover, to illuminate what may be considered the fundamental and finally insoluble intellectual dilemma that confronted Chinese liberals seeking an indigenous authority for their ideals.

The Chinese tradition of political speculation does not naturally encompass the concept of limited government—the notion, that is, that the government can be at the same time essential and yet less than all-powerful. Chinese thinkers were disposed on this question to assert one extreme view or another. The Legalist claimed that the interests of ruler and state were identical in their magnitude and substance. The Confucian equated government, broadly speaking, with the totality of human social and moral aspiration. The philosophical Taoist denied the relevance of government entirely, viewing it as an artificial hindrance to the natural and spontaneous workings of the Way. These perceptions found their way into our own time, if only as what might best be called cultural instincts. So, as we have seen, Taoist scepticism communicated itself to the quasi-anarchist subtradition that was from the beginning a part of the revolutionary movement; and, as we have also noted, Confucianism shared with revolutionary socialism a vision of the state as an all-encompassing community of faith.

But the view that the government is merely an agency of the community, exercising necessary functions but not in itself to be mistaken for the ends which it serves or invested with a transcendent personality—for this view there was no precedent, no cultural resonance, however faint. The state, wrote Harold Laski in 1925, "is judged not by what it is in theory, but by what it does in practice. The State, therefore, is subject to a moral test of adequacy. There is no *a priori* rightness about its decisions."[26] Hu Shih, Lo Lung-chi, and other persevering liberals measured the governments of their day against this standard and found them woefully lacking. But the combination of prevailing circumstance and lingering prejudice made it impossible to translate into terms sufficiently compelling or practical the idea of a government so limited in its legitimate claims. In respect to its political (as distinct from its social or its educational) program, it was this more than anything else, perhaps, that rendered liberalism not only alien to China, but unassimilable. For in the transition from Confucianism to Communism, from one all-encompassing world view to another, the Chinese held finally to the belief that political processes are the creations, not the creators, of political values.

Hu Shih's defense of democracy in the 1930s provoked as much derision as did his case against dictatorship. Whether they spoke as apologists for the Nanking regime or expressed an educated social and political analysis of China's situation, the advocates of dictatorship uniformly argued that democratic government would demand a much higher level of political experience, social cohesion and intellectual sophistication than the Chinese people possessed or could reasonably aspire to. Hu responded by turning this argument on its head. Democracy, he said, is "kindergarten government," while dictatorship—at least the kind of "modern" or "idealistic" dictatorship that T. F. Tsiang and Ting Wen-chiang and others called for—is "graduate school government." Efficient authoritarianism, Hu insisted, presupposes not only greater social discipline and a higher level of technical administrative competence than China can boast, but also, if it is to achieve the ends that its proponents have in view, a leader, or a party, or an ideology that can attract and sustain mass enthusiasm and generate the attitudes necessary to maintain at all times a high degree of participation in the political life of the community. "Enlightened despotism signifies government by the specially outstanding," Hu wrote; democracy, on the other hand, is "the government of every-day common sense," a government that leaves it to the individual to "muddle through" on his own, politically engaged only to the extent that the management of his own affairs requires it, and, in the process, receiving a political education far more meaningful in relationship to his particular situation than endless hours of Party indoctrination. "In a country like ours, lacking a politically trained population, the best possible political education is a democratic constitutional government which can gradually enlarge the base of political authroity."[27] Hu was no more than rephrasing here an opinion he had expressed nearly twenty years earlier, in furious response to the condescending foreign view that Yuan Shih-k'ai's imperial schemes established beyond dispute that the Chinese are a race incapable of governing themselves democratically. "Young China believes in democracy," he had written then; "it believes that *the only way to have democracy is to have democracy.* Government is an art, and as such it needs practice. I would never have been able to speak English had I never spoken it. The Anglo-Saxon people would never have had democracy had they never practiced democracy."[28]

By temperament and education, Hu Shih was as much an elitist as any of the participants in the 1930s debate on democracy and dictatorship. But, faced by the alternative so starkly portrayed by his opponents, he chose to remain faithful to the liberal side of his beliefs. It was, of course, an academic debate, with little force either to moderate or to undermine the character of the Nanking regime. But the affirmation that democracy is, in the final analysis, simply the right and the ability to order one's life in terms that are relevant to it, a power and a talent that become real as they are exercised—such an affirmation is not lightly to be dismissed. It marks a significant step in the direction of a demythologized ideal of government, whether the myth be that of the superior man who occupies a position of moral ascendancy over society at large; or that of the man of "special competence" whose ascendancy is a matter of intellect and the mastery of technique; or that of the enthusiastic ideologue. And the chasm between ruler and ruled vanishes when the two are united into one, however circumscribed may be the kingdom thus established.

Before we discount too easily the practical value of such an affirmation, we would do well to take account of the uses to which it was put—not by the liberals, but by the Communists, as China's vast social upheaval moved into its climactic stages in the 1940s. Traveling through the Liberated Areas of North China in 1946 and 1947, an American reporter had occasion to inquire of his Red Army guide how the people whom he witnessed practicing an uncomplicated but effective kind of village democracy had been prepared to assume such responsibilities. The answer he received, deep in the northwest hinterland, strikes the ear like a remarkable echo: "It is utterly useless to train the people for democracy beforehand. . . . If the people lead a democratic life, their habits will naturally be transformed. Only through the practice of democracy can you learn democracy."[29]

Epilogue

THROUGHOUT THE DECADES AND THE CENTURIES that we have surveyed here, we have heard those Chinese whose thoughts inclined to speculative consideration of the great issues of their polity expressing their grief and their alarm because of the distance that they perceived dividing the ruler from the ruled. We have seen their perception of the problem change, in response to a flood of unfamiliar experiences and unprecedented ideas, bringing in train a sense both of greater peril and greater possibility. But the concern itself has remained, felt more urgently, perhaps, by the Chinese than it might have been by thinkers whose inherited philosophy did not stress to the same degree the ideal of the moral community. Three times in the last hundred years, the radical disjunction between the claims of those who govern and the condition of those who have borne the burden of being governed has brought the Chinese to the point of attempting revolutionary solutions: in 1911, against the autocracy of the Manchus; in the mid-1920s, against the oppressive anarchy of warlordism; and in the late 1940s, against the failing regime of the Nationalists. (One might add to this list a forth event: the Great Proletarian Cultural Revolution of the 1960s. But this upheaval involved issues of ideology, policy, and personality too complex to digest within the scope of the present discussion.)

The promise of "a democratic life" expressed so matter-of-factly in the late 1940s seemed to vindicate the aspirations of three generations of forward-looking Chinese. But it has been a pledge only half honored. The Chinese Communists early and firmly accepted the view that a morally coherent political order must incorporate the masses as active participants in its constitution. The remarkable organizational apparatus that has been created in the People's Republic is designed not merely to enforce political and social discipline, but also to provide the means

351

whereby popular participation can be mobilized, and through which it can be manipulated. Political participation has itself become a form of political discipline. And for those to whom the ideal of democracy signifies not only the right of access to political processes, but also the freedom to set the terms on which that right will be exercised, this appears as a part of the promise of democracy left unredeemed.

In the first half of the twentieth century, those who have figured in this account as "reformers," "progressives," "radicals," "liberals," or "revolutionaries" demanded, in the changing idiom of changing times and circumstances, liberation from the all-embracing constraints of traditional orthodoxy. They denounced as a tyranny over mind, spirit, and community the totality of political authority, social regulation, and intellectual conformity which constituted the old Chinese order. This demand for liberation expressed itself, however, in two distinct forms. The first of these accepted the inherited premise that human nature is conditioned by environment, but revised the view of the ultimately decisive environmental forces that shape human character. The second, and more radical, expression of the demand for liberation was an attempt to break out of the framework of totalistic assumptions entirely, by asserting that human beings create their own character and, in the process, create the cultural environment in which they live. Behind the New Culture attack upon Confucianism was an attack upon the belief that men are no more than the creatures of a culture over which they have no control.

For reformers like Liang Ch'i-ch'ao and others of his generation, and for "conservative" intellectuals of the 1920s and 1930s, Chinese culture—that is, the collective personality of the nation and the people—was still largely identified with the high culture of old China. Such thinkers might reject the elitist social implications of Confucianism, and the authoritarian political assumptions on which the monarchy rested; but they found it impossible to repudiate the old culture without at the same time undermining the legitimacy of China's claim to nationhood. The New Culture radicals offered an escape from this impasse. Culture is created by people, they proclaimed; therefore, the historically significant cultural mode must be popular. In other words, China's genuine cultural personality is not merely the product of the social and political elite, created and perpetuated from motives of self-interest. China's true culture encompasses also expressions of the popular spirit found in a variety of hitherto neglected or despised social, artistic, and intellectual forms.

It was the New Culture academics, in the course of their scholarly excavations, who disclosed the foundations of this popular culture, barely discernible beneath the debris of the decaying structure of Confucianism; and it was they who sketched the preliminary design for a new culture to rise on the site thus reclaimed. But it was the Chinese Communists who exploited the discovery by turning it to revolutionary purposes. In their understanding, culture is a primary ideological category, as essential in its explanatory significance as are material factors in the shaping of social character. "We Communists of China have for years been struggling not only for the political and economic revolutions, but also for the cultural revolution," declared Mao Tse-tung in 1940. "The aim of all our efforts is the building of a new society and a new nation of the Chinese people. In such a new society and new nation, there will be not only a new political organization and a new economy, but a new culture as well." The content of this culture is accordingly determined: it must be a revolutionary culture embodying the aims of the regime and the society—or, in Mao's words, "The new-democratic culture is the anti-imperialist and anti-feudal culture of the broad masses."[1]

Totalism, not pluralism, is thus the hallmark of China's revolutionary culture. The new regime moved purposefully to satisfy the nationalistic and social aspirations that had impelled it to power. It moved with equal purpose to eradicate the liberal view that state and culture are divisible, and that culture is finally a private responsibility and accomplishment. It established an order in which the demand for collective ideological enthusiasm overwhelmed individual intellectual confidence.

The measure to which liberal ideas may be translated into political and social conduct necessarily reflects the existence and extent of a consensus: common social expectations; a shared confidence that reasonable hopes may be realized within the community; self-limits commonly agreed upon and acknowledged. Such a consensus cannot be imposed, nor can it evolve out of lives too distantly situated, in terms of day-to-day experience, to share a language of aspiration and determination. A liberal consensus presupposes, in fact, a liberal culture—and herein lay the paradox of liberalism in China, and the liberals' dilemma. The dilemma was twofold: how to translate the values of a few into the expectations of the multitude; and how to secure opportunity and protection for the kind of social behavior which those values justify, and which in turn justifies those values. These were problems to which there was no solution in the context of China's public life in the first half of the twentieth century.

The liberals, cosmopolitan offspring of an evolving modern and urban culture, had no access to China's political and social resources. They could cohere only among themselves, in academic and professional congregations vulnerable to repression or neglect. Chinese politics made no natural place for them; they were themselves, in principle and by temperament, incapable of the kind of organized militancy that might have turned them from petitioners into power-brokers. Theirs was a generation that traversed the desert of despair to reach, in the late 1940s, the wastelands of desperation. They entered China's "new-democratic culture" in 1949—barring the few who, like Hu Shih, sought refuge in exile—sharing something of the pride that its nationalist victory engendered, hopeful of a revival of civic vigor, but on the whole reserving judgment on the new regime, and ill prepared to defend themselves against its claims upon their reputations, their talents, and their minds.

The relationship that has existed between Chinese intellectuals and the government of the People's Republic since 1949 does not properly lie within the scope of this narrative. Encountering responsibilities of a magnitude and complexity for which its years in the wilderness had hardly prepared it, the new government relied perforce on the technical and management skills of the "old-style intellectuals"—but on its own terms, which did not tolerate suspended judgment. The 1950s were a hazardous and cruel time for intellectuals compelled to renounce the accomplishments and values of their vocation, and to denounce the friendships of a lifetime. Few resisted: Liang Shu-ming was one who did, and who somehow survived. Most made the confessions and self-criticisms called for, but many found themselves even so unsuitably situated. Lo Lung-chi, who to his subsequent regret took advantage of the false spring of the Hundred Flowers in 1957 to press again his case for "expert administration," complained that "among higher intellectuals there are returned students from England who make their living as drag-coolies, and returned students from the United States who run cigarette stalls."[2] Lo himself, who had until that time played a fairly prominent non-Party role in the administration, was soon relegated to the obscurity in which he died in 1965.

By the mid-1960s, when the country was seized by the convulsions of the Great Proletarian Cultural Revolution, most of the "old-style intellectuals" were old in fact; many had died; over the next decade, some were driven to death. In this vast, ungovernable attempt to make revolution a way of life, an ongoing experience rather than a historical turning-point, there was no place for intellectualism or professionalism. Even the structures of secular education were leveled in the cause of ideological enthusiasm. In the aftermath of this great tempest, earlier motives have reemerged: a concern for industrial and agricultural productivity, for technology and education—even if this means the abandonment of the principle of "socialist egalitarianism," and the encouragement of elitist motives. Under the rubric of the "Four Modernizations," the Chinese leadership has undertaken what looks, on first appraisal, suspiciously like a "Self-strengthening" movement. Under the sponsorship of cultural exchange programs, students are dispatched abroad to immerse themselves preponderantly in technical specializations; foreigners are invited to teach English and similarly exotic subjects in provincial normal schools and universities; contracts are out for the translation of textbooks on a massive scale, from Japanese and other languages; precious foreign exchange is committed to the purchase of industrial and military hardware (and software)—the "machinery and mathematics" of the late twentieth century.

"*Plus ça change . . .* " is, of course, a popular parlor entertainment among historians. None play it more skillfully, perhaps, than those whose study has been the seductive history of the "changeless" Chinese. Matching the present off against the past in this fashion may, indeed, reveal something of the perdurable tensions that beset the relationship between what was once a splendid, self-contained, and condescending civilization, and remains today a self-contained and condescending revolutionary culture, on the one hand; and, on the other, an aggressive, energetic, possessive and, in many ways, culturally unstable intruder.

But it is essentially an ahistorical diversion, likely to obscure more than it reveals. It obscures the fact that between the 1870s and the 1970s China experienced a process of political disintegration and reintegration that left virtually no individual particle of the whole untouched—though we cannot know for sure with what consequences at the level of individual self-perceptions. It obscures the fact that China has undergone, and apparently survived, a century-long social and cultural trauma painful and profound to a degree that is, to us, literally incomprehensible. It obscures the fact that China's political leaders today are masters of their own house as the Self-strengtheners of the 1870s, shoring up a crumbling edifice, were not—the heirs and in part the architects of a triumph over the adversities of social and political anarchy, civil strife, and cultural disorientation such as their predecessors could hardly have envisioned.

This, then, is not a story to which we can set a conclusion. An epilogue must suffice.

In December, 1978, on Peking's "Democracy Wall," a manifesto appeared, a "big-character poster" entitled "The fifth modernization: democracy." It was signed by one Wei Ching-sheng: twenty-nine years old, a junior-highschool graduate who had become, at the age of sixteen, a Red Guard; who had subsequently served as a platoon commander in the People's Liberation Army; and who was employed, in 1978, as an electrician in the Peking public parks administration, with no Party affiliation. A modern young man, one might say, born as the revolution came to power, one of the numberless victims of the "ten lost years" of the Cultural Revolution, a common young man of the new order.* But a young man with ideas uncommonly heard, as it turned out, who in his

---

* For the story of "Democracy Wall," and for Wei Ching-sheng's enormously moving personal history, see Roger Garside, *Coming Alive: China after Mao* (McGraw-Hill Book Co., 1981), especially chapters 10–12.

off-time edited a mimeographed underground newspaper called *Explorations* (*T'an-so*), in which his manifesto had also appeared. This is part of what Wei Ching-sheng had to say in his message posted on a Peking wall:

> In the course of history, dictators have spoken in many languages and have used varying methods, but they have all lectured their good people on the same theme: because we live in society, society's interests must come first. . . .
>
> Man *is* pre-eminently a social being, and has always lived in a given society, but society is made up of different individuals and each individual, despite his contact with other people, maintains his existence independently, in accordance with his own particular nature. Thus, the social character of humanity stems from a convergence of these numerous, different common points and inerests, and the structure of society must be conditioned by the existence of the individuals who compose it. We have to conclude, therefore, that if individuality and sociability are the two main components of human nature, individuality comes first.
>
> However the difference between totalitarianism and democracy cannot be reduced to an equation between individuality and sociability. It is a difference of mode. If totalitarianism is to exist at all, it can only do so through the suppression of individuality. That is why it is essentially a form of professional slavery. Democracy on the other hand implies a cohesion of individuals and that is why it is in essence a form of cooperation. No one can point to a totalitarian society which does not oppress the individual, and no one can cite a democracy which does not encompass some kind of compatibility between its citizens. Democracy is founded on individual needs. Do you prefer to live free or enslaved? For the majority of Chinese this is a superfluous question.[3]

In the spring of 1979, Wei Ching-sheng was arrested; six months later he was tried and found guilty of "counter-revolutionary crimes of a serious nature." He was sentenced to fifteen years imprisonment, and the loss of his political rights for an additional three years; his appeal was denied. "You have read it yourself," the prosecutor said. "It is decreed in our Constitution that there is freedom of belief. You can believe or not believe in Marxist-Leninism and the thoughts of Mao Tse-tung as you wish, but you are absolutely not permitted to oppose them. . . . If your power had the power to seize our power . . . what power would our nine hundred million people have left to speak of? In a class society, the law and the country are the same. . . ."[4]

It would be presumptuous to suppose that we have, in the preceding pages, adequately assessed the motives that lay behind these different messages. It is at least evident, however, that the great issues of individual and collective identity with which the Chinese have contended in their long struggle to come to terms with their past and their present, their place in history, and in the world at large, are issues neither resolved, nor yet forgotten. It is not presumptuous to hope that the second voice will not silence the first.

Notes

Chapter 1: The Inheritance (pp. 1–23)

1. Arthur Waley, *Translations from the Chinese* (New York: Alfred A. Knopf, 1941), p. 242.
2. Arthur Waley (trans.), *The Analects* (London: Allen and Unwin, 1938), p. 222.
3. Henry Yule and Henri Cordier, *Cathay and the Way Thither* (London: Hakluyt Society, 1913–1916), vol. III, p. 74.
4. Quoted in Tse-tsung Chow, "The Anti-Confucian Movement in Early Republican China," in A. F. Wright (ed.), *The Confucian Persuasion* (Stanford: Stanford University Press, 1960), p. 292.
5. Chan Wing-tsit, *A Sourcebook in Chinese Philosophy* (Princeton: Princeton University Press, 1963), p. 69.
6. Burton Watson (trans.), *Hsun Tzu: Basic Writings* (New York: Columbia University Press, 1963), p. 171.
7. Chan, *Sourcebook*, p. 36.
8. Ibid., p. 32.
9. W. A. C. H. Dobson (trans.), *Mencius* (Toronto: University of Toronto Press, 1963), p. 166.
10. See H. G. Creel, *Confucius: The Man and the Myth* (New York: John Day, 1949), especially chapters 10 and 15 and the Postscript.
11. Dobson, *Mencius*, p. 166 (last phrase modified).
12. Ibid., p. 66. The phrase, "Heaven sees . . ." etc. is found in the Shu ching; see James Legge (trans.), *The Chinese Classics*, V. 1. ii. 7.
13. Waley, *The Analects*, p. 214.
14. Ibid., p. 199.
15. Dobson, *Mencius*, p. 147; and Chan, *Sourcebook*, p. 76.

16. Watson, *Hsun Tzu*, p. 162.
17. Ibid., pp. 18–19.
18. Chan, *Sourcebook*, p. 98.
19. Ibid., p. 112.
20. Ibid., p. 101.
21. *Lun-yü* 2:12.
22. Chan, *Sourcebook*, p. 100.
23. Ibid., p. 87.
24. Waley, *The Analects*, p. 88.
25. S. Wells Williams, *The Middle Kingdom* (New York: Charles Scribner's Sons, 1895) vol. I, pp. 382–383.
26. Burton Watson (trans.), *Records of the Grand Historian* (New York: Columbia University Press, 1961), vol. I, p. 121.
27. William Theodore de Bary and others (eds.), *Sources of Chinese Tradition* (New York: Columbia University Press, 1960), p. 175.
28. René Grousset, *The Rise and Splendor of the Chinese Empire* (Berkeley and Los Angeles: University of California Press, 1953) p. 61. A more restrained translation of the same passage is found in De Bary, *Sources*, p. 259.
29. Harold L. Kahn, *Monarchy in the Emperor's Eyes* (Cambridge, Mass.: Harvard University Press, 1971), pp. 115–116.
30. Waley, *Translations from the Chinese*, p. 142.
31. Chang Chung-li, *The Chinese Gentry* (Seattle: University of Washington Press, 1955), p. xix.
32. John Dewey, "What Holds China Back?" *Asia*, May 1920; reprinted in *Characters and Events* (New York: Henry Holt & Co., 1929), vol. I, p. 212.
33. Karl Mannheim, "Conservative Thought," in Kurt Wolff (ed.), *From Karl Mannheim* (New York: Oxford University Press, 1971), p. 173. For a discussion of "conservatism" and "traditionalism" see J. G. A. Pocock, "Time, Institutions and Action: An Essay on Traditions and Their Understanding," in *Politics and Experience: Essays Presented to Professor Michael Oakeshott on the Occasion of His Retirement* (Cambridge: Cambridge University Press, 1968), pp. 209–237.
34. Mircea Eliade, *Cosmos and History* (New York: Harper & Row, 1959), p. 95 and *passim*. It should be noted, however, that the absence from the Chinese historical sense of the "cosmogonic act" differentiates the Chinese from those cultures which Eliade characterizes as "primitive" or "archaic." For a study of Chinese historical stereotypes, see Arthur F. Wright, "Sui Yang-ti: Personality and Stereotype," in A. F. Wright (ed.), *The Confucian Persuasion*, pp. 47–76.
35. Eliade, *Cosmos and History*, p. 89.
36. Benjamin I. Schwartz, *In Search of Wealth and Power: Yen Fu and the West* (Cambridge, Mass.: Harvard University Press, 1964), p. 18.
37. Jonathan Spence, *Emperor of China* (New York: Alfred Knopf, 1974), pp. 72–75.
38. Teng Ssu-yü and John K. Fairbank (eds.), *China's Response to the West* (Cambridge, Mass.: Harvard University Press, 1964), p. 18.
39. Ibid., p. 87; translation substantially modified.

Chapter 2: Confucian Criticism (pp. 24-47)

1. *Lun-yü* 2:3
2. De Bary, *Sources of Chinese Tradition*, pp. 481-486.
3. Waley, *Translations from the Chinese*, p. 324.
4. Louis J. Gallagher, S.J. (trans.), *China in the Sixteenth Century: The Journals of Matthew Ricci 1583-1610* (New York: Random House, 1953), p. 55.
5. Quoted in Adolf Reichwein, *China and Europe: Intellectual and Artistic Contacts in the Eighteenth Century* (New York: Alfred A. Knopf, 1925; reprinted Taipei: Ch'eng-wen Publishing Co., 1967), pp. 80-81.
6. Ibid., p. 89.
7. Voltaire, *Philosophical Dictionary*, translated, with an introduction and glossary by Peter Gay (New York: Basic Books, 1962) vol. I, pp. 169-170.
8. Reichwein, *China and Europe*, p. 95.
9. *The Wealth of Nations*, Chapter VIII.
10. *On Liberty*, Chapter III.
11. Edward A. Ross, *The Changing Chinese: The Conflict of Oriental and Western Cultures in China* (New York: The Century Co., 1911), p. 57.
12. James Matheson, *The Present Position and Prospects of the British Trade with China* (London, 1838), quoted in Peter Ward Fay, *The Opium War* (Chapel Hill: University of North Carolina Press, 1975), p. 121.
13. Gallagher, *China in the Sixteenth Century*, p. 26.
14. Peter Gay, *The Enlightenment: An Interpretation: The Rise of Modern Paganism* (New York: Alfred A. Knopf, 1967), chapter 7 *passim* and p. 419.
15. F. W. Mote, "China's Past in the Study of China Today" *Journal of Asian Studies* 33.1:107-120 (Nov. 1972).
16. Burton Watson (trans.), *Cold Mountain: 100 Poems by the T'ang Poet Han-shan* (New York: Columbia University Press, 1970), p. 100.
17. *Lun-yü* 8:13.
18. In the discussion of the thought of Huang Tsung-hsi, Ku Yen-wu, and Wang Fu-chih that follows I have relied in the first instance largely on translations that appear in De Bary, *Sources of Chinese Tradition*, chapter 22 ("The Late Harvest of Confucian Scholarship"), pp. 582-629. In most cases, however, I have modified the wording in accordance with my reading of the original texts (using for this purpose the Kuo-hsueh chi-pen ts'ung-shu edition published in Taipei under the general editorship of Wang Yun-wu), or the very useful annotated Japanese translations by Gotō Motomi and Yamanoi Yū in *Min-matsu Shin-sho seiji hyōron shū* (An Anthology of Late-Ming Early-Ch'ing Political Criticism) published in 1972 by Heibonsha, Tokyo. Where I have relied on other texts or translations, that fact is noted.
19. Liang Ch'i-ch'ao, *Intellectual Trends in the Ch'ing Period*, translated with introduction and notes by Immanuel C. Y. Hsü (Cambridge, Mass.: Harvard University Press, 1959), p. 38.
20. David S. Nivison, *The Life and Thought of Chang Hsueh-ch'eng (1738-1801)* (Stanford: Stanford University Press, 1966), p. 16.
21. Liang Ch'i-ch'ao, *Intellectual Trends*, p. 38.

22. Hsiao Kung-ch'üan, *Chung-kuo cheng-chih ssu-hsiang shih* (A History of Chinese Political Thought) (Taipei, 1954), p. 637.
23. *Aphorisms Concerning the Interpretation of Nature and the Kingdom of Man*, number 36.
24. The remark is by Chang Tung-sun, appended to Liang Ch'i-ch'ao's "Jen-sheng-kuan yü k'o-hsueh" (The Philosophy of Life and Science) in *K'o-hsueh yü jen-sheng-kuan* (Science and the Philosophy of Life) (Shanghai, 1923).
25. The forty-seventh aphorism.
26. Hu Shih, *The Chinese Renaissance* (Chicago: University of Chicago Press, 1934), pp. 70–71.
27. Joseph R. Levenson, *Confucian China and its Modern Fate: The Problem of Intellectual Continuity* (London: Routledge and Kegan Paul, 1958), p. 13.
28. *Social Contract: Essays by Locke, Hume and Rousseau*, with an introduction by Sir Ernest Barker, (London, New York, Toronto: Oxford University Press, 1947), p. 300.
29. Roger D. Masters, *The Political Philosophy of Rousseau* (Princeton: Princeton University Press, 1968), p. 355.

Chapter 3: The Nineteenth Century: Rebellion and Restoration (pp. 48–76)

1. Edict of December 28, 1776. Translated in L. C. Goodrich, The *Literary Inquisition of Ch'ien Lung*, 2nd ed. (New York: Paragon Reprint Corp., 1966), p. 144.
2. H. B. Morse, *The Chronicles of the East India Company Trading to China, 1635–1834* (Cambridge, Mass., Harvard University Press, 1926), vol. II, p. 245.
3. J. L. Cranmer-Byng, "Lord Macartney's Embassy to Peking, 1793" *Journal of Oriental Studies* 4.1&2:164 (1957–58, published 1960).
4. William Theodore de Bary, "A Reappraisal of Neo-Confucianism," in A. F. Wright (ed.), *Studies in Chinese Thought* (Chicago: University of Chicago Press, 1953), p. 98. The sentiments are those of Ch'eng Hao (1032–1085).
5. Liang Ch'i-ch'ao, *Intellectual Trends in the Ch'ing Period*, p. 78.
6. Quoted in Chang Hao, *Liang Ch'i-ch'ao and Intellectual Transition in China, 1890–1907* (Cambridge, Mass.: Harvard University Press, 1971) p. 30.
7. Teng Ssu-yü and J. K. Fairbank (eds.), *China's Response to the West*, p. 31.
8. William Theodore de Bary (ed.), *Sources of Chinese Tradition*, p. 678.
9. Fred W. Drake, *China Charts the World: Hsu Chi-yü and His Geography of 1848* (Cambridge, Mass.: East Asian Research Center, 1975), p. 189.
10. Ibid., pp. 35–36.
11. *The Missionary Herald* (Boston), vol. 38, p. 336 (August 1842).
12. Stuart Creighton Miller, "Ends and Means: Missionary Justification of Force in Nineteenth Century China," in J. K. Fairbank (ed.), *The Missionary Enterprise in China and America* (Cambridge, Mass.: Harvard University Press, 1974), p. 263.

13. Ibid., p. 264.
14. Masataka Bannō, *China and the West, 1858-1861: The Origins of the Tsung-li Yamen* (Cambridge, Mass.: Harvard University Press, 1964), p. 10.
15. Mary C. Wright, *The Last Stand of Chinese Conservatism: The T'ung Chih Restoration, 1862-1874* (Stanford: Stanford University Press, 1957), p. 38.
16. Ibid., pp. 261-263.
17. William Milne, Jr., quoted in Peter Ward Fay, *The Opium War*, p. 88.
18. Jen Yu-wen, *The Taiping Revolutionary Movement* (New Haven and London: Yale University Press, 1973), p. 27.
19. Peter Duus, "Science and Salvation in China: The Life and Work of W. A. P. Martin," *Papers on China* (Cambridge, Mass.: East Asia Program of the Committee on Regional Studies, Harvard University) vol. 10, p. 103 (1956).
20. T. T. Meadows, *The Chinese and Their Rebellions* (Stanford, Calif.: Academic Reprints, 1953), p. 446. (Originally published in 1856.)
21. Vincent Shih, *The Taiping Ideology: Its Sources, Interpretations, and Influences* (Seattle and London: University of Washington Press, 1967), p. 417.
22. Bannō, *China and the West*, p. 237.
23. Shih, *The Taiping Ideology*, p. 406.
24. Ibid., p. 76.
25. A modification of translations in Jen, *The Taiping Revolutionary Movement*, p. 231 and Shih, *The Taiping Ideology*, p. 398.
26. Wright, *The Last Stand of Chinese Conservatism*, p. 63.
27. Knight Biggerstaff, *The Earliest Modern Government Schools in China* (Ithaca: Cornell University Press, 1961), p. 95.
28. Teng and Fairbank, *China's Response to the West*, p. 83.
29. Dun J. Li, *The Essence of Chinese Civilization* (Princeton, Toronto and London: D. Van Nostrand Co., 1967), pp. 351-355.
30. Wright, *The Last Stand of Chinese Conservatism*, p. 141.
31. Teng and Fairbank, *China's Response to the West*, pp. 76-77.
32. Feng Kuei-fen, "Chih yang ch'i i" (On the Manufacture of Foreign Weapons), in Shih Chün (ed.), *Chung-kuo chin-tai ssu-hsiang shih ts'an-k'ao tzu-liao chien-pien* (A Survey of Source Materials on Modern Chinese Intellectual History) (Peking, 1957), pp. 143-144. A different translation may be found in Teng and Fairbank, *China's Response to the West*, pp. 52-54.
33. Feng Kuei-fen, "Ts'ai hsi-hsueh i" (On the Adoption of Western Learning), ibid., p. 139. See also Teng and Fairbank, *China's Response to the West*, pp. 51-52.
34. See Chan Wing-tsit (trans.), *Instructions for Practical Living and Other Neo-Confucian Writings by Wang Yang-ming* (New York and London: Columbia University Press, 1963), *passim* and, in the second instance, p. 273.
35. Teng and Fairbank, *China's Response to the West*, p. 51.
36. De Bary, *Sources of Chinese Tradition*, pp. 714-717.
37. John K. Fairbank, Katherine Frost Bruner, and Elizabeth MacLeod Matheson (eds.), *The I. G. in Peking: Letters of Robert Hart, Chinese Maritime Customs, 1868-1907* (Cambridge, Mass.: Belknap Press of Harvard University, 1976), vol. I, p. 119 (letter of August 26, 1873).

Chapter 4: The Nineteenth Century: Reform (pp. 77–132)

1. *The Emperor Kuang Hsü's Reform Decrees, 1898,* reprinted from the *North China Daily News* (Shanghai: North China Herald, 1900), p. 11.
2. Teng Ssu-yü and J. K. Fairbank (eds.), *China's Response to the West,* p. 177.
3. K'ang Yu-wei's seventh memorial (February 1898), quoted in Don C. Price, *Russia and the Roots of the Chinese Revolution 1896–1911* (Cambridge, Mass.: Harvard University Press, 1974), p. 46.
4. This somewhat florid translation is from *The Emperor Kuang Hsü's Reform Decrees,* true to the meaning of the Chinese text but a pretty free rendering of it. See *Kuang Hsu ch'ao tung-hua lu,* compiled by Chu Shou-p'ing (1909), edited and punctuated by Chang Ching-lu and others (Peking, 1958), p. 4189 (= 24th year of Kuang Hsu, p. 173).
5. Hsiao Kung-ch'üan, *A Modern China and a New World: K'ang Yu-wei, Reformer and Utopian, 1858–1927* (Seattle and London: University of Washington Press, 1975), p. 406.
6. Both quotations from K'ang Yu-wei's autobiographical account, translated in R. C. Howard, "K'ang Yu-wei (1858–1927): His Intellectual Background and Early Thought," in A. F. Wright and Denis Twitchett (eds.), *Confucian Personalities* (Stanford: Stanford University Press, 1962), pp. 301–302.
7. Letter dismissing Captian Elliot (1841), in H. B. Morse, *The International Relations of the Chinese Empire* (London: Longmans, Green & Co., 1910–18) vol. I, p. 642.
8. S. Wells Williams, *The Middle Kingdom,* vol. I, p. 172.
9. *The Travels of Marco Polo,* translated and introduced by Ronald Latham (London: The Folio Society, 1968), p. 179.
10. Rhoads Murphey, *Shanghai: Key to Modern China* (Cambridge, Mass.: Harvard University Press, 1953), p. 9.
11. Shih Chün (ed.), *Chung-kuo chin-tai ssu-hsiang shih ts'an-k'ao tzu-liao chien-pien,* p. 138.
12. Murphey, *Shanghai: Key to Modern China,* p. 6.
13. Williams, *The Middle Kingdom,* vol. I, p. 108.
14. W. A. P. Martin, *A Cycle of Cathay* (Edinburgh and London: Oliphant Anderson and Ferrier, 1896), p. 298.
15. Jonathan Spence, *To Change China: Western Advisers in China, 1620–1960* (Boston and Toronto: Little, Brown & Co., 1969), pp. 142–143.
16. Ibid., pp. 148–150.
17. Howard, "K'ang Yu-wei," p. 305.
18. *The Autobiography of Fukuzawa Yukichi,* revised translation by Eiichi Kiyooka (New York and London: Columbia University Press, 1966), p. 247.
19. Spence, *To Change China,* pp. 152–156.
20. Martin, *A Cycle of Cathay,* pp. 299–301.
21. Spence, *To Change China,* p. 150.
22. Quoted in Donald W. Treadgold, *The West in Russia and China: Religious and Secular Thought in Modern Times. Volume 2: China, 1582–1949* (Cambridge: Cambridge University Press, 1973), p. 65.
23. W. A. P. Martin, *Hanlin Papers, or Essays on the Intellectual Life of the*

Chinese (1880), cited in Spence, *To Change China*, p. 139.

24. Adrian A. Bennett and Kwang-Ching Liu, "Christianity in the Chinese Idiom: Young J. Allen and the Early *Chiao-hui hsin-pao*, 1868–1870," in J. K. Fairbank (ed.), *The Missionary Enterprise in China and America*, p. 192.

25. Roswell S. Britton, *The Chinese Periodical Press, 1800–1912* (Shanghai: Kelly & Walsh, Ltd., 1933), p. 23.

26. Ibid., p. 53.

27. Ibid., p. 42; Paul A. Cohen, *Between Tradition and Modernity: Wang T'ao and Reform in Late Ch'ing China* (Cambridge, Mass.: Harvard University Press, 1974), p. 77.

28. Britton, *The Chinese Periodical Press*, pp. 64–65.

29. Quoted in Harold Quigley, *China's Politics in Perspective* (Minneapolis: University of Minnesota Press, 1962), p. 22. See also Williams, *The Middle Kingdom*, vol. I, p. 420.

30. Cohen, *Between Tradition and Modernity*, p. 11.

31. Ibid., p. 15.

32. Hsiao, *A Modern China and a New World*, pp. 510–511, quoting Fryer's *Tso-chih chu-yen* (Homely Words to Aid Government, 1885).

33. Cohen, *Between Tradition and Modernity*, pp. 122–125.

34. Ibid., pp. 205, 203, 207.

35. Ibid., p. 200.

36. Ibid., p. 225.

37. Ibid., p. 183.

38. Cheng Kuan-ying, "Hsi hsueh" (Western learning), in Shih, *Ssu-hsiang shih . . .* , p. 232.

39. Cheng Kuan-ying, "I-yuan shang" (On Parliamentary Government), ibid., pp. 238–239.

40. Ho Kai and Hu Li-yuan, "Hsin cheng lun-i" (A Discussion of Political Reform), ibid., p. 198.

41. Ibid., p. 174.

42. Cohen, *Between Tradition and Modernity*, p. 207.

43. Frederic Wakeman, Jr., *The Fall of Imperial China* (New York: The Free Press, 1975) pp. 165–168.

44. Cohen, *Between Tradition and Modernity*, p. 221.

45. Ho Kai and Hu Li-yuan, "Hsin cheng lun-i," in Shih, *Ssu-hsiang shih . . .* , p. 216.

46. Quoted in T'ang Chih-chün, *Wu-hsu pien-fa jen-wu chuan kao* (Draft Biographies of Personalities Involved in the Reform Movement of 1898) (Peking, 1961), pp. 59–60.

47. K'ang Yu-wei's autobiographical account, in Lo Jung-pang (ed. and trans.), *K'ang Yu-wei: A Biography and a Symposium* (Association for Asian Studies/University of Arizona Press, 1967), p. 38.

48. Ibid., pp. 41–42.

49. See James Legge, *The Chinese Classics*, vol. V, pp. 55–57 and Prolegomena, p. 56.

50. Joseph R. Levenson, "Liao P'ing and the Confucian Departure from History," in Wright and Twitchett (eds.), *Confucian Personalities*, p. 319.

51. Liang Ch'i-ch'ao, *Intellectual Trends in the Ch'ing Period*, pp. 93, 99.

52. Fung Yu-lan, *A History of Chinese Philosophy*, trans. by Derk Bodde (Princeton: Princeton University Press, 1952–1953), vol. II, pp. 129–130.

53. Ibid., p. 675.

54. Ibid., p. 683 (translation modified).

55. Hsiao, *A Modern China and a New World*, pp. 202–203.

56. K'ang Yu-wei's autobiographical account, in Lo, *K'ang Yu-wei*, p. 143.

57. Translated in Hellmut Wilhelm, "Poems from the Hall of Obscured Brightness," in Lo, *K'ang Yu-wei*, p. 328.

58. George Kateb, *Utopia and Its Enemies* (Glencoe: The Free Press, 1963), pp. 9, 11.

59. Hsiao Kung-ch'üan, "K'ang Yu-wei's Excursion into Science: *Lectures on the Heavens,*" in Lo, *K'ang Yu-wei*, p. 387.

60. J. K. Fairbank and others (eds.), *The I. G. in Peking*, vol. I, p. 500 (letter of November 18, 1883).

61. Cohen, *Between Tradition and Modernity*, pp. 242–243 and Part IV *passim*.

62. Joseph R. Levenson, "'History' and 'Value': The Tensions of Intellectual Choice in Modern China," in A. F. Wright (ed.), *Studies in Chinese Thought*, pp. 146–194. This is an early statement of an interpretation more fully developed in Levenson's later scholarship.

63. Fairbank (ed.), *The I. G. in Peking*, vol. II, p. 1070 (letter of June 21, 1896).

Chapter 5: The Revolution of 1911: Intellectuals as Political Entrepreneurs (pp. 133–202)

1. Philip C. Huang, *Liang Ch'i-ch'ao and Modern Chinese Liberalism* (Seattle and London: University of Washington Press, 1972), p. 74.

2. Hu Shih, *Hu Shih liu-hsueh jih-chi* (Hu Shih's Diary of His Years as a Student Abroad) (Taipei, 1959), p. 122.

3. Karl Mannheim, *Ideology and Utopia*, trans. by Louis Wirth and Edward Shils (New York: Harcourt, Brace & World, 1955), p. 9.

4. Both quotations are from William L. Langer, *The Diplomacy of Imperialism* (New York: Alfred A. Knopf, 2nd ed. 1951), pp. 505, 508.

5. Edict of Janurary 29, 1901, in *Kuang Hsu ch'ao tung-hua lu* p. 4601. (26th year of Kuang Hsu, p. 135.)

6. Yuan Shih-k'ai, *Yang-shou-yuan tsou-i chi-yao*, edited by Shen Tsu-hsien (Memorials and papers from the Garden for the Cultivation of Longevity) (Hsiang-ch'eng: Honan, 1937), *chüan* 35, pp. 2b–3b.

7. Donald Keene, "The Sino-Japanese War of 1894–95 and Its Cultural Effects in Japan," in D. Shively (ed.), *Tradition and Modernization in Japanese Culture* (Princeton: Princeton University Press, 1971), p. 143.

8. This account of Chinese students in Japan is based primarily on the following: Sanetō Keishū, *Chūgokujin Nihon Ryūgaku Shi* (A History of Chinese Students in Japan) (Tokyo, rev. ed., 1970); and Fang Chao-ying, *Ch'ing-mo Min-ch'u yang-hsueh hsueh-sheng t'i-ming-lu ch'u-chi* (A first Collection of Records of Students Studying Abroad in the Late Ch'ing and Early Republican Period) (Nankang, 1962). Information concerning examination quotas is taken from

Chang Chung-li, *The Chinese Gentry* (Seattle: University of Washington Press, 1955.)

9. Liang Ch'i-ch'ao, *Hsin Ta-lu yu-chi chieh-lu* (A Brief Account of Travels in the New World), in *Yin-ping-shih ho-chi* (Collected Works from the Ice-Drinker's Studio) (Shanghai, 1936), Chuan-chi *chüan* 22, p. 36. (Hereafter YPSHC/CC [Chuan-chi] or YPSHC/WC [Wen-chi].)

10. Sanetō, *Chūgokujin Nihon Ryūgaku Shi*, pp. 193–194. It is worth noting that this little book was written not by Japanese, but by Chinese anxious to spare their compatriots confusion and embarrassment.

11. G. B. Sansom, *The Western World and Japan* (London: The Cresset Press, 1950), p. 428.

12. Tozama Masakazu, "On the Principles of Sociology," trans. in Donald Keene, "The First Japanese Translations of European Literature," *The American Scholar* 45.2:276–277. (Spring 1976).

13. T. H. Huxley, *Evolution and Ethics and Other Essays*, quoted in William Irvine, *Apes, Angels and Victorians: The Story of Darwin, Huxley, and Evolution* (New York: McGraw-Hill, 1972), p. 348.

14. Hou Lin, "Yen Fu ti fan-i" (The Translations of Yen Fu), reprinted in Chang Ching-lu (ed.), *Chung-kuo chin-tai ch'u-pan shih-liao, erh pien* (Materials on the History of Modern Chinese Publishing, second collection) (Peking, 1957), p. 115. The Chinese for the last line reads: "I li chin fen-ming, tsao-hua yuan wu kuo."

15. Benjamin I. Schwartz, *In Search of Wealth and Power: Yen Fu and the West* (Cambridge, Mass.: Belknap Press of Harvard University Press, 1964), p. 99.

16. Hu Shih, *Ssu-shih tzu-shu* (A Self-Account at Forty) (Taipei, 1959), pp. 49–50.

17. Sanetō, *Chūgokujin Nihon Ryūgaku Shi*, p. 494.

18. Mary B. Rankin, *Early Chinese Revolutionaries: Radical Intellectuals in Shanghai and Chekiang, 1902–1911* (Cambridge, Mass.: Harvard University Press, 1971), p. 66.

19. Tsou Jung, *Ko-ming chün* (The Revolutionary Army), ed. published in Hong Kong in 1903, reprinted in John Lust, *The Revolutionary Army: A Chinese Nationalist Tract of 1903* (The Hague/Paris: Mouton & Co., 1968), pp. 1, 5.

20. Chang Ping-lin, "Po K'ang Yu-wei lun ko-ming shu" (In Refutation of K'ang Yu-wei's Discussion of Revolution), in Shih Chün (ed.), *Chung-kuo chin-tai ssu-hsiang shih ts'an-k'ao tzu-liao chien-pien*, p. 602.

21. For Liang's self-appraisal see Liang Ch'i-ch'ao, *Intellectual Trends in the Ch'ing Period*, pp. 98–107.

22. Ting Wen-chiang (comp.), *Liang Jen-kung hsien-sheng nien-p'u ch'ang-pien ch'u-kao* (A Preliminary Chronology of the Life of Liang Jen-kung [Ch'i-ch'ao]) (Taipei, 1959), p. 15.

23. Liang Ch'i-ch'ao, "*Ch'ing-i pao* i pai ts'e ch'u-tz'u" (Commemorating the One Hundreth Issue of *Ch'ing-i pao*), YPSHC/WC 6.54.

24. Edict of February 14, 1900, in *Kuang Hsu ch'ao tung-hua lu* pp. 4470–4471. (26th year of Kuang Hsu, pp. 4–5.)

25. Quoted from a contemporary Japanese account in Marius B. Jansen, *The Japanese and Sun Yat-sen* (Cambridge, Mass.: Harvard University Press, 1954), p. 80.

26. Liang Ch'i-ch'ao, *Hsin min shuo* (On the New People), "Lun kuo-chia ssu-hsiang" (On Nationalist Sentiments), YPSHC/CC 4.16.

27. Ibid., "Lun chin-pu" (On Progress), YPSHC/CC 4.58.

28. Ibid., "Lun tzu-yu" (On Freedom), YPSHC/CC 4.40.
29. Liang Ch'i-ch'ao, "Lun chuan-chih cheng-t'i yu pai hai yü chun-chu erh wu i li" (Autocracy is a Hundred Times Worse Than Monarchy, and in No Way Better), YPSHC/WC 9.101.
30. *Hsin min shuo*, "Lun ch'üan-li ssu-hsiang" (On the Idea of Political Rights), YPSHC/CC 4.39.
31. Ibid., "Lun chin-ch'ü mao-hsien" (On Stalwartly Taking Risks), YPSHC/CC 4.23 and 29–30.
32. Liang Ch'i-ch'ao, "Shih chung te-hsing hsiang-fan hsiang-ch'eng i" (Ten Moral Categories: Differences and Similarities), YPSHC/WC 5.48–49.
33. Headline of a story that ran in *The Boston Herald*, May 26, 1903, is quoted from Joseph R. Levenson, *Liang Ch'i-ch'ao and the Mind of Modern China* (London: Thames and Hudson, 2nd rev. ed. 1959), p. 71. I am indebted to Professor David M. Deal for calling my attention to the headline in the *Walla Walla Union* of August 29, 1903.
34. Liang Ch'i-ch'ao, *Hsin Ta-lu yu-chi chieh-lu*, YPSHC/CC 22.124. Other quotations concerning Liang's American tour are from the same source, *passim*.
35. Liang Ch'i-ch'ao, "Cheng-chih-hsueh ta-chia Po-lun-chih-li chih hsueh-shuo" (The Theories of the Great Political Scholar Bluntschli), YPSHC/WC 13.86.
36. Liang Ch'i-ch'ao, "K'ai-ming chuan-chih lun" (The Theory of Enlightened Autocracy), YPSHC/WC 17.50.
37. "Cheng-chih-hsueh ta-chia Po-lun-chih-li chih hsueh-shuo" YPSHC/WC 13.69.
38. T'an Ssu-t'ung, *Jen hsueh* (A study of Humane Affection) (Taipei, 1958), p. 56. Liang Ch'i-ch'ao quotes this passage in his *Intellectual Trends . . . ,* and quite specifically includes the Ch'ing dynasty in T'an's indictment; see YPSHC/CC 34.68.
39. Liang Ch'i-ch'ao, *Wu-hsu cheng-pien chi: T'an Ssu-t'ung chuan* (A Record of the 1898 Reforms: The Biography of T'an Ssu-t'ung), YPSHC/CC 1.109.
40. Chang Ping-lin, "Po Chung-kuo yung wan-kuo-hsin-yü shuo" (In Refutation of the Proposal that China Should Use Esperanto), *Min pao*, no. 21, p. 70.
41. Lu Hsun, "Some Recollections of Chang T'ai-yen [Ping-lin]," *Selected Works* (Peking: Foreign Languages Press, 1956–60), vol. IV, pp. 266–268.
42. Charlotte Furth, "The Sage as Rebel: The Inner World of Chang Ping-lin," in C. Furth (ed.), *The Limits of Change: Essays on Conservative Alternatives in Republican China* (Cambridge, Mass.: Harvard University Press, 1976), pp. 117, 149.
43. Chang Ping-lin, "Ssu huo lun" (On the Four Varieties of Humbug), *Min pao*, no. 22, pp. 1–3.
44. Harold Z. Schiffrin, *Sun Yat-sen and the Origins of the Chinese Revolution* (Berkeley and Los Angeles: University of California Press, 1968), p. 365.
45. Sun Yat-sen, "Fa-k'an tz'u" (Dedication), *Min pao*, no. 1.
46. Cited in Shimada Kenji and Ono Shinji, *Shin-gai Kakumei no Shisō* (The Intellectual Background of the 1911 Revolution) (Tokyo, 1969), p. 148.
47. Ch'en T'ien-hua, *Ching-shih-chung* (The Tocsin), in *Hsin-hai ko-ming* (The 1911 Revolution; edited by Chung-kuo shih-hsueh hui, 8 vols) (Shanghai, 1957), vol. II, p. 121. Cf. text in Ono and Shimada, op. cit. pp. 99–100.

48. "Ch'en Hsing-t'ai [T'ien-hua] hsien-sheng chüeh-ming shu" (Ch'en T'ien-hua's Last Letter), *Min pao*, no. 2, p. 1.

49. Ch'en T'ien-hua, "Lun Chung-kuo i kai-ch'uang min-chu cheng-t'i" (That It Is Appropriate for China to Establish a Democratic Form of Government), *Min pao*, no. 1, p. 48.

50. Wang Ching-wei, "Min-tsu ti kuo-min" (Race and Citizenry), *Min pao*, nos. 1 and 2; quotes here from no. 2, p. 18 and no. 1, p. 31.

51. Hu Han-min, *"Min pao chih liu ta chu-i"* (The Six Great Principles of *Min pao*), *Min pao*, no. 3, pp. 9–11. Cf. text in *Hsin-hai ko-ming*, vol. II, pp. 262–264.

52. Cited in Michael Gasster, *Chinese Intellectuals and the Revolution of 1911: The Birth of Modern Chinese Radicalism* (Seattle and London: University of Washington Press, 1969). p. 140.

53. Wang Ching-wei, "Po *Hsin-min ts'ung-pao* tsui-chin chih fei ko-ming lun" (In Refutation of the Most Recent Anti-Revolutionary Arguments of *Hsin-min ts'ung-pao*), *Min pao*, no. 4, p. 30.

54. "Chün cheng-fu hsuan-yen" (Manifesto of the Military Government), *Hsin-hai ko-ming*, vol. II, p. 16.

55. Ch'en T'ien-hua, "Lun Chung-kuo i kai-ch'uang min-chu cheng-t'i," *Min pao*, no. 1, p. 49.

56. Feng Tzu-yu, "Min-sheng-chu-i yü Chung-kuo cheng-chih ko-ming chih ch'ien-t'u" (Socialism and the Future of China's Political Revolution), *Min pao*, no. 4, pp. 105–109.

57. Chu Chih-hsin, "Lun she-hui ko-ming tang yü cheng-chih ko-ming ping hsing" (That the Social Revolution Should Be Undertaken Together with The Political Revolution), *Min pao*, no. 5, p. 50.

58. Hu Han-min, *"Min pao chih liu ta chu-i,"* *Min pao*, no. 3, pp. 11–12.

59. Liang Ch'i-ch'ao, "Ta mou-pao ti-ssu-hao tui-yü *Hsin-min ts'ung-pao* chih po-lun" (In Response to Criticisms of *Hsin-min ts'ung-pao* Appearing in the Fourth Issue of a Certain Journal), YPSHC/WC 18.98–99.

60. Crane Brinton, *The Anatomy of Revolution* (New York: Vintage, rev. ed., 1952), pp. 153–154.

61. Ting, *Liang Jen-kung nien-p'u*, p. 228.

62. Edict of September 1, 1906, as translated in Meribeth Cameron, *The Reform Movement in China, 1898–1912* (Stanford: Stanford University Press, 1931), p. 103.

63. K. S. Liew, *Struggle for Democracy: Sung Chiao-jen and the 1911 Chinese Revolution* (Berkeley and Los Angeles: University of California Press, 1971), pp. 71–72.

64. J. K. Fairbank and others (eds.), *The I. G. in Peking*, vol. II, pp. 1528–1533 (letters of February 3, May 18, and September 29, 1907).

65. Calvin W. Mateer, in the first instance, and in the second, Douglas Story, *Tomorrow in the East* (London, 1907); both quoted in Mary C. Wright, "The Rising Tide of Change," in M. C. Wright (ed.), *China in Revolution: The First Phase, 1900–1913* (New Haven: Yale University Press, 1968), pp. 1, 30.

66. See Hans Kohn, *The Idea of Nationalism* (New York: The Macmillan Co., 1956), p. 19.

67. Wang Ching-wei, "Lun ko-ming chih ch'ü-shih" (On Revolutionary Trends), *Min pao*, no. 25, p. 3.
68. Quoted in Don C. Price, *Russia and the Roots of the Chinese Revolution*, p. 208 (translation slightly modified).
69. Wang Ching-wei, "Tsa po *Hsin-min ts'ung-pao*" (In Refutation of *Hsin-min ts'ung-pao* on Several Counts), *Min Pao*, no. 12, p. 5.
70. Wu Yueh, "Wu Yueh i-shu" (Posthumously Published Writings of Wu Yueh), printed in *T'ien-t'ao* (April, 1907), pp. 7–8, 27.
71. Ch'iu Chin, "Fan Tung-hai ko" (Adrift on the Eastern Sea), *Hsin-hai ko-ming*, vol. III, p. 210. This account of Ch'iu Chin's career draws heavily on Mary Rankin's *Early Chinese Revolutionaries*; my translation of these lines, however, differs considerably from hers, as found on pp. 45–46.
72. Liang Ch'i-ch'ao, "Yueh luan kan-yen" (Reflections on the Canton Uprising), YPSHC/WC 27.66–67.

Chapter 6: The New Culture Movement: Intellectuals as Political Amateurs (pp. 203–279)

1. Both quotations cited in William A. Lyell, *Lu Hsün's Vision of Reality* (Berkeley: University of California Press, 1976), pp. 74–75.
2. These descriptions are extracted from the Annual Report for 1917 submitted by H. Picard-Destelan, Co-Director-General of the Chinese Post Office, May 1918, and published in H. T. Montague Bell and H. G. H. Woodhead, *China Year Book 1919–1920* (London: George Routledge & Sons Ltd.), pp. 267–276. The year was selected more or less at random: 1917 was not infamously worse, nor conspicuously better, than other years. It is worth noting, perhaps, that the postal service was one of the unifying factors that contributed to the sense of national cohesion throughout the period of warlord separatism.
3. Thomas Hobbes, *Leviathan*, Part I, Chapter 13.
4. Reginald Johnston, "A League of the Sacred Hills," *The Nineteenth Century and After* 73.432: 306 (February 1913).
5. Ibid., *passim*. The Russell quote is taken, with the author's permission, from Suzanne Ogden, "Russell's Influence on China's Social Reconstruction in the 1920s" (unpublished MS.); for Levenson's opinions, see *Confucian China and Its Modern Fate*, vol. 3, p. 76 and *passim*.
6. The most comprehensive work on this subject in English is Y. C. Wang, *Chinese Intellectuals and the West, 1872–1949* (Chapel Hill: University of North Carolina Press, 1966). My discussion also draws on Shu Hsin-ch'eng, *Chin-tai Chung-kuo liu-hsueh shih* (A History of Chinese Students Abroad in Modern Times) (Shanghai, 1927); and Lin Tzu-hsun, *Chung-kuo liu-hsueh chiao-yü shih 1847–1975* (Chinese Study Abroad, 1847–1975) (Taipei, 1976).
7. See Y. C. Wang, *Chinese Intellectuals and the West*, Appendix C, p. 516. The figures are based on a sample of 578 returned students listed in the 1925 edition of the English-language publication, *Who's Who in China*.
8. Barry Keenan, *The Dewey Experiment in China: Educational Reform and*

Political Power in the Early Republic (Cambridge, Mass.: Harvard University Council on East Asian Studies, 1977), *passim;* the quotations are taken from p. 30 and p. 18.

9. Quoted in Hsü Kai-yü. "The Life and Poetry of Wen I-to," *Harvard Journal of Asiatic Studies,* vol. 21, p. 147 (1958).

10. Y. C. Wang, *Chinese Intellectuals and the West,* p. 371.

11. Ibid., pp. 365–367. See also Shu Hsin-ch'eng (ed.), *Chung-kuo chin-tai chiao-yü shih tzu-liao* (Materials on the History of Modern Chinese Education) (Peking, 1961; 3 vols.), vol. I, pp. 375–376.

12. Edict of June 11, 1898; *Reform Edicts,* p. 11.

13. L. C. Arlington and William Lewisohn, *In Search of Old Peking* (Peking: Henri Vetch, 1935), p. 123.

14. H. S. Brunnert and V. V. Hagelstrom, *Present Day Political Organization of China* (Shanghai, 1912), pp. 223ff. But *caveat lector:* this source describes the Imperial University as it existed on paper in the last years of the dynasty; the extent to which this description conforms to reality remains uncertain.

15. Shu Hsin-ch'eng, *Chung-kuo chin-tai chiao-yü shih tzu-liao,* p. 383.

16. Ts'ai Yuan-p'ei, "Chiu-jen Pei-ching ta-hsueh hsiao-chang chih yen-shuo" (Speech on the Occasion of Assuming the Presidency of Peking University [January 9, 1917]), in *Ts'ai Yuan-p'ei hsien-sheng ch'üan-chi* (Collected Works of Ts'ei Yuan-p'ei) (Taipei, 1968), pp. 721–722.

17. Ts'ai Yuan-p'ei, "Pei-ching ta-hsueh Chin-te hui chih chih-ch'ü shu" (The Essential Significance of the Society for the Promotion of Moral Rectitude at Peking University), ibid., p. 469.

18. Ts'ai Yuan-p'ei, "Ta Lin Ch'in-nan [Shu] han" (In Response to Lin Shu's Letter), ibid., pp 1087–1088.

19. Ku Hung-ming, *Letters from a Viceroy's Yamen* (Shanghai, 1901), pp. 94–96.

20. Richard C. Kagan (trans.), "Ch'en Tu-hsiu's Unfinished Autobiograhy," *China Quarterly,* no. 50 (April–June 1972), p. 303.

21. Ch'en Tu-hsiu, *Ch'en Tu-hsiu tzu-shu* (Ch'en Tu-hsiu's Autobiography) (Tainan, 1968), pp. 40–41.

22. This is the phraseology of the advertisement that ran in successive issues of *Hsin ch'ing-nien;* the magazine was published by the China Science Society (Chung-kuo k'o-hsueh she), established by Chinese students in the U. S. in 1914. Chow Tse-tsung lists, and briefly describes, 604 periodicals that appeared for the first time from 1915 to 1923. Many of these were short-lived, but a few became more or less permanent fixtures in prewar intellectual life— like *Science,* which continued to publish until the eve of the Sino-Japanese War. See Chow Tse-tsung, *Research Guide to the May Fourth Movement* (Cambridge, Mass.: Harvard University Press, 1963), pp. 26ff.

23. Ch'en Tu-hsiu, "Ching-kao ch'ing-nien" (Appeal to Youth), *Hsin ch'ing-nien,* vol. I, no. 1 (September 1915).
    (*Hsin ch'ing-nien* hereafter abbreviated HCN.)

24. Ch'en Tu-hsiu, "Wo-chih ai-kuo chu-i" (My Patriotism), HCN vol. II, no. 2 (October 1916).

25. Kao I-han, "I-chiu-i-ch'i nien yü-hsiang chih ko-ming" (The Revolutionary Forecast for 1917), HCN vol. II, no. 5 (January 1917).

26. Lu Hsun, "Silent China," *Selected Works* vol. II, p. 321.

27. Hu Shih, untitled autobiographical essay in *Living Philosophies* (New York: Simon & Schuster, 1931), p. 251.

28. These are excerpts from several essays written over a period of several years. See Jerome B. Grieder, *Hu Shih and the Chinese Renaissance: Liberalism in the Chinese Revolution, 1917–1937* (Cambridge, Mass.: Harvard University Press, 1970), chapter III *passim*.

29. Hu Shih, *Chung-kuo hsin wen-hsueh yun-tung hsiao shih* (A Short History of the New Literature Movement in China) (Taipei, 1958), p. 14.

30. Ch'en Tu-hsiu, "Wen-hsueh ko-ming lun" (On the Literary Revolution), HCN vol. II, no. 6 (February 1917).

31. Ch'ien Hsuan-t'ung, "Chung-kuo chin-hou chih wen-tzu wen-t'i" (The Language Question in China from Now On), HCN vol. IV, no. 4 (April 1918).

32. Wu Chih-hui, "*K'o-hsueh chou-pao* pien-chi hua" (Science Weekly: The Editor's Column), no. 4 (May 4, 1924); reprinted in *Wu Chih-hui hsien-sheng hsuan-chi* (Selected Works of Mr. Wu Chih-hui) (Taipei, 1964, 2 vols.), vol. I, p. 262.

33. Lin Shu, "Lun ku-wen pu-tang fei" (Why the Old Literature Should Not Be Destroyed), quoted by Hu Shih in the correspondence section, HCN vol. III, no. 3 (May 1917); and Lin Shu, "Lun ku-wen pai-hua chih hsiang hsiao-chang" (On the Relative Merits of the Classical and the Vernacular Languages), in *Chung-kuo hsin wen-hsueh ta-hsi* (The Genesis of China's New Literature) (Shanghai, 1935–1936, under the editorial supervision of Chao Chia-pi, 10 vols.), vol. II, Wen-hsueh lun-cheng chi (Literary Polemics, edited by Cheng Chen-to), p. 81.

34. Yen Fu, "Shu-cha liu-shih-ssu" (Letter Sixty-Four), ibid., pp. 96–97.

35. Chang Shih-chao, "P'ing hsin wen-hsueh yun-tung" (A Critique of the New Literature Movement), ibid., p. 223.

36. Cited in Howard Boorman (ed.), *Biographical Dictionary of Republican China* (New York: Columbia University Press, 1967–1971, 4 vols.), vol. III, p. 443.

37. Mei Kuang-ti, "P'ing t'i-ch'ang hsin wen-hua che" (A Critique of Those Who Advocate the New Culture), *Hsueh-heng*, vol. I, no. 1 (January 1922); reprinted in *Chung-kuo hsin wen-hsueh ta-hsi*, vol. II, pp. 127–132.

38. Hu Shih, *The Development of the Logical Method in Ancient China*, (Shanghai, 1922), Introduction, pp. 6–7.

39. See Chow Tse-tsung, *The May Fourth Movement: Intellectual Revolution in Modern China* (Cambridge, Mass.: Harvard University Press, 1960), pp. 239–242; and Grieder, *Hu Shih and the Chinese Renaissance*, pp. 189–193.

40. José Ortega y Gasset, *The Revolt of the Masses* (New York: Norton College ed., 1957), p. 42, note 2.

41. Hu Shih, "Hsin ssu-ch'ao ti i-i" (The Significance of the New Thought), HCN vol. VII, no. 1 (December 1919); and "Hsin sheng-huo" (The New Life), *Hsin sheng-huo tsa-chih* (The New Life Magazine), no. 1 (August 24, 1919).

42. Hu Shih, author's preface to the Taipei edition of *Chung-kuo ku-tai che-hsueh shih* (A History of Ancient Chinese Philosophy) (Taipei, 1958), p. 5; and "Chieh-shao wo tzu-chi ti ssu-hsiang" (Introducing My Own Thought), the

author's preface to *Hu Shih wen-hsuan* (Selected Works) (Shanghai, 1930), p. 13.

43. Ting Wen-chiang, "Hsuan-hsueh yü k'o-hsueh" (Metaphysics and Science), *K'o-hsueh yü jen-sheng-kuan* (Science and the Philosophy of life) (Shanghai, 1923, 2 vols.), vol. I, pp. 20–21.

44. Charlotte Furth, *Ting Wen-chiang: Science and China's New Culture* (Cambridge, Mass.: Harvard University Press, 1970), p. 111.

45. D. W. Y. Kwok, *Scientism in Chinese Thought, 1900–1950* (New Haven: Yale University Press, 1965), p. 21.

46. Richard Hofstadter, *Social Darwinism in American Thought* (New York: George Braziller, Inc., 1959), pp. 46–48.

47. Ibid., p. 31.

48. Quoted in Benjamin I. Schwartz, *In Search of Wealth and Power*, p. 132.

49. Yen Fu, "P'i Han" (*Contra* Han [Yü]), in Shih Chün (ed.), *Chung-kuo chin-tai ssu-hsiang shih ts'an-k'ao tzu-liao chien-pien*, pp. 480–481.

50. Quoted in Schwartz, *In Search of Wealth and Power*, p. 219.

51. Chiang Meng-lin, "Ch'u tao Pei-ching ta-hsueh shih tsai hsueh-sheng huan-ying-hui chung chih yen-shuo" (Speech Delivered at a Student Welcoming Reception on the Occasion of [Chiang's] Arrival at Peking University), *Kuo-tu shih-tai chih ssu-hsiang yü chiao-yü* (Thought and Education in a Transitional Period) (Shanghai, 1933), p. 395.

52. Chiang Monlin, *Tides from the West* (New Haven: Yale University Press, 1947), p. 123. This is the gist of the speech noted above as Chiang recollected it in his English reminiscences.

53. Chiang Meng-lin and Hu Shih, "Wo-men tui-yü hsueh-sheng ti hsi-wang" (Our Hopes for the students), *Kuo-tu shih-tai chih ssu-hsiang yü chiao-yü*, pp. 156ff. This was drafted by Hu Shih.

54. Hu Shih, "A Plea for Patriotic Sanity," *Chinese Students Monthly*, 10.7:425–426 (April 1915).

55. Hu Shih, *Hu Shih liu-hsueh jih-chi*, pp. 821, 842–843.

56. Hu Shih, "Wo-men k'o-i teng-hou wu-shih nien!" (We Can Wait Fifty Years!), *Tu-li p'ing-lun* (The Independent Critic), no. 44 (April 2, 1933); and "Ch'en-mo ti jen-shou" (Silent Endurance), *Tu-li p'ing-lun*, no. 155 (June 16, 1935).

57. HCN vol. I, no. 1 (September 1915).

58. Hu Shih, "Hsin ssu-ch'ao ti i-i," HCN vol. VII, no. 1 (December 1919); and "Shih-yen-chu-i" (Experimentalism), HCN vol. VI, no. 4 (April 1919).

59. John Dewey, "Science and Social Philosophy," *Lectures in China, 1919–1920* (edited and translated from the Chinese by Robert W. Clopton and Tsuin-chen Ou) (Honolulu: University Press of Hawaii/East–West Center, 1973), pp. 62–63.

60. Quoted in Schwartz, *In Search of Wealth and Power*, p. 235; I have slightly modified the translation.

61. Liang Ch'i-ch'ao, "Ou-yu hsin-ying lu" (Impressions of Travels in Europe), YPSHC/CC 23.1–38 *passim*.

62. Ting Wen-chiang, "Hsuan-hsueh yü k'o-hsueh," p. 22.

63. T'ao Meng-ho, "Ou-chou chih kan-hsiang" (Impressions of Europe) HCN vol.

VII, no. 1 (December 1919); and "Ou Mei lao-tung wen-t'i" (The Labor Problem in Europe and America), HCN vol. VII, no. 2 (January 1920). See also *Meng-ho wen-ts'un* (Collected essays of [T'ao] Meng-ho) (Shanghai, 1925), pp. 65–95 *passim*.

64. Chan Wing-tsit, *A Sourcebook of Chinese Philosophy*, p. 107.

65. Henri Bergson, *Creative Evolution*, chapter III, quoted in Morton White, *The Age of Analysis* (Boston: Houghton Mifflin Co., 1962), pp. 498–501.

66. Chang Chün-mai, "Jen-sheng-kuan" (The Philosophy of Life), in *K'o-hsueh yü jen-sheng-kuan*, vol. I, pp. 1–2 *passim*.

67. Ting Wen-chiang, "Hsuan-hsueh yü k'o-hsueh," p. 20.

68. *K'o-hsueh yü jen-sheng-kuan*, Hu Shih's preface, p. 20.

69. Chang Chün-mai, "Tsai lun jen-sheng-kuan yü k'o-hsueh, ping ta Ting Tsai-chün [Wen-chiang]" (Another Discussion of the Philosophy of Life and Science, and a Rejoinder to Ting Wen-chiang), *K'o-hsueh yü jen-sheng-kuan*, vol. I, pp. 81–82.

70. On Liang Chi see Lin Yü-sheng, "The Suicide of Liang Chi: An Ambiguous Case of Moral Conservatism," in Charlotte Furth (ed.), *The Limits of Change*, pp. 151–168; and Guy Alitto, *The Last Confucian: Liang Shu-ming and the Chinese Dilemma of Modernity* (Berkeley: University of California Press, 1979), chapters I and II.

71. Alitto, *The Last Confucian*, p. 109.

72. Both quotations are from Dewey's lecture on "Science and Knowing," the tenth in a series of sixteen lectures on "A Philosophy of Education" delivered in Peking in the autumn of 1919, with Hu Shih serving as platform interpreter. See *Lectures in China*, p. 247.

73. For Liang Shu-ming's comments on Dewey and Russell, see *Tung Hsi wen-hua chi ch'i che-hsueh* (The Cultures of East and West and Their Philosophies) (Shanghai, 1922), p. 176.

74. Bertrand Russell, "Chinese and Western Civilisations Contrasted," *Selected Papers of Bertrand Russell* (New York: Modern Library, 1927 [1955]), pp. 208–224 *passim*.

75. Liang Shu-ming, *Tung Hsi wen-hua chi ch'i che-hsueh*, pp. 152–153.

76. Quoted in Alitto, *The Last Confucian*, p. 129.

77. Liang Shu-ming, *Tung Hsi wen-hua chi ch'i che-hsueh*, chapter V, *passim*.

78. Ts'ai Yuan-p'ei, "Wu-shih nien lai Chung-kuo chih che-hsueh" (Chinese Philosophy During the Last Fifty Years [1923]), *Ts'ai Yuan-p'ei hsien-sheng ch'üan-chi*, p. 573.

79. Hu Shih, "Wo-men tui-yü Hsi-yang chin-tai wen-ming ti t'ai-tu" (Our Attitude Toward Modern Western Civilization), *Hsien-tai p'ing-lun* (Contemporary Review), vol. IV, no. 83 (July 10, 1926).

80. Hu Shih, "Hsieh tsai K'ung-tzu tan-ch'en chi-nien chih hou" (Written after the Commemoration of Confucius' Birthday), *Tu-li p'ing-lun*, no. 117 (September 9, 1934).

81. Hu Shih, "Pien-chi hou-chi" (Editor's Note), *Tu-li p'ing-lun*, no. 142 (March 17, 1935); and "Shih-p'ing so-wei 'Chung-kuo pen-wei chih wen-hua chien-she'" (A Critique of What Is Called "Cultural Reconstruction on a Chinese Basis"), *Tu-li p'ing-lun*, no. 145 (April 7, 1935).

82. Hu Shih, "Ta Ch'en Hsü-ching hsien-sheng" (A Reply to Mr. Ch'en Hsü-ching), *Tu-li p'ing-lun*, no. 160 (July 21, 1935).

83. Lu Hsun, author's preface to *Na-han* (A Call to Arms), *Lu Hsun ch'üan-chi* (Collected Works of Lu Hsun) (Peking, 1956, 10 vols.), vol. I, pp. 5–8.

84. William A. Lyell, *Lu Hsün's Vision of Reality*, p. 26.

85. Lu Hsun, "K'uang-jen jih-chi" (A Madman's Diary), *Lu Hsun ch'üan-chi*, vol. I, pp. 12–19.

86. Lu Hsun, "Tsai chiu-lou shang" (Upstairs in a Wineshop), *Lu Hsun ch'üan-chi*, vol. II, pp. 28–33.

87. Lu Hsun, author's preface to *Na-han*, *Lu Hsun ch'üan-chi*, vol. I, p. 8.

88. Chiang Meng-lin, "She-hui yun-tung yü chiao-yü" (The Social Movement and Education), *Hsin chiao-yü* (The New Education), February 1920; reprinted in *Kuo-tu shih-tai chih ssu-hsiang yü chiao-yü*, pp. 178–179.

89. Hu Shih, "I-pu-sheng-chu-i" (Ibsenism), HCN vol. IV, no. 6 (June 1918).

90. John Dewey, "America and Chinese Education," *The New Republic* March 1, 1922; reprinted in *Characters and Events: Popular Essays in Social and Political Philosophy* (New York: Henry Holt and Co., 1929; edited by Joseph Ratner, 2 vols.), vol. I, p. 306.

91. Chiang Meng-lin, "Hsueh-feng yü t'i-kao hsueh-shu" (Academic Character and the Elevation of Learning), *Ch'en-pao fu-k'an* December 2, 1922; reprinted in *Kuo-tu shih-tai chih ssu-hsiang yü chiao-yü*, pp. 184–188.

92. Quoted in Alitto, *The Last Confucian*, pp. 141–142.

93. John Dewey, "The New Leaven in Chinese Politics," *Asia*, April 1920; reprinted in *Characters and Events*, vol. I, p. 253.

Chapter 7: The Claims of Ideology (pp. 280–325)

1. P'eng Te-tsun, "K'a-nei-chi chuan" (Biography of Carnegie), HCN vol. I, no. 1 (September 1915).

2. Ch'en Tu-hsiu, "T'an cheng-chih" (Talking Politics), HCN vol. VIII, no. 1 (September 1920).

3. Mao Tse-tung, quoted by Edgar Snow in *Red Star Over China* (New York: Random House, 1938), p. 132; and "Speech Made at the Yenan Forum on Literature and Art," May 2, 1942, text in Conrad Brandt, Benjamin Schwartz and J. K. Fairbank (eds.), *A Documentary History of Chinese Communism* (Cambridge, Mass.: Harvard University Press, 1952), pp. 410–411.

4. Michael Walzer, *The Revolution of the Saints: A Study in the Origins of Radical Politics* (New York, Athaneum, 1970), p. 19.

5. Bernard Crick, *In Defense of Politics* (Baltimore, Penguin Books, 1964), p. 39.

6. This and the following quotations from Shils are taken from *The Intellectuals and the Powers and Other Essays* (Chicago and London: University of Chicago Press, 1972), pp. 29–31.

7. Lucian Pye, *The Spirit of Chinese Politics: A Psychocultural Study of the*

Authority Crisis in Political Development (Cambridge, Mass.: MIT Press, 1968), p. 31.

8. Hannah Arendt, *On Revolution* (New York, Viking Press, 1965) p. 55.

9. Ch'en Tu-hsiu, "O-lo-ssu ko-ming yü wo kuo-min chih chueh-wu" (The Russian Revolution and the Awakening of Our People), HCN vol. III, no. 1 (April 1917).

10. Quoted in F. J. Raddatz, *Karl Marx: A Political Biography* (Boston and Toronto: Little Brown, 1979), p. 48.

11. See, *inter alia*, E. H. Carr, *The Bolshevik Revolution, 1917–1923* (New York: Macmillan, 1953), vol. III, pp. 501ff.

12. Quoted in ibid., p. 538, from K. S. Weigh, *Russo-Chinese Diplomacy* (Shanghai, 1928), p. 313.

13. Lenin's "Report to the Second Congress of the Communist Organizations of the Peoples of the East," in Hélène Carrère d'Encausse and Stuart R. Schram, *Marxism and Asia* (London, Penguin Press, 1969), pp. 168–169.

14. Lin Yü-sheng, *The Crisis of Chinese Consciousness: Radical Antitraditionalism in the May Fourth Era* (Madison: University of Wisconsin Press, 1979), p. 78.

15. Ch'en Tu-hsiu, "Ching-kao ch'ing-nien" (Appeal to Youth), HCN vol. I, no. 1 (September 1915).

16. Ch'en Tu-hsiu, "Hsien-fa yü K'ung-chiao" (Constitutionalism and the Confucian Religion) HCN vol. II, no. 3 (November 1916).

17. Ch'en Tu-hsiu, "Ching-kao ch'ing-nien," loc. cit.

18. Hu Shih, *Hu Shih liu-hsueh jih-chi*, p. 332.

19. Translation, with slight modifications, from Kevin Fountain (ed.), *Ch'en Tu-hsiu: Lifetime Oppositionist*, the Fall 1979 issue of *Chinese Law and Government* (vol. XII, no. 3), p. 27.

20. Ch'en Tu-hsiu, "Ou-hsiang p'o-huai lun" (On the Destruction of Idols) HCN vol. V, no. 2 (August 1918).

21. Ch'en Tu-hsiu, "Wo chih ai-kuo chu-i" (My Patriotism) HCN vol. II, no. 2 (October 1916); and "Chin-tai Hsi-yang chiao-yü" (Modern Western Education) HCN vol. III, no. 5 (July 1917).

22. D'Encausse and Schram, *Marxism and Asia*, p. 47.

23. *Mei-chou p'ing-lun*, no. 25, June 8, 1919.

24. "Hsin ch'ing-nien hsuan-yen" (Manifesto of The New Youth) HCN vol. VII, no. 1 (December 1919).

25. Ch'en Tu-hsiu, "Shih-hsing min-chih ti chi-ch'u" (The Foundations for the Realization of Democracy) HCN vol. VII, no. 1 (December 1919).

26. Ch'en Tu-hsiu, "K'o-lin-te p'ai" (The Von Ketteler Monument) HCN vol. V, no. 5 (November 1918).

27. Quoted in d'Encausse and Schram, *Marxism and Asia*, pp. 223–224.

28. "An Open Letter to All Comrades," translated in Fountain, *Ch'en Tu-hsiu*, quoted here with slight modifications.

29. Fu Ssu-nien, "Ch'en Tu-hsiu an" (The Case of Ch'en Tu-hsiu), *Tu-li p'ing-lun* (The Independent Critic), no. 24, October 30, 1932.

30. Ch'en Tu-hsiu, "Wo-ti ken-pen i-chien" (My Basic Ideas), November 1940 (or 1941?), in *Ch'en Tu-hsiu tsui-hou tui-yü min-chu cheng-chih ti chien-*

chieh (Ch'en Tu-hsiu's last thoughts on democracy) (Taipei, 1959), pp. 25–26.

31. Ch'en Tu-hsiu, "Kei S ho H ti hsin," ibid., p. 30.

32. Li Ta-chao, "Ch'ing-nien yü lao-jen" (The Young and the Old), HCN vol. III, no. 1 (April 1917).

33. Li Ta-chao, "Bolshevism ti sheng-li" (The Victory of Bolshevism), HCN vol. V, no. 5 (November 1918); the translation here follows, with some modifications, that found in Teng and Fairbank (eds.), *China's Response to the West*, pp. 246–249.

34. Liang Ch'i-ch'ao, in letters to his children in America, in Ting, *Liang Jen-kung nien-p'u*, pp. 719–722.

35. Mao Tse-tung, "Report on an Investigation of the Peasant Movement in Hunan (February 1927)," in Brandt, Schwartz and Fairbank (eds.), *A Documentary History of Chinese Communism*, pp. 80, 83.

36. Li Ta-chao, "Ch'ing-nien yü nung-ts'un" (Youth and the Village), originally published in *Ch'en-pao*, February 20–23, 1919; reprinted in *Li Ta-chao hsuan-chi* (Selected Works of Li Ta-chao) (Peking, 1962), p. 150.

37. Ibid., p. 149.

38. Maurice Meisner, *Li Ta-chao and the Origins of Chinese Marxism* (Cambridge, Mass.: Harvard University Press, 1967), p. 86.

39. *Li Ta-chao hsuan-chi*, p. 237.

40. Ibid.

41. Li Ta-chao, "Lu Yü Shan teng-sheng ti Hung-ch'iang-hui" (The Red Spear Society in Shantung, Honan, Shensi, and Other Provinces), *Li Ta-chao hsuan-chi*, pp. 569–570. Written in 1926, this was Li's last published essay.

42. Li Ta-chao, "Yen-shih-hsin yü tzu-chueh-hsin" (Pessimism and Self-Consciousness), a letter to the editor of *Chia-yin*, August 10, 1915; in *Li Ta-chao hsuan-chi*, pp. 29–30.

43. Li Ta-chao, "Wu-chih pien-tung yü tao-te pien-tung" (Material Change and Moral Change), *Hsin-ch'ao*, vol. II, no. 2 (December 1919).

44. Li Ta-chao, "Yu ching-chi shang chieh-shih Chung-kuo chin-tai ssu-hsiang pien-tung ti yuan-yin" (An Economic Explanation of the Transformation of Modern Chinese Thought), HCN vol. VII, no. 2 (January 1920).

45. Li Ta-chao, "Jen-chung wen-t'i" (The Race Problem), translated in D'Encausse and Schram, *Marxism and Asia*, pp. 220–222.

46. Ts'ai Ho-sen's letter to Ch'en Tu-hsiu is reprinted in *Tu-hsiu wen-ts'un* (Collected Works of [Ch'en] Tu-hsiu), vol. IV, p. 298.

47. L. S. Feuer (ed.), *Marx & Engels: Basic Writings on Politics and Philosophy* (Garden City: Doubleday, 1959), pp. 108–109, 398.

48. Li Ta-chao, "Chin" (Now), HCN vol. IV, no. 4 (April 1918).

49. Li Ta-chao, "Wei-wu shih-kuan tsai hsien-tai shih-hsueh-shang ti chia-chih" (The Value of the Materialist Concept of History in Modern Historiography) HCN vol. VIII, no. 4 (December 1920); text corrected in *Li Ta-chao hsuan-chi*.

50. Li Ta-chao, "Wu-chih pien-tung yü tao-te pien-tung," loc. cit.

51. Li Ta-chao, "Wei-wu shih-kuan tsai hsien-tai shih-hsueh-shang ti chia-chih," loc. cit.

Chapter 8: The Dilemmas of Modernity: Intellectuals
as the Victims of Politics (pp. 326–350)

1. Ch'en Tu-hsiu, letter to Wang Shu-ch'ien, HCN vol. II, no. 1 (September 1916).
2. Ch'en Tu-hsiu, letter to Ku K'o-kang, HCN vol. III, no. 5 (July 1917).
3. Hu Shih, "To yen-chiu hsieh wen-t'i, shao t'an hsieh chu-i" (Study More Problems, and Talk Less about Theories), Mei-chou p'ing-lun, no. 31 (July 20, 1919).
4. This and the following quotations are drawn from Li Ta-chao, "Tsai lun wen-t'i yü chu-i" (Another Discussion of Problems and Theories), Mei-chou p'ing-lun, no. 35 (August 17, 1919).
5. Hu Shih, "Wo-men tsou na-i t'iao lu?" (Which Road Shall We Follow?), Hsin yueh (The Crescent), vol. II, no. 10 (December 1929).
6. Maurice Meisner, Li Ta-chao and the Origins of Chinese Marxism, pp. 109ff.
7. Hu Shih, "San lun wen-t'i yü chu-i" (A Third Discussion of Problems and Theories), Mei-chou p'ing-lun, no. 36 (August 24, 1919).
8. Ch'en Yün, "How to be a Communist Party Member," in Brandt, Schwartz, and Fairbank, A Documentary History of Chinese Communism, pp. 334–335.
9. See Liu Shao-ch'i, How To Be a Good Communist (Peking: Foreign Languages Press, 4th ed. rev., 1964), p. 48; and James T. C. Liu, "An Early Sung Reformer: Fan Chung-yen," in J. K. Fairbank (ed.), Chinese Thought and Institutions (Chicago: University of Chicago Press, 1957), p. 111.
10. Quoted in Harriet C. Mills, "Lu Xun: Literature and Revolution—From Mara to Marx," in Merle Goldman (ed.), Modern Chinese Literature in the May Fourth Era (Cambridge, Mass. and London: Harvard University Press, 1977), p. 201.
11. Mao Tse-tung, "On the New Democracy," Selected Works, vol. II (Peking: Foreign Languages Press, 1965), p. 372.
12. Hu Shih, "Chih nan, hsing i pu-i" (Knowledge is Difficult, but Action Is Not Easy Either), Hsin yueh, vol. II, no. 4 (June 1929).
13. On this subject see Jerome B. Grieder, Hu Shih and the Chinese Renaissance, pp. 239ff.
14. Chiang T'ing-fu [T. F. Tsiang], "Chih-shih chieh-chi yü cheng-chih" (The Intelligentsia and Politics), Tu-li p'ing-lun (The Independent Critic), no. 51 (May 21, 1933).
15. Harold Laski, A Grammar of Politics (New Haven: Yale University Press, 1925), pp. 35, 379–431 passim.
16. John Dewey, "Public Opinion in Japan," The New Republic, November 11, 1921.
17. Lo Lung-chi, "Wo tui tang-wu-shang ti 'chin-ch'ing p'i-p'ing" (My "Respectful Criticism" of Party Affairs), Hsin yueh, vol. II, no. 8 (October 1929).
18. Lloyd Eastman, The Abortive Revolution (Cambridge, Mass.: Harvard University Press, 1974), p. 2, quoting Charles E. Gauss, U.S. chargé d'affaires.
19. Lo Lung-chi, "Wo-men yao shen-mo-yang ti cheng-chih chih-tu?" (What Kind of Political Institutions Do We Want?"), Hsin yueh, vol. II, no. 12 (February 1930).

20. Quoted in Eastman, *The Abortive Revolution*, pp. 147–148.
21. Ch'ien Tuan-sheng, "Min-chu cheng-chih hu? Chi-ch'üan kuo-chia hu?" (Democratic Politics? Or a Unified Nation?) *Tung-fang tsa-chih* (The Eastern Miscellany), vol. XXXI, no. 1 (January 1, 1934).
22. Ting Wen-chiang, "Min-chu cheng-chih yü tu-ts'ai cheng-chih" (Democratic Politics and Dictatorial Politics), *Tu-li p'ing-lun*, no. 133 (December 30, 1934); and "Tsai lun min-chu yü tu-ts'ai" (Another Discussion of Democracy and Dictatorship), *Tu-li p'ing-lun*, no. 137 (January 27, 1935).
23. Eastman, *The Abortive Revolution*, p. 148.
24. Chiang T'ing-fu [T. F. Tsiang], "Ko-ming yü chuan-chih" (Revolution and Authoritarianism), *Tu-li p'ing-lun*, no. 80 (December 10, 1933); and "Lun chuan-chih, ping ta Hu Shih-chih hsien-sheng" (On Authoritarianism, in Reply to Mr. Hu Shih-chih), *Tu-li p'ing-lun*, no. 83 (December 31, 1933).
25. Hu Shih, "Ts'ung nung-ts'un chiu-chi t'an tao wu-wei ti cheng-chih" (From a Discussion of Rural Relief to a Discussion of *Wu-Wei* Government), *Tu-li p'ing-lun*, no. 49 (May 7, 1933).
26. Laski, *A Grammar of Politics*, p. 28.
27. Hu Shih, "Tsai lun chien-kuo yü chuan-chih" (Another Discussion of National Reconstruction and Authoritarianism), *Tu-li p'ing-lun*, no. 82 (December 24, 1933).
28. Hu Shih, "China and Democracy," written for *The Outlook* in 1915, and reprinted in *Hu Shih liu-hsueh jih-chi*, pp. 746–747.
29. Jack Belden, *China Shakes the World* (New York: Harper & Brothers, 1949), p. 89.

Epilogue (pp. 351–356)

1. Mao Tse-tung, "On the New Democracy," in Brandt, Schwartz and Fairbank (eds.), *A Documentary History of Chinese Communism*, pp. 263–264, 272.
2. *Jen-min jih-pao* (The People's Daily), March 23, 1957.
3. Wei Jingsheng [Ching-sheng], "The Fifth Modernization: Democracy," extract published in *Index on Censorship*, vol. 8, no. 5 (September–October 1979), p. 10.
4. "The Complete Text of the Investigation of Wei Jing-sheng's Case," typescript, pp. 74, 78.

Bibliography

In respect to its sources, intellectual history is an undiscriminating subdiscipline. Not ideas and individuals only, but anything that contributes to an understanding of the context in which ideas had, or have, their particular meanings, is grist to the mill of the intellectual historian.

The bibliography that follows, however, is perversely selective. It is not intended to serve as a research guide, nor does it pretend fully to encompass the existing literature on any of the topics on which it touches. Its modest purpose is to enable an interested reader to pursue at least one step further some of the major issues or personalities with which we have been concerned in the preceding pages, or to see them from a different perspective. Only published works are listed. Some collections of scholarly articles are included, but articles published in scholarly journals (such as *The Journal of Asian Studies*, *The China Quarterly*, *Modern China*, *Philosophy East and West*, etc.) are excluded.

I. General and Background Reading

There are several collections of Chinese source materials in translation, with well-informed and useful commentary. See especially William Theodore de Bary and others (eds.), *Sources of Chinese Tradition* (Columbia, 1960); Chan Wing-tsit, *Sourcebook in Chinese Philosophy* (Princeton, 1963); and John K. Fairbank and S. Y. Teng, *China's Response to the West* (Harvard, 1954).

Arthur Waley, *Three Ways of Thought in Ancient China* (Allen & Unwin, 1939) and Frederick W. Mote, *Intellectual Foundations of China* (Knopf, 1971) provide, in very different ways, an excellent introduction to the various schools of classical Chinese thought. Donald J. Munro, *The Concept of Man in Early China* (Stanford, 1969) and Vitaly A. Rubin, *Individual and State in Ancient China* (Columbia, 1976) explore specific themes in broad terms.

Jonathan D. Spence, *Emperor of China: Self Portrait of K'ang Hsi* (Knopf, 1974) offers, in somewhat unorthodox style, a compellingly vivid and vigorous sense of the political and intellectual world "at the top" in the early Ch'ing period. Etienne Balazs, *Political Theory and Administrative Reality in Traditional China* (University of London/SOAS, 1965) treats briefly but with great insight the seventeenth-century dissidents and their world.

Stimulating explorations of some of the great themes of culture and polity, difficult but rewarding, are Joseph R. Levenson, *Confucian China and Its Modern Fate* (California, 1958, 1964, 1965); Thomas A. Metzger, *Escape from Predicament: Neo-Confucianism and China's Evolving Political Culture* (Columbia, 1977); and Laurence A. Schneider, *A Madman of Ch'u: The Chinese Myth of Loyalty and Dissent* (California, 1980).

Donald W. Treadgold, *The West in Russia and China: Religious and Secular Thought in Modern Times; Volume II: China, 1582–1949* (Cambridge, 1973) is a provocative interpretation, in some ways contentious, but substantial.

Two general surveys, useful because they treat individuals otherwise generally neglected, are Chün-tu Hsüeh (ed.), *Revolutionary Leaders of Modern China* (Oxford, 1971); and Chester C. Tan, *Chinese Political Thought in the Twentieth Century* (Doubleday, 1971).

II. The Nineteenth Century

There is a large literature on the decline of the Ch'ing, but as yet not very many books that treat directly the intellectual history of this complex phenomenon.

On the Taiping Rebellion, viewed from the perspectives of its intellectual significance, see Vincent C. Y. Shih, *The Taiping Ideology: Its Sources, Interpretations, and Influences* (Washington, 1967); and Jen Yu-wen, *The Taiping Revolutionary Movement* (Yale, 1973).

Mary C. Wright, *The Last Stand of Chinese Conservatism: The T'ung-Chih Restoration* (Stanford, 1957) conveys with remarkable sympathy and erudition a sense of the integrity of Confucian self-confidence, its reasonableness, and its vulnerability.

Fred W. Drake, *China Charts the World: Hsu Chi-yü and His Geography of 1848* (Harvard/EARC, 1975) explores China's first recognition of the larger world beyond its inherited frontiers. Adrian Bennett, *John Fryer: The Introduction of Western Science and Technology in 19th Century China* (Harvard/EARC, 1967) carries the story further. Paul A. Cohen, *Between Tradition and Modernity: Wang T'ao and Reform in Late Ch'ing China* (Harvard, 1974) provides, in addition to a biography of this uncommon personality, a provocative thesis concerning the nature of the reformist impulse and the ways in which it was acted upon. In this connection, see also Paul A. Cohen and John E. Schrecker (eds.), *Reform in Nineteenth-Century China* (Harvard/EARC, 1976).

Several different views of the motives and accomplishments of the missionary endeavor in the nineteenth and twentieth centuries, and reactions to it, are found in John K. Fairbank (ed.), *The Missionary Enterprise in China and America* (Harvard, 1974).

The major work on K'ang Yu-wei (and much else besides) is Hsiao Kung-ch'üan, *A Modern China and a New World: K'ang Yu-wei, Reformer and Uto-*

pian, 1858–1927 (Washington, 1975). See also Lo Jung-pang (trans. and ed.), *K'ang Yu-wei: A Biography and a Symposium* (Arizona/AAS, 1967); and Laurence G. Thompson (trans.), *Ta T'ung Shu: The One-World Philosophy of K'ang Yu-wei* (Allen & Unwin, 1958), an abridged translation.

Finally, much information on the substance and significance of intellectual trends can be culled from what is destined to become the standard history of the decline of the Ch'ing: *The Cambridge History of China: Volume 10—Late Ch'ing, 1800–1911, Part 1* (edited by John K. Fairbank; Cambridge, 1978); and *Volume 11—Late Ch'ing 1800–1911, Part 2* (edited by John K. Fairbank and Kwang-Ching Liu; Cambridge, 1980). The bibliographic essays and bibliography are indispensable to the serious student.

III. Reformers and Radicals at the Turn of the Century

Influenced, perhaps, by the views of the participants, much Western scholarship on the 1911 Revolution and its antecedents has emphasized its intellectual (rather than its social or political) origins.

Michael Gasster, *Chinese Intellectuals and the Revolution of 1911: The Birth of Modern Chinese Radicalism* (Washington, 1969) surveys the principal actors and issues. Important background studies include Martin Bernal, *Chinese Socialism to 1907* (Cornell, 1976); Don C. Price, *Russia and the Roots of the Chinese Revolution* (Harvard/EARC, 1974); and James R. Pusey, *China and Charles Darwin* (Harvard/EARC, forthcoming).

Liang Ch'i-ch'ao is one of very few Chinese intellectuals whom one can approach through the interpretations of several scholars, notably Joseph R. Levenson, *Liang Ch'i-ch'ao and the Mind of Modern China* (Harvard, 1953); Chang Hao, *Liang Ch'i-ch'ao and Intellectual Transition in China, 1890–1907* (Harvard, 1971); and Philip Huang, *Liang Ch'i-ch'ao and Modern Chinese Liberalism* (Washington, 1972).

Yen Fu is the focus of Benjamin I. Schwartz's magisterial study of some of the most compelling cultural and intellectual issues that confronted Chinese reformers; see *In Search of Wealth and Power: Yen Fu and the West—Western Thought in Chinese Perspective* (Harvard, 1964).

None of the intellectuals who figured in the early phases of the revolutionary movement has yet been the subject of a full-scale study. Charlotte Furth, "The Sage as Rebel: The Inner World of Chang Ping-lin," in Charlotte Furth (ed.), *The Limits of Change: Essays on Conservative Alternatives in Republican China* (Harvard, 1976), is a perceptive and imaginative brief study of a difficult subject. The volume in which it appears is an important contribution to the intellectual history of China from the turn of the century into the 1930s. What *can* be said about the intellectual dimensions of Sun Yat-sen's early career is expertly examined in Harold Schiffrin, *Sun Yat-sen and the Origins of the Chinese Revolution* (California, 1968).

Charlton M. Lewis, *Prologue to the Chinese Revolution: The Transformation of Ideas and Institutions in Hunan Province, 1891–1907* (Harvard, 1976) examines a crucially important area in a pivotal time. Mary Backus Rankin, *Early Chinese*

Revolutionaries: Radical Intellectuals in Shanghai and Chekiang, 1902–1911 (Harvard, 1971) looks at the personalities, ideas, and organizations of China's first activist generation.

Against this background, William Ayers, *Chang Chih-tung and Educational Reform in China* (Harvard, 1971) conveys a sense of the conservative/monarchical position in the waning years of the Ch'ing dynasty.

IV. The New Culture

The New Culture movement, understandably, has attracted the attention of many scholars interested in intellectual history. The following is a sampling of the considerable literature thus generated.

The *magnum opus* on the May Fourth movement—its political and social ramifications as well as its intellectual inspiration—is Chow Tse-tsung, *The May Fourth Movement: Intellectual Revolution in Modern China* (Harvard, 1960); *Research Guide to the May Fourth Movement* (Harvard, 1963), by the same author, contains much information on New Culture periodicals in the years 1915–1924, and an extensive bibliography. Benjamin I. Schwartz (ed.), *Reflections on the May Fourth Movement: A Symposium* (Harvard/EARC, 1972) offers several interpretive essays written to commemorate the fiftieth anniversary of the event. Lin Yü-sheng, *The Crisis of Chinese Consciousness: Radical Antitraditionalism in the May Fourth Era* (Wisconsin, 1979) interprets the ideas of several of the protagonists of the New Culture movement (Ch'en Tu-hsiu, Hu Shih, Lu Hsun) quite differently from the way they are treated in this book.

No full-scale studies have yet been published on several of the major proponents of the New Culture—e.g., Ts'ai Yuan-p'ei and Ch'en Tu-hsiu. Some sense of the individual and collective personality of the movement may be derived from the studies that are available, including: Jerome B. Grieder, *Hu Shih and the Chinese Renaissance: Liberalism in the Chinese Revolution, 1917–1937* (Harvard, 1970); Charlotte Furth, *Ting Wen-chiang: Science and China's New Culture* (Harvard, 1970); Laurence A. Schneider, *Ku Chieh-kang and China's New History: Nationalism and the Quest for Alternative Traditions* (California, 1971); Guy Alitto, *The Last Confucian: Liang Shu-ming and the Chinese Dilemma of Modernity* (California, 1979).

William A. Lyell, Jr., *Lu Hsün's Vision of Reality* (California, 1976) gives a vivid description of its subject's early life, and assesses the inspiration and structure of his art as a short story writer. Lu Hsun is also at the center of several brief but solid essays in Merle Goldman (ed.), *Modern Chinese Literature in the May Fourth Era* (Harvard, 1977); and in T. A. Hsia, *The Gate of Darkness: Studies on the Leftist Literary Movement in China* (Washington, 1968). Both these volumes contain much else of substance on the emergence of a modern Chinese literature. Leo Ou-fan Lee, *The Romantic Generation of Modern Chinese Writers* (Harvard, 1973) is concerned with a number of important writers whose perspectives were more individual than social. C. T. Hsia, *A History of Modern Chinese Fiction, 1917–1957* (Yale, 1961) is a well-rounded general survey, and includes a useful bibliography of works both in Chinese and in translation.

The New Culture period is the turning point for several studies that are more broadly framed, including Y. C. Wang, *Chinese Intellectuals and the West, 1872-1949* (North Carolina, 1966), which presents an essentially traditionalist assessment; and D. W. Y. Kwok, *Scientism in Chinese Thought, 1900-1950* (Yale, 1965), which treats Wu Chih-hui, Ch'en Tu-hsiu and Hu Shih as major protagonists, together with a number of less celebrated Westernizers.

V. From the New Culture to the People's Republic

The culminating phases of China's revolutionary experience have been dealt with more fully in terms of the social and ideological strategies of the revolution than in terms of its intellectual history. Useful in this connection, both for documentation and commentary, are such collections as C. Brandt, B. Schwartz, and J. K. Fairbank, *A Documentary History of Chinese Communism* (Harvard, 1952); and Hélène Carrère d'Encausse and Stuart R. Schram, *Marxism and Asia: An Introduction with Readings* (Penguin, 1969).

Maurice Meisner, *Li Ta-chao and the Origins of Chinese Marxism* (Harvard, 1967) is a very important interpretation of the man, and of the manner in which Marxist categories came to encompass Chinese aspirations. No comparably insightful study of Ch'en Tu-hsiu has yet been published.

Of the numerous biographies of Mao Tse-tung, Jerome Ch'en, *Mao and the Chinese Revolution* (Oxford, 1965) is perhaps the most sensitive to the problems which interest an intellectual historian. Frederic Wakeman, Jr., *History and Will: Philosophical Perspectives of Mao Tse-tung's Thought* (California, 1973), though not purporting to be a biographical study, is a stimulating (and structurally difficult) interpretation of the genesis and logic of Mao's ideas. Dick Wilson (ed.), *Mao Tse-tung in the Scales of History* (Cambridge, 1977) contains a number of useful contributions to an understanding of the many facets of "Maoism."

Some sense of the ideology of Nationalism, and of intellectual conditions during the Nanking decade, can be gained from the relevant chapters in Lloyd Eastman, *The Abortive Revolution: China Under Nationalist Rule, 1927-1937* (Harvard, 1974); and James C. Thomson, Jr., *While China Faced West: American Reformers in Nationalist China, 1928-1937* (Harvard, 1969). Arif Dirlik, "T'ao Hsi-sheng: The Social Limits of Change," in Furth (ed.), *The Limits of Change*, examines the ideas of one of Nationalism's more interesting thinkers.

The student movement, more in its political than in its intellectual aspect, is examined in John Israel, *Student Nationalism in China, 1927-1937* (Stanford, 1966); for the fate that overtook some members of that generation, see John Israel and Donald W. Klein, *Rebels and Bureaucrats: China's December 9ers* (California, 1976).

Suzanne Pepper, *Civil War in China: The Political Struggle, 1945-1949* (California, 1978), contains long chapters on the intellectuals' assessment of the postwar crisis, otherwise a little studied subject.

The frequently tense and troubled relationship that has existed between Chinese intellectuals and the regime which came to power in 1949 is a subject that lies chronologically outside the scope of this book and this bibliography. Following are a few titles that touch, albeit randomly, on aspects of this enormous topic: Merle Goldman, *Literary Dissent in Communist China* (Harvard, 1967); Robert Jay Lifton, *Thought Reform and the Psychology of Totalism: A Study of "Brainwashing" in China* (Norton, 1961); Theodore H. E. Chen, *Thought Reform of the Chinese Intellectuals* (University of Hong Kong, 1960); Mu Fu-sheng, *The Wilting of the Hundred Flowers: The Chinese Intelligentsia Under Mao* (Praeger, 1962); Joseph R. Levenson, *Revolution and Cosmopolitanism: The Western Stage and the Chinese Stages* (California, 1971); Donald Munro, *The Concept of Man in Modern China* (Michigan, 1979); Chen Jo-hsi, *The Execution of Mayor Yin, and Other Stories from the Great Proletarian Cultural Revolution* (Indiana, 1978).

Index

The index proper is followed by a list of *pinyin* transliterations and their Wade–Giles counterparts, omitting terms that are identical in both systems (e.g., Wei Yuan) or in which the only difference is the use of the hyphen in the Wade–Giles transliteration (e.g., Hu Hanmin, Hu Han-min).

Conversion of *pinyin* to Wade–Giles transliteration

pinyin	Wade–Giles
Aiguo xueshe	Ai-kuo hsueh-she, *see* Patriotic Academy
Baihua	Pai-hua, *see* Vernacular literature movement
Baohuang hui	Pao-huang hui, *see* Society for the Protection of the Emperor
Beida	Peita, *see* Peking University
Bo Juyi	Po Chü-i
Cai Yuanpei	Ts'ai Yuan-p'ei
Chen Baozhen	Ch'en Pao-chen
Chen Duxiu	Ch'en Tu-hsiu
Chen She	Ch'en She
Chen Tianhua	Ch'en T'ien-hua
Chen Zhi	Ch'en Chih
Chunqiu	*Ch'un-ch'iu, see Spring and Autumn Annals*
Cixi	Tz'u Hsi
Daizhen	Tai Chen
Daoguang	Tao Kuang
Datong shu	*Ta-t'ung shu*
Daxue	*Ta hsueh, see The Great Learning*
Ding Wenjiang	Ting Wen-chiang
Dongfang zazhi	*Tung-fang tsa-chih, see Eastern Miscellany*
Donglin	Tung-lin
Dong Zhongshu	Tung Chung-shu
Duanfang	Tuan-fang
Duli pinglun	*Tu-li p'ing-lun, see Independent Critic*
Feng Guifen	Feng Kuei-fen
Feng Ziyou	Feng Tzu-yu
Fu Sinian	Fu Ssu-nien
Gao Yihan	Kao I-han
Geming jun	*Ko-ming chün, see Revolutionary Army*
Gong	Kung (Prince)
Gongyang	*Kung-yang* (commentary)
Guancha	*Kuan-ch'a, see The Observer*
Guangfu hui	Kuang-fu hui, *see* Restoration Society
Guangxu	Kuang Hsu
Guan Zhong	Kuan Chung
Gu Hongming	Ku Hung-ming
Gu Jiegang	Ku Chieh-kang
Guomindang	Kuomintang
Guwen	*Ku-wen, see Old Text school*
Gu Yanwu	Ku Yen-wu
Hong Xiuquan	Hung Hsiu-ch'üan
Ho Qi	Ho Ch'i, *see* Ho Kai
Hu Shi	Hu Shih
Huang Xing	Huang Hsing
Huang Zongxi	Huang Tsung-hsi
Jiang Fangzhen	Chiang Fang-chen
Jiang Menglin	Chiang Meng-lin
Jiaqing	Chia Ch'ing
Jiayin zazhi	*Chia-yin tsa-chih, see Tiger Magazine*

pinyin	Wade–Giles
Jingbao	*Ching-pao, see* Peking Gazette
Jingshi	Ching-shih, *see* Statecraft
Jinwen	*Chin-wen, see* New Text school
Jizi	Chi-tzu
Kangxi	K'ang Hsi
Kang Youwei	K'ang Yu-wei
Lan Gongwu	Lan Kung-wu
Liang Ji	Liang Chi
Liang Qichao	Liang Ch'i-ch'ao
Liao Ping	Liao P'ing
Li Dazhao	Li Ta-chao
Li Hongzhang	Li Hung-chang
Liu Shipei	Liu Shih-p'ei
Liu Xin	Liu Hsin
Lunyu	*Lun-yü, see* Analects
Luo Jialun	Lo Chia-lun
Luo Longji	Lo Lung-chi
Lu Xun	Lu Hsun
Mao Zedong	Mao Tse-tung
Mei Guangdi	Mei Kuang-ti
Meizhou pinglun	*Mei-chou p'ing-lun, see Weekly Critic*
Minbao	*Min pao, see People's Report*
Mingyi daifang lu	*Ming-i tai-fang lu, see* "Propositions for a More Propitious Age"
Nuli zhoubao	*Nu-li chou-pao, see* Endeavor
Qianlong	Ch'ien Lung
Qiangxue hui	Ch'iang hsueh hui, *see* Society for the Study of National Strength
Qian Xuantong	Ch'ien Hsuan-t'ung
Qingyibao	*Ch'ing-i pao, see Journal of Disinterested Criticism*
Qiu Jin	Ch'iu Chin
Shenbao	*Shen-pao*
Sheng Xuanhuai	Sheng Hsuan-huai
Shijing	*Shih ching, see Classic of Poetry*
Shiwubao	*Shih-wu pao*
Siku quanshu	*Ssu-k'u ch'üan-shu*
Sima Qian	Ssu-ma Ch'ien
Shujing	*Shu ching, see Classic of History*
Shunzhi	Shun Chih
Song Jiaoren	Sung Chiao-jen
Su Shi	Su Shih
Tan Sitong	T'an Ssu-t'ung
Tansuo	*T'an-so, see Explorations*
Tao Menghe	T'ao Meng-ho
Tao Xingzhi	T'ao Hsing-chih
Tianyan lun	*T'ien-yen lun*
Tongcheng	T'ung-ch'eng
Tongmeng hui	T'ung-meng hui, *see* Revolutionary Alliance
Tongwen guan	T'ung-wen kuan
Tongzhi	T'ung Chih

pinyin	Wade–Giles
Wang Anshi	Wang An-shih
Wang Jingwei	Wang Ching-wei
Wang Fuzhi	Wang Fu-chih
Wang Tao	Wang T'ao
Wanguo gongbao	*Wan-kuo kung-pao*
Wei Jingsheng	Wei Ching-sheng
Woren	Wo-jen
Wu Yue	Wu Yueh
Wu Zhihui	Wu Chih-hui
Xiandai pinglun	*Hsien-tai p'ing-lun, see Contemporary Review*
Xianfeng	Hsien Feng
Xinchao	*Hsin ch'ao, see Renaissance*
Xing Zhong hui	Hsing Chung hui, *see* Revive China Society
Xin jiaoyu	*Hsin chiao-yü, see New Education*
Xinmin congbao	*Hsin-min ts'ung-pao, see New People's Miscellany*
Xinmin shuo	Hsin-min shuo, see "On the New People"
Xin qingnian	*Hsin ch'ing-nien, see New Youth*
Xinyue	*Hsin yueh, see Crescent*
Xue Fucheng	Hsueh Fu-ch'eng
Xueheng	*Hsueh heng, see Critical Review*
Xu Jiyu	Hsu Chi-yü
Xunzi	Hsun-tzu
Yan Fu	Yen Fu
Yan Ruoju	Yen Jo-chü
Yao Hongye	Yao Hung-yeh
Yishibao	*I-shih pao*
Yijing	*I-ching, see Book of Changes*
Yuan Shikai	Yuan Shih-k'ai
Yu Pingbo	Yü P'ing-po
Zeng Guofan	Tseng Kuo-fan
Zhang Binglin	Chang Ping-lin
Zhang Dongsun	Chang Tung-sun
Zhang Junmai	Chang Chün-mai
Zhang Shizhao	Chang Shih-chao
Zhang Yuanji	Chang Yuan-chi
Zhang Zhidong	Chang Chih-tung
Zheng Guanying	Cheng Kuan-ying
Zhongyong	*Chung-yung, see Doctrine of the Mean*
Zhou Shuren	Chou Shu-jen, *see* Lu Hsun
Zhuangzi	Chuang-tzu
Zhu Ciqi	Chu Tz'u-ch'i
Zhu Xi	Chu Hsi
Zhu Zhixin	Chu Chih-hsin
Zongli yamen	Tsungli yamen
Zou Rong	Tsou Jung
Zuo	*Tso* (commentary)
Zuo Zongtang	Tso Tsung-t'ang

Printed in the United States
By Bookmasters